READER'S DIGEST

BACK ROADS
AND
GETAWAY
PLACES
OF CANADA

BACK ROADS
AND
GETAWAY PLACES
OF CANADA

Reader's Digest

The Reader's Digest Association (Canada) Ltd.
Montreal

Back Roads and Getaway Places of Canada

PROJECT EDITOR:
Andrew R. Byers

DESIGNER:
Andrée Payette

MAP DESIGNER:
Lucie Martineau

EDITORS:
Sandy Shepherd, and Deirdre Gilbert,
Philomena Rutherford, Agnès Saint-Laurent

PICTURE EDITOR:
Rachel Irwin

ART SUPERVISOR:
John McGuffie

COPY EDITOR:
Joseph Marchetti

RESEARCH EDITOR:
Wadad Bashour

COORDINATOR:
Susan Wong

PRODUCTION:
Holger Lorenzen

EDITORIAL ASSISTANCE:
Elizabeth Eastman

CONTRIBUTORS

CONTRIBUTING RESEARCH EDITOR:
Enza Micheletti

CONTRIBUTING WRITERS:
See list, pages 392-393

CONTRIBUTING EDITORS:
Geneviève Beullac, Patricia Derrick,
Grace Deutsch, Gillian Foss, Douglas How,
Susan Lawrence, Mike McGarry

INDEXER:
Judy Yelon

CARTOGRAPHY:
Hatra, Westmount, Que.

The credits and acknowledgments that appear on pages 392-393
and 400 are hereby made part of this copyright page.
Copyright ©1994
The Reader's Digest Association (Canada) Ltd.
All rights reserved. Unauthorized reproduction,
in any manner, in whole or in part, in English
or other languages, is prohibited.

Canadian Cataloging in Publication Data
Main entry under title:
Back roads and getaway places of Canada
1st Canadian edition
Includes index
ISBN 0-88850-000-9
1. Canada — Guidebooks — I. Reader's Digest
Association (Canada). II. Title: Back roads and
getaway places of Canada.
FC75.B33 1994   917.104'67   C93-090453-2
F1017. B33 1994

Reader's Digest and the Pegasus logo are registered
trademarks of The Reader's Digest Association Inc.

Printed in Canada

94 95 96 97 98 / 5 4 3 2 1

ACKNOWLEDGMENTS
The publisher acknowledges with thanks the assistance of the
following organizations and individuals:

Parks Canada
Environment Canada
Canadian Wildlife Service

Tourism British Columbia
Tourism Association of Southwestern British Columbia
Tourism Association of Vancouver Island
Alberta Economic Development and Tourism
Saskatchewan Tourism
Travel Manitoba
Travel Ontario (Ontario Ministry of Culture, Tourism and Recreation)
Ontario Heritage Foundation
Festival Country Travel Association
Peterborough Tourism Bureau
Ottawa Valley Tourist Association
Huronia Tourism Association
Southwestern Ontario Travel Association
Sunset Country Travel Association
Near North Tourism Association
Presqu'Ile District Tourism and Commerce Association
Tri-Town Chamber of Commerce
James Bay Frontier
Algoma Country Travel Association
Grey Bruce Tourism Association
Rainbow Country Travel Association
Muskoka Tourism Association
York Region Tourism Marketing Agency
Quinte's Isle Tourism Association
Ontario East Travel Association
National Capital Commission
Ministère du Tourisme du Québec, Accueil et renseignements touristiques
Association touristique de l'Abitibi-Témiscamingue
Association touristique de l'Outaouais
Association touristique des Laurentides
Association touristique de Lanaudière
Association touristique du Cœur-du-Québec
Association touristique de Charlevoix
Association touristique du Saguenay–Lac-Saint-Jean
Association touristique de la Montérégie
Association touristique de l'Estrie
Association touristique de Chaudière-Appalaches
Association touristique du Bas-Saint-Laurent
Association touristique de la Gaspésie
Association touristique des Îles-de-la-Madeleine
New Brunswick Economic Development and Tourism
Prince Edward Island Marketing Agency
Nova Scotia Department of Tourism, Culture and Recreation
Newfoundland Department of Tourism and Culture

Ruth Allen	Gayle Ferguson	Rod McFayden
Neville Atkinson	Vicky Haberl	David McGrew
Elinor Barr	Larry Halverson	Susan McNamee
Jacques A. Brunet	David Harley	Étienne Marquis
Dan Bulloch	Tom Hince	Florence Miller
Sandra Chabot	Dan Hinde	Liz Poulton
Ernie Christmas	Carol Horne	Maxime Saint-Amour
Rod Cotton	Jerry Ives	Bruce Shoenhals
Jennifer Corbett	Juanita Keel-Ryan	Fryzee Shuhood
Kay Coxworthy	Doug Kielau	Al Smith
Robert Davidson	Diane Lamoureux	David Steele
Everett DeJong	Carol Livingstone	Judy Sutherland
Erin Downey	Peter McFadden	Debbie Thorne
Rod Drew	Al McFayden	Wayne Zimmer

Thanks is also expressed to provincial parks departments, city and municipal offices
across Canada, the Council of Haida Nations, and Ducks Unlimited.

Foreword: An abundant choice of destinations and drives...

A pale crescent moon hovers in the clear night sky above a silhouette of high, rugged peaks in Waterton Lakes National Park, Alberta (page 90).

*B*ACK ROADS AND GETAWAY PLACES OF CANADA offers an abundant choice of destinations and drives across this vast country of ours. A considerable number are near or within reasonable distance of the major cities and larger communities where most Canadians live. Some are ideal for relaxing day-trips and weekend escapes. The wealth of travel possibilities and the wide range of detail and information in the book will help you put together longer journeys with varied attractions, activities, and events. It will also ensure that you pick the best places to see and the most exciting things to do in distant parts of the country.

Back Roads and Getaway Places of Canada celebrates an unspoiled and uncrowded country. In general, this 400-page travel guide highlights little-known and offbeat places—secluded beaches and campsites, quaint villages

A mill of times past spruced up for today at Flesherton (page 184)   *A sandy strand at Lac Philippe, a Gatineau Park getaway (page 258)*

and historic forts, gardens and ghost towns, and much, much more. (In treating some of our best-known attractions—our national parks, for example—the book focuses on the unfamiliar features of these sites.) This guide also takes you on drives along country lanes and wilderness roads. Most drives can be traveled in a day, but some are challenging expeditions in remote areas. Here, too, you will also find suggestions for travel by boat, train, and plane.

For reliable, on-the-spot background information about the sites and drives, we approached more than 180 knowledgeable local writers, whose contributions form the basis of this travel guide. (For a complete list of our contributors, please see pages 392-393.) We also contacted countless municipal, regional, and provincial travel experts, who generously confirmed facts and added extra details.

An array of sailboats finds peaceful anchorage along the waterfront at Mahone Bay, a maritime community on the Atlantic coast (page 363).

Altogether *Back Roads and Getaway Places of Canada* contains detailed descriptions of 340 sites and 26 national park close-ups, as well as driving instructions for 56 drives. The informative text is complemented by more than 400 photographs, which were specially commissioned for this guide. Some 76 maps pinpoint specific regions and routes. Other features include special-events boxes and easy-to-scan symbols pinpointing recreational activities. (For more details, see "How to use the book" on pages 12-13.)

Back Roads and Getaway Places of Canada is designed for those looking for quiet, unhurried vacations in appealing and unusual places across our vast land. Its descriptions and photographs make this guidebook a delight for those who wish to know more about the many little-known byways and corners of this country. *The Editors*

Contents

Symbols for "Places to see"

🏺	Antiques, crafts	👣	Hikes, walks	🐟	Deep-sea fishing
🚲	Cycling		Horseback riding		Diving
∧	Campsites	↗	Rock hounding		Swimming
🪑	Picnic sites	⚙	Winter sports	❋	Special attractions
	Bird-watching	⛵	Sailing		Whale-watching
	Climbing		Canoeing	📷	Nature photography
	Golfing	🐟	Freshwater fishing	⌂	Accommodations

Symbols for "Roads to explore"

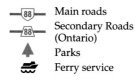

—88—	Main roads
—88—	Secondary Roads (Ontario)
▲	Parks
⛴	Ferry service

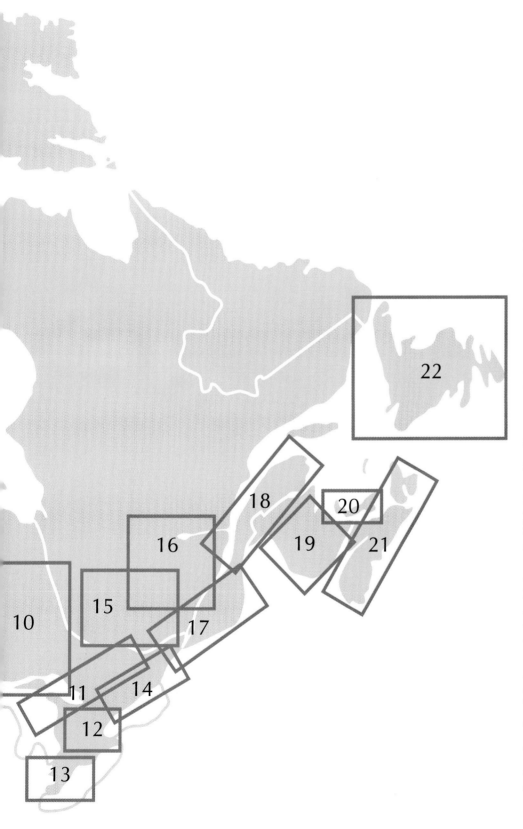

How to use the book

Back Roads and Getaway Places of Canada divides our country into 22 regions, which are arranged west to east from Vancouver Island to Newfoundland. The incidence map (*left*) locates these regions. A two-page scenic photograph, followed by a two-page regional map, introduces each chapter. A table of contents, listing "Places to see," "Roads to explore," and "National park close-ups," accompanies each regional map.

"Places to see"—the detailed site descriptions—are number-keyed on the regional map. Each site description begins with the symbols (see opposite page) for relevant recreations and facilities. A tinted box listing special events in the area is at the end of many descriptions.

Sidebars in each chapter appear in italics in the "Places to see" list. They provide extra information about the number-keyed sites, or about remote or unusual places and things.

"Roads to explore"—the suggested drives in each region—appear in large tinted boxes. Each drive offers a route map and point-to-point directions. (See opposite page for the key to the symbols on the route maps.)

Opening times for museums and other sites mentioned in the site descriptions and drives are in italics. The information tells you which sites are admission free.

"National park close-ups" on beige-tinted pages describe the park and offer details about activities and accommodations.

CENTRAL BRITISH COLUMBIA

3

CENTRAL
BRITISH COLUMBIA

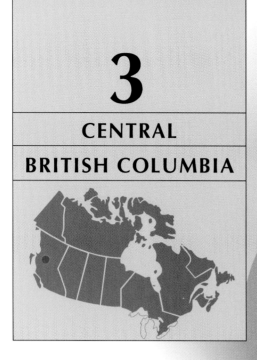

Places to see
Queen Charlotte Islands
Naikoon Provincial Park
Port Edward
Hazelton
Fort St. James
Cottonwood House Provincial
Historic Park
Barkerville Historic Town
Bowron Lake Provincial Park
Williams Lake
Tweedsmuir Provincial Park
Bella Coola
Gang Ranch
Clinton
Lillooet
Ashcroft

Roads to explore
Houston–Ootsa Lake–Burns Lake
Williams Lake–Horsefly–Likely
Clinton to Williams Lake

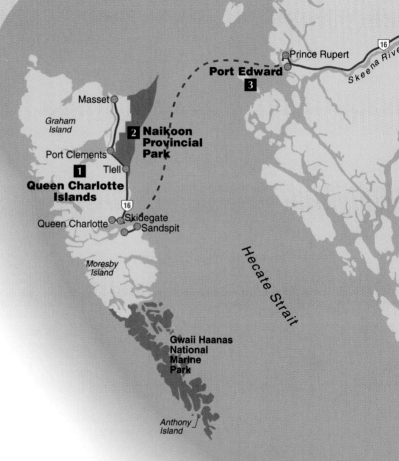

Previous pages:
Rainbow over Highway 27, near Fort St. James

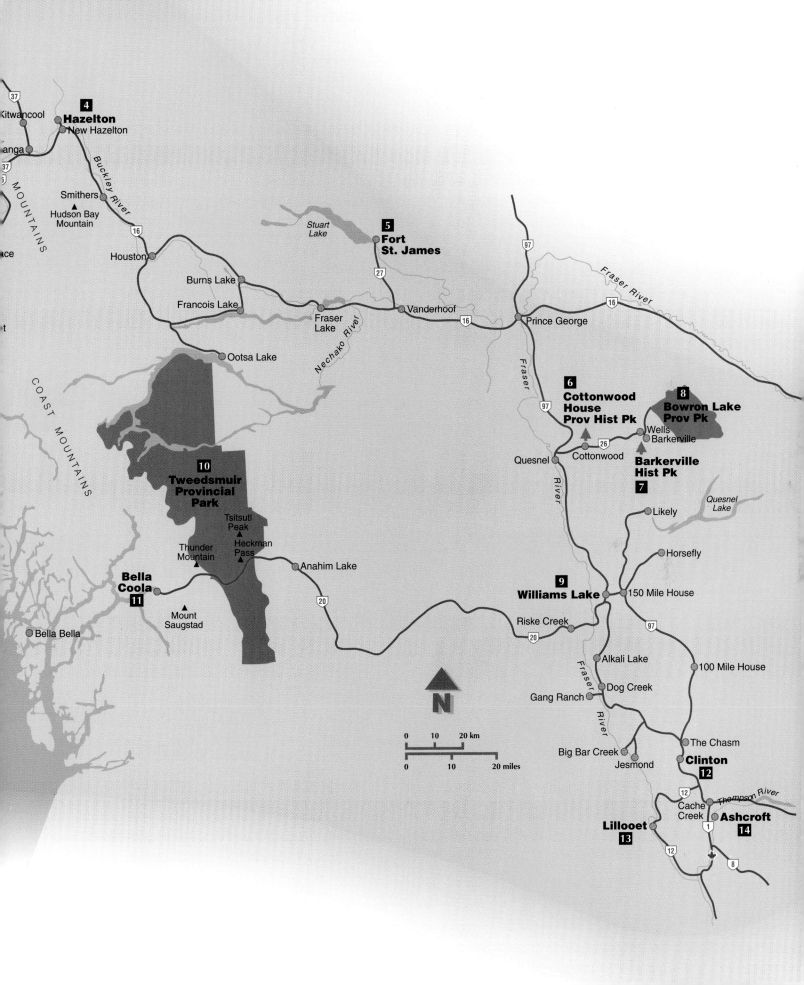

37
Kitwancool

4 **Hazelton**
New Hazelton
anga

37

MOUNTAINS

Smithers
▲ Hudson Bay Mountain

Buckley River

Stuart Lake

5 **Fort St. James**

97

Fraser River

16

Houston

Burns Lake

Francois Lake

Fraser Lake

Vanderhoof

16

Prince George

16

Nechako River

COAST MOUNTAINS

Ootsa Lake

Fraser

97

6 **Cottonwood House Prov Hist Pk**

8 **Bowron Lake Prov Pk**

Wells
Barkerville

26

10 **Tweedsmuir Provincial Park**

Quesnel

Cottonwood

River

Barkerville Hist Pk

7

Tsitsutl Peak ▲
Thunder Mountain ▲

Heckman Pass ▲

Anahim Lake

Quesnel Lake

Likely

Horsefly

Bella Coola

11

Mount Saugstad ▲

20

9
Williams Lake

150 Mile House

Riske Creek

97

Bella Bella

20

Fraser River

Alkali Lake

100 Mile House

Gang Ranch

Dog Creek

N

The Chasm

0   10   20 km

Big Bar Creek

Jesmond

Clinton

12

0   10   20 miles

12

Thompson River

Cache Creek

Lillooet

13

1

Ashcroft

14

12

8

1 Queen Charlotte Islands

Enveloping fogs and mists heighten the sense of mystery and remoteness associated with the "Misty Islands," the Queen Charlotte Islands. To the Haida Indians, the 250-km-long crescent of 150 islands sitting some 90 km offshore has been their *Haida Gwaii* (homeland) for thousands of years.

At 9,033 km², Graham and Moresby make up the bulk of the archipelago. Graham Island (about 6,400 km²) is the largest and the most populous: most communities are located here. Population is sparse on Moresby. The southern three-quarters of the island has been designated Gwaii Hanaas National Park Reserve.

A six-hour ferry ride brings visitors from Prince Rupert to Skidegate on Graham Island, and there are scheduled flights from Prince Rupert and Vancouver to the Sandspit airport on Moresby Island. A ferry links the two islands. Highway 16 connects Graham Island's main communities and attractions: Queen Charlotte City, Skidegate, Port Clements, Masset, Haida, the Delkatla Bird Sanctuary and Naikoon Provincial Park.

Queen Charlotte City (pop. 950) is the unofficial capital of Graham Island. Incorporated in 1908, and known locally as Charlotte, it was the first registered townsite on the islands. This seaside community has a fine collection of quaint wooden dwellings. A 1909 schoolhouse is among examples of turn-of-the-century architecture. The renovated Premier Hotel, built in 1910, retains its original facade. The town has bed-and-breakfast and hotel accommodation, and a campground.

Skidegate stretches along an expansive gravel beach overlooking Rooney Bay. Strolling here between late April and June, you may glimpse gray whales offshore. The mammals feed and calve here during their annual migrations between Mexico and Alaska.

A beach walk leads to the Skidegate Band Council Office, which is built in the traditional longhouse style. It is easy to spot because of the 16.5-m totem pole out front. This is the work of internationally known sculptor Bill Reid and local artist Guujaaw. A canoe shed near the Haida Gwaii Watchman Building displays Reid's 15-m-long oceangoing *Loo Taas* (Wave Eater), a replica of a Haida cedar canoe, commissioned for the 1986 World's Fair at Vancouver. Reid casts in bronze, carves in silver, gold, wood, and argillite, a black slatelike stone found in the Queen Charlottes. His major work, *The*

Across from the shore lights at Skidegate Landing on Graham Island rises the blue outline of the mountains on Moresby Island.

Black Canoe—The Spirit of Haida Gwaii— stands outside Canada's embassy in Washington, D.C.

The cedar-log Queen Charlotte Islands Museum, beside the Haida Gwaii Watchman Building, contains a major collection of Haida totem poles and argillite carvings, and a pioneer gallery and gift shop. *Open June to August, Monday to Friday, 10 am to 5 pm, weekends, 1 to 5 pm; winter hours vary.* Haida carvings, paintings, and weav-

NEWFOUNDLAND AND LABRADOR

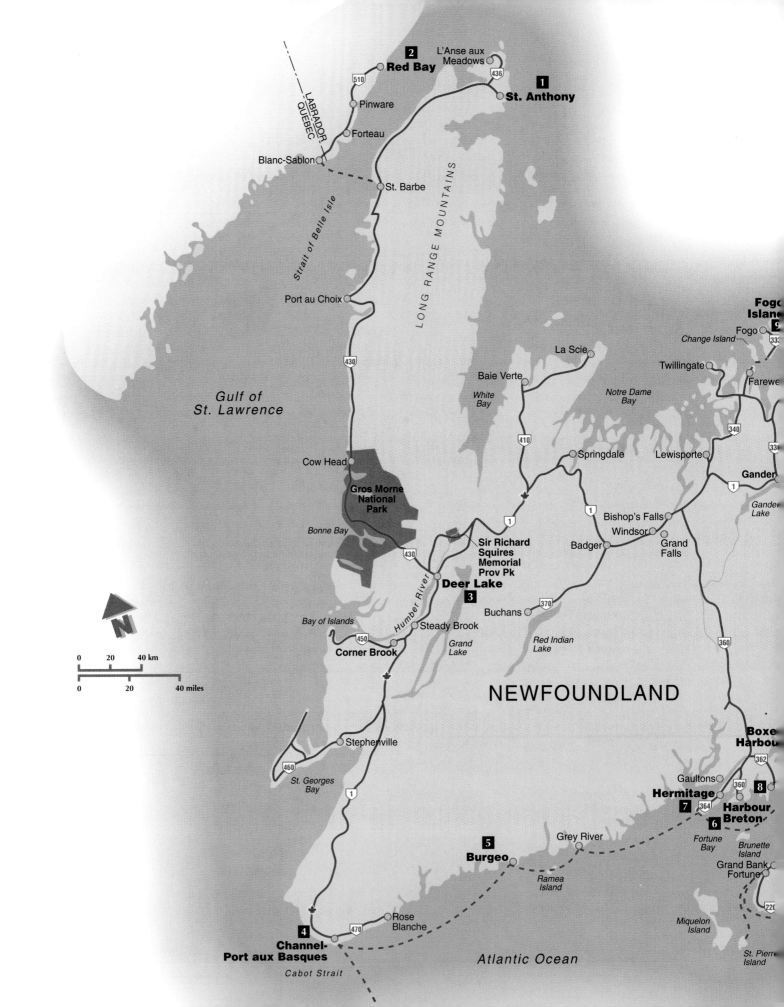

VANCOUVER ISLAND

1

VANCOUVER

ISLAND

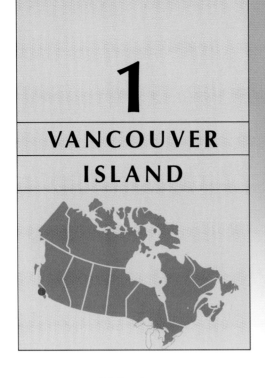

Places to see
Port Hardy
Alert Bay
Cape Scott Provincial Park
Telegraph Cove
Quadra Island
Strathcona Park
Nootka Sound (boat trips)
Gold River
Cumberland
Denman and Hornby Islands
Ucluelet
Tofino
Bamfield
Gabriola Island
Lake Cowichan
Salt Spring Island
Galiano Island
Pender Island
Mayne Island

Roads to explore
Port Hardy to Holberg
Around Lake Cowichan

National park close-up
Pacific Rim

Previous pages:
Whaling Station Bay, Hornby Island

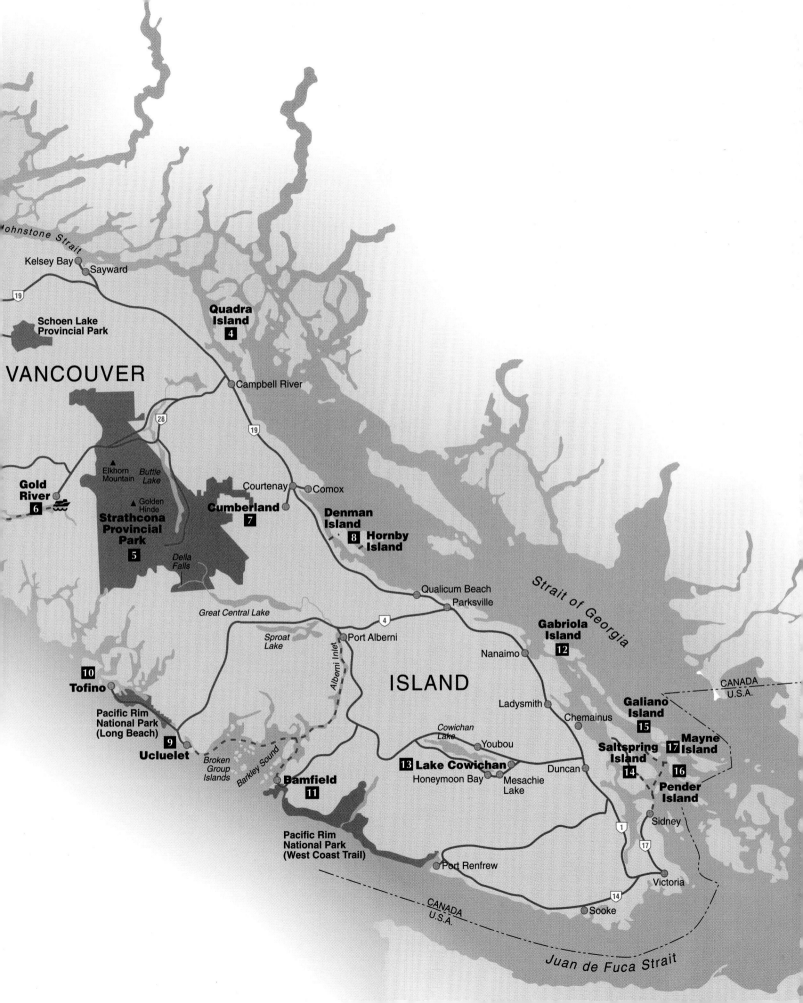

Johnstone Strait

Kelsey Bay Sayward

19

Schoen Lake
Provincial Park

**Quadra
Island**
4

VANCOUVER

28

Campbell River

19

▲ Elkhorn   *Buttle
Mountain   Lake*

**Gold
River**
6

▲ *Golden
Hinde*

Courtenay Comox

Cumberland
7

**Strathcona
Provincial
Park**
5

*Della
Falls*

**Denman
Island**

**Hornby
Island**
8

Qualicum Beach
Parksville

Great Central Lake

4

Strait of Georgia

*Sproat
Lake*

**Gabriola
Island**
12

Alberni Inlet Port Alberni

ISLAND

Nanaimo

10
Tofino

Pacific Rim
National Park
(Long Beach)

CANADA
U.S.A.

Ladysmith

**Galiano
Island**
15

Chemainus

9
Ucluelet

*Broken
Group
Islands*

Barkley Sound

*Cowichan
Lake*

Youbou

**Saltspring
Island**
14

**Mayne
Island**
17

13 **Lake Cowichan**

16

Bamfield
11

Honeymoon Bay

*Mesachie
Lake*

Duncan

**Pender
Island**

1

Sidney

17

Pacific Rim
National Park
(West Coast Trail)

Port Renfrew

Victoria

CANADA
U.S.A.

14

Sooke

Juan de Fuca Strait

1 Port Hardy

The gateway to the Inside Passage—the marine route north to mainland Prince Rupert—and the base for exploring northern Vancouver Island is the town of Port Hardy (pop. 5,082).

It has been accessible by paved road since 1979 when the Island Highway was completed, after an aggressive lobbying campaign by North Islanders. The campaign is puckishly commemorated by Carrot Park, after the islanders asked the government "Do you carrot all?" In the park, a heritage plaque adorned by a carved wooden carrot claims the spot as "Mile 0, Trans-Carrot Highway."

Battling is in Port Hardy's blood: it was named after Vice-Admiral Sir Thomas Masterman Hardy, R.N. (1769-1839), who fought at Nelson's side at the Battle of Trafalgar.

Walking is a pleasure in this town, especially along the seawall by the busy harbor alive with fishing boats, sailboats and floatplanes. This is "King Coho Country," where the Coho salmon abounds.

The highlight of the Port Hardy Museum, which exhibits the area's history, is a display from an 8,000-year-old archaeological site in Bear Cove, on the other side of the bay from Port Hardy. *Open year-round, but the hours are variable. Contact the museum first.*

A short distance before you enter Port Hardy is the Quatse River Tidal Marsh, a bird sanctuary at the mouth of the Quatse River, where shorebirds, ducks, herons, and geese can be observed from trails.

At nearby Fort Rupert, visitors can see Kwakiutl totem poles. Or they may visit, by appointment, The Copper Maker, a workshop and gallery. In Fort Rupert, a chimney is all that remains of the old Hudson's Bay Company coal-mining operation and trading post that was established there in 1849.

For those interested in a two-day round-trip cruise, a ferry sails from Port Hardy to Prince Rupert through the Inside Passage. Passengers are frequently rewarded with a close look at eagles, whales, and porpoises.

Port Hardy's welcoming gateway sign

Special events
Filomi Days (July)

Roads to explore: From a "Home for Lost Soles" to a Danish settler's garden

Distance (approx.): 67 km/42 miles

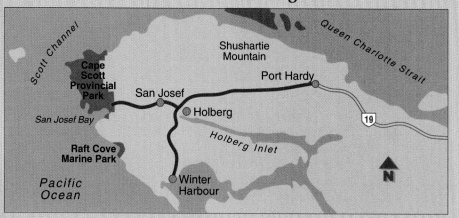

Just outside Port Hardy is the logging road that provides access to the remote northern tip of Vancouver Island. Drive west from Port Hardy on Highway 19. About 3.5 km from town, pavement turns to gravel, and the logging road winds through hilly terrain.

● At Kains Lake, about 20 km along, on the right side of the road, is the Shoe Tree, a "home for lost soles," as a sign explains. Hundreds of pairs of shoes and boots nailed to the tree trunk encircle it to a height of 2 m.

● Some 15 km later, the road passes Nawhiti Lake, a B.C. Forest Service recreation site set among tall, mossy, second-growth trees. Just a little farther on, the road climbs a steep hill that has a sweeping view of Nawhiti Lake and the surrounding forest.

● Drive on to Holberg (pop. 200), at the end of a 33-km fjord. Holberg was settled by Danish immigrants from Minnesota, who had aban-

The Shoe Tree, Kains Lake

doned the nearby Cape Scott area. It was named after 18th-century Danish writer Baron Ludvig Holberg.

Holberg itself was abandoned by 1916, until logging began there around 1942. A logging community was established, on a floating log boom, complete with homes, electricity and water services. It was said to be the largest floating camp on the west coast of North America.

The community's logging heritage is kept alive at the community park where axe-throwing, log-bucking (sawing), and log-birling competitions are held during the Loggers' Sports Days, in mid-June.

● At the intersection 3.9 km outside Holberg, turn right for the San Josef campsite, 20 km away. Just before the San Josef River, a short side road leads to Ronning's Garden, a Danish settler's garden, currently being restored. Continue to the campsite, and the trailhead to Cape Scott Provincial Park.

● Alternatively, turn left at the intersection outside Holberg and drive 26 km to the village of Winter Harbour. The fishing hamlet offers excellent fishing, forest walks and wildlife, including a chance to see the rare elephant seal. It also has a campsite.

2 Alert Bay

⋀ 🎣 ‼ ▱ ❋ ✈ 📷

As you approach Cormorant Island on the ferry from Port McNeill, wooden buildings become visible, set on pilings over the water. This is the settlement of Alert Bay (pop. 628), the heart of Kwakiutl Indian culture.

Alert Bay has been a shipping stop for fuel since the late 1800s. It gets its name from the first vessel that put into the bay.

At either end of Alert Bay's main street are two testaments to the island's Kwakiutl culture: the Nimpkish Burial Ground, at the south end of Fir Street (turn right off the ferry ramp), and the U'Mista Cultural Centre, at the north end of Front Street.

Alert Bay's historic Anglican church, built in England, was reassembled here in 1879.

A RUGGED RAIN FOREST ON A WINDSWEPT CAPE

Cape Scott Provincial Park's challenge is legendary. To reach its 1,507 km² coastal rain forest, drive 67 km east from Port Hardy along an unpaved logging road to San Josef Bay and Cape Scott trailhead parking. The only access to the park is by foot, along rough and demanding trails (some are more than 20 km long). They head through an ancient, mossy forest of red and yellow cedar, lodgepole pine, hemlock, and fir.

Moss and mushrooms, Cape Scott

Hikers in this park are nothing less than determined. They crawl through openings in the thick undergrowth of salmonberry, huckleberry, salal, and fern, sometimes using tunnels left behind by black bears. It takes six hours to reach the 2.4-km strip of fine-textured sand at Nels Bight, and another two hours to reach Cape Scott. The cape is named after David Scott, a Bombay merchant who financed the first trading voyage along the Pacific coast in 1786.

River otters, cougars, deer, elks, and wolves can be seen here. Sea lions and seals bask along the park's 64-km coastline. Sandhill cranes and herons wade in its coves. An estimated 10,000 Canada geese rest here on their way south from the Queen Charlotte Islands along the Pacific flyway.

The park is one of the rainiest areas on the continent—with records of up to 500 cm a year. Violent storms defeated Danish attempts to settle the Hansen Lagoon region in 1897 and 1910 and forced almost 80 families to retreat. They left behind place-names such as Frederiksen Point and Eric Lake. Before the Danes, Kwakiutl Indians occupied Cape Scott. Some experts believe the region was their original homeland.

The burial ground is guarded by aging memorial totem poles carved with striking Kwakiutl motifs. It is a sacred site, and visitors are asked not to walk in the graveyard.

Visitors are welcome, however, at the U'Mista Cultural Centre, built in traditional longhouse style. The centre houses an impressive collection of potlatch masks and ceremonial artifacts confiscated in the 1920s by federal government agents, but since restored to the community.

Outside the Big House, where potlatch ceremonies are held, is the world's tallest totem pole, 53 m high. It was erected in 1973. The designs up the pole, and the sun motif that crowns it, tell the tale of the Kwakwak'awakw nation to which the Kwakiutl tribe belongs.

European history has been preserved in Alert Bay as well. The Anglican Christ Church, founded in 1879, is a little chapel built in England and brought to Alert Bay for reassembly. Crosses along the peak of its roof and the gables make it look like a gingerbread house.

Totem pole, Alert Bay

On the ridge overlooking Alert Bay is Gator Gardens Ecological Park. There are no alligators here, however. It is a swamp filled with salal bushes higher than a man's head, and hemlock and pine trees hung with bright green "witches'-hair" mosses. A 225-m boardwalk meanders through skunk cabbage and stone grey cedar snags, all that remain of the forest that once covered the area.

Special events

Indian Sports Day (June)

Cormorant Sea Festival (August)

A boardwalk is the main street in Telegraph Cove, a much admired Pacific beauty spot.

3 Telegraph Cove

⋀ ⛺ 🚐 ❄ 🛠 📷

Wharves, boats, and clapboard houses on top of pilings overlook the harbor of Telegraph Cove (pop. 25). A long boardwalk connects the waterside buildings and serves as the main street.

Telegraph Cove was established in 1911 as the terminus of a telegraph line strung tree-to-tree up the east coast of Vancouver Island from Campbell River. From Telegraph Cove, morse messages were relayed to Alert Bay on Cormorant Island, just to the north of the cove.

The cove is the starting point for tours to whale-watching grounds in nearby Johnstone Strait and in Robson Bight, 20 km away. The bight is a 1,250-ha ecological reserve, frequented by killer whales, or orcas, which con-gregate there during the summer. The reserve includes "rubbing beaches," where the whales take turns rubbing their bellies and sides against submerged rocks. No boats are allowed inside the reserve, though tour boats do take sightseers close to the whales.

At Beaver Cove is the Canfor dryland log sort, where logs from the Nimpkish Valley are sorted for lumber, plywood, shingles and pulp mills. The yard is open to visitors. In the bay, the busy 5.5-m "sidewinder" tugs maneuvring the logs are an intriguing sight.

Visitors can take a ride on the Englewood Railway, which runs

Wharf sign, Telegraph Cove

through mountains and forests. The railway belongs to one of the last rail-logging outfits in British Columbia, and the engine that pulls the trains is a steam locomotive. The train leaves from Woss Camp, in the interior.

Special events
Boardwalk Craft Fair (August)

4 Quadra Island

Λ ⛺ ⛽ ⛴ 🐟 🚶

The largest island in Discovery Passage is Quadra Island, some 24 km long, reached by ferry from Campbell River. It was named for the 18th-century Spanish explorer Bodega y Quadra.

A pleasure craft anchors in sheltering, azure waters off Rebecca Spit, Quadra Island.

Quadra is far less built-up than most of the southerly islands in the Gulf of Georgia. Its pace is low-key, and it offers world-class salmon fishing, deep forests to explore, and mountain trails.

The provincial park at Rebecca Spit has breathtaking views across Sutil Channel to the mainland's Coast Range mountains. The only camping sites are in the adjacent We-Wai-Kai Campground, run by the Cape Mudge Indian Band. Ancient petroglyphs depicting masks and mythological creatures can be seen on boulders along the high tide line at We-Wai-Kai Beach. They are among the most important petroglyphs on the Pacific coast.

The Kwakiutl Museum and Cultural Centre at Cape Mudge displays sacred potlatch regalia, including rattles, masks, and headdresses. *Open year-round, Monday to Saturday, from 10 am to 4.30 pm; Sunday, only in summer, from 12 pm to 4.30 pm.*

On the island trails you might come across black-tailed deer and Douglas squirrels, or see river otters, harbor seals and sea lions. Wolves and cougars are more rare. Thick mosses, salal, oregon grape, and wildflowers grow among the trees, some of which are huge original-stand cedars and firs. Woodpeckers, tanagers, thrushes and red-winged blackbirds fly overhead.

Oysters and clams can be dug up on the shores. If saltwater fishing is your interest, first purchase a license, available at most stores and lodges.

Quathiaski Cove and Whiskey Point, at the south end of the island, are two of the best scuba-diving sites in North America. The underwater life includes octopuses, sea urchins, sea anemones, and even sharks (though not the deadly species).

In the northern part of the island are the ruins of the Lucky Jim Gold Mine, once a gold and copper mine.

Special events
May Days (May)
Salmon Barbecue (June)
Fall Fair (August)

Della Falls spills over the pine-clad slopes of "Nine Peaks," Strathcona Provincial Park.

5 Strathcona Park

Λ ⛽ ⛴ 🚣 🐟 🚶 📷

Strathcona Park is British Columbia's oldest provincial park, created in 1911. It is also the island's largest park, covering more than 2,226 km². Its headquarters are at Miracle Beach, between Courtenay and Campbell River.

A world of snow-capped mountains, glaciers, and old-growth forests, most of Strathcona is accessible only to those girded for backwoods survival. But there are equipped campgrounds around the park and gentle trails, particularly around Buttle Lake, Ralph River, Forbidden Plateau, Paradise Meadows and Strathcona Park Lodge. Since the roads in the park are used by giant logging trucks, be sure to park right off the road.

From the Buttle Lake area, trails lead to: Lupin Falls (a 20-minute walk through cool forest dotted with plants such as candy stick and Indian pipe); Lady Falls (another 20-minute walk); and Karst Creek (a 45-minute walk past sculpted limestone, sinkholes and waterfalls). From Ralph River Campground there is a 20-minute circular walk through forest and stands of wild ginger.

A scenic paved road near the outlet of Buttle Lake travels south along the lakeshore. At the end of the lake are Myra Creek and the Westmin Resources mine. From there, trails lead to Myra Falls and Cream Lake.

Forbidden Plateau was said by Indians to be inhabited by evil spirits who devoured women and children.

RIDING THE WAVES TO REMOTE INLETS

Traveling at a steady speed of 12 knots, the *Uchuck III* plies the remote Nootka and Kyuquot sounds on the northwest Pacific coast of Vancouver Island. This 41.5-m-long wooden vessel—a converted Second World War minesweeper—delivers everything from groceries to culverts and transports local passengers bound for isolated ports and work camps. It also welcomes vacationers on its regularly scheduled trips to Nootka Island, the mill town of Tahsis, and Kyoquot Sound.The departure point the Gold River dock, is located at the end of Highway 28 on Muchalat Inlet.

During July and August, the *Uchuck III* takes vacationers along the Muchalat Inlet, one of Nootka Sound's three arms, which extends inland to Strathcona Park. The ship stops at Resolution Cove, where Capt. James Cook first dropped anchor on this coast in 1778. It continues on to Friendly Cove (Yuquot) on the southeast corner of Nootka Island, also visited by Cook who made contact here with the local Indians. Friendly Cove is the ancestral home of the Mowachaht and the site of an ancient settlement (possibly 4,000 years old). The band now permits short guided tours, for a fee.

The *Uchuck III* skirts Blight Island and the mouth of Tlupana Inlet (another arm of Nootka Sound) on its journey up the long, narrow Tahsis Inlet to the community of that name. Tahsis has been called "The Birthplace of British Columbia," for it is here that Cook met the Indian chieftain Maquinna at his Indian quarters.

The two-day journey to Kyuquot covers the same route as the trip to Tahsis. But the *Uchuck III* continues on to the Pacific via Esperantza Inlet and rides the ocean waves until it reaches Kyuquot. (The ship docks offshore at Walter's Island.) During spring voyages to Kyuquot, vacationers may see gray whales, whose migratory route parallels this stretch of the Pacific coast. (All *Uchuck III* trips require reservations.)

The cool, spacious depths of Upana Caves, near Gold River, call to adventurous spelunkers.

The area is reached by gravel road from Courtenay. The trailhead to Paradise Meadows is reached along the Fletcher Challenge logging road off the same road. From Paradise Meadows, there are trails to Mount Becher (2 hours), Douglas Lake and MacKenzie Lake (3 hours), Kwai Lake (6 hours), Battleship Lake (1 hour) and Loop Trail (45 minutes).

Strathcona Park Lodge, just outside the park where Buttle turns into Upper Campbell Lake, offers guided activities including rock climbing, mountaineering, skiing, trout fishing, heli-hiking, wildflower study, and photography, as well as some Elderhostel courses for seniors. It also has flat-water and white-water kayaking.

6 | Gold River

At the junction of the Gold and Heber rivers is the mill town of Gold River (pop. 2,200). It is at the centre of a white water area that draws adventure seekers from around the world. The world's best kayakers and white-water rafters brave Gold River's powerful current and spinning whirlpools and the Big Bend, a 90-degree turn in the Gold River. Onlookers can watch from the Big Bend Park picnic area just off Highway 28.

Serious spelunkers can explore nearby Quatsino Cave or visit the Upana Caves, just north of town. Other attractions include a tour of the Gold River Pulp Mill at the end of Highway 28 on Muchalat Inlet.

Charter floatplanes are available to the remote fishing resorts of Nootka Sound, where Captain Cook made contact with West Coast natives in 1778. A converted minesweeper runs day-trips to Nootka and Kyuquot sounds.

Special events
Gold River Days (June)

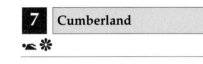

7 Cumberland

The small town of Cumberland (pop. 2,200) is quiet now, but in the early years of this century it bustled with merchants and miners and hummed with intrigue.

The main street, lined with elegant 19th-century buildings, leads to the Cumberland Museum in the Cumberland Cultural Centre. The museum's exhibits tell the town's coal-mining history and of the disastrous fire that burned down whole blocks of houses. They include photographs of its Japanese communities, and a walk-through model of a coal mine. *Open daily, mid-May to mid-October, and Monday to Saturday, mid-October to early May, from 9 am to 5 pm.*

During the 1920s, Cumberland had 10 coal mines and a population of 15,000, made up of segregated communities of blacks, British, Chinese, Italians, and Japanese. The last mine locked its gates in 1966, and most of the town's inhabitants drifted away. The only Chinatown cabin still standing can be seen a mile out of town, on the road to Comox Lake, a glacier-fed stretch of water perfect for a swim.

Every year, on Miners' Memorial Day in June, labor movement representatives come to Cumberland to visit the grave of Albert "Ginger" Goodwin, a union activist. He had been fighting to improve hazardous mine conditions when, in 1918, he was suddenly conscripted into the army. Sensing a government trap, he headed for the Cumberland Hills. Teams of police set off to find him. Among them was bounty-hunter Daniel Campbell, who shot Goodwin to death. Goodwin's funeral procession in Cumberland stretched more than a kilometre, and his death prompted the day-long Vancouver General Strike.

Special events
Empire Days (May)
Miners' Memorial Day (June)
Comax Lake Days (July)

8 Denman and Hornby Islands

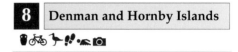

Most visitors taking the ferry from Buckley Bay on Vancouver Island stream across Denman Island to catch another ferry to Hornby Island. However, while Denman's beaches are less spectacular or sandy than Hornby's, they are quieter and offer excellent beachcombing.

Beachcombers search for seashore souvenirs at Whaling Station Bay, Hornby Island.

At Boyle Point Provincial Park, for example, a short hike can yield a bounty of clams and oysters. A wooded track leads to the rocks and their treasure. A license is not needed to take shellfish for your own use, but there are daily limits. And do not pick from the well-marked commercial spots.

Sea lions frequent the area in February, when massive schools of herring gather to spawn in Lambert Channel, between Denman and Hornby islands. The huge mammals, drawn by the appetizing herring, themselves become a food source for killer whales. Occasionally, visitors can witness dramatic encounters of predator and prey.

Cycling can be an excellent way to see both islands. Traffic is light, most roads are paved, and the climate is mild. Both islands have cycle shops which rent or repair cycles. For mountain bike enthusiasts, several trails lead to the top of Hornby's Mount Geoffrey.

On Hornby, there are hiking trails up the mountain from the ferry slip to Ford's Cove. And there is a 4-km loop around Helliwell Park, which leads from deep Douglas fir woods to the top of south-facing black cliffs. Hundreds of eagles, cormorants, gulls, great blue herons, and dozens of species of ducks feed, mate, and nest there.

Hornby's beaches are excellent for children, with gradual sloping beaches and almost no undertow. On the beach west of Tralee Point, ancient Indian petroglyphs are carved into the rock, and fossils can be found off Phipps Point. Another natural wonder is the myriad reefs off Ford's Cove, a favorite with scuba divers. Kayak rentals and tours of some of Hornby's marine areas are available year-round.

If the day is too cool for the beach, jaunting from artist's studio to studio can make a memorable day on either of the two islands. There are potters, sculptors, carvers, basket weavers, jewellers, and producers of stained glass.

Special events
Hornby Festival of the Performing Arts
(August)

9 Ucluelet

At the Western entrance to Barkley Sound is the village of Ucluelet (pop. 1,500), home to the third largest commercial fishing fleet in British Columbia. It was built around a natural harbor and in fact "Ucluelet" is a native word meaning "safe harbor." The community has been connected by road to the rest of Vancouver Island only since 1959, when the Port Alberni-Ucluelet Highway was completed.

A colorful landmark in the village is a floating fishing resort called the *Canadian Princess*, a 70-m former hydrographic survey ship, which plied the coast for 43 years before being berthed on Peninsula Avenue in 1977. She now heads a fleet of 13-m powerboats which carry thousands of visitors to the fishing grounds each year.

At the foot of Main Street is the first store built in Ucluelet, in 1908. It now houses a souvenir and stationery shop,

but its floor, shelving, and front counter are original.

At the end of Peninsula Road is Amphitrite Point lighthouse station, around which tours are conducted during the summer. It consists of a vessel traffic monitoring system, the Tofino Coast Guard Radio Station, and an Emergency Response Building, which was completed following a tragic oil spill on the coast in 1989.

The many beautiful flower gardens in the village were inspired by Scottish horticulturist George Fraser, who settled in the village in the 1800s and cleared a garden plot out of the coastal rain forest to plant rhododendrons, azaleas, heathers and various hybrids.

As Fraser gained world fame, his garden on the banks of Ucluelet inlet became a frequent stopover for steamer passengers. In 1991, the village dedicated a small garden on Peninsula Drive to his memory.

Ucluelet was a bustling sealing centre before the turn of the century, and has since prospered as a logging and fishing community. Sports fishermen are attracted to the rich fishing grounds there, which yield salmon, cod, halibut, red snapper, and hake. Ucluelet also offers naturalists whale-watching and nature cruises, and excellent scuba diving.

> **Special events**
> Whale Fest (March)
> Pacific Rim Music Festival (July)
> Ukee Days (August)

10   Tofino

The beaches of the wild, open Pacific flank Tofino (pop. 1,100) on one side, the numerous islands and waterways of Clayoquot Sound on the other. In the midst of this wilderness, Tofino is a little beacon of civilization. It has several art galleries and restaurants. Its waterfront bustles with commercial boats unloading salmon, shrimp and her-

The glory of a perfect Pacific day greets the fishing vessels tied up at Tofino's docks.

ring. Whale-watching zodiacs and fishing charters put out to sea from here. It is also a base from which to explore nearby sites.

Hot Springs Cove is at the entrance to Sidney Inlet, about 40 km from Tofino by boat. It is a 20-minute hike from the cove to the hot springs through forest on well-maintained cedar walkways. The hot spring water, which can reach a comfortable 50⁰C, tumbles down a 3.5-m waterfall into a series of small pools before reaching the sea.

Vargas Island, only 20 minutes by charter boat from Tofino, is covered with largely unspoiled rain forest and edged with remote, white beaches, some of which face the open Pacific. It offers excellent hiking, beachcombing, and wilderness camping.

The view from downtown Tofino across the waters of Browning Passage is dominated by the green and lush Meares Island and its twin peaks, Lone

Pacific Rim

Where roaring surf meets soundless rain forest on the west coast of Vancouver Island, the contrasts can be quite eerie. This is Pacific Rim National Park. Inside the tightly woven barrier of trees, silence engulfs everyhing, including the massive evergreens whose tops soar out of sight.

Pacific Rim, established in May 1970, encompasses three separate land-and-sea sections. The northernmost section is Long Beach, an 11-km strip of off-white, hard-packed sand with a backdrop of evergreen forest. It can be reached by Highway 4 from Port Alberni. About 20 km southeast of Long Beach, the Broken Group Islands, a cluster of some 100 rocky isles in Barkley Sound, form the second section. The MV *Lady Rose* sails from Port Alberni to the islands, and to Ucluelet and Bamfield on the mainland to the north and south of Barkley Sound. The third section, the 77-km-long West Coast Trail, stretches between Bamfield and Port Renfrew, at the mouth of the Strait of Juan de Fuca. An unrestricted logging road from Port Alberni and a restricted one from Lake Cowichan lead to Bamfield. It is advisable to check with the logging company for time restrictions on the second road.

The West Coast Trail was cut between 1907 and 1912, and cabins were constructed along it equipped with telephones, as havens for sailors shipwrecked in the treacherous Strait of Juan de Fuca. Without the trail and the cabin refuges, those who survived shipwreck died from exposure, unable to penetrate the rain forest. The trail is accessible from Bamfield or Port Renfrew, and runs southeast for about 77 km. It takes roughly a week to complete and is recommended for experienced hikers only, from May 1 to October 1. Reservations are required and there is a fee for hikers. Visitors who wish for a taste of the trail without walking its length can take a short walk to the trailhead at Brady Beach or along the trail to Topaltos Bay near Cape Beale.

The three forests

Long Beach and the West Coast Trail are lined with three distinct ribbons of forest. Closest to the ocean are stands of Sit-

Seagulls crowd a wave-battered beach on the West Coast Trail, Pacific Rim.

ka spruce, with twisted boughs and bent trunks that attest to the strength of the buffeting winter storms, and the stamina of the trees themselves. Somewhat shorter trees signal the beginning of the second ribbon, shore pine bog. The trees grow in clumps, like heads of cauliflower, on stagnant, moss-covered bogs at least 10,000 years old, and in places 9 m deep. In the third ribbon, the trees are so dense that the canopy virtually blots out the sun and almost no light reaches the forest floor. The most common tree is western hemlock, although the largest and oldest species is western red cedar. A 1,000-year-old specimen measures 19 m around; its crown is 43 m in the air. Eight hiking trails in the Long Beach area, ranging from less than 1 km to 5 km in length, take walkers into this dense, dark world.

Few animals are visible in this dank, murky habitat. There are garter snakes that slither silently, lungless salamanders that breathe through their skins, and the small Pacific tree frog. Small animals of the undergrowth—red squirrels, mink, martens, and raccoons—find adequate sustenance, but they are few in number and make little noise. There are not even many large mammals under the rain forest's canopy, apart from black-tailed deer, which graze in glades among Sitka spruce. This absence is partly due to the forest's density, and partly due to the Strait of Georgia: its strong, chilly currents have deterred some species, such as chipmunks and moose, from crossing from the mainland. A few large species, however, did manage to swim across to Vancouver Island, and reach park environs. The park's black bears are larger than their mainland counterparts; their coats are pure black—with none of the brown or cinnamon tints found elsewhere. And cougars inhabit the dark rain forest undergrowth. But these solitary felines are rarely seen.

A seashore circus

A fascinating assortment of creatures lives in the park's waters. In the intertidal areas along the rocky shoreline, algae and plankton tint the rocks with hues of red and brown. As the tide ebbs, huge boulders emerge with clusters of barnacles, limpets, and mussels clinging to them. In the larger tide-pools, darting sculpins mingle with those vagabonds of the crustacean world, the hermit crabs, which inhabit discarded shells rather than grow their own covering. There are more than 20 different sea stars or starfish here, more than anywhere else in the North Pacific.

Spiny sea urchins, colorful sea anemones, and sea slugs with brilliant orange, yellow, and white skin, brighten the bottom of Barkley Sound. Several octopus species can also be found. The largest—and the largest in the world—is *Octopus dofleini*, known commonly as the giant Pacific octopus. When spread like a spider, it can measure as much as 6 m across. However, most specimens are only about half that size.

This range of marine creatures provides a well-stocked larder for many sea mammals, which can be seen from the shore or a boat. On Sea Lion Rocks, off the shore of Long Beach, northern sea lions bask, their growls rivaling the surf in decibel level. In sheltered Barkley Sound, harbor seals poke their whiskered heads above the surface to scan for predators—in particular their deadly enemy, the killer whale.

The most impressive animal drawn to this food supply, and the one that attracts throngs of visitors during the spring, is the Pacific gray whale—a 14-m giant. The park is a stopover between the whales' summer feeding grounds in Arctic waters and their winter calving grounds off Mexico. But a small number, perhaps 50, remains in the area all summer, in Clayoquot Sound, joining southbound pods in the fall. The whales can be seen from

A cluster of colorful sea anemones, Pacific Rim

the shore or from a boat—whale-watching excursions leave from Tofino and Ucluelet.

Of the approximately 250 species of birds spotted in the park, half are water birds. Thousands of plovers, sandpipers, and turnstones stalk the beaches and tide pools for their invertebrate meals. Myriad gulls and diving ducks gather in April to feed on the spawning herring. Wintering elsewhere and moving into the park to breed are the penguinlike divers, with wonderful names such as ancient murrelet and rhinoceros auklet, which approach land only between dusk and dawn. Bald eagles, too, favor the park, scouting the coast for crabs and cast-up fish. Ever the opportunists, they scavenge seal and sea lion corpses, when they are not robbing ospreys of their hard-won meals.

PARK INFORMATION

Visitors' centres: *For Long Beach, on Highway 4 just inside the park boundary. For the West Coast Trail, at Pachena Bay, south of Bamfield.*
Camping: *At Long Beach, the year-round Green Point campground with facilities offers 94 sites. A primitive walk-in campground, at the end of 1.2-km Schooner Trail at Long Beach's north end, has 100 sites and is open year-round. Both operate on a first-come first-serve basis. The maximum stay is seven days. In the Broken Group Islands, there are designated sites on eight islands. Campgrounds on Gibraltar, Dodd and Willis islands, where the waters are protected, are recommended for novice boaters.*
Activities: *At Long Beach, fishing and surf-fishing, scuba diving, hiking and nature walks , whale-watching. Wickaninnish Centre offers an interpretive program. The Broken Group Islands, accessible by boat only, offers anchorages for large vessels. The inner channels of the islands are suitable for canoes and kayaks.*

Cone and Mount Colnett. The old-growth forest of Meares Island, laced with hiking trails and abundant with wildlife, was declared a Tribal Park in 1984 by Clayoquot and Ahousaht native bands. This was done to prevent it from being logged, and in recognition of the fact that the Clayoquot Sound forests are only one of three old-growth temperate rain forests left in the world. The other two are in New Zealand and Chile. Even so, the future of the island's forests is still uncertain.

On Meares Island, 8 km up the eastern shore of Lemmens Inlet, which almost divides the island in two, are the remains of Fort Defiance. It was the winter quarters of Capt. Robert Gray, the first American to circumnavigate the globe. He built his 14-m sloop there, during the winter of 1791-92. The ruins were declared a protected archaeological site in 1967.

Special events
Whale Fest (March)
Clayoquot Days (August)
Pacific Rim Music Festival (July)

11 Bamfield

An inlet along the south coast of Barkley Sound splits the community of Bamfield (pop. 200) into two. It is linked only by a boardwalk, which hugs the shoreline. East-side residents can easily drive out of the village, but west-side residents must use boats to reach their cars parked on the east side. The west side is a tranquil West Coast Venice, with no traffic.

Before 1900, Bamfield was an Indian village. Ruins of an ancient Ohiaht village still remain and Execution Rock, off Second Beach, is where the Ohiahts threw invading enemies over the cliffs to their deaths.

Ocean waters skim the sand and stones of Brady's Beach at Bamfield, near Pacific Rim's rugged West Coast Trail.

Today, Bamfield is the northern access point for the rugged West Coast Trail, which runs through part of the Pacific Rim National Park. The path was hacked out of the wilderness in 1906 after 126 passengers drowned when the SS *Valencia* was wrecked off the rocky shore. The path, called the Life-Saving Trail, was developed so that those whose ships had sunk could find their way back from this "graveyard of the Pacific." Each year, more than 4,000 visitors walk the 77-km trail from Port Renfrew to Bamfield.

Visitors to Bamfield can leave their vehicles in Port Alberni and travel to the community aboard the MV *Lady Rose*. Most summertime visitors, however, drive along the gravel logging road from Port Alberni, a 93-km drive that takes about two hours.

Bamfield is a popular destination for sports fishermen hoping to catch trophy-sized fish in Barkley Sound. It also offers bird- and whale-watching, canoeing, sailing and kayaking.

The Bamfield Marine Station's biological laboratories were originally the terminus for a trans-Pacific submarine cable system, which linked all the Commonwealth countries. Every weekend in summer, the Marine Station offers tours of its laboratories. The MacMillan laboratory contains the 8-m-long skeleton of a mighty gray whale.

Special events
Annual Fire Week (July)
Bamfield Marine Research Station
Open House (October)

---

12 Gabriola Island

The ferry from Nanaimo takes you to Gabriola Island (pop. 3,500) in the Strait of Georgia. Spanish settlers are said to have named the island, from the word *gaviola*, meaning "seagull." They left their mark in some of the island's place-names, too, such as Des-canso Bay. This is where the ferry docks. The island can be toured along the circular South Road, which in the north becomes North Road.

The island's sandy beaches are perfect for picnicking and watching shore life. Brickyard Beach, for example (so named for the brick fragments that wash up on the beach from a factory that operated there in the early part of the century), is a favorite feeding spot for water birds. And seals can be seen in the narrows between Gabriola and Mudge islands.

Gabriola has inherited some fascinating petroglyphs from the Coast Salish Indians that used to live there. At Degnen Bay, a petroglyph of a marine creature is visible at the far end of the bay when tides are low. It is a stone carving, depicting "spirit" faces.

At Lock Bay in the north, Sandwell Provincial Park has a series of worn petroglyphs etched in large rocks at the high tide line. Kitchen refuse, or middens, containing oyster and clam shells left over from Indian feasts, can also be found in Lock Bay.

Gabriola also has some incredible sandstone formations carved in the cliffs by the wind and waves. At Drumbeg Provincial Park, there are unusual rock formations, including spherical holes in the sandstone on the beach. Just 3 km from the turnoff to Drumbeg, look out for the solid-log St. Martin's Church of the Anglican/Catholic Eucharist, on the left-hand side of the road.

Off North Road, a public path between houses leads to the island's northernmost tip and the Malaspina Galleries. This is a strip of sandstone, 90-m-long and 4-m-high, eroded in the shape of giant waves, overhung by a few stunted trees.

Cyclists might consider this trip, since there are only a few steep hills to conquer.

Special events
Salmon Barbecue (August)

---

13 Lake Cowichan

The tall stands of trees that surround the town of Lake Cowichan (pop. 2,500) almost shout their importance to its existence. Forestry has sustained the community for almost one hundred years, since it was first settled in 1887. It still does, although there is only one mill left, at Youbou, 16 km west of Lake Cowichan.

In the middle of the village is Saywell Park. It overlooks the lake and has picnic areas, but also contains the Kaatza Station Museum. The museum is housed in the E & N Railway station, built in 1913, and has exhibits from the community's past such as a 1918 caboose, and a display on the West Coast pioneer days. *Open daily, mid-May to Thanksgiving, from 9 am to 4 pm; Thanksgiving to mid-May, except Monday, from 1 pm to 4 pm.*

A Gulf Islands car ferry slips past the forested islands in the peaceful Strait of Georgia.

Roads to explore: Nurseries, wildflowers, and satellites

Distance: 80 km / 50 mi

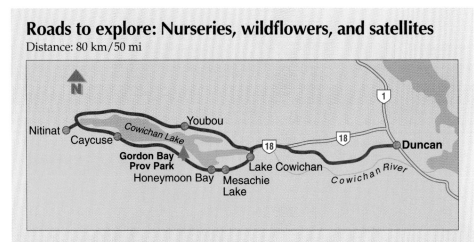

The village of Lake Cowichan is the start of a drive on Highway 18, which circles the sparkling lake with the same name.
● Drive along the waterfront South Shore Road southwest of the village for 5 km, to Mesachie Lake, and the Lake Cowichan Research Station. The station researches improved strains of trees for the coastal forests. Call ahead for guided tours. There are a number of demonstration forests on Highway 18, with trees at every stage of growth, from seedlings in newly planted areas to sturdy adult Douglas firs. Since the Lake Cowichan region is logging country, drivers should travel with care: giant logging trucks use this road, too.
● Just a few kilometres farther on is the sawmill settlement of Honeymoon Bay, named after a landowner who left town in the late 1800s to find a bride. He never returned, but the name stuck. The paved road stops here; the recommended speed limit on the gravel road is 50 km/h.
● Beyond Honeymoon Bay are the Marsh Meadows Golf Course and Gordon Bay Provincial Park. Just less than 1 km farther on is a wildflower reserve with typical flowers of a West Coast rain forest.
● At Caycuse is the BC Forest Products campsite, where you can go hiking, camping, fishing, and boating. Beyond Caycuse, the road winds and becomes mountainous as it curves around the western edge of the lake and travels along the northern shore.
● About 16 km before Lake Cowichan village, at Youbou, is the only sawmill in the lake area that still works. Tours are available in summer. Near Lake Cowichan village is the Teleglobe Canada Satellite Earth Station. Tours are sometimes available, and the giant satellites can be seen in the compound.
● North of Lake Cowichan village is historic Meade Creek, where gold was first found in the 1800s. Today, visitors can try their luck and pan for gold in the creek's waters.

Putting at Marsh Meadows Golf Course, Honeymoon Bay

Next to the museum is the Bell Tower School, built in 1925. Also in Saywell Park is the Fletcher Challenge weir, built in 1957 to supply a local pulp and paper plant with water. The company runs free summer tours of its nearby logging operations.

A walk through the village will take you past rows of small shops with two-story false fronts that make them look bigger than they are. Across the green bridge that spans the river is the Riverside Hotel, rebuilt in 1929, once an exclusive retreat for wealthy hunters and fishermen.

Special events

Lake Days (June)

Youbou Regatta Days (August)

---

14 Salt Spring Island

Salt water trickling from a small hill at the north end of this island provoked Hudson's Bay officials to name it "Salt Spring" in the 1850s.

Travelers from Vancouver Island land at Fulford Harbor. From there they can go to Ruckle Park, where there are exceptional views of the Strait of Georgia and walks along the rocky shoreline. Henry Ruckle's farmhouse, built in the 1870s, can be seen in the valley just beyond the park entrance. It is not open to the public.

The Burgoyne Valley, on the arterial road linking Fulford and Ganges, is dotted with historic farmhouses and churches. The valley was settled by the Akerman family in the mid-1860s. The family-owned log-house museum, on the right side of the road just past the Fulford Community Hall, has a collection of Coast Salish Indian artifacts. *Open weekdays during the summer, 1 pm to 4 pm.*

Woods, fields, and a patch of sweet peas sum up the rustic appeal of Salt Spring Island.

The jagged cliff that looms above Burgoyne Bay is Mount Maxwell. The mountaintop is accessible from Cranberry Road, near Ganges, but use a four-wheel drive in winter. The peak has spectacular views of Burgoyne Valley and Vancouver Island.

Ganges, the island's main commercial centre, was named after the flagship of the Royal Navy's Pacific Squadron (1857-60). It has several galleries and craft shops, and hosts the weekly Saturday Farmers' Market in the centrally located Centennial Park. Handcrafted goods are for sale and local musicians provide lively performances.

From a terminal in Vesuvius, the island's other commercial centre, the Vesuvius-Crofton ferry links travelers with the Duncan area of Vancouver Island. Just before the terminal is Sunset Drive, which winds through farmlands around the north end of the island. Seashore-hugging North Beach Road is another popular scenic drive.

The performing and creative arts are well represented throughout the year. There are numerous arts and craft shops on Salt Spring Island, which is well-known for its artists and artisans. Local theatrical groups keep entertainment alive year-round.

Special events

Round the Island Race (May)

Sea Capers (mid-June)

Fulford Day (mid-August)

Fall Fair (late September)

Festival of Lights
(late November)

15 Galiano Island

🎒⛺🚴⛴🛶📷

Galiano Island's evergreen forests, clamshell beaches, and abundant wildlife must look much as they did when Spanish explorer Dionisio Alcala Galiano landed there in 1792. Galiano is said to be the most scenic of the Gulf Islands.

Cyclists stop for a picnic beside a vivid mural outside a store on Galiano Island.

On the eastern rim of British Columbia's Gulf Islands, the island stretches northwest for more than 26 km along the western edge of the Strait of Georgia. Despite its length, its total land area is only 57 km²—it is just over 3 km across at its widest point. Most of Galiano's 900 residents live on the south end, close to the B.C. Ferry Terminal at Sturdies Bay. As the first stop on the ferry from Tsawwassen to the Gulf Islands, Galiano is relatively easy to reach from the mainland.

Protected from Pacific rains by Salt Spring and Vancouver islands, Galiano is the driest of the Gulf Islands. Water can be scarce, so if you come for just a day, bring your own drinking water. Fire is always a problem, and campfires are allowed only in designated areas of Montague Harbor Marine Park.

There are several good fishing spots in Galiano waters, particularly in Active Pass, between Galiano and Mayne islands, and Porlier Pass, between Galiano and Valdes islands. The scuba diving is excellent, and there are numerous opportunities to see bald eagles, harbor seals and, occasionally, killer whales.

At the far end of the island is Dionisio Point Provincial Park on Coon Bay, reached along a lane. It goes through a high, reforested area with impressive views across the Strait of Georgia to the mainland. The lane ends at a parking lot on Dionisio Point. From here, visitors can hike through a mature forest of cedar, fir, and arbutus, or walk the beaches along the Strait of Georgia and Porlier Pass.

Along Porlier Pass Road, there are superb views of Trincomali Channel, Salt Spring and nearby smaller islands, with the mountains of Vancouver

Island beyond. Galleries and craft shops are scattered along the road.

In south Galiano is Montague Harbor Marine Park, with camping facilities, and there is a spectacular view of Active Pass from Galiano Bluffs.

Special events
Strawberry Tea (June)
Galiano Weavers Exhibit and Sale (July and November)
North Galiano Jamboree (early July)
Artists' Guild Exhibition and Sale (July)
Poetry Festival (July)
Blackberry Festival (October)

16 Pender Island

No one is sure anymore if Pender Island is one island or two, but there is no doubt that it started out as one. In 1903, when the shortest route between Pender's east and west side was by portaging over a rocky isthmus, is-

A deer peers out of the grass on Mayne Island, the most secluded of the Gulf Islands.

landers had the government dig a channel across the isthmus, creating two islands and making it easier to sail from one to the other. By 1950, however, cars were more common, so the government built a bridge and reconnected the Penders.

Pender (pop. 1,400) is a delightful place to visit, with a Mediterranean climate (40 to 55 cm of rain a year), many beaches, scenic bays and inlets, rolling valleys and open country.

North Pender is the most populated part of the island and is where the ferry from Vancouver Island docks, at Otter Bay. Its numerous small bays and coves are excellent for boating and fishing, and there is plenty of access to the sea for canoeists and kayakers. There is a 9-hole golf course, and the area offers many forest hikes and seaside walks. In summer, tours are conducted around a Salish Indian archaeological site, on the north side of the bridge.

Just over the bridge, on South Pender, is a public beach (most of the beaches on South Pender are privately owned). From Gowlland Point there are splendid views of Boundary Pass,

the American San Juan Islands, and Mount Baker in Washington State. Killer whales are occasionally spotted in the offshore waters.

The highest point on Pender Island is Mount Norman, which can be climbed, although in places it is quite steep. From the top you look over Bedwell Harbor to Boundary Pass, the San Juans, and the Strait of Juan de Fuca, where a steady stream of ships and tankers passes over the horizon.

Special events
Salmon BBQ and Fish Derby (July)
Pender Yacht Race (August)
Fall Fair (August)
Weavers' Sale (late November)

17 Mayne Island

Midway between Vancouver and Victoria is Mayne Island (pop. 781), where scenic roads pass madrona and fir-covered crags, promontories and sandy beaches.

The ferry to the island docks in Village Bay, near Miner's Bay, the main settlement on the island and one of the oldest settlements on any of the Gulf Islands. Vancouver miners stopped here on their way to the Fraser River goldfields across the Strait of Georgia, in 1855, giving the settlement its present name.

Miner's Bay is a little less raucous today, but it still has remnants of its past: a 100-year-old hotel; St. Mary Magdalene Church, built in 1896; a jail dating from 1893; and a community centre built in 1899. The jail, now the Mayne Museum, houses pictures and memorabilia of island life. *Open July and August, Friday, Saturday, and Sunday, from 11 am to 3 pm.*

From Miner's Bay, the Georgina Point Road travels along the seashore to Georgina Point Lighthouse, built in 1885. It has spectacular views of Active Pass and Strait of Georgia.

The open portal of the departing car ferry theatrically frames the sunset and the twinkling lights of the Mayne Island terminal.

The best beach is at Campbell Bay. The path that leads to it is about 2 km from the Fernhill Road turnoff. On Fernhill Road is Fernhill Lodge, a hotel with rooms decorated in Moroccan, Jacobean, Oriental, and other styles. In summer, the lodge serves "historical" dinners based on menus from second-century Rome to Victorian England.

Visitors interested in wildlife and scenery should not miss two island walks. The first, Helen Point, starts 1 km from the ferry terminal. After a leisurely hour and a half, the trail opens onto a moss-covered point which is perfect for picnicking or watching the seals, sea lions, and bald eagles. The whole peninsula is an Indian reserve and visitors must keep to the paths and leave no litter.

The second walk starts 600 m east of the Helen Point Trail. This gravel road on the south side is a private access road to Mount Parke. Leave the car on the main road and walk the 3 km to the summit. The spectacular views from the top of Mount Parke are worth the climb.

Special events
Fall Fair and Parade (mid-August)

Springwater Salmon Derby
(late August)

Salmon Barbecue (early September)

Arts and Crafts Fair (mid-November)

AROUND VANCOUVER

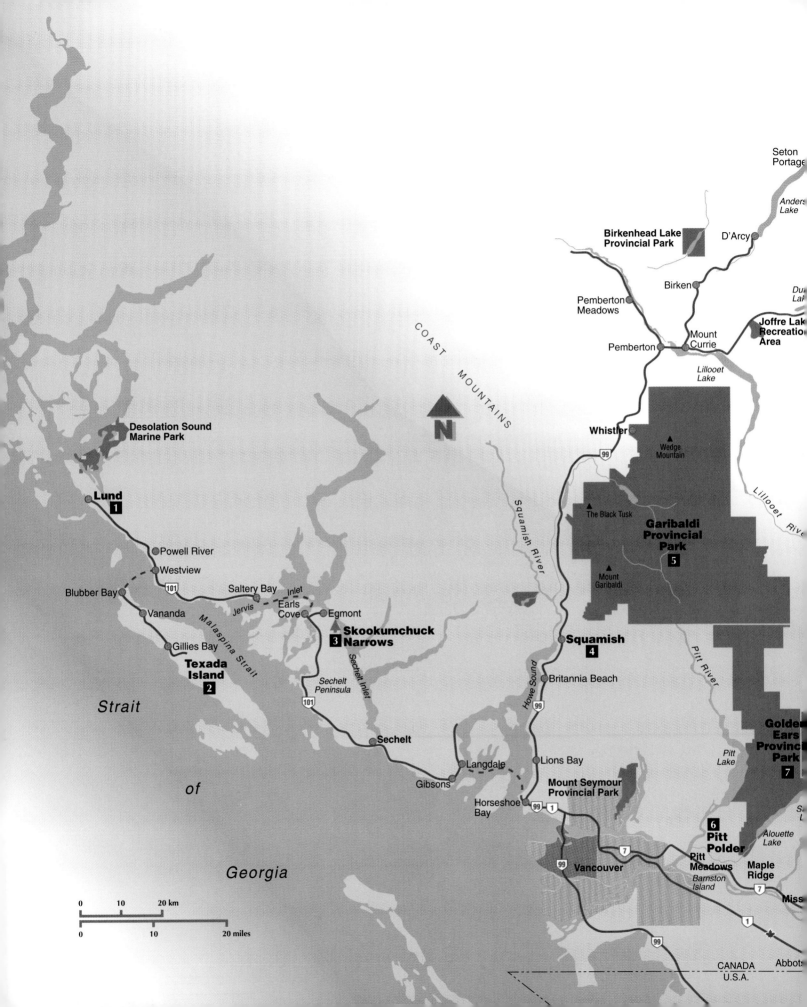

Seton
Portage

Anders
Lake

Birkenhead Lake
Provincial Park

D'Arcy

Birken

Du
Lak

Pemberton
Meadows

Mount
Currie

Joffre Lake
Recreation
Area

Pemberton

Lillooet
Lake

COAST MOUNTAINS

N

Whistler

99

Wedge
Mountain

Lillooet River

Desolation Sound
Marine Park

The Black Tusk

Garibaldi
Provincial Park

5

Lund
1

▲ Powell River

Westview

101

Saltery Bay

Inlet

Blubber Bay

Jervis

Earls
Cove

Egmont

Mount
Garibaldi

Vananda

Malaspina Strait

▲ **Skookumchuck**
3 Narrows

Squamish
4

Gillies Bay

Texada
Island
2

Sechelt
Peninsula

Sechelt Inlet

Britannia Beach

Pitt River

Pitt
Lake

Strait

101

Howe Sound

99

Golde
Ears
Provinc
Park

7

of

Sechelt

Lions Bay

Langdale

Gibsons

Horseshoe
Bay

99 1

Mount Seymour
Provincial Park

Alouette
Lake

6
Pitt
Polder

Georgia

99

Vancouver

7

Pitt
Meadows

Barnston
Island

Maple
Ridge

7

Miss

0   10   20 km

0   10   20 miles

1

CANADA
U.S.A.

99

Abbots

Seton
Lake

Lillooet

12

osh River

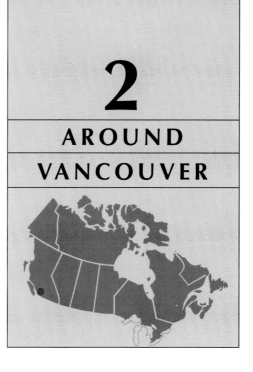

2

AROUND
VANCOUVER

Places to see
Desolation Sound
Provincial Marine Park
Lund
Texada Island
Skookumchuck Narrows
Squamish
Garibaldi Provincial Park
Pitt Polder
Golden Ears Provincial Park
Sasquatch Provincial Park
Barnston Island
Cultus Lake Provincial Park
Hope
Coquihalla Canyon Recreational Area:
Othello/Quintette tunnels
Manning Provincial Park

Roads to explore
Pemberton to D'Arcy
Pemberton to Lillooet
Along the Chilliwack River valley

Previous pages:
Lower Joffre Lake, Joffre Lakes Recreation Area,
just off the Duffey Lake Road,
between Pemberton and Lillooet

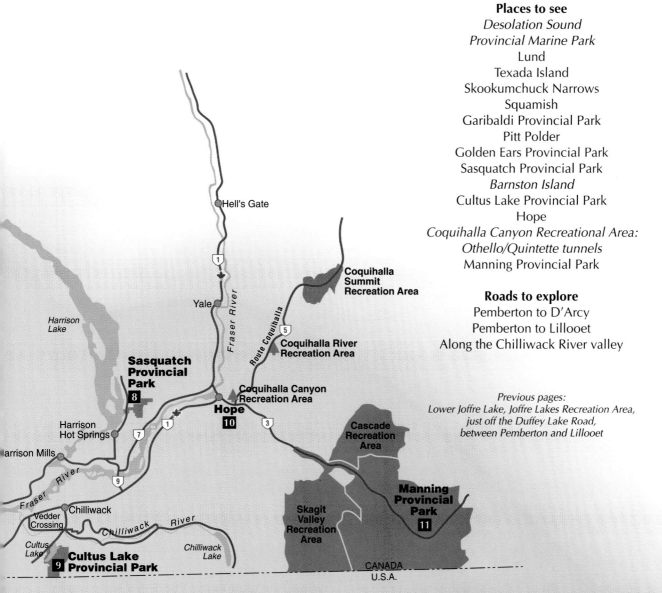

Hell's Gate

1

**Coquihalla
Summit
Recreation Area**

Yale

Fraser River

Route Coquihalla

5

**Coquihalla River
Recreation Area**

Harrison
Lake

**Sasquatch
Provincial
Park**

8

**Coquihalla Canyon
Recreation Area**

Hope

10

3

1

Harrison
Hot Springs

7

**Cascade
Recreation
Area**

arrison Mills

Fraser River

9

Chilliwack

Vedder
Crossing

Chilliwack River

**Manning
Provincial
Park**

11

Cultus
Lake

**Cultus Lake
Provincial Park**

9

Chilliwack
Lake

**Skagit
Valley
Recreation
Area**

CANADA
U.S.A.

A BOATER'S PARADISE IN A PARK OF SHELTERED BAYS

Despite its forbidding name, Desolation Sound, situated north of Lund on the east side of Malaspina Peninsula, is a place of beauty. It is one of the channels of the Pacific that reach into British Columbia's mountainous mainland. The 5,600-ha Desolation Sound Provincial Marine Park protects more than 60 km of its southern shore. The park's waterways are accessible by pleasure craft or chartered boat from Lund or Powell River.

Malaspina Peninsula shelters Desolation Sound from the winds off the Strait of Georgia. The sheltered bays and inlets offer havens for boaters. Popular anchorages include Grace Harbour, Tenedos Bay (in the heart of the park), and Prideaux Haven (on its northwest extremity). Here, swimmers plunge into waters warmed to 24°C by the summer sun. Malaspina Inlet, Tenedos Bay, and the open waters of the sound provide catches of chinook and coho salmon.

Although the park is a boater's paradise, its interior of falls, lakes, and mountains (some more than 2,400 m high) is an imposing setting for camping, hiking, and freshwater fishing. A rewarding combination of these three activities can be found on the hiking trail leading from Tenedos Bay to Unwin Lake (the park's largest inland freshwater lake).

A blue heron, denizen of the waters of Desolation Sound

Desolation Sound has a rich diversity of wild life. Islets such as Sky Pilot Rock in Otter Bay sustain crowded seal rookeries. Blue floats on Malaspina and Lancelot inlets mark commercial oyster beds. Red sea cucumbers and pale crabs grow in profusion alongside oysters at Theodosia Inlet. In winter, visitors come here at night to unearth littleneck and manilla clams from beaches. (This is the only time of year the tide retreats far enough to reveal their hideways.) The sound is also a haven for bald eagles, blue herons, Canada geese, kingfishers, and other birds.

At sunset, a flotilla of cruisers at Lund awaits another day of deep-sea fishing and diving.

1 Lund

Highway 101—the longest stretch of road in North and South America—begins in Puerto Monte, Chile, and ends at the fishing village of Lund (pop. 350). As the village comes into view at the end of the road, you pass houses with overgrown fruit trees and an aged bus slumped in someone's yard.

Lund is typical of many coastal communities: fishing vessels bob alongside sleek pleasure craft tied up at the government dock, and there are signs everywhere for boat rentals, charters, and salvage. Behind a marine engine shop, boat ways can take ships up to 10 m long out of the water for repairs. It is not uncommon to see a fishing boat or tug under construction. At the end of the boardwalk is a coffeehouse and studio, built on pilings. The wood-carving studio is open to visitors during the summer.

The old hotel building, with an air of lapsed gentility, dates from 1911. It stands on the north shore of Lund harbor, facing the Strait of Georgia and Savary Island. The village post office is run from the hotel lobby. Back in the hotel's heyday, Union Steamships stopped twice a week at the hotel, and the bar was frequented by fishermen and loggers from Desolation Sound. In those days, the general store sold everything from sewing needles to log-boom chains. At the present-day store, attached to the hotel, you can find basic provisions as well as axes and other essentials for roughing it outdoors.

Several firms offer rentals and charters for fishing, scuba diving, and sightseeing tours to local destinations such as Desolation Sound Marine Park on the far side of the Malaspina Peninsula. In summer, a water-taxi service runs to nearby Savary Island, with its white sandy beaches.

Special events
Lund Days (August)
Lund Bluegrass Festival (mid-August)

2 Texada Island

Just off the mainland across Malaspina Strait, the blue silhouette of Texada Island rises from the waters of the Strait of Georgia. Some 48 km long and 8 km wide, Texada is the largest and most northerly of the Gulf Islands.

A ferry leaves from the marina at Powell River for the north end of the island about every hour and a half, taking only 20 minutes to cross Malaspina Strait. Despite this close connection, Texada is a remote and rugged place. Travelers on the island's logging roads are advised to use sturdy vehicles.

The uninhabited east side of Texada rises steeply from the Malaspina Strait. The shoreline reveals a layered fringe of balsam and Douglas fir, cedar, spruce and west coast maple, broken by occasional logging cuts. Underneath the rocky ground run rich veins of copper, gold, iron, and marble.

Through the years, many companies have mined Texada. It is still possible to stumble on mining relics, such as the rock crusher near one of the island's abandoned quarries in the north, with bits of ore rusted into its gears.

There are three active mining operations left. In Vananda, the biggest community on the island, reminders of the past linger on in street signs for Copper Queen Street and Smelter Avenue. In its heyday, this community boasted the largest opera house north of San Francisco.

On the island's west side is a residential and summer-cottage area at Gillies Bay, with a general store and art studios, and a stretch of sandy beach at low tide. Shelter Point Regional Park, south of Gillies Bay, is a picnic and camping spot with a pebbly beach and a view of Vancouver Island's mountains across the Strait of Georgia.

3 Skookumchuck Narrows

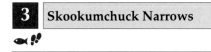

Four times a day, at the 200-m-wide entrance to landlocked Sechelt Inlet, tides squeeze through Skookumchuck Narrows to create one of the largest saltwater rapids in the Pacific. Skookumchuck is Chinook for "turbulent water" or "rapid torrent."

During the biggest tidal changes, waves rise a metre high, huge whirl-pools form, and a wall of water 2 m high charges through the rapids at a speed of 30 km/h. There are only about 15 minutes of relatively slack water between tide changes. Tales of boats and log booms lost to the rapids are legion.

The best views of the rapids are from 123-ha Skookumchuck Narrows Provincial Park. Access is from the road just north of Egmont and along a 4-km trail through magnificent towering forest dappled with filtered sunlight.

The hike along the western edge of the Narrows takes an hour and leads to viewing spots at Roland Point and Narrows Point. There, sitting on the gently sloping rock, you may glimpse sunfish darting in the clear water, or see a seal challenging the rapids at high tide.

Inexperienced boaters are advised not to venture into the Narrows.

4 Squamish

Two heights of land dominate the town of Squamish (pop. 12,000)—Mount Garibaldi to the northeast, and the Stawamus Chief to the southwest. At 610 m, the Stawamus Chief is one of the largest granite monoliths in the world. Its jagged outline resembles the profile of a sleeping Indian chief.

The Squamish area is a mecca for rock climbers. A number of schools here prepare rock-climbing beginners for the trails on nearby Smoke Bluffs. The experienced climbers are more attracted by Stawamus Chief.

Shannon Falls Provincial Park, 4 km south of Squamish on Highway 99, has Canada's third largest falls. At 335 m, Shannon Falls is five times higher than Niagara. The surrounding 87-ha park also attracts rock climbers.

About 15 km south of Squamish is Britannia Beach (pop. 500), where Bri-

Highway 99 to Squamish skirts the sheer mountainous cliffs along Howe Sound.

tannia Mines produced 56 million tonnes of copper ore between 1905 and 1974. Today, visitors can don a hard hat and board a covered mining train for a guided tour through the underground shafts and tunnels.

Porteau Cove, 20 km south of Squamish on Highway 99, is a marine provincial park where scuba divers can explore two sunken ships. The wrecks attract marine life of all sizes. The park also has a campground.

During the summer, a pleasant way to reach Squamish is by the *Royal Hudson*, a restored 1940s excursion steam train that runs between North Vancouver and Squamish from early June to mid-September. Alternatively, take a round-trip on the MV *Britannia*.

Special events
Discovery Day, Britannia Beach (early May)
Squamish Loggers' Sports Day
(late July or early August)
Squamish Open Air Regatta (early August)
Indian Summer Art Festival (August)
Octoberfest (October)

Roads to explore: Two wilderness byways that follow in the footsteps of miner and logger

1. PEMBERTON TO D'ARCY
Distance: 37 km (one way)/23 miles

Snow-capped peaks encircle the village of Pemberton (pop. 550) at the northern end of Highway 99. The valley in which the village is located is famed for seed potatoes. The village has long been a mecca for campers, hikers, and fishermen, and is a base for two short wilderness drives (Pemberton to D'Arcy and Pemberton to Lillooet), which might be combined into a day-long excursion.

● Take the paved road from Pemberton to Mount Currie and turn north onto the road to D'Arcy. This is part of the Douglas Trail, which was built from Fort Langley to Lillooet during the gold rush of the 1860s. It was abandoned when the Fraser Canyon was opened up in 1864.

● About 4 km northeast of Mount Currie, turn right at the hydroelectric substation to reach the Forest Service Recreation Area at Owl Creek. The large open area comprises two campsites: one on Owl Creek, the other on Birkenhead River. Beyond this point, the road runs along the winding Birkenhead River.

● Continue to the recreation area at Spetch Creek, located halfway across Hindoo Flats, 12.6 km from Mount Currie. It offers overnight camping.

● The road turns northeast, following the Gates River past the community of Birken, about 26 km from Mount Currie.

● Turn west on Blackwater Creek Road to Birkenhead Lake Provincial Park. On the gravel road to the park, stop at the Forest Service recreation area on Blackwater Lake, which offers boating and fishing.

● Continue to Birkenhead Lake Provincial Park, amid the snowy Coast Mountains. The 6-km-long lake attracts fishermen, who angle for kokanee and trout. Hiking trails encourage visitors to explore this remote setting. There are camp and picnic sites.

● Return to the main road, and drive north to D'Arcy at the south end of Anderson Lake, where there are campgrounds. Once known as Port Anderson, the community was the site of a Hudson's Bay Company trading post during the gold rush of the 1860s.

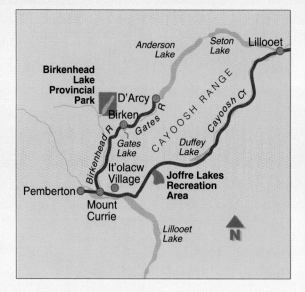

2. PEMBERTON TO LILLOOET
Distance (approx.): 100 km/62½ miles

The Duffey Lake Road to Lillooet follows a logging and wilderness road, which was paved in 1990.

● Head east from Pemberton toward Mount Currie and turn right at the church. After 9 km of gravel, paved road recommences at Lillooet Lake.

● Drive to the Joffre Lakes Recreational Area, run by the province. Joffre Lakes Trail leads along Upper Joffre Creek, past three glacial lakes, and offers a view of 2,390-m-high Mount Matier, just east of the park.

● Heading north from the park, follow the road along Cayoosh Creek all the way to Lillooet, traveling on the south shore of Duffey Lake.

Along the way, you will pass a number of picturesque spots worth a brief stop. One of them is a boat launch ramp about 19 km north of Joffre Lakes. Another is Seton Lake Reservoir Recreation Area, about 6 km south of Lillooet. This heart-of-the-wilderness spot is ideal for swimming and picnicking.

● At the end of the road is the town of Lillooet, the gold rush capital of the 1860s, and the southern end of the Cariboo Wagon Road that led to the Cariboo goldfields.

5   **Garibaldi Provincial Park**

Thistles thrive by B.C. roads in summer.

A true backcountry preserve, Garibaldi Provincial Park is 1,958 km² of wilderness with 2,678-m Mount Garibaldi at its heart. No vehicles are allowed into the park, and access to its mountainous interior is only by five trailheads, reached from Highway 99.

The first trailhead is the Diamond Head or Elfin Lakes Trail, northeast of Squamish. Turn right on Mamquam Road and continue for 16 km on a steep, winding gravel road to the trailhead parking lot. From there, hike or mountain bike 11 km to the Elfin Lakes ranger station, where an overnight shelter can sleep 34. There is also a free campground. No campfires are permitted in the park. However, propane stoves are available at several cooking shelters, though visitors must provide their own cooking gear.

The second trailhead is Black Tusk or Garibaldi Lake, 37 km north of Squamish. This section is off-limits to mountain bikes, and visitors must hike the 9-km trail. There are two camping areas: Taylor Meadows (7.5 km up the trail) and the Garibaldi Lake ranger station. From the campgrounds, visitors can hike 7 km to the 2,315-m Black Tusk Mountain. Farther along the trail is azure-blue Garibaldi Lake, with the Sphinx and Sentinel glaciers on its eastern shore.

The third trailhead is 2.5 km south of Whistler at Cheakamus Lake. The 3-km hike to lake is across relatively flat terrain. The site has no cooking facilities, but there are some undeveloped camping areas.

The Singing Pass trailhead can be reached through the Village Square parking lot in the popular ski-resort town of Whistler. The 7.5-km trail has spectacular views of mountains, glacial lakes, and alpine floral meadows. From Singing Pass, visitors can hike a further 2 km to Russett Lake for overnight camping.

The fifth trailhead is Wedgemount Lake, 13 km north of Whistler on Highway 99. The rigorous 7-km hike is for experienced hikers. There is an undeveloped campground and a small overnight hut. Mountaineers often use this as a staging area for climbing surrounding peaks, including the 2,891-m Wedge Mountain, the highest in the park.

6 Pitt Polder

In Pitt Polder, Katzie Marsh dike restrains Pitt Lake and creates a refuge for water birds.

This secluded pocket of land in the Fraser River valley is both a remarkable land reclamation project and a natural habitat for wildlife. The 1,600 ha of reclaimed land is on the eastern bank of the Pitt River, the last major tributary of the Fraser before it flows into the Strait of Georgia. Its source is Pitt Lake, which is subject to ocean tides. It is the only freshwater tidal lake in the world.

Polder, in Dutch, means "land reclaimed from the flood." That is what Dutch immigrant Dr. Jan Blom did when, in 1949, he decided to recover the land destroyed by a disastrous flood in 1948, which covered half the Fraser Valley.

Spider's web, Pitt Polder

Blom supervised the draining, diking, and clearing of 2,754 ha. To farm the land, he called upon a dozen Dutch families, who settled here and created a small world of meadows and barns reminiscent of Holland—all within view of the lofty, snow-crested Coast Mountains.

Today, the rich soils of the polder meadows produce a carpet of lush grass that makes this area one of the best in the Fraser Valley to raise cattle and dairy herds.

But not all of Pitt Polder is farmland. Visitors can explore the region by hiking or cycling along the roads running on top of the dikes, or by canoeing through the marshes.

By 1972, the northernmost holdings, near Pitt Lake, became too costly to reclaim. These 1,296 ha were sold to the British Columbia provincial government to establish a green belt and wildlife area. Today, the Pitt Polder Green Belt and Wildlife Management Area, at the south end of Pitt Lake, is one of two key waterfowl refuges in the Fraser Valley. A wide variety of ducks and geese, including the rare greater sandhill crane, inhabit Pitt Polder. Bald eagles abound, and ospreys nest here in summer. Animals such as otters, beavers, coyotes, deer, raccoon, bobcats, and bears also roam the Green Belt area.

The Pitt Polder has numerous nature and hiking trails. The most popular dikes to walk are the Perimeter, Circular, Mountainside and Crane Reserve.

There are lookout towers and pavilions on the trails and in the marshes. Most trails begin at Pitt Lake.

Travel by canoe allows visitors a much closer view of the Green Belt marshes. Widgeon Creek is a popular waterway for canoeists. Canoe rentals are available at Pitt Lake. Fishermen will find that carp, trout, and salmon abound in the Green Belt and Pitt Lake.

Special events
Pitt Meadows Day (early May)
Blueberry Festival (August)

7 Golden Ears Provincial Park

As the sun sets, the twin peaks of Golden Ears Mountain glint a golden color, from which the mountain and this 550 km² park take their name. Early

A mountain goat monument marks the entry to Golden Ears.

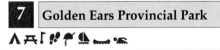

GOLDEN EARS PARK

surveyors of the area mentioned "the beautiful peaks known as the Golden Ears," but this majestic 1,706-m-high mountain is only one of many in the coast range enclosed within the park's boundaries.

Access to Golden Ears is through the municipality of Maple Ridge, 41 km east of Vancouver on Highway 7. Follow the park signs north from the highway at the communities of Haney or Albion.

Alouette Lake, ringed by lofty mountain peaks, entices swimmers and boaters at Golden Ears Provincial Park.

From its southern boundary, Golden Ears extends 55 km northward through mountain wilderness to the southern boundary of Garibaldi Provincial Park. The two parks are separated by a barrier of rugged mountains.

Alouette Lake, the recreational centre, is at the south end of the park. The two main campgrounds are among the biggest in British Columbia. Alouette Lake has 205 fully equipped camping units; Gold Creek, just up the road, has 138. Most trailers and recreational vehicles can be accommodated, although there are no hookups. There is a large picnic area on Alouette Lake.

The lake itself is good for swimming, although its waters fed by glaciers are always cold.

Golden Ears is a hiker's paradise. The Mike Lake Trail is one of the easiest and most scenic in the park. It is a one-and-a-half hour round-trip. The trail is also used for horseback riding. The 10-km Alouette Mountain Hiking Trail is a five-hour hike (one-way), which rewards the effort with a spectacular view of Alouette Lake. The most difficult trail is the 12-km Golden Ears hike, which can take seven hours (also one-way), an overnighter for all but the most experienced.

The Spirea Nature Area has sundew flowers that trap flies, and milk-white Indian pipe grows in the dense forest nearby. Many species of mushrooms and fungi sprout on the forest floor in the fall. As for wildlife, herds of deer are frequently seen grazing at the side of the road and campers may hear the howls of coyotes at night. Black bears seldom visit the campgrounds, but just in case, store food inside vehicles overnight.

8 Sasquatch Provincial Park

The name of this 1,220-ha park on the shores of Harrison Lake honors an enduring legend of the mountainous West. Many tales are told about a giant, apelike survivor of the snowy summits. The legendary creature, known as Bigfoot or Sasquatch, appears elsewhere under other names—the Yeti of Tibet may be a distant relation. Through the years, Sasquatch sightings have occurred in the northwest United States and in British Columbia. Some who claim to have seen the Sasquatch say it is 3-m tall and weighs more than 140 kg. But little solid evidence of this elusive being exists.

While a few visitors to the park may hope for a glimpse of the Sasquatch, most come here for the pleasures of the three picturesque campgrounds. The campgrounds are situated on Deer and Hicks lakes. Mountain ranges encircle shimmering Deer Lake, in the northeast of the park. It offers some of the best fishing in the park, although all powerboats are banned (except those with electric motors). Deer Lake has two campgrounds: Bench (64 units) and Lakeside (42).

The campground at Hicks Lake, located in the park's southwest sector, provides 71 units. The site is complemented by fine beaches, walking trails, and canoeing routes. Powerboats with engines of 10 hp or less are permitted on the lake.

Bicyclists disembark from the ferry after a day's trip on Barnston Island (in the background).

BY A SPRAWLING CITY, A SECLUDED ISLAND GETAWAY

Three of the fastest growing municipalities in the Vancouver area—Surrey, Maple Ridge and Pitt Meadows—lie close to Barnston Island (pop. 150) in the Fraser River. Yet this island remains remarkably untouched by urban development. The stretch of river separating it from mainland Surrey has helped preserve the island's rustic charm—the weathered fishing boats on the shores, the timeworn dairy barns overgrown with thistles.

The island can be reached by a 5-minute ferry ride across the Fraser River from Surrey's 104th Avenue. The ferry is a small barge hooked up to a powerful tug. The trip is free, but there is no schedule. Park at the end of the ramp and honk your horn to summon the ferry.

From the ferry you can see the industry spawned by the Fraser River: the riverside sawmills and log booms tied to the mainland and the shore of Barnston Island. Small tugs work around the logs under tow or in the booming areas, while larger fishing boats pass by on their way to farm the rich waters.

Once off the ferry, a 10-km paved route circles Barnston Island. The island is a small, flat crescent only 5 km long and about 3 km across, the land so low that it was constantly flooded until a dike was built. This dike is now the roadbed for the round-the-island drive.

Mixed farming and fishing are the main occupations on Barnston. Most of the population lives along the southeastern shore. Many residents are fishermen who can walk from their gardens onto the wharves where their boats are tied up and their fishnets laid out to dry.

Keep an eye out, especially early in the year, for bald eagles attracted by the salmon runs. The eagles perch high in the cottonwood trees that dot the island. Blue herons are also part of the island scene, preferring to roost in the moist pastures at the island's centre. For cycling, walking, jogging, or driving, Barnston Island promises a refreshing day-long adventure in the country, just a half-hour excursion away from the city.

While on the island, remember there are no tourist facilities, and no public land except for the road. Try to park off the thoroughfares, and be prepared to take your garbage with you when you leave.

Green Point, near the park entrance and information centre, is an enchanting picnic site beside Harrison Lake, once a water route for gold seekers heading for British Columbia's interior in the 1860s.

Trout Lake, just a short distance from the information centre, is a tiny body of water, known to yield "keeper-sized" trout. (No powerboats are allowed.)

To reach Sasquatch, travelers pass through the village of Harrison Hot Springs, famous for its hot spring baths. Waters bubbling from a spring in the lake's depths may reach 60°C. The hot spring pool at the centre of town is less scalding, because the water is cooled to 38°C for the comfort of bathers. The high sulfur content of the water is said to be health-giving.

Natural hot springs abound in the nearby forest, usually in primitive surroundings. You can reach them on foot or by four-wheel-drive vehicle.

9 | Cultus Lake Provincial Park

Since the 1890s, Cultus Lake, between the International Ridge to the southeast and Vedder Mountain to the northwest, has been a popular summer getaway.

Early Indians called Cultus Lake *See-ehl-chah* or *Tsowallie*. The present name is a Chinook word derived from the Salish *kul* meaning "bad or worthless." This beautiful spot may have been called bad because of an Indian taboo. But Cultus Lake has been mentioned in many tall tales. Some tales claim the lake is bottomless, with underwater caverns and tunnels leading to the Fraser River. Others say it has a resident monster—a giant two-headed snake.

A ptarmigan, a bird of British Columbia's slopes

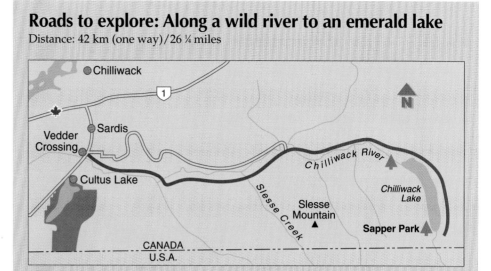

Roads to explore: Along a wild river to an emerald lake

Distance: 42 km (one way)/26 ¼ miles

The half-day trip to Chilliwack Lake begins at the two-lane bridge over the Vedder/Chilliwack River at Vedder Crossing. (The one river becomes the other at this point.) This back road—a gentle but steady climb eastward—skirts and crosses the turbulent Chilliwack River and its many smaller tributaries. Spring runoffs from the nearby mountains reshape the wild river every year. The roadside is deeply forested, rich with ferns, mushrooms, and mosses. The far-off snow-crested peaks, such as 2,429-m Slesse Mountain, rise sheerly from the Slesse Valley, a tributary of the Chilliwack Valley.

● Just a little farther on is the home of the Canadian Olympic Kayak team. Team members and kayakers from around the world test the Chilliwack

At Chilliwack Lake, the soft sand and cool water are ideal for a soothing promenade.

River, renowned for its challenging white waters.

● The Thurston Meadows Recreation Site, 18 km from the start, is the perfect rest stop, with barbecue pits and picnic tables on the riverbanks.

● Just 4 km farther on is the government-operated Chilliwack River Salmonid Enhancement Facility, which aims to introduce 260,000 coho, chinook, chum, steelhead and trout into the Chilliwack River each year. The river is considered one of British Columbia's best for salmon fishing. *The hatchery is open daily, 8 am to 3:30 pm.*

● About 30 km from the start, the road turns from asphalt to hard-packed, well-maintained gravel. Just before Chilliwack Lake is the Post Creek Recreational Site on the left side of the road. A winding, stone-filled lane leads to a parking area, the starting point for the trails to Lindeman, Greendrop, and Flora lakes. The lovely Lindeman Lake, an easy 1.2-km walk away, is a good place to hike or bird-watch.

● Chilliwack Lake's deep, emerald-green waters lure fishermen seeking trout, lake trout, and Dolly Varden. Chilliwack Lake Provincial Park, situated where the river leaves the lake, has more than 100 campsites. There are also picnic sites and a boat launching ramp.

● For unsurpassed views of the lake, take the unmaintained forestry road that cuts through stands of giant cedar trees and follows the lake to its south end. There, the Royal Engineers built Sapper Park, a primitive campground, where you might pause and enjoy your lunch before the return trip.

On the rugged road to Chilliwack Lake, the afternoon sun gilds fence, field, and forest.

The 556-ha Cultus Lake Provincial Park has four excellent campgrounds: Clear Creek, 80 units; Delta Grove, 58; Entrance Bay, 52; Maple Bay, 106. Beaches are found at Delta Grove and Entrance, Maple, and Spring bays.

A park interpreter is available from June to August to assist visitors. The park has many activities for children, ranging from daytime nature hikes to star gazing in the evenings.

Whereas the lake is abuzz with ski boats, skiers, and jet skis, the surrounding woods are filled with many quieter, natural sights and sounds.

The Teapot Hill Trail, which begins at Honeymoon Bay, for example, is a 5-km hike to Teapot Hill which takes about one hour each way. The Seven Sisters Trail between Entrance Bay and Clear Creek is through beautiful forest and a group of seven mammoth Douglas firs. A horseback riding trail, also used by hikers, links the north end of the park at Edmeston Road with the south end at Road 918 near Maple Bay picnic grounds.

A self-guiding, interpretive trail from Maple Bay parking lot takes the visitor past many of the park's natural sights, while the 40-minute Giant Douglas Walk from Delta Grove campground on the Columbia Valley High-

way passes some mighty Douglas firs.

August is the busiest month at Cultus Lake, the highlight being the Krafty Raft Race. Every year do-it-yourselfers build and race rafts made out of anything that floats.

10 Hope

The town of Hope (pop. 6,500) is the southern gateway to the Fraser River canyon. Although many travelers pass through this community in summer, not all of them stop. Those who do find it an excellent base for tours and wilderness outings. Hope itself has

A BREATHTAKING SCENE BY A MIGHTY GORGE

Five railway tunnels and two bridges in the 130-ha Coquihalla Canyon Recreational Area, just 10 km east of Hope, provide excitement in the splendor of a secluded setting. Here, the abandoned Othello/Quintette railway tunnels and bridges skirt the Coquihalla River, whose turbulent waters have sliced a 90-m-deep gorge through solid granite.

To reach the site, head east from Hope along Kawkawa Lake and Othello roads. Turn right at Tunnels Road, and drive to the parking lot next to the site. A 2.8-km walk leads through the tunnels and across the bridges. Bring a flashlight to examine the tunnels, which are still black from the smoke of coal-burning locomotives.

As you leave the first tunnel, you enter a breathtaking world where shrubs and trees cling tenaciously to tiny niches on the sheer canyon walls. At the exit of the second tunnel, you cross a bridge high above the swirling, raging Coquihalla River. The puzzle of the site is the whereabouts of the fifth tunnel, because you really pass through only four. A window in the third tunnel is counted as the fifth member of the quintette. Watch for it.

This secluded gorge, which thrills today, challenged the railway engineers building a route between Merritt and Hope in 1914. The chief engineer, Andrew McCulloch, decided to traverse the gorge by tunnel and bridge. McCulloch's admiration for Shakespeare's plays inspired the names of his projects. In this case, he chose Othello.

The end result was an impressive feat, but a practical failure. Snow and ice blocked the rails here, which remained impassable for much of the year. When this stretch of the railway was closed in 1959, it was handed over to British Columbia for preservation.

Coquihalla Canyon Recreational Area, open spring to fall, offers picnicking and fishing for steelhead trout.

The hoary marmot is a creature of the craggy slopes in Manning and other western parks.

some interesting attractions. There is the Japanese Friendship Garden, a tribute to Japanese Canadians who were interned at the Tashme Camp, just east of Hope, during the Second World War. The region's more distant past can be glimpsed at Hope Museum, in artifacts of the Sto:Lo Nation peoples who first inhabited this area, the fur trade, and the 1860 Fraser River gold rush.

Beside Highway 3, 16 km east of Hope, lie massive boulders, evidence of the Hope Slide. On 9 January, 1965, a side of Johnson Peak plunged into the valley below, burying the road in 45 m of rubble. A plaque by the highway marks the site of the disaster.

Highway 1, north of Hope, passes by incredible scenery: the churning waters of the Fraser River, jagged canyon walls, and forest-clad mountain slopes.

On Highway 1, 21 km north of Hope, is Yale (pop. 300), once the biggest town north of San Francisco and west of Chicago. While the gambling houses and stern-wheelers are just memories, evidence of this settlement's colorful past, such as gold pans, a scale for weighing nuggets, and a model of a stern-wheeler, are on display at the Yale Museum. *Open June to September, Wednesday to Sunday, 9:30 am to 5:30 pm.*

Marriage in a truly picturesque church is the goal of many visitors to

Yale, who exchange their vows at St. John the Divine Anglican Church. Built in 1859-1860, it is the oldest church on its original site on the mainland of British Columbia, and contains many of its original furnishings.

Special events

Fraser River Barrel Race, Yale (August)

Hope Brigade Days (September)

Salmon Spawning Run (October)

11 Manning Provincial Park

Hosts of wildflowers carpet Manning Provincial Park in July and August. During this brief, frost-free period, alpine meadows burst into bloom along Highway 3.

The western entrance to the park leads to Rhododendron Flats, one of the few sites in British Columbia where rhododendrons grow in the wild. The flowers reach their peak in about mid-June.

Follow the Skagit River along Highway 3 to Manning Park Lodge. Just across from the lodge, there is a paved road, open July through September, which climbs to the Cascade Lookout. From here, you can admire the towering Cascade Mountains.

From the lookout, a 6-km gravel road leads to 2,063-m-high Blackwall Peak. The 1-km self-guiding Paintbrush Trail begins at the Alpine Naturalist Hut.

The 21-km Heather Trail starts at the nearby parking lot. During the summer, the meadows it cuts through become a floral carpet up to 24 km long and 5 km wide.

West of Manning Park Lodge are the Lightning Lakes, aptly named Strike, Flash, Thunder and Lightning. Several trails branch off here: the 9-km Lightning Lake Loop; the 12-km Lightning Lake Chain; the 20.4-km Skyline I Trail, and the challenging 29.2-km Frosty Mountain Loop. The view of the North Cascades at the top of Frosty Mountain (2,408 m), the park's highest peak, is stunning.

On Manning's western boundary is the 32,570-ha Skagit Valley Recreation Area. It offers some of the finest fly-fishing in North America.

To the north is the Cascade Recreation Area. History buffs may choose to hike the old Dewdney, Whatcom or Hope Pass trails. They were built in the late 1800s as routes to the British Columbia interior, and sustained the gold rush traffic and the drive to settle the Okanagan Valley.

A backdrop of far-off mountains sets the scene for a picnic in a meadow bordered by pines at Manning Provincial Park.

2 Naikoon Provincial Park

This 726-km² park embraces beaches, bogs, and forests. Naikoon—a corruption of *Nai-kun*, the Haida word for "long nose"—describes Rose Spit, a 5-km slip of land at the northern tip.

From Highway 16 you enter the park at Tlell, which is about 40 km north of the Skidegate ferry terminal. There are entrances also at Mayer Lake and close to Masset. The park headquarters are near the Tlell River Bridge. From the picnic area beside this bridge a 5-km self-guiding trail leads to the beach and the shipwrecked *Pesuta*, a wooden cargo ship that ran aground during a 1928 storm. The trail follows the windswept north bank of the serpentine Tlell, a river renowned for coho salmon and steelhead trout.

Mayer Lake also has boating, picnicking, and wilderness camping, as well as fishing for cutthroat trout. Misty Meadows Campground near the park headquarters has 30 sites.

The central section, known as the Argonaut Plain, is mostly flat bogland, much of it covered in stunted spruce, pine, and cedar, and fringed with forests of lodgepole pine, and red and yellow cedar. Pacific storms pound the rocky western shoreline; beautiful beaches rim the mainland-facing eastern coast. The 90 km of beaches in the park are dotted with driftwood that is smoothed and sculpted into tortuous shapes by the sea. White dunes, stabilized by vegetation, creep inland.

Legend says that 109-m-high Tow Hill on the north shore is a giant whale that was turned into stone while fighting the Haida hero Tow. To reach this volcanic outcrop, drive east from Masset on the gravel road that

Mushroom, Naikoon Provincial Park

ings may also be purchased from a gift shop in the museum at the entrance to Skidegate.

About 1 km north of the village, a well-traveled pathway leads down to a rocky beach and to Balance Rock, a huge boulder resting precariously on bedrock littered with ancient fossils.

Some 107 km north of Skidegate, the village of Old Masset (pop. 672) lies at the tip of Graham Island. The Ed Jones Culture and Education Museum there exhibits Haida artifacts. A 12-m-high Bear Mother totem pole stands in front of St. John's Church. Carved in 1969 by world-acclaimed Haida artist Robert Davidson, it is the first totem pole raised in memory of Masset elders of earlier generations.

Anthony Island, at Moresby's southernmost tip, has the world's finest display of Haida mortuary poles. They are found at the village site of Ninstints, a United Nations World Heritage Site. Get permission from the Skidegate or Masset Band Council Office before visiting this or any unoccupied village site.

Special events
Hospital Day at Queen Charlotte City (June)
Skidegate Day (June)

begins at the mouth of the Hiellen River. The road passes the Delkatla Wildlife Sanctuary—a stopover for trumpeter swans, sandhill cranes, and other wildfowl. The sanctuary is also a haven for speedy peregrine falcons, hairy woodpeckers, and saw-whet owls. The Tow Hill Ecological Reserve, farther east along the road, preserves the dunes, ancient beaches, and peat

At Naikoon Provincial Park, Cape Fife Trail leads through a rain forest's trees and tangle.

bogs near Yakan Point. Trails veer off into swampy bogs where homesteaders tried—but failed—to farm in the early 1900s.

The road ends at Agate Beach. The campground here has 21 sites with fire pits and picnic tables. Between May and September, campers must pay an overnight fee.

From the Agate Beach parking lot, walk west along the west bank of the Hiellen River. Take the trail's left fork to climb Tow Hill for a sweeping view of Dixon Entrance. On a clear day you can see Alaskan islands.

The trail's right fork leads to the beach, which is littered with small shells and varicolored stones polished to perfection by the sea. Retreating tides reveal craggy twists of rock. Finger holes and deep pockets mark the surface of the ancient basalt slabs. The sandy corridors and alleyways between rocks are great places for beachcombing.

In early summer the dunes are blanketed with wild strawberries in full flower and later by bright yellow beach tansy. Look for scallops, cockles, butter clams, and razor clams, which the local people harvest from May to September. Black-tailed deer, seals, sea lions, peregrine falcons, soaring bald eagles, and pods of killer and gray whales add to the spectacular scenery.

From the Tow Hill parking lot, visitors can head out in other directions too. One excellent two-to-three-day walking trip crosses 10 km to Fife Point on the east coast. A 21-km loop takes hikers across to Rose Spit, an ecological reserve set aside for scientific research and the preservation of the dunes, their birds, and vegetation. You may not camp, hunt, or fish there, but it is excellent for bird-watching, a vantage point for seeing birds southbound on the Pacific flyway. You can enjoy the salty breeze and crashing surf as you return to Tow Hill along the hard-packed sand of North Beach.

3 Port Edward

🐟 ⌨ ❄ ⌂

More than 30 canneries once operated at the mouth of the Skeena River. At Port Edward (pop. 700), the North Pacific Cannery Village Museum recalls those boom years. In operation from 1889 to 1968, it is the oldest surviving

fish processing plant on British Columbia's coast and a national historic site.

When the cannery was built, Port Edward was an isolated fishing village, accessible only by boat. Today you can reach the village by following a 10-km side road from Highway 16.

The North Pacific Cannery is built on pilings sunk in the mud of Inverness Passage. It is a living museum, containing a processing plant with the original canning line, and equipment and displays reflecting fishing village life in the 19th and early 20th centuries. Boardwalks link buildings, many of them built on platforms extending out over the fast-flowing water. The mist-covered Coast Mountains provide a scenic backdrop.

During a tour, guides explain the exhibits or show how they work. A hit with summer visitors is the cannery's one-man show, *The Skeena River Story*, a series of historical vignettes about the fishing industry. During the show, the performer rapidly changes costumes to depict some 20 characters. Slide projections of period scenes re-create the atmosphere of bygone days in this area.

More than 2,500 people lived at the North Pacific Cannery during peak seasons. To accommodate its employees, the company built family housing

and bunkhouses. One large bunkhouse has recently been converted into a bed-and-breakfast inn for visitors.

4 Hazelton

🏺🏕️🥾🐟❄️📷⛺

The snowcapped peaks of the Rocher Déboulé Range dominate the horizon at Hazelton—the dwelling place of the Gitksans, the people of the Skeena, for more than 8,000 years. The dense forests and mountains within a 65-km radius of Hazelton (pop. 486) are the sacred precinct of these peoples.

Longhouses and totems at 'Ksan Indian Village reveal the heritage of the Gitksan.

The 'Ksan Indian Village, located just outside Hazelton, is a showplace of Gitksan art and culture. The village comprises seven tribal longhouses: the Fireweed House of Masks and Ropes, the Frog House of the Distant Past, the Wolf House of our Great Grandfathers, the House of Wood Carving, the Silk-Screening Studio, the 'Ksan Gift Shop, and the Northwest National Exhibition Centre. *'Ksan Indian Village is open daily, mid-May to mid-October, 9 am to 6 pm. Hours vary the rest of the year. Guided tours are available on the hour.*

The Northwest National Exhibition Centre is a combination museum and art gallery. It displays 'Ksan blankets, masks, and baskets. *Open daily from*

Roads to explore: A drive to a distant lake chain

Distance: 181 km (with side trips)/112 ½ miles

The Lake District, midway between Prince George and Prince Rupert, is the site of some of British Columbia's largest lakes. Stuart, Takla, and Babine lakes lie north of Yellowhead Highway 16, Francois and Ootsa lakes are to the south.
● The backroad from Houston to Burns Lake via Francois and Ootsa lakes is worth exploring. Ootsa is a combination of smaller lakes, and this loop drive on mostly gravel roads is ideal for anyone in the mood for backcountry exploration, fishing, and camping.
● Stock up on fuel and supplies before you head out. The first leg of the trip leaves Yellowhead Highway 16, 3.5 km west of Houston, and heads south on the Morice River Forest Road.
● A scarred hillside covered with fireweed 21 km from the highway junction marks one of B.C.'s worst forest fires. The 1983 blaze destroyed 185 km² of forest and a handful of homes.
● The junction with the Morice-Owen Forest Road 27 km on is an opportunity for a side trip: Morice Lake and excellent fishing lie to the west; Owen Lake and a spacious campground can be found to the southeast. The road to the left continues toward Ootsa Lake through marshes and across the Nadina River. About 2.5 km southeast, a short side road leads down to the small lakeside Francois West Forest Service Recreation Site.

● Just past the recreation site, the gravel road swings south, away from Francois Lake and over the Shelford Hills. There is another small Forest Service Recreation Site at Rainbow Lake.
● A side road leads south to a picnic site at Wistaria Provincial Park, and another side road, opposite the Wistaria Community Club, leads 1.5 km south to a boat launch and small wharf on one of Ootsa Lake's many sheltered bays. The Wistaria boat ramp is a jump-off point for northern Tweedsmuir Provincial Park.
● The road continues eastward through grainfields paralleling the north shore of Ootsa Lake to the Ootsa Landing Forest Service Recreation Site, 44 km from Noralee.
● The community of Ootsa Lake is 2 km east of the recreation site. The nearby Nechako Reservoir Spillway has campsites and boat wharves.
● Backtrack to Ootsa Lake and follow the signs for the 63-km drive north, on pavement, to Burns Lake. At a junction 20 km north of Ootsa, drive 19 km north to the Southbank ferry terminal on Francois Lake.
● The ferry, which makes the crossing in 20 minutes, leaves the south side on the

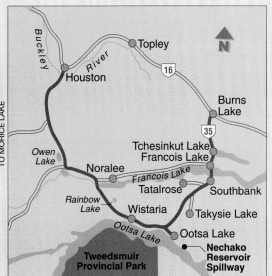

hour. Logging trucks, visitors, and residents share this free link to the north shore and the centres along Yellowhead Highway 16. Along the remaining 24 km from Francois Lake to Burns Lake and Highway 16, you will find resorts and campgrounds at Tchesinkut Lake and Agate Point.
● The loop drive from Houston to Burns Lake via Ootsa Lake takes about four hours, but allow a day for side trips. Although tourist facilities are limited on the Houston-Ootsa section, there are resorts and campgrounds on the Ootsa to Burns Lake section.

mid-May to mid-October from 10:30 am to 4:30 pm. Closed Tuesdays and Thursdays in winter.

The House of Wood Carving contains the Kitnmaax School of Northwest Coast Indian Art. The works of native artists trained at the school are found in collections around the world. Visitors can see student artists hard at work carving cedar. Their creations are sold in the 'Ksan Gift Shop. *Open daily from 9 am to 6 pm, mid-May to mid-October.*

Images of eagles, bears, and other creatures adorn the totem poles at 'Ksan Village.

The longhouses recount different aspects of Gitksan life. Some describe traditional methods of making clothes and utensils, or display costumes and handicrafts. Others show the preparations surrounding traditional feasts. The walls of the longhouses, handmade with traditional tools, are decorated with images of mythical figures.

The village preserves an impressive group of totem poles. In fact this entire area is noted for outstanding collections, many of them featured in the paintings of Emily Carr. The combined Hazelton and neighboring Kitwanga regions have the largest concentration of totem poles in British Columbia. Some of the best groupings are at Kispiox Village (25 km north of New Hazelton), Kitwanga (40 km west of New Hazelton), and Kitwankool (35 km north of Kitwanga).

Special events

Kispiox Rodeo (June)

Pioneer Days (August)

5 Fort St. James

Fort St. James (pop. 2,058) is one of the oldest, continuously occupied settlements west of the Rocky Mountains. In July 1806, the fur trader and explorer Simon Fraser and his crew beached their birch-bark canoes on the shores of Stuart Lake where the present village now stands. They immediately set about building a lakeshore trading post, which endured for more than a century.

Fraser christened the huge region served by Fort St. James "New Caledonia," possibly because it reminded him of his mother's description of the Scottish Highlands. The similarities are striking: wild open lakes surrounded by ancient smoothed mountains and cloaked in forest of spruce, pine, and hardwoods.

Fort St. James National Historic Site, on Kwah Road by Stuart Lake, has Canada's largest collection of fur-trade buildings kept on their original site. The fur warehouse, fish cache, men's

Fort St. James's General Warehouse displays fur pelts and trade goods of yesteryear.

house, trade store, officers' dwelling, and the grounds have been restored to their 1896 condition. A costumed staff re-creates the spartan life of this isolated post. *Open daily, July and August, 9:30 am to 5:30 pm; mid-May, June, and September, 10 am to 5 pm.*

Another reminder of this region's past is Our Lady of Good Hope Catholic Church. A 3-km drive from the national historic site, the simple little church looks out across Stuart Lake. Built in 1873, it is one of British Columbia's oldest churches. Evening services are still held there in summer.

The community of Fort St. James—called the Fort by local people—retains an informal frontier spirit. It hugs the southeastern corner of Stuart Lake. The 1,472-m-high bulk of Mount Pope provides a majestic backdrop. The road through the town never strays far from views of Stuart Lake. This splendid but moody expanse of water is about 12 km wide at Fort St. James and 100 km long. It is part of a system of lakes and rivers extending some 300 km northwest of Fort St. James.

In the 1930s and 1940s, the bush plane was essential transportation in this sparsely settled region. From the 1930s through the 1970s, Fort St. James

At Fort St. James, the repository for furs was the General Warehouse, built in the 1880s.

was an important floatplane base serving northern miners, foresters, hunters, and trappers. A one-third scale model of a Junker W-34 floatplane in Cottonwood House Provincial Historic Park commemorates early aviation at the fort. The whine of small aircraft still echoes across Stuart Lake, since nowadays the fort is a favored jumping-off point for fly-in adventure in northern British Columbia.

Two provincial parks on the southern shore of Stuart Lake provide a base from which to explore the back roads around Fort St. James. Paarens Beach Provincial Park, which has 36 campsites, is about 15 km west of Fort St. James. Sowchea Bay Provincial Recreation Area, which is just 5 km beyond Paarens Beach, has 30 campsites.

6 Cottonwood House Provincial Historic Park

The treasure of this 10-ha historic park is the two-story Cottonwood House, the last complete surviving roadhouse on the Cariboo Wagon Road. The gold rush road of the 1860s extended 610 km from Yale north to Barkerville. Highway 26 (the road today's traveler takes to each Barkerville) follows the final stretch of that historic road. Cottonwood House welcomed its first stagecoach visitors in 1865, offering room and meals to passengers, as well as fodder and shelter for pack animals and coach horses. Period furnishings include desks, chests, reclining chairs, a barrel stove, and a kitchen stove with two ovens. *Open daily, May to Labor Day, from 10 am to 4 pm.*

7 Barkerville Historic Town

This 65-ha historic town re-creates the gold rush atmosphere that gripped this place during the 1860s. Meticulously restored saloons, stores, hotels, and restaurants of the late 19th century line the main street leading to the simple wooden structure of St. Saviour's Church. The ornate Theatre Royale stages the music, songs, and bittersweet humor of the gold fields. The uneven boardwalks lead around the town to 127 historic buildings. Staff in period costume perpetuate a convincing illusion of Barkerville's booming bygone days. *Site open year-round from 8 am to dusk. The visitor reception centre is open daily from June to Labor Day. Administration offices open Monday to Friday from 8:30 am to 4:30 pm.*

The town takes its name from Billy Barker, a British riverboatman turned miner. In 1862 Barker and his partners discovered gold after drilling a 12-m shaft near Williams Lake. The claim yielded $600,000 worth of gold. Barker married a widow with expensive tastes, who spent his money and left him when it ran out. He died in Victoria in 1894 with nothing but memories and was buried in a pauper's grave.

In 1868 the town burned down, but it was rebuilt within a month. As gold petered out, the miners departed, and Barkerville became a backwater. In 1958 British Columbia declared it an historic park. The town was then restored to its 1858-1885 appearance.

Another local gold rush in the 1930s created the fortunes of the mining town of Wells, some 8 km west. Despite the depression, Wells thrived during the development of an underground gold mine. Today the main street with its false fronts and wooden sidewalks looks a little bit like a set for a Wild West movie.

Special events
Great Canadian Hill Climb (March)
Official Opening (June)
Dominion Day Celebrations (July)
Wells Heritage Festival (September)
Invitational Horse Carriage Races (September)
Snowmobilers' Yamafest (November)
Victorian Christmas (pre-Christmas weekend)

8 Bowron Lake Provincial Park

This 1,216-km² park is in the remote Cariboo Mountains, where some of the majestic peaks reach more than 2,000 m. The impressive feature of the park is six major lakes—Isaac (at 38 km the longest), Indianpoint, Lanezi, Sandy, Spectacle, and Bowron—linked by rivers, creeks, and portages. This chain—as it appears on a detailed map—resembles a slightly askew rectangle. The park takes its name from John Bowron, a settler and gold commissioner at nearby Barkerville during the gold rush boom of the 1860s.

Bowron Lake Provincial Park is accessible by gravel road from Highway 26, which passes Cottonwood House, Wells, and Barkerville. The registration centre and a campground are on the northeast corner of Bowron Lake. Two private campgrounds offering canoe rentals are near the park entrance.

Since it was established in 1961, the park has been a mecca for backcountry canoeists. Every year more than 4,000 canoeists and kayakers paddle its circuit of lakes and rivers. (A reservation system ensures there is no overcrowding.) A leisurely paddle might take 7 to 10 days, with time out for sudden squalls on the long, narrow mountain lakes. Canoeists with limited time and experience can take the west side of Bowron Lake to the head of Spectacle Lake—an easy 24-km journey without portages.

Only Bowron Lake is open to motorboats. All other lakes and rivers are reserved for canoeists.

The park is also a wildlife sanctuary for moose, bear, deer, and beaver. At the higher elevations, there are caribou, mountain goat, and grizzly bear. The interior of the park is undeveloped, except for patrol cabins, portages, and designated campsites with food caches (to prevent thefts by hungry bears).

East of Williams Lake, a road at Likely leads to Quesnel Lake, the largest in the Cariboo area.

9 Williams Lake

The first name for Williams Lake (pop. 10,500) was *Columneetza*—a Shuswap Indian word meaning "gathering place of the princely people." There are two stories about the origin of the present name. It may honor Chief Will'yum, a Shuswap who kept the peace between the Indians and local settlers, or William Pinchbeck, a wealthy rancher of the pioneer days.

The town came into its own only when the railway reached there in 1919. Today the rail station—the oldest building in Williams Lake—still serves passengers bound for Vancouver and the coast and houses the Station House Art Gallery. The adjoining Williams Lake Museum focuses on the area's ranching and rodeo history. Photographs chronicle the local stampede from its beginnings in 1919. The museum has an extensive collection of cowboy equipment: saddles, hats, spurs, and chaps. *Open from early June to mid-September, Monday through Saturday from 11 am to 4:30 pm. Tours are available by appointment in winter.*

The community is a jumping-off place for those wishing to explore the 8,000 lakes and forests of the Cariboo Region to the east and the ranching country of the Chilcotin to the west. Every July, the famous Williams Lake Stampede celebrates the cowboy's traditional skills—bronco riding, calf roping, steer wrestling, wild-horse racing, pony express, and bull riding.

A 3-km trail on the north side of town leads to a superb viewpoint at Signal Point.

Special events
Trail Riders Show (May)
Williams Lake Stampede (July)
Loggers' Sports Festival (July)
Sugarcane Finals Rodeo (September)
Cariboo Fall Fair (September)
B.C. Rodeo Association Finals (September)
Medieval Fair (November)

Roads to explore: Where the gold rush began

Distance (approx.): 210 km (round-trip)/130½ miles

A circular drive of 210 km from Williams Lake through 150 Mile House to the communities of Horsefly and Likely passes through the rugged Cariboo Country where the gold rush of the 1860s began.
● From Williams Lake, head 16 km east on Highway 97 to 150 Mile House (that's 150 miles north from the start of the Cariboo Gold Rush Wagon Road at Lillooet). Turn northeast and drive 5 km to the junction of the Horsefly and Likely roads. Keep to the right through ranching country for some 50 km until you reach the hunting and fishing community of Horsefly (pop. 400).
● On the left is Harper's Lake, named after a founder of the huge Gang Ranch. Miners renamed the town after being bitten by horseflies.

The ghostly remnants of Quesnel Forks, near Likely

● At Horsefly Community Hall, cross the single-span river bridge and drive 500 m to man-made sockeye salmon spawning beds on both sides of the road. In the fall, salmon also spawn in the river by the bridge. Gold was found around Horsefly in 1859 and it was that strike that began the gold rush in Cariboo Country. Horsefly's Jack Lynn Museum contains displays about those early years. *Open July and August, or by appointment.*
● Horsefly Lake Provincial Park, about 12 km along the road, has camping, swimming, picnic sites, boating, and fishing.
● Head back through Horsefly and follow the signs to Mitchell Bay Landing Road, which veers east and then north. The next 50 km is gravel. For the first 18 km, it runs close to the Horsefly River. Watch for sandbars in the river where the first gold was found. Try panning.
● The road continues to the junction of Mitchell Bay Landing with the Horsefly/Likely forest roads. Turn left on the bumpy forestry road that crosses the moun-

tainside for 28 km (a 1-hour drive) until it reaches Likely Road.
● Some 11 km along the road, you will see Quesnel Lake, the largest lake in the Cariboo. It has 500 km of scenic shoreline, and a picnic site with hiking trails. A 1-km trail leads to a Chinese blast oven where coke was produced for blacksmiths' shops during the gold rush.
● At the 18 km marker, there is a turnoff to Polley Lake and a forestry campsite. The trail continues until it becomes the paved Likely Road, 2 km from the town.
  Likely (pop. 500) has a number of heritage sites. Antiques line the walls of one: "The Most Popular Pub in B.C." Visitors can pan for gold at the nearby ghost town of Quesnel Forks, the first gold camp in the Cariboo.
● Head back over the bridge and continue southwest on the Likely Road. Drive 45 km until you reach 150 Mile House. From there, travel back to Williams Lake.

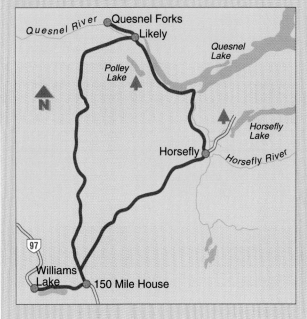

---

10   Tweedsmuir Provincial Park

⋀ ⛺ ♨ 🛶 ⚓ 🐟

At 9,810 km², Tweedsmuir is the largest of the 385 provincial parks in British Columbia. It is a huge and remote wilderness of snowcapped peaks, glaciers, deep canyons, swift-flowing rivers and mighty waterfalls. But few of these natural wonders are

accessible by road. Only one road—Highway 20 from Williams Lake to Bella Coola—bisects the southern sector. This gravel road enters the park at Heckman Pass and zigzags for more than 20 km into the valley of the Atnarko River. Because of the steep grades and switchbacks on this section—known as "the Hill"—you might want to avoid it if you are towing a trailer. The paved road resumes at the

end of "the Hill." The park headquarters are some 2 km farther on.
  Along the highway, several trails offer a glimpse of the park's interior. Near Stuie, the Kettle Pond Trail is a 30-minute to 1-hour loop walk. The Burnt Bridge Trail, at the western boundary of the park, climbs over the Mackenzie Heritage Trailhead to a lookout over the Bella Coola Valley. This can become a 2-hour loop walk if

Near Gang Ranch, sprinklers supply water that turns parched land into verdant fields.

you continue up the Burnt Bridge Creek Crossing and return by walking downstream to the parking lot.

Just west of Heckman Pass, an 8-km trail leads north toward the Rainbow Range, also called the *Tsitsutl* (the painted mountains) in the Bella Coola dialect of the local Nuxalk Nation. The peaks astonish with their array of red, lavender, violet, and yellow tints. At the end of the 8-km trail, you come to an unnamed lake. Trails beyond this point lead to a wilderness that only those experienced in hiking and surviving in the wild should explore.

The park has many challenging trails, including part of the 420-km Mackenzie Heritage Trail. The Hunlen Falls Trail starts 2 km east of park headquarters. In a vehicle with high clearance, drivers can take the Atnarko Tote Road for about an hour to the trailhead. A moderate 1-hour hike leads to Stillwater Lake. Another 6 to 8 hours of strenuous hiking leads to viewpoints—210 m above the Atnarko River—near the 260-m-high Hunlen Falls, the third highest uninterrupted waterfall in Canada.

11 Bella Coola

⛺ 🚐 ⛵ 🐟 ❄ ⌂

This fishing and lumbering village (pop. 900) stands where the Bella Coola River flows into the north arm of Burke Channel, an extension of the Pacific Ocean. The village is at the western end of a 64-km-long valley, bounded on the east by Tweedsmuir Provincial Park and 2,500-m-high snowcapped mountains of the Coast Range.

The valley has long been home to the Nuxalk Nation. The first Europeans were fur traders of the 1860s. B. F. Jacobsen, a Norwegian collector of Indian artifacts, arrived in 1884 and wrote about the region's similarity to his homeland's fjords and mountains. Inspired by his descriptions, 84 Norwegians led by the Reverend Christian Saugstad settled the western end of the Bella Coola Valley in 1894. Norwegians from Minnesota followed, some settling in Hagensborg, 20 km to the east.

Bella Coola Museum, built in 1898 as a schoolhouse, recounts the history of the Nuxalk Nation and Norwegian settlers. *Open daily from late June to early September, 9 am to 5 pm.* Floods forced the villagers and the Nuxalks to relocate on the south side of the river in 1936. Their diverse cultures give Bella Coola its special character. Some buildings are painted with Nuxalk whales and eagles. Totems stand guard at the Nuxalk Nation Band Office. Carvings and paintings adorn the Adwsalcta First Nation School in the newer section of the Nuxalk Reserve, some 6.5 km east of town. Ask the band office for permission to see the petroglyphs above Thorsen Creek.

On Walker Island, 10 km east of Bella Coola, two parks with cedar groves offer hiking trails and horseback riding. Farther east, you can visit the Snootli Creek Fish Hatchery, which raises chinook, coho, and steelhead salmon stock for release in local rivers. Some original hand-built, square timbered Norwegian buildings can still be seen in Hagensborg, where The Sons of Norway Heritage House is furnished as a typical Norwegian home of the early 1900s.

Special events

Nuxalk May Day Festivities and Sports Day (May)

Salmon Queen Festival (July)

Fall Fair and Loggers Sports (September)

Roads to explore: Ranches, canyons, and deserts

Distance: 200 km / 124 miles

The 200-km Clinton-to-Williams Lake route, once an old gold rush trail, takes at least four hours to drive, largely on gravel roads. By exploring its many attractions, travelers can turn this drive into a weekend or a week-long jaunt. Near Riley Lake, drivers unwilling to go the full distance can return by one of two roads to Highway 97.

● From Clinton, travel southwest on the Pavilion-Clinton Road through Cutoff Valley toward Kelly Lake.

● Just beyond the Kelly Lake Hydro-electric Substation, leave the Pavilion-Clinton Road and head north up Jesmond Road.

● Continue north through Porcupine Creek Valley. A low wooded mountain range, known as the Edge Hills, separates this valley from the steep-walled Fraser Canyon.

● Circle H Mountain Lodge is 24 km north of Kelly Lake. This family-run guest ranch offers rides up into the nearby Limestone Mountains.

● The next major landmark is 2,243-m Mount Bowman, one of the highest peaks in this region. You will pass it on the way to Jesmond.

● Just beyond Jesmond, turn west on the Big Bar Road leading to a ferry crossing on the Fraser. The ferry has been in operation since 1894 and serves ranches and homesteads on the west side of the river.

● The 19-km gravel road is a steady 800-m descent to the ferry crossing. The first 14-km stretch follows Big Bar Creek through a beautiful, sheltered valley. Near the Fraser, the vistas change to multicolored clay and rock formations. Here, the switchback descent becomes hazardous. Be prepared to use your low-est gear on the way down to the ferry crossing and back to the main route.

● About 5 km north of the junction with the ferry road, Big Bar Guest Ranch offers family vacations, supervised trail rides, hiking, and even gold panning.

● North of Big Bar Guest Ranch, the road dips into a hollow that shelters the weathered buildings of the abandoned OK Ranch.

● At Riley Lake, there is camping at a Forest Service recreation site 1 km east of the road. Big Bar Lake Provincial Park, 12 km east, has 33 campsites, a picnic area and boat launch. At this point, you return by the side road passing Big Bar Lake to Highway 97, 46 km to the east.

● North of Riley Lake, the gravel road winds through the scrub timber parkland. Remnants of the last Ice Age—drumlins, eskers, and giant boulders—form part of the landscape. After about 10 km, the river road meets the Meadow Lake Road, another side road returning to Highway 97 at 59 Mile.

● From this junction, the road continues northwest and exits through a narrow canyon to the broad, irrigated fields of Canoe Creek Valley.

● The view here is panoramic. The almost limitless cattle country of the Gang Ranch appears on the horizon across the Fraser. Pulpit Rock, a landmark to rafters, rises from the muddy river.

● The road follows the canyon to a suspension bridge across the Fraser River, which provides access to the Gang Ranch.

● The Gang Ranch headquarters, 8 km west of the bridge, comprises a one-room school, a store and post office, and village amenities.

● Beyond Gang Ranch Bridge, the road snakes up the walls of the canyon in hairpin turns. Where the zigzags end, it winds northward, skirting wine-red cliffs of lava deposited eons ago.

● Near Dog Creek (Circle S Ranch), the road descends again to another sheltered oasis of green fields.

● Giant boulders, fallen from sheer volcanic cliffs, create a moonscape on the hillside north of Dog Creek Valley. The road climbs up to the benchland high above the Fraser Canyon. Look west across the river to the grasslands stretching to the horizon. Islands of aspen mark the natural springs and creeks that carry water to the Fraser.

● Eventually the road swings away from the Fraser to follow Alkali Creek. A wildlife sanctuary on the shores of Alkali Lake protects the nesting grounds of the white pelican.

● A short distance beyond Alkali Lake, you see the red buildings of Alkali Ranch, reputedly the province's oldest ranch.

● Between Alkali Lake and Williams Lake lies the community of Springhouse. A signpost marks the Springhouse Trails Ranch, where you can enjoy a night at a guest ranch and campground.

● The final stop is Williams Lake, the gateway to the Chilcotin and the start of the road to Bella Coola.

An abandoned farm building at Meadow Lake on the road to Alkali Lake

A WARM WELCOME AT A WORKING RANCH

Traveling from Clinton to Williams Lake through Chilcotin Country, you can visit Gang Ranch, British Columbia's largest working ranch: at 400,000 ha almost half the size of Prince Edward Island. The property stretches 48 km east to west from Big Creek to the Fraser River and 96 km north to south from the Chilcotin River to the Coast Mountains. Ranch headquarters are about 8 km west of the junction of the Empire Valley and Gang Ranch roads. The main access is by a suspension bridge used by miners and ranchers to ford the Fraser River. Almost like a small village, the ranch has its own general store and post office.

Sunflowers grow in Chilcotin ranch and farm gardens.

Thaddeus Harper and his brother Jerome, U.S. cattlemen who came to British Columbia during the gold rush of the 1860s, founded the ranch in 1883. When established, it encompassed roughly 1.5 million ha, and was one of the largest ranches in the world. The Harpers named it after the double-furrowed gangplow; they were the first to use the plow in British Columbia. Their H or JH-connected brand is one of the original brands still in use in the province.

Bev and Larry Ramsted manage Gang Ranch today, welcoming visitors who drop in to chat in the store or to send cards from the post office. (Gang Ranch has its own postmark.) There are no visitor accommodations but, with luck, especially in the off-season, you might meet genuine cowboys. (They are rarely at headquarters during summer.) The ranch has unusual geological formations, rugged scenery, and varied wildlife. One of the world's largest herds of California bighorn sheep roams the site.

12 Clinton

During the gold rush days of the 1860s, Clinton (pop. 662) was known as Junction. The settlement was the crossroads of the Fraser Canyon and Cariboo roads. Although no one ever discovered gold here, every miner seeking his fortune passed through the settlement. In 1863, at the completion of the Cariboo, it was given its present name in honor of Henry Pelham Clinton, 5th Duke of Newcastle, and British colonial secretary from 1859 to 1864.

Although the gold rush brought the "Wild West" to Clinton, the community had its "proper" side. In the winter of 1867, Mrs. Mary Smith, a leader of local society, launched the formal week-long Clinton Ball. At one time it attracted guests from as far away as San Francisco. The ball, with dancers in period costume, is still held the weekend following the Victoria Day weekend.

For years, the ball was held at the Clinton Hotel, which burned down in 1958. Some mementos, including wine decanters from the hotel bar, are displayed at the South Cariboo Historical Society Museum, located near the visitors' information centre. *Admission free; donations accepted. Open daily, May and June, 10 am to 6 pm; July and August, 9 am to 8 pm.*

Painted Chasm is some 15 km north of Clinton on Highway 97. Turn right at Chasm Road and follow the road for 8 km to a viewpoint and picnic spot. The canyon—1.5 km long and more than 120 m deep—was carved by glacial meltwaters some 10,000 years ago. The glittering rock layers of rusty pink and brown are best seen near sunset. There are several trails in the area. One leads to the bottom of the chasm, where you can follow a path along a creek past several small waterfalls.

Special events
Medieval Days (August)

13 Lillooet

The broad main street of Lillooet (pop. 1,850) was made for wagon drivers of the early 1860s. Since oxen cannot back up, drivers needed the width to turn around double-freight wagons pulled by teams of 20 oxen. In those gold rush days, the community was the southern departure point of the Cariboo Road. It was Mile "0," the first stagecoach rest stop (mile house) on the way to the goldfields. A rock cairn on Main Street marks where the road began. (Later the road started at Yale to the south.) The settlement was named for a trail connecting Lillooet Lake to the Fraser River. Some say the name is an Indian word for wild onion; others translate it as meeting of the waters, or trail's end.

You enter Lillooet over the Bridge of the 23 Camels (on the Fraser River), near where the combined Seton and Cayoosh creeks empty into the muddy Fraser. The bridge is named for the gold seeker Frank Laumeister who imported camels to carry his mining gear to the goldfields. It replaced a 1911 suspension bridge which still stands 3 km upstream. Both spans figure in a 10-km self-guiding tour, *Walking the Bridges.* You can get the pamphlet from the Lillooet Museum (and visitors' information centre) in the former St. Mary's Anglican Church. The museum displays artifacts and photographs of local history. *Admission is free, but donations are accepted. Open daily, July to September from 9 am to 6 pm; May 15 to June 30 and September 30 to October 31, from*

Sparsely forested hills surround Lillooet, which is set in the midst of a semidesert.

noon to 4 pm. The walking tour passes such sites as the newspaper office where "Ma" Murray wrote her outrageous editorials, the Miyazaki Heritage House, and the Old Log Cabin Theatre, once used as a camel barn.

A 12-m-high ponderosa pine in Hangman's Tree Park served as a gallows more than 100 years ago. Nearby rock pilings mark where miners panned for gold.

Lillooet's history is celebrated with Only in Lillooet Days the second weekend in June. That's when local folk, playing the part of outlaws, rob a passenger train and "kidnap" a judge. Visitors can dress up as gold seekers and join the fun.

Special events
Indian Band Annual Powwow (January)

Begbie Night (June)

Only in Lillooet Days (June)

Lillooet Lake Rodeo (September)

Black Powder Shoot
(Thanksgiving weekend)

14 Ashcroft

∧ ‼ ⊷ ⌁ ❄ ⌂

Here, in 1862, Clement Francis Cornwall and his brother Henry established a ranch they called Ashcroft Manor after the family home in England. Across the arid scrubland, the Cornwalls—both keen fox hunters—pursued coyotes with hounds imported from England. At a roadhouse, they provisioned miners heading north on the Cariboo Road. Today this roadhouse—a two-story frame dwelling shaded by elm trees—is just south of Ashcroft. It continues the tradition of conviviality.

From the manor, a 5-km drive on Cornwall Road leads from a high benchland of sagebrush and bunchgrass to Ashcroft (pop. 1,950), nestling in greenery on the Thompson River.

With the arrival of the CPR in 1884, Ashcroft became the railhead for Cariboo Country and northern British Columbia. Stagecoaches sped north with

passengers and mail; freight wagons carried goods and equipment to Cariboo Country and returned with gold. Barnard's Express (later the B.C. Express)—the BX—was distinguished by its red-and-yellow coaches. (The Historic Hat Creek Ranch, 22.5 km north of town, displays a BX coach.) Ashcroft thrived with stables and blacksmith shops, but its importance faded when the railway linked Vancouver to the Cariboo Country just before the First World War. The last stagecoach from Ashcroft left for the northern interior in 1919.

At the stampede every June, Ashcroft remembers its ranching and stagecoach days. Exhibits at the Ashcroft Museum chronicle the years between the arrival of the CPR and the

Once a place of pioneer hospitality, Ashcroft Manor is still popular with today's travelers.

First World War. *Admission free; donations accepted. Open daily early April to late September from 10 am to 6 pm.* A self-guiding walking tour, available at the museum, directs you to several handsome turn-of-the-century homes.

Ashcroft claims to be "Copper Capital of Canada." Highland Valley Copper Mine, on Highway 97C, 40 km south, has one of the world's largest open-pit mines. Twice-daily tours are available between early May and late August. Reservations are advisable.

Special events
B.X. Daze (August)

Ashcroft Fall Fair (September)

SOUTHEASTERN BRITISH COLUMBIA

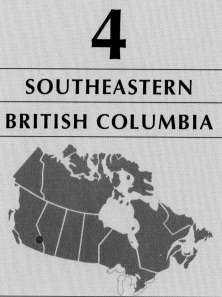

4

SOUTHEASTERN
BRITISH COLUMBIA

Places to see
Nicola Lake
Salmon Arm
Sicamous
Grand Forks
Nakusp
New Denver
Nelson
Creston
Kimberley

Roads to explore
Kettle and Okanagan valleys
New Denver to Ainsworth Hot Springs
Kimberley–Cranbrook–Fort Steele

National park close-up
Mount Revelstoke and Glacier
Yoho and Kootenay

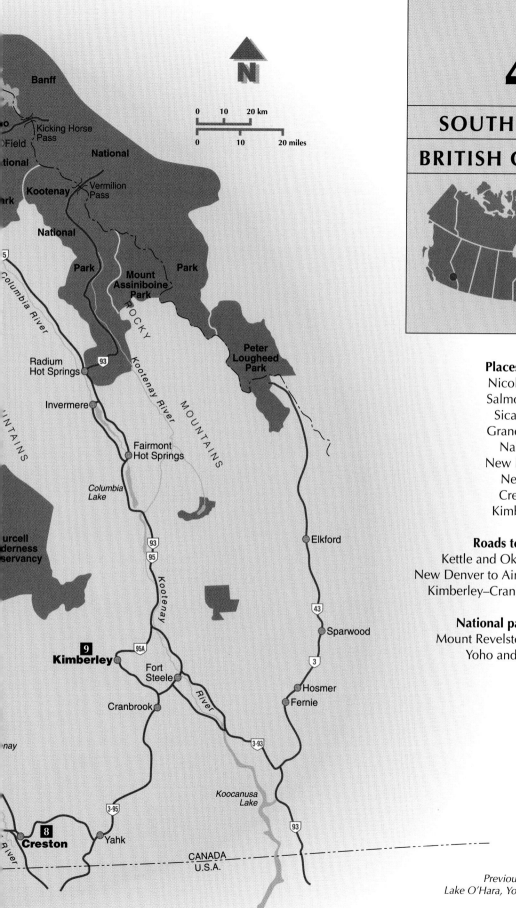

N

0   10   20 km

0   10   20 miles

Banff

Kicking Horse
Pass

Field

National

tional

Kootenay

Vermilion
Pass

rk

National

Park

Park

Mount
Assiniboine
Park

ROCKY

5

Columbia River

Peter
Lougheed
Park

93

Radium
Hot Springs

Kootenay River

MOUNTAINS

INTAINS

Invermere

Fairmont
Hot Springs

Columbia
Lake

Elkford

urcell
derness
servancy

93
95

Kootenay

43

Sparwood

95A

9

3

Kimberley

Fort
Steele

Hosmer

Cranbrook

River

Fernie

3-93

nay

Koocanusa
Lake

3-95

93

8

Creston

Yahk

River

CANADA
U.S.A.

Previous pages:
Lake O'Hara, Yoho National Park

1 Nicola Lake

Nicola Lake lies in the Nicola Valley, at the heart of the vast grasslands of southern British Columbia. Because the peaks of the Coast and North Cascade mountain ranges block the eastward flow of rain-bearing clouds from the Pacific, the valley seldom gets more than 25 cm of rain, most of it in late spring.

Sagebrush, bunchgrass, ponderosa pine, and prickly pear cactus thrive here. And so do cattle. Every year

The elegant Quilchena Hotel on Nicola Lake is a survivor of the Edwardian era.

ranchers ship some 15,000 head of cattle. The 220,000-ha Douglas Lake Cattle Company, 25 km east of Nicola, is one of Canada's largest cattle ranches.

Nicola Lake is known for its rainbow trout. But the 22-km-long lake contains 25 other varieties of fish, such as kokanee, Dolly Varden, char, and freshwater lingcod.

The lake also offers some of the finest opportunities for windsurfing in the British Columbia interior. The nearby hills are ideal terrain for hiking and backpacking and, in winter, cross-country skiing.

At Quilchena, on the lake's southeastern shore, stands the gracious Quilchena Hotel, built by pioneer rancher Joseph Guichon. When the hotel opened in 1908, it was hailed as one of the finest in the British Columbia interior. Polo games, horse racing, and rodeos were held on the nearby meadowland.

Prohibition closed the bar and the hotel in 1919, but it did not go to ruin. In 1958, Guy Rose, Guichon's grandson, reopened it and transformed the polo field into a golf course. The hotel is open from May to October.

Campers will find Monck Provincial Park, with its 71-unit campground on the north shore, an excellent summer base for exploring Nicola Lake. Access is via the 11.2-km-long Monck Park Road that leaves Highway 5A, some 11 km northeast of Merritt.

Within the park, a resident naturalist will explain its unusual features. The trails run through a wealth of dry-country wildflowers. Expect sightings of wildlife, too. Trails on the hillside overlooking the park lead to an ancient volcanic outcropping.

On Labor Day weekend, Merritt holds the Nicola Valley Memorial Rodeo and Fall Fair, with street dancing, pancake breakfasts, old-time fiddling contests, as well as the rodeo.

2 Salmon Arm

Shuswap Lake in the heart of British Columbia's interior is a scenic but oddly shaped body of water with four sprawling arms: Salmon Arm, Anstey Arm, Seymour Arm, and Shuswap Arm. It has nearly 1,000 km of rugged shoreline for boaters to explore.

The town of Salmon Arm (pop. 12,115) is the largest community on the lake. Its waterfront is famous as a nesting site for the rare western grebe, which performs a fascinating mating dance on the surface of the lake.

One of the most popular trails in the area is at Margaret Falls, near Herald Provincial Park, 25 km to the north of Salmon Arm. A comfortable 10-minute

Roads to explore: On Okanagan byways

Distance (approx.): 310 km/193 ¾ miles

This circle drive through the Kettle and southern Okanagan valleys begins at the junction of highways 33 and 97, just outside Kelowna in Rutland, and covers mountainous backcountry, scrubland, orchards, and vineyards. With an overnight stopover at a wayside campsite, you might manage the trip in two days.

● From the junction, head east on Highway 33, which turns south and passes through Beaverdell. Some 80 km after the junction, you can turn west on a 16-km gravel road that leads to the 24 campsites at Conkle Lake Provincial Park. Or you can go to the 49 campsites at Kettle River Recreation Area, 15 km south of the Conkle Lake turnoff.

● Rock Creek, only 5 km from the United States border, lies at the southern end of Highway 33. Swing west, along Highway 3, which runs parallel to the border. About 7 km west of Rock Creek, Johnstone Creek Provincial Park offers a 16-unit campground.

● After this point, Highway 3 climbs Anarchist Mountain. Its name recalls a local figure of bygone days, Richard Sidley, whose outspoken views cost him his job as a justice of the peace.

● Highway 3 snakes down to Osoyoos Lake. Haynes Point Provincial Park's

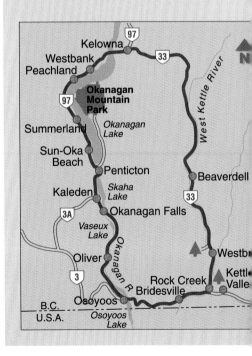

Gray clouds darken the skies above the fields, hills, and scrubland of the arid Osoyoos area.

walk leads to the base of the 30-m-high waterfall and a small cave hidden behind a veil of cold mountain water.

Just 50 km northwest of Salmon Arm, Roderick Haig-Brown Provincial Park spans both sides of the Adams River. In October, you can stroll along riverside trails to watch sockeye salmon journeying upstream to spawn.

You can also enjoy the thrill of white water rafting on the rough-and-tumble waters of the Adams River. A local company based in Scotch Creek organizes excursions.

Near Magna Bay, some 25 km east of Roderick Haig-Brown Provincial Park, an annual bluegrass festival attracts music lovers in mid-July.

3 | Sicamous

This Shuswap Lake community (pop. 2,000) claims to be the houseboat capital of Canada. According to local houseboat operators, the vessels—designed for floating holidays—are easy to run. You can rent one in Sicamous; operators give you brief instruction before you take over.

Around Shuswap Lake, there are more than 20 provincial parks, and over 100 different beaches and public areas where houseboaters can tie up overnight. Imagine cruising to four lakeshore golf courses, or mooring offshore for horseback riding, swimming, and hiking.

Paddle-driven Phoebe Ann *carries passengers and mail to Shuswap Lake destinations.*

36-unit campground sits on a sandspit that parallels the highway crossing of Osoyoos Lake.
● From Osoyoos, drive south on Highway 97 to see the Osoyoos kettles, two giant potholes left by glaciers. Turn back and drive north on 97, through lush orchards and past the community of Oliver.
● Vaseux Lake Provincial Park, 15 km north of Oliver, encloses one of Canada's few deserts. Nearby is a bird and bighorn sheep sanctuary. You may glimpse California bighorns from the roadside.
● Okanagan Falls, at the south end of Skaha Lake, has two parks: Christie Memorial, a day-use park on the lake, and Okanagan Falls Park, a 20-unit campground near the Okanagan River.
● Some 5 km north of Okanagan Falls on Highway 97, the Okanagan Game Farm contains 1,000 animals of 130 species. *Open year-round, from 8 am to dusk.*
● The next stop is Penticton (pop. 24,400), the largest community in the southern Okanagan area, which provides access to beaches on Skaha and Okanagan lakes.
● From Penticton, head north on Highway 97 along the western side of Okanagan Lake. Near Sun-Oka Beach, stop at the Summerland Agricultural Research Station, which is open to the public.
● North of Summerland, signs to Sumac Ridge Estate Winery point the way to one of the many small enterprises of this kind in the Okanagan region. The wineries welcome visitors and provide tours.
● Farther along, Okanagan Lake Provincial Park is a base for sailing on Okanagan Lake. It also has 156 vehicle campsites.
● After the park, Highway 97 first passes Westbank and then Westside (across Okanagan Lake from Kelowna). Bear Creek Provincial Park, 7 km north of Westside, offers hiking trails and 80 campsites.
● The final stop is Kelowna (pop. 65,000), the largest Okanagan community. Its attractions include the floating bridge and the Kelowna Centennial Museum. A return to the junction of highways 33 and 97 in Rutland marks the end of the trip.

During July and August, the 45-passenger paddle wheeler MV *Phoebe Ann* sails from Sicamous carrying mail, supplies, and passengers. The most popular trip is the mail run to the small community of Seymour Arm. The *Phoebe Ann* leaves Sicamous early in the morning and, after making stops and deliveries along the lake, arrives around noon at Seymour Arm, the northernmost point on Shuswap Lake. During the one-hour stopover, you can lunch at the Seymour Arm Hotel, or take a dip at Silver Beach Provincial Park, the setting for one of the most beautiful beaches on Shuswap Lake.

4 Grand Forks

The rolling, green hills of the Kootenays ring Grand Forks. During its boom years early this century, three railways hauled out gold, silver, and copper produced by nearby mines. The town was also a staging point, or gathering place, for prospectors who converged on the Granby Valley and the Kettle Valley farther west.

Today Grand Forks is a community of more than 3,500, which attracts hikers, cyclists, and cross-country skiers, and local-history enthusiasts.

Clearly marked hiking trails around Phoenix and Thimble mountains to the west and Christina Lake to the east (one of British Columbia's warmest lakes) lead to superb views, rewarding nature walks, and sandy beaches.

Grand Forks is a treasure trove for history buffs. The Boundary Museum takes you back to the time when Grand Forks had the largest copper smelter in the British Empire. *Open daily, June to September, and Monday to Friday, the rest of year, 9:30 am to 4:30 pm.*

Within a short walking distance of the museum, just off the highway at 5th Street, are a dozen restored homes

The snowy heights of the Selkirk Mountains dwarf Nakusp on Upper Arrow Lake.

In a shaded stream of the Granby Valley, a lone swimmer enjoys a secluded, refreshing dip.

and many buildings dating from the gold rush era.

The Doukhobors, persecuted in Russia for their religious beliefs, settled in the Granby Valley in 1909. The town is home to the headquarters of the Canada's Orthodox Doukhobors. The Doukhobor heritage is reflected in the restaurants, which serve traditional Russian dishes.

A 17-km stretch of road along the Granby Valley, north of town, provides a pleasant side trip. From the Boundary Museum, turn right onto Highway 3, cross the bridge and take the next left on Granby Road. Follow the Granby River north, past the "slag piles" of black tailings from the old smelter, and on to Smelter Lake, created by a hydroelectric dam.

Along the highway are the remains of mining camps and towns. Cross the Granby River at Humming Bird Bridge, and then return to Grand Forks. The North Fork Road, north of the bridge, leads to a wilderness area, known as the Upper Granby River watershed. This rugged region is strictly for experienced hikers, naturalists, and white water kayakers.

Ward Lake, a waterfowl refuge 2 km to the northwest of Grand Forks, offers a quiet place to picnic.

5 Nakusp

The busy logging village of Nakusp (pop. 1,600) lies between the Monashee and Selkirk ranges on the eastern shore of Upper Arrow Lake. This mountainous region is blessed with hot springs where waters bubble to the surface from the depths of the earth.

A walk along Nakusp's waterfront provides a sweeping view of Upper Arrow Lake, Saddleback Mountain, and the other mighty peaks of the Monashee Mountains, farther west. The Arrow Lakes comprise 518 km² of fishable water, in which rainbow and Dolly Varden trout, lingcod, whitefish, and kokanee salmon are plentiful. Many of the small mountain lakes near Nakusp are good for fly-fishing and, in winter, ice fishing.

Down by the village waterfront is the Leland Hotel, one of the longest operating hotels in British Columbia. Some parts of the hotel date from 1892, the year Nakusp was founded.

More than 100 years ago, the village was a frontier boomtown and shipbuilding port on the Arrow Lakes–Columbia River steamboat route. It also served as the railhead for the

Mount Revelstoke and Glacier

The Columbia Mountain system, ancient even when the Rockies were born, contains some of Canada's most awesome and most rugged scenery—massive steep-walled mountains, narrow, avalanche-scarred valleys, boulder-strewn glaciers and perpetual ice sheets. One of its ranges—the Selkirk Mountains—rises in the 260-km² Mount Revelstoke National Park and in the larger Glacier National Park, which covers 1,350 km². Glacier's eastern boundary is formed by the Purcell Range.

Mount Revelstoke National Park was founded in 1914 after a group of local citizens, so impressed with its beauty, urged its preservation. Glacier National Park was established in 1886, only a year after the Canadian Pacific Railway crossed Rogers Pass, which cuts through the Selkirks.

Winter rules this landscape with a special power. Every winter, moisture-laden air from the distant Pacific rolls up against the mountains, and releases huge quantities of snow —there can be up to 23 m of snowfall in a year. But the snow cannot cling to the impossibly steep slopes for long. With a loud resounding crack, a large fissure rips across the high slopes above the snow-plastered trees. Instantly, the whole slope starts sliding, picking up speed with every second. Hundreds of tonnes of snow, which moments before rested peacefully on the slopes, are transformed into one of nature's greatest forces, a frothing white cloud hurtling through the air at speeds of more than 320 km an hour. Avalanches such as these are most frequent from November to May.

On routes such as the Trans-Canada Highway, which borders Mount Revelstoke and bisects Glacier National Park, giant snowsheds protect the road against avalanches and forecasters regularly monitor the snow buildup. Whenever the accumulation of snow seems likely to get out of hand, artillery gunners train howitzer cannon on the danger spots, dissipating their full force. Winter travelers should enquire about the safety of the road, at information centres in Revelstoke and Golden, before entering the parks.

The rain forest valleys

Deep in the mountain valleys, giant western red cedars have endured the assault of winter for at least 800 years. From bases up to 4 m in diameter, they taper skyward, weather-beaten spikes that reach 46 m above the snow. On their wooden elbows, in the damp world beneath the canopy, hang rich mats of feathery moss and convoluted lungwort lichen.

Birds live in these valleys for the brief summer only. By the time the snows come, the eerie twangs of the varied thrush and the long melodies of the winter wren are gone. However, thousands of small mammals—mostly shrews, voles, and mice—live here throughout the year. In winter they scurry in search of food, in the twilight of tunnels under the snow. Few creatures remain above the snow's surface. Among them are the mountain caribou, snow-country specialists, with feet that act like snowshoes and a digestive system partial to tree lichens. Black bears, visible in summer, spend the period of cold curled up inside hollow cedars.

The snow forest

Toward the summits, the forest changes to a wet belt of mountain hemlock, Engelmann spruce, and subalpine fir. Snowfall is more prodigious in this subalpine region, and the winter here can seem lifeless. But gray jays, common ravens, and hawk owls, usually summer regulars, are seen here in winter. And occasionally the tin whistle of golden-crowned kinglets and the buzzy phrases of the boreal chickadees break the silence. You may see the prints of a pine marten on the surface of the snow, bounding parallel to the tracks of its prey, a red squirrel.

In the alpine reaches, the forests are broken by meadows. When the snow disappears from these clearings, late in July, the meltwater swirls with the minuscule bodies of golden snow fleas. Gray jays and mountain chickadees time their nesting so that their young are just out of the nest at this brief moment of plenty. And young ground squirrels busy themselves gathering food to hoard and fatten themselves up for the next winter sleep.

Wildflowers rush to flower and set seed at this time. The meadows turn white and gold with spring beauties and glacier lilies, to be covered only two weeks later by lupine, mountain valerian, Indian paintbrush, arnica, and heather. These are the meadows that have made Mount Revelstoke Park, in particular, famous. You can see them from the 26-km Summit Parkway that starts just inside the park's western entrance and climbs to the 1,938-m height of Mount Revelstoke itself. You can also get a good view from trails through the park, accessible from the Parkway or the Trans-Canada Highway. Hikers should be warned that Mount Revelstoke Park has no campgrounds, although Glacier has two.

The treeless zone

Above the tree line, long slopes of sparse, ground-hugging vegetation stretch along low ridges. And where recent rock-slides have shaken the mountains, lichen-crusted boulder fields lie in unstable repose. This landscape has been carved by ice sheets that have formed, melted, and reformed in the region over the millennia.

In Glacier National Park, glaciers have cut deeply into the valleys and crafted the classic matterhorn formation of Mount Sir Donald and the fortress towers of Mount Tupper. The park has more than 400 glaciers. One of the most visible

The magnificent but precipitous slopes of the Selkirk Mountains in Glacier National Park pose challenges to even the most experienced skiers.

is the Illecillewaet Glacier, which can be seen from trails leading from the Illecillewaet campground. Other glaciers and snow-mantled crags can be seen along the Trans-Canada Highway, particularly along Rogers Pass, one of the world's most beautiful stretches of mountain road.

In Mount Revelstoke the ice sheets have created the Clachnacudainn Icefield, which dominates the park's centre, and a permanent patch of ice known as the Icebox, enclosed by rock walls. You can reach the Icebox along the 1-km-long Meadows-in-the-Sky Trail, which leads from the Summit Parkway. Another 6-km-long one-way trail from the summit leads to Eva and Miller lakes. Eva Lake sits on a ledge that, a few metres from the lakeshore, plummets over 100 m to the valley below.

Although the tundra is a harsh environment, it is far from lifeless. Caribou, wolverines, grizzly bears, and mountain goats thrive here. So do microscopic creatures. In late spring, when the cold loosens its grip on the alpine zone, the snows turn watermelon pink. This spectacular display marks the invasion of red algae. These organisms multiply in the melt-water, propelled by whiplike tails. In the last stages of the snow's disintegration, blood-red veins of algae streak the mountains, a flamboyant gesture against winter.

PARK INFORMATION
Access: The Trans-Canada Highway.
Visitors' centres: Revelstoke, just outside Mount Revelstoke National Park; Rogers Pass, in Glacier National Park.
Accommodation: Two campgrounds with 76 sites in Glacier National Park. Glacier Park Lodge at Rogers Pass provides year-round accommodation.
Summer activities: Hiking, interpretive programs and self-guiding trails.
Winter activities: Mount Revelstoke offers cross-country skiing and snowshoeing. Skiing in Glacier National Park is challenging and can be hazardous. Before setting out, skiers in both parks should check conditions; skiers in Glacier have to register with the park warden services before setting off down the slopes.

Roads to explore: Spectral settlements of a silver boom

Distance (approx.):
80 km/50 miles

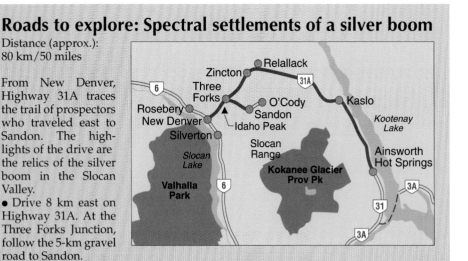

From New Denver, Highway 31A traces the trail of prospectors who traveled east to Sandon. The highlights of the drive are the relics of the silver boom in the Slocan Valley.

● Drive 8 km east on Highway 31A. At the Three Forks Junction, follow the 5-km gravel road to Sandon.

In 1897, six years after silver was discovered in this region, Sandon was a boomtown of 5,000. Nearby Sandon Creek yielded the world's largest galena (silver-lead ore) nugget, weighing more than 120 tonnes and valued at $20,000. Today, the village contains 52 heritage buildings, but most of them are empty—only 10 to 20 hardy individuals still live around here.

● Return to the Three Forks Junction and continue east on Highway 31A through the Valley of Ghosts. Here are abandoned mining communities such as Zincton and Retallack. You can see the remains of mine workings, aerial tramways, and railway tracks along the 47-km route to Kaslo.

● The next stop is Kaslo on the western shore of Kootenay Lake. In 1889 this sawmill community was a major supply and transportation outpost for American interests competing for business in the Slocan silver boom.

At the east end of the village's busy main street is the 50-m lake stern-wheeler *SS Moyie*, now a museum. Built in 1898, this elegant steamer served Kootenay Lake until 1956. The Langham Hotel, a restored heritage site, is also a museum and cultural centre. Kaslo's 1897 city hall is one of the oldest wood-frame city halls still in use in Canada.

● Highway 31 winds along the cliffs and lakeshore for 17 km to the town of Ainsworth Hot Springs. Established in 1882 and originally called Hotsprings Camp, it was the first mining settlement in the Kootenays. The hot mineral waters at Ainsworth flow from a cave, now part of a commercial complex. The Silver Ledge Hotel, with a small museum, and Fletcher's General Store, both built in 1896, retain Ainsworth's original character.

● About 15 km from the town, on a gravel road that leads west from Highway 31, are the Cody Caves. Their features include the "Throne Room," a 38-m² limestone gallery of stalactites and stalagmites, an echo room, and an underground creek.

ambitious, reward efforts with superb alpine views. For the longer mountain trails, you can hire guides from Nakusp, who will lead you to the heights on foot, or by horseback or llama. The docile llamas, skilled at negotiating mountain trails, are imports from the Andes of South America.

In late August and September, mushroom lovers converge on the forests around the village of Nakusp where they pick the pine and chanterelle varieties.

In winter, Nakusp is a popular cross-country skiing centre. You can savor the Wensley Creek Ski Trail just west of town on Highway 6 and a number of other trails north of town along the Hot Springs Road.

Special events

Minto Days Heritage Festival
(late June)

Fishing Derby (early June)

Annual Slo-pitch tournament
(August long weekend)

Fall Fair (late September)

6 New Denver

When silver was discovered in nearby Slocan Valley in 1891, this village was first named Eldorado—the fabled city of riches. The name was later changed by miners who hoped that the town would surpass the mining centre in Colorado called Denver.

Within five years of the silver discovery, New Denver grew from a prospectors' camp into a mine-claim and supply base. Today it is a picturesque village of 571 inhabitants.

The glory and hardship of pioneer days is the subject of the Silvery Slocan Museum, built in 1897 as a Bank of Montreal. Local historical artifacts include a sample of galena (silver-lead ore), a 4560 Winchester shotgun, and objects from the Japanese-Canadian internment in the 1940s. *Open daily, late June to mid-September, 10 am to 4 pm.*

Nakusp and Slocan Railway, which ran east to the rich mines of Sandon in the Slocan Valley.

Nakusp's museum chose the unusual and the bizarre as the theme for its historical collection. Its curiosities include a pig preserved in a small jar, a deer bone around which a cedar stump had grown, and snowshoes for a horse.

Nakusp's hot springs, just 12 km from town, have two outdoor pools filled with odorless mineral water. One of the pools is piping hot (42°C);

the other is a little cooler for more comfortable soaking.

Several other hot springs are located in scenic wilderness settings, within easy reach of town. Getting to these springs requires a little legwork, but the hike is usually worthwhile. The Halcyon, Halfway and St. Leon springs are probably the best-known natural springs. Ask at the Nakusp visitors' centre for maps and descriptions.

Near Nakusp, a number of hiking trails, ranging from the easy to the

Another village memorial, the Nikkei Internment Memorial Centre, commemorates the transportation during the Second World War of more than 21,000 people of Japanese origin to the ghost towns and remote communities of British Columbia's interior. More than a third were resettled around New Denver.

The horizons here glow with the snowcapped peaks of the encircling Valhalla, Slocan, and Kokanee ranges. One of the grandest is the 2,280-m Idaho Peak, whose summit is reached up a steep trail. The view of Slocan Lake from the top is spectacular.

7 Nelson

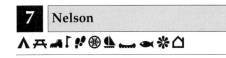

The forested slopes of the Purcell Mountains cradle Nelson (pop. 8,700). This "Queen City of the Kootenays"

A blaze of wildflowers and a fine view of Slocan Lake await hikers atop Idaho Peak.

is situated on the Kootenay River and overlooks the west arm of Kootenay Lake, one of British Columbia's largest lakes.

Nelson began as a mining boom-town of the late 1880s. By 1904, it had grown into the largest centre between Vancouver and Winnipeg. When the silver boom died in the early 1920s, Nelson switched from mining to lumbering, and fruit growing, ranching, and into its role as the area's administrative centre.

Baker Street, the town's main thoroughfare, was restored in the 1980s. There are more than 300 heritage buildings here, some built before 1910. They include the restored art deco Capitol Theatre, built in the 1920s. Vancouver and Victoria are the only British Columbia cities with more heritage architecture.

The self-guiding heritage tours of Nelson begin at the city hall, where you can obtain three tour brochures published by the Nelson Heritage Advisory Committee. The Heritage Cemetery Tour takes you through Nelson's cemetery on Falls Street, at the very top of a hill. One of the graves is that of Frederick Niven (1878-1944), a Scottish-Canadian novelist who wrote sketches of Canadian pioneer life.

In summer, visitors can ride some of Nelson's history, on the town's 1899-vintage streetcar No. 23. Board it at the east end of Lakeside Park, after waiting on the south side under the trees, or on the sandy beach.

The Nelson Museum at the east end of Anderson Street displays Indian artifacts, old mining equipment and the restored *Ladybird Speedboat*, which set the world speed record for its class in 1933. *Open daily, May to September, 1 pm to 6 pm; winter months, Monday to Saturday, 1 pm to 4 pm.*

Nelson is a good base for recreation. Ambitious hikers and backpackers can test their mettle in neighboring Valhal-

Nelson's ivy-draped stone courthouse is one of the town's handsome heritage structures.

la Wilderness Provincial Park, Purcell Wilderness Conservancy and Kokanee Glacier Park. These wilderness parks are within a two-hour drive of the city.

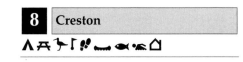

Special events

Kootenay Summer School
of the Arts (July-August)

Nelson Midsummer Curling Bonspiel
(early July)

8 Creston

Flanked by orchards and farms, Creston (pop. 4,200) lies in a verdant valley between the Purcell and Moyie mountains to the east and the Selkirk Range to the west. Tours are available from here to such diverse spots as a local brewery and a candle-making plant.

In 1863, the Dewdney Gold Rush Trail between Hope and

Peach orchards thrive in Creston.

A series of masterful murals depict the early development of Creston's logging industry.

Wild Horse Creek cut across this area. In the 1880s, mining, forestry, and agriculture spurred the growth of the community. With the arrival of the railway in the 1890s, the settlement acquired its original name, Seventh Siding.

A heritage revitalization program is helping to renew Creston's downtown buildings. Some of these are Edwardian in design, but most are art deco buildings, dating from the 1930s. The two grain elevators gracing the downtown area—an unusual sight in southern British Columbia—are justified by bountiful harvests.

The town is enlivened by large colorful murals at five different sites, depicting local themes such as logging, wildlife, and wildlife management. The "Creston Valley Four Seasons" mural decorates one wall of a department store. Creston Valley Museum displays pioneer and Indian objects such as the Kootenay Canoe, whose bow and stern come to a point at or under the waterline. The only other similar design is found in the Amur River region in Siberian Russia. *Open daily, April to October, 10 am to 3:30 pm; October to March, open by appointment.*

About 1 km from town is the Wayside Gardens and Arboretum. One of its gardens rises through three levels, then follows a stream in a formal design against a backdrop of mountains and orchards. *Open daily, year-round, 9 am to 5 pm.*

About 5 km north on Highway 3A, a picnic pavilion overlooks the valley. A plaque here commemorates the 85 km of diking that protects 10,000 ha of farmland from river flooding.

Across the river valley, in the Creston Valley Wildlife Management Area,

Roads to explore: A rail museum, a Rockies fort

Distance (approx.): 90 km/56 ¼ miles

Take a drive around the Kimberley-Cranbrook section of the Rocky Mountain Trench. This great valley, flanked in this area by the Rockies on the east and the Purcell Mountains to the west, is a great valley stretching 1,400 km from the United States border almost to the Yukon.

● From Kimberley, take Highway 95A to Cranbrook. As you head south, you can turn west onto Highway 44. This 75-km summer route, known locally as the Gray Creek Pass Road, crosses the Purcell Mountains to Kootenay Lake and Creston Valley. It is a gravel forestry road with sharp switchbacks and grades on the descent to Gray Creek. If you take this route, travel slowly on the downgrade. Check the road's condition with a local information centre before setting out.

● At Cranbrook (pop. 16,000) stop at the Canadian Museum of Rail Travel, on the highway at Baker Street. Restored cars of the 1929 Trans-Canada Limited recall days of luxurious cross-country rail travel. You can order tea in the dining car.

● Take Highway 3/95 to Cranbrook's eastern boundary, and keep left on the 3/95 route signposted to Invermere and Radium. Directly ahead are the Rocky Mountains.

● Some 12 km on, the road crosses the Kootenay River, and travelers can see the giant waterwheel of Fort Steele on the east bank.

● The turnoff to the Fort Steele Historic Site is just ahead on the left. This famous settlement was originally known as Galbraith's Ferry, since it was a ferry crossing that served prospectors in the nearby Wild Horse Creek gold rushes of 1863 and 1884.

When the prospectors left, the settlers moved in. Land disputes between the settlers and the local Indians forced the RCMP to send Superintendent Sam Steele to the community to ease the tension. He set up the first post east of the Rockies and resolved the arguments within a year. In his honor the settlement was renamed Fort Steele.

Bypassed by the railway in 1904, Fort Steele then became a ghost town, until its reconstruction some 70 years later. Now it is a Heritage Town with 60 restored buildings, and train and stagecoach rides. *Open daily, year-round, 9:30 am to dusk.*

● From Fort Steele, continue north on Highway 93/95, passing the Kootenay

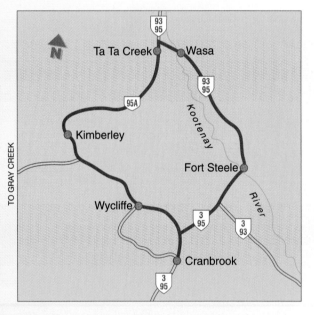

River wetlands, an important habitat for migratory waterfowl. Wasa Lake Provincial Park, 21 km from Fort Steele, has a shallow lake with camping and picnic areas, a beach, boat-launching facilities, and nature trails.

● Highway 93/95 crosses the Kootenay River, some 2 km north of Wasa Lake, and then meets Highway 95A. Turn south on Highway 95A, which rises steadily toward the Purcell Mountains and the town of Kimberley.

the wetlands welcome thousands of migrating birds in spring and fall, including tundra swans. From these birds, the valley gets its name "Valley of the Swans." Some 250 species of birds, such as ospreys and bald eagles, nest here.

You can take guided canoe tours through the marshes in summer. Almost 1 km of boardwalk is accessible to wheelchairs, as is a further 6.5 km of trail in the immediate area; another 48 km of dikes is open to hikers. From the campground west of the wildlife centre, a suspension bridge over Summit Creek leads to the 5-km marked Dewdney Hiking Trail.

Special events
Blossom Festival (May)
Fall Fair (early September)

9 Kimberley

Wilkommen is the greeting in Kimberley (pop. 7,000), a Bavarian-style community in the mountains of southeastern British Columbia. Originally a mining centre and site of the world's largest silver-lead-zinc mine, Kimberley, Canada's highest city, has become a recreational centre for all seasons.

In the Platzl, the bricked pedestrian street in the city centre, the world's largest cuckoo clock keeps time. The Platzl fronts shops and outdoor cafés in the Bavarian style, complete with strolling accordion players.

The Heritage Museum, with its collection of mining artifacts, is located on the Platzl, above the Public Library. The International Arts Centre is a block from the Platzl.

The Bavarian City Mining Railway, a few minutes drive away, runs on a 2.5-km track. Its first stop is a viewpoint of the surrounding Thousand Peaks. The train passes over a 7.6-m-high, 61-m-long timber trestle, from which passengers can see the entrance to the huge Sullivan Mine. Artifacts

The church of St. Eugene, near Kimberley, is one of the finest wooden churches in the area.

from that mine line the route. A wildlife sanctuary and a golf course lie nearby.

Mining began here in 1892, with four men staking claims which they sold to a mining company that later became Cominco. Today the company maintains the 1-ha Cominco Gardens, which is open to visitors.

From the centre of Kimberley, follow the 6-km Rotary/Lions Walkway along Mark Creek, which leads to the village of Marysville, a delight for antique and curio lovers. St. Mary's River courses through Marysville. The Marysville Falls on Mark Creek, just off the main

street of the village, can be reached by boardwalk.

An appealing site of this region is the 1897 Gothic-style church of the St. Eugene mission, situated in the secluded St. Mary's River valley. Drive some 15 km east of Kimberley on Highway 95A and turn south on the old airport road to reach the church.

Special events
Cranbrook Sam Steele Day
(late June)
Julyfest (late July)
Kimberley International Old Time
Accordion Championships (mid-July)

Yoho and Kootenay

Lake O'Hara, one of Yoho Park's most dazzling landmarks, glows with emerald brilliance in a setting of imposing peaks and tumbling falls.

They are siblings: one is brash and unruly, the other genteel and slightly inhibited. Yoho and Kootenay national parks share family likenesses in their Rocky Mountain geography, but each has a distinctive personality. They also form part of the Canadian Rocky Mountain Park World Heritage Site that includes Banff and Jasper national parks.

Yoho is the older, born when Canada's first transcontinental railway was conquering the Rockies. It has one of the most dramatic landscapes in Canadian parks. Yoho's mountains are brawny and sheer, its valleys deep, its waterfalls among Canada's highest. The boisterous Kicking Horse River courses through mud and crumbling glacial till. And snowslides bury the rail line and highway every winter.

In contrast to this wild turbulence, Kootenay is gracious and subdued. This narrow park on the west side of the Continental Divide is bisected by both the Banff-Winder-

mere Highway and the long, relatively gentle valleys of the Vermilion and Kootenay rivers. It is a striking blend of hot springs, cold lakes, deep canyons, and twisting glaciers.

Even the names set a certain tone. Yoho is a Cree word meaning "inspiring awe," whereas Kootenay is named for the entrepreneurial Kootenay Indians. Before the bison herds were decimated in the mid-19th century, the Kootenays crossed the Rockies each spring to hunt the animals. In the late 18th century they introduced horses to the Plains Indians, trading the stock for implements that the Peigan and Blackfoot Indians had acquired through the fur trade.

The Kootenay Indians developed a small industry around iron-rich clay found at Ochre Creek, a tributary of the Kootenay River. The place, just inside the northern entrance to the park, is known today as the "Paint Pots." By firing the yellow and orange earth in bonfires, they reduced it to a readily transportable vermilion ochre, which was in great demand among both Plains and Woodland peoples.

Yoho's robust charms

As soon as the railway was built, Yoho's robust charms attracted all sorts of sightseers, including painters. During a visit to the park, J.E.H. MacDonald, one of Canada's Group of Seven, wrote: "I have waterfalls and glaciers and mountain brooks, and meadows, and rockslides, and snowy peaks; and there are trees, the spruce and the balsam and the plumy Lyall's larch—and August went out with Christmas card weather with the larches all drooping in a sparkle of snowy boughs and sunlight."

The Lyall's larch he wrote about grows on the margins of the timberline meadows, about 2,000 m above sea level. A relative of the tamarack and western larch, Lyall's larch loses its needles in late September, but only after they have turned a bright cadmium yellow. Against the clear blue skies and white snow-bearing clouds, or beside the milky blue and bright emerald lakes of the Rockies, this conifer commands attention, whether in its summer green or autumn yellow.

MacDonald also described Emerald Lake: "It is emerald and malachite and jade and rainbow green, and mermaid's eyes, and the beads of Saint Bridget, and the jewels of St. Patrick's crown, and anything else the imagination can ascribe to it." Emerald Lake can be reached by road off the Trans-Canada Highway, a short distance from the town of Field, the park's administrative centre.

One of Yoho's most oustanding features—the Burgess shale fossil bed of Mount Wapta—was discovered in 1909 by Dr. Charles Doolittle Walcott, an American paleontologist. Walcott was guiding his horses along a mountain ridge when he split open a shard of shale, and in it found the fossilized remains of several soft-bodied organisms. Being a scientist, he recognized what he had found—rocks of the Middle Cambrian period, some 500 million years old. The area, protected by park authorities, has since yielded examples of about 120 species of marine invertebrates, all preserved in exquisite detail in the ancient muds. The Burgess Shale is reached on foot, on a fairly strenuous 22-km round-trip. Access is restricted and a place on the hike must be reserved in advance.

Southwest of the fossil bed, on the edge of the park, are Wapta Falls, which tumble down 30 m to Kicking Horse River, swelling its width at that point to 60 m.

A roadside park

Just as Yoho was a child of the railway, so Kootenay was sired by the first road built across the central Canadian Rockies. It was created in 1920, nine years after the road through Vermilion Pass was constructed, part of the Banff-Windermere Highway, the first road linking eastern British Columbia to the Prairies, which was opened in 1923.

The park's upper edge abuts the Great Divide and its lower limit is marked by a narrow portal, once called the Iron Gates. This opens onto the Rocky Mountain Trench, a great valley separating the Rockies from the Columbia Mountains. The park's sinuous extent follows the Vermilion and Kootenay rivers. The northern sector is guarded by glacier-hung Storm Mountain and Stanley Peak, a short distance from Vermilion Pass. In the south, the deep rust rocks of Sinclair Canyon splash bold colors. At one extremity it is a larch-bearing paradise. Elsewhere, the forests give way to meadows dotted with carpets of such high-altitude beauties as white mountain heather, dwarf willow, and bog laurel.

In the Canadian Rockies, spring does not reach the alpine zone until June. In July, when the lower-region grasses are developing seed heads, bright yellow spring avalanche lilies are still bursting through the snowpack in the glacier-hung highland meadows. Spring is an especially good time to explore Kootenay's extremes. In the bright warmth of an April morning, you can cross-country ski on crusty snow and later, near Radium Hot Springs, stroll through budding poplar trees, or swim in a naturally hot outdoor pool.

In 1968, lightning struck near the park's northeastern boundary, igniting a fire that burned for four days. By the time the flames were extinguished, a vast expanse of forest had been destroyed. But within days the charred area had started to regenerate. For even as it razed the trees, the fire restored forest vitality, culling aged and dying trees, opening up rangeland for grass eaters such as elk and deer, and clearing the way for berry shrubs and bushes, an important food source for black and grizzly bears. A short walk among the blackened trunks around the Vermilion Pass, at the northern entrance to the park, will reveal a wealth of ground cover flourishing in the ash-enriched earth—bunchberry, false huckleberry, twinflower, bright yellow arnica, and the showy-pink fireweed that has lent its name to this walk, the 800-m Fireweed Trail.

Because many of Kootenay's visitors just drive through the park without stopping, they miss some of the most spectacular sights—larch-edged Floe Lake nestling beneath the sheer cliffs of the Rock Wall, and the easily accessible cirque in which Stanley Glacier sits. Others who explore some of the hundreds of short, easy trails off Highway 93 will come upon sights such as the rock formation near Sinclair Summit resembling a head-dressed Indian chief, and the unusual view of Mount Assiniboine from Kootenay Crossing.

PARK INFORMATION
Access: The Trans-Canada Highway in Yoho Park; Highway 93, in Kootenay Park.
Visitors' centres: Field in Yoho Park; and Radium Hot Springs in Kootenay Park.
Accommodation: In Yoho: 5 campgrounds with 315 campsites, only 2 semi-serviced; reservations required for Lake O'Hara campground. In Kootenay: 5 campgrounds with 476 sites: 1 for groups, 1 for winter use; 3 are semi-serviced only.
Summer activities: Moutaineering, rafting (in Kootenay only), hiking, horseback riding and canoeing are among the many available activities.
Winter activities: Skiing, snowshoeing, ski touring, and ice climbing.

SOUTHERN ALBERTA

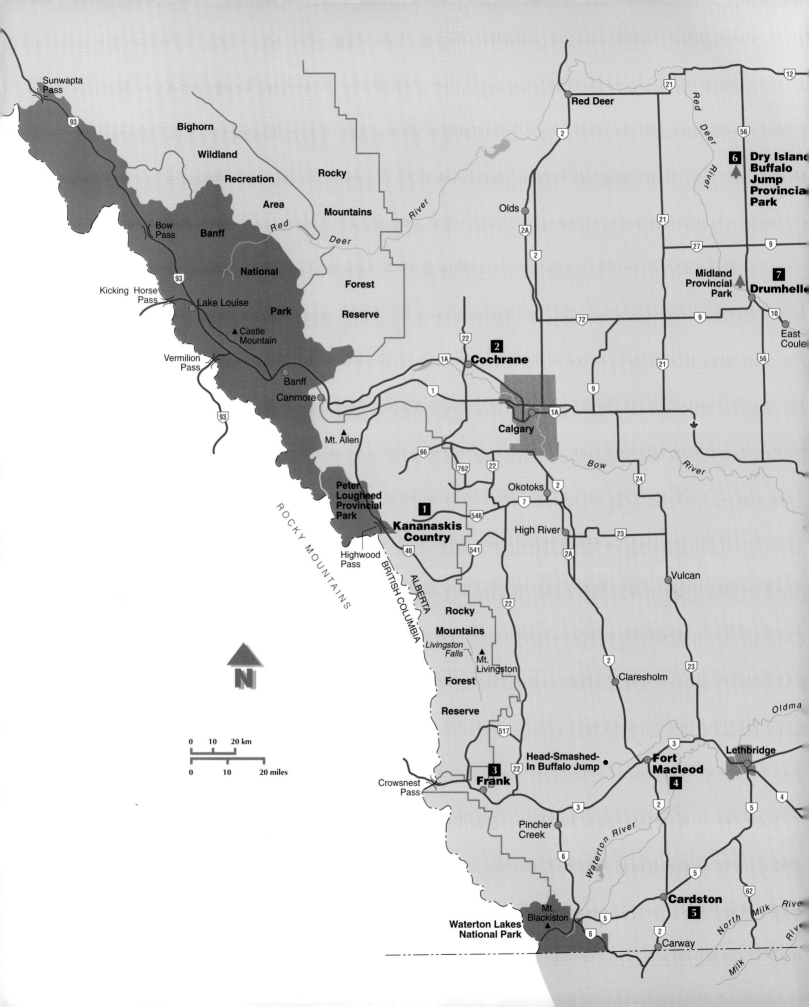

Sunwapta
Pass

93

Bighorn

Wildland

Recreation

Area

Bow
Pass

Banff

Rocky

Mountains

Red

National

93

Kicking Horse
Pass

Lake Louise

Park

Deer

River

Forest

Reserve

▲ Castle
Mountain

Vermilion
Pass

Banff

93

Canmore

▲ Mt. Allen

ROCKY MOUNTAINS

Peter
Lougheed
Provincial
Park

Highwood
Pass

ALBERTA
BRITISH COLUMBIA

Red Deer

2

21

12

2A

6 Dry Island
Buffalo
Jump
Provincial
Park

Olds

2

27

9

56

9

72

Midland
Provincial
Park ▲

7
Drumheller

2
Cochrane

1A

21

9

56

10

East
Coule

1

21

1A

66

Calgary

1
Kanananskis
Country

762

22

Bow

River

24

Okotoks

2

546

7

High River

23

2A

40

541

Vulcan

22

Rocky

Mountains

Livingston
Falls

▲ Mt.
Livingston

Forest

Reserve

Claresholm

2

23

Oldma

517

Head-Smashed-
In Buffalo Jump ●

22

Fort
Macleod

3

Lethbridge

3

3
Frank

4

Crowsnest
Pass

2

5

4

3

Pincher
Creek

6

Waterton River

5

Cardston

5

62

River

North Milk River

Waterton Lakes
National Park

Mt.
Blackiston ▲

6

5

Carway

Milk River

N

0   10   20 km

0   10   20 miles

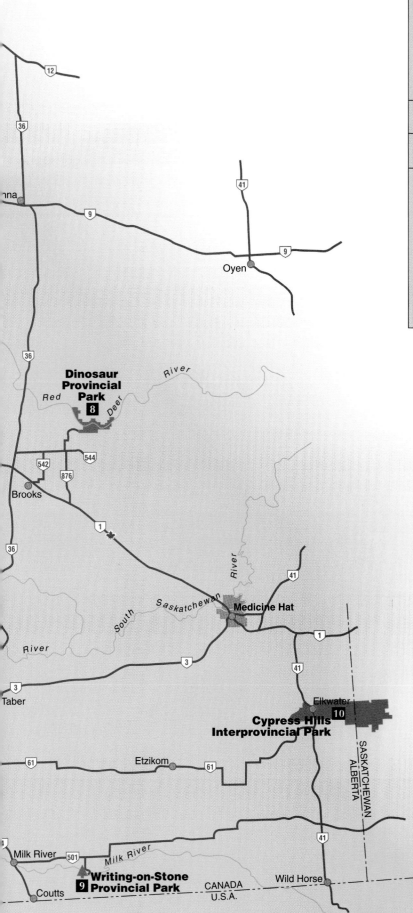

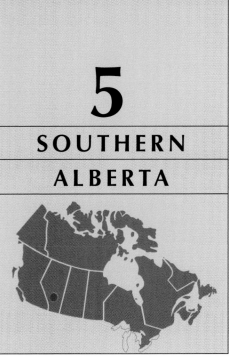

5

SOUTHERN

ALBERTA

Places to see

Peter Lougheed Provincial Park

Kananaskis Country

Cochrane

Frank Slide

Frank

Fort Macleod

Cardston

Head-Smashed-In Buffalo Jump

Dry Island Buffalo Jump

Provincial Park

Drumheller

The Royal Tyrrell Museum

Dinosaur Provincial Park

Writing-on-Stone Provincial Park

Rock carvings and paintings

at Writing-on-Stone

Cypress Hills Interprovincial Park

Roads to explore

Crowsnest Pass

East Coulee Drive

Dinosaur Trail

National park close-up

Banff

Waterton Lakes

Previous pages: Elkwater Lake,
Cypress Hills Interprovincial Park

A PARK ON THE EDGE OF THE CONTINENTAL DIVIDE

Rugged mountain wilderness and some of the most breathtaking scenery in Canada have been preserved and made accessible in Peter Lougheed Provincial Park. Alberta's largest provincial park—508 km^2 within the western flank of Kananaskis Country—allows you to drive to the edge of untamed lands and the mighty rock wall of the Continental Divide. Originally Kananaskis Provincial Park, it was renamed Peter Lougheed to honor the Premier who created Kananaskis Country.

Enter the park on Highway 40 and turn on to the Kananaskis Lakes Trail 52 km south of the Trans-Canada Highway, Route 1. Descend through dense stands of jack pine and spruce into a broad, bowl-shaped valley carved by glaciers only 10,000 years ago. The windswept slopes, home to bighorn sheep, mountain goats, and grizzly bears, curve gently up to halt abruptly at the near vertical incline of the Rocky Mountains reaching far overhead.

Stop at the visitor information centre, 4 km from the Highway 40 turnoff, and see hands-on interpretive displays of the human and natural history of the area.

The road ends between Upper and Lower Kananaskis lakes, which are an astonishing turquoise hue, glacier fed, and icy cold.

As you return, look out for a large marsh on your right with an active beaver lodge and, with luck, you may see great blue herons feeding along its edge. This marks the head of the Pocaterra hiking and cycling trail, named for George Pocaterra, a young Italian aristocrat who came to Canada in 1903 and became the first white man to see the Kananaskis Lakes from the south.

Rejoining Highway 40, turn south to the Highwood Pass, which runs through a unique example of high arctic tundra. (It is closed from mid-December to June.)

You can leave the park by the 64-km Smith-Dorrien Trail, a gravel road that runs along the broad Smith-Dorrien Creek and then narrows and winds through forests of giant pines.

1   Kananaskis Country

In 1977 the Alberta government marked out an area of superb natural beauty three-quarters the size of Prince Edward Island as a recreational utopia.

The 4,250-km^2 area of Kananaskis Country—as they called it—encompasses wildlife sanctuaries, ecological reserves, and three provincial parks. Vast wilderness areas are preserved in pristine entirety; in other spots, ski hills, golf courses, hotels, and campgrounds let visitors enjoy the sight of the magnificent scenery.

Stretching from the outskirts of Calgary to the British Columbia border, the terrain here encompasses the timeless rock and ice of the high alpine peaks, glacial valleys of evergreen and aspen forest, meadows of wildflowers, and gentle flats where prehistoric bison hunters sheltered and pioneers set up some of Alberta's first ranches.

Kananaskis Country has millions of visitors a year. But since it also has myriad trails—roughly 1,500 km of them—you are unlikely to meet many of those visitors. You may, however, be lucky enough to catch a glimpse of elks, moose, bighorn sheep, mountain goats, beavers, deer, or bears.

A common access point is by the Kananaskis Trail, or Highway 40, which runs south from the Trans-Canada Highway about 90 km west of Calgary. Make your first stop at the Barrier Lake Information Centre, 6 km from the Trans-Canada Highway, Route 1, for trail maps and information pamphlets.

Another 18 km along this dramatically beautiful route is Kananaskis Village with its three hotels, and the Nakiska Ski Resort, site of the 1988 Olympic downhill races. Just past the village, the Mount Kidd and Mount

At 2,206 m, spectacular Highwood Pass on Highway 40 in Peter Lougheed Park is the highest stretch of paved road in Canada.

Lorette 18-hole public golf courses, designed by Robert Trent Jones, lie at the base of their majestic namesakes.

During the summer, some boaters launch their craft on the Spray, Barrier, and Upper and Lower Kananaskis lakes, while others go canoeing, rafting, and kayaking on the Kananaskis River. You can rent mountain bikes or book white-water rafting trips at the Village, and take horse rides from Boundary Stables just across the highway. Anglers will find stocked and native fish in high mountain and valley lakes.

In winter, Kananaskis Country becomes a silent wonderland of frozen waterfalls and snowy meadows. Most popular of the five cross-country ski areas is the Canmore Nordic Centre, home of the 1988 Olympic biathlon and cross-country events, 1.8 km south of Canmore. Its cedar-beamed lodge, with massive stone fireplace, has a spectacular view of snow-topped Mount Rundle.

2 Cochrane

A traveler leaving the newly built Canadian Pacific Railway station at this western frontier settlement some 100 years ago would have been as likely to find countesses and senators whiling away time on the polo field as cowboys in the local saloon.

In today's Cochrane (pop. 5,000), the polo field has made way for the rodeo grounds and the gentry has ceded to a flourishing artists' community, but traces of former glory still linger.

A 20-km drive west from Calgary, Cochrane nestles on the southwestern slope of the Big Hill, called in Cree *Manachaban* (the place where you get bows). The Bow River, with some of the best opportunities for trout fishing in North America, runs along the

Three-flowered avens, or prairie smoke, blossoms of Alberta's drylands

town's southern outskirts.

To see how the gentler pioneers once lived, visit the elegant Fisher House, now the Mount St. Francis Catholic Retreat, some 2.5 km north of downtown. Charles Wellington Fisher (1871-1919), Alberta's first Speaker of the House, was a wealthy rancher who brought stonemasons from England to build his house on the Big Hill's western face looking out to the Rocky Mountains. Wellington and his wife hired English maids and cooks for their lavish parties and capped off the local social season with an autumn wolf hunt.

The ranching that gave the town its start still thrives around Cochrane, and you can sample the cowboy way of life at the Cochrane Ranch Provincial Historic Site. Here in the 1870s Quebec Senator Matthew Henry Cochrane (1824-1903), backed by wealthy eastern businessmen and politicians, took advantage of bargain land prices offered by the Dominion of Canada to encourage settlement of the west.

For just one cent an acre, Cochrane leased 109,000 acres and, in 1881, was the first to drive huge herds of cattle north from Montana. Poor herding practices and bitterly cold winters decimated his stock after only two years and the lease was divided. Despite its failure, the Cochrane Ranch marked the beginning of Alberta's beef cattle industry. At the interpretive centre, you can learn about early herding, branding, and bronco busting, and see how the ranchers lived. *Open daily, mid-May to Labor Day, 10 am to 6 pm.*

At Studio West, on Second Avenue and Bow Street, sculptor Don Beggs casts the bronzes of ranchers, cowboys, and Indians that grace civic buildings and art galleries from Fredericton to Victoria.

Special events
Heritage Days (August)

85

Banff

In 1883, workmen laying track for the Canadian Pacific Railway noticed steam rising from a fissure in Sulphur Mountain, near the present-day Banff townsite. When they investigated it they found a cavern containing hot, sulfurous water. The workmen erected bathhouses at the spot, but an owner-ship dispute soon followed, and the federal government was called in to settle it. An order in council was passed in 1885 reserving the springs for the "advantage of the public," and a 26-km² area around the springs was declared Hot Springs Reserve and, later, as Canada's first national park, Rocky Mountains Park. In 1930, the name was changed again to Banff National Park.

A gray jay perches on the snow-laden bough of a larch tree in Banff National Park.

Today, Banff encompasses some 6,641 km². Even so, it is only about half the size of its northern neighbor Jasper National Park. Banff also adjoins Yoho and Kootenay national parks on its western flanks, and the four parks form a world heritage site. Their combined area ensures large and en-dangered species—grizzly bears, for example—have enough room to live in peace within the protective boundaries that only national parks can provide. The grizzly population is now estimated at 80 to 100 in Banff (and 110 in Jasper). In spring and summer they can be seen grazing and searching for food under rocks and logs along quiet park roads.

Hot springs and ghost towns

The hot springs responsible for Banff's creation are all fed by waters beneath 2,451-m Sulphur Mountain, just south of Banff townsite. Surface waters trickle down more than 2 km underground, where they are turned to steam by the heat from the earth's core. Under pressure, the steam shoots up through a fault in the rock and emerges at the hot springs. A stone bathhouse, built in 1887, the swimming pool, and the original 1914 stone structure of Cave and Basin are open to the public. It is also possible to soak at Upper Hot Springs. Warm water from the springs flows down Sulphur Mountain to the Cave and Basin Marsh below, creating a microclimate with lush vegetation that stays green all year, streams that seldom freeze, some birds that have given up migration, and tropical fish. The fish were deposited there by Banff residents as an experiment to see how they would thrive. Illegal though this "stocking" was, the exotic species are doing very nicely in their mountain stream. However, they may have contributed to the demise of the once rare and endangered long-nose dace, a species of minnow. A promenade built into the marsh makes it possible to watch the diverse wildlife of this unusual wetland.

Not far from Banff townsite, on the Lake Minnewanka Road, are the remains of Bankhead, a coal-mining town once larger than Banff itself. Now only foundations and rusting machinery remain. In the ruins rises tall-stemmed wild rhubarb, which es-caped from gardens originally planted by Chinese laborers and seeded itself all over the site. The town expanded after the CPR opened a mine at nearby 2,998-m Cascade Mountain in 1903 to provide fuel for its steam engines. But the expense of mining the brittle coal in solid mountain rock, as well as miners' strikes, forced the mine to close. By 1922 Bankhead had become a ghost town.

Another mining town in the park was Silver City. After silver and copper were shown to a local prospector, the railway was extended here in 1883 and Silver City was born. But it too was short-lived, since there proved to be no silver. The site is worth visiting for the little-known Silverton Falls. An easy 2.5-km hike from the Bow Valley Parkway leads to the picturesque falls.

Banff's glacial beauty

Glaciers carved the deep valleys and depressions and mold-ed the jagged peaks and ridges of the massifs that make Banff so awesome. They still bulldoze their way down slopes, scouring the land and feeding lakes and icy rivers along their way. The best route through this landscape is the Bow Valley Parkway (1A), which has far less traffic than the Trans-Canada Highway (1), and the Icefields Parkway (93 North), which stretches from Lake Louise north to the Co-lumbia Icefield Centre and Jasper. But the beauties of Banff are best seen on foot and there are many trails that reveal the park's splendors. From the shore of Lake Louise an easy 6.4-km trail takes walkers to the Plain of Six Glaciers. The trail runs above moraine and gravel fields to one of two surviving teahouses built in the park by the CPR at the turn of the cen-tury. Beyond the teahouse is a ridge of moraine that offers a breathtaking view of the surrounding mountains and six glaciers: Upper and Lower Victoria, Upper and Lower LeFroy, Aberdeen, and Pope.

A moderately steep 2.4-km trail goes to Larch Valley from the Moraine Lake Road. The trail climbs to subalpine mead-ows overlooking Moraine Lake, a blue-green jewel set in the valley of the Ten Peaks. In autumn, when the larch trees turn gold, this walk is particularly beautiful. Another 2.4-km climb from the meadows takes you to the top of Sentinel Pass, one of the highest passes in the park, at an elevation of 2,611 m. To cross it, walkers need a pair of sturdy boots.

Below Sentinel Pass is the Giant Steps Cascade. Access is by a trail that starts at the Paradise Creek parking lot, also on the Moraine Lake Road. The trail follows a loop through Paradise Valley to the rock stairway.

The lakes of the Rockies are renowned for their milky-emerald color caused by glacial "rock flour" suspended in the water. One of the most beautiful is Lake Louise, cupped in an ice-scooped basin where it reflects the scoured mountains around it. There is a stunning view of Lake Louise from above Lake Agnes, a lake in a hanging valley flanked by two unmistakable mountains—Little and Big Beehive. The short

8-km hike to Lake Agnes and back goes past Bridal Veil Falls and up a stairway cut into the cliffs to a teahouse.

Also renowned for their color are the Inkpots, clear green pools fed by underground springs that keep the water at a constant temperature of 10°C. In summer, the best way to get to them is along Johnston Canyon, from the Bow Valley Parkway. The trail passes seven waterfalls that have carved deeply into the walls of the limestone canyon. In winter the Inkpots can be reached from Moose Meadows parking lot by a cross-country skiing trail that bypasses the canyon.

PARK INFORMATION
Access: Trans-Canada Highway (1), Bow Valley Parkway (1A), and Highway 93.
Visitors' centres: Banff townsite and Lake Louise.
Accommodations: 14 campgrounds, two of which are year-round; the rest are open from May or June to September. Sites available on a first-come, first-served basis. Group camping also available. Hotels and lodges.
Summer activities: Hiking, camping, spelunking (with a permit only), power-boating (on Lake Minnewanka only), rafting, canoeing, kayaking, golfing, horse riding, trail biking (on designated trails), fishing (with a permit only), swimming.
Winter activities: Camping, cross-country skiing, and alpine skiing.

The motionless surface of Banff's Lake Louise reflects Victoria Glacier (far left) and the snowy peaks of the mountains on its northern flank.

MEMORIAL TO A CALAMITY IN A MOUNTAINOUS PASS

Just after 4 am on April 29, 1903, Turtle Mountain's east face broke away, and 90 million tonnes of limestone roared over the two-year-old mining town of Frank. Giant boulders buried buildings, the main road and railway tracks. One hundred people were in homes in the path of the slide, and 70 died. Only 12 bodies were recovered, and injured survivors had to be dug out from layers of rock and debris. Stone crashed onto the mine, blocking the entrance and trapping 17 miners who later tunneled to safety.

The 500 people left in Frank, where the new mine already produced 1,000 tonnes of coal a day, eventually carried on. Mine clearing took almost two months, but most of the town's commercial buildings were undamaged and business resumed. It was not until after government surveyors decided in 1912 that another fall was possible that the town was moved to safety, across what is now Highway 3.

Causes of the massive slide are still debated, but theories suspect such culprits as mountain structure, mining operations, earthquake, and pressures within the rock from freezing water. Scientists now monitor movement with lasers and seismic apparatus, but no major shifts have been recorded here.

Frank Slide was made a provincial historic site in 1977, and a year-round interpretive centre opened eight years later, giving visitors marvelous views of Turtle Mountain, the Crowsnest Valley and the slide itself. Displays, interpretive programs and a 20-minute audiovisual presentation tell of development of the five Crowsnest Pass towns, coal-mining techniques and theories of why the 1903 disaster happened. A self-guiding walk on the 1,500-m trail through the fallen rocks, many containing fossils, has 17 stops of interest to geologists, historians, and photographers. *Open daily, May 15 to Labor Day, 9 am to 8 pm; the rest of the year, 10 am to 4 pm.*

3 Frank

❋

Once a bustling coal-mining town, historic Frank (pop. 194), site of one of the world's most massive rockslides, is now a peaceful village in its second home in the Crowsnest Pass.

Frank was founded in 1901 by Montana businessman H. L. Frank, who bought the coal-rich land at the foot of Turtle Mountain that was mined until 1918. The town had to be moved in 1912, however, after government surveys warned of a possible repeat of the devastating mountain slide of 1903.

Today's Frank has architecture from both sites, including miners' cottages. The art gallery at the Crowsnest Pass Arts Association building was the school and community hall of "new" Frank; the two-story building next to it is a store from the original town.

An unmarked trail 500 m west of Frank leads to the sulfurous cold springs that provided supposedly curative baths at two sanatoriums here. The 1906 gravel Old Frank Road loops south of the town, passing between the immense gray boulders of the 3-km² slide and allowing a glimpse of the first townsite in basement depressions and a rusted fire hydrant.

Special events
Harvest Festival (September)

4 Fort Macleod

⋀ Γ ⋙ ⋙ ❋

Frontier days are recalled at Fort Macleod (pop. 3,110). The town is southern Alberta's oldest settlement. On the outskirts is the Fort Macleod Museum, a reconstruction of the original North West Mounted Police fort built in 1874. It was the first outpost of the NWMP, the forerunners of today's Mounties. They drove whiskey traders and outlaws from the southern prairies.

Roads to explore: Mines and ruins of a Rockies gateway
Distance (approx.): 142 km/88 miles

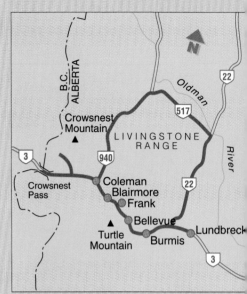

Crowsnest Monument marks the mountain pass of the same name.

The Rocky Mountains seem impenetrable here, west of Lundbreck, but they are cut through by Highway 3 to British Columbia, and by the 1,350-m-high Crowsnest Pass, discovered in 1873. The CPR railway came through in 1898, followed by mining companies in search of the area's rich coal seams.

● From Lundbreck, drive west on Highway 3 and climb the rolling grassland foothills to the lonely ruins of Leitch Collieries, the only Canadian-owned mine in the pass. It was active from 1907 to 1915. *Guided tours available daily, mid-May to early September, 9 am to 5 pm. Self-guiding tours, the rest of the year.*

● An information stop 3 km farther west gives magnificent views of Turtle and Crowsnest mountains, which were visited by native peoples 10,000 years ago.

● Bellevue's east entrance leads to the town's main street, access point for a 366-m underground mine tour. The Bellevue Cafe gained fame in 1920 when a shootout here between train robbers and police left three dead.

● At Hillcrest Cemetery, south of Bellevue, mass graves contain 150 of the 189 victims of Canada's worst mine disaster, a massive underground explosion in 1914. A rough, steep trail, west of the Hillcrest Trailer Court, leads to the overgrown ruins of the mine's surface plant.

● Drive on to Frank through the towering boulders of the 1903 rockslide. Head west to Blairmore.

● Blairmore's east access turns onto 20th Avenue, rich with 1920s commercial buildings. The town, now the pass's major business centre, began as a railway siding in 1893. The park bandstand was used as a meeting place by striking miners in the turbulent 1920s and 1930s.

● Exit west of town for Coleman, founded with the American-owned International Mine in 1903. Turn left at the east access and drive 1.4 km to the main street, site of scenes in the Disney movie *The Journey of Natty Gann.*

Behind Coleman's Grand Union Hostel stands the building that housed the *Coleman Journal* from 1921 to 1970. Opposite the hostel is the Crowsnest Museum. At the former police barracks at 7809 18th Avenue, now a private home, a constable was shot by rum runner Emilio Picariello in a 1933 Prohibition confrontation.

South of the main street are a few derelict coke ovens last used in the 1950s;

in 1905 more than 200 used to blaze around the clock.

Go north to Flumerfelt Park and walk the Miner's Path to the graceful waterfall of Nez Perce Creek. Miners heading to work at the 1909 McGillivray Mine crossed the creek by a wooden stairway still visible through the undergrowth.

● Travel 16 km to the British Columbia border, past peaceful Crowsnest Lake. At the valley bottom, an inn straddling the border and a few houses are the only remains of the CPR town of Crowsnest.

● Return to Coleman and refuel before turning north on Highway 940, a 1940s gravel forestry road built for fire-fighting access. This wilderness route twists through thick coniferous forest, home to moose, deer, elks, and bears.

● At 35 km take the right fork to Highway 517 through The Gap, a deep canyon piercing the Livingstone Range, through which the Oldman River plunges to the prairies. The former native trail and wagon road winds to Maycroft, a turn-of-the-century farming community.

● When you turn south on Highway 22 to join Highway 3 west of Lundbreck, do not miss Lundbreck Falls, a thundering 12-m drop of the Crowsnest River.

A tiny chapel at a campground near Bellevue is open to worshippers and wayfarers.

Log buildings and exhibits at Fort Macleod Museum tell of the Mounties' life in 1874.

The museum has displays of authentic NWMP pistols and carbines. Some of the early police buildings, include a blacksmith's shop and a medical centre with a primitive 1910 X-ray machine. Covered wagons and Indian tepees on the grounds re-create the feeling of bygone days. *Open daily, May to late June, and Labor Day to mid-October, 9 am to 5 pm; early July to Labor Day, 9 am to 8:30 pm; mid-October to end April, weekends, 9:30 am to 4 pm.*

You can take a self-guiding tour along the main street of the town, lined by some 30 heritage buildings. Among them are frame buildings dating from the 1890s. The restored 1910 Empress Theatre, the oldest working theatre in Alberta, is one of several brick and sandstone buildings from the turn of the century.

5   Cardston

Charles Ora Card, a son-in-law of Brigham Young, brought 10 families here from Utah in 1887 and founded Canada's first Mormon settlement. His log dwelling has been restored and refurnished with handmade furniture. *Admission free, donations accepted. Open Monday to Saturday, April to Labor Day, 10 am to 5 pm.*

The tranquil community of Cardston (pop. 3,480) now houses one of

Waterton Lakes

When Lt. Thomas Blakiston first came upon the Waterton Lakes in the fall of 1858, he described a "grand and picturesque" scene, with mountaintops of "very curious shapes," "cascades of snow water falling down the narrow gullies" and "magnificent cliffs." Blakiston was a naturalist and surveyor with the Palliser expedition, exploring the prairies and looking for a railway route through the Rockies. He was so impressed with the chain of three lakes—until then, the Kootenai Lakes for the Indians who camped there—that he renamed them after the noted but eccentric British naturalist Charles Waterton. It was an appropriate choice. Waterton Lakes National Park is as different from the other Rocky Mountain parks as its namesake was from most men of his time. In fact, part of Waterton Lakes is not in the mountains at all.

A fly-fisherman retrieves his line at Cameron Lake in Waterton Lakes.

The park, originally set aside as a forest reserve in 1895, became a park in 1911. Its 525-km² area protects a diversity of landforms, wildlife and plants peculiar to the blending of prairie and mountain habitats found nowhere else in our national park system.

You enter the main road into the park from Alberta Highway 6, passing the Maskinonge Wetlands. Just past the old park gate building, now boarded up, stop to observe a pair of ospreys, their nest of twigs perched on a pole overlooking the marsh. Every day during the summer they can be seen flying over the wetlands to catch fish. As you drive farther along the parkway, the rich wetland changes to arid prairie meadows. In late spring and early summer the flats are bright with blue lupines, mariposa lilies, and balsam roots.

Despite its comparatively small size, Waterton has more plant varieties than Banff and Jasper together, including more than 800 species of wildflowers. An interesting way to see them is to drive up the Red Rock Canyon Road, stopping for short hikes and explorations along the way. The road runs westward, following the Blakiston Valley, which provides a natural division between prairie and mountain landscapes. On the drier south-facing slopes you will find fescue, oat grass, yarrow, and sticky geranium, all typical prairie vegetation. You may on occasion be lucky enough to see some of the park's many bears, black and grizzly, foraging on the plants and grubs. Across the valley and Blakiston Creek, lodgepole pine and forest wildflowers provide more luxuriant scenery. About halfway up the 15-km drive is the turnoff to the Crandell Mountain Campground and a good hike to Crandell Lake, about an hour each way.

At Red Rock Canyon itself, take time for another stroll to witness the forces of water carving the red and green mudstone for which Waterton is noted.

Upper Waterton Lake is the heart of the park. The deepest lake in Alberta and in the Canadian Rockies, its clear, cold waters reach 148 m down. Although barely 500 m wide, it runs south almost 11 km from Waterton townsite to Goat Haunt Landing in Glacier National Park, Montana. The lake lies almost equally in Canada and the United States. A wooden-hulled cruise ship, the *International*, built in 1927, takes passengers from Waterton townsite to its southern end. Visitors wishing to spend the night in Glacier Park must register with U.S. park rangers at the landing.

The natural elements of these parks operate as though the international boundary did not exist. Wolves, cougars, moose, and bears wander the valleys in search of food, inadvertently carrying seeds from one country to the other.

Parks' staff often lead hikes across the border or discuss the co-operative improvement of wildlife or fire management policies. To commemorate this peaceful co-operation and to recognize the natural unity of the two parks, Waterton and Glacier were made the world's first International Peace Park in 1932. In the late 1970s, they became one of the United Nations' biosphere reserves, worldwide standards by which to measure man's impact on the environment.

PARK INFORMATION
Access: Highways 5 and 6.
Visitors' centre: Waterton townsite, a full-service centre open May through September; limited facilities from October to April.
Accommodations: 3 campgrounds in the park and 3 on nearby land. Open May to October. One winter camping site. Hotels and motels.
Summer activities: Hiking, camping, climbing, canoeing, and rowing (motorized boats only on Middle and Upper Waterton lakes), golf, fishing (with permit only), horse riding, cycling and trail biking, windsurfing, scuba diving, tennis.
Winter activities: Cross-country skiing.

Alberta's newest and perhaps grandest interpretive displays, the Remington Alberta Carriage Centre.

In the 1950s Cardston's Don Remington started to collect and restore horse-drawn vehicles. By the early 1980s, running out of space for his evergrowing collection, he offered the carriages to the province if the government would exhibit them in his hometown. Remington died a few years before the opening of the centre on Cardston's main street—renamed Carriage Lane—but he did live to see the complex begun and his dream fulfilled.

The centre takes visitors back to the turn of the century, with staff clothed as the drivers, street cleaners, stable hands, or wealthy carriage riders of the period. Stroll through the townsite built in the main showroom to experience the sights, sounds—and even smells—of an age before the automobile reigned.

Some 66 of the more than 200 carriages in the collection are displayed in vignettes that show how they were used and how carriage salesmen and tack shops operated. Working wagons, stage coaches, and fire-fighting vehicles share the streets with elegant velvet-lined conveyances.

You may recognize the two-wheeled Hansom cab as the type that rattles along the foggy cobblestone streets of London in Sherlock Holmes movies. An Irish touring cart is similar to one that carried John Wayne in *The Quiet Man*. The royal coaches are those actually used by Queen Elizabeth and other royal family members during visits to southern Alberta.

In the grounds outside, a highlight of your visit will be riding in some of the carriages, drawn by the centre's matched teams of black quarter horses, sturdy Clydesdales, or Canadian-breed carriage horses. You can watch workmen reconstructing carriages in the restoration and blacksmithing area, tour the stables and tack rooms to see the grooms harnessing the teams, and even try your hand at driving, through

WHERE THE PLAINS INDIANS RELIVE THEIR VIVID PAST

Thousands of years of Plains Indian cultural and spiritual history are brilliantly captured at Head-Smashed-in Buffalo Jump, just 18 km west along a newly paved access road from the historic town of Fort Macleod.

A lookout on top of the cliffs at the site provides a view of the Oldman River valley to the east, the territory of the Peigan and Blood Nations to the south and the flat plains extending north along the foothills of the Rocky Mountains. This astonishing vista spreads out from one of the largest of the jumps where for more than 5,000 years Plains Indian hunters drove thundering herds of buffalo down narrowing paths and over the cliff edge to their deaths.

The Head-Smashed-In Buffalo Jump (declared a World Heritage Site by UNESCO in 1981) has a wide-ranging interpretive centre built right into the cliff walls. Staff include Blood and Peigan Indian guides who can answer all questions about their heritage—in Blackfoot, if you ask them—as they take you through the five-level centre or along the upper or lower trails.

Whether you choose a guided tour or browse through the centre on your own, take the elevator to the top and work your way downward. The top three levels show how Plains Indians lived, hunted the buffalo that sustained them, and moved freely across the plains. The next shows the impact of the arrival of the horse about 1750, and the effects of the arrival of Europeans and the gradual disappearance of the buffalo. The last level explains what has been learned from the digs at the site.

Lighting and sound effects vividly depict the methods used at kill sites, from the drive to skinning and preparing the animals. The history of the Plains people is illustrated by tools, weapons, tepees, and clothing.

A state-of-the-art laser disc show runs hourly in the 80-seat theatre, and visitor-operated laser disc videos throughout the centre help to bring this

Skulls and bones collected 10 m deep at the foot of the cliff over which buffalo herds were driven.

fascinating history to life. Special weekend events throughout the year include a powwow and tepee village in July, where hundreds of native dancers perform grass, traditional, chicken, and jingle dances. At other times visitors can learn how to make arrowheads, spear tips or pemmican, or do the intricate beadwork that decorates Indian clothing. In summer, at the excavations below the cliffs, you can hold arrowheads, buffalo bones, and other artifacts—some dating back 6,000 years—as workers explain their meaning and age.

The centre has parking areas for all vehicles, with a special shuttle service up the hill to the centre's main doors. *Open daily, mid-May to Labor Day, 9 am to 8 pm. The rest of the year, Tuesday to Sunday, 9 am to 5 pm.*

computer simulation. The centre has carriages from Calgary's Glenbow Museum and Heritage Park, as well as the Don Remington Collection. *Open daily, mid-May to Labor Day, 9 am to 8 pm; the rest of the year, 9 am to 5 pm.*

6	Dry Island Buffalo Jump Provincial Park

Citizens of Huxley, Alta., battled for years to preserve a canyon 20 km east of the hamlet, rich with animal and plant life and echoes of Indian history. In 1970 the Alberta provincial government declared this lovely steep-sided valley Dry Island Buffalo Jump Provincial Park.

The Red Deer River twists its way through the bottom of the canyon. Some of the province's best freshwater fish fossils have been found in a coulee near the Big Valley stream that enters the river from the east.

On the west side of the park is the 45-m-high buffalo jump, its cliff face still holding white bone fragments from ancient hunts. Tools, pottery fragments, Indian graves, and fire pits found near the bottom of the jump indicate that this was a ceremonial ground for at least one tribe.

The Dry Island, 3 km north of the jump, is 8 ha of tabletop hill, a natural wonder carved out by wind and rain, but never surrounded by water.

The prairie buffalo and wild horses that once roamed the canyon are long

At Dry Island, the Red Deer River snakes through a canyon where plants of badlands, prairie, and northern forest mingle.

gone, making way for more than 425 flowering plant species, 22 types of mammals, and 150 transient or nesting bird groups, such as golden eagles and short-eared owls. Tall, lush fescue grows only on the Dry Island, but look for pin cherry, willows, hawthorn, silverberry, buffalo berry, buckbrush, rose and cinquefoil shrubs scattered through the canyon. Junipers thrive on the uplands, poplars and shrubs populate the lower valley near the river, and aspen, balsam poplars, and willows stand at the northeast side.

Badgers and white-tailed and mule deer feed here all year, and long-eared and small-footed bats live in the canyon's caves. Goldeye, lake chub, long-nose dace, northern pike, spotted shiner, and northern redhorse all glide through this stretch of the river.

You can drive down a winding road to the parking area at the bottom of the 200-m-deep canyon, but leave trailers at the top. There are a number of walking paths and picnic areas.

7 Drumheller

The city of Drumheller (pop. 6,277) lies in a valley carved into the spectacularly eerie badlands of southern Alberta's Big Country. The first homesteader found his way here in 1902, and the city, named after entrepreneur Samuel

Drumheller, was established in 1910. Coal mines and a 1913 rail link to Calgary attracted the first immigrants. Oil and gas discoveries followed as coal demand dwindled, and ranching and farming flourished in the valley.

Today Drumheller, in the land where dinosaurs roamed, provides access to 50 attractions within a 100-km radius. The life-sized replica of *Tyrannosaurus*

Roads to explore: Driving through dinosaur country

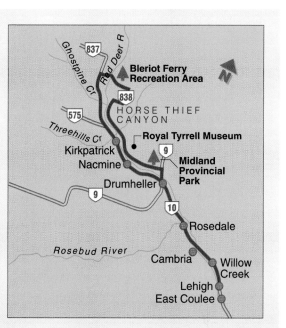

1. EAST COULEE DRIVE
Distance: 25 km/15½ miles

Head southeast from Drumheller along the East Coulee Drive to find vanishing hoodoos and a time when coal was king. The drive begins at the junction of highways 9 and 10.

● The first stop is not advised for those with a weak stomach. The Star Mine Swinging Bridge, in the hamlet of Rosedale, lets visitors experience one of the daily routines of a local coal miner. The original 117-m-long suspension bridge, now replaced, was built in 1931 and miners trudged across it to work until the mine closed in 1957.

● About 7 km east of the bridge, stop to examine the hoodoos. Looking like giant mushrooms with their caplike tops, these soft sandstone pillars have been formed by erosion through countless years. Indians thought them petrified ogres who moved by night. Geologists forecast that within a hundred years the elements will complete their work and the hoodoos will be gone.

● Drive another 7 km east to the town of East Coulee and explore high school life in the 1930s at the School Museum. A restored classroom has the original maps, desks, and books, as well as school photographs of children who once sat here. Another schoolroom offers a nostalgic look at the once thriving coal-mining communities with mine photographs and miners' clothing and equipment.

● Before returning to Drumheller, visit the Atlas Coal Mine Museum, also in East Coulee. The mine, built in 1936 and closed in 1979, has the last standing ore-sorting machinery of its kind in Canada.

2. DINOSAUR TRAIL
Distance: 48 km/30 miles

To unearth the modern and prehistoric splendors of the Drumheller Valley, start out west from Drumheller on Highway 838, along the Dinosaur Trail.

● The Homestead Museum, located just 1 km west of the city, is your first stop. The Quonset structure looks unprepossessing but houses first-class displays of Indian artifacts, clothing from the 1890s to 1920s, and turn-of-the-century machinery.

● Travel west for 4 km and discover the Royal Tyrrell Museum of Paleontology, which displays a world-famous collection of dinosaur skeletons.

● The World's Biggest Little Church can be spotted another 1.5 km down the Trail. The church was built by Drumhellerite Tig Seland during the 1960s, but vandalism and weather damage made it necessary to rebuild the tiny structure. In 1991 the task was completed, detail for detail, at the Drumheller Correctional Institution. Take the whole family in for a look, but remember it only holds six people at a time.

A fountain set in a pond greets visitors at the entry to the Royal Tyrrell Museum.

● Continue west to the Dinosaur Trail Golf and Country Club. The nine-hole course, framed by the natural beauty of the badlands to the north and the Red Deer River to the south, has a driving range and miniature golf.

● About 8 km farther down the trail is the Horse Thief Canyon. A self-guiding walk following information signs past oyster beds and embedded fossils takes approximately 45 minutes. Afterward, you can relax at the picnic area.

● Cross the Red Deer River by the Bleriot Ferry, one of the last in Alberta still operated by cable, then drive east on Highway 837 until you reach Drumheller's city limits.

● Just outside the city, uncover even more of the badlands' hidden secrets at the Prehistoric Parks Walk along shale paths past several life-sized replicas of dinosaurs, then stop at Ollie's Rock and Fossil Shop for a cool drink and enjoy the many exhibits.

RECONSTRUCTED GIANTS OF THE ROYAL TYRRELL

Experience a walk through more than 4 billion years of earth's past at the only museum in Canada solely devoted to studying dinosaurs. Opened in 1985, the Royal Tyrrell Museum of Paleontology, 6 km northwest of Drumheller in Midland Provincial Park, is already one of the world's most famous.

Geologist Joseph B. Tyrrell found the first dinosaur remains in the area in 1884. The building named in his memory now houses one of the world's largest collections of dinosaur skeletons, some two stories tall. Here are 30 life-sized replicas of dinosaurs, hundreds of exhibits and dioramas, an indoor garden with more than 100 plant species and computer programs to challenge your dinosaur and fossil knowledge. A window built into one of the main laboratories lets you watch (when work is in progress) the painstaking reconstruction of dinosaur skeletons from fossilized bones. Allow several hours to explore. *Open daily, Victoria Day to Labor Day, 9 am to 9 pm. Winter hours: 10 am to 5 pm, Tuesday to Sunday.*

A reconstructed dimetrodon skeleton, Royal Tyrrell Museum.

rex standing next to an 8-m waterfall in the city's Centennial Park has itself been photographed by countless awed visitors through the years.

One of the most exciting ways of exploring the Drumheller region is by hovercraft on the Red Deer River. The hovercraft takes passengers on a 45-minute "flight," year-round, through a land where creatures of the Cretaceous age roamed 75 million years ago.

> **Special events**
> Music Festival (March)
> Broncosaurus Days (late June-early July)

8 Dinosaur Provincial Park

⋀ ⛺ 🍴 🐟 ❋ 📷

Lush tropical forests covered a coastal plain here 75 million years ago. Crocodiles lazed in the warm waters, dinosaurs roamed the lowlands, and winged reptiles owned the skies.

Today, 48 km northeast of Brooks, where the vast prairie falls away to reveal the 6,600-ha Dinosaur Provincial Park, a stripped-down sculpted landscape has compressed and fossilized the evidence of those times. Among the sandstone towers and valleys lie beds of fossilized bones, remains of the 120 million years of dinosaur rule.

Since geologist and explorer Joseph Burr Tyrrell unearthed the first skeletal evidence in the early 1880s, more than 35 species and 150 complete specimens have been extracted in this arid area and exhibited around the world. Here was the first confirmed mass extinction of a large herd of dinosaurs, where some 80 tri-horned *Centrosaurus* have been excavated. Littering the grave site are

Once a swampy domain of giant beasts, Dinosaur Provincial Park is now a parched and eroded badland.

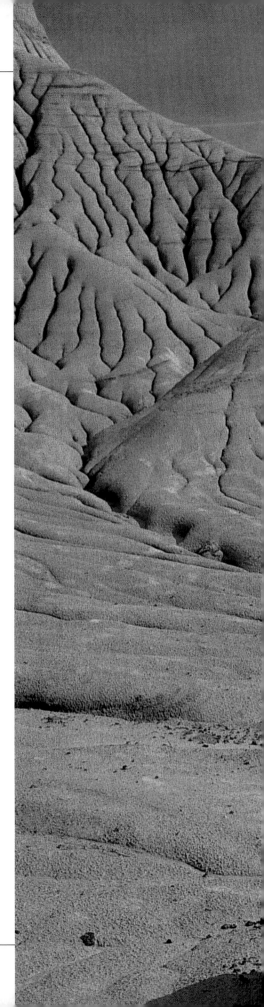

the scarred bones and teeth of visiting carnivores.

The park, established in 1955, was declared a United Nations world heritage site in 1979 as one of the world's richest sources of late Cretaceous dinosaur fossils. At the field station of the Royal Tyrrell Museum of Paleontology, you can watch technicians prepare fossils for the main museum in Drumheller. *Admission to the field station is free, but donations are accepted. Open daily, mid-May to Labor Day, 9 am to 9 pm; reduced hours the rest of the year.*

Guided walks, children's programs, audiovisual presentations, and bus tours into the park are provided in the summer, as well as site tours of any active bone quarries. Visitors can browse through fossil display buildings and the 1900 rustic cabin of pioneer black cowboy John Ware, moved here from its Red Deer River site in the 1950s.

Interpretive trails take you through the badlands and along the plant-rich riverbanks, where you may spot yellow warblers, golden eagles, prairie falcons, and mountain bluebirds.

The summer sun traditionally bakes the park's floor to 40°C—uncomfortable for some humans but ideal for the odd rattlesnake or scorpion.

9 Writing-on-Stone Provincial Park

Λ ⚷ ‼ ⚓ ⛵ ❊

In the Milk River valley, close to the southern end of Alberta, about 8 km from the United States border, rise the sandstone cliffs of Writing-on-Stone Provincial Park. Just over the border, in Montana, the Sweetgrass Hills, green and lush even in mid-summer, dominate the horizon and seem to belong to another world.

Red-tailed hawk, Writing-on-Stone Provincial Park

A park guide explains the possible myth and meaning of the Writing-on-Stone petroglyphs.

VISIONS OF BATTLES, SPIRITS OF THE NIGHT

Writing-on-Stone Provincial Park contains a wonder of native art and history. It was to this sacred place of mystery and magic that people of the Blackfoot, Assiniboine and Gros Ventres tribes came for hundreds of years to leave their stories in the stone. The sheer cliffs of the park still bear echoes of these visits in pictures carved into the rock (petroglyphs) or painted on its surface (pictographs). The park has one of the largest concentrations of rock inscriptions in North America.

Archaeologists say all drawings are the handiwork of Indian artists. The Indians themselves attributed at least some of them to spirits who worked under cover of darkness, leaving carvings to reveal the future to those who read them.

Petroglyph artists used bones, rocks, or metal to depict events from hangings to battles. The different styles of human portrayals—rounded figures carrying spears, circular-shaped warriors, and men with square shoulders and pointed shoulders—give hints at the period when the drawings were made. Many pictures represent everyday objects such as the sun, wildlife, or horses. Ceremonial scenes and battle records are also common. More fantastic figures include a walking spear, and still others are abstract designs born of visions and dreams.

One of the most famous and complex of the petroglyphs records a battle between the Peigan (Blackfoot) and the Gros Ventres in the first half of the 1800s. Legend claims that on the eve of the battle a Peigan warrior dreamed about the attack of Gros Ventres, and carved his vision into the valley wall enabling his people to rout the enemy. Visitors can see these fragile works only on guided archaeological tours from mid-May to September.

Indian peoples chose this eerie, brittle landscape to record their memories in the walls. Here, too, centuries of environmental forces, including southern Alberta's famed winds, have carved into the valley's soft cliffs. Curved and bulbous shapes have pushed together to form a flowing natural architecture. Balls of stone sit on towers that shoot into the air; tiny caves have been scooped out of the rock by wind and rain.

Richardson's ground squirrels, Writing-on-Stone Provincial Park

Wild animals such as coyotes and deer frequent the park, and the plants range from the ball cactus to a diversity of vivid wildflowers. The well-kept 4.4-km Hoodoo Trail, for which a self-guiding map is supplied, takes you through the unique rock formations—but watch out for the park's thriving rattlesnake population. At lookout points on the trail you can see a replica of the North West Mounted Police outpost built in 1889 to control the whiskey trade. *The park is open year-round. Guided walks are available mid-May to early September.*

10 Cypress Hills Interprovincial Park

The Cypress Hills spring up about 600 m above the seemingly interminable prairie here with little warning, looking to unsuspecting travelers as if they had just sprouted from the earth.

In truth, they were formed about 50 million years ago, starting out as a giant deposit of pebbles and cobbles at the bottom of a prehistoric lake. This eventually turned into conglomerate, a kind of natural cement that held firm as the lake dried and weather wore down the surrounding area. A geological upheaval helped the process million of years later, and passing glaciers carved the hills into severe lines. Today these dramatic promontories with their dense greenery—they get more rain than anywhere else in the area—are the main feature of Cypress Hills Interprovincial Park, the Alberta and Saskatchewan parks that were joined in 1989 by the first agreement of its kind in Canada.

In Alberta, just west of the town of Irvine, take Highway 41 south into the park. Elkwater townsite is about 40 km down the road, and 5 km farther on look for signs to Reesor Lake on the Battle Creek Road that links the parks. The Battle Creek Road, much of it gravel and dirt, is for dry weather travel only; rains and winter condi-

Vacationers soak up the sun at Elkwater Lake in the heart of Alberta's Cypress Hills.

tions make it impassable.

In the early 1960s, the federal government created Reesor Lake by damming up the nearby Battle Creek, and flooding two tiny lakes.

A greater fritillary, a Cypress Hills butterflly

Famous among fishermen for its liberal stocks of rainbow trout, the lake also has a 40-site campground and glorious scenery.

Between Reesor Lake and the Saskatchewan border are two more campgrounds at Graburn and Battle creeks,

both in marvelous surroundings. A walk from the Battle Creek campground takes you to Graburn Cairn, marking an early North West Mounted Police detachment.

The park also has a motel, restaurant, beaches, boat rentals and a golf course nearby. Cycling and hiking trails throughout the park lead visitors among many varieties of wildflowers, including orchids. Elks, beavers, and moose lodge here, while sharp-shinned hawks, dusty flycatchers, and ruby-crowned kinglets skim the sky.

One thing you will not find in these hills is a cypress tree. French-Canadian explorers misidentified the area's lodgepole pines, and a cypress (*cyprès* in French) has never grown here.

CENTRAL ALBERTA

6

CENTRAL
ALBERTA

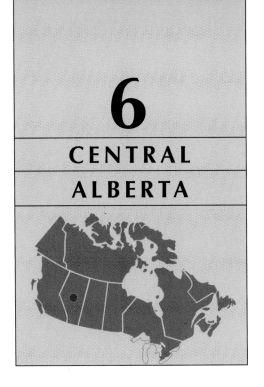

Places to see
Willmore Wilderness Park
Grande Cache
William A. Switzer Provincial Park
Rocky Mountain House
Markerville
Wetaskiwin
Alberta Prairie Railway Excursion
Stettler
Ukrainian Cultural Heritage Village
Smoky Lake
Lac La Biche
Cold Lake

Roads to explore
Hinton to Edson
Lakeland Country:
Cold Lake–Bonnyville–St. Paul–
Elk Point–Frog Lake

National park close-up
Jasper
Elk Island

Previous pages:
Old Fort Point, Jasper National Park

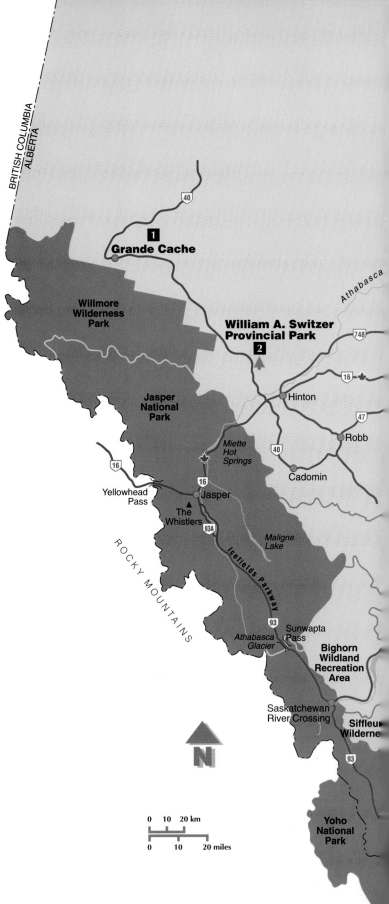

BRITISH COLUMBIA
ALBERTA

40

1
Grande Cache

Willmore
Wilderness
Park

Athabasca

**William A. Switzer
Provincial Park**
2

748

Hinton

16

Jasper
National
Park

*Miette
Hot
Springs*

40

Robb

47

Cadomin

16

16

Yellowhead
Pass

Jasper

93A

*Maligne
Lake*

The
Whistlers

R O C K Y   M O U N T A I N S

Icefields Parkway

93

Sunwapta
Pass

*Athabasca
Glacier*

**Bighorn
Wildland
Recreation
Area**

Saskatchewan
River Crossing

**Siffleu
Wilderne**

93

N

0   10   20 km

0   10   20 miles

**Yoho
National
Park**

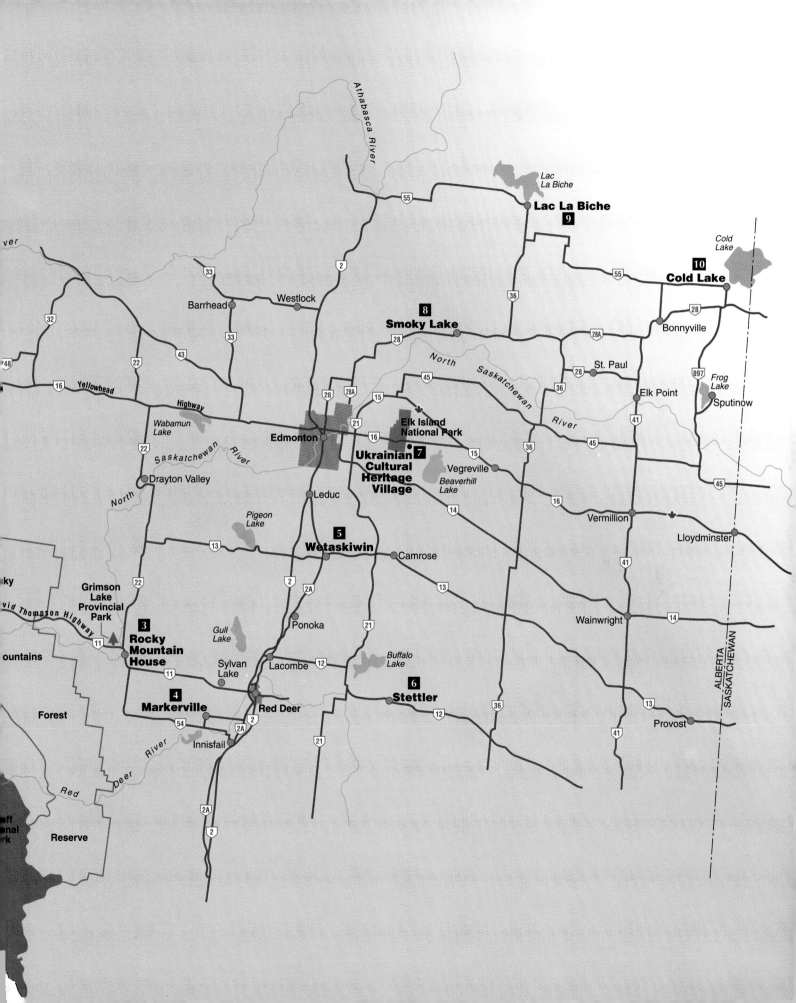

A PRISTINE WILDERNESS FOR HIKERS AND RIDERS

At 4,664 km², Willmore Wilderness is the largest park of its kind in Alberta. Its southern border touches Jasper National Park. Its northern border reaches almost to Grande Cache. At its eastern border is Rock Lake Recreation Area, some 42 km from William A. Switzer Provincial Park. Both Grande Cache and Rock Lake provide access to this remote park.

Willmore Wilderness is virtually pristine. The mineral wealth has been little exploited. The wildlife that once sustained the local Indians and enriched the fur traders is now protected. The scenery embraces snowy peaks, forest-clad slopes and alpine meadows, steep-walled valleys, chains of lakes, fast-flowing rivers, and marshy floodplains.

All journeys here are made on foot or by horseback. Since there are no roads, visitors leave their vehicles at the park's perimeter. A 750-km network of trails—the joy of adventurous hikers and riders—traverses the wilderness. The trails skirt the major rivers—the Smoky, Berland, Muskeg and Wildhay—and lead through deep forests of fir and spruce. Experienced adventurers usually call on guides and outfitters at Grande Cache to arrange hiking, fishing, or camping trips in Willmore's formidable wilds.

Near Grande Cache, there are a number of trails and day-trips suitable for visitors who wish to explore the wilderness with a minimum of effort. One of the easiest trails is a 6-km (round-trip) hike from the Hell's Gate staging area to Eaton Falls. To reach this point, drive 6 km north of Grande Cache and turn left on a 7.5-km gravel road. (The staging area is ideal for a picnic or a barbecue.) The trail to Eaton Falls offers superb views of Hell's Gate and other surrounding mountains.

Another 200-m hike from the staging area brings you to the Hell's Gate cliffs, which overlook a 200-m-high gorge where the Sulphur and Smoky rivers meet. The gorge forms part of the boundary of the Willmore Wilderness.

1 Grande Cache

In the early 19th century, trappers left their furs in storage at a staging post on the slopes of Grande Mountain. Here, furs awaited shipment to eastern Canada. The name of this staging post—"grande cache"—was conferred on the northern Alberta town built nearby in 1960 to house miners who were working on local seams of coal.

Today, the coal mines are closed, but Grande Cache (pop. 3,700) is a recreational centre and the gateway to the Willmore Wilderness Park.

Grande Cache is a paradox—a modern town surrounded by mountain wilderness. Sometimes the wilderness encroaches, when elk, deer, and occasionally a bear wander within the town's boundaries.

But this wilderness is inviting. Hiking and horse-riding trails encircle Grande Cache. Fishing is permitted in season. There is also a nine-hole golf course with a breathtaking setting.

The nearby rivers—Smoky, Sulphur, Wildhay, Kakwa

Bighorn sheep thrive in Alberta's parks.

—and Sheep Creek offer white-water canoeing and kayaking. Canoe and kayak rentals are available. Visitors eager for adventure will enjoy the guided white-water rafting tours.

Along Highway 40, outside of town, a number of campsites and picnic areas have spectacular surroundings. Fireman's Park on high banks overlooking the Sulphur River has an enclosed barbecue shelter, as well as playgrounds and horseshoe pits. A town-operated camp on Pierre Grey Lake provides six cabins and a main lodge.

Grande Cache Lake, northeast of town, is popular with windsurfers, boaters, and fishermen; Victor Lake, west of town, is for fishing and canoeing only.

2 William A. Switzer Provincial Park

In the foothills of central Alberta, William A. Switzer Provincial Park marks the transition between the northern (boreal) forest and Rocky Mountains. The park is located on a stretch of Highway 40 that passes panoramic views of the Athabasca River valley.

The 2,686-ha park encompasses a chain of five lakes—Jarvis, Blue, Cache, Graveyard, and Gregg. Its mountain and forest vegetation supports waterfowl and moose, elks, mule and white-tailed deer, bears, wolves, eagles, hawks and many songbirds.

Geologically, the park shows the effects of glacial movement during the last Ice Age and, later, the flow of the Athabasca River through the valley. These effects can be examined by hiking the park's 19-km network of trails.

The most comprehensive of the trails is the 3.5-km Valley Trail, which starts from Gregg Lake campground, and leads through the main geological and wildlife areas. The 10.6-km Jarvis Lake

Roads to explore: Caves, coal towns, and glacial lakes

Distance (approx.):
258 km/160 miles

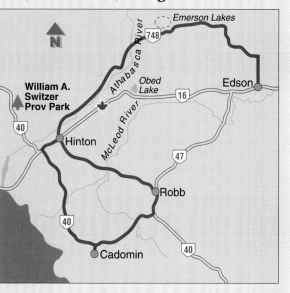

This is a lopsided figure-eight drive along what was the Grand Trunk Railway's Coal Branch linking small mining towns in the Athabasca Valley.

● Head southeast from Hinton on Route 16 to Highway 40. Turn left and drive south for 52 km through forested land and across swift-flowing rivers to Cadomin.

● Until the 1940s, Cadomin was a thriving coal-mine town with a population of 2,500. This has since dwindled to 107, because only two coal mines now operate in the adjacent area.

The Mountain Road General Store, and the adjoining Hole-in-the-Wall Cafe share a building with a gas station and a post office. The general store retains a traditional backwoods atmosphere. Visitors here may sense a remoteness of place and time when they see advertisements for bygone products still posted up. The cafe's walls display photographs chronicling the area's history.

The cafe is the meeting place for anyone interested in a guided tour of Cadomin Cave, 1.5 km southwest of the town. (No one should enter the cave without an experienced guide.) The total length of its known passages is 3 km. Since the cave is chilly and muddy, visitors are advised to bring suitably warm clothing, boots, and a hard hat. Contact the national park administration office in Jasper for a place on the cave tour.

● Heading east from Cadomin on Highway 40, you pass two campgrounds: Watson Creek with 36 campsites, and Coal Spur with 8. There is good fishing at both campgrounds. Just past Coal Spur is the junction with Highway 47. Go north on 47 to the small community of Robb, where there is a chance to replenish supplies. Then head northwest on the forestry road to Hinton. The McLeod River campground, with 22 sites, lies about halfway along this road.

● About 42.5 km up the forestry road is the Bighorn Trail. At the gravel crossroad, turn left and travel about 500 m to the trailhead, which is on the left. The

20-km trail was one of the original pack trails, and has scenic views of the Athabasca Valley and Rocky Mountains.

● From the trail's parking area, return to the road and continue north toward Hinton. Once you get to the traffic lights at the bottom of the hill, turn right and drive for 5 km, then turn onto Forestry Road 748. The road leads to Emerson Lakes, 56 km northeast of Hinton, and the Emerson Lakes campground, with 11 campsites. The glacial Emerson Lakes are popular for hiking, and a trail leads around five small lakes where visitors can observe moose, mule deer, white-tailed deer, elks, and black bears.

● Down the road, about 8 km along, is the trailhead for the Wild Sculpture Trail. This relatively easy walk is about 9 km long and follows the lakes' shores until it reaches the sculptured "hoodoos," rocks with intriguing shapes formed by the last Ice Age, which loom 15-20 m above the trail. In winter a groomed cross-country ski trail leads to the rocks.

● The area between here and Edson is open country for cross-country skiing, snowshoeing, and ice fishing. Edson can be reached by driving east along Forestry Road 748 for another 31 km.

● Edson, once the CN railway's "Gateway to the Last Great West" and now a hunting centre, has a two-day summer sidewalk jamboree with street dancing, auctions, arts and crafts displays. From Edson, head west along the Yellowhead Highway back to Hinton.

Trail and the 4.7-km Cache Lake–Gregg Lake Trail also serve as cross-country ski trails in the winter.

Trail information can be obtained at the park's office, located in Kelley's Bathtub at the north end of Jarvis Lake.

Switzer Park has five campgrounds: some are rustic, some are partly serviced. Trout, whitefish and pike fill the lakes, and there is a canoe route down meandering Jarvis Creek.

The park is busy in winter, too. Roads are kept open, and you can ice-fish on Jarvis, Cache, and Gregg lakes, and skate on Jarvis Lake at Kelley's Bathtub. An adjoining day-use area is available for barbecues and bonfires. Cross-country skiers and snowshoers are welcome, although there are no specific snowshoe trails.

3 | Rocky Mountain House

Buffalo herds graze peacefully at the entrance to the Rocky Mountain House National Historic Site, 7 km west of Rocky Mountain House (pop. 5,400) on Highway 11A.

Guided tours for groups are available at the site from May to October, with the emphasis on the early explorers, Indians, and the fur trade. Visitors can also take self-guiding walks.

Native Indian objects and trade goods, as well as archaeological artifacts, are exhibited at the visitors' centre. From the centre, you have a choice of two scenic trails—one 3.2-km long, and the other a mere 900-m run along the banks of the North Saskatchewan River. They lead to the sites of four forts built between 1799 and 1875 by fur-trade

An Indian tunic, Rocky Mountain House Museum

Jasper

In the mid-1700s, European fur traders ventured into the Rockies seeking a route across the mountains to the west coast. By 1813, the North West Company had established a supply depot (later called Jasper House after its clerk, Jasper Hawse) in what is now Jasper National Park. For years afterward, pelts from the west were exchanged for goods from the east around a pond in the Athabasca Pass called The Committee's Punch Bowl. Today, hikers hardy enough to retrace the traders' route up the Whirlpool River will find a plaque commemorating those dauntless explorers of long ago.

Jasper National Park was created in 1907, when transcontinental railways were pushing through this part of the Rockies. It is the largest park in the Rockies, covering 10,878 km². It is also part of a World Heritage Site comprising Banff, Yoho, and Kootenay national parks. The park's headquarters and most of the park's facilities are within Jasper townsite. The townsite lies at the junction of Highway 16 (the Yellowhead Highway), which cuts across the park, and Highway 93 (the Icefields Parkway), which runs down to Banff National Park.

Glacial heritage

The Icefields Parkway gets its name from the Columbia Icefield, which straddles the Continental Divide at the Banff-Jasper boundary. It is the largest ice cap south of the Arctic Circle, covering 325 km²; it is frozen to a depth of about 365 m. Six major glaciers creep from the icefield. The most accessible is the Athabasca Glacier. Trails to the snout of the glacier lead from the parkway through glacial debris and moraines and past a meltwater pond—the melting snout has been receding since the 1800s and now retreats at a rate of 1-3 m a year. In summer it is bright with red snow algae and the glowing blue of exposed ice. You will need warm clothes near the glacier, even in summer, because the winds blowing off this tongue of ice can get quite chilly. The best views of the glacier can be seen from the 4-km Wilcox Pass Trail that climbs above the highway and leads to Wilcox Pass.

Golden-mantled ground squirrel, a denizen of western parks.

You can get a good view of an interesting hanging glacier from Cavell Meadows Hike, in the southwestern part of Jasper, off Highway 93A, at the end of the Mount Edith Cavell Road. An 8-km loop zigzags above Cavell Valley up to subalpine meadows. Across Cavell Valley, the Angel Glacier spreads its "wings" before flowing over the lip of 3,368-m-high Mount Edith Cavell down the cliffs to the valley below. The air is often filled with the sounds of the glacier cracking and of avalanches down its slopes.

Jasper's glaciers have left their mark in the park's rivers and lakes. Glacial debris mixed with ice and particles of rock have been ground down in the river waters and the resulting sand has created dunes along the eastern shore of Jasper Lake and beyond the park's eastern boundary. On dry, windy days when Jasper Lake is low, the sands blowing from it fill the air like gray smoke.

The constant inflow of glacial sand and silt has left Jasper Lake sterile. In contrast, Talbot Lake, lying just behind the dunes, is rich in nutrients. It is an excellent place to see waterfowl, which feed off the insects and organisms that thrive in the lake's waters. Elk (or wapiti) and mule deer are among the animals that nibble on the dune grasses.

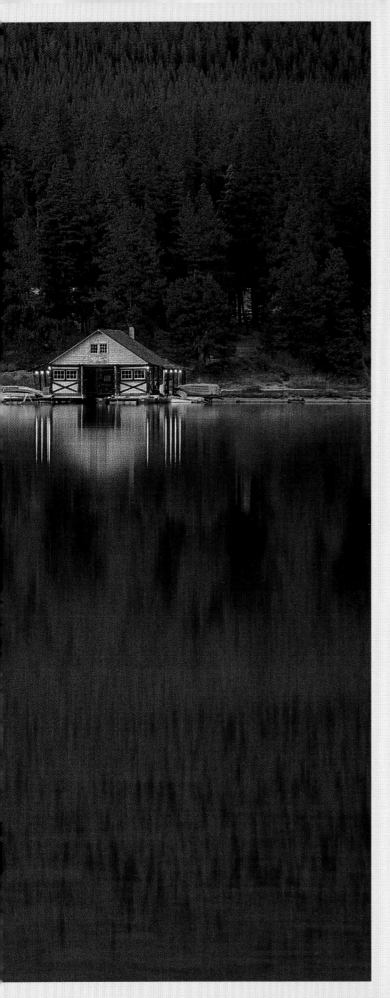

You can also see such animals on the many trails that weave around Jasper townsite. It takes only an hour or less to stroll some of the shorter trails. One of these, the paved, 2.4-km-long Clifford E. Lee Trail, runs around Lake Annette, a purple and blue-green jewel of a mountain lake. For a longer circuit, you can walk 30 minutes out of town to the 6.5-km-long Old Fort Point. Some think the trail's name refers to Henry House, a trading post established by fur trader William Henry. From a grassy knoll at the point, hikers have sweeping views of the Athabasca Valley, Mount Edith Cavell and the red-orange Pyramid Mountain. It is not unusual to come face-to-face with bighorn sheep, which graze in the aspen and spruce groves on the trail.

The disappearing lake

One of Jasper National Park's most extraordinary features is Medicine Lake. The rushing waters of the Maligne River tumble into the southern end of this lake—which appears to have no outlet. In fact, an underground gully runs from the lake down the Maligne Valley. Some 16 km along the valley, just below Maligne Canyon, the waters reappear as great boiling springs in the Lower Maligne River. This is not their only outlet, however. Dye tests have shown, intriguingly, that Medicine Lake waters also find their way to Lac Beauvert, and to other small lakes nearby, leading to speculation that there is a vast labyrinth of rivers underground.

Medicine Lake sits on a bed of limestone rock perforated by underground tunnels. In summer, when the lake is fed by melting ice and snow, it is 8 km long and 18 m deep. When autumn sets in and the summer runoff dwindles, the water level starts to drop. By November, the lake bed is nearly dry.

Upstream from Medicine Lake is the aquamarine Maligne Lake. The finest views of this spectacular lake are seen from the trail to the Bald Hills Lookout. It is a 5.2-km walk uphill along an old fire road through the subalpine forest to timber-line meadows and the site of what was once a fire lookout station. From there the Opal Hills and the pale gray Queen Elizabeth Range are also visible. In summer, caribou herds feed in the area.

PARK INFORMATION
Access: Highway 16 (Yellowhead Highway) and Highway 93 (Icefields Parkway).
Visitors' centres: Jasper townsite (year-round); Icefield Information Centre (May to September).
Accommodation: 10 campgrounds, open from May to September or October; 1,772 sites available on a first-come first-served basis. Some campgrounds have facilities for the disabled. Hotels and hostels and accommodation in private homes.
Summer activities: Walking, hiking, backcountry camping (for which a park-use permit is needed), white-water rafting, kayaking, rowing, and canoeing on all lakes and ponds except Cabin Lake; powerboating on Pyramid Lake only; fishing with a permit only, swimming in hot springs, horse riding, golfing, trail biking, windsurfing, tennis, climbing, wildlife watching, museums.
Winter activities: Downhill skiing, cross-country skiing, ice climbing, snow boarding, skating, sleigh riding, ice fishing (with a permit only), snowshoeing, and canyon crawling.

The blurred image of a boathouse shimmers in the mirror of Jasper's Maligne Lake, the largest glacier-fed lake in the Canadian Rockies.

rivals, the North West and the Hudson Bay companies. Signs along the trails describe some of the plants in the area that were used for medicinal and other purposes. Also on the trails are a York boat and a Red River cart, which exemplify 19th-century transportation.

The Rocky Mountain Native Friendship Centre displays native and Métis crafts, paintings, videos, and a tepee. The Rocky Mountain House Museum has displays and artifacts from turn-of-the-century settlers and forestry workers. *Open daily, May to Labor Day, 10 am to 8 pm; Labor Day to Thanksgiving, Monday to Friday, 8:30 am to 5 pm, weekends and holidays, 10:30 am to 6 pm; the rest of the year, 10 am to 5 pm.*

A 5-km trail goes through Rocky Mountain House, and another 3-km trail through Riverside Park by the North Saskatchewan River at Highway 11A. The town has two campgrounds. Golfers might want to try an 18-hole golf course, 6 km to the west.

Just after dawn, a dock jutting into Crimson Lake invites swimmers to take an early dip.

A replica of a century-old fur-trading store at Rocky Mountain House Museum proffers axe-heads, blankets, and provisions.

At 344-km² Crimson Lake Provincial Park (16 km to the northwest of Rocky Mountain House on secondary Highway 756), you have 166 campsites to choose from. Crimson Lake is an ideal spot for boating, waterskiing, and windsurfing. A 17-km trail system through the forest provides excellent paths for cycling or hiking, and cross-country skiing in winter.

Summer bird-watching tours offer sightings of owls, loons, woodpeckers, and sandhill cranes. Some 15 species of orchids grow at Crimson Lake.

Neighboring Twin Lakes has some 46 campsites and a 30-site group-camping area. Trout fishing is excellent. (Powered craft are forbidden on the lakes.)

Reservations for a number of different kinds of North Saskatchewan River excursions are available at Rocky Mountain House. In summer, you can pick horseback trail rides and voyageur canoe trips; and, in winter, dog-sled adventure tours.

Special events

Rocky Rodeo and Exhibition (June)

David Thompson Days Country Fair (August)

Sunchild Reserve Powwow (August)

4 Markerville
❋

The largest cream can in the world (2.75 m high and 5 m tall) and a memorial to "the poet of the Rocky Mountains" draw visitors to Markerville (pop. 55) on the banks of the Medicine River.

The giant can—topped with barley stalks—is a centennial tribute to the pioneers who opened the hamlet's historic creamery. Markerville was established by 50 Icelanders who left the drought-stricken prairies in the northwestern United States in 1888. A cooperative of 34 farmers founded the creamery in 1897, and it was later run by the Danish Morkeberg family, who remained butter makers at the creamery until 1972. The creamery, now the only registered dairy museum in Alberta, exhibits dairy and butter-making equipment from the 1930s. Icelandic food is served here, and an art gallery and a gift shop display the work of local artists. *Open daily, Victoria Day to Labor Day, 10 am to 5:30 pm. Admission free; donations are accepted.*

Across the Medicine River, in the Memorial Picnic Grounds, a monument honors the Icelandic-Canadian poet Stephan G. Stephansson, who lived in Markerville. In 1920, seven years before his death, Iceland declared Stephansson its greatest poet since the 13th century.

Stephansson House, 3 km northwest of Markerville off Highway 592, has the original desk and chair where the "poet of the Rocky Mountains" spent endless nights working by the light of a coal-oil lamp. Here he wrote volumes of poetry and tracts on social issues. Guides in period garb take visitors on tours through the house. *Open from Victoria Day to Labor Day, 10 am to 6 pm. Admission is free, although donations are accepted.*

The only remaining building recalling Markerville's Icelandic heritage is the 1907 wooden Lutheran church, two blocks north of the creamery.

Dickson (pop. 70), the first Danish settlement in western Canada, lies 15 km southwest of Markerville off Highway 54. Its history is remembered in the Dickson Store Museum, opened by Denmark's Queen Margrethe II in 1991. The store, built 80 years before this dedication, is now a provincial historical site restored to the 1930s period. The interior displays provisions and hardware and reconstructed living quarters, and includes a gift shop. *Open mid-May to Labor Day, Monday to Saturday, 10 am to 5:30 pm, Sunday 12:30 to 5:30 pm. Admission is free, but donations are accepted.*

Some 6 km east of this community, Dickson dam has created Glennifer Lake, a perfect spot for fishing, boating, camping, and picnicking. The dam—11 km long and 2 km wide—is the largest in Alberta.

Off Highway 54, south of Raven, the Medicine River Wildlife Rehabilitation Centre cares for injured and orphaned wild animals. Every year, the nonprofit centre treats some 100 different species before returning those that are healthy enough to the wild.

At the main building, visitors can observe the animals under care. *Open daily, year-round, from 8 am to 5 pm. Admission free; donations are accepted.*

Special events

Icelandic Picnic (mid-June)

Markerville Pioneer Days (late June)

Tombola Festival at Stephansson House (late July)

Cream Day at the Creamery (early August)

Harvest Festival at Dickson (October)

5 Wetaskiwin

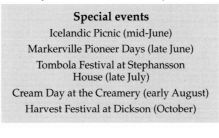

In a fertile mixed-farming area where gas and oil are also found lies the city of Wetaskiwin (pop. 10,000). Originally Siding #16 on the Calgary-Edmonton railway, Wetaskiwin became a village

"Donkey head" pumps, near Wetaskiwin and other Alberta towns, work night and day to siphon off underground oil deposits.

in 1892 and Canada's smallest city in 1906. The name *Wee-Tas-Ki-Win-Spati-now* is Cree for "hills (or place) of peace." A cairn on Highway 2A north of the city commemorates the end of an ancient feud between Cree and Blackfoot Indians.

More modern legends abound in the Reynolds-Alberta Museum of Transportation, Aviation and Agriculture, one of the most important transportation museums in Canada, which displays vintage cars and aircraft. Visitors are invited to watch the restoration of

ALL ABOARD FOR DINOSAUR JUNCTION!

The Alberta Prairie Railway Excursion revives the experience of train travel across prairie and badland. The train leaves from Stettler and stops along the way to let passengers get off and inspect some of the spots. An authentic 1920 Baldwin steam locomotive (or a 1950s CWR diesel engine) pulls a collection of old-time passengers cars. Musicians and entertainers dressed in period costume accompany travelers.

Travelers have three trip choices: a 75-km northbound trip to Ferlow Junction; a 145-km eastbound trip to Consort; and a 70-km southbound trip to Dinosaur Junction. Trips take place on weekends from June to September; five times a week in July and August.

Each of the excursions has its highlights. The northbound trip stops at Donalda (pop. 250), where travelers can admire a collection of more than 750 antique lamps at the local museum. One of the gems of this collection is the sparking lamp—the timepiece of courtship in bygone days.

The eastbound train passes Botha, Gadsby, and Halkirk, and stops at Castor (pop. 935). Here travelers can inspect another local museum, located in the village's old CPR station. Displays include dental equipment from the early 1900s. The trip continues to Coronation (pop. 1200)—the site of Fantasy Lane. This collection of bizarre wooden figurines and monsters is the creation of a local man.

The southbound train heads for Big Valley (pop. 300), once an important railway terminal. Today, the station and roundhouse are part of a railway museum and interpretive centre.

Other southbound stops include: Rumsey (pop. 90), which is the site of the Moraine Ecological Reserve, and Rowley (pop. 17), which is proud of its Old West station and Sam's Saloon. The final stop on this trip is Morrin (pop. 375), where lunch or dinner is served, before the return to Stettler.

Elk Island

In the strictest sense, Elk Island National Park is not really an island. Rather than a land encircled by water, it is a 195-km² area of hills surrounded by flatlands, a refuge for endangered species like bison, elk, and trumpeter swan. Geologic relics—hollows, knobs, and gullies—further emphasize its separateness from the grain fields along the park's perimeter.

Winter steals into the park in November, reminding thousands of waterfowl to head south. White-tailed deer, elk, and moose seem to be everywhere, simply because the leafless forest exposes them to view.

Beavers huddle inside their lodges while their muskrat cousins who are active all winter make their home in frozen clumps of shoreline grass. The tracks on the snow show red

Delicately interlaced aquatic plants decorate the shallows of Astotin Lake, Elk Island.

tree squirrels commuting from their warm nests to spruce-cone caches buried around tree roots. Long-tailed weasels, snowshoe hares and deer mice are up and about too.

On clear moonlit nights, the coyotes begin their chorus: short, sharp barks followed by long, drawn-out howls. Often they can be seen crossing Astotin Lake, tiny figures against the huge expanse of frozen water.

Blizzards persist into March, but by April the worst is over. The prairie crocus pushes through the forest floor followed by clumps of violets, purple-stemmed asters, and wild roses. In all, some 250 different kinds of flowering plants contribute to Elk Island's glorious palette.

The bluebirds' mating choruses announce the arrival of songbirds: warblers and thrushes take up residence in the poplar forest; flycatchers and kinglets are seen in the spruce forest; blackbirds and marsh wrens chatter in the marshes.

At the first sign of open water, flocks of coots, ducks, geese, and other waterfowl land on the ice-free stretches. Motionless on stiltlike legs, great blue herons wait in small ponds for a juicy fathead minnow or stickleback. Tundra swans, Canada geese, red-headed ducks, pintails, loons, and red-necked grebes are among more than 20 varieties that summer at Elk Island.

On a tree-covered knoll overlooking the lake you may spot a moose browsing on tender, hazelnut shoots. His passage through the aspen poplar understory is easy to trace; the vegetation has been trimmed back, as if by shears. The forest, over 70 percent of the park, is home to hoary bats, porcupines, northern orioles, yellow-rumped warblers, and hairy woodpeckers. Saskatoon, bunchberry, prickly rose, red-osier dogwood and sarsaparilla provide them with abundant food.

The *chat-chat-chat* of the red squirrels echoes in the silence of the white spruce forest. The spruce are survivors of many fires that have swept through Elk Island, the last one in 1895. In their cool greenery, the yellow-bellied sapsuckers and pileated woodpeckers probe for carpenter ants, and ruffed grouse feed on wild raspberries. Scattered stands of bleached white aspen shade plains bison grazing contentedly while their calves gambol in the grass.

By August's end the first frosts are nipping at any lingering flowers. Almost overnight, the park's deciduous trees burst into brilliant reds, yellows, and oranges. Fall is the rutting season and the clashes of mature bull elks echo through the misty hills.

Thousands of ducks, coots, loons, Canada geese, and tundra swans pack the lakes. Then, as arctic air moves farther south, the great migration is resumed. The final stragglers finally lift off about mid-November, just as the last patches of water freeze. Now winter rules the park once more.

PARK INFORMATION
Access: Highways 16 from the south; Highway 15 from the north.
Visitors' centre: Located 800 m north of Highway 16, inside the park.
Accommodation: 112 semi-serviced sites at Sandy Beach campground in the Astotin Recreation Area, and a more primitive campground at Oster Lake Group Tenting Area. Stays limited to two weeks. Group and winter camping in the Astotin Recreation Area. Astotin Interpretive Centre is open year-round.
Year-round activities: Wildlife observation; bird-watching (the park is on a major flyway).
Summer activities: Hiking, picnicking, biking, boating (all motorized boats prohibited), sailing, golfing. Both fishing and swimming are prohibited.
Winter activities: Cross-country skiing, snowshoeing.

these vehicles. The old-time cars and bicycles, as well as agricultural and industrial machines in the museum collection, are kept in such good shape that they often appear in parades.

The Reynolds-Alberta Museum also houses Canada's Aviation Hall of Fame, which hosts different exhibitions every month. The museum is located opposite Wetaskiwin airport, 2 km west of the city on Highway 13. *Open daily, mid-May to Labor Day, 9 am to 9 pm. Winter months, open daily, 9 am to 5 pm. Admission free on Tuesdays.*

Wetaskiwin is blessed with another aviation museum, the Reynolds Museum, where visitors can see hundreds of vintage machines such as a 1919 Reynolds sport monoplane powered by a model T Ford engine, and a 1945 paratrooper's folding motorcycle. *Open daily, mid-May to early September, 10 am to 5 pm.*

Wetaskiwin offers walking tours to its 1891 train station, 1908 courthouse, and the Wetaskiwin and District Museum in the 1908 Electric Light Building. The museum houses re-creations of the life of the early settlers. *Open summer months, Tuesday to Friday, 10 am to 5 pm; weekends, 1 pm to 5 pm; winter months, Tuesday to Friday, 1 to 4 pm.*

Wetaskiwin's surroundings include a waterfowl sanctuary and Pigeon Lake Recreation Area west of the city, an outdoor playground with golf, fishing, and hiking trails.

6 | Stettler

∧ ₮ ╷ •☜ ❋ ⌂

A Swiss settler called Stettler persuaded a group of his countrymen to start farming in the Red Deer River valley in 1905. They prospered here and, in gratitude, honored Stettler by giving his name to the community (pop. 5,000) when it became a town

in 1906. Stettler Town and Country Museum salutes its pioneers with a collection of buildings from the 1890s and early 1900s: a courthouse, post office, harness shop, a 1908 church, and a 1911 railway station. *Open daily, May to September, 9 am to 5 pm; open the rest of the year by appointment only.*

Originally Stettler was a community serving local farmers. The discovery of oil in 1949 transformed the community. Within a short time, 6,700 oil wells sprouted in the nearby farmlands. Stettler is still an important oil-producing hub.

7 | Ukrainian Cultural Heritage Village

❋

A horse-drawn hay wagon clip-clops past an onion-domed church, thatched barns, and simple wooden houses. On the dusty streets of the village, women wearing brightly colored kerchiefs go about daily chores, while men work in the fields and gardens. This is the Ukrainian Cultural Heritage Village Provincial Historic Site, which proudly preserves the sights, sounds, and sym-

A beaming girl in traditional garb plays a part in re-creating the past at the Ukrainian Cultural Heritage Village.

bols of the first four decades of Ukrainian culture and experience in western Canada.

The east-central region of Alberta—covering 8,000 km² from Fort Saskatchewan to Vermilion—is one of the main areas of Ukrainian settlement in Canada. In 1892, the first Ukrainians came to the Edna district 65 km northeast of Edmonton, lured by the promise of 65 ha of farmland for the affordable sum of $10. The ensuing wave of immigration brought a quarter of a million Ukrainians to new homes and communities not only in Alberta, but also to the vast fertile tracts of central Saskatchewan and western Manitoba.

The 130-ha Ukrainian Cultural Heritage Village contains over 30 buildings, which re-create the life of the immigrants, from impoverished beginnings to relative prosperity in the 1920s and the 1930s.

One of the most touching re-creations at the village is the temporary dugout-type dwelling, called a *burdei* (or, sometimes, a *zemlianka*), which was usually the first prairie home for thousands of immigrants. A *burdei* was hardly larger than a bedroom in a modern house. Wives and children often lived in this meagre habitation throughout the cold and lonely prairie winter, while their husbands worked elsewhere to provide money for their support.

The change from subsistence farming to commercial farming is the story told at the village, where five farmsteads with various improvements trace the material progress of the Ukrainian farmers. After the *burdei*, a home like the 1919 Slemko house must have seemed luxurious—although a family of seven children lived in one room and slept in one bed.

Throughout the village, costumed guides play the roles of settlers and recount the experience of coming to a new land. Cultivators in the fields use historic methods and machinery. In the kitchens, cooks prepare traditional Ukrainian dishes for the delectation of visitors. Musical entertainments and games give a picture of the lighter side of an otherwise harsh existence.

The Ukrainian Cultural Heritage Village offers a variety of programs and special events throughout the year. Notable events are Ukrainian Day and a harvest fair (both held in August), and a farmers' market on the weekends. To tour the village properly, set aside a few hours. *Open daily, Victoria Day to*

Victoria Settlement Provincial Historic Site preserves a modest 1906 Methodist church.

Labor Day, from 10 am to 6 pm daily, and from Labor Day to Thanksgiving from 10 am to 4 pm. Group tours only are admitted during the rest of the year by appointment. Admission is free on Tuesdays.

8 Smoky Lake

The Plains and Woodland Cree Indians called this stretch of water Smoking Lake for the smokelike vapor that emanated from its waters and concealed the opposite shore. The name has stuck, shortened by settlers. In spring and fall, the lake is home to thousands of migrating geese, ducks, and other waterfowl.

The first Ukrainians in Canada settled around the North Saskatchewan River flowing northeast from Edmonton. The town of Smoky Lake (pop. 1,057) typifies the communities they established. The most prominent features are the churches, crowned with a cluster of onion domes and decorated inside with the richly embellished altar icon screens.

Smoky Lake's Holy Trinity Russo-Greek Orthodox Church, the second on this site, was built in 1904 in the shape of a cross, with an open central dome; a bell tower was added in 1928. The church has one of the largest Ukrainian cemeteries in Alberta.

The Ukrainian Cultural Heritage Village contains a replica of a barn once built by settlers.

Evening falls at Lac La Biche, once plied by canoes laden with cargoes of northern furs.

Across the highway, the Smoky Lake Museum houses the original tools, tapestry, and clothing of early Ukrainian pioneers. *Open Victoria Day to Thanksgiving, Saturday, 10 am to 4 pm; Sunday, 1 pm to 5 pm, or Monday to Friday by appointment.*

Just to the south of Smoky Lake is the Victoria Settlement Provincial Historic Site, one of Alberta's oldest settled communities, dating back to the 1860s. Victoria's name was changed to Pakan at the turn of the century, to honor the Indian chief who prevented his Cree followers from joining the second Louis Riel rebellion.

In 1919, the railway was built 15 km to the north, through Smoky Lake, and most of Victoria was moved there, including its hospital. Decades later, in 1974, the original site of Pakan was declared an important historic resource. In 1981 it was opened as the Victoria Settlement Provincial Historic Site. The Hudson's Bay Company had built a fort there in 1864, and the clerk's quarters still stand, the oldest building in its original location in Alberta. The Methodist church still stands, too. These days, visitors to the church watch slide shows on the history of the settlement. *Admission is free. Open from mid-May to Labor Day, with costumed interpreters in attendance.*

Pine Ridge Forest Nursery, 19 km east of Smoky Lake just off Highway 28, is a provincially owned tree nursery. Some 35 million seedlings are grown here, and 15 million seeds planted, annually. One of the greenhouses is the size of two football fields. *Tours are available by appointment only.*

Almost 10 km south of Smoky Lake, on secondary Highway 857, is SS. Peter's and Paul Russian Orthodox Church at Dickiebush. It was built by Stephen Rosichuk who could neither read nor write, but who remembered how his church had looked in his homeland.

Some 8 km north of Smoky Lake, a 28,000-ha buffalo ranch, called the Inn at the Ranch, keeps one of Alberta's largest private herds and offers bed-and-breakfast accommodation.

Special events
Smoky Lake Stampede, Heritage Days, Parade and Cultural Show (August)

Fort Victoria Days (August)

Smoky Lake, Pumpkin Capital of Alberta Weigh-Off (October)

9 Lac La Biche

The fur trade is the key to the story of Lac La Biche (pop. 2,737), which in French means Doe Lake. It is at the origin of two northern river systems—the Athabasca/Mackenzie and the Churchill River basins—that flow in

A boardwalk curves through a leafy glade at Sir Winston Churchill Provincial Park.

different directions (north and east respectively) to the Arctic Ocean. Both systems served as fur-trade routes. The growth of the trade ensured the development of Lac La Biche, one of the oldest communities in Alberta.

Settlers came with the Alberta and Great Waterways Railway in 1915. One of the most enterprising was J. D. McArthur, builder of the Lac La Biche Inn, a grand railway hotel. It was one of the few structures here to survive a 1919 forest fire so fierce that townfolk had to take refuge in the lake.

Every August Indians and Métis get together near the town for a four-day powwow and celebration, during Lac La Biche Heritage Days. The fish derby draws anglers from all parts of the area. The celebration also features a parade, traditional Indian contests, dancing, and a baseball tournament.

Lac La Biche Mission, a national provincial historic site, is located 10 km west of town. The mission, established in 1853, set up Alberta's first printing press, which produced books in English, French, and Cree. The gristmill built there in 1862 still stands, as does the sawmill, erected in 1871, the first sawmill in Alberta. *Open daily, July 1 to Labor Day, 10 am to 6 pm. The rest of the year, visits by appointment.*

About 12 km east of town on secondary road 881 is 234-ha Sir Winston Churchill Provincial Park, on the largest of eleven islands in Lac La Biche. A causeway crosses to the island park, which is a haven for 200 bird species. Visitors will find two well-marked hiking trails here, as well as sandy beaches and 72 campsites.

10 Cold Lake

The angler who plans to catch a lunker of a lake trout should head for the town of Cold Lake (pop. 4,017). Its 373-km^2 lake of the same name has a reputation for yielding tasty trout. Some catches have weighed as much

Expansive Cold Lake is a fishing paradise with generous supplies of trout and pike.

as 23.9 kg. Northern pike and walleye also reside in its cool waters.

The town of Cold Lake was founded in 1905 as a commercial fishing site. In 1954, an RCAF station opened here. Heavy-oil project and other petroleum interests have bolstered the economy.

Much of the town is within easy walking distance from the boardwalk at the marina, where 250 boats can berth, and boats can be rented. A local landmark is nearby Clark's General Store, which still keeps the decor of a 1920s ice-cream parlor.

The totem poles near the marina are the work of Chief Ovide Jacko, of the Cold Lake Indian Reserve. They were placed here in 1966-1967 as symbols of goodwill to the town of Cold Lake from local Indians.

The 398-ha Cold Lake Provincial Park, 4 km northeast from the marina, provides a taste of northern camping, boating, and hiking for families and groups. More than 115 campsites are available from May until late Septem-

ber, with some year-round sites. The park has more than 9 km of walking and cross-country ski trails.

The Cold Lake region is close to two important bird-watching sites. Moose Lake, 40 km south on Highway 28,

The yellow-shafted flicker inhabits Alberta's wooded river valleys.

shelters more than 40 species, including Canada geese and white pelicans. Jessie Lake in Bonnyville has viewing platforms and trails that enable visitors to observe some 200 species of birds, such as whooping cranes, bald and golden eagles, and yellow rails.

Special events

Rodeo Days, Grand Centre
(early June)

Aqua Days (late July-early August)

Alberta Air Show
(An event held every other July)

Roads to explore: UFO's, flyways, and fur-trading posts

Distance (approx.): 250 km/156 miles

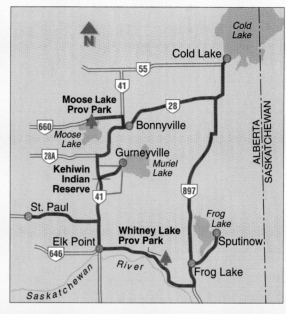

Heading out from Cold Lake, 300 km northeast of Edmonton, at the junction of highways 55 and 28 close to the Saskatchewan border, this drive goes through the Lakeland Country in northeastern Alberta.

● First stop is the farming community of Bonnyville (pop. 5,150), 50 km southwest of Cold Lake on Highway 28. The town is surrounded by recreational lakes. In town, Jessie Lake is an ideal place for nature hikes and bird-watching. Two major flyways for migratory birds intersect at the lake, and rare species often land on its marshy shores.

● Just to the west is the turnoff on Highway 660 to Moose Lake Provincial Park, which offers a sandy beach, opportunities for sailing and fishing, and hiking trails along Deadman's Point.

● Continuing south on Highway 28, take the Gurneyville turnoff east to the Kehiwin Indian Reserve. Descendants of the great chiefs Poundmaker and Big Bear live at Kehiwin. Visitors can tour a steel plant and a weaving workshop that makes blankets, shawls, and shoulder bags interwoven with Plains Indian symbols.

● Returning to Highway 28, head south for 10 km to where Highway 28 turns abruptly west to the town of St. Paul (pop. 5,021), famous for its 1967 Centennial project: a 12-m-high flying saucer launching pad. Since 1993, the pad has had its own UFO—a visitors' centre—placed neatly on the pad by an earthbound crane.

● Returning from St. Paul east along Highway 28, head back to where Highway 41 goes due south and follow it for 9 km until you reach Elk Point.

● Elk Point (pop. 1,400) has a 30-m-high mural with images that trace the events of the North-West Rebellion of 1885 that took place nearby and left its mark on the heritage of the community.

● East of town, 16 km along Highway 646, visitors can tour the Canadian Salt Plant, which produces some 400 tonnes of salt daily.

● On Elk Point's north hill is a 10-m chain-saw statue of Hudson Bay surveyor Peter Fidler, who immersed himself in the Indian culture in the 1790s. About 11 km southeast of town, at Fort George-Buckingham House Provincial Historic Site, an interpretive centre tells the history of two rival 1792 fur-trading posts, forts George and Buckingham. *The interpretive centre is open daily, from mid-May to Labor Day, 10 am to 6 pm.*

● From Elk Point, take secondary Highway 646 east past Lindbergh. The entrance to the 1,335-ha Whitney Lakes Provincial Park is on Highway 646, 27 km east of Elk Point. This wilderness park has four lakes. There are nature trails and campgrounds at Ross and Whitney lakes.

● Continue along Highway 646 to Route 897, and then turn due north for Frog Lake, which can be reached on a side road on the east of the highway. Frog Lake has a cairn and trail that commemorate the massacre of Métis during the North-West Rebellion of 1885.

● Leaving Frog Lake, head north on Highway 897 for the return drive to Cold Lake. At the northern end of the highway, turn onto Highway 28 for Cold Lake.

SASKATCHEWAN

7

SASKATCHEWAN

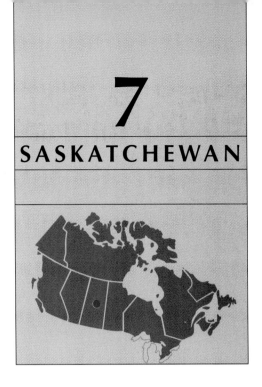

Places to see

The Great Sand Hills
Meadow Lake Provincial Park
Maple Creek
Cypress Hills Interprovincial Park
Batoche National Historic Site
Wanuskewin Heritage Park
Lake Diefenbaker
Buffalo Pound Provincial Park
Wood Mountain Post Provincial Park
Grasslands National Park
St. Victor's Petroglyphs Provincial Park
Fort Qu'Appelle
Motherwell Homestead National Historic Site
Canora
Moose Mountain Provincial Park
Cannington Manor Provincial Park

Roads to explore
Batoche to Fort Carlton Provincial Park
Willow Bunch to Ogema

National park close-up
Prince Albert

Previous pages:
Saskatchewan Landing Provincial Park
on Lake Diefenbaker

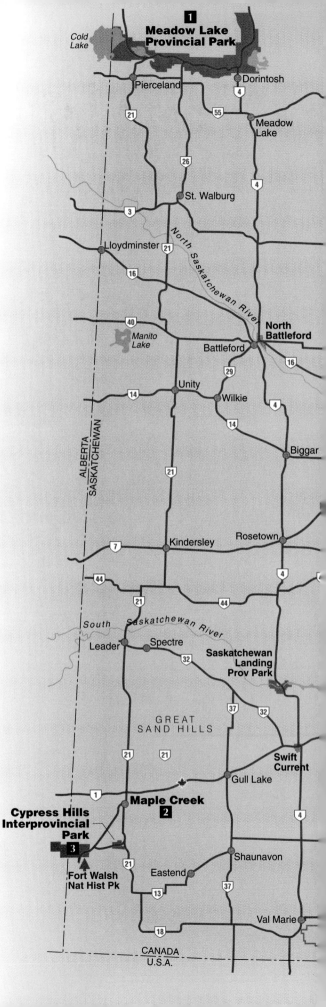

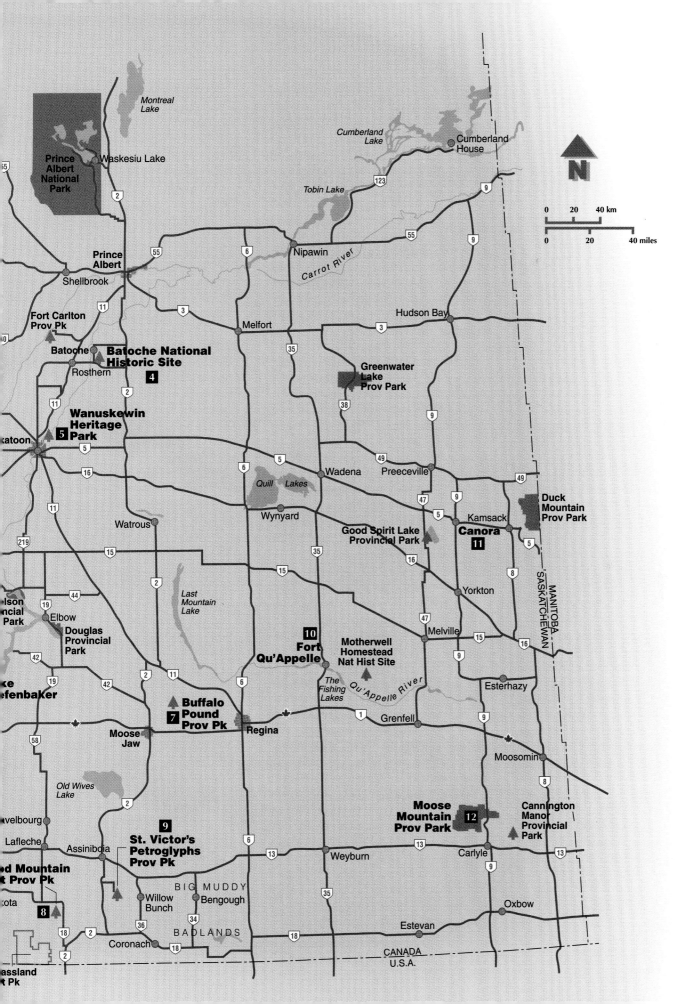

SAND AND SAGEBRUSH

Pronghorns of the Saskatchewan prairies

North of Maple Creek, shifting sands move restlessly across a 1,900-km² region known as the Great Sand Hills. This desertlike region lies north of the Trans-Canada Highway and extends to Highway 32.

The dunes of the Great Sand Hills originate with the last Ice Age. About 14,000 years ago, retreating glaciers left behind heaps of grit and fine white sand. The prevailing west-by-northwest winds whip this residue into the dunes—some more than 1.6 km long and 15 to 20 m high—and drift them eastward at a rate of 3 to 4 m every year.

You can drive into the Great Sand Hills on the "Straw Road" just outside Sceptre (pop. 167). Local people will be glad to show you the way. You will discover the Great Sand Hills are by no means barren. The dunes support groves of aspen, birch, and willow, and shrubs such as wild rose, saskatoons, chokecherry, and silver sagebrush. The aridity is perfect for prickly-pear and pincushion cacti. Lance leaf and lemonweed with 12- to 15-m-long roots also thrive here. (Pioneers used these wiry roots as binder twine.) The region is home to pronghorn antelope, mule deer and sharp-tailed grouse.

Before you explore the dunes, stop at Sceptre's Great Sand Hills Museum. A mural on the exterior facade depicts the dunes; another, inside the museum, the humble beginnings of the settlers who first made their homes in this arid region.

1 Meadow Lake Provincial Park

Meadow Lake is one of Saskatchewan's largest and most northerly provincial parks, covering some 1,600 km² of mixed boreal forest. It has more than 25 lakes, all ideal for camping, canoeing, and fishing. The park was set up in 1959 from a provincial forest previously used for trapping, commercial fishing, logging, and farming.

Stands of aspen trees grow here to impressive heights of 15 m or more. On bright summer days the trees turn some of the park's winding roads into cathedral arches of green and white. Green light filters down through the leaves between the slender white pillars of the tree trunks. Also scattered through the woods are clusters of white birch, spruce, and jack pine.

In summer, tamarack trees blend in with the evergreens, but in fall their feathery deciduous needles create a stunning contrast of reddish gold and yellow. Wildlife—moose, deer, elk, and bear—abounds here. The call of loons, coyotes and wolves is the campers' lullaby. At night, above the campsites, the aurora borealis, or northern lights, may draw its shimmering curtains of cool green and pink across the sky.

To appreciate the boreal forest, walk the 2-km White Birch Nature Trail, also near Flotten Lake. It leads past the Flotten River, through a white birch grove and a jack pine forest, before emerging onto a bog via a boardwalk.

At the other end of the park, south of Pierce Lake, is the Humphrey Lake Trail. This easy half-day hike ends at a height of land which has a lookout platform with a view of the nearby lakes and forest. An important part of the life cycle of the forest can be seen north of Kimball Lake, where a fire swept through the forest during the early 1980s. As the ravaged forest heals, the verdant undergrowth and the slender, young trees slowly envelop its blackened stumps.

One of the scenic sights in the park is the Salt Creek valley, north of Flotten Lake. A roadside turnoff presents a superb view of the rugged, densely wooded valley, which plunges 120 m below the surrounding countryside.

2 Maple Creek

A dozen crewmen, laying steel rails across the prairies for the CPR in 1882, stopped work for the winter, but decided to stay on rather than to return home. They put up a log cabin on the banks of a nearby creek where a cluster of luxurious maples grew—a strange sight in this treeless region. Like the maples, the settlement took root—and the name has endured.

Although present-day Maple Creek (pop. 2,297) also calls itself "an old cow town," ranching is still big business. It is worth stopping here to soak up the spirit of small western town, before heading on to Cypress Hill Interprovincial Park or the Great Sand Hills.

The Old-Timers' Museum on Main Street preserves Indian arrowheads, antique rifles and pistols, cowboy gear, and other mementos from Maple Creek's rambunctious pioneer past.

Jasper Cultural and Historical Centre, just a block south of the museum, occupies a converted brick school, where theme rooms display

Prince Albert

Prince Albert National Park lies between two worlds: to the south are quarter sections, combines, and grain elevators; to the north are traplines, timber berths, and uranium mines. It is reached from highways 263 and 264 to the east, near Waskesiu Lake townsite, and at the junction of highways 263 and 240 near Sandy (Halkett) Lake to the southeast.

The glaciers that shaped the park's boreal landscape left gently rolling hills, expansive lakes, and rivers snaking through muskeg and bog. Within this landscape, there are several forests, each with a character of its own. Aspen thrives on well-drained uplands, jack pine grows along the sandy ridges, and black spruce and tamarack prefer depressions and bogs.

Each hiking trail in the park offers a sample of the forest mosaic. The 3-km-long Narrows Peninsula Trail on the north shore of Waskesiu Lake begins in a mixed-woods forest of aspen, birch, and white spruce. Sunlight streams through the high canopy to a forest floor brightened by wild rose, highbush cranberry, sarsaparilla, and bunchberry. The trail descends to the lakeshore along a beach ridge covered in jack pine. At the trail's end you walk waist deep in the gracefully nodding fronds of ostrich ferns growing amid horsetails, wild mint, and currants.

This is a balsam fir forest where white spruce grows to more than 1 m in diameter—dimensions unusual for the boreal forest. It is one of the oldest forests in the park.

Prince Albert's tree mosaic is complemented by an equally rich tapestry of waterscapes. These account for a third of the park's 3,875 km^2. Three large glacier-gouged lakes—Waskesiu, Kingsmere, and Crean—sprawl across the centre of the park, where rivers follow old glacial channels. Imprisoned by ice for six or seven months of the year, the park's lakes erupt with life during the brief boreal summer. The spectacle begins at the Narrows of Waskesiu, where bald eagles, ospreys, loons, mergansers, and grebes come to fish in the season's first open water. Once the weather has been warm and sunny for a few days, the white pelicans return from wintering grounds on the Gulf of Mexico to Lavallée Lake near the park's north boundary. There, nearly 7,000 nest in cramped closeness on a small island. (The breeding colony is off-limits to visitors.)

One of the park's most intriguing environments is muskeg, a dense mat of waterlogged vegetation that oozes menacingly among islands of stunted black spruce and tamarack. There are great expanses of muskeg in the park, but only the area skirting the 1-km-long Boundary Bog Nature Trail at the park's east boundary is readily accessible. From the security of a boardwalk, you can explore muskeg dotted with pitcher plants, cloudberry, bog rosemary, and the tiny sundew, which captures its insect prey in sticky, red spikelets radiating from its diminutive leaves.

The conservationist and writer Grey Owl lived his last seven years beside Ajawaan Lake, a small body of water tucked into the forest north of Kingsmere. There, with his wife, Anahareo, Grey Owl raised a pair of beaver kits, recounting their antics in *Pilgrims of the Wild* and *Tales of an Empty Cabin*. Until his death in 1938, Grey Owl was thought to be an Indian. Then it was discovered that his real name was Archibald Stansfeld Belaney, and that he had emigrated to Canada from his native England in 1906. His grave is in the park and his cabin on the far shore.

PARK INFORMATION
Access: Highways 263, 264 and 240.
Visitors' centre: Waskesiu Lake.
Accommodations: Year-round accommodation in cabins and motels in Waskesiu Lake townsite; seasonal accommodation in the Waskesiu International Hostel, and in some nearby 500 serviced and rustic campsites along Highway 263 at Sandy, Namekus, and Trappers lakes. Group tenting sites at Trappers and Kingsmere lakes.
Summmer activities: Swimming, fishing, picnicking, hiking, boating, and canoeing. Riding stables, tennis courts, lawn bowling greens, an 18-hole golf course, and boat and canoe rentals, as well as launching and mooring facilities at three marinas.
Winter activities: Cross-country skiing and snowshoeing.

Bison, Prince Albert National Park

old-time phonographs (designed for cylinder records), horseshoes of different styles, and other treasures of the town's yesterdays.

Special events

Maple Creek Cowtown Rodeo (late May)

Jasper Jamboree Ranchmen's Rodeo (early July)

Light Horse Show (mid-August)

Cowboy Poetry Gathering (late September)

---

3 Cypress Hills Interprovincial Park

∧ ⛺ ↑ ↓ ↑ ⚙ ♨ ⇆ ☀

Rising 610 m above the grassy plains, the Cypress Hills region is a forested plateau, the highest point of land between the Rocky Mountains and Labrador. This 2,600-km² region—a remnant of a larger prehistoric up-land—is crisscrossed by coulees and valleys. Alberta and Saskatchewan share the Cypress Hills and preserved portions of the region in separate provincial parks. In 1989 the two provinces united the parks to form Cypress Hills Interprovincial Park, the first of its kind in Canada.

The Saskatchewan portion of the Cypress Hills park has many unusual features. It is the only area in Saskatchewan where lodgepole pine grows. The park combines prairie and mountain habitats. Birds common only in northern forests of the Rockies nest here. At least 18 species and two varieties of orchids flourish in the hills. Pronghorns graze here, on one of the few remaining fescue grasslands in Canada.

The Saskatchewan park is divided in two by The Gap, a 16-km-wide valley. The 44-km² centre block, south of Maple Creek, can be reached by High-

Historic Fort Walsh huddles within a wooden palisade at the foot of the Cypress Hills.

way 21. After visiting the centre block, travel the Gap Road, across the top of the hills, to Lookout Point and Bald Butte. The road leads to the park's 176-km² west block and Fort Walsh National Historic Park. This unpaved route is unsuitable for driving in rainy weather. Instead, take Highway 271 to Fort Walsh. This all-weather road, running southwest from Maple Creek, bypasses the centre block completely.

Fort Walsh, situated just south of the western block, was an important North West Mounted Police post and centre for trade from 1875 until 1883. The present palisade fort faithfully reconstructs the original with barracks, guardroom, powder magazine, stable, and workshops. It also has a visitors' centre. *Open daily, mid-May to Thanksgiving, 9 am to 6 pm.*

Buses connect the fort to Abe Farwell's trading post. This was the site of the Cypress Hills Massacre of 1873, during which American hunters killed a group of Assiniboine Indians after a dispute about stolen horse. The massacre led to the creation of the North West Mounted Police, who brought law and order to the area. *Open daily, mid-May to Labor Day, 9 am to 5 pm.*

4 | Batoche National Historic Site

For four days in May 1885 a battle raged at Batoche on the banks of the South Saskatchewan River. It was the main battle and the last act of the North-West Rebellion of 1885. A force of 300 Métis and Indians led by Louis Riel and Gabriel Dumont confronted about 900 men led by Maj.-Gen. Frederick Middleton who were armed with cannons and Gatling guns.

On May 12, 1885, Middleton's troops defeated the Métis and put an end to their dream of a separate nation on the prairies. Riel was tried for treason and hanged in Regina, and buried at St. Boniface, Man. The Batoche battlefield is now a 182-ha national historic park of poignant memory.

The park's visitor reception area outlines the life of the Métis, and the conflict at Batoche and its historic consequences. An exhibit hall displays mementos of the past, such as Métis clothing of the time and uniforms and equipment used by the Canadian government forces. Mock-ups of the battlefield and the Métis camp re-create the stages of the conflict. Staff in Métis costume also describe the confrontation on tours of the battlefield. Trenches and rifle pits are still visible here.

Maps and signs explain the ruins of the Métis village of Batoche on the other side of the South Saskatchewan—just a ferry crossing away—and a historic trail used by Métis and Middleton's government forces.

Away from the battlefield stands the white clapboard mission of St. Antoine

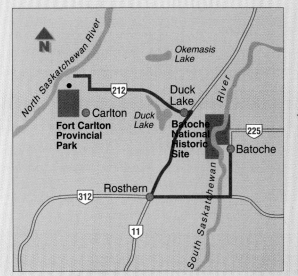

Roads to explore: Battlegrounds in wheat country
Distance (approx.): 60 km/37 miles

From Batoche, travel south on Highway 225 along the South Saskatchewan River to Highway 312, and head west to Rosthern (pop. 1,560). This town in the heart of wheat country greets visitors with a 13-m-high sculpture of wheat sheaves.

The Station Arts Centre/Seager Wheeler Place is named after one of the town's founding fathers, Seager Wheeler. It displays grain varieties Wheeler developed in the 1890s. *Admission free, donations accepted. Open year-round, Tuesday to Saturday, 10 am to 4 pm.*

The history of German Mennonite immigrants to Rosthern is told at the Mennonite Heritage Museum. On display are photographs, furniture and medical instruments. *Open May to October, Friday, 10 am to 12 pm and 1 pm to 4 pm; Sunday, from 2 pm to 5 pm.*

● Just north of Rosthern on Highway 11 is Valley Regional Park, equipped with camping facilities. *Open May to October.*

● Some 30 km north of Rosthern on Highway 11 is Duck Lake (pop. 517), a town which has painted its history in mural form on its buildings. The colorful paintings depict the 1876 signing of Treaty No. 6 between Indians and government representatives, the faces of Sir John A. Macdonald, and Métis leaders Louis Riel and Gabriel Dumont. Thirty-seven buildings in Duck Lake are considered heritage properties, and have been restored to the style of the 1800s.

● Duck Lake's Regional Interpretive Centre lies just off Highway 11. It features more than 2,000 artifacts including Indian costumes, religious articles and pioneer tools, and a film theatre that shows documentaries of the area's history. A 24-m tower gives a bird's-eye view of the ground where Indians, Métis, and North West Mounted Police battled in 1885.

● From the Interpretive Centre, travel west on Highway 212 through the Beardy's and Okemasis Indian Reserve to reach Fort Carlton Provincial Park. At the fort, built by the Hudson's Bay Company in 1810, are the remains of a fur-trading post. It was one of the sites of the signing of Treaty No. 6, which ensured the peaceful opening of the west. A fur provisions store on the site displays pelts, and the Trading Depot exhibits goods used in the 1800s. The Carlton Trail on the fort grounds meanders along the riverbank and through woods and hills. *Open daily, Victoria to Labor Day, 10 am to 6 pm.*

Night work on Saskatchewan's wheatland

de Padoue, once the Métis "capital." The church and the nearby rectory are furnished in the style of the 1890s. The church has religious statues, oil paintings and crystal chandeliers, and a box stove that warmed the congregation.

Just a few metres from the church is the rectory, still scarred by bullet holes received during the battle. Among the exhibits here are Gabriel Dumont's .44 revolver and his bridle of horsehair and leather. Some of Louis Riel's personal belongings are also displayed.

A short walk from the rectory is the graveyard where Gabriel Dumont now lies, alongside many of those who died in the battle. He fled the area after the battle, but later returned to Batoche, where he died in 1906.

Admission free. Open daily, May and June, and September to mid-October, 9 am to 5 pm; July and August, 10 am to 6 pm.

5 Wanuskewin Heritage Park

At Wanuskewin Heritage Park, just outside Saskatoon, archaeologists have unearthed some of the most exciting finds in North America, which reveal the prehistoric way of life of nomadic Northern Plains Indians. The 100-ha park has yielded 19 sites, dating from 5,000 to 8,000 years. Wanuskewin (pronounced *Wah-nus-kay-win*) is a Cree Indian word, which loosely translated means "living in harmony."

At the interpretive centre, displays emphasize the importance of the buffalo as a source of meat and hides, clothing and ornaments. The archaelogical equipment used to dig up the past is part of an exhibit that encompasses piles of buffalo bones, pottery fragments and other objects.

The oldest object excavated at Wanuskewin is a spearpoint believed to be 8,000 years old. Despite the impressive finds, archaeologists cannot identify Wanuskewin's first inhabitants because no burial grounds that might provide clues have come to light.

Nevertheless enough is known to provide visitors with a feeling for the life of the early Indians. At the storyteller's tepee, you can select (with the help of a computer) a legendary story of prehistoric times. The toolmaker's tepee displays spears and other weapons made from animal bone. A family tepee shows the place where each family member—an elder, the father, mother and children—sat in the tent.

The centre also houses a restaurant offering native cuisine such as buffalo steak and bannock (not the Scots cake, but a flour-and-water unleavened bread, which remains a staple of many native peoples' diet).

On the grounds outside the centre, 15 stone cairns mark part of a drive lane used by Indians 2,300 years ago to drive stampeding buffalo to a buffalo jump. Marked trails lead to historic and symbolic remnants of the Indians' past. The Sunburn Tepee Rings shows the circular layout of ancient camps. The purpose of the Medicine Wheel, a 1,500-year-old ring of sacred stones, remains a mystery. *Open daily, year-round, 9 am to 5 pm; Victoria Day to Labor Day, 9 am to 9 pm.*

6 Lake Diefenbaker

This 200-km-long lake is never more than 2 or 3 km wide. In the 1960s, it was blasted out of the South Saskatchewan River valley to provide irrigation and electricity for the surrounding semiarid farmland. Its name honors John Diefenbaker, the first Saskatchewan resident to become Canadian Prime Minister (1957-1963).

The project created nearly 800 km of lakeshore, now the site for three attractive provincial parks. The small communities of Elbow and Riverhurst are the best jumping-off spots from which to explore this man-made lake.

Douglas Provincial Park, just southeast of Elbow, has the 2.5-km Juniper Nature Trail that crosses aspen wood-

The five towers atop the boulder-packed Gardiner dam house the gates that control the water flow of Lake Diefenbaker.

land and grasslands. A feature of the park is the Big Dune, a haven for mule deer and coyotes. More than 1 km long, this height of land rises 30 m from the prairie floor.

Northeast of Elbow, Danielson Provincial Park abuts east and west sides of Gardiner dam. You can tour the 5-km-long and 64-m-high earth-fill dam—the largest of its kind in Canada. (It was named for Saskatchewan Premier and Diefenbaker political rival, J. C. Gardiner.) Houseboats for lake holidays are for rent here.

From Riverhurst, a small ferry—a transportation novelty in the midst of the prairies—provides a shortcut across the lake. Riverhurst itself has a 2-m-high war memorial, embedded with rifles from the Boer War and First World War, and weapons from the last big battle between the Cree and Blackfoot. Indian and pioneer weaponry are exhibits at the Fred T. Hill Museum. *Open daily, mid-June to September, 2 to 5 pm and 7 to 9 pm.*

At the western end of the lake is Saskatchewan Landing Provincial Park. Government troops used this crossing in 1885 to transport supplies for troops who suppressed the Metis uprising at Batoche. A stone house, built at the turn of the century by Frank Goodwin of the North West Mounted Police, houses the visitors' centre.

7 Buffalo Pound Provincial Park

A herd of purebred plains buffalo—28 at the last count—roam an 81-ha enclosure in this park on the shores of Buffalo Pound Lake. At Pound Cliffs, the Indians once stampeded buffalo to death for food and clothing. The numbers killed by spear and club were few compared to the millions that once thundered across the plains. But with

the advent of firearms in 1750, the slaughter ended only when the buffalo was almost extinct. Now parks like this are the only domains of the buffalo.

A 7.5-km road from the park entrance leads to an enchanting marshland—1,040-ha Nicolle Flats, which is located at the eastern end of Buffalo Pound Lake. It takes only minutes to walk the Nicolle Flats Marsh boardwalk, the best spot to glimpse the 40 different species of birds of this area, or to smell the perfumes wafting from prairie flowers.

Near the boardwalk is the 2-km Bison Trail. Here binoculars are a must for a close-up view of the buffalo sheltering in the adjoining park.

Three successive trails encircle the marshland. The 3-km Nicolle Flats Trail offers a never-ending wildlife spectacle. In spring and fall, ducks,

Cattails enclose Nicolle Flats Marsh boardwalk, Buffalo Pound Provincial Park.

geese, and other migratory birds stop here on their flight along the Central flyway, which stretches from the Mackenzie River delta to the Gulf of Mexico. Great blue herons flit between cattails, bulrushes and duckweed. Other marsh birds include yellow-headed blackbirds, American bitterns, coots, shovelers, and grebes.

The Nicolle Flats Trail passes the homestead settled by Charles and Catherine Nicolle in 1881. The 1903 stone farmhouse still stands, an enduring tribute to their pioneering spirit The trail continues onto the 1.5-km Valley Trail, a scenic pathway along the Moose Jaw River.

More ambitious hikers can carry on along the 8-km Dyke Trail, which skirts the Moose Jaw and Qu'Appelle rivers.

Special events

South Saskatchewan Wildlife Association Fish Derby (Victoria Day weekend)

Nicolle Flats Nature Festival (early June)

8 Wood Mountain Post Provincial Park

A bench of prairie interrupted by high buttes and wooded valleys in southern Saskatchewan forms the Wood Mountain Uplands. The focus of the uplands

Reconstructed barracks at Wood Mountain Post recall the days when the Mounties brought law and order to Saskatchewan.

is Wood Mountain Post Provincial Park and the adjacent Wood Mountain Regional Park.

Wood Mountain became a North West Mounted Police post in 1874. At Wood Mountain Post Provincial Park, displays in a reconstructed barracks and mess hall describe how 4,000 Sioux and their chief, Sitting Bull, fled here in 1877, after defeating the legendary American general George C. Custer, at Little Bighorn. *Admission free; donations accepted. Open late May to Labor Day, 10 am to 4 pm. Daily in July. In June, closed Wednesdays; in August and September, Tuesday and Wednesday.*

A 4-km road links the park with Wood Mountain Regional Park. It is also possible to walk along the path which crosses Wood Mountain Creek. The white pillars mark the trail that was used in the 1870s and 1880s by the North West Mounted Police as they traveled back and forth between Wood Mountain and Fort Walsh.

At the regional park visitors may picnic, camp, swim, pick berries, or hike. A short walk to the top of Sitting Bull Hill brings you to a stone cairn commemorating the Sioux chief. A plaque on the cairn explains that the Sioux camped in the Wood Mountain district for four years. The hill once

GRASSLANDS: A PRAIRIE PARK IN PROGRESS

Grasslands National Park opened in 1989. It is the only park of its kind in North America to preserve a tract of mixed-grass prairie and its rare, often endangered creatures. It comprises two blocks of land covering about 450 km². Future plans call for a park twice this size. The Grasslands information centre and administrative offices are based in Val Marie, at the junction of highways 4 and 18. *The centre is open daily, late May to early September, 8 am to 6 pm. The rest of the year, Monday to Friday, 8 am to 4:30 pm.*

Nearby West Block is a high tableland bisected by the Frenchman River valley. Retreating glaciers—and centuries of erosion—have shaped the gently rolling hills, grassy coulees, and steep-sided ravines, which border the wide valley. The serpentine river twists and turns as it flows through this arid land.

The East Block, southwest of Wood Mountain, contains the Killdeer Badlands, whose lofty sandstone and shale pinnacles, buttes, moraines, and turtlebacks are also the legacy of glacial action. Because stabilizing vegetation here is sparse, the earth crumbles easily under the impact of extreme temperature, wind, and water. Even the small, transitory streams in rills and gullies continually change the appearance of this area. *Information about the East Block is on display at the Rodeo Ranch Museum, Wood Mountain Regional Park.*

The first pioneers described the Prairies as a "sea of grass." Today, Grasslands National Park—true to its name—preserves blue grama, spear, june, and dozens of other grass varieties. At first sight, the sparse grassy mantle

Buffalo once scratched their hides on Grasslands' rubbing stones.

may seem a withered hue. But a closer look at hillside and plain reveals the subtle colors of hundreds of wildflowers and plants, such as wolf willow, lemon-yellow prickly pears, mauve pincushion, and the pungently aromatic sagebrush.

Remnants of Indian culture decorate the high crests of hills and plateaus in the park. Tepee rings (rocks used to anchor tents), burial cairns, and stone medicine wheels remain undisturbed.

Buffalo once roamed here in vast herds. Rubbing stones and wallows—used by the mighty beasts for scratching and rolling—are strewn across plain and slope.

Under the wide expanse of a clear summer sky, a peregrine falcon cavorts in the updrafts. The endangered bird keeps company here with other rare creatures, such as the pronghorn antelope, the ferruginous hawk, and the short-horned lizard. All these creatures are well adapted to the rigors of the area's harsh climate, where rainfall is less than 40 cm and temperatures soar to 40°C. Cacti and other succulents thrive by storing the limited water ration.

Among Grasslands' survivors are the gregarious black-tailed prairie dogs, which construct networks of underground burrows, known as "colonies" or "towns." The West Block is the site of the largest of these in Canada. Prairie-dog habitations— if abandoned—shelter other threatened species, such as the whimsical-looking little burrowing owl and the prairie rattlesnake.

Major Walsh's spartan but elegant office at Wood Mountain Post is as it was in 1874.

surveyed Sioux lodges on the nearby plains, the winter cabins of Métis hunters and fur traders in the coulees, and the North West Mounted Police post, where crude log buildings clustered inside a stockade along a creek. A rodeo arena, ranch houses, barns, and corrals have long since replaced the lodges and cabins.

At the base of Sitting Bull Hill, the Wood Mountain Rodeo and Ranching Museum recounts the story of ranching in the area. *Open daily, mid-May to mid-August, 10 am to 6 pm.*

Visitors can join a trail ride or a cattle drive by talking to one of the local bed-and-breakfast services.

Special events

Wood Mountain Country Music Jamboree
(early June)

Wood Mountain Stampede (mid-July)

Wood Mountain Cowboy Poetry
Gathering (early August)

9 St. Victor's Petroglyphs Provincial Park

⛺ ⛱ 🐾 ❋ 📷

St. Victor (pop. 41) is situated in the St. Sylvain Valley. It typifies the Saskatchewan village, except for one thing. The nearby hills contain mysterious sandstone carvings, or petroglyphs.

The images incised in sandstone at a lofty site near St. Victor mystify experts.

St. Victor's Petroglyphs Provincial Park preserves the carvings on a 123-m-high cliff that overlooks the village. A 165-step stairway built into the cliffside leads to the summit where the petroglyphs are located. One of the rewards of the climb to this lofty site is the breathtaking 40-km view of the surrounding prairie.

The petroglyphs are a series of images incised horizontally in sandstone. This only adds to their mystery because petroglyphs usually run vertically. Only four other sites similar to St. Victor exist in Canada.

No one knows the exact date of the petroglyphs. But, as no images of horses appear here, some experts assume carving occurred before 1750, when the horse was first introduced on the Canadian prairies.

Some of the glyphs clearly depict human heads and hands, and animals—pronghorn antelopes, grizzly bears, turtles, deer, and elk. According to archaeologists, the carvers may have been ancestors of the Sioux and Assiniboine Indians. But what prompted the early peoples to create the carvings eludes the experts.

The petroglyphs are best viewed in the morning (before 10 am), late afternoon, or early evening. At these times the angle of the sunlight sharpens the outlines of the images. In September and October, the Friends of the Petroglyphs sponsor night viewings, when

Roads to explore: Buttes, bluffs, and buffalo jumps

Distance (approx.): 270 km/168 miles

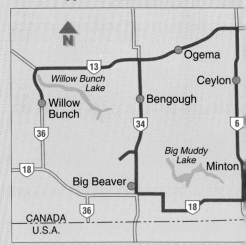

Travel north of Willow Bunch on Highway 36, turn east on Highway 13 for 40 km and then south on Highway 34 through Bengough (pop. 516). The flatland drops down into a 56-km stretch of valley dotted with sagebrush and craggy buttes. This is Big Muddy Valley.

Rugged hills on the valley floor form a backdrop for the "72" Ranch. A gravel road, just before the ranch, heads west toward Castle Butte, a 60-m-high landmark once used by settlers, Indians, and outlaws as they crossed through the area. As you drive, beware of the cattle along the road to the butte.

Throughout the valley there are hundreds of tepee rings and other evidence of the many Indian tribes that stayed there. The valley's canyons and gulches

also made good hideouts for horse thieves, cattle rustlers and outlaws. In the late 1800s the Outlaw Trail, a highly organized outlaw escape route, ran from the Big Muddy to New Mexico.

● Drive on to the intersection of highways 34 and 18 and turn west to the hamlet of Big Beaver (pop. 10), nestling in a coulee. A general store on Big Beaver's Main Street displays the motto: "If we don't have it, you don't need it." But what you will need if you are going to continue on the drive is food and refreshments.

The Big Beaver Museum and Nature Centre houses local historic curiosities. The centre is not open on a regular basis,

At sunset in the Big Muddy Badlands

but, at the Rural Municipality Office at the north end of Main Street, visitors can make arrangements to see it.

● From Big Beaver, travel east on Highway 18, which dips in and out of the valley before reaching Highway 6. Turn north to the hamlet of Minton (pop. 115). To explore local buffalo jumps and caves, get permission from the rural municipality office on Minton's Main Street.

● Head back toward Big Beaver and Bengough to camp out for the night, or carry on north to the junction of highways 13 and 6. Drive west to Ogema (pop. 397) and the Deep South Pioneer Museum, a reconstructed pioneer village of 23 buildings. *Open Sundays and statutory holidays, May 1 to October 31, 1 pm to 5 pm.*

A FARMSTEAD OF YESTERYEAR

Among the large, mechanized farms of Saskatchewan, one 3.5-ha farmstead still uses the equipment and practices of the pre-First World War period. This is the Motherwell Homestead. Now a national historic site, it was built in 1896 by William Richard Motherwell, who began farming here in 1882. Mother-well eventually became Saskatchewan's first agriculture minister (1905-1918) and later a federal minister with the same portfolio.

Victorian pitcher and basin, Motherwell Homestead

The homestead comprises the four distinct areas—as it did in 1912. The Dugout Quadrant contains the water reservoir; the Garden Quadrant, the family vegetable patch. The largest L-shaped barn in the area dominates the Barn Quadrant, the centre of farming operations. But the showpiece of the site is the House Quadrant, where ornamental trees, flowerbeds, and a tennis lawn frame Motherwell's 1896 stone dwelling.

The Victorian style prevails in the back parlor, which was used only on formal occasions. The decor includes large black leather armchairs and sideboards with china and silverware. In the front parlor, an upright piano takes pride of place. On Sunday afternoons, the Motherwells and their hired hands gathered here for song and prayer.

Today staff at the Motherwell Homestead churn butter, bake bread, and perform bygone chores. They also work the fields with a Hart-Parr tractor, an Oliver gangplow, and other vintage agricultural equipment. Most of the farm animals—Clydesdale horses and Plymouth Rock chickens—are the same kinds raised in the early 1900s. *Admission free. Open daily, Victoria Day to Thanksgiving, 10 am to 5:30 pm.*

flashlights are used for illumination.

Next to St. Victor's Provincial Historic Park, Sylvain Valley Regional Park offers camping, barbecuing, and swimming facilities. The historic feature of the park is the McGillis Pioneer Home, a sod house built in 1889 by Angus "Catchoo" McGillis, St. Victor's first pioneer. *Open daily, July to September, 9 am to 5 pm.* Part of St. Victor's Roman Catholic Church, built in 1914, has been transformed into a religious museum. *Open daily, late June to late August (and on civic holidays), 10 am to 12 pm and 2 pm to 4 pm.*

10 Fort Qu'Appelle

A ghostly Indian legend inspired the name of the scenic Qu'Appelle River valley. According to the legend, an Indian brave returning home from the hunt heard a voice call his name. After repeatedly answering "Qu'appelle?" ("Who calls?" in French) and receiving no reply, the brave hastened home where he learned that his beloved had died. With her last breath, she had called his name.

Fort Qu'Appelle (pop. 1,879) was originally a Hudson's Bay Company post, established in 1864 at the height of the great buffalo hunts on the plains. The post prospered as a centre for a roaring trade in buffalo hides.

Fort Qu'Appelle and its museum have exhibits and sites that recall the drama of Saskatchewan's past. One of the Hudson's Bay post buildings—preserved at the musem—served as Maj.-Gen. Frederick Middleton's temporary headquarters and base of operations. Middleton was on his way to Batoche to quell the North-West Rebellion of 1885. *Open daily, July and August, 10 am to 12 pm and 1 pm to 5 pm.*

The community's Treaty Park marks the site of the signing of the Indian Treaty No. 4, the most important of 10 Indian treaties negotiated with the British Crown. It was signed here on September 15, 1874. Under its terms, the Indians handed over about 75,000 sections of land in south Saskatchewan to the British. Every September the Treaty No. 4 Gathering commemorates the signing. The week-long occasion is organized to create heightened awareness of the Indians' culture and issues.

In 1876 the North West Mounted Police established an outpost in Fort Qu'Appelle on the present site of the Echo Ridge Golf Course, at the edge of town. Here Chief Sitting Bull appeared in 1881 to plead to the NWMP for a Canadian refuge for his Sioux people, who had fled their territory in the United States. A cairn and an interpretive centre mark the site.

Today, prairie vacationers prize Fort Qu'Appelle as a summer destination. The community is the jumping-off point to a string of nearby lakes—Pasqua, Echo, Mission, and Katepwa—hidden on the verdant floor of the Qu'Appelle Valley. The Fishing Lakes—as their collective name suggests—offer great catches. Other pleasures include water-skiing, camping, picnicking, swimming, and hiking.

Special events

Standing Buffalo Powwow (early August)

Treaty No. 4 Gathering
(mid-September)

Qu'Appelle Valley International
Walleye Cup (mid-September)

The expanse of the four Fishing Lakes, near Fort Qu'Appelle, is a prairie summer playground.

11 Canora

The statue of a woman in Ukrainian dress, bearing bread and salt, traditional gifts of welcome, greets visitors to Canora (pop. 2,466). It proclaims the town's Ukrainian origins. In 1897, 180 families from the western Ukraine settled in the area, and named the town after the *Canadian Northern Railway*, which had transported them here. Today, 60 percent of the district's population is Ukrainian.

Unique in Canada is Canora's Holy Trinity Ukrainian Orthodox Church, built in 1928. Its slender black domes and spires contrast with the massive, onionlike golden domes on many of Ukrainian Orthodox churches of the prairies.

The National Doukhobor Heritage at Veregin, about 20 km east of Canora, remembers the Russian Doukhobors, or "spirit wrestlers," who, after burning their armaments in a symbolic gesture of pacifism in 1897, moved to Canada to continue their communal life-style. The heritage village contains a museum; the original home of their leader, Peter "The Lordly" Veregin; a functional bakery with a *peche*, or clay oven; restored barns, homes, and work sheds, and a communal bathhouse. Surveying the village is a statue of Leo Tolstoy. The Russian writer is honored for having donated proceeds from his 1899 novel *Resurrection* for the Doukhobors' relocation.

12 Moose Mountain Provincial Park

In the southeastern corner of Saskatchewan, a line of birch- and aspen-covered hills rises more than 100 m above the prairies. The area is known as the Moose Mountain Uplands. The park of that name contains a 388-km^2 portion of the uplands.

Elegant domes of black slate crown the Holy Trinity Ukrainian Orthodox Church at Canora.

A MANOR ON THE PLAINS

After Edward Michell Pierce lost his fortune in England during the early 1880s, he sailed for Canada intending to rebuild his wealth and to establish a family estate on the wide open spaces of Saskatchewan.

Cannington Manor Provincial Park preserves remnants of Pierce's dream. It pays a poignant tribute to settlers who struggled to set up a kind of uppercrust English colony in a land unsuitable for the purpose.

Pierce responded to a Canadian government advertisement, which offered tracts of cheap western farmland. In 1882, Pierce and his family arrived at his prairie domain, and donated some of his land to found the community of Cannington Manor for fellow English settlers. For two decades, the Pierces, their dependents and hangers-on attempted to live up to the finest traditions of English country life. There was horse-racing, cricket and tennis matches, billiards, and a hunt club. In this round of pleasure, farming—vital for survival—was a secondary pursuit.

By 1900, Cannington Manor was an abandoned village. Some settlers, wearied by the harshness of prairie life, returned to England. Others drifted away after the CPR redirected a promised railway line elsewhere.

In 1965, the remains of the village became the core of the present provincial historic park. A walk along the 500-m-long village street passes a cluster of old-time stores and businesses. All Saints Anglican Church—consecrated in 1885—is the only structure now used as it was originally. Maltby House and other properties are furnished in late-19th-century styles. Staff in Victorian garb guide visitors and do workaday tasks of yesteryear. They may ask you to make rope and saw wood, or join in croquet, horseshoes, and other diversions once enjoyed by the Manor pioneers. A visitors' centre is located at the entrance of the village. *Open daily, from Victoria Day to Labor Day, 10 am to 6 pm.*

The landscape is the creation of the last Ice Age. The receding glaciers shaped the hills and embedded ice in the soil. Later, the icy deposits melted and formed the more than 400 pocket-sized lakes and ponds, which are a distinctive feature of the park.

Kenosee Lake, the largest of these lakes, is the centre for activities such as boating, swimming, and water-skiing. The lake, with an ample supply of perch, is popular with anglers. The visitors' centre—a stone Elizabethan-style structure—was built when the park opened in 1931. Its displays introduce visitors to the park's diverse plant and animal life.

Altogether, about 100 species of animals, birds, and reptiles are found in Moose Mountain Provincial Park. Some of these can be seen a short distance from the visitors' centre on two marked trails—the 4.5-km Beaver Lake Trail and the 2-km Wuche Sakaw Trail— that lead into an inviting, easy-to-explore wilderness.

MANITOBA

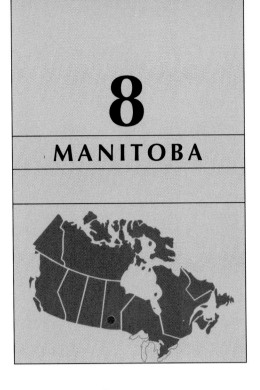

8
MANITOBA

Places to see
Duck Mountain Provincial Park
Turtle Mountain Provincial Park
Neepawa
International Peace Garden
Spruce Woods Provincial Heritage Park
Morden
Oak Hammock Marsh
Hecla Provincial Park
Grand Beach Provincial Park
Steinbach
Elk Island Heritage Park
Sandilands Provincial Forest
Whiteshell Provincial Park

Roads to explore
Pembina Valley
River Road Heritage Parkway
to Oak Hammock Marsh

National park close-up
Riding Mountain

Previous pages:
A field of sunflowers near Holland, southwest of
Spruce Woods Provincial Heritage Park

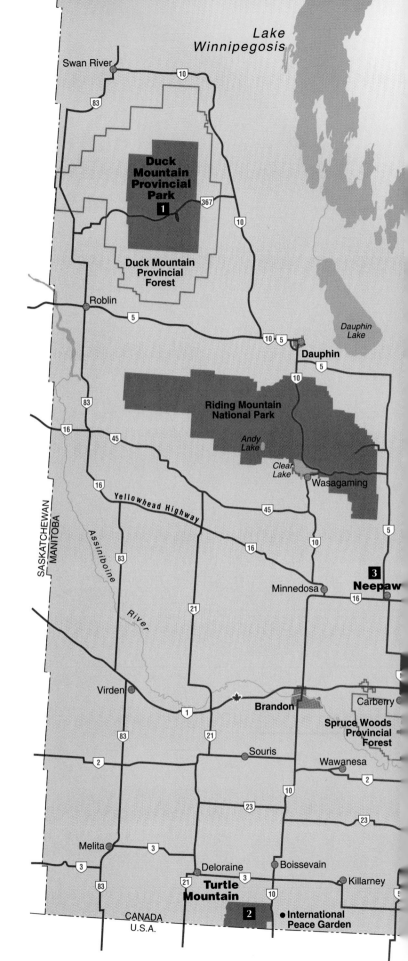

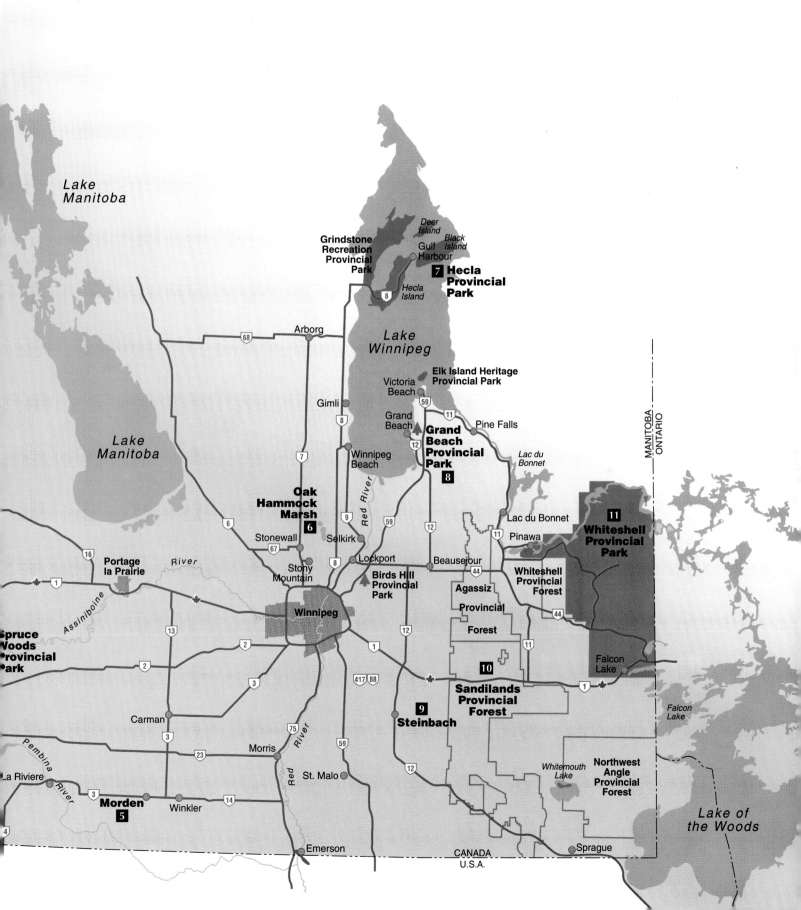

Lake Manitoba

Lake Manitoba

Grindstone Recreation Provincial Park

Deer Island

Black Island

Gulf Harbour

7 **Hecla Provincial Park**

Hecla Island

Lake Winnipeg

Arborg

68

Gimli

8

7

Victoria Beach

Elk Island Heritage Provincial Park

59

11

Grand Beach

Grand Beach Provincial Park

8

Pine Falls

Winnipeg Beach

12

Oak Hammock Marsh **6**

9

Red River

59

12

Lac du Bonnet

6

Stonewall

67

Selkirk

Lac du Bonnet

11

Pinawa

11 **Whiteshell Provincial Park**

16

Portage la Prairie

River

Stony Mountain

8

Lockport

Beausejour

Whiteshell Provincial Forest

1

Assiniboine

Birds Hill Provincial Park

44

Agassiz Provincial Forest

44

Spruce Woods Provincial Park

Winnipeg

13

2

12

1

11

Falcon Lake

2

3

417 88

1

Carman

10

Sandilands Provincial Forest

Falcon Lake

Pembina

La Riviere

River

3

Morris

75

Red River

59

9 **Steinbach**

Whitemouth Lake

Northwest Angle Provincial Forest

23

3

14

St. Malo

12

Morden **5**

Winkler

4

Red River

Emerson

Sprague

CANADA U.S.A.

Lake of the Woods

The tranquil waterways of Duck Mountain Provincial Park are ideal for leisurely canoeing.

1 | Duck Mountain Provincial Park

Duck Mountain Forest Reserve encloses a provincial park of the same name, an Eden for outdoor enthusiasts. Two provincial roads—366 and 367—bisect the park, which encompasses 1,274 km² of some of the most beautiful scenery in western Canada.

In the southeast corner of Duck Mountain Provincial Park is Baldy Mountain, the highest point in Manitoba at 831 m. A 12-m-high tower on the mountain overlooks the Grandview Valley and the northern fringes of Riding Mountain National Park. The tower is a superb vantage point to survey the park's forest in its spring finery or spectacular fall colors.

More than 70 lakes—many suitable for family canoeing—dot Duck Mountain's dense forest. Within a 30-km radius of the Blue Lakes—the park's geographic centre—there are 15 lakes accessible by road. East and West Blue lakes, and Childs Lake offer snorkeling and scuba diving; Childs, East Blue, and Wellman lakes are ideal for swimming. Many of the park's lakes entice fishermen with catches of rainbow, brook, lake and brown trout, walleye, perch, pike, and smallmouth bass.

Naturalists can enjoy a gentle hike on the 2.2-km Pine Meadows self-guiding interpretive trail. This begins at the Duck Mountain Forest Center, which is located at the intersection of provincial roads 366 and 367. During the hike, you may glimpse white-tailed deer, majestic elk or moose, porcupines, rabbits, bears, squirrels, foxes or woodchucks. The park's many birds include the boreal and great gray owls, and golden and bald eagles.

For winter sports enthusiasts there are cross-country ski trails, from novice to expert, as well as 80 km of groomed snowmobile trails.

Special events

The Swan Valley Sport Fishing Enhancement Pike Tournament (late May)

Swan River Northwest Round-up (late May)

2 | Turtle Mountain Provincial Park

From a distance, the wooded hills of Turtle Mountain region of Manitoba look like turtle shells. It may be this likeness that gave the region its name. Or it may be the abundance of western painted turtles, with their brilliant orange, yellow, and green undersides,

found in the area. The creatures are more plentiful here than in anywhere else in Manitoba.

Established in 1961, Turtle Mountain Provincial Park covers 180 km² of forest and wetland, and its hills rise 180 to 245 m above the prairies. It contains nearly 400 lakes and marshes.

Adam Lake, close to Highway 10, is the site of the park's most accessible campground and beach. Within the park, there are campsites at Max and Oscar lakes. A walking trail at Adam Lake Beach includes a mini-obstacle course for fitness enthusiasts. A nearby tower gives visitors a chance to watch moose meandering about distant lakes or marshes.

Much of Turtle Mountain is wilderness but some of it is accessible by car. The West Main Road is a gravel byway that crosses the park. It branches off the Oskar Lake Road near Max Lake, passes Breadon Lake, and cuts through a mature spruce plantation before emerging at the park's west gate, 1 km from Canada Corner on Highway 450. The road can be forbiddingly slippery and sticky after heavy rains, but presents few problems when dry.

In the park's forest, trembling aspen coexists with birch, oak, ash, and Manitoba maple. Northern pike, pickerel, rainbow and brown trout lure anglers at Bower and other lakes. Muskrats, foxes and coyotes lurk in the woods. You may spot a skunk family, a porcupine, a white pelican, a loon, or a silent lone blue heron. During the summer, you can rarely go through the park without catching sight of a white-tailed deer. And you will certainly see the painted turtles, ambling through the park or perching on logs in the many shallow lakes, which also contain beaver lodges and dams.

Manitoba parks shelter white pelicans.

3 Neepawa

Ⲁ Ⲑ ⊕ ⧫ ⚊ ⚏ ⚕ ✻

Neepawa (pop. 3,600) nestles in the foothills south of Riding Mountain National Park. This farming community was first settled by traders from Ontario who traveled on the North Fort Ellice Trail, a trade route that linked Winnipeg to Fort Edmonton. The town was named for a Cree word meaning abundance. The fer-

Davidson Memorial, "the stone angel" of Margaret Laurence's novel of that title.

tile area around the town was christened Beautiful Plains, a designation that today identifies everything from the school division to the local bakery.

The arrival of the Manitoba and Northwestern Railway in 1883 sparked the town's rise to prosperity. The early years saw the construction of some handsome civic structures, such as the Beautiful Plains County Court Building (1884), the J.A. Davidson Block (1889), Knox Presbyterian Church (1892), the Odd Fellows Hall (1903) and the Hamilton Hotel (1904). All these buildings are still standing. The County Court is the oldest operating building of its kind on the prairies and Manitoba's second oldest public building. Both this building and Knox Church are provincial historic sites.

Neepawa was the girlhood home of the novelist Margaret Laurence (1926-1987), who lived at 312 First Avenue. The brick house, named in her honor, now houses an art gallery, offices, art studios, and many of her personal possessions, including her green portable typewriter. *Open daily, early May to mid-October, but hours vary. Open weekends, mid-October to early May, 1 pm to 5 pm.*

Laurence's fictional town, Manawaka, was loosely modeled after the

AT THE HEART OF A CONTINENT, A GARDEN OF GOODWILL

At the International Peace Garden, the four columns of the 35-m-high Peace Tower thrust into the vast prairie sky. At the base of the tower, a landscaped garden with flowers, pools, and walkways straddles the international boundary between Manitoba and North Dakota. The garden commemorates the enduring goodwill between Canada and the United States, which share the longest unfortified border in the world. This is mid-point on the border between the Pacific and the Atlantic. The garden is a formal oasis set in the midst of the hills, woods, and lakes of the Turtle Mountain region, which overlaps both countries. The 586-ha Canadian sector of the garden was carved from a forest reserve. The 360-ha American sector is situated 72 km directly north of Rugby, North Dakota—the geographic heart of North America.

At the opening of the International Peace Garden on July 14, 1932, more than 50,000 local people came here to celebrate the event—and caused the biggest traffic jam the region has ever

At sunset, sunken pools reflect the columns of the Peace Tower, which dominates the International Peace Garden on the Canada-United States border.

known. (In the same year, a similar project was undertaken when Waterton Lakes National Park in Alberta and Glacier National Park in Montana became an international peace park.) Today, the garden contains many attractions: The Peace Chapel with its three encircling stone walls engraved with quotations from the world's great peacemakers; the Errick F. Willis Memorial Pavilion, and the 2,000-seat Masonic Auditorium. *Open year-round. Staff is on duty only from mid-May to mid-September.*

Riding Mountain

Amid a sea of agriculture, Riding Mountain National Park preserves habitats characteristic of northern, western, and eastern Canada—boreal forest, grasslands, and deciduous woodlands — and offers wildlife such as the white pelican, great gray owl, and eastern cougar a chance of survival. Rife with bogs, marshes, and dense woodland when settlers first headed west, this section of the Manitoba Escarpment, which rises 320 m above the prairie, was a natural barrier to oxcarts and canoes. Those travelers who could crossed on horseback—thus the name Riding Mountain.

Streams incise deep canyons in this prairie mountain, which is composed primarily of hard beds of shale and limestone, capped by glacial debris. Ancient Lake Agassiz formed as the last of the glacial ice melted along the escarpment 12,000 years ago. Successive beach ridges, now easily detected under bands of bur oak paralleling the foot of the escarpment, mark receding water levels as the lake drained off to Hudson Bay some 8,000 years ago.

Riding Mountain nurtures more than 5,000 members of the deer family (moose, elk, white-tailed deer), some 10,000 beavers, hundreds of black bears, and more than 150 species of nesting birds. Eastern hardwood forests predominate near the base of the escarpment. Fertile soil and ample moisture create favorable conditions for Manitoba maple, American elm, and green ash. Sarsaparilla and poison ivy carpet the forest floor with a uniform verdure. At migration time, broad-winged, red-tailed, and rough-legged hawks circle on air masses bubbling up from the escarpment.

The Ochre River flows through the largest and most spectacular valley in the eastern region of the park. Henry Youle Hind of the Assiniboine and Saskatchewan Exploring Expedition of 1858 was the first to describe its ocher deposits, from which local Indians made clay pipes. Hind's Indian guides were reluctant to cross the valley, fearing the devils who were said to live there. Modern-day poachers are not at all impressed by the old myths and superstitions. They regularly enter the area on illegal hunting forays.

To the west, the Birdtail Creek meanders through a broad, curving valley, flanked by riverbanks from an ancient glacial watercourse. North-facing hills are covered with aspen, balsam poplar, and white birch; those facing south are clothed in rough fescue, native Kentucky bluegrass, and june grass.

A restaurant in a wooded glade, Riding Mountain

Few ecosystems are as highly productive as grasslands, where 1 m² of rich soil can yield up to 30 species of grasses and wildflowers. Small wonder such grasslands once supported thousands of bison on the southern Manitoba plains. By the early 20th century, agriculture had all but wiped out the bison. Now they are found mainly in protected areas such as Riding Mountain. Its herd of 30 animals is in a small enclosure at the heart of the park.

Despite the tread of bison hooves, a display of prairie wildflowers waxes and wanes throughout the summer. For a few brief days in spring, prairie crocuses—legendary ears of the earth and the official floral emblem of Manitoba—unfold their pale lavender blooms. The orange colors of hoary puccoon splash the grasslands in early summer. Later the prairie heat rouses a succession of blossoms: wispy-pink, three-flowered avens, northern bedstraw, fiery-red wild bergamot, meadow blazing star, and blue giant hyssop.

The south-central portion of the Riding Mountain plateau is speckled with potholes. Shallow catch basins amid gravelly knob-and-kettle relief, these watering holes are regarded as the duck factories of North America. Nutrient rich, bubbling with aquatic invertebrates and small fish, and surrounded by willow and aspen, they are ideal breeding grounds for waterfowl, such as canvasbacks, redheads, and hooded mergansers.

Deep in this pothole country lies Whitewater Lake, its shallow depth mostly controlled by beaver dams on the periphery. Bald eagles nest nearby, and threatened white pelicans loaf in groups during hot summer days. During spring migrations, more than 24 species of waterfowl can be seen in one day. In spring, common loons and red-necked grebes echo their mating diatribes from all corners of the lake.

A pack of timber wolves, one of several in the park, roams the fringes of the lake. But you will rarely see these powerful hunters. Often only their tracks, or perhaps a half-eaten carcass, reveal their presence.

Throughout the park, white spruce communities, pure aspen stands, and mixed spruce and aspen vie for light, moisture, and the upper hand. Heavily used animal trails crisscross the aspen forests. Like corridors in a well-designed home, these trails connect meadows, feeding areas, and watering holes.

The park's rolling plateaus are most splendid in the fall. Tamarack trees blaze in the valley bottoms and balsam poplar and trembling aspen glow golden on the slopes. Raspberries, hazelnuts, highbush cranberries, rose hips, saskatoon berries, pin cherries, and hawthorn berries satisfy the insatiable appetites of large numbers of black bears. Proud bull elks roar beneath the aspen canopies, herding their harems of cows, and occasionally splitting the stillness of frosty mornings with the crack of their antlered rivalry. Thousands of honking snow geese and Canada geese sweep southward along the central flyway.

The aspen parkland is part of what is known as the mixed-wood section of the boreal forest. Different plant communities succeed each other over time, the present one being predominantly aspen. Extremely harsh, dry winters with temperatures dropping to –30°C for several weeks at a time, snow cover for almost half a year, and short, moist summers create the climate needed for this parkland tapestry.

Wasagaming, Cree Indian name for "Lake of Clear Waters," is a seasonal resort townsite on the south shore of Clear Lake, the jewel which first prompted Manitobans to lobby for the establishment of a national park. Development of the park provided work for 1,000 destitute men of the 1930s. Under relief-work schemes, they built roads, a golf course,

Clear Lake's crystal beauty spurred the creation of Riding Mountain.

cottage subdivisions, and national park buildings. Immigrant craftsmen from Scandinavia masterfully constructed a number of log structures, expressive of their home country architecture. English cottage gardens beautified the townsite. There is now also a small reserve belonging to the Keeseekooweenin First Nation on the west shore.

German prisoners of war were detained at Whitewater Lake from 1943 to 1945. Yet such camp relics as remain—old foundations, dugout canoes fashioned in spare time, and cultivated peonies and baby's breath—all symbolize harmony and peace. The conservationist Grey Owl lived in the park for six months in 1931. His solitary cabin can be seen on Beaver Lodge Lake.

PARK INFORMATION
Access: Highway 10, which cuts through the park, and Highway 19.
Visitors' centre: Wasagaming.
Accommodations: 800 sites in six campgrounds; 14 picnic sites.
Summer activities: Fishing, swimming, boating and canoeing (boats and canoes can be rented at the main pier on Clear Lake); hiking, biking, and riding (bicycles and horses can be rented); tennis; golfing; slide shows and films at several locations; naturalist-led car caravans. More than 100 km of trails.
Winter activities: Ice fishing at Clear Lake, snowshoeing, cross-country skiing, and downhill skiing at Agassiz Ski Hill.

137

White spruce forests compose only one of the environments in Spruce Woods Provincial Park.

Neepawa where she grew up. The "stone angel" from which the second novel in the Manawaka series draws its title is the Davidson Memorial in Riverside Cemetery. The soulful figure of a woman, leaning on a cross and carrying a wreath, remembers John Davidson, a town founder.

Neepawa's Beautiful Plains Museum is located in the former Canadian National Railways Station building. Most of the exhibits in the museum, such as a turn-of-the-century general store, were obtained when local merchants modernized their businesses. *Open daily from late May to late August, 9 am to 5 pm Monday to Friday and 1 pm to 5 pm on weekends.*

Special events

Annual Summer Fair (early June)

Manitoba Holiday Festival of the Arts (early July)

Antique Market (early September)

4 Spruce Woods Provincial Heritage Park

Farms, fields of grain, and rural towns surround the island of wilderness that is Spruce Woods Provincial Heritage Park. In the 1880s, the renowned naturalist Ernest Thompson Seton (1860-1946) described the area as "a land possessing a crop of priceless treasures." The image is still true. The park contains some of Manitoba's most spectacular landscapes, as diverse as shifting sand dunes, quicksand, tall-grass prairie, bogs, coniferous forests, and dramatic river valleys.

Some 10,000 years ago, the region between Brandon and Portage La Prairie was a sandy delta of prehistoric Lake Agassiz. Eventually forests of white spruce—for which the park is named—stabilized its shifting sands. In 1964 almost 250 km² of this region was set aside as a park.

Visitors enter Spruce Woods Park by Highway 5, which leads to the Kiche Manitou Campground and a day-use area. There are numerous established trails through the park's varied landscapes. Three trails lead into the Spirit Sands, one of the park's most fascinating and fragile features. They take hikers directly from century-old spruce forests into a desert with dunes reminiscent of the Sahara.

The 1.4-km Isputinaw Trail goes up the bank of the Assiniboine River, through a marshy wetland and on to an arid ridge. At the top of the ridge there is a panorama of desert dunes and coniferous forests.

On-site signs assist walkers to explore the Marsh Lake Trail, which leads to an oxbow lake. The wide variety of plants makes this 1.5-km hike a botanist's delight.

Signs along the 1.2-km Springridge Trail explain how the Assiniboine River and underground springs shaped the land. Backcountry camping is possible along the rugged Epinette Trail system, and return trips may vary from a comfortable 4 km to a tougher 40 km.

On these trails hikers may spy creatures unique to Spruce Woods—lizards called northern prairie skinks, or western hognose snakes so named for their upturned noses, with which they burrow for toads.

Early adventurers have left their mark in this region. At the confluence of Pine Creek and the Assiniboine River, are the remains of Pine Fort, a trading post established in 1768 by two English fur traders from Montreal.

5 Morden

In 1882, the Canadian Pacific Railway decided to run a branch line through Morden, because the settlement lay near a vital water supply—Deadhorse Creek. The outlying communities of Nelsonville and Mountain City—and their buildings—relocated here, and the town was born.

Many of the moved buildings can still be seen along Stephen, Mountain, and Nelson streets in Morden. In 1984 the community beautified Stephen Street, by creating brick sidewalks and decorating its historic houses with flower boxes.

Morden has several claims to fame. Its museum has the largest collection of marine reptile fossils in North America. These giants once swam the waters of a shallow inland sea that stretched from Canada to the Gulf of Mexico. *The Morden and District Museum is open daily, May to August, 2 pm to 5 pm; weekends only, September to April, 2 pm to 5 pm.*

Roads to explore: Indian mounds, prairie museums

Distance: 110 km/68 miles

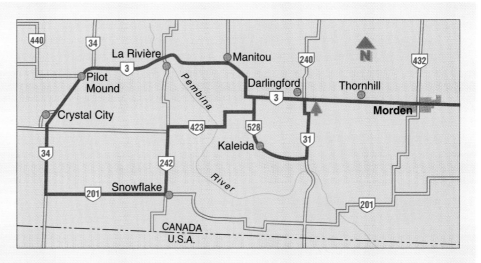

From Morden, drive west on Highway 3 through the steeply banked Pembina River valley to the village of Darlingford. At the junction of highways 3 and 31 is LaVerendrye Wayside Park, marking the overland route taken by the French explorer Pierre de La Vérendrye in his search for a great western sea.

● Continue on Highway 3 past Manitou. A sign on the right marks the Archibald Historical Museum. It honors former Manitoba MLA Nellie McClung, an outspoken writer and reformer who led women in their fight for the right to vote.

The museum features an 1878 furnished log cabin, where McClung lived as a teacher at a nearby rural school. It is furnished as described in her book *Clearing in the West*, which is displayed here. The museum area also contains a 1908 farm home, a three-story barn with an old country store, and agricultural artifacts. *Open daily, mid-May to Labor Day, 12 pm to 8 pm.*

● Farther west on Highway 3, the road dips into the Pembina Valley and the La

Gold-tinged oaks and dark green conifers line a winding Pembina Valley back road.

Rivière area, a haven for deer and wild turkey.

● From La Rivière, follow Highway 3 to Highway 34 and turn south to Pilot Mound—a 35-m-high mound visible 25 km away. Assiniboine Indians used the mound as a cardinal point to orient themselves during buffalo hunts.

● A further 7 km away is Crystal City, which has a printing museum with old presses still in use. *Open year-round, Monday through Friday, 9 am to 5:30 pm.*

● Follow Highway 34 south to a road junction marked Snowflake. Turn left on the gravel road, usually well-main-

tained, for about 15 km to Star Mound School Museum, housed in an 1886 schoolhouse built on the site of an Indian burial ground. *Open daily, late April to October, dawn to dusk.*

● From Snowflake, turn north up Highway 242 and continue past the junction with Provincial Road 423. Turn east on the next road, marked Pembina Crossing, which leads to another vantage point of the Pembina River valley. The road winds slightly northeast for a few kilometres, then turns east to Highway 528. Turn north on Highway 31, east on Highway 3 and return to Morden.

Situated in the shadow of the Pembina Hills, Morden enjoys the longest frost-free period of any place on the prairies. This has enabled the foundation of the Agriculture Canada Research Station, which works to improve strains of local crops, ornamental shrubs, trees, and flowers. Visitors may tour the grounds, which contain more than 3,000 species of plants, a fish pond, and an arboretum, which provides a gene pool of plants for research. *Admission free. Open year-round, dawn to dusk.*

Camping, swimming, and boating are possible at Lake Minnewasta, just to the west of the town. Minnewasta Golf and Country Club has an 18-hole golf course.

Special events
Blossom Week (May)
Cripple Creek Music Festival (July)
The Morden International Triathlon (July)
Corn and Apple Festival (August)

6 Oak Hammock Marsh

Every year, thousands of ducks and Canada geese flock to the wetlands of the Oak Hammock Marsh Wildlife Management Area, a prairie oasis just 40 km north of Winnipeg. These migratory birds feed and linger in the tallgrass together with pelicans, grebes, prairie falcons, gray partridge and some 260 other water birds.

Bird-watchers and wildlife photographers come here in May and June to witness bird courting rituals. In August, clumsy ducklings can be seen attempting maiden flights over the marsh. And in late September, tens of thousands of Canada geese, snow geese, and ducks touch down in the pastures on their way south to warmer winter climes.

Signpost, Oak Hammock Marsh

A century ago the marsh, known at that time as St. Andrews Bog (or "the Bog"), covered 47,000 ha. It stretched from the Red River just north of Winnipeg to the Teulon area, and was one of Manitoba's largest prairie marshes. But settlers drained and farmed all but a 250-ha remnant of the marsh.

Plans to restore the wetlands began in the late 1960s. By 1973, Oak Hammock Marsh earned its official title. Today it covers a 36-km^2 area of reclaimed land. There are 28 km of dikes and boardwalks, as well as many nesting islands. It also encloses 225 ha of native prairie, the largest tract of tallgrass prairie in Manitoba. From June to late August the tallgrass glows with orange prairie lilies, blazing stars, and other wildflowers.

A 300-m boardwalk and earthen walkways lead to an observation mound. Along the way is a duck-shaped pond, originally a borrow pit used to build nearby dykes. Large wading birds are seen only in pastures around the north mound area. Nearby are artesian wells, the source of much of the marshland water.

The Oak Hammock Conservation Centre opened in 1993. It comprises the national office of Ducks Unlimited and the marsh interpretive centre, which offers tours and workshops. *Open daily, year-round.*

7 Hecla Provincial Park

In Lake Winnipeg are islands that were once part of Iceland—New Iceland, that is. In 1875, Mount Hekla, Iceland's largest volcano, erupted violently, driving many people out of their land. They came to Canada. Land was set aside by the Canadian government as a self-governing colony where Icelandic fishermen and farmers could speak their language and hold on their customs. The 172-km^2 Hecla Island was one of four regions in the Republic of New Iceland.

Roads to explore: A heritage parkway and a quarry park

Distance: 85 km/53 miles

From Winnipeg, go north on Main Street, which becomes Highway 9. About 8 km north of the Perimeter Highway interchange, turn east and take the River Road Heritage Parkway.
• This 12-km road, lined by stone houses, hugs the widening Red River. Look for the modest Scott House, built by boatman William Scott. It is typical of the area, combining Manitoba limestone with Scottish and French-Canadian building techniques. Farther along

tamed the Red River rapids since 1915. The dam, which controls the river's uneven flows with a series of adjustable wooden curtains, is the only one of its kind in North America.

Cross to the east side of Lockport Bridge, where archaeologists have unearthed artifacts dating back to 1000 BC. The Kenosewun Museum and visitors' centre houses displays about the Indian cultures that flourished here. *Open daily, July and August, 11 am to 7 pm.*

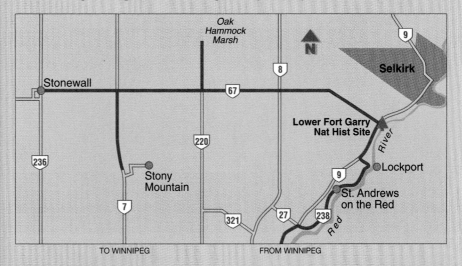

is Twin Oaks, built in the mid-1850s as the residence for a girls' school.
• Drive on for 6 km to the black-steepled St. Andrews on the Red Anglican Church, the oldest stone church west of the Great Lakes. Built in 1832, the church is still used for worship. It still has some of its original furnishings, such as buffalo-hide kneeling benches.
• St. Andrew's Rectory, opposite the church, is now a national historic park. Its main floor contains exhibits depicting the early days of the settlement. *Open daily, mid-May to early September, 10 am to 6 pm; the rest of September, Saturday and Sunday only.*
• A few hundred metres farther on, the Captain Kennedy Museum and Teahouse (1866) overlooks the river and a fine garden. *Open May to September.*
• The parkway ends at Lockport (pop. 1,500). The town is centred around the St. Andrews dam and locks that have

• North of Lockport is Lower Fort Garry National Historic Site, built in 1831. It was the major provisioning centre for the fur trade in Western Canada in the mid-1880s. Learn about the fur trade and the surrounding settlements, and witness daily life of the time at the bakery and the blacksmith shop. In summer there are reenactments of the past, complete with booming cannon. *The grounds are open year-round; the buildings are open daily, mid-May to September.*
• From the fort, drive 16 km to Oak Hammock Marsh, one of Manitoba's major staging grounds for migratory waterfowl.
• Another 15 km farther on, the town of Stonewall (pop. 3,000) has created a park out of a century-old quarry. Quarry Park features a beach, campground, and trails. Take a break in Stonewall's ornate May House tea room.
• From Stonewall, double back 5 km to Highway 7, and drive 16 km south to the North Perimeter Highway and return to Winnipeg.

The black steeple of St. Andrews on the Red, framed by Capt. Kennedy's garden

A veranda view takes in the historic Icelandic village of Hecla, settled in the late 19th century.

viewing birds and moose. There are boardwalks and hiking trails for birders and several viewing towers for spotting other wildlife.

Hecla village features several restored buildings, including a typical home, the church, fish station, school, and community hall—all as they were in the 1920s and 1930s.

During the summer, visitors can see demonstrations of traditional Icelandic commercial fishing methods, from setting and pulling the nets to smoking and drying the fish.

Gull Harbor, at the northern tip of the island, is the island's recreational centre, with a beach, tennis courts, an 18-hole golf course, and hiking and cross-country trails. The trails range from the 3-km lighthouse walk on the narrow spit that forms the harbor to the 12-km West Quarry Trail, where you may spot moose moving ponderously through the woods and sloughs.

8 Grand Beach Provincial Park

Fine white sand, rolling sand dunes as high as 8 m, and a lagoon populated with birds (including a pair of rare piper plovers) make up Grand Beach Provincial Park. The 4-km beach along the eastern shore of Lake Winnipeg lives up to its name—it is rated among the best in North America. The park offers spacious campgrounds, walking trails, and facilities for windsurfing and fishing.

Gull Harbor serves as the prime resort and base for recreation in Hecla Provincial Park.

In 1969, the island became part of 865.4-km² Hecla Provincial Park, which opened six years later. Since then, only a small group of Icelandic descendants have continued to live here. But their legacy can be seen in the restored Icelandic fishing village of Hecla, some 26 km from the Grassy Narrows causeway that connects Hecla to Provincial Highway 8 on the western shore of Lake Winnipeg.

The winding road to Hecla village passes a coastline more reminiscent of the Maritimes than the Prairies. There's a breathtaking view across the water to the dark and shadowy Black Island, an area of great spiritual importance to the Saulteaux and Ojibwa Indians. Here, the sacred midewiwin ritual for the ordination of medicine men was once performed. Ceremonies are still conducted on this island every July.

Just before the park entrance, the Grassy Narrows Marsh provides one of the best places in the province for

The Grand Beach resort was boosted by the arrival of the Canadian Northern Railway in 1914 and the resort's official opening in 1916. A dance hall (according to local boosters, it was one of the largest in the British Commonwealth), a hotel, a boardwalk and a merry-go-round combined to light up nights at the beach with a carnival atmosphere. When the passenger trains stopped in 1961, cars took their place, bringing thousands of weekend revelers here between May and September.

It is undoubtedly quieter on the park's trails. Among them is the self-guiding Ancient Beach Trail, which takes hikers on an hour's walk to different levels of the shoreline of long-gone Lake Agassiz, an Ice Age lake that once covered most of Manitoba. As you climb the trail you can see evidence of three distinct shorelines, the oldest dating back 10,000 years.

9 Steinbach

⌐ ❋ ⌂

In 1874, 18 families from a tiny Anabaptist Mennonite sect left their villages in southern Russia and established the settlement of Steinbach, on the eastern edge of the Canadian prairie. Since then, Steinbach (pop. 9,000) has grown into an industrious and prosperous town.

Steinbach's Mennonite Heritage Village celebrates the area's religious and secular history. Situated at the town's northern outskirts, the 16-ha site is laid out in the pattern of a traditional Mennonite village, with homes and other buildings facing a neat central street and fields stretching out behind them. The dominating structure is Canada's only wind-powered gristmill, a replica of the first mill built here in 1877.

Visitors strolling down the Heritage Village street can see early prairie housing, including a *semlin* (a shelter made from soil, sod, wood, and grass), a log house similar to those built in 1877, and a traditional house-barn in

More than a replica, the windmill at Steinbach's Mennonite village still grinds grain.

the style of Mennonite homes on the Russian steppes.

The grounds also contain a barn with petting zoo for children, a blacksmith's shop, a printer's, and a general store. Monuments to Johann Bartsch and Jakob Hoeppner, who led a migration from Prussia to Russia in the late 1780s, were shipped here from Russia. The Bartsch monument arrived complete with bullet marks—a legacy of the Russian Revolution.

The Village Centre and Artifacts Building houses a gallery illustrating the Mennonite experience from the 16th century to the present. Traditional foods, such as *borscht* (cabbage soup), *pluma moos* (a cold fruit soup), and *pyrohy* or *perogies* (filled dumplings), are served at the Livery Barn Restaurant. Visitors can sample Mennonite cuisine at several local restaurants. *Open May to September, Monday to Saturday, 10 am to 5 pm; Sunday, noon to 5 pm. From June and August, Monday, 9 am to 7 pm; Sunday, noon to 7 pm.*

> **Special events**
> Pioneer Days (early August)

A WALK ON A WILD ISLAND

The sunny exuberance of Grand Beach contrasts with the peacefulness of its neighbor, Victoria Beach, just to the north on Lake Winnipeg. A longtime ban on cars in summer preserves the gentle pace of life that first attracted cottagers here in the early 1900s. Summer visitors who venture into Victoria Beach from Highway 59 can leave their cars in the community parking lot before going for a stroll around town or a swim at the public beach.

North of Victoria Beach is Elk Island Heritage Park—an untouched and beckoning wilderness about 2 km from the mainland. Its pine-covered cliffs rise some 30 m from the waters of Lake Winnipeg. The island can be reached by canoe from the spot where Highway 504 ends. (This road, just east of Victoria Beach, is an extension of Highway 59.) Visitors park here and paddle across. Sometimes an adventurous adult will try to wade across when the waters of Lake Winnipeg are low.

An old-growth jack pine forest mantles much of Elk Island. In the shade of the 9- to 12-m-high pines, the undergrowth is sparse, which makes strolling or hiking easy. Several unmarked trails traverse the island, but the ridgeways and beaches also offer attractive pathways. If you follow the shore, you can circle this out-of-the-way

American goldfinch

island without risk of going astray.

Elk Island is one of the best spots in Manitoba for bird-watchers, who come to see goldfinches and other species common to this part of Manitoba. From May to September, rare cliff swallows congregate on the island's northeast side. Here, in the high sand cliffs, they dig holes for nesting.

10 Sandilands Provincial Forest

Λ ⍋ ⁉ ⊛ ◐ ⚲ ✳

In 1923, the 2,772-km² Sandilands Provincial Forest was established to ensure timber resources for future generations. Lumbering was once vital to the economy of Piney, Sprague, and other communities on the fringes of the forest. (At the southern end of the forest, near Piney, local residents have created the 712-ha Spurwoods Heritage Reserve to honor their logging forebears.)

Sandilands Provincial Forest stretches about 90 km from the Trans-Canada Highway to the Canada-United States boundary. The Trans-Canada Highway cuts through the northern sector, crossing seven sand ridges, once the shores of prehistoric Lake Agassiz. Along the highway, there are hiking trails, which lead into a wilderness containing towering jack pines and low-lying cedar and tamarack swamps.

At the 120-ha Sandilands Forest Centre, near Hadashville, visitors can tour a museum where the theme is forests and forestry. (The centre is located 2.5 km south of the junction of the Trans-Canada and Highway 11.) An identification display describes the region's trees: alder, balsam fir, cedar, jack and red pine, oak, cottonwood and ash. Other attractions include a fire tower, with fire fighting equipment, and a CPR "tree-planting" coach, once used by forestry officials to explain the benefits of forestation on the prairies. *Open daily in summer, 2:30 to 7 pm.*

The centre is the starting point of two self-guiding loop trails, the 0.8-km Old Beaver Dam Trail and the 0.75-km Sagimay Trail. A picturesque feature of the Old Beaver Dam Trail is Beaven Bridge, which spans the scenic Whitemouth River. It is one of the few suspension bridges in Manitoba.

Just off Manitoba's main highways, beckoning back roads cut across a checkered prairie.

Some 5 km east of the centre is the Pineland Forest Nursery, which grows millions of conifer seedlings annually. Visitors sometimes receive a tiny pine tree as a reminder of their tour. *Open year-round, 8:30 am to 4 pm.*

11 Whiteshell Provincial Park

Λ ⍋ ⅄ ⁉ ⚹ ⌁ ⊛ ⛴ ▭ ⚲ ✳

Whiteshell was created in 1962 as Manitoba's first provincial park. It embraces 2,590 km² and contains some

Cycling is another way of exploring trailside attractions in many Manitoba parks.

200 lakes. The name is related to an Indian belief that the small, white shell of this area was the shell with which the creator breathed life into the first humans. Traces of Indian settlement in this region date back 4,000 years. The Bannock Point site, east of Rennie River on Road 307, preserves stone effigies (known as "boulder mosaics") in the shapes of turtles and snakes, placed here at least 1,000 years ago by Saulteaux and Ojibwa Indians.

The jack pines that tower over the rock faces are typical of the Whiteshell forests. The islands and gently sloping rocks on a myriad of lakes make excellent spots for camping and shore lunches. Wild rice flourishes in the sheltered corners of the lakes, and in the late summer months Indians harvest the delicacy. One of the most popular activities on the Whiteshell lakes is sports fishing. About a quarter of Manitoba's fishing lodges are located here.

Highway 307 cuts across the western sector of the park past Nutimik and Brereton lakes. At the southern end of the park is its principal resort, Falcon Lake, accessible from highways 1 and 44. Just north of Falcon Lake is another popular getaway, West Hawk Lake. The lake is 110 m deep—the deepest in Manitoba. It is believed to have been created by a meteorite.

Some of the more accessible hiking trails in Whiteshell Provincial Park include the 1.5-km Picket Creek Trail at Nutimik Lake, the 4-km Amisk Trail at Brereton Lake, the 2-km Falcon Creek Trail near the entrance to Falcon Lake, and the 4-km McGillivray Falls Trail near Caddy Lake. At Nutimik Lake, a converted log cabin houses the Whiteshell Natural History Museum, which contains Indian artifacts and displays about the park's ecology. *Open Saturday and Sunday, May and June; and daily, July to Labor Day, from 9 am to 12 pm and 1 pm to 5 pm.*

Near the village of Rennie on Highway 44 is the Alf Hole Goose Sanctuary where you can see geese from the grounds and galleries of the visitors' centre. The best times to visit the sanctuary are May and June and again in September. The geese can also be seen along the 1.5-km self-guiding Alf Hole Trail around Goose Pond.

The best way to experience the park's lakes is by canoe. The Whiteshell Canoe Route begins at the Caddy Lake boat launching facility 8 km north of West Hawk Lake on Highway 44. The 20-km canoe route—ideal for beginners—follows the passage taken by French explorer Pierre de La Verendrye on his 1733 expedition to Red River.

NORTHWESTERN ONTARIO

9

NORTHWESTERN
ONTARIO

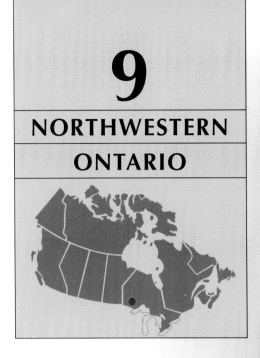

Places to see
Red Lake
Kenora
Keewatin
Woodland Caribou Provincial Park
Rainy River
Sioux Lookout
Ignace
White Otter Lake: McOuat's Castle
Quetico Provincial Park
Kakabeka Falls Provincial Park
Sleeping Giant Provincial Park
Ouimet Canyon Provincial Park
Nipigon
Lake Nipigon Provincial Park
Nirivian Islands
Longlac

Roads to explore
Rainy River to Fort Frances
Kakabeka Falls to Thunder Bay

National park close-up
Pukaskwa

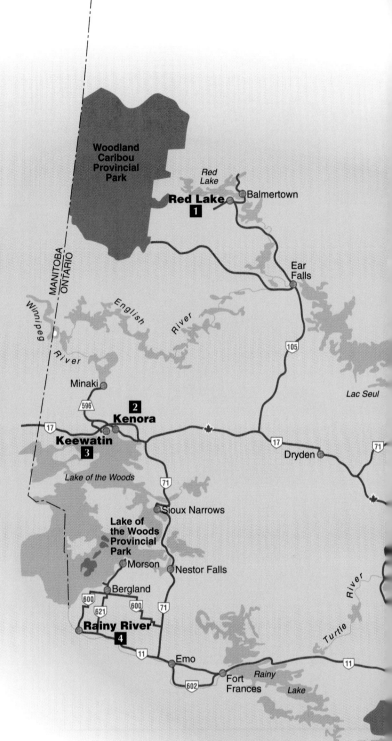

Previous pages:
Water lilies on the shores of Rainy Lake,
near Fort Frances

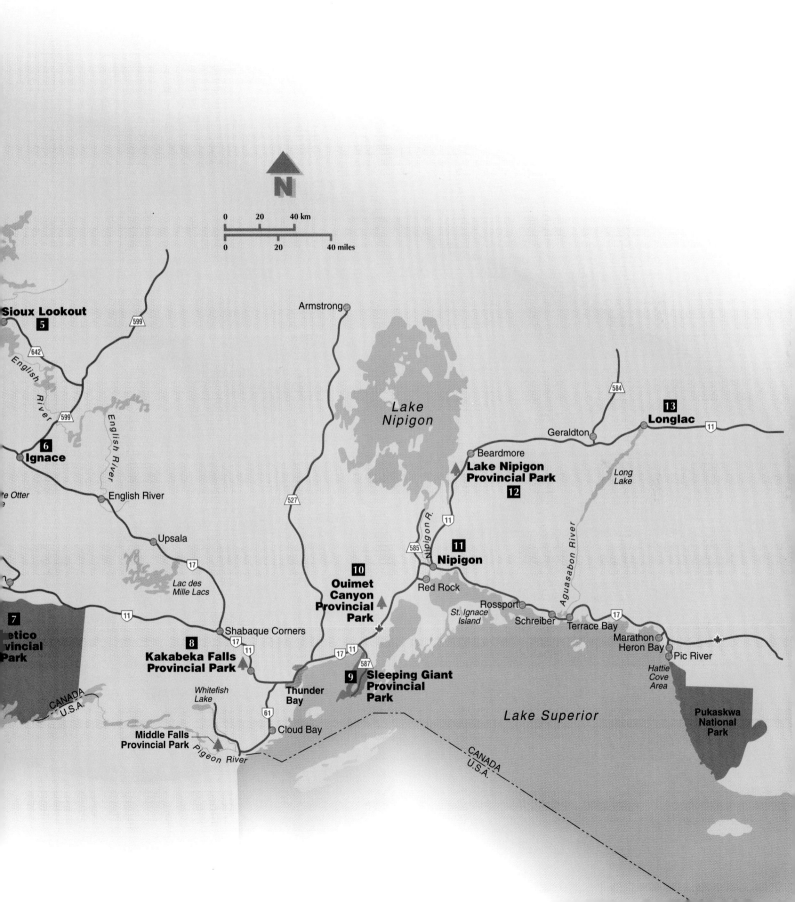

Sioux Lookout
5

599

642

English River

English River

599

Ignace
6

English River

e Otter

Upsala

17

Lac des
Mille Lacs

11

7
etico
vincial
Park

Shabaque Corners

11

8
Kakabeka Falls
Provincial Park

61

Whitefish
Lake

Middle Falls
Provincial Park

Pigeon River

Cloud Bay

Armstrong

527

10
Ouimet
Canyon
Provincial
Park

17 11

587

9 **Sleeping Giant**
Provincial Park

Thunder
Bay

CANADA
U.S.A.

Lake
Nipigon

Nipigon R.

585

11

11
Nipigon

Red Rock

St. Ignace
Island

Rossport

Schreiber

Terrace Bay

Beardmore

Lake Nipigon
Provincial Park
12

Geraldton

Aguasabon River

17

Marathon
Heron Bay

Hattie
Cove
Area

Pic River

CANADA
U.S.A.

Lake Superior

Pukaskwa
National
Park

584

13
Longlac

11

Long
Lake

1 Red Lake

Indian folklore relates that two hunters killed an old moose they thought was an evil spirit in disguise, and its blood stained the nearby lake. They called the place Misque Saigon (Blood Red Lake), a name later shortened to the form used today.

Red Lake (pop. 5,000) was settled first by the Sioux, then the Ojibwa. In 1790 it became a fur-trading post. Once Ontario's most northwesterly settlement accessible by road, it was often referred to as "the end of the road." But Red Lake suddenly became very accessible after July 25, 1925. That was when the Howey brothers, spurred on by a favorable geological report, stumbled on a rich vein of gold. The discovery spawned an epic gold rush that produced close to $400 million in gold. The town still produces more than 350,000 ounces of gold a year.

The history of the gold rush days is told in the Red Lake Museum, housed in two historic homes. *Open 11 am to 7 pm, Monday to Friday, May to mid-June; daily, late June to September.* Mine tours are conducted on Thursdays, from June to August. And the many abandoned mine sites offer exciting possibilities for avid rock hounds.

A centre for outdoor enthusiasts, Red Lake offers a variety of activities.

A Red Lake monument salutes the Norseman floatplane, the north's "workhorse."

The recently built Norseman Theme Park on the lakeshore is a memorial to the Norseman aircraft known as "the original Canadian workhorse." It was once the principal means of bringing miners and supplies to Red Lake. As if in flight, a vintage aircraft tops a pedestal on the shore of Howey Bay.

The large deep lake has exceptional sportfishing, opportunities for boating, and several supervised beaches, ideal for children. In winter it is popular with snowmobilers and cross-country skiers.

Special events
Red Lake and Golden Trappers' Festival
(late February)

2 Kenora

The border between Manitoba and Ontario once ran through a settlement at the north end of Lake of the Woods. In those days—the late 1870s—it was a lumber milling community called Rat Portage. At about the same time that the railway line between Winnipeg and Rat Portage was completed, in 1881, gold was discovered in the area. The discovery prompted a four-year provincial boundary dispute between Manitoba and Ontario. It was settled in 1884 by the British Privy Council, which decreed that the border should be moved some 48 km to the west.

Rat Portage was renamed Kenora in 1905, amalgamating the first two letters of the neighboring communities of Keewatin, Norman, and Rat Portage. Kenora (pop. 9,800) is now a pulp and paper town and lake resort.

Just east of Main Street, Hennepen Lane marks what was once the interprovincial border. The Lake of the Woods Museum on Main Street South has displays of Indian artifacts and the history of pioneer times in Rat Portage. In the summer months, it displays work by local craft people. *Open daily, July and August, and the rest of the year, Tuesday to Saturday, from 10 am to 5 pm.*

McLeod Park downtown is home to Kenora's landmark, Husky the Muskie. The 13-m-high wood, steel, and fiberglass statue is a symbol of the record-breaking catches that have made this area a mecca for anglers.

The regional archaeologist's office on Second Street exhibits native and European artifacts. And on Lakeview Drive is a railway museum in a converted caboose. The Lake of the Woods Cultural Centre on Airport Road, in nearby Jaffray Melick, has a collection of Ojibwa objects.

The pulp and paper company Boise Cascade conducts tours through the local paper mill and wood-harvesting operations. (Children under 12 are not allowed on the tours.)

At Redditt, 20 minutes north of Kenora, on Highway 658, you can see a house made entirely of bottles. In 1973 Frank Deverall built it for his wife's doll collection.

Recreational opportunities are many on Lake of the Woods, which has more than 14,000 islands and 6,000 km of shoreline bordered by four provincial parks. (Rushing River Provincial Park, some 21 km east of Kenora, is the most accessible and contains a picturesque cascade.) The lake offers excellent fishing for walleye and muskie, swimming, sailing, canoeing, hiking, and golfing. At Sioux Narrows, ancient Indian rock paintings mark the rocks along the lakeshore.

The lake is known for its houseboats, some of which have been on the water for more than 80 years.

Husky the Muskie, Kenora landmark

These vessels are a relaxing way of enjoying the lake's back channels and cruising past the moose, bear, deer, blue herons, bald eagles, and white pelicans that live on the lake.

Special events

Rat Portage First Nation Traditional Powwows (late May and late July)

Lake of the Woods Multicultural Festival (early June)

Harbourfest (July-August)

Kenora International Bass Tournament (early August)

Lake of the Woods International Sailing Association Regatta (early August)

3 | Keewatin

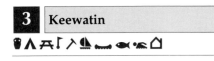

Ontario's most westerly town, Keewatin (pop. 2,000) lies on the northern shore of Lake of the Woods.

The town contains an interesting piece of history: the Mather-Walls House at 1116 Ottawa Street. Built in 1889, it is a fine example of the Queen Anne style. The Mather family founded the Keewatin Lumber Company in 1879, to supply crossties to the CPR, and David Mather, the grandson of the company's founder, later became president of the CPR. The house was one of three designed locally for the family (the other two can still be seen). John Walls, a foreman with the lumber company, bought the house in 1906. His daughter preserved it almost unchanged until the Ontario Heritage Foundation acquired it in 1975. Painstakingly restored, it now showcases a bygone era. *Open July to Labor Day; Monday to Friday, 10 am to 3 pm; weekends, 1 pm to 4 pm.*

From the veranda of the house you can see the Keewatin Boat Lift, built on the site of the former Keewatin Milling Company's spillway. A wooden platform operated by electric winches carries boats over the 7-9-m elevation from Lake of the Woods to the Winnipeg River system. Boaters should

Few rapids disrupt the maze of canoe routes in the wilds of Woodland Caribou Provincial Park.

CENTURIES-OLD CANOE ROUTES IN A REMOTE PARK

On the Berens River plateau, hugging the Ontario-Manitoba boundary, is Woodland Caribou Provincial Park. This 4,500-km^2 park contains more than 1,800 km of canoe routes, the best means of exploring the park, so it is popular with adventurous canoeists. There are no roads into the park, but it can be reached by portage from one of the surrounding forestry roads or by charter plane from Ear Falls or Red Lake. Information and permits are available from the Red Lake district park office. Canoe rentals are available from local outfitters.

The park's topography is typical of the Canadian Shield—elongated lakes and massive outcrops of bedrock. But what makes it so spectacular are the headwaters of six major river systems, and a mix of boreal, woodland, and prairie vegetation. Stands of 60- to 100-year-old jack pine are interspersed with black spruce swamps and small stands of trembling aspen and white birch. The park abounds with species of prairie plants, rare in Ontario, such as prairie crocus, parsley fern, floating marsh marigold, prairie spikemoss and prairie gray-stemmed goldenrod.

Dry hot summers and thin sandy soil contribute to a large number of forest fires in the park. But the fires have a positive effect—the jack pines need to be burned periodically to release the seeds from their cones. In addition, many flowering plants thrive in the burned areas among the young saplings, including fireweed, blueberry, Bicknell's geranium, hooked-spur violet and crimson-fringed bindweed.

The park's richly diverse plant life enables a variety of animals to live there. The jack pine supports dense clumps of *Cladina* lichen, the main food of woodland caribou. A herd of about 120 of these animals lives in the park and gave it its name. Rare animals such as Franklin ground squirrels, red-sided common garter snakes and snapping and painted turtles live alongside moose and black bears. The park is also visited by white pelicans and bald eagles.

The park's waterways were traveled for centuries and are consequently marked with evidence of the region's early inhabitants. Among such relics are well-preserved collections of rock art. Artery Lake has one of the largest sites. Others are scattered, mainly by the Bloodvein, Gammon, and Oiseau rivers.

Both the Hudson's Bay and North West companies established trapping areas here, using the rivers as routes to transport furs and supplies. Today, backwoods enthusiasts and avid naturalists travel the waterways.

At Rushing River Provincial Park, near Kenora, swimmers revel in a roily cascade.

check ahead for weight and size restrictions.

Another curiosity is the Potholes, a group of four spherical depressions, from 75 cm to 1 m across and 1 m or more deep, in the rock on Sixth Street, just one block south of Highway 17. A viewing area overlooks the potholes. It is not known what formed them—they remain Keewatin's mystery.

Keewatin's Portage Bay Recreation Area offers many outdoor activities, including fishing and hunting.

4 Rainy River

In the 1800s, the Rainy River valley's namesake community was a hub of commercial activity for boats coming down the river and trains that stopped there with supplies. As traffic down the river diminished, so did the importance of Rainy River (pop. 1,000) itself.

Today, however, the community's waterfront life has been revived with the construction of a marina, riverside campgrounds, and picnic shelters. The old CNR station has also been renovated and boasts a restored 4008 steam locomotive. The town celebrates its prosperous past every year in a festival called "Railroad Daze."

A border crossing point from Baudette, Minn., Rainy River is at the heart of superb hunting and fishing territory. The area is noted for walleye.

Special events
Railroad Daze (mid-July)

5 Sioux Lookout

Although Highway 72 to Sioux Lookout is a quiet stretch of road with few amenities, travelers can be assured of a warm welcome when they reach this

Near Keewatin, boathouses and docks line the scenic bays and coves of Lake of the Woods.

remote town. Situated on the northern shore of Pelican Lake, this community of 3,311 is a major jumping-off point for many of northwestern Ontario's 22,000-odd lakes. The name Sioux Lookout refers to a nearby hill, where the Ojibwa spied the approach of their enemies, the Sioux. According to le-

At Sioux Lookout, a sign proclaims the part the town plays in northwestern Ontario.

gend, their foresight was rewarded with the successful ambush of their opponents, whose skulls are said to lie downstream near Pelican Narrows.

Outfitters at Sioux Lookout offer custom-made vacations on the region's premier attraction, the waterways of English River–Lac Seul, which stretch from a point east of Ignace to the Manitoba border. The waterways were once used by fur traders and explorers heading west.

There are few roads to take travelers to the region's many scenic getaways. However local outfitters operate fly-in vacations to distant fishing and hunt-

ing camps. You can even rent your own lake or wilderness island. Back home, fishermen brag about this area's amazing catches of walleye, northern pike, muskellunge, and lake trout. Hunters point with pride to a moose head on the wall and say they shot it here.

Sioux Lookout Museum chronicles the town's origins in 1906 as a survey camp for the Grand Trunk Railway and its gold boom of the 1920s. When gold was discovered at Red Lake and Pickle Lake, prospectors used newfangled airplanes to explore the distant corners of the region. Such pioneer flights made Sioux Lookout North America's

A CNR steam locomotive and caboose at Drew P. Jeffries Park commemorates the railway's role in developing Sioux Lookout.

second busiest aviation centre during the 1930s. *The museum is open daily from early June to late August, 9 am to 6 pm.*

Ojibway Provincial Park, just 25 km southwest of Sioux Lookout on Little Vermilion Lake, has 50 campsites, a beach, and 11 km of hiking trails.

Special events
Blueberry Festival (late July–early August)

6 Ignace

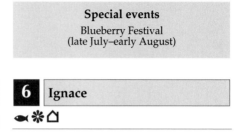

On the shore of Lake Agimak, just one piece in a mosaic of lakes, is the mining town of Ignace (pop. 2,300). In the 1700s it was a summer settlement for Ojibwa Indians, who harvested blueberries and wild rice along the lakeshore. A century later, construction crews for the Canadian Pacific Railway arrived, to make the settlement a junction between Kenora and Thunder Bay. The town was named for Ignace Mentour, Iroquois guide to the CPR's chief engineer, Sandford Fleming, and famed for his strength and endurance. According to one tale, Ignace ran more than 6 km in 29 minutes, wearing snowshoes.

When the last train passed through in the late 1950s, Ignace as a railway town was dead. But mining, forestry, and tourism revived it. The old CPR station is now an historic site.

The Ignace Regional Travel Centre on Main Street has exhibits recounting the origin and history of the community, and describing mining, forestry, and forest fire management. *Open daily; 8 am to 8 pm, June to August; 8 am to 4:30 pm, October to May.* Logging and mining equipment will be showcased at a heritage museum planned to open in 1994 alongside the travel centre.

Because Ignace has wilderness all around, wild game is often seen nearby. Moose and deer appear at dawn and dusk along the roadside; and in the fall, black bears roam the area. In season, the game attracts hunters, just as the lake's trophy-sized trout, walleye, northern pike, and smallmouth bass attract anglers.

Roads to explore: From farmland to Shield

Distance (approx.): 120 km/75 mi

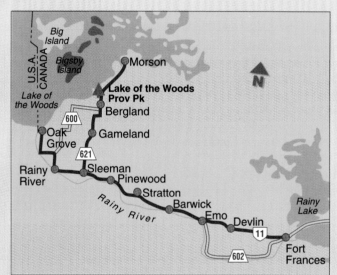

The Rainy River valley extends from a level farming landscape, bordering the Lake of the Woods, into terrain marked with the rocky remnants of the last Ice Age, at the edge of the Canadian Shield.

The drive along the valley begins at Oak Grove, at the mouth of the Rainy River, on Lake of the Woods. Oak Grove Camp was formerly the Hudson's Bay Company's camp known as Hungry Hall. Ancient native burial mounds and artifacts found in the area predate by 600 years the coming of the Europeans. Many of the artifacts are displayed at Oak Grove Camp.

● About 1.6 km down River Road, a large fenced area encloses a herd of nearly 200

The end of a fine day's fishing, at Morson, on the reedy shores of Lake of the Woods

wild bison, visible at several points for the next 10.5 km.

● Turn right onto Highway 600 and then left onto Highway 11 through the town of Rainy River.

● Continue east on Highway 11 to Sleeman.

● Take a side trip north about 35 km up Highway 621, to Lake of the Woods Provincial Park, or to the vacation getaway of Morson. Or, if the direct route is your choice, continue along the valley for 50 km, passing through several small agricultural communities, to Emo, the site of the region's annual August Agricultural Fair.

Emo also boasts one of the smallest churches in the world, with seating for eight. At the Women's Institute Museum, pioneer artifacts, musical instruments, war memorabilia, and clothing from the early 1900s are on display. *Admission free. Open daily from mid-May to early October, 10 am to 5 pm.*

● A further 30 km east completes the valley drive to Fort Frances, once called Fort St. Pierre. The Fort Frances Museum and Cultural Centre depicts the area's Indian fur trade and pioneer life. *Open daily, June to August, 10 am to 8 pm; August to June, 10 am to 5 pm.* The town's Boise Cascade speciality paper plant conducts tours by reservation.

● Pithers Point Park, 2.4 km east of town, has a replica of Fort St. Pierre, a restored logging tug, *The Hallett*, and the Lookout Tower Museum, which overlooks Fort Frances and neighboring International Falls, Minn., on the American side of the Rainy River.

● Highway 11 takes you to the Noden Causeway, which straddles a scenic chain of islands east of town.

A WILDERNESS CASTLE AT WHITE OTTER LAKE

Trapper Jimmy McOuat (pronounced *McKewitt*) was in his mid-forties when he came to White Otter Lake in 1903, having lost all he owned by prospecting for gold. Single-handedly, he began to build a log castle complete with a tower. This slight man did everything himself. He cut and hauled red pine logs to the site. Later, he grooved, chinked, and dovetailed them. Each was left rounded on the outside, and squared on the inside.

McOuat's solitary labors ended in 1914. His dwelling in the deep forest rose three stories, about 30 m from the lakeshore. Its rustic frame was punctuated with 26 sash windows. The feature that truly transformed McOuat's home into a castle was the imposing four-story tower, which was capped by a gambrel roof.

Why McOuat built such a grand structure in such a remote setting is a mystery. Its secret drowned with him in 1918, while he was netting trout for his winter reserves. But he often cited a childhood prank: He threw a corncob at a blacksmith and hit him on the ear. The irate man shouted: "Jimmy McOuat, ye'll never do no good. Ye'll die in a shack!"

During the 1980s, Ignace and Atikokan undertook the restoration of McOuat's castle, which for decades had been considered a derelict backwoods curiosity. The site is inaccessible by road. In summer, it can be reached by a boat tour from Atikokan, or by floatplane from Ignace, Atikokan, and Fort Frances.

McOuat's Castle, illuminated at night

Northern Ontario's wilderness lakes reflect the abstract shapes and colors in rocky outcrops.

Agimak Lake is the starting point for a 15-portage, 37-km canoe route to White Otter Lake. The route takes canoeists past sandbanks that were formed some 11,000 years ago by glacier lakes. The other attraction on these lakes is ancient red-ochre pictographs, thought to have been created between 600 and 1,000 years ago. They depict human figures, canoes, moose, and turtles and may be markers for successful hunting and fishing grounds. They were probably made by ancestors of the area's Cree and Ojibwa Indians.

Special events
White Otter Days (August)

7 | Quetico Provincial Park

Sheer granite cliffs, foaming rapids, flower-scented waterways, and a lacy pattern of lakes make up Quetico Provincial Park. The park's name is thought to mean "a benevolent spirit dwelling in regions of beauty."

Covering 4,750 km², the park contains more than 1,500 km of canoe routes, the best means of really exploring its wilderness. The park's entry points can be reached only by canoe, except for the Dawson Trail Campground at French Lake. The many lakes are connected by portages, which average 400 m.

The waterways wind through forest which boasts a surprising range of trees, from black spruce to white pine to red maple, oak, elm, and birch. More than 90 species of birds live here. They include ospreys, bald eagles, and barred owls. Chipmunks, beavers, and red squirrels are easy to spot. In early July, moose are often seen feeding among lily pads and bulrushes. Timber wolves are common but rarely seen, as are black bears and the secretive lynx.

The waterways also flow past ancient pictographs drawn onto the sheer

cliff faces. The red-ochre drawings were made centuries ago by the ancestors of the Ojibwa Indians. There are more than 30 pictographs in the park, depicting moose and caribou, canoes and abstract marks. The clearest are near Lac LaCroix.

The first European to open up the Quetico area was Jacques de Noyon, in 1688. French fur traders followed along the routes established by explorers LaVérendrye, Fraser, and MacKenzie. Simon Dawson first surveyed its waterways, in 1857, to plot a settlers' oxcart, steam tug, and canoe route to the west.

Today the visitors' centre at the Dawson Trail Campground has displays, slide shows, lectures, a research library, and knowledgeable staff on hand.

There are seven interpretive trails in the campground area. The more adventurous hikers can enjoy a 10-km round-trip on The Pines Trail from French Lake to a Pickerel Lake campsite with a fine beach and towering red pines. The Pines is an extension of the circular Whiskey Jack Trail, gateway to the interior wilderness.

Although park facilities do not operate off-season, it is possible to enjoy the park during the winter, by snowshoe, cross-country skiing, or dogsled.

---

8 | Kakabeka Falls Provincial Park

True to their Ojibwa name, "sheer cliff falls," the Kakabeka Falls plunge 39 m over slate cliffs into the Kaministiquia River gorge below. They are the highlight of the Kakabeka Falls Provincial Park, and spectacular at any time of the year. In winter the freezing winds mix with the moisture-filled air to cover the gorge with fantastic white shapes. Spring and summer sunshine

A distant view shows Kakabeka Falls—"Niagara of the North"—dropping into its gorge.

touch the mist-cloaked falls and cliffs with rainbows. In fall, a breathtaking spectacle of brilliantly colored foliage frames the cascading water.

A convenient parking lot off Highway 11-17 provides easy access to a view of the falls. Wooden walkways and viewing platforms with interpretive displays extend along both sides of the gorge, which was carved by turbulent meltwater from retreating glaciers, and by continuing erosion.

The falls blocked the route of early voyageurs, who were forced to carry their fur-laden canoes along the Mountain Portage on their way to Old Fort William, at the mouth of the river. Even soldiers of the Wolseley expedition, moving westward to suppress the Riel Rebellion, had to endure the portage. Today you can walk a 2-km stretch of the historic Mountain Portage Trail and explore the 3-km Little Falls Trail. From the trails you can see the rock above the falls, which contains ancient marine sediments with fossils that are 1.6 billion years old—some of the oldest fossils on earth.

The park has a well-equipped campground with sandy beaches. A hydroelectric dam above the falls poses a danger to swimmers who do not heed the caution to stay inside the roped areas. Children should be supervised.

In winter, 13 km of groomed trails are available for cross-country skiing. The 10-km River Terrace Trail offers a fine bluff-top view of the valley.

9	Sleeping Giant Provincial Park

From the city of Thunder Bay, if you look across the water, you can see the profile of a "sleeping giant." It is in fact the 40-km-long Sibley Peninsula and Sleeping Giant Provincial Park. The name refers to the legendary Ojibwa figure Nanibijou (the Giant), who was turned to stone by the Great Spirit for having led the white man to a deposit

Roads to explore: Where echoes of Finland are still heard

Distance: 190 km/118 miles

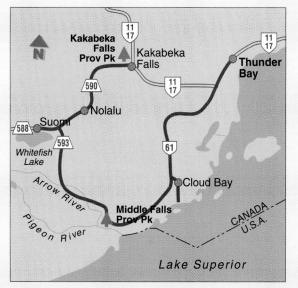

From Kakabeka Falls Provincial Park, travel down Highway 11-17 for a short distance to the crossroads and turn west onto Highway 590. The highway bends south to the quaint village of Nolalu, snuggling into the banks of the Whitefish River.

● Travel west on Highway 588 out of the river valley and past fertile farmland and rolling hills. About 17 km farther on is the hamlet of Suomi. Many of the farms and fields in this area were first cleared by Finnish settlers, and their language is still commonly heard here. Beautiful Whitefish Lake is situated close by; it provides excellent fishing and boating. Legend has it that the lake has two bottoms, and the fish swim back and forth between them.

● Go back along Highway 588 to the junction with Highway 593 and turn right. Highway 593 is a 52-km road that winds south and then east. This excellent paved highway, which is called the Devon Road, skirts both the Arrow and Pigeon rivers for much of its length. Intensive logging took place here in the early 1930s, and both rivers were used by logging companies to run the gigantic white and red pine logs. A few uncut pines can still be seen along this road, as can a healthy stand of white birch.

● Continue to Middle Falls Provincial Park, on the banks of the Pigeon River. Voyageurs once had to carry 7-m birch-

bark canoes and 40-kg packs over this stretch of river. Enjoy a relaxing picnic and take in the beauty of the 6-m-high falls.

● Travel north on Highway 61. There are a number of hikes in the area, including a trail to the High Falls. The falls are located 1.6 km west of Highway 61 and tumble 28 m into the tumultuous Pigeon River gorge. The high rock ridge that parallels the road is a mesa that was created 1.1 billion years ago when a dark volcanic rock was pushed into the sedimentary rock.

● Continue up Highway 61 to Cloud Bay. Turn south onto Cloud Bay Road—a dirt road—and drive 4 km through a lush forest of poplar and evergreen trees. Take the right fork in the road to the Little Trout Bay Conservation Area. There is direct access to Lake Superior here, and the view down the mountain-rimmed, aquamarine bay is spectacular. Pause to picnic, hike, boat, or fish.

● Return to Cloud Bay and continue for 35 km to Thunder Bay. Before you reach Thunder Bay, the highway crosses a bridge that spans the mighty Kaministiquia River. This waterway drains most of the lakes and streams crossed during this particular drive. At the height of the fur trade, this river was an important link to the west. Several kilometres upstream from the Highway Bridge, off Rosslyn Road, is a reconstruction of Old Fort William—the North West Company's major fur depot. The fort re-creates life as it was lived here in the 1820s, when adventurers, fur traders, and voyageurs wheeled and dealed at this site.

Red columbine, a flower of Ontario's northland

of silver on the rugged shores of Lake Superior. The peninsula rises 244 m above the waters of the lake.

The best way to appreciate the park is on foot, hiking along some of its 70 km of trails. The main route is the 40-km Kabeyun Trail, which extends along the park's western shore from Thunder Bay Lookout, 137 m above the lake. This trail leads to the full height of the Sleeping Giant before rounding the tip of the peninsula, where it drops down to Tee Harbour. On top of the Giant, just west of the "chimney" cleft high above Lehtinen's Bay, is a 130-m-deep chasm, with a lookout view unequaled in northwestern Ontario. To walk the entire trail takes two to three days and requires wilderness provisions and sturdy footwear.

There are several easier trails, which can take an afternoon or a day. The park's 80-km Capsule Tour can be enjoyed by car or bicycle. In winter, there are 30 km of groomed wilderness cross-country ski trails.

Whether you choose to walk, ride, ski, or drive, look out for the great variety of animals. More than 190 species of birds have been recorded here. It also has unusually diverse plants, which include arctic cloudberries, but-

On the roadside in Sleeping Giant Provincial Park, a fearless and inquisitive red fox is caught on the prowl by a visitor's camera.

terwort, British Columbia thimbleberries, and two species of rare orchid.

The Marie Louise Campground has an interpretive centre with interactive cultural and natural history exhibits.

10 Ouimet Canyon Provincial Park

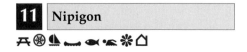

Bracing air and eerie silence strike you as you survey the scene from the rim of Ouimet Canyon and look down the 100-m drop to the bottom. The canyon and the provincial park that contains it are named after Canadian soldier, politician and judge, Joseph Aldéric Ouimet. The park is a nature reserve, which has been set aside for authorized natural history research.

Wooden platforms that jut out from the cliff face create the sensation of being suspended in space when you stand on them. They provide an unimpeded view of the cliffs opposite, 150 m away, and of the sheer cliffs extending to the north, as well as a distant vista of Lake Superior, framed by the canyon's southern entrance.

The platforms are reached along a 1-km-long marked trail, posted with interpretive signs. The trail runs through mixed boreal forest—jack pine, balsam fir, white birch, and black and white spruce—along the edge of the canyon. (Due to the risk posed by high cliffs, deep crevices, and the potential for rock falls, you are advised to keep to the established trail and use the designated lookout areas. Careful supervision of children is essential.)

Geological features reveal the natural history of this area. The flat-topped mesas, on which you walk above the vertical rock faces, are 1,142-million-year-old igneous rock intrusions into older sedimentary rocks. Huge boulders at the bottom of the canyon are evidence of the power of seasonal freezing and thawing of water in joints along the rock face. The talus slopes of broken rock along the canyon floor

speak of slow, timeless erosion. Some columns of rock resist breaking away: one of them, a pinnacle on the west side of the canyon, aptly named "Indian Head," can be seen from a nearby platform.

Late spring snowmelt and the lack of sunlight make the canyon very cold. Ice may even remain year-round beneath the giant boulders on the canyon floor. For this reason, only subarctic plants grow there, among collapsed sections of the canyon wall. To safeguard the sensitive vegetation in this area, visitors are not permitted on the canyon floor.

11 Nipigon

The name of this town just above Lake Superior's north shore is a corruption of the Ojibwa *Annimigon* meaning "the lake you cannot see the end of."

From the scenic lookout just west of the Nipigon River Bridge, on Highway 11-17, you can see Lake Superior, Nipigon Bay, the mouth of the Nipigon River, and the town nestling in the river valley.

Nipigon (pop. 2,400) is a small town—most of its shops are situated on Front Street, just south of the train tracks. But with some 450,000 travelers passing through the community each year, the stores are usually bustling. Follow the signs on tree-lined Front Street down to the newly renovated waterfront. Boating enthusiasts from all over the Great Lakes tie up here, and a stroll around the docks to admire the wide range of vessels is a pleasant way to spend an hour or two.

From the waterfront, to the east you can see a high cliff—known as the Palisades—jutting up from the shore of Lake Superior. A boat can be hired for a closer look at the rock, which is marked with several Ojibwa pictographs dated between 400 and 1,000 years old. They include the squatting figure known as Maymaygwayshi,

From a lookout perched on a sheer stone wall, visitors peer into Ouimet Canyon's cool depths.

which means "ghost," or "merman," or "spirit." Visitors often leave tobacco here, for good luck.

To enjoy the upper Nipigon River, drive north up Highway 580, the Pine Portage Road. This drive winds 36 km through the hills of the Nipigon River valley and skirts three hydroelectric dams. In the fields around Cameron and Pine Portage dams, remnants of the villages that sprang up to build these huge structures are visible. Their once carefully tended gardens have since run wild and some popular garden variety flowers flourish in the most unexpected places.

Several clearly marked turnoffs lead along the west edge of the river to the Nipigon watershed and good picnic sites. Several logging roads located east of Highway 580 provide a chance for hiking and, if the road ends at a lake, fishing.

> **Special events**
> Nipigon Falls Fishing Festival
> (September)

12 Lake Nipigon Provincial Park

A beach of black sand marks the site of Lake Nipigon Provincial Park, on the eastern shore of the largest body of water entirely inside Ontario. The sand is what remains of ancient volcanic rock weathered by wind, rain, and ice.

The park site was once an Ojibwa settlement and the black sand beach has given up a rich cache of their tools and jewelry. The Woodland Indian artist Norval Morriseau was born in the local settlement, which was abandoned in the late 1930s.

The lake's cold clear water is legendary for its trout fishing (there is a boat ramp at the provincial park). The world record speckled trout, a 7-kg giant, was caught in 1916, to the south, in the Nipigon River. Near the mouth of the river is Orient Bay, where several sports lodges are situated. A stone fireplace, a few weathered cottages, and an icehouse mark the site of the CPR's Royal Windsor Lodge, a landmark hostelry from 1913 to 1974, when it burned down. Among its famous guests was the Prince of Wales, Prince Edward, who fished here in 1924.

If you do not have a boat, charter fishing can be secured from the Hook Shop, a tackle store in Beardmore (pop. 503), to the north of the provincial park. Beardmore was born when gold was discovered in the nearby hills, at the turn of the century. There are few remaining vestiges of the gold rush days, save the Miner's Inn, a dining lodge and hotel. In the 1960s this building was the headquarters of the Leitch Mine, the oldest and richest mine in Canada at the time. When the lodes of gold ran out, so did the town's prosperity, and much of its population.

To get a good view of Lake Nipigon, drive north from Beardmore on Highway 11, and west on Highway 580 to the Poplar Point campsite. To the west you will see an array of islands in the distance, the largest of which is Shakespeare Island. Logging once took place on these remote islands, and teams of horses provided much of the power. Poplar Point is an ideal spot for camping, picnicking, bird-watching, and boating.

> **Special events**
> Beardmore Fish Derby
> (June)

AN ISLAND "NATION" ON SUPERIOR'S NORTH SHORE

In October 1979, three men landed on St. Ignace Island, off the north shore of Lake Superior, and planted a flag on it, declaring the new "nation" of Nirivia. The nation encompasses 59 islands and was "established" by local residents and naturalists, in a bid to protect their natural beauty. The Nirivian Island Expedition Ltd., Thunder Bay, runs the only organized tours and maintains camps on the islands, which can also be visited independently.

The Nirivian islands are accessible only by water, from Nipigon and Rossport. The largest of the islands is St. Ignace, which Jesuit priests named after Ignatius Loyola—founder of the Jesuits—when they explored the 410 km² island in the 17th century.

Named for the Cree word for "far-off enchanted place," Nirivia is truly magical. Many of the islands are covered with black spruce forests that vibrate with the trills of birds. St. Ignace alone has about 100 lakes and ponds, many waterfalls, and the tallest mountain on the Great Lakes, Mount St. Ignace, at 503 m above sea level. Among the islands' other treasures are the fjordlike Woodbine and Morn harbors on Simpson Island, the mighty cliffs of Talbot and Agate islands, and the rock formation of the "Arch" on Hope Island. Paradise Island, which rises only 15 m above Lake Superior, has an ancient cobble beach covered with lichens, tiny, twisted white birch, and carpets of mountain cranberry, a shrub also known as lingonberry.

The islands have 125 km of trails, some of them easy, some quite rugged. The Mountain Trail, a 38-km round-trip, leads from Armour Harbour, on the south side of St. Ignace, to the tip of Mount St. Ignace. From there the view can stretch 42 km southwest toward Black Bay and encompasses many of Nirivia's smaller islands.

Wildlife is abundant on the islands, particularly moose, deer, squirrels, snowshoe hares, and countless species of birds. There are also bears on the larger islands. St. Ignace's lakes and the Moffat straits on the east of the island have trout, northern pike, bass, perch, and walleye. On the southern end of the straits is St. Ignace Harbour, a favorite camping area.

At sunset, the islands of Superior's north shore become bold, black outcrops in a silvery lake.

13 Longlac

∧ ⚑ ⇌ ⌗ ❋

On the northern tip of Long Lake is the lumbering community of Longlac (pop. 2,073). As the town's name suggests, it has a French past, but it also has a French present—as you stroll down the town's streets you will hear French-Canadian accents. More than half of Longlac's residents are francophone.

The town's French history dates back to the arrival of the first *coureurs des bois*, before the mid-1700s. By 1800, the North West Company had established a fur-trading post on the west side of Long Lake. The original post is thought to have stood at Gauthier Point, a spot locals can direct you to.

Soon afterward, in 1813, the Hudson's Bay Company opened a rival post, at the north end of Long Lake. (The two posts were merged in 1821.) Ojibwa and Cree Indians came to Long Lake post to trade furs for knives, pots, and beads. The two bands still live near Longlac. During the 1800s, the post served as a stopover on the winter packet route from the Red River in Manitoba to Montreal.

The building of the National Transcontinental Railway in the years before the First World War linked Longlac to the outside world and opened this region for lumbering and gold mining.

Today, Longlac offers excellent hunting, fishing, and wilderness canoeing. Long Lake and the Kenogami River are known for their pickerel, lake trout, and pike. The waterfront has a marina, fishing platforms, and docks. There is a public beach at Jeff Gauthier Memorial Park, and there are campgrounds, tennis courts, picnic sites, and hiking trails. There are 50 km of groomed cross-country skiing trails around Longlac, and hundreds of kilometres of snowmobile trails.

Special events
Summerfest (July)

Pukaskwa

Until the Trans-Canada Highway reached Lake Superior's rugged northeastern shore in the 1960s, much of the area was accessible only by train, plane, or canoe. For the most part the railway followed the coastline, as did the highway. But between Wawa and Marathon, both swung across a stubby peninsula shutting off more than 1,800 km² of spectacular coastline and boreal hinterland between the highway and the world's largest body of freshwater. As a result, the area continued to be as remote as it was when the first Europeans set eyes on it some 300 years ago.

Even today there is no year-round habitation. But, since 1983, there is a national park, Pukaskwa (pronounced *Puck-a-saw*), a splendid wilderness cradled between the Pic and the Pukaskwa rivers.

The landscape is pure Canadian Shield, that massive rock formation cast in the cauldrons of billion-year-old volcanoes. Tip Top Mountain, the park's highest hill and the second highest point in Ontario, rises 640 m above sea level, 457 m above Lake Superior's surface.

At the end of the last Ice Age, glacial meltwater raised Superior's water level to great heights. The flooding receded slowly, leaving beaches of boulders and sand, some as much as 130 m above sea level.

About 100 circular and oval stone structures known as the Pukaskwa Pits are found in and around these beaches. The Pits are recognized as

Black bears are part of Pukaskwa's wildlife population.

sacred sites by the First Nations people of the area and are respected for their connection with the spirit world. Excavation of some pits has produced few artifacts—mostly pottery fragments, fish bones, and pieces of copper.

The white bark and broad leaves of birch and trembling aspen often mark the valley edges and shorelines of inland lakes while white spruce, balsam fir, and jack pine are predominant on the rocky hummocks and slopes. In early summer, bunchberry and lily-of-the-valley form a white patchwork in the woods.

In no time, these flowers are overshadowed by the yellow blooms of clintonia, the blue petals of tall lungwort, and the red moccasin flower. By mid-June the coralroots and delicate

twinflowers have blossomed. Asters and bedstraws have come and gone by August, when the ghostly white Indian pipes appear.

The exposed headlands and coastal islands harbor spruce trees stunted by surf-drenched winds and their level sections are covered by mats of chin-high bearberry (*kinnikinnick*) and blueberry. The flat ground is dotted with single plants of encrusted saxifrage, one of a group of arctic plants that survive along Lake Superior's rugged coastline due to its cool summer winds and turbid fogs.

The spectacular 80-km-long Pukaskwa River drops 260 m from its headwaters at Gibson Lake to Schist Falls, the last gorge on its journey to Superior's shore. During spring runoff, the river offers challenging canoeing, although the turbulent water at Ringham's Gorge should be attempted only by experienced canoeists. Others should take the 2-km Two Pants portage.

The river also has many peaceful stretches, where common mergansers and loons fish the deeper pools, and mallards, teals, and black ducks splash about in the shallows. Kingfishers and northern water thrushes feed along its banks, where great blue heron stand and wait for a stickleback or shiner.

Around the turn of the century, loggers penetrated what is now parkland, leading to the founding of a bustling logging settlement called Pukaskwa Depot. But after timber prices fell, the depot closed in 1930.

Now, with new growth clothing the forested slopes, caribou once again fearlessly trek the Cascade River hills. And wolf and moose, lynx and snowshoe hare, gray owl and ermine, safe from man's depredation, are left to their own devices as predator or prey.

PARK INFORMATION
Access: Route 627 south of Marathon.
Visitors' centre: Hattie Cove. Picnic sites and parking available.
Accommodations: 67-site campground, three sand beaches on Lake Superior.
Summer activities: Backcountry hiking and short hikes near Hattie Cove; boating on Lake Superior; wilderness canoeing; fishing.
Winter activities: Snowshoeing and cross-country skiing on a 6-km trail near Hattie Cove.

NORTHEAST ONTARIO / NORTHWEST QUEBEC

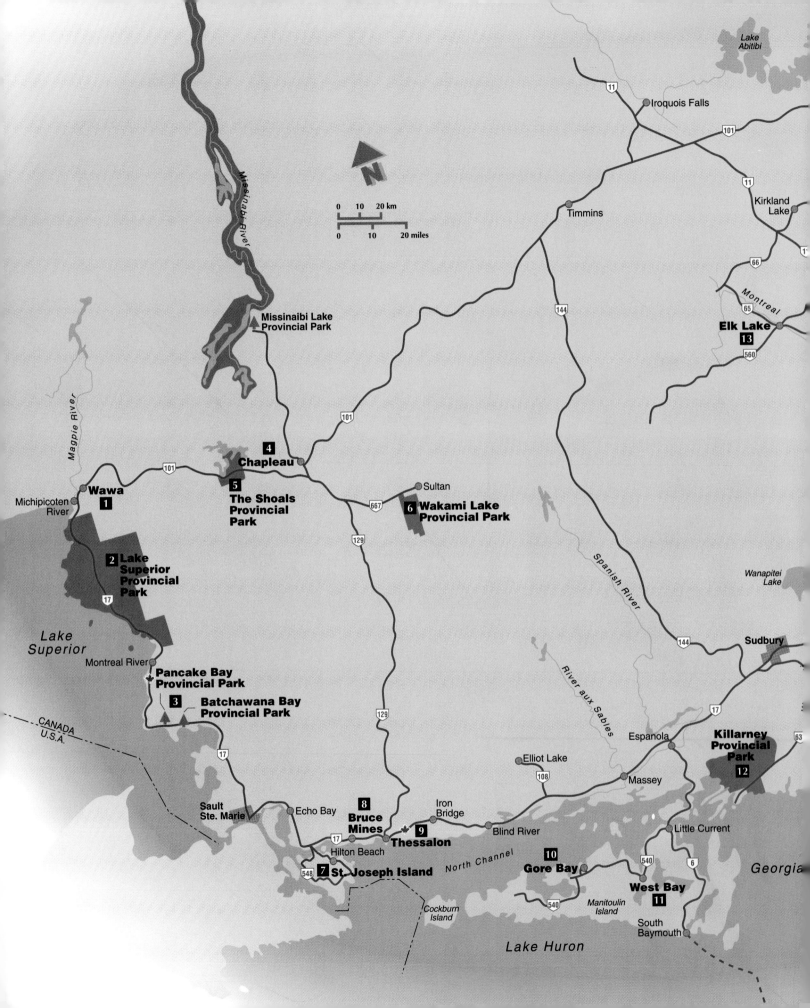

18 Parc de cons. d'Aiguebelle

Lac Malartic

19 Val-d'Or

Malartic

Rouyn-Noranda

101

117

66

QUEBEC
ONTARIO

101

391

glehart

Notre-Dame-du-Nord

65

Angliers

iskeard
aileybury

Ville-Marie

Cobalt

chford

17

11

Lake Timiskaming

14

Temagami

Lake gami

101

Témiscaming

15

Marten River

63

Ottawa River

64

11

Lake Talon

Mattawa River

Mattawa

16

North Bay

17

Sturgeon Falls

Callander

Lake Nipissing

French River

ay

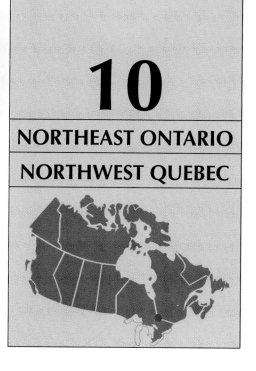

10
NORTHEAST ONTARIO
NORTHWEST QUEBEC

Places to see
Wawa
Lake Superior Provincial Park
Pancake Bay and Batchawana Bay
Provincial Parks
Chapleau
The Shoals Provincial Park
Wakami Lake Provincial Park
St. Joseph's Island
Bruce Mines
Thessalon
Gore Bay
West Bay
Killarney Provincial Park
Elk Lake
Temagami
Marten River Provincial Park
Mattawa
Cobalt
Parc d'Aiguebelle
Val d'Or

Roads to explore
Manitoulin Island
Around Lake Timiskaming

Previous pages:
George Lake, Killarney Lake Provincial Park

1 Wawa

The 8.5-m-high steel "Wawa Goose," poised for flight at the junction of Highways 17 and 101, marks the turnoff to this community of 5,000. Wawa, meaning "wild goose" in the Ojibwa tongue, occupies the southwestern end of a small and picturesque lake of the same name. Although the town was settled in the 1890s, its downtown core retains a frontier character. A major landmark, the Lakeview Hotel, has occupied the same site for more than a hundred years. The present hotel replaced the original hostelry in the 1940s.

Wawa began as a transit camp for shipments from Lake Superior during the building of the Canadian Pacific Railway in the 1880s. The rails were shipped to Michipicoten Harbour on Lake Superior and hauled to Wawa Lake. Then they went by boat to the other end of the lake, about 8 km away, and were hauled overland again to the Missanaibi area at the railhead.

In 1898 the wife of a local Indian known as William Teddy showed him a handful of yellow stones she had found in the lake. Teddy knew that miners were interested in such stones—and so began Wawa's "gold rush."

A mosaic of pebbles, Lake Superior Provincial Park

Gold continued to play a role in the area for a time. But the real source of the regional economy was something more prosaic—iron ore. The height of land north of the town was found to be a "mountain" of iron ore, which was mined at the turn of the century. Today Wawa supplies iron ore to its own sinter plant and to the steel mills of Sault Ste. Marie. Tours are conducted to the iron ore mine and sintering plant, and an abandoned open-pit mine.

Some 8 km south of Wawa on Highway 17, a signpost points west to Michipicoten River Village. Known locally as The Mission, the village is the area's original settlement, founded by 17th-century fur-trading voyageurs. The Michipicoten River was the main canoe route from the upper Great Lakes to Hudson's Bay.

At the village crossroads, a right turn leads to a wooden bridge with Upper Silver Falls on the right and Lower Silver Falls on the left. The road continues to Michipicoten Harbour, once a busy port with a 90.5-m-long docking facility for the Great Lakes ships, or "lakers."

A left turn at the crossroads takes you to a marina where you can board a sailing charter to explore the mystery of Michipicoten Island, a few kilometres up the coast. A site believed by the Indians to harbor evil spirits, it was avoided for centuries and remains uninhabited. Today rockhounds search its beaches for agates.

Boisterous waves pound the lonely beach on Agawa Bay, Lake Superior Provincial Park.

One of the most spectacular natural attractions of the region lies approximately 5 km south of Wawa, off Highway 17. Here the Magpie River cascades 23.5 m into a rocky gorge. A viewing platform, hiking trails, and picnic sites make it well worth a visit.

2 Lake Superior Provincial Park

Some 96 km of Lake Superior's rugged shore form the western boundary of Lake Superior Provincial Park. Soaring headlands, forest-cloaked hills, steep-walled canyons, and about 500 inland lakes make it one of the most splendid parks in Ontario.

Algonquian-speaking Indians frequented this area from about 9000 B.C. They came in summer to the sheltered coves from where they could fish or go

inland to hunt and pick berries. The Indians left their mark in the form of rock paintings. The totems of three Ojibwa clans—the caribou, lynx, and pickerel—are the most frequently depicted images. Others were painted for a religious purpose. Still others were a record of important events, such as the large painting on Agawa Rock. It depicts the journey to Agawa Bay of four or five canoes from Carp River on the south shore, led by Chief Myeengun and guided by Misshepezhieu—the Great Lynx and a god of the lake.

Devil's Chair Island, just north of Cape Gargantua, was said to have been the resting place of Nanabush after he jumped over the lake. Nanabush was the god who protected the Ojibwa. There may have been an ochre mine on the island, where the Indians prepared the colors that they used for rock paintings and to paint their bodies with.

In the 18th and early 19th centuries fur posts were established here, but by the 1840s beavers became almost extinct here. Traders abandoned their posts, and most of the Indians left. Now the 1,540-km² park, one of Ontario's largest, is visited by hikers, canoeists, anglers, and campers. The hardwood and coniferous forests are home to more than 250 species of birds, small mammals such as red squirrels, red foxes, minks, and martens, and moose and black bears. On Montreal Island, in the south of the park, woodland caribou have been reintroduced.

| 3 | **Pancake Bay and Batchawana Bay Provincial Parks** |

Local folklore says that once a year voyageurs camped here on the last night of their journey back from the west to Sault Ste. Marie. With supplies almost gone they turned the remains of their flour into batches of pancakes. And so Pancake Bay was named. Prevailing winds, wave action, and two protective promontories have created the 3.2-km stretch of fine sand where you would expect a rocky shoreline. This makes the bay perfect for swimming (if you like refreshing temperatures in the range of 15-20°C).

In the park, the Journey Through the Past Trail provides an opportunity to see the area's varied ecology, geology, and heritage. The 3.6-km nature walk is made up of 12 posts of detailed information. It takes you past a mighty boulder, called an erratic, that was deposited by a glacier; a post that describes the tragic wreck of the *Edmund Fitzgerald*—the large freighter that went down 24 km southwest of the bay in 1975; and a 224-m boardwalk across the Black Bog—a cedar swamp—which is joined by nearby Black Creek, where beavers entertain onlookers with their antics.

This trail and the others in the park take walkers through a special fusion of vegetation where many species are at their northernmost limit. Yellow birch and sugar maple predominate in the forests, whereas pines are more prevalent along the shoreline. Chipmunks, squirrels, beavers, muskrats, and cranes have been spotted, and robins, blue jays, and pileated woodpeckers are often heard nearby. And there is a plentiful supply of wild berries and hazelnuts along the way.

A recreation park, Pancake Bay also offers fishing and cycling, and a large play area for children.

About 12 km south of Pancake Bay is Batchawana Provincial Park. It is made up of some 170 ha of mixed forest and a 2-km-long stretch of sandy beach on Lake Superior. *Batchawana* is an Ojibwa word, which means "narrows

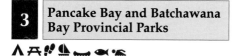

A red fox, a denizen of park woods

and swift waters." It refers to the fast-flowing waters that course through the narrow mouth of the bay when pushed by the strong Superior winds.

The bay's waters are shallow and excellent for swimming. They are sheltered by some of the highest hills in Ontario, with peaks reaching 632 m above sea level.

Fly-in wilderness fishing trips, and hunting trips for moose, bear, partridge, geese, and ducks, are available.

At the entrance to the park is an information centre, where staff will instruct you how to find the 36.5-m-high Chippewa Falls, which has a pedestrian walkway and a fish-viewing platform. They will also tell you about trails to forgotten mines, the best places for birdwatching, where to hunt for agates, and where to find the most superb scenery.

4 Chapleau

Once a Hudson's Bay post, the settlement of Chapleau became permanent in 1882-83 with the arrival of the Canadian Pacific Railway. This was its only link with the outside world before 1950, when Highway 129 was completed. The town (present pop. 3,400)

was named for Sir Joseph Adolphe Chapleau, who was Premier of Quebec from 1879 to 1882.

On Monk Street is the Chapleau Centennial Museum and Tourist Information Centre. The museum recalls the area's history with exhibits such as a huge stuffed timber wolf, railway memorabilia, furnishings that adorned a country home early in this century, a handmade birchbark canoe, and a wilderness exhibit with a replica of a trapper's cabin. Outside the museum is a wood and steel sculpture that represents the cultures that make up Chapleau, and its lumber and railway industries. *Open daily from Victoria Day to Thanksgiving, 9 am to 7 pm.*

On Young Street is a beautiful Victorian building erected in 1919 by a local lumber baron in memory of his son, killed in World War I. The building now houses the Harry Searle Branch 5 of the Royal Canadian Legion. Also on Young Street, backing onto the Chapleau River, is the Anglican Church, built in 1905.

Downtown, toward the banks of the Nebskwashi River, are the old Protestant and Catholic cemeteries. Louis Hémon, author of the novel *Maria Chapdelaine*, is buried in the Catholic cemetery. He died in 1913 when he was struck by a train near Chapleau.

The many forests, lakes, and rivers nearby offer good fishing, hunting, and other recreational activities.

5 The Shoals Provincial Park

The Shoals Provincial Park is set amid evergreens and bogs in the heart of Ontario's boreal forest. Its many lakes offer campsites in tranquil settings, excellent fishing, and canoeing. Trails run through the forests and some of the 28 different plant habitats.

Much of the park's 10,644 ha were created by retreating ice sheets. There are four eskers in the park, ridges of sand and gravel left behind by melting glaciers. Two of these are in Little Wawa Lake, forming the sand shoals that gave the park its name.

In 1885, the Canadian Pacific Railway came to the shores of Windermere Lake, and logging was started there. The town of Nicholson developed on the lakeshore, and by 1916 was the largest supplier of railway ties in Canada. But the supply of timber became depleted and, with the Great Crash of 1929 and a 1931 fire that destroyed the sawmill, the town of 350 people collapsed. The buildings that remain are overgrown and decaying.

Canoeists can explore the park along the South Loop, which takes a day and goes through seven small lakes, or along the North Loop, which is a two-day trip that ends at Prairie Bee Lake.

Alternatively, hike through the park. You will see most wildlife along the marshy areas. On other trails you may also come across the shy timber wolf, red fox, lynx, or marten. The lakes are full of northern pike, whitefish, perch, walleye, and trout.

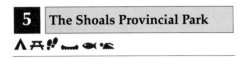

CPR steam engine No. 5433 and a plaque honoring Louis Hémon appear on the grounds of Chapleau Centennial Museum.

The floatplanes of northern Ontario's skies fly visitors to remote hunting and fishing lodges.

6 Wakami Lake Provincial Park

∧ ⊼ ⵏⵏ ⛺ 🚣 ⚓ 🐟 ❋

The Ojibwa Indians who came to the lake in summer to hunt and fish called it *Wakamagaming*, which means "still and clear." This beautiful site of 8,762 ha is surrounded by steep hills clothed with jackpine forests, interspersed with islands of southern deciduous trees, such as yellow birch, sugar maple, and white pine.

The lake lies on the Arctic watershed, known as The Height of Land. It divides the waters that flow north to the Arctic from those that flow to the Great Lakes and the Atlantic Ocean.

In the early years of this century, the lake was dammed and its forests were logged. Remnants of this industry can still be seen, at the Historic Lumbering Exhibit. A 1-km trail leads round this outdoor site, past old logging equipment and lumbering buildings.

Visitors can swim, picnic, boat, canoe, fish, and hike in the park. The 65-km Wakami Loop canoe route takes about three days to complete, and the Wakami River route, about nine days. The Height of Land Hiking Trail circles around Wakami Lake for 78 km.

The shorter trails include the Beaver Meadow Trail, which leads around an esker and an abandoned beaver pond, and the Transition Trail, through pockets of southern deciduous forest.

Wakami Lake has abundant fish, including yellow pickerel and northern pike. There is a fish smoker between Brown's Bay and Maple Ridge campgrounds. The park is open from early May to late September.

Special events
Woodsmen's Days (July)
Pancake Breakfast (August)

7 St. Joseph's Island

⊼ 🐕 ∧ ❋

In the early 19th century, the most westerly outpost of British North America was Fort St. Joseph, on St. Joseph's Island. The island is reached by bridge from Highway 17. As you drive onto the island, if you take the right turn onto Highway 548, you will reach the village of Richard's Landing and Sailor's Encampment, a good spot to watch freighters sailing by. Look out for moose and deer on the roads—they wander freely on the island.

At the southern tip of the island are the ruins of Fort St. Joseph. The fort was built from 1798 to 1803 to protect the trade route from Montreal to the upper Great Lakes and to maintain the British alliance with various native nations. A village grew up around the fort sustained by trade, canoe-building, and other enterprises. The fort was attacked by American forces in 1814, two years after it was abandoned by the British, and it was never rebuilt.

Today, interpretive signs lead visitors to the main points of interest. The visitors' centre displays objects, such as tools, furs, and military uniforms, uncovered in archeological digs. The centre also has reconstructions of daily life in the fort. Films on the fur trade and the archeology of the site are shown daily. *Open daily, Victoria Day weekend and Labor Day to Thanksgiving, 10 am to 5 pm; Canada Day to Labor Day, 10 am to 6 pm.*

Trails run through a dense maple forest around the fort area, and through a 324-ha bird sanctuary. Visitors wishing to hike around the island should ask permission, since most of the land is privately owned.

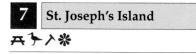

A mallard, a summer resident of Ontario waters

At the junction of Highway 548 and 5th Sideroad is Adcock's Woodland Garden. Route 548 also passes through Hilton Beach, which has a marina, restaurants, and shops. About 6 km before the bridge to the mainland is the St. Joseph Island Museum Village. The site includes an 1880 log cabin, an 1878 schoolhouse, and other pioneer buildings. *Open June, weekend afternoons only, July 1 to early September, daily.*

The island offers good fishing, and minerals abound for rockhounds.

Special events
Maple Syrup Festival (April)
Cornfest (late August)

8 Bruce Mines

Canada's first successful copper mines were Bruce Mines, on the north shore of Lake Huron. Although the mines are now closed, the town (pop. 565) that grew up around them still exists. Many of its earliest settlers were tin miners from Cornwall, in England.

South of the highway and just east of the downtown core, is the Bruce Mines Museum, housed in a former Presbyterian church of 1892. The museum, founded in 1955, contains exhibits of the town's life since its settlement in 1847. A variety of displays recall the community's connection with the Marquess of Queensbury. A son of the formulator of the Queensbury rules of boxing, he was once the Bruce Mines' manager. A recent acquisition is a *yakaboo*, a one-man boat that sailed in the Caribbean between 1908 and 1918. *Open daily from mid-May to June and mid-September to October, 9 am to 3 pm; late June to Labor Day, 9 am to 7 pm.*

Just across the highway from the museum is an open-air mine shaft, now open only for tours. A mining scene re-created in the open pit reflects the technology of 1840s. *Open daily, July and August, 9 am to 7 pm.*

Bruce Mines also has a marina and facilities for fishing. In fall visitors enjoy scenic tours, hunting, and fall fairs. Winter sports include snowmobiling, ice fishing, and cross-country skiing.

Special events
Four and Friends Art Show (mid-July)

9 Thessalon

Thessalon (pop. 1,444) is situated on the mouth of the Thessalon River and surrounded on three sides by water. This lumber town is a base for hunters, anglers, and boaters. Reflected in the gentle river are the homes of the original, late 19th-century settlers, whose lumbering activity sent many a log between the river banks.

In Lakeside Park, just across the highway is a historic plaque which commemorates the capture of two American schooners during the War of 1812. There is also a sandy beach ideal for a relaxing stroll or sun-bathing.

Just 2 km north of Thessalon are the hamlet of Little Rapids and the Thessalon Township Heritage Park and Museum. The buildings of the park tell the heydays of the region's lumbering era. *Open daily, July 1 to Labor Day, 10 am to 5 pm.*

Midway between Thessalon and Chapleau is a spectacular spot on the Mississagi River, just 1.6 km off Highway 129. The Aubrey Falls drop 39 m amid wild and beautiful scenery. The water runs from Victoria Day to Thanksgiving, and is diverted to a hydroelectric dam nearby, for the rest of the year.

10 Gore Bay

The town of Gore Bay (pop. 800) on Manitoulin Island hunches down between two tree-covered bluffs and looks out toward the North Channel of Lake Huron. In its early years the settlement was called *Pushk-dinong* (Barren Hill) by the local Ottawa Indians. This was probably due to the great fire of a century before, which had laid waste the whole island. The name was changed later and may have originated from a steamship called the *Gore*, which became trapped by ice in the bay during the 1850s and was forced to overwinter there.

In 1870 a few Scottish settlers came to the area. The community prospered, and Gore Bay eventually became a busy port. In 1889 it was made the judicial capital of Manitoulin Island. The Western Manitoulin Historical Society Museum, in a restored jail and jail-keeper's house, exhibits marine ar-

tifacts from the town's heyday. *Open year-round, Monday to Saturday, 10 am to 4:30 pm; Sunday, 2 pm to 4 pm.*

A walk through the heart of Gore Bay, with its Victorian homes and limestone churches, recalls the town's rich history. Its thriving business sector and striking waterfront development promise continuing prosperity.

At the Pavilion, on the boardwalk, visitors can pick up tourist information, grab a bite in the Tea Room, watch local artisans, or climb the spiral stairs to enjoy a superb view from the lookout. For a picnic spot with a view, follow Hall Street to East Bluff Road which leads up the escarpment.

The rugged Cup and Saucer Trail offers sweeping views across Manitoulin Island.

Just beyond the town, at the mouth of the bay, is Janet Head lighthouse, built in 1880, and thought to be named after a daughter of Lieutenant Bayfield, surveyor of Lake Huron.

The waters around Gore Bay abound with bass, pike, lake trout, and muskellunge.

Special events
Annual Carp Derby
(third weekend of June)
Lions' Fest (July)
Blooper Ball Tournament (August)

11 West Bay

A century and a half has passed since the community of West Bay, originally called *M'Chigeeng* (Place of the Fish Harpoon), was settled. It was part of an experiment in 1848 by the Canadian government to make Manitoulin Island a refuge for Ojibwa Indians from Minnesota who wanted to live here. The village (pop. 800) is the hub of West Bay First Nation Reserve 22.

West Bay is well known as a mecca for Indian artists, some of whose work is displayed at Kasheese Studio at the intersection of highways 540 and 551.

An architectural feature of West Bay is the 12-sided, tepee-shaped Immaculate Conception Catholic Church, on Highway 551. Rebuilt in 1972 following a fire, it features works by Leland Bell and other native Indian artists. Near the church stands the Ojibwa Cultural Foundation and Gallery. An educational and resource centre for native people in the region, it is also a showcase and retail outlet for their artists and artisans.

Two trail networks are close by. The M'Chigeeng Trails consist of 8 km of trails. The Cup and Saucer Trail, 5 km east of West Bay on Highway 540, offers 10 km of pathways. Both trail networks offer challenging climbs, which culminate at a 351-m-high lookout, the highest on Manitoulin Island.

Special events
West Bay Powwow (mid-July)

12 Killarney Provincial Park

The white quartzite hills and crystal lakes of Killarney Provincial Park on the north shore of Lake Huron's Georgian Bay have inspired some of Canada's best landscape artists—among them A. Y. Jackson, Frank Carmichael, Arthur Lismer, and A. J. Casson of the Group of Seven. So great was Jackson's passion that he and the Ontario Society of Artists (O.S.A.) lobbied hard to preserve Killarney's "big old pine trees" and unspoiled beauty. In 1964 the Ontario government agreed to set aside 345 km² of wilderness—and the "crown jewel" of Ontario provincial parks was born.

For some of the best hiking in Ontario, try the Silver Peak Trail (35 km), or the Baie Fine Trail (13 km), which are segments of the 100-km La Cloche Silhouette Trail. A shorter walk is the 4-km return Cranberry Bog Trail. They all offer views of the hardwood forest around George Lake, the rocky Georgian Bay coastline, and the white hills of the La Cloche Mountains—one of the most unusual alpine formations east of the Rockies.

Along the way are sugar maples, yellow birch, and trees rarely found this far north—black cherry and American beech. At their feet bloom white trailing arbutus, red and white trilliums, and delicate summer orchids. Occasionally, tracks are left by moose, whitetail deer, otter, and wolf.

Most visitors to the park prefer to travel through by canoe, using portage routes that link its 280-odd lakes and ponds. Leaving from the main campground at George Lake, canoeists can discover Killarney Lake's inlets and wooded islands, the crystal waters of

Sportsman's Inn at the village of Killarney (just outside the provincial park) provides a base for exploring this scenic wilderness.

Roads to explore: Byways of the biggest island in a lake

Distance (approx.): 220 km / 137 ½ miles

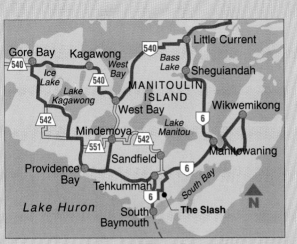

Manitoulin Island is the world's biggest island in a lake. For a one-day island trip, head south from Gore Bay on Highway 542. Just after Long Bay, turn east on Perivale Road, rejoining Highway 542 at Spring Bay.

● Take Highway 551 east to sandy Providence Bay, to view the harbor centre's historic, archeological, and environmental displays, or book a fishing charter.

● Continue east on the Government Road, then on to Tehkummah, to visit quaint Ward's General Store. From here, tour Blue Jay Creek Fish Culture Station at the junction of the Government Road and Highway 542. A side-trip north on Highway 542 takes in the government fish hatchery at Sandfield.

● Leaving Highway 542, turn right on Highway 6 for the daily ferry from South Baymouth to Tobermory, or back-track 2 km to Lakeshore Road. Here the provincial Fisheries Research Unit welcomes visitors. Follow scenic Lakeshore Road (best in dry weather) until the road ends at The Slash. Take the Slash Road back to Highway 6.

Bridal Veil Falls, Manitoulin Island

● Turn right on the highway until you reach the town of Manitowaning. The Assiginack Museum, St. Paul's Anglican Church, and S.S. *Norisle* Heritage Park here are rich with history. Horse races are held on the first weekend in July.

● Now take the road to Wikwemikong Unceded Indian Reserve, traditional home of the Odawa Nation, and the Holy Cross Mission begun by the Jesuits in the 1600s. The village has an unusual eagle-shaped health centre. The popular powwow, held over the August holiday weekend, features traditional native dancers. The Wikwemikong-based De-ba-jeh-mu-jig professional theatre also holds summer performances. Continue via Kaboni back to Manitowaning.

● In town, turn left to return to Highway 6, and about 4 km farther on, turn left on Bidwell Road. At Green Bay, take the scenic gravel road above Bass Lake to Sheguiandah, home of the Sheguiandah First Nation. The local museum contains ancient fossils, tribal artifacts, and old tools. *Open year-round, Monday to Sunday, 10 am to 4:30 pm.*

● North on Highway 6 for 10 km brings you to Little Current, where a rustic, single-lane swing bridge offers the only road off the island. Visitors can enjoy the community's unusual shops, and the Haweater Festival, held on August holiday weekend.

● From Little Current, follow Highway 540 west through the community of West Bay to scenic Bridal Veil Falls at Kagawong, a good place for a rest before completing the trip past Ice Lake back to Gore Bay.

O.S.A. Lake, and countless channels clogged with beaver lodges. The lucky might hear the lone cry of a bald eagle or spot the black wings of a turkey vulture soaring high above the ridges.

13 Elk Lake

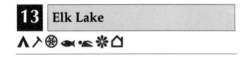

A tranquil, small lakeside town at the junction of the Montreal and Makobe rivers, Elk Lake (pop. 524) has the serenity that comes after a full life.

Centuries before Europeans arrived here, the lakes and rivers in the area were trade routes established by native Indians. They left pictographs painted onto rocks at several points on their canoe routes, such as at Beaver House Lake, and settlements whose remains are still being uncovered.

The Cree named Elk Lake for the herds of elk that browsed on its shores. When European fur traders moved to the area, followed by lumber camps in

The unspoiled beauty of Killarney Provincial Park has inspired many Canadian painters.

headframes are rusting monoliths in the bush. The Gowganda and Area Museum, in the Old Union Hall, contains Indian and pioneer artifacts, a large collection of early photographs, and an outdoor exhibition of mining equipment and a log cabin. *Open Monday to Friday, mid-May to mid-September, 9 am to 5 pm.*

Gowganda's main attraction these days is its fishing. The word *gowganda* is Ojibwa for "pickerel's tooth." Appropriately, Gowganda Lake is kept stocked with pickerel. Boating, camping and swimming are also popular pastimes here.

14 Temagami

On the tip of the northeast arm of Lake Temagami, a body of water shaped like a six-tentacled octopus, is the town of Temagami (pop. 1,100). This entire region is blessed with natural beauty. The last Ice Age left behind scores of glacial lakes, which today are fringed with some of Ontario's last stands of old-growth red and white pine, and studded with cedar- and pine-covered islands.

Lake Temagami (its name is Ojibwa for "deep waters by the shore") is more than 77 m deep, 50 km long, but a mere 8 km at its widest point.

The possibility that the settlement of Temagami might be a getaway for "city-choked, dust-laden" vacationers was considered in

An old-world facade of stucco, stone, and timber greets visitors at Temagami's station.

the early 1890s. With the arrival of the railway in 1905 and the construction of the road from North Bay in 1920, it developed as a summer resort.

the 1870s and the railway at the turn of the century, the elk and the resident caribou moved away to the north.

In 1907, silver was discovered at Gowganda, about 45 km away. An instant village of tents sprang up on both sides of the Montreal river, as Elk Lake became a dormitory town. Elk Lake's population swelled to between 5,000 and 10,000. To accommodate this influx of desperate prospectors, hotels and boarding houses mushroomed. In the space of two years, banks, a hospital, a newspaper, a post office, and a power company were established in the town. Its mayor at this time was Jack Monroe (1875-1942)—prospector, war hero, football player, heavyweight boxer, and writer.

Most of Elk Lake's old buildings have gone, but its colorful past is remembered in the Elk Lake Museum and Heritage Centre, housed in a for-

mer Roman Catholic church built in 1909, during the town's heyday. Furnished interiors of the time include a saloon, classroom, general store, blacksmith's forge, and a domestic kitchen. Equipment and clothing used by miners and trappers, early photographs, and antiques also form part of the display. *Admission free, donations accepted. Open July and August, Tuesday to Thursday, 11 am to 5 pm, Friday to Sunday, 10 am to 5 pm.*

Today, Elk Lake draws visitors to its lakes and rivers for fishing—northern pike, pickerel, lake and speckled trout, whitefish, bass, and perch abound—and canoeing. In season, hunters may shoot moose, bear, and birds. In summer, the surrounding countryside invites camping, boating, water-skiing, swimming, and rockhounding. And in winter, snowmobiling, cross-country skiing, and ice fishing are possible.

Most of the mines at Gowganda (pop. 139) are silent now, the mine buildings are empty, and the gaunt

A view from a plane captures the maze of islands, lakes, and woods near Temagami.

In the early days, tourist steamboats churned the waters of the lake. Today, canoes glide along 20 routes, up hundreds of wilderness waterways. If a paddle isn't to your liking, a pair of hiking boots will get you up the 1-km trail on Caribou Mountain to the panoramic view of Temagami, or any of the other scenic trails. You can also drive deep into the forest on the network of long-established, well-maintained gravel logging roads.

In winter, groomed trails at James Lake, Wanapitei, and Jumping Caribou attract cross-country and alpine skiers.

Just half a kilometre south of Temagami, on the lake, is Finlayson Point Provincial Park. It has camping facilities, good beaches, and a plaque that commemorates the writer and conservationist Grey Owl.

Special events
Grey Owl Festival (Canada Day weekend)
Lake Temagami Lake Trout Derby
(early September)

15 Marten River Provincial Park

Once massive pine forests covered almost all of Ontario. But civilization and logging have depleted them and remnants of the forests are scattered far and wide. However, some old-growth stands remain in Marten River Provincial Park, where towering white pines can be found that are more than 300 years old.

The park lies within a transitional zone between northern and southern forest. Its northern species include black spruce which mingles with pockets of southern species such as yellow birch. The 5-km Forest Hiking Trail takes you past these and other species as well as majestic ancient white pines. Along the way you may see moose, foxes, otters, and snowshoe hares.

The way of life of the men who cut down these forests is remembered in the Logging Camp Exhibit in the park. A restored camp, complete with an office, bunkhouse, kitchen, meat house, scaler's shack (the scaler measured the diameter of the trees that were cut and calculated the volume of timber produced), stable, and blacksmith's shop, re-creates what it was like to be a lumberjack from 1915 to 1920. *Tours are conducted from mid-June to early September, Monday to Friday at 1:30 pm and on weekends at 10:30 am and 1:30 pm.*

The park also offers plenty of opportunity for canoeing, swimming, boating, cycling, and fishing for yellow pickerel, bass, lake trout, and pike. And in winter there are groomed trails for cross-country skiing, snowmobiling, and snowshoeing.

16 Mattawa

The 23-m-high steeple of St. Anne's Roman Catholic Church rises above tree-lined streets and pierces the sky over Mattawa, "the meeting of the waters," at the confluence of the Mattawa and Ottawa rivers.

For over 200 years explorers, missionaries, voyageurs, and fur traders traveled these rivers. The early 1800s brought a Hudson's Bay post, loggers, and the first settlers. And the early 1890s saw the arrival of the Canadian Pacific Railway.

Today, Mattawa (pop. 2,413) continues its tradition as a meeting-place, from the day-to-day merging of its French and English population to its mixture of the present with the past. On the north banks of the Mattawa, at the site of the Hudson's Bay Company trading post, a red-pine log cabin houses the Mattawa and District Museum. Its displays interpret the early settlement of the Mattawa area. *Open daily, June to August, 9 am to 5 pm.*

The museum lies within a waterfront park. Nearby is a marina for boats traveling the 260-km Lake Timiscaming-Ottawa River Waterway.

The natural surroundings that attracted the fur traders and loggers now draw outdoor enthusiasts. Walkers can hike the Eau Clair Gorge, visit Brent Crater, said to be the second largest meteorite crater in Canada, or explore nearby Algonquin Park. Canoeists can trace many of the paths followed by the early explorers and fur traders, and anglers can enjoy the well-stocked waters. In winter skiers can race down Mount Antoine.

Outside Mattawa is the Samuel de Champlain Provincial Park, whose heritage centre shows films and exhibits from voyageur life, such as a reconstructed voyageur freight canoe.

Special events
Northeastern Ontario Fiddling and Step-Dancing Championships (mid-August)
North Bay–Mattawa Canoe Race (mid-August)

17 Cobalt

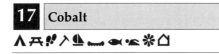

According to legend, in 1903 a blacksmith, Fred LaRose, threw a miner's hammer at a nosey fox. The hammer missed the fox but hit a rock, and exposed the world's richest silver vein. The rush was on, and the town of Cobalt (present pop. 1,481) was born.

Willet Green Miller, the provincial geologist who gave the town its name, reported seeing pieces of silver as "big as stove lids or cannon balls lying on the ground." Cobalt sprang into existence almost overnight, as prospectors, claim-jumpers, and fortune hunters streamed into the area. The townsite around Cobalt Lake soon sprouted hotels, stores, restaurants, an opera house, and a theatre. Between 1908 and 1910 Cobalt was home to as many as 10,000 people.

In 1910, Cobalt opened the first electric street car system north of Toronto. Later it boasted the first northern stock exchange. The mines still produce silver, but its fluctuating value has forced Cobalt to seek other forms of income.

Today, Cobalt is a town of winding streets that guide visitors past period buildings to a turn-of-the-century mining camp.

The town also boasts three museums. The Northern Ontario Mining Museum has an extensive collection of old photos, mining equipment, dis-

An old mine elevator on Cobalt's Heritage Silver Trail is a monument to a mining past.

plays, mining lore, and what is claimed to be the world's largest collection of native ore specimens. *Open daily, June to September, 9 am to 5 pm; October to May, Monday to Friday, 9 am to noon.*

The Bunker Military Museum, located in the 1910 railway station, has a military collection dating back to the 1880s. *Open daily, June to August, 9 am to 5 pm; September to May, visits by appointment only.*

The Cobalt-Coleman Firefighter Museum documents the many disastrous fires suffered during the early 1900s, as well as the fire of 1977, which gutted almost a third of the town. *Open daily, June to September, 9 am to 4 pm.*

The Township of Coleman municipal offices occupy Cobalt's oldest "prefab." This wooden building, built in British Columbia and reassembled here in 1905 to house the Canadian Bank of Commerce, became a prototype for the bank's branches in other mining communities.

The Heritage Silver Trail, located just off Highway 11B, is one of the area's most popular attractions. This 6-km self-guiding driving/hiking tour visits five vintage 1900s mine sites. By means of billboards, site signs, and information points, visitors can travel through the past and experience the history of the Cobalt camp. Each stop illustrates a different aspect of mining, and is complete with picnic tables, lookout, and side trails.

Special events
Miners' Festival (early August)

18 Parc d'Aiguebelle

This 243-km² park is the largest in Quebec's Abitibi-Témiscamingue region. Some 10,000 years ago, Ice Age glaciers sheared away the 2.5-billion-year-old rock to reveal layers of the earth's crust. At the same time, they carved more than 80 lakes contained in the park. The name of the region—

Abitibi (from the Algonquin "place where the waters separate")—takes on full meaning here. A watershed within the park separates the rivers that run south to the St. Lawrence from those that flow north to James Bay.

A forest of black spruce, balsam fir, jack pine, and paper birch dominates Aiguebelle. But rarer species such as yellow birch, black ash, cedar, larch, red maple, and white pine also thrive in the park. Blueberries, raspberries, wild cherries, and hazelnuts abound here too. The park's natural wealth remained untouched by development largely because of its poor soils and its inaccessibility.

A beaver dam breaks the course of a placid stream near Lac La Haie, Parc d'Aiguebelle.

The most easily accessible entrance to Parc d'Aiguebelle is at Mont-Brun on the south side of the park, which can be reached from Route 117. Mont-Brun is the site of the visitors' bureau and interpretive centre. The western entrance is at Destor (accessible from Route 101); and the northern gate is at Taschereau (from Route 111).

Most of the park facilities are near Sault and La Haie lakes, although there are campsites elsewhere. The Abijévis campground, at Lac Matissard near Mont-Brun, has 47 campsites. Remote Lac de la Muraille has a number of rustic campsites that appeal to the more adventurous campers.

A 30.8-km network of hiking trails throughout the park leads through a

Roads to explore: Stately mansions and a magical forest

Distance (approx.): 90 km / 56¼ miles

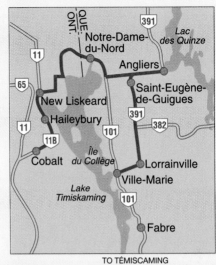

TO TÉMISCAMING

Lake Timiskaming, whose name is Algonquian for "deep waters," is one of the deepest lakes in Ontario. It forms a natural boundary between Ontario and Quebec, near Cobalt. The drive around the lake starts at Cobalt.

● Head north on Highway 11B to Haileybury (pop. 4,900), where stately homes built by mining magnates grace the lakeshore.

● Just over 3 km north of Haileybury is one of the best views of the lake and its many islands. Slightly to the northeast is Chief Island, and to the southeast, Burnt Island, reputed to offer excellent pickerel fishing.

● Follow Highway 11B into New Liskeard (pop. 5,500). On Whitewood Avenue is the limestone Public Library, built with a grant from the American Carnegie Foundation early this century. Follow Whitewood south to Fleming Drive, which runs along the waterfront. Two nearby marinas bristle with boats. In summer, the Timiskaming Tour Boat, which cruises around the lake, leaves twice daily.

● From New Liskeard, take Highway 11B across the Wabi River, and then Highway 65E into Quebec. Don't miss the interesting artifacts displayed at the Saugeeng Algonquin Handy Craft Shop. Stop to admire the view of the Quinze River as you leave on Route 101.

● On Route 101, look for the junction where a country road will lead you to Route 391, then on to Angliers, a charming community on the shores of Lac des

Quinze. Visit the *T.E. Draper*, a wooden tugboat, and the interpretive centre with its re-creation of logging life.

● Follow Route 391 south, past St.-Eugène-de-Guigues, through flat farmland to Lorrainville, where you take Route 382 to Ville-Marie (pop. 2,700). The oldest community in the Abitibi-Témiscamingue region, the town was established in 1886 by Oblate priests. Enjoy the view from the stairs at the end of Notre-Dame-de-Lourdes Street. Farther along the street you come to the town hall where La Salle Augustin-Chenier offers summer theatre. Beside the town hall is a square-log cabin built in 1881, now an historic site.

● Visit nearby Fort Témiscamingue National Historic Site, where attractions include the remains of a trading post dating from 1720, an interpretive centre, a beach, and the Enchanted Forest, with its glade of curiously twisted pines. *Admission free. Tours mid-May to early September, Monday 1 pm to 5 pm, Tuesday to Sunday, 9 am to 5 pm.; September to mid-November, open by appointment.*

● The drive onward to old-world Île du Collège, just north of Ville-Marie, passes through a beautiful landscape of gentle hills, cosy inlets, and modest farms.

● South of Ville-Marie, Route 101 follows the shore past Fabre, Laniel, and Lac Kipawa, a fisherman's paradise. The drive ends 40 km farther south, at the town of Témiscaming.

Enchanted Forest, Fort Témiscamingue

land of rock-strewn valleys, lakes, and waterfalls. There are also 7.2 km of interpretive trails. A number of lookouts and a 64-m-long suspended bridge at Lac La Haie provide superb views. In winter, 32 km of groomed trails attract cross-country skiers.

The lakes, rivers, and brooks of Parc d'Aiguebelle are ideal for canoeing and fishing enthusiasts. There is a good supply of northern pike and walleye at Lois, Matissard, and Patrice lakes, and speckled and gray trout at Sault and La Haie lakes. Lois and Matissard lakes offer opportunities for swimming, sailing, and windsurfing.

19 Val d'Or
✳ ⌂

A gold rush second only to the Klondike occurred here in the mid-1930s, and nine gold mines still operate around Val d'Or (pop. 35,000).

The first mine in this community was Sigma—dubbed "Queen of Gold Valley"—at the entrance to the city. It opened in 1937 and is still working. In summer, tours of Sigma's gold-refining plant and the region can be arranged through the visitors' centre at Val d'Or.

The first major community in the area was Bourlamaque. In 1923, Robert C. Clark and Gabriel Commanda discovered the rich vein of gold that sparked the Val d'Or boom. Ten years later, the Teck Corporation built simple wooden dwellings for its employees working at the nearby Lamaque Mine. The settlement became the village of Bourlamaque. At its peak, the village had about 2,000 residents, mostly miners and their families. The Lamaque Mine eventually closed in 1989, after yielding $220,000,000 worth of gold. By that time, Bourlamaque had been incorporated into Val d'Or.

The Quebec government recognized Bourlamaque as an historic site in 1979. The Bourlamaque Miners' Village is an unusual historic site because it is still an active community; its 85 small

Bourlamaque Miners' Village, still an active community, has been designated an historic site.

houses, mainly located along St. Jacques between Perry Drive and Rue Perrault, are occupied. In one of the houses open to the public, at 123 Rue Perrault, the furnishings re-create the life of the first miners.

As you stroll through the Miners' Village, you will pass different sites: the bunkhouse, the mine manager's house, the police station, the dispensary, and the cafeteria. *Open daily, late June to early September, 9 am to 9 pm. The*

rest of the year, Monday to Friday, 9 a.m. to 5 p.m. Weekends by appointment.

In Val d'Or, at the end of Boulevard des Pins, a 20-m-high lookout tower provides a sweeping view of the Cadillac Fault, where the mines are located.

Malartic Mining Museum, 30 km west of Val d'Or on 117, simulates the descent into a mine. *Open daily, early June to mid-September, 9 am to 5 pm. The rest of the year, Monday to Friday, 9 am to 5 pm. Weekends by appointment.*

CENTRAL ONTARIO

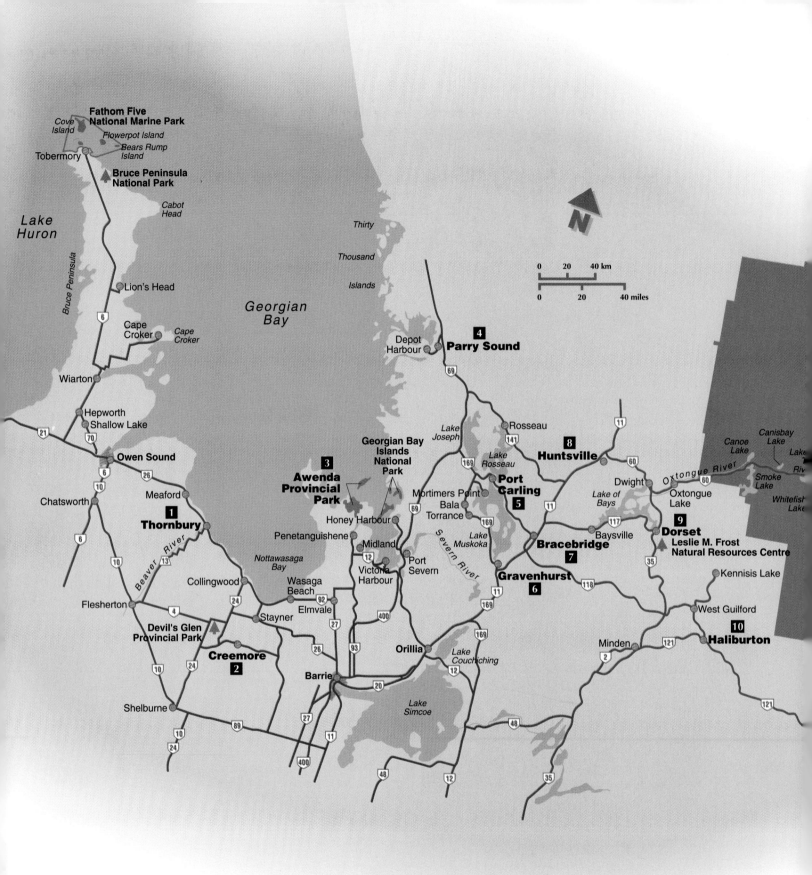

Fathom Five National Marine Park
Cove Island
Flowerpot Island
Bears Rump Island
Tobermory
Bruce Peninsula National Park
Cabot Head
Bruce Peninsula
6
Lion's Head
Cape Croker
Cape Croker
Wiarton
Hepworth
Shallow Lake
21
70
6
Owen Sound
26
10
Chatsworth
Meaford
6
1
Thornbury
Beaver River
13
10
4
Flesherton
Devil's Glen Provincial Park
24
10
24
Creemore
2
Shelburne
10
24
89

Lake Huron

Georgian Bay

Thirty Thousand Islands

Depot Harbour
4
Parry Sound
69

Lake Joseph
Rosseau
141
8
Huntsville
169
Lake Rosseau
Port Carling
5
Mortimers Point
Bala
Torrance
69
169
Gravenhurst
6
Bracebridge
7
Baysville
11
Lake of Bays
117
11
Dwight
Oxtongue River
60
Oxtongue Lake
9
Dorset
Leslie M. Frost Natural Resources Centre
35
118
Kennisis Lake
West Guilford
10
Haliburton
Minden
121
2
121

Canoe Lake
Canisbay Lake
Smoke Lake
Whitefish Lake
Lake
Riv

3
Awenda Provincial Park
Georgian Bay Islands National Park
Honey Harbour
Penetanguishene
Midland
12
Victoria Harbour
Port Severn
Severn River
Lake Muskoka
400
Orillia
Lake Couchiching
12
169
Nottawasaga Bay
Collingwood
24
Wasaga Beach
Stayner
92
Elmvale
27
26
93
Barrie
20
Lake Simcoe
48
27
11
400
48
35

0   20   40 km
0   20   40 miles
N

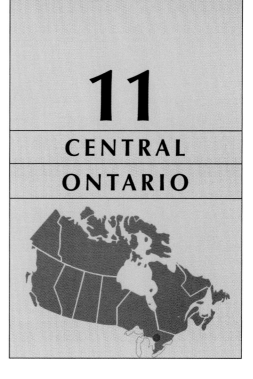

11

CENTRAL
ONTARIO

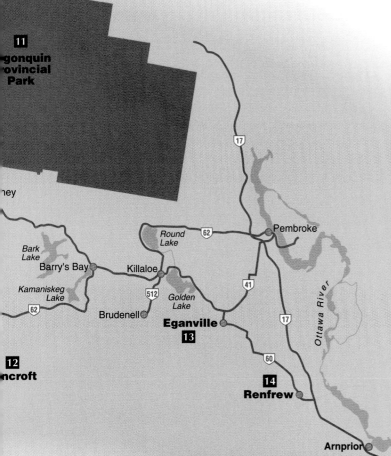

11
Algonquin
Provincial
Park

Bark
Lake

Barry's Bay

Kamaniskeg
Lake

62

Brudenell

512

Golden
Lake

Round
Lake

62

Killaloe

Eganville
13

41

60

14

Renfrew

17

Pembroke

17

Ottawa River

Arnprior

17

12
ncroft

ney

Places to see
Thornbury
Creemore
Awenda Provincial Park
Parry Sound
Thirty Thousand Islands (boat trip)
Port Carling
Gravenhurst
Bracebridge
Huntsville
Dorset
Haliburton
Algonquin Provincial Park
Bancroft
Eganville
The Opeongo Line
Renfrew

Roads to explore
Beaver Valley: Thornbury to Flesherton
Around the Lake of Bays
The Opeongo Line:
Renfrew–Dacre–Foymount–Brudenell–
Wilno–Killaloe

National park close-up
Fathom Five
Bruce Peninsula
Georgian Bay Islands

Previous pages:
Hogs Falls in Beaver Valley, near Flesherton

1 Thornbury

With Georgian Bay in front of it and the Niagara Escarpment rising behind it, Thornbury (pop. 1,500) has an exquisite setting that promises much in the way of recreation.

In its early days the town was a port for Great Lakes steamships. The Beaver River provided numerous sites for sawmills. But the advent of the railway, good roads, and cars ended Thornbury's old industries. Now the harbor caters to pleasure boaters, and the CNR line, with its wooden trestle over the river, is today the 32-km Georgian Cycle and Ski Trail.

The town was first surveyed in 1833 and by 1887 was a thriving agricultural and business centre. An example of the prosperity of some former citizens

An aerial view shows the bountiful apple orchards bordering the town of Thornbury.

is the nursing home, once the house of lumber baron Henry Pedwell. It was built in 1900, and used a windmill to pump water into an attic tank, which provided the luxury of running water and indoor plumbing.

The Victorian brick mansion on the banks of the millpond belonged to Thornbury's first reeve, Thomas Andrews. It too was built in 1900.

The old milldam's "fish lock" is the centrepiece of the community. It operates much like a canal lock, lifting the fish 7 m over the dam into the millpond from where they can reach the upper Beaver River. Every spring and fall the river is a fishermen's paradise, filled with trout and salmon. It also draws spectators who enjoy watching salmon battle to reach the spawning grounds upstream.

The unusually mild climate between Georgian Bay and the Niagara Escarpment makes the Beaver Valley one of Ontario's largest apple-producing areas. The valley has more than 175 com-

In summer, some of Thornbury's gracious dwellings lodge bed-and-breakfast guests.

mercial orchards. At the Farmers' Market on Highway 26, apple pies, candy apples, and fresh cider are for sale.

Special events
Annual Southern Georgian Bay Chili Cook-off (mid-July)

Georgian Bay Sailing Regatta (late July)

Georgian Triangle Spring Trout Derby (mid-April)

Fathom Five

A necklace of 19 islands on 130 km of cold, clear, crystal-blue Lake Huron form Fathom Five, Canada's first national marine park. From Cove Island to Bear's Rump Island, the rocky outcrops are links in the chain of a massive limestone ridge—the Niagara Escarpment—that arcs from upstate New York to Wisconsin. In 1990, Fathom Five and neighboring Bruce Peninsula National Park received international recognition when the United Nations designated the Niagara Escarpment and both parks a world biosphere reserve.

Fathom Five is also the freshwater diving capital of the world. Twenty-one ships are known to have been wrecked off the treacherous Bruce Peninsula during the late 19th and early 20th centuries, on shoals with such telling names as Bad Neighbor and the Spur. The ships have made these waters a dramatic underwater museum. Among the doomed ships was the *Philo Scoville,* which ran aground on the north shore of Russel Island in 1889.

The visitors' centre and divers' registration office are found in Tobermory, a small fishing village nestling between the Big and Little Tub harbors. From Tobermory, boats set sail for trips round the shallow waters of Big Tub Harbour. Below the surface, the deck of the 36-m sailing ship *Sweepstakes,* which sank in 1885, lies in clear view, and nearby is the steamer *City of Grand Rapids,* which sank in 1907 after it caught fire.

One regular stop on boat trips is Flowerpot Island, a small piece of land only 2.2 km across, named for the two massive sea stacks along its east shore. Legend says the island was avoided by the local Algonquin Indians, who believed that its mysterious caves and unearthly rock formations were shrouded in ancient taboos. Today Flowerpot remains the only island in the park with public facilities: six campsites

Divers search for sunken shipwrecks in the depths of Fathom Five.

mounted on platforms skirt Beachy Cove, and two sheltered docks offer moorings for tour boats and private craft.

A two-hour hike along the looped trail on Flowerpot Island takes in its landmarks. More than 8,000 years ago, two huge stacks of rock started forming from the escarpment bluff. Water and frost wore away the rock much like a lathe, and formed the majestic flowerpot pillars, which today are 11.5 m and 6 m tall. Steps up the bluff lead to a hanging cave, carved by wave action before lake levels dropped dramatically after the last Ice Age.

At Castle Bluff, on the island's eastern tip, the Flowerpot light has marked the main shipping channel between Georgian Bay and Lake Huron since 1896. Cliffs on the north shore conceal a honeycomb of caverns, once used by lighthouse keepers as cold storage for perishable foods.

The island slopes gently to the lower west shore, where the delicate pink, yellow, and white calypso orchid flourishes in the limestone-rich soil, beside the brilliant striped coral root and rare Alaskan orchid.

Another way to experience the park is from the giant ferry *Chi-Cheemaun* (Big Canoe), which makes regular round-trips daily, between Tobermory and Manitoulin Island, and passes Cove Island Beacon. Finished in 1858, this lighthouse is the oldest in the Upper Great Lakes.

PARK INFORMATION
Access: Tobermory, or Ontario Northland ferry, during spring, summer and fall. Also accessible by private boat.
Visitors' centre: Tobermory.
Accommodation: Six campsites on Flowerpot Island. Additional accommodation available on mainland.
Summer activities: Glass-bottomed boat tours, fishing and diving charters, guided hikes on Flowerpot Island, daily interpretive programs, swimming, camping, hiking, scuba diving and snorkeling, fishing, boating, nature photography.

Roads to explore:
Beautiful vistas of the Beaver River valley

Distance (approx.): 90 km/56¼ miles

The road along the Beaver River between Thornbury and Flesherton is a delightful, little-known rural route. From Thornbury, drive west on Highway 26 to the Collingwood–St. Vincent Township Line. Turn left to drive up a steep hill to the top of Niagara Escarpment.

● At the top of the hill, turn left and stop to enjoy the views of apple orchards near Thornbury and the deep blue waters of Georgian Bay to the east. Beyond the Beaver Valley, the Blue Mountains rise some 219 m to meet the horizon.

● Continue on the township line to the second stop sign and turn right onto the Clarksburg Sideroad, which descends into Clarksburg. Before entering the village, look for a narrow gravel road on the right, halfway down the hill. Follow it for about 500 m for a side trip to the Clendenan Dam.

● Go back to the Clarksburg Sideroad and turn right. Just before the arch bridge is Firemen's Park. Here you can see remnants of the Haines Mill dam. The rapids below the dam are a popular place for kayak and canoe racing.

● Cross the bridge into the village. Turn left at County Road 13 to visit the Beaver Valley Military Museum, with armaments and equipment from 1880 to the present day.

● Head south on County Road 13 (Beaver Valley Road) to the heart of the valley, following it through Heathcote to the village of Kimberley. To the west of the village are Talisman Mountain Resort and Bowles Bluff, and to the east, Old Baldy, an outcrop of rock rising 180 m above the valley.

● For a closer look at Old Baldy and a bird's-eye view of Kimberley, walk the

Eugenia Falls, a Beaver Valley attraction

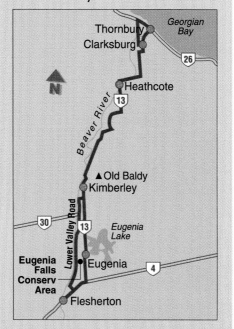

Bruce Trail loop. Park at the Old Baldy parking lot, on the 6-7 Sideroad. The trail loop starts here and goes south along the cliffs, drops into the valley and climbs the other side before turning north to return to 6-7 Sideroad. Complete the loop by walking back to the parking lot.

● Continue south through Kimberley on County Road 13 to the top of the hill on the other side of the village, where a picnic site provides a view of the valley.

● Just south of Kimberley is the village of Eugenia. Cross the Beaver River bridge and turn right, following the signs to the Eugenia Falls Conservation Area. Here the river drops over a 30-m cliff of the Niagara Escarpment into a wilderness gorge called Cuckoo Valley, where an 1852 gold find turned out to be only pyrite—fool's gold.

● From Eugenia, continue south until County Road 13 meets Highway 4. Drive west to Flesherton, a town noted for its numerous antique shops.

● To complete the drive and return to Thornbury, leave Flesherton by Highway 4, traveling east. Turn north on the Lower Valley Road past the Eugenia hydroelectric generating station.

● Continue north along the Lower Valley Road until it connects with County Road 13 near Kimberley.

2 | Creemore

Bigger is definitely not better in the village of Creemore (pop. 1,200), home of a micro-brewery and the smallest jail in North America.

Roadside greeting, Creemore

The founders of Creemore Springs Brewery have maintained the character of their 100-year old building at 139 Mill Street. The brewers use local spring water to make their distinctive beer, and produce small batches using an open-fired kettle, according to the Bavarian Purity Laws of 1516. *Tours of the brewery can be arranged by reservation.*

Creemore's jail, built in 1882, is a 3.5-m-by-6-m stone structure with three cells and a hallway. It was last used in the early 1940s to detain drunks, but it was renovated in 1971 so that visitors can "do time" in the jail.

Creemore Springs Brewery uses a copper kettle and follows a time-honored Bavarian tradition to prepare its distinctive beer.

Creemore's shops offer crafts and collectibles, such as this clock smith's antique selection.

The surrounding hills were originally colonized by Loyalists, but by 1842 more settlers had arrived to open up the farmlands below, where the Mad and Noisy rivers meet.

This village has retained its 19th-century charm. A number of Creemore artisans, such as a potter, clock smith, and a carver of wooden signs, work at their long-established crafts in heritage buildings on Mill Street. Farther along this street, shaded by a canopy of maples, are stately brick homes built at the turn of the century. A memory of horse-and-buggy days—the village's last hitching post—is at 232 Mill Street.

The downtown Sovereign Restaurant, built as a hotel in the 1870s, was converted in 1979 to its current form. St. Luke's Anglican Church, a block west on Louisa Street, dates from 1887.

Visitors can either drive or hike to enjoy the surrounding countryside. Take the Ganaraska Trail along the Mad River from the village of Avening, 3 km southeast of Creemore. The trail leads through Creemore to Glen Huron where it joins the Bruce Trail at a scenic lookout above a waterfall.

Devil's Glen Provincial Park, on the Niagara Escarpment, makes a good base for exploring the area. The glen is a steep gorge, down which the Mad River drops 300 m on its way to meet the Nottawasaga River. The park's Mad River Trail, a 2.5-km section of the Bruce Trail, runs steeply down the escarpment face.

Special events

Classic Car Show
(early June)

3 Awenda Provincial Park

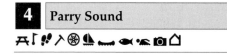

Awenda Provincial Park sits on the tip of the Penetanguishene Peninsula, which juts into the waters of Georgian Bay. The 1,935 ha of this natural environment park comprise a peaceful and diverse landscape of cobble beaches, sand dunes, boulder fields, kettle lakes, and deciduous forest. In summer, some 200 campsites offer shade and seclusion in the cool, thick woods.

About 30 km of trails lead through the trees, past wetlands, and along the top of Nipissing Bluff, which plunges 60 m down to the shore. In winter, the trails are groomed for cross-country skiing. Four beaches on Georgian Bay provide opportunies for picnicking, swimming, and sunbathing.

Beavers and deer can be spotted here. Colorful birds, such as cerulean warblers, ruby-throated hummingbirds, and yellow-throated vireos are also denizens of the park.

South of the park, at Penetanguishene (pop. 5,300), lies the Historic Naval and Military Establishments, a reconstructed 19th-century naval dockyard and military base. *Open daily, Victoria Day to Labor Day, 10 am to 5 pm.*

Farther south, on the edge of Midland (pop. 12,100), is Sainte-Marie-Among-the-Hurons, a replica of a Jesuit mission that stood on the site from 1639 to 1649. Near the mission is the Wye Marsh Wildlife Centre, with nature trails, a floating marsh boardwalk, and interpretive programs.

On the opposite side of the highway, the Martyrs' Shrine honors the Jesuits killed between 1642 and 1649.

In Midland itself are the Huron Indian Village, a full-scale replica of a 16th-century village, and the Huronia Museum, with displays of Indian and pioneer life. *Open daily, Victoria Day to Thanksgiving; January to mid-May, mid-October to December, Monday to Friday, 9 am to 5 pm.*

4 Parry Sound

Windswept pines crowning hills that rise from island-studded waters are just part of Parry Sound's beauty, made famous in the paintings of the Group of Seven. The town (pop. 6,052) faces the heart of Georgian Bay dotted with 30,000 islands.

Parry Sound sits at the junction of old Indian canoe routes and the route

A quiet beach promises unruffled summer pleasure at Waubuno Park, near Parry Sound.

Bruce Peninsula

At the northern end of the slender limestone finger that separates Georgian Bay from Lake Huron is the Bruce Peninsula National Park, a study in natural contrasts. White limestone cliffs, reaching heights of 50 m, tower above the turquoise-blue water of the bay on the peninsula's eastern side. Yet less than 10 km away to the west, the sandy, low-slung shores of Lake Huron extend into lush fens and woodlands.

The Niagara Escarpment, a lofty, jagged ridge of limestone that winds for 725 km through southwestern Ontario, hems the eastern border of the park, then drops beneath the waters of Georgian Bay to reemerge as the islands of Fathom Five National Park, off the tip of the peninsula. More than 400 million years ago, this region was covered by a shallow tropical sea. Massive reefs of sedimentary rock formed from the skeletons of ancient marine creatures. When the sea retreated, glaciers, wind, and water carved the dramatic rock formations seen today. In 1990 the United Nations designated the entire escarpment and the two parks one of only six world biosphere reserves in Canada.

Limestone cliffs line the Bruce Peninsula's east coast.

To explore Bruce Peninsula, begin at Cyprus Lake, the park's only campground, 11.2 km south of Tobermory. The Head of Trails, at the lake's northern end, opens up three 2-km routes that lead to the Georgian Bay shoreline, where they intersect with the Bruce Trail. This trail runs along the cliff tops and ends at Tobermory. One of the three trails, the Georgian Bay Trail, travels over the remains of ancient coral reefs and an underground river, before emerging to a breathtaking view of the bay. A kilometre offshore, the waters reach depths of 170 m, Georgian Bay's deepest point.

Heading west along the cliffs, the trail descends to a boulder beach, composed of innumerable cobblestones. It is an excellent place to hunt for marine fossils. A short hike farther west brings you to the Natural Arch and the Grotto, a cave pounded 20 m into the depths of the cliff by waves. Hikers who climb down may be surprised to come face to face with scuba divers who swim in through subterranean passages leading from the bay.

The trail then leads to Overhanging Point, where the continuous erosion of the underlying, softer limestone layer has left a thin sheet of the more durable dolomite rock suspended, so that explorers can descend under the escarpment's lower edge through Lord Hunt's Tunnel. Along the ridge, gnarled white cedars cling tenaciously to the limestone rock face, part of an ancient first-growth forest. Some of Canada's oldest trees, they have been documented at more than 1,000 years old. The sheerness of the cliffs protected these trees from the fires and logging that ravaged much of the Bruce Peninsula in the late 1800s.

More than 40 orchid species, the largest concentration north of Florida, bloom on the peninsula in spring and early summer, attracting naturalists and photographers. For the best sight of Bruce Peninsula's wildflowers, turn west off Highway 6, just north of the entrance to Cyprus Lake, onto the Dorcas Bay Road. The 6 ha of wetlands and woods along the beach are an ideal habitat for the showy lady's slipper, ram's-head lady's slipper, dwarf lake iris, insectivorous sundews, and pitcher plants. While walking here you might come across the Massasauga rattlesnake. The Bruce Peninsula is one of the last strongholds of this, Ontario's only poisonous snake. It is brown, with a mottled back, and measures 45-99 cm. The timid Massasauga shies away from well-traveled trails; if seen, it is best left to slither away unmolested.

South of the entrance to Cyprus Lake is the Emmett Lake Road. Take the left fork at the end of the road to the parking lot and walk an old logging track, marked by blue blazes. About 900 m farther on is the beach called Halfway Log Dump. This route to Georgian Bay was cut by loggers in the early 1900s. On the boulder beach, logs were stockpiled through the winter and then floated to local sawmills each spring.

Nearby is Cave Point where, according to local folklore, bootleggers concealed a forbidden whisky still. The whisky was made from wheat and corn salvaged from ships that ran aground along the shore. Many inhabitants of the Bruce frowned on the making of unlawful liquor. All the same, it is said that the bootleggers ran a bustling trade.

PARK INFORMATION
Access: Tobermory, or the Ontario Northland ferry, in spring, summer and fall. Also accessible by private boat or plane.
Visitors' centre: Tobermory.
Accommodations: Camping at Cyprus Lake Campground; at Birches for trailers and at Poplars and Tamarack for tents.
Summer activities: hiking, camping, scuba diving, snorkeling, fishing, swimming, picnic areas, boating, nature photography, interpretive programs.

The rocky coves on Georgian Bay, once the haunt of smugglers, now provide a playground for divers, swimmers, and sunbathers.

AN ISLAND CRUISE ON GEORGIAN BAY

During the summer, the cruise ship *The Island Queen* slips out of Parry Sound Harbour twice a day on a 3-hour trip around some of the 30,000 islands off the eastern shores of Georgian Bay. The 64-km voyage circles around the substantial bulk of Parry Island, the site of the Wasauksing First Nation Indian Reserve. Many of the islands here are merely humps of bare gray stone rising just above the surface of the bay. Some, however, are roomy enough to hold clusters of wind-twisted pine or to provide rocky bases for picturesque summer cottages. All these islands were once summits of ancient hills, later rounded by glaciers of the Ice Age.

During its journey, *The Island Queen* passes a number of unusual island sites. At Huckleberry Island, the cruise ship must negotiate a tight squeeze through a geological formation known as the Hole-in-the-Wall. Afterwards, it crosses an open stretch of the bay to reach the peninsula where Killbear Point Provincial Park is located. Once a Nipissing Indian hunting ground, the park still has some bears, which may be glimpsed from the boat deck. The ship continues past Wall, or Skull, Island. This was an ancient Indian burial ground, where human remains have been found wrapped in birch bark, laid in crevices, and covered with stones.

After rounding Parry Island, *The Island Queen* weaves between the rock islets and edges past Devil's Elbow. It passes the ruins of Depot Harbour, Ontario's largest ghost town (it was abandoned only in the late 1940s) and sails by a wooden swing bridge at Rose Point, before returning to Parry Sound Harbour.

On midsummer evenings, *The Island Queen* dons a theatre cloak. The Festival of the Sound plays a series of nighttime galas aboard the ship throughout July and August. On the mainland, Parry Sound's Rainbow Theatre stages its *Murder on the Island Queen* mysteries.

Seguin River swirls around the pillars of Parry Sound's historic CPR trestle bridge.

of the early voyageurs on their way from the St. Lawrence to fur-rich regions of Canada's north and west. The Sound itself was named in honor of the English explorer William Parry, in 1820. About 30 years later, the townsite was exchanged by the Ojibwa for Parry Island.

The West Parry Sound Museum on Tower Hill features the town's logging and shipping history. *Open July to Labor Day, Saturday to Wednesday, 10 am to 6 pm, Thursday and Friday, 10 am to 9 pm; Labor Day to July, Tuesday to Sunday, 10 am to 4 pm.* Visitors can climb to the top of a nearby observation tower for a superb view of Parry Sound.

Local historic sites include the 86-year old CPR trestle straddling the mouth of the Seguin River; the first District Court House in northern Ontario, designed in 1871; the Parry Sound Pumphouse, built in 1892; and the Rose Point Swing Bridge to Parry Island, all that is left of the western terminus of the Ottawa-Arnprior-Parry Sound Railway.

Glacial action has left a large number of nearby lakes and rivers, where there are opportunities for boating, swimming, or fishing. In winter, eight snowmobile clubs offer 800 km of connecting trails. The Seguin Trail and the Rotary and Algonquin Regiment Fitness Trail are used by cross-country skiers.

Special events
Snowfest Carnival (February)

Christmas in July

Festival of Sound
(mid-July–early August)

Jazz Festival (August)

boat had protected and retractable propellers that could be raised in shallow waters.

The Muskoka Lakes Museum, on Port Carling Island, is reached from the mainland by a pedestrian ramp. It displays settler artifacts, items from the boatbuilding era, and an 1875 log house, called Hall House. *Open early June to Thanksgiving, Monday to Saturday, 10 am to 5 pm; Sunday, 12 pm to 4 pm. Closed Mondays and Tuesdays in September.*

On Port Carling Dock is the Port Carling Pavilion, an open-sided structure with wooden roof shingles and a distinctive coxcomb ridge line. Also known as the "Freight Shed," because it was used as a warehouse and shelter during the days of steamboat travel, it is now a heritage building preserved by the Ontario Historical Society. The pavilion roof still offers passersby protection from pouring rain.

In summer months, visitors can enjoy outdoor arts and crafts shows.

Special events
Annual Heart of Muskoka (early July)
Annual Muskoka Antique Show (late July)
Hub of the Lakes Heritage Festival (mid-September)

5 Port Carling

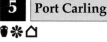

Canal locks made the village of Port Carling (pop. 5,498) one of the most vital centres for the region's early transportation and commerce. Now it is a hub for visitors heading for the Muskoka lakes.

The locks operate during boating season, allowing small and large boats on their way to and from the lakes to bypass the rapids on Indian River.

The area was once famous for its boatbuilding, and boats are still treasured. Seasoned residents fondly remember the Disappearing Propeller Boat Company, which, between 1916 and 1924, produced the "dippy." This

Hollyhocks and yarrows luxuriate by the Muskoka Lakes Museum, Port Carling.

6 Gravenhurst

Once a logging community on an inlet of Lake Muskoka, Gravenhurst (pop. 8,500) became a town and lakeside resort in Victorian times.

The town's Victorian charm is evident in several buildings. Among them is the Opera House, built in 1901, where the Muskoka Summer Festival Theatre performs in season.

The Bethune Memorial House, on John Street, was the manse of a Presbyterian church and the birthplace of Norman Bethune (1890-1939), whose father was the minister. Bethune became a doctor, and during the Spanish Civil War, established the first mobile blood service on the battlefield. He then went to China to organize hospital care and train army doctors. He died there in 1939 of blood poisoning.

Part of the Bethune Memorial House is furnished as it was at the time of Bethune's birth. The second floor is a museum honoring his achievements. *Open daily, excluding holidays, June to Labor Day, 9 am to 6 pm; the rest of the year, 10 am to 5 pm.*

Gravenhurst offers many opportunities for recreation. Down at the wharf is a restored Victorian steamship, RMS *Segwun*, which takes visitors on lake cruises, from June to October. Muskoka Bay has a public park and beach. Offshore is Eleanor Island, a nesting site for great blue heron. And on the shores of Gull Lake you can picnic beneath century-old white pines or swim in their dappled shadows. On Sunday evenings in summer, music wafts from a barge on the lake.

7 Bracebridge

Situated on the Muskoka River, which flows down a series of chutes to Lake Muskoka, Bracebridge (pop. 12,308) took the obvious course and became a

Georgian Bay Islands

Georgian Bay Islands National Park consists entirely of islands, 59 in total. Virtually all are granite mounds that lie scattered among the 30,000 islands along Georgian Bay's eastern shoreline.

A billion years ago, these islands were the great peaks of a mountain range taller than the Rockies. Now they are no more than the rounded roots of that ancient range, veined and clotted with brightly colored quartz and feldspar and darker-hued hornblende and biotite. Here, the scattered giant boulders are erratics, dumped by the ice sheet that covered this area, and almost all of Canada, some 12,000 years ago.

The rocks are relatively smooth and flat, broken by clusters of vegetation growing in the thin soil found in clefts and depressions. Juniper, bearberry, oak, and the white pine— the park's symbol—all survive here. Exposed to the prevailing west winds, the pines lean to the east, unbroken in root or trunk. This stirring sight seems to have had a mystical pull on Canada's most famous artists, the Group of Seven. Again and again, A.Y. Jackson, Lawren Harris, and others returned to capture this scenery on canvas.

Most of the Georgian Bay islands are within a stone's throw of each other and of the mainland, which allows many species to wander freely in and out of the park. In winter, large herds of deer regularly cross the ice to browse on the park's stands of cedar.

But perhaps the park's most fascinating inhabitants are its amphibians and reptiles. Some 33 species of frogs, toads,

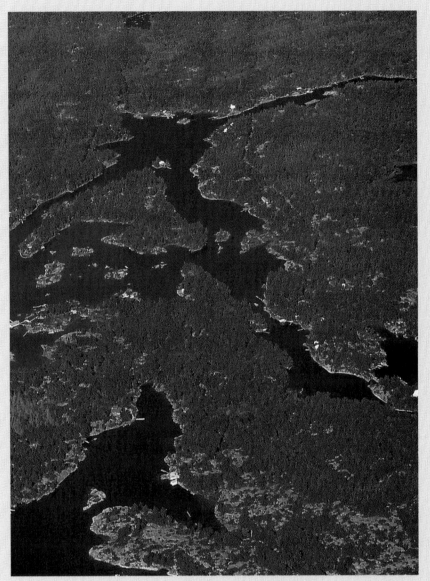

Jagged islands like pieces of a jigsaw puzzle lie scattered along Georgian Bay.

lizards, snakes, turtles, and salamanders have been identified on the islands— more than in any other national park in Canada. One of the prettiest creatures is the spotted turtle, which sports bright yellow or orange dots on its dark shell. The park is one of the few remaining refuges for the fox snake and the massasauga rattlesnake.

That 29 amphibian and reptile species have been found on Beausoleil Island suggests that it is indeed as sunny as its name implies. It is the largest island in the park and lies just a short boat ride from Honey Harbour. It has evidence of human occupation dating back 1,000 years. But even more unusual is the meeting of Canada's southern hardwood forest with the northern evergreens on this island. Nowhere else in the country can you observe the change so readily. The abrupt crossover from the forest of beech and maple clothing the southern half of the island to the large expanses of bare granite and the white pines of the northern half is best seen from a boat offshore.

PARK INFORMATION
Access: By boat only. Launching ramps, boat rentals and water taxis available at Midland, Penetanguishene and Honey Harbour.
Visitors' centre: Cedar Spring on Beausoleil Island. Park administrative office at Honey Harbour.
Accommodations: 15 campgrounds, 13 on Beausoleil Island, with 200 sites available on a first-come, first-served basis. Stays limited to two weeks. Limited docking available to visitors at all use areas. Maximum tie-up at any dock is 72 hours. Facilities for 1-day docking at 9 sites.
Summer activities: fishing, swimming, snorkeling, picnicking, hiking.
Winter activities: camping, snowshoeing, cross-country skiing, snowmobiling.

resort town. The river and the lake offer excellent boating, fishing, swimming, and canoeing. You can also take a summer cruise through the waterways. And several galleries in the town display the work of the many artists attracted here by the scenery.

Woodchester Villa is one of the most intriguing sights in Bracebridge. Built in 1882, it is one of some 30 surviving octagonal houses in Ontario (at one time the province boasted more than

100). This poured concrete residence had indoor plumbing, forced-air heating, and electric lighting—novelties in the late 19th century. *Admission free, donations accepted. Open Tuesday to Sunday, July 1 to Labor Day, 9 am to 5 pm.*

A reconstruction of Bracebridge's Presbyterian church on the grounds is now used as an art gallery. *Open year-round, Tuesday to Saturday, 10 am to 1 pm, 2 pm to 5 pm; July 1 to Labor Day, also open Sunday, 1 pm to 4 pm.*

8 Huntsville

The gateway to the Lake of Bays and the western entrance of Algonquin Provincial Park, Huntsville (pop. 11,500) is undoubtedly a resort town. Opportunities for hunting, fishing, canoeing, and camping abound here.

But there are also interesting historical sites not far away. Just 6 km south

Roads to explore: A lakeshore drive in scenic Muskoka
Distance (approx.): 68 km / 42½ miles

This half-day drive around the Lake of Bays offers an entrancing glimpse of Muskoka, long a popular Ontario playground. The starting point is Huntsville.
● From Main Street, follow King William Street to Highway 60. Drive east for about 3 km, passing Fairy Lake on your right, until you reach Muskoka Road 23. Turn right and follow Canal Road for about 6 km to North Portage Road. The world's shortest railway—known as The Portage Flyer—once ran for 2 km parallel to this road to South Portage. The train operated from 1903 until 1958.
● Take Muskoka Road 9 to South Portage. On the right you pass Westermain Woods, a wilderness area created in 1979.
● Continue south on Road 9, following the western shore of the lake, until it becomes Road 2 which will bring you to the

village of Baysville. Settled in the late 1800s, it still has an old-world feel and it is worth browsing here. (Or cross the bridge and turn right onto Heney Road to the dam on the North Branch of the Muskoka River, for a picnic break.)
● Take Highway 117 east to Dorset. Watch for the left turn onto the "old" Highway 117, which runs by the lake. Along the way, you will glimpse Bigwin Island, named after native leader Chief Bigwin, who died in 1940 at the ripe age of 101.
● Turn left onto Glenmount Road, leading to Norway Point, for a view of the remains of Bigwin Inn and a superb view of the lake. The island inn was a palatial resort of the 1930s and 1940s. The red roofs of the rotunda building and observation tower are visible from the shore.
● Return to Highway 117 and drive on to Dorset. Then follow Highway 35 along the eastern shore toward Dwight. Just before Birkenhead, a side road leads to beautiful Ten Mile Bay and the 1897 Sea Breeze Church.
● Return to Highway 35 and continue on to Dwight, where you can browse in the Indian Trading Post and antique shops. Turn left at the beach road for a picnic spot by the lake.
● Take Highway 60 west, through the hamlets of Hillside and Grassmere, back to Huntsville.

At sunrise, mist shrouds Muskoka's Lake of Bays.

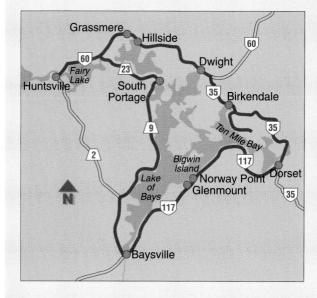

of Huntsville is the Madill Log Church. The Irish immigrant John Madill was drawn to the area by promises of a land grant, and as one of the first settlers here, donated a small portion of his grant for the church and cemetery.

Neighboring settlers helped him cut down trees and build the square-timbered church, in 1872-1873. There are several log churches in Ontario, but none is so well preserved or still used. The United Church of Canada congregates at Madill once a year.

On the Brunel Road within Huntsville, in a pretty wooded setting, is the Muskoka Pioneer Village, containing several restored and furnished settler houses and buildings, from the period 1860-1910. Its museum exhibits items from Muskoka's history. *The village is open from late June to September, 10 am to 5 pm; October to Thanksgiving, 11 am to 4 pm. The museum building is open year-round, Monday to Friday, from 10 am to 4:30 pm.*

About 11 km northeast of Huntsville, near Williamsport, is the Dyer Memorial. The 13-m-high memorial stands at the heart of a botanical garden, which covers 4 ha and overlooks the East River. It was erected by an American lawyer, Clifton G. Dyer, in memory of his wife, Betsy.

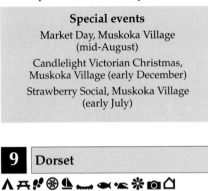

Special events

Market Day, Muskoka Village (mid-August)

Candlelight Victorian Christmas, Muskoka Village (early December)

Strawberry Social, Muskoka Village (early July)

9 Dorset

A one-way road bridge connects the two halves of the village of Dorset (pop. 500), which is bisected by Trader Bay, on the eastern arm of the Lake of Bays. The village was first settled in 1859, and by the 1880s it began to flourish as a logging community. Now it prospers as a mooring-point for pleasure boaters. If you cross the bridge on foot, linger awhile to watch the pleasure craft coming in to anchor where lake steamers docked in bygone days.

For a spectacular view of Dorset and Trading Bay on Lake of Bays, head for the Dorset Observation Tower, just north of Dorset. A short distance out of the village, look for the road sign for the road to the tower. Turn left and drive up to the top of the hill, where parking is available.

Once a ranger's tower, the 30-m steel structure sits atop a 150-m-high hill. Railings line both sides of the 118 steps that take the adventurous all the way to the top. Here, in the fall, is the best panoramic view of the rolling, flame-colored Haliburton Highlands. Picnic tables at the site make the stop all the more pleasant. *Open during the summer, 8 am to 8 pm, and from Labor Day to Thanksgiving, 8 am to 7 pm.*

South of Dorset on Highway 35 is the 24,000-ha Leslie M. Frost Natural Resources Centre, on the shore of Lake St. Nora. This residental education centre for the management of natural resources includes a model sawmill, nature exhibits, demonstrations, and lectures. And more than 27 km of skiing and hiking trails offer nature enthusiasts an excellent opportunity to

A riverside restaurant attractively situated by the dock tempts boaters to disembark at Dorset.

A hillside vista reveals Haliburton Village on Head Lake encircled by rugged woodland.

explore landscapes typical of the Haliburton Highlands. *Open Monday to Friday, 8 am to 5 pm.*

Special events
Dorset Snowball (February)

Canada Day Fireworks (July 1)

Baysville to Dorset Canoe Race
(August)

Country Market
(every Sunday in summer)

10 Haliburton

Haliburton, on the shores of Head Lake, is an ideal base for visitors with recreation in mind. This village of 1,800 is surrounded by the Haliburton Highlands, an accessible wilderness playground with more than 600 lakes and dense forest.

In 1861, the Canadian Land and Emigration Company endeavored to settle the area with English farmers.

When that failed, lumber became the main industry, from the 1870s to the 1960s. This past is relived every Wednesday at 10.00 a.m, from July 1 to Labor Day, when groups of interested people gather at the Government dock for the heritage walk, led by a local resident.

The walk begins at St. George's Anglican Church, built in 1922. The original church, built in 1864, was the first local landmark. Over the decades, fire has claimed many of the town's original wooden buildings, but some of the survivors can be seen on the walk. These buildings include the Dysart Town Hall, Bank's Heritage Store and the yellow-brick Lucas House built in 1907, with the village's first plumbing and electric lighting.

The Rail's End Gallery, located in the old railroad station, houses memorabilia from the station's working days. It is now the centre of activities for the Haliburton Guild of Fine Arts. The village's visitors' centre is based inside a picturesque CNR caboose.

On the lake's north shore, Haliburton Highlands Museum recalls the area's early days with exhibits that chart Haliburton's evolution from a struggling farming community to a thriving lumber town. On the grounds are the Reid House, built in the late 1870s and now restored to turn-of-the-century decor, a blacksmith's shop, and a log cabin from "Rackety Ranch," an early homestead on Gull River. *Open daily during the summer, and in winter from Tuesday to Saturday, from 10 am to 5 pm.*

Haliburton's abandoned 17-km rail link to Kinmount is fast becoming a popular trail. It is open to hikers, cyclists, and horse riders. For a picnic, stop by the Ritchie Falls near Lochlin.

The 20,235-ha Haliburton Forest and Wildlife Reserve, 20 km north of nearby West Guilford, is a private reserve that has been turned into a working model of "sustainable development." The reserve follows traditional practices of logging and hunting, but

emphasizes recreation—fishing, camping, hiking, and mountain biking.

Special events
Haliburton County Highland Games
(early July)

Country Good Times, Wilberforce
(mid-July)

Annual Summer Art Exhibition and Sale
(late July to early August)

Haliburton Rotary Carnival
(early August)

Bluegrass Festival (early August)

Haliburton County Studio Tour
(early October)

11 Algonquin Provincial Park

Maple-covered hills, rocky ridges, pine forests, spruce bogs, and myriad lakes, ponds, and streams cover the 7,700-km² preserve that is Algonquin Provincial Park. It is Ontario's oldest provincial park, founded in 1893. The beauty of its unspoiled nature is captured in the work of the painter Tom Thomson, who drowned in Canoe Lake in 1917.

The park's visitors' centre, 43 km east of the West Gate, stands on a rocky ridge overlooking Sunday Creek val-

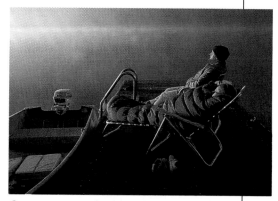

Campers cocooned against dawn's chill see the sunrise at Algonquin Provincial Park.

ley. It houses the Park Museum, which has 28 dioramas depicting wildlife habitats and aspects of park history. From the centre, there are views of hardwood and coniferous forest and a

Cut amethyst, a Bancroft treasure

spruce bog. *Open daily, late May to late June, 10 am to 6 pm; late June to early September, 9 am to 9 pm; mid-September to mid-October, 10 am to 6 pm; mid-October to late October, 10 am to 5 pm; November to mid-May, weekends only, 10 am to 4 pm.*

The Logging Museum, by the East Gate, has an audiovisual program and exhibits that include a re-created caboose camp, a steam-powered log tug, and a working log dam and chute. *Open daily, late May until mid-October, 10 am to 6 pm.*

The best way to discover the wild beauty of Algonquin Provincial Park is by canoe or on foot, choosing from more than 2,400 km of canoe routes or 16 interpretive hiking trails.

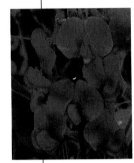

Wild sweet pea, Ontario roadside

Several short trails are easily accessible from Highway 60, which cuts through the southern sector of the park. The 1.9-km Lookout Trail and the 2-km Beaver Pond Trail are the most popular. The Mizzy Lake Trail, an 11-km round-trip, passes many lakes and ponds. For those who like something more rugged, the overnight backpacking Highland and Western Uplands trails have loops that range from 19 km to 71 km. These demand stamina and experience.

More than 250 species of animals have been identified in the park. The creatures to watch for are moose (seen most often in the morning or evening), white-tailed deer, and black bears.

Staff provide guided canoe outings, hikes, evening programs, and museum sessions for children. In August the Wolf Howl is a major attraction. An interpretive lesson on wolf packs is given before visitors are led by car to a site where they send out a wolf howl and wait for a response. It is a night to remember.

In winter, more than 80 km of cross-country ski trails and numerous snow-shoe trails wind over hardwood hills. Winter camping is permitted.

Special events

Ski Loppet (February)

Wolf Howl (August)

12 Bancroft

🗑️🏕️🎣🏹❄️⊕🐟🛶✳️📷⌂

The "Mineral Capital of Canada," Bancroft (pop. 2,500) is set amid rugged hills where geological forces have produced some 300 varieties of semiprecious stones and other minerals, such as blue sodalite, magnetite, and biotite. In August, Bancroft celebrates its natural wealth at the four-day International Rockhound Gemboree.

Many disused mine sites around the town are evidence of earlier mining activity. They are easily accessible to rock collectors and amateur mineralogists.

The town was hewed from the wilderness by loggers in the 1800s, and was established in 1861 as York River, after the river on whose banks it stands. But the trees that were cut down were not replaced, and the lumbermen left.

The railway too has come and gone, and the old station now houses the

Rock hounds inspect boxes of semiprecious stones at the annual Gemboree at Bancroft.

A climber, using crampons to secure a hold on the sheer rock, clings to the face of the Eagle's Nest Lookout, near Bancroft.

Information Centre, the Bancroft Art Gallery, and the Bancroft Mineral Museum. A mining display and a collection of more than 500 ore and gem samples are exhibited at the musem. *Open year-round, Monday to Saturday, 9 am to 4 pm.*

The Bancroft Historical Museum, contained in a mid-19th century log house in York River Centennial Park, depicts local pioneer life and features antique logging equipment. *Open daily, early July to Labor Day, 10 am to 5 pm.*

Just about 2 km north of town, on Highway 62, is the Eagle's Nest Lookout, at an elevation of 152 m. A picnic site at the top of the cliff provides a bird's-eye view of the York River valley, which is quite stunning in the fall. The intrepid can reach it by climbing the rock face, using rope and crampons. For the more cautious, there is a road to the top. The lookout is also a good place to collect minerals and, in season, pick blueberries.

Also to the north is Baptiste Lake, with its annual canoe race, and to the south is Paudash Lake. Both are ideal for fishing and water sports.

The area is well equipped for winter sports. A network of snowmobile trails radiates from Bancroft. The Mineral Capital Luge Club has a 750-m track. There is nordic skiing on the groomed trails at Silent Lake, and downhill skiing on the Madawaska Ski Hill.

Special events

Frosty Frolics (February)

Bancroft Sled Dog Races
(mid-February)

Kinsmen Home & Recreation Show
(early June)

Baptiste-to-Bancroft Canoe Race (June)

Party in the Park (July)

Arts and Crafts Festival
(late July)

Summer Crafts Fair (late July)

Rockhound Gemboree
(Civic Holiday weekend)

Coe Hill Fair
(weekend before Labor Day)

Maynooth Madness (Labor Day)

13 Eganville

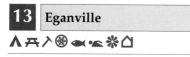

The tranquil, steepled village of Eganville (pop. 1,300) lies deep in the heart of the Bonnechere Valley. In this tree-lined community, the greatest commotion you will hear is the roar of the Bonnechere River as it rushes along its tumultuous course through town and down the Fifth Chute.

The river has bisected Eganville since the town's earliest days, when John Egan built the first sawmill here in 1837. Irish lumbermen were lured by work in the sawmill. The Protestants chose to settle in the hills on the north side of the Bonnechere. The Catholic families congregated on the south side, over the bridge. For more than a century, the town's prosperity depended on the timber trade.

Today Eganville is best known for the Bonnechere Caves, some 8 km southeast of town. Over time, water has carved out enormous chambers in the limestone bedrock. Today, some of the bigger caves are hundreds of me-

tres deep. You can descend into them by way of a wooden stairway.

Guides decipher the geological formations that decorate the caves. In the depths, stalactites dangle from the cave ceiling like huge icicles; stalagmites rise from the floor; and flowstone covers walls and floors. Flowstone is a rippled layer of stone created where thin sheets of water have deposited calcium and other minerals.

The guides will also show you fossils of sea creatures that lived here some 500 million years ago, when the limestone tunnels formed the bed of a vast tropical sea. This was long before the first dinosaurs roamed the earth.

As you explore the caves, you are constantly accompanied by the distant roar of the Bonnechere River. Even in this underground world, part of the river winds its way through the deepest caves. *Guided tours daily, from late May to early September (and weekends until Thanksgiving).*

The waters of the Bonnechere River mirror the stone Victorian structures of Eganville.

ECHOES OF THE PAST
ON A PIONEER ROAD

The road known as the Opeongo Line (see the facing page) leads across level farmland that stretches from the Ottawa River to Renfrew to Dacre. (*Opeongo* in Algonquin means "shallow narrows.") Beyond Dacre, the road climbs to a land of steep hills and superb vistas. The Opeongo Line was one of a number of colonization schemes begun in the mid-1850s by Canada West—the Ontario government of the day—to open remote regions for settlement. The government offered free land to settlers (aged 18 or over), who promised to build a dwelling and to cultivate at least 12 acres within four years.

Advertisements described the land along the Opeongo Line as "a sandy loam... deep and rich." The Irish and Scots settlers found much of the land thin and rocky, but they stayed on. Some 200 families were living here by the time the road was completed in 1858. The first arrivals were later joined by Germans and Poles. (Wilno, the first Polish settlement in Canada, was established in 1864.)

Because settlers could barely make a living from farming, they worked as lumbermen during the winter. After 1860, lumber companies thrived here by harvesting the vast local stands of white pine. Teams of horses hauled huge loads of timber; drivers competed to see whose teams could pull the biggest loads. Stopping places provided blacksmith shops and inns for lumbermen, where liquor, song, and tall tales kept things lively. Some of these spots, such as Barry's Bay and Dacre, became large communities.

In 1893, after the opening of a railway from Ottawa to Parry Sound, the lumber companies shifted away from the Opeongo Line. The boom times ended when the last white pines were cut down in the early 1900s. Today the Opeongo Road is a scenic route of quiet hamlets and farms that retains echoes of the pioneer past.

Children seek adventure on rocky outcrops by the restless Bonnechere River, near Renfrew.

14 Renfrew

The Bonnechere River plunges down several waterfalls, known as chutes, on its way to join the Ottawa River. The settlement of Second Chute later became Renfrew, named by Scottish immigrants after the ancestral home of their Stuart kings. They were drawn here by advertisements issued by the government of the time to attract farmers to the area.

Today, Renfrew (pop. 8,300) is a modern industrial town. But remnants of early farming and industrial activity in this region can be seen in the McDougall Mill Museum. This collection is housed in a handsome three-story stone gristmill, built in 1855, overlooking the river, in O'Brien Park. Pioneer clothing, military uniforms, and artifacts and tools from 19th-century Ottawa River valley farms are displayed. The old swing bridge just outside the museum adds a pleasing touch to this riverside site. *Tours of the museum are conducted daily from mid-June to Labor Day, 9:30 am to 4:30 pm.*

Storyland, 13 km north of Renfrew off Highway 17, displays some 200 fairy-tale characters in a woodland setting. You can survey the Ottawa River valley from the 122-m-high Champlain Lookout in the park. *Open daily, late May to early November.*

Special events
Lumber Baron's Festival
(late July)
Renfrew Fall Fair (early September)

Roads to explore: On the Opeongo Line

Distance: 163 km/102 miles

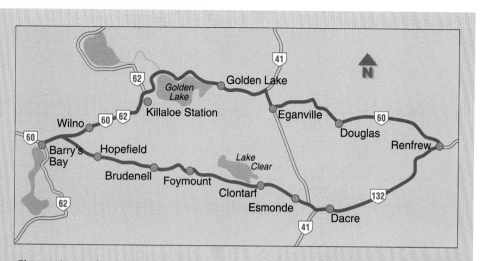

To explore the Opeongo Line, head southwest from Renfrew for 27 km on Highway 132, through Ferguslea and Shamrock to Dacre. Here you can visit Two Island Marble, for an exhibition and sale of pieces of local dolomite.

● Three kilometres past Dacre is the junction with Highway 41. About 1 km to the south of the junction is a "magnetic" hill where cars seem to defy gravity by freewheeling uphill—an optical illusion. Continue north on 41 about 250 m until you see the Opeongo road sign.

● Turn left for the 25-km drive to Foymount, up the steep sides of the Black Donald Mountains.

● Stop for a picnic at the Opeongo Line Park. Just beyond, on the right, is a freshwater spring. Farther on, the Roman Catholic church, St. Joseph's on the Opeongo, marks Esmonde. The village was originally known as the Curry Settlement, after Irishman Thomas Curry.

● The road continues to skirt the ridge, following the Mount St. Patrick fault line. The green-trimmed, white frame of St.

A highlight of this Opeongo Line drive is the Bonnechere Caves, near Eganville.

Clement's Anglican Church announces Clontarf. Just past the settlement is Opeongo Maple Products, where you can sample syrups and candy and see pioneer equipment and Indian artifacts.

● Climb through open fields, past century-old log-and-frame farmhouses with snake rail fences and strings of barns, and past St. John's Lutheran Church (1850). The road then travels up Plaunt's Hill. Canny Xavier Plaunt anticipated the lumber traffic along the Opeongo Line and built a hotel to serve the shantymen and settlers that passed through. The hotel is now a private home and farm.

● When you reach Foymount, take a brief detour left up the 1,650-m-high elevation for a spectacular view over the Bonnechere River valley. To the west is Round Lake, ahead is Golden Lake, and to the right, Clear Lake.

● Continue to the ghost town of Brudenell. All that remains of this once-bustling crossroads settlement are Costello's Hotel, a wood-frame building with a decorative gingerbread trim around its veranda; Our Lady of the Angels Roman Catholic Church (1870); and the graveyard opposite with headstones dating from 1815.

● Drive on to Hopefield crossroads, where the road turns to gravel and winds round gray granite hills divided by gullies. Turn left at Highway 60/62 to Barry's Bay. Across from the wood-frame J. R. Booth Railway Station (1900) is the Balmoral Hotel, once patronized by lumber barons.

● Go back along Highway 60/62 for 10 km to Wilno, established in 1864 as Canada's first Polish settlement. The Wilno Tavern that flourished as a hotel in its early days still provides a warm welcome and excellent Polish dishes. The Wilno Craft Gallery sells a range of crafts, from quilts to decoys. The twin spires of St. Mary's Church (1936) dominate Wilno's landscape. It was dedicated to Our Lady Queen of Poland in 1937.

● Continue past Killaloe Station. In the 1970s, Killaloe and its pretty environs attracted people who set up communes

Illumination inside the Bonnechere Caves reveals a fascinating subterranean world.

and lived a back-to-the-land existence. Several communes still thrive there.

The remains of a 19th-century gristmill can be seen on the banks of Brennan's Creek in Old Killaloe.

● At Golden Lake is an Algonquin Indian reserve with a museum. Its displays feature birch-bark canoe construction. Drive on to Eganville, built on the fifth chute of the Bonnechere River. The Bonnechere caves are 8 km to the southeast.

● To complete the loop, continue on Highway 60 for the last 29 km back to Renfrew.

AROUND TORONTO

Nottawasaga Bay

Trent Canal
15 **Kirkfield**
Gamebridge
Talbot R.
48
121
Balsam Lake
Fenelon Falls
35

Beaverton
Sturgeon Lake

Lake Simcoe
Lindsay

400
11
Barrie

48

Jacksons Point
Sutton
Sibbald Point Provincial Park
7
Lake Scugog
Scugog Island

27
400
11
12
7A

Bradford West Gwillimbury
Holland Landing
14 **Sharon**
Uxbridge
18 **Port Perry**

25
24
10
Mono Centre
Nottawasaga River
11 **Tottenham**
1 **Hockley** **10**
9
Schomberg **12**
Newmarket
Aurora
47
Stouffville
35
115

6
Orangeville
Alton **9**
25
Belfountain
Inglewood
13
Kleinburg
Richmond Hill
400
11
7
Markham
Pickering
12
Oshawa
Bowmanville
Whitby

River

5 **Elora**
6 **Fergus**
Cheltenham
Terra Cotta
10
Ajax
2

Grand
86
24
8 **Rockwood**
Acton
7
Brampton
901
Lake Ontario

St. Jacobs
4
Georgetown
25
5
2
Agglomération de Toronto

7
Guelph
Credit
10

Waterloo
Kitchener
7 8
401
Campbellville **7**
River
Port Credit
Mississauga

6
Oakville

Cambridge
CANADA
U.S.A.

401
Burlington

3 **Paris**
St. George **2**
Dundas
Ancaster
Hamilton
8
Niagara-on-the-Lake

2 53
53
Queen Elizabeth Way
Niagara River

Brantford
6
Stoney Creek
Grimsby
Beamsville
St. Catharines
55

Jordan **1**

20
North Pelham
Thorold
Niagara Falls

Grand

River
6
Queen Elizabeth Way

Kawartha
17 Petroglyphs Provincial Park
• Stonyridge
28
16 Bobcaygeon
Buckhorn Lake
Stony Lake
Lakes
Pigeon Lake
• Lakefield
Chemong Lake
Otonabee River
Peterborough
7
7
2
• Hastings
Trent River
20 Keene
Trent Canal
Serpent Mounds Provincial Park
Rice Lake
48
4
3
28
401
2
• Trenton
2
21 Brighton
• Colborne
Port Hope 19
Cobourg
Presqu'ile Provincial Park

N

0   20   40 km
0   20   40 miles

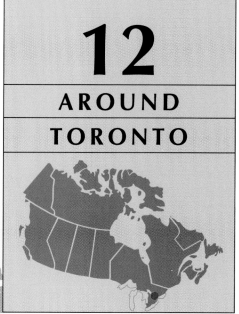

12
AROUND
TORONTO

Places to see
Jordan
St. George
Paris
St. Jacobs
Elora
Fergus
Campbellville
Rockwood
Alton
Hockley
Tottenham
Schomberg
Kleinburg
Puck's Farm
Sharon
Kirkfield
Bobcaygeon
The rocks that teach
Petroglyphs Provincial Park
Port Perry
Port Hope
Tyrone Mill
Keene
Brighton
Serpent Mounds Provincial Park

Roads to explore
Niagara Peninsula: Grimsby to North Pelham
Credit River Valley: Norval to Orangeville
Tottenham to Tyrone Mill

Previous pages:
Vineland Estates Winery, near Vineland,
Niagara Peninsula

Ball's Falls Conservation Area takes its name from this falls, located in a woodland setting.

9 m long. Tea is served on Tuesday afternoons. *Open daily, mid-April to late November, 1 to 5 pm; July and August, 10 am to 5 pm.*

Just a few minutes walk along Main Street is an old pink and gray winery, which now houses the Jordan Antiques Centre and the Cave Spring Cellars, one of the area's award-winning wineries. The long fortresslike building also contains the On the Twenty Restaurant, and the Jordan Museum Gift Shop, where you can buy tinware and pewter ware, jewelry, old-fashioned toys, children's clothing, and homemade jams and jellies.

At the junction of Main Street with Regional Road 81 and 19th Street is an 1850s red-brick house (now an antique lighting shop) that used to be a smithy. The stagecoach from St. Catharines to Toronto would make its first stop at the blacksmith's forge, where the driver would change his tired horses for newly shod ones.

Ball's Falls Conservation Area and Historic Park is located nearby. Once a 19th-century industrial hamlet, the site features an historic flour mill, as well as a lime kiln and fruit-drying shed. *Open early April to Victoria Day and Labor Day to October, Sunday to Thursday; Victoria Day to Labor Day, daily; November, Monday to Friday, 10 am to 4 pm.*

From the early days of the village, its crafts people and weavers created high-quality items, and the name Jordan became synonymous with fine crafts. Today, antique hunters value such rare items as Grobb furniture, woven coverlets from the Fry family and Orth and Moyer pottery made from the local reddish clay.

Special events

Victorian At Home Day
(August)

Pioneer Day (October)

Ball's Falls Thanksgiving Festival
(mid-October)

¹ Jordan

In the late 18th century, many settlements in the Niagara Peninsula were established by Loyalists crossing the United States border. The settlements were named according to their location in miles from the border. The area in which Jordan (pop. 400) was founded was known as The Twenty.

Twenty-Mile Creek runs through the village. And on Main Street is the Jordan Historical Museum of the Twenty. The museum complex includes the Pennsylvania Dutch-style Jacob Fry House (1815), a stone schoolhouse built in 1859, and the Mennonite churchyard, where headstones mark the graves of the first Mennonites known to settle in Canada. There is also a rare early 19th-century fruit press, made by the Fry family, which is

Roads to explore: Orchards, vineyards, and museums
Distance (approx.): 104 km/65 miles

Baskets of freshly picked fruit, Vineland

The Grimsby-to-Vineland stretch of this route skirts picturesque orchards and vineyards at the base of the 200-m-high Niagara Escarpment. Side roads ascend the escarpment and lead to the heart of the Niagara fruit-growing belt.

● Grimsby (pop. 16,996) is the starting point. Visit the Grimsby Museum, at the junction of Highway 8, Elm and Murray streets. The museum's elegant front door once opened to wayfarers at the Marlatt Tavern, a vanished Grimsby hostelry of the mid-19th century. One of the treasured items in the museum is a Windsor side chair belonging to Col. Robert Nelles, a prominent Loyalist settler in this area. *Open Thanksgiving to Victoria Day, Wednesday to Sunday, 1 pm to 5 pm; Victoria Day to Thanksgiving, Tuesday to Saturday, 10 am to 5 pm, Sunday, 1 to 5 pm.*

From the museum, continue along Elm for one block, turn right onto Mountain Road, and carry on for 3 km to Quarry Road. Follow the signs to Beamer Memorial Conservation Area at the top of the Niagara Escarpment. The lookout is an ideal spot for observing spring and fall hawk migrations.

● Leave Grimsby and drive east on Regional Road 81 toward Vineland. Along the roadside, at peach, apple, cherry, and pear orchards, signs invite passersby to "Pick your own fruit."

● Some 9 km farther east of Grimsby (just after Beamsville), turn right onto the Cave Springs Road, leading to the Cave Springs Conservation Area. Explore the cave, where ice forms even on the hottest day.

● Return to 81 and drive another 5 km. Turn right (south) onto Cherry Avenue,

HOTELS/MOTELS/COTTAGES

	No. of Cottages	No. of Rooms	Air Conditioning	Television	In-House Movies	Housekeeping Units	Major Credit Cards	Pets Allowed	Babysitting Services	Tour Guides	Boat Rentals	Car Plug-In	Beach	Pool	Dining Lounge	Coffee Shop
LAKESHORE DRIVE PROPERTIES																
12. Ambassador Motel, 666 Lakeshore Dr. P1a 2G2 472-3340		10		●			●	●	●				●			
4. Arizona Motel, 1078 Lakeshore Dr. P1A 2H3 472-0800		19	●	●			●	●	●							
13. Balsam Cottages, 651 Lakeshore Dr. P1A 2G1 474-4883	5			●			●	●	●			●	●	●		
19. Bayshore Motel, 566 Lakeshore Dr. P1A 2E6 472-5350	12	●	●	●		●	●						●			
9. Best Western, 700 Lakeshore Dr. 474-5800 P1A 2G4 1-800-461-6199		130	●	●	●		●	●	●			●		●	●	●
26. Bonny Vu Motel, 377 Lakeshore Dr. P1A 2E4 472-9870		15	●	●			●					●				
10. Comfort Inn by Journey's End, 676 Lakeshore Dr. P1A 2G4 4949444 1-800-228-5160		81	●	●			●	●				●				
20. Dolphin Motel, 549 Lakeshore Dr. P1A 2E5 472-5370	9	10	●	●			●	●	●		●	●				●
1. Fifth Wheel Country House, Pinewood Park Dr. P1A 8J8 476-2372		11	●	●			●	●				●			●	●
23. Franklin Motel, 444 Lakeshore Dr. P1A 2E1 472-1360		16	●	●			●	●	●			●		●		
6. Glen Garry Motel, 785 Lakeshore Dr. P1A 2G7 472-1085	8	6		●			●	●			●	●	●			
22. Glenwood Motel, 467 Lakeshore Dr. P1A 2E2 472-1644	3	12	●	●			●	●	●			●				
24. Holiday Plaza Motel, 416 Lakeshore Dr. P1A 2C6 474-1431		13	●	●			●	●				●				
18. Kingsdale Inn, 570 Lakeshore Dr. P1A 2E6 495-4551		50	●	●	●	●	●					●				
27. Lancelot Inn, 295 Lakeshore Dr. P1A 3N8 476-0200		27		●			●					●	●			
17. Lincoln Motel, 594 Lakeshore Dr. P1A 2E6 472-3231 Apt."s (1)		26		●			●	●	●			●				●
8. Manitou Motel & Store, 710 Lakeshore Dr. P1A 2G4 472-1900	3	16	●	●			●	●	●			●				
11. Maple Grove Motor Crt. & Cottages, 673 Lakeshore Dr. P1A 2G1 476-4312	15	10	●	●			●					●	●			
3. Pine Hill Motel, Pinewood Park Dr. P1B 8J8 472-2130		12	●	●			●					●				
15. Pine Point Log Cabins, 12 Mowat P1A 1X7 472-0572 or 472-3224	5			●		●			●				●			
2. Pinewood Park Inn, Pinewood Park Dr. P1B 8J8 472-0810, 1-800-461-9592		118	●	●	●		●	●	●	●		●		●	●	●
5. Rock Haven Motel, 812 Lakeshore Dr. P1A 2G8 472-6470		8		●			●	●								
21. Shady Maple Villa, 468 Lakeshore Dr. P1A 2E1 472-7028	9			●			●		●			●				
25. Star Motel, 405 Lakeshore Dr. P1A 2C5 472-3510		14		●			●					●	●			
16. Sunset Park Motel & Cottages, 641 Lakeshore Dr. P1A 2E9 472-837	6	14	●	●			●	●		●	●	●	●			
14. Torbay Cottages, 585-589 Banner Ave. P1A 1X7 476-0076	6			●		●						●	●			
7. Venture Inn, 718 Lakeshore Dr. P1A 2G4 472-7171, 1-800-387-3933		77	●	●			●	●				●				
CENTRAL PROPERTIES																
31. Days Inn, 255 McIntyre St. P1B 2Y9 W. 474-4770, 1-800-DAYS INN		46	●	●	●		●	●				●				
32. Baywood Motor Hotel, 307 Algonquin P1B 4W1 474-3610		45	●	●			●		●						●	●
29. Howard Johnson Hotel, 425 Fraser St. P1B 3X1 472-8200, 1-800-I-G -HOJO		95	●	●								●			●	●
30. Comfort Inn by Journey's End, 1200 O'Brien St. P1B 9B3 476-5400		60	●	●			●	●				●				
...25 ...mour St. P1B 8G4 495-1133 1-80 -578-7878		100	●	●	●		●	●				●		●		

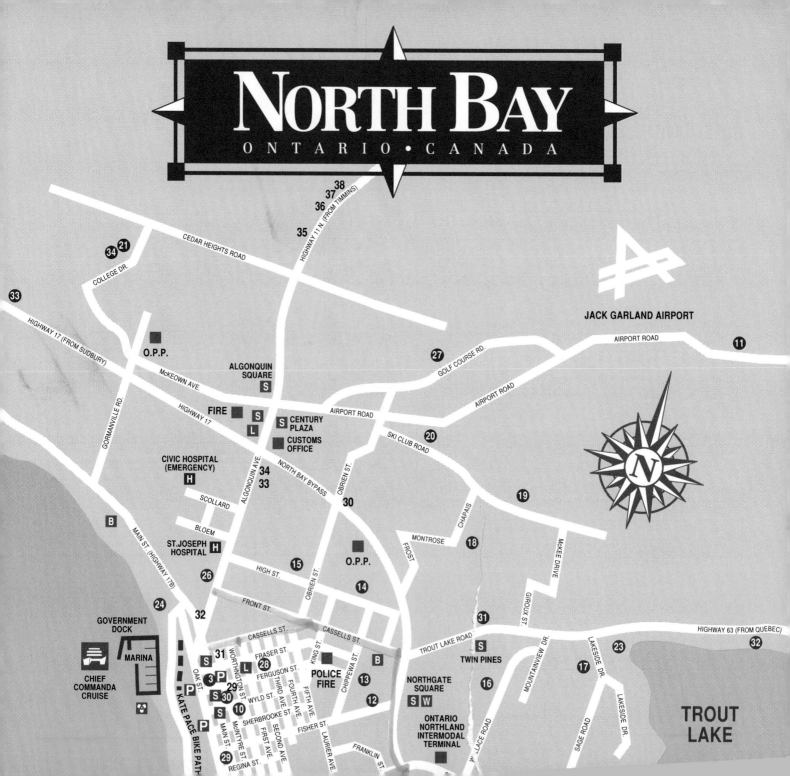

NORTH BAY
ONTARIO · CANADA

JACK GARLAND AIRPORT

CEDAR HEIGHTS ROAD

COLLEGE DR.

HIGHWAY 11 N. (FROM TIMMINS)

38
37
36
35

34 21

33

HIGHWAY 17 (FROM SUDBURY)

O.P.P.

McKEOWN AVE.

GORMANVILLE RD.

HIGHWAY 17

ALGONQUIN SQUARE
S

FIRE
S
L

CENTURY PLAZA
S

CUSTOMS OFFICE

AIRPORT ROAD

AIRPORT ROAD

GOLF COURSE RD.

AIRPORT ROAD

27

11

SKI CLUB ROAD

20

CIVIC HOSPITAL (EMERGENCY)
H

ALGONQUIN AVE.

34
33

NORTH BAY BYPASS

OBRIEN ST.

30

SCOLLARD

BLOEM

B

ST. JOSEPH HOSPITAL
H

MAIN ST. (HIGHWAY 17B)

26

HIGH ST.

15

OBRIEN ST.

O.P.P.

14

19

MONTROSE

FROST

CHAPAIS

18

McKEE DRIVE

24

32

FRONT ST.

GOVERNMENT DOCK

MARINA

CHIEF COMMANDA CRUISE

CASSELLS ST.

CASSELLS ST.

31

GIROUX ST.

TROUT LAKE ROAD

MOUNTAINVIEW DR.

HIGHWAY 63 (FROM QUEBEC)

LAKESIDE DR.

23

32

KATE PACE BIKE PATH

P

S 31
OAK ST.

WORTHINGTON ST.

FRASER ST.
L
28

FERGUSON ST.

KING ST.

CHIPPEWA ST.

B

TWIN PINES
S

MOUNTAINVIEW DR.

16

LAKESIDE DR.

SAGE ROAD

17

P
3
S
29
S 30
S
10

McINTYRE ST.

MAIN ST.

WYLD ST.

THIRD AVE.

SHERBROOKE ST.

FOURTH AVE.

FIFTH AVE.

SECOND AVE.

FIRST AVE.

FISHER ST.

POLICE FIRE

13

12

NORTHGATE SQUARE
S W

ONTARIO NORTHLAND INTERMODAL TERMINAL

W. LACE ROAD

TROUT LAKE

P

29
REGINA ST.

LAURIER AVE.

FRANKLIN ST.

#	Establishment	Rooms													
33.	Voyager Motel Hotel, 123 Delaware Ave. P1B 6Z6 472-1490, 1-800-461-9531	80	•	•	•		•	•		•			•		•	•

HIGHWAY 11 NORTH

#	Establishment	Rooms								
35.	Bomark Motel, Highway 11 North P1B 8G3 474-3100	12	•	•			•	•		•
36.	White Fawn Motel, Highway 11 North P1B 8G3 497-3150	12		•			•	•		•	•
37.	Bay Motel, Highway 11 North P1B 8G3 472-7422	9		•			•			•	•
38.	North Highway Inn, Highway 11 North P1B 8G3 495-0722	10		•		•				•	•

TENT/TRAILER PARKS

	No. of Sites	Hook-Ups	Additional Space	Store	Washrooms	Showers	Laundry	Pets Allowed	Babysitting	Pool	Beach	Opening Date	Closing Date	Acreage
40. Champlain Tent & Trailer Park, 1202 Premier Rd. 474-4669	55	42		•	•	•	•	•			•	May 1	Oct. 31	3
41. Dutchies Trailer Park, 670 Lakeshore Dr. 497-0170	42	34	30		4	4						May 1	Oct. 15	
42. Fairview Park, Box 395, Riverbend Rd. 474-0903	34	25	50	•	•	•	•			•		May 1	Oct. 31	15
23. Franklin Motel, Tent & Trailer Park, 444 Lakeshore Dr. 472-1360	55	55	39	•	•	•	•		•	•		May 1	Oct. 31	39

DESTINATIONS

Amelia Field	9	Lee Park	8
Armstrong Beach	23	Marathon Beach	24
Armstrong Field	17	Memorial Gardens	13
Arts Centre	30	Nipissing University	34
Birchaven Cove	22	North Bay & Area Museum	3
Canadore College	21	North Bay Golf Course	27
Canadian Forces Base	11	North Bay Public Library	10
Centennial Park	18	#1 Nautilus Fitness Centre	29
City Hall	10	Optimist Club Fields - Peter Handley / Jim Kelly Field	16
CG's Fitness Centre	28	Peter Palangio Arena	16
Champlain Park / Beach	5	Pinewood Park Golf Course	4
Chippewa High School	14	Silver Beach	25
Duchesnay Falls	33	St. Joseph Scollard Hall	15
Ecole Secondaire Algonquin	26	Sunset Park	1
Fischer Field	12	Troy Field	12
Float Plane Base	32	Tweedsmuir Park	6
Granite Curling and Tennis Club	31	West Ferris Arena	6
Johnson Field	12	West Ferris Secondary School	2
Laurentian Ski Hill	19	Widdifield Secondary School	20
Lee Field	7	YMCA	13

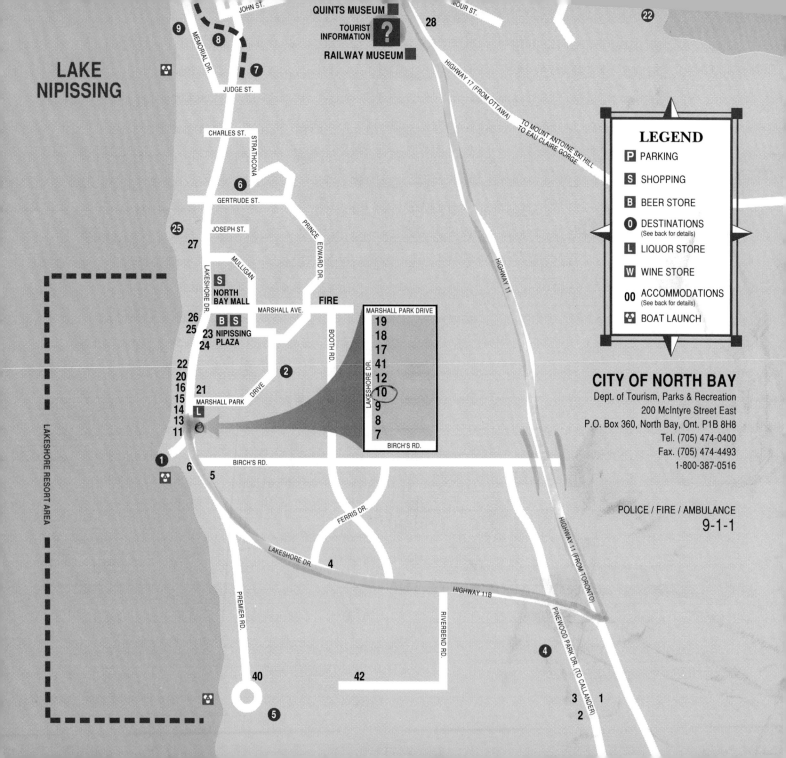

LAKE
NIPISSING

QUINTS MUSEUM
TOURIST
INFORMATION ?
RAILWAY MUSEUM

28

22

JOHN ST.

SEYMOUR ST.

HIGHWAY 17 (FROM OTTAWA)

TO MOUNT ANTOINE SKI HILL
TO EAU CLAIRE GORGE

9
8
7

MEMORIAL DR.

JUDGE ST.

CHARLES ST.

STRATHCONA

6

GERTRUDE ST.

25

JOSEPH ST.

27

PRINCE EDWARD DR.

MULLIGAN

LAKESHORE DR.

S
NORTH
BAY MALL

MARSHALL AVE.

FIRE

26
25

B S

23 NIPISSING
24 PLAZA

2

BOOTH RD.

HIGHWAY 11

22
20
16
15
14
13
11

21

MARSHALL PARK

DRIVE

L

1

6

BIRCH'S RD.

5

LEGEND

P PARKING

S SHOPPING

B BEER STORE

0 DESTINATIONS
(See back for details)

L LIQUOR STORE

W WINE STORE

00 ACCOMMODATIONS
(See back for details)

BOAT LAUNCH

MARSHALL PARK DRIVE

19
18
17
41
12
10
9
8
7

LAKESHORE DR.

BIRCH'S RD.

CITY OF NORTH BAY

Dept. of Tourism, Parks & Recreation
200 McIntyre Street East
P.O. Box 360, North Bay, Ont. P1B 8H8
Tel. (705) 474-0400
Fax. (705) 474-4493
1-800-387-0516

POLICE / FIRE / AMBULANCE
9-1-1

LAKESHORE RESORT AREA

FERRIS DR.

LAKESHORE DR.

4

HIGHWAY 11B

HIGHWAY 11 (FROM TORONTO)

PINEWOOD PARK DR. (TO CALLANDER)

4

PREMIER RD.

RIVERBEND RD.

40

42

5

3 1
2

which passes Lakeview Cellars, one of the newest of Niagara's wineries.

● Stay on Cherry Avenue. Turn left on Moyer Road to visit Vineland Estates Winery.

● Return to Cherry Avenue and drive up to Regional Road 73 (Fly Road), which runs across the top of the Niagara Escarpment. Along the way, stop at the Sugar Bush. When the sap runs in March, visitors stop here on weekends to sample pancakes and fresh maple syrup. From Regional Road 73, turn left onto Regional Road 24.

● Another kilometre brings you to Sixth Avenue. Turn left to Ball's Falls Conservation Area and walk to the falls. Opposite the park is a cluster of pioneer buildings, including an 1809 flour mill, the old Ball House (1850), and a church built in the 1860s and still used for weddings. Tours bring these sites to life. (For times, see Jordan, opposite page.)

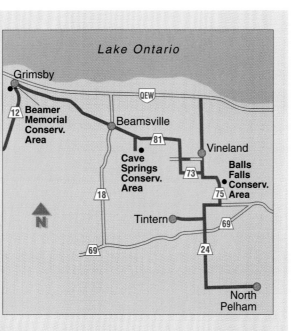

● Once out of the park, turn left back to Regional Road 24 and left again. Continue south along Regional Road 24. Turn right (west) on Spring Creek Road to visit the tiny hamlet of Tintern and the Tintern Not So General Store, which offers hand-decorated clothing and accessories.

● Return to 24 and continue to Uncle Porky's Farm, whose homemade sausage is famous throughout the area, and where you can enjoy a horse-drawn hay (or a sleigh ride, during the winter months).

● Continue on 24 a few more kilometres to Metler Road. Turn left (east) toward the small village of North Pelham. On the left, you pass Little Lake Poultry Farm, where the owners keep a surprising variety of exotic animals and delight in showing them to visitors.

● Farther along, on the right, there is a sign pointing to the Comfort Maple. In a field just off the road stands what is said to be Canada's oldest living sugar maple. The 400-year-old tree was named for a local family called Comfort. Legend says, if you hug the maple (some 27 m high and 26 m wide) and make a wish, your wish will come true.

● At Short Hills Trout Farm, some 4 km after the Comfort Maple, you can catch and cook your lunch, or just buy it and have it cooked for you. Enjoy a picnic on the grounds. From the farm, turn left onto Regional Road 24 and return to Vineland and the Queen Elizabeth Highway.

Wine tasting is one of the pleasures of a visit to the Niagara Peninsula's vineyards.

2 St. George

Stately homes sit side by side with apple orchards, thoroughbred horse ranches and million-dollar dairy farms in the area around St. George (pop. 1,000). The town was once predominantly a farming community. Today, its Victorian Main Street is lined with antique stores, gift shops and boutiques.

The 1888 South Dumfries Township Hall is a pretty sight, with its rose beds, shaded lawn and Victorian gazebo, where you can often hear free musical entertainment in summer. For those who love flowers, the Joseph Smith Lily Garden, one of the largest in the province, has rare species of lilies.

West of town is the winding Grand River. Following its banks are trails, laid on the bed of a railway track and passing through wetlands and rare Carolinian forest. The vegetation includes a mix of oaks, hickories, wild licorice, sycamores and water hemp. The wetland vista at the west end of the forest is a well-kept secret among birders. Naturalists may want to bring binoculars to catch sight of rare species such as Acadian flycatchers and Louisiana water thrushes.

Red and pink cosmoses run riot outside a quaint house in St. George.

North of St. George, on Howell Road, there are apple orchards that supply much of southwestern Ontario. Every fall Farrow Orchards, Howell's Orchards, and Orchard Home welcome visitors with explanations of how apples are cultivated and cider is produced.

On Blue Lake Road, just west of Highway 24, is the restored childhood dwelling of Adelaide Hunter-Hoodless (1857-1910). In 1897, Hoodless founded the Women's Institute, an organization

The treasures of an antique store in St. George's Main Street tempt a browser to window-shop.

for rural women that quickly spread across the country, and introduced the teaching of domestic science into Ontario schools. Inside the charming two-story white house are 19th-century kitchen implements, such as a spoon made from a cow horn, as well as costumes and antiques, which can be seen on a guided tour. *Open late February to late December, Monday to Friday, from 10 am to 4 pm; between Victoria Day and Thanksgiving, also Sunday, from noon to 5 pm.*

Special events

St. George Lily Festival
(early July)

St. George Antique Fair and Sale
(Labor Day weekend)

Apple Harvest (late September)

3 Paris

⌐ ✳ ⌂

In the early 1800s, an American industrialist called Hiram Capron founded a town in the valley of the Grand River, near his gypsum mine. Capron called the town Paris, after the plaster of paris the gypsum was used to make.

Paris (pop. 7,907) is unusual in that several of its buildings are faced with cobblestones. The style is seen more often in New York State. The builder Levi Boughton came to Paris in the 1830s from Rochester in New York. He brought with him a construction technique that had been originated by the Romans. Rounded pebbles, which lay in abundance in the fields around Paris, were passed through a standard ring to select stones of the same shape and size. They were then laid in horizontal rows between courses of masonry, giving the buildings an attractive "knitted" appearance.

Paris has 12 houses, two churches and several walls from previous buildings that are cobbled. One of the finest examples is the Paris Plains Church, built in 1845. The church and other cobbled buildings, such as the Levi Boughton House, can be seen on a self-guiding walking tour.

Robert White's Boot and Shoe Store was where Alexander Graham Bell received the first "long-distance" phone call. It was sent from Brantford, 12 km away, where Bell used to live. A plaque marks the site of his home, at 94 Tutela Heights Road.

4 St. Jacobs

👢 👣 ✳

The "village of many Jacobs," or Jakobstettel, as St. Jacobs was once called, was settled more than a century ago by Mennonites. This Protestant group was originally established in Europe in the 16th century and scattered across Europe and North America to escape persecution.

Over the years this area has maintained its Mennonite way of life. Even today, in and around St. Jacobs (pop. 1,300), you can often see Old Order Mennonites—the most conservative group—driving along peacefully in horse-drawn buggies. They wear dark 19th-century-style clothing—the men and boys wear broad-brimmed black hats, the women and girls are in long skirts, high-necked blouses, black boots and bonnets. They eschew smoking, drinking alcohol, and many 20th-century necessities (cars, electricity, phones, and TV). The only visible signs of modernity seem to be sunglasses and the fluorescent orange triangular signs on the rear of their buggies that warn approaching motorists of slow vehicles. Farms with windmills instead of electrical wires are a sure sign of an Old Order Mennonite family.

Mennonite farmers sell fresh produce, sausages, and maple syrup from the end of their driveways (but not on Sundays). St. Jacobs Farmers' Market is open on Thursdays and Saturdays year-round, and on Tuesdays from June to August. (Handmade crafts and furniture are also sold at the market.)

To dig further into the Mennonite story, visit The Meetingplace, a modern multimedia museum at 33 King St. A 30-minute documentary film, *Mennonites of Ontario*, colorfully illustrates their history and the differences between subgroups of the 25,000 Ontario Mennonites, most of whom are not of the Old Order. There is also a replica of a Mennonite meetinghouse and a cave, where the early Mennonites in

Silos rise like sentinels over the fields near St. Jacobs, the heart of Mennonite Ontario.

Europe gathered to worship. *Admission by donation. Open from early May to late October, Monday to Friday, 11 am to 5 pm; Saturday, from 10 am to 5 pm; Sunday from 1:30 to 5 pm; early November to late April, Saturday, 11 am to 4:30 pm, Sunday, 2 pm to 4:30 pm.*

Another St. Jacobs attraction is the Maple Syrup Museum of Ontario, in a renovated factory on Spring Street South. A wide collection of artifacts related to the production of maple syrup is on display; there are sugaring-off demonstrations, and a variety of maple sugar and maple syrup products for sale. *Open daily, excluding Mondays, from January to May, 10 am to 6 pm.*

The village has several craft shops, where locally made pottery, blown glass, and weaving are for sale, and a blacksmith's shop.

Special events
The Art of the Craft Show and Sale
(late August)

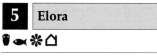

5 | **Elora**

Over the centuries, the Grand and Irvine rivers have carved out a spectacular 30-m-deep limestone gorge. Here, a retired British officer founded Elora in 1832, naming it after the Ellora caves in India, to which his sea-captain brother had traveled.

The town's past can still be seen on Mill Street, the main street of Elora (pop. 3,200), in well-preserved 19th-century shops faced with stone.

A cat painted on a door greets the passerby in Elora.

At the eastern end of the gorge, an island of rock called the Tooth of Time stands immovable as the Grand River hurtles by on both sides. The dramatic rock is now an Elora landmark. But in 1903, local councillors considered blowing it up because it caused ice jams and floods. Recent councillors have chosen to make the rock more secure: the Tooth of Time now has cement fillings in its base to protect it from the continuous action of the water. At the Elora Mill Inn, an 1838 gristmill that has been refurbished as an inn and restaurant, you can get a superb view of the Tooth and hear the constant roar of the waterfall above it.

Decorative features beautify the facade and door at the entrance to a dwelling in Elora.

West of the town is the Elora Gorge Conservation Park, where picnicking, camping, swimming, hiking, and white water kayaking are possible. At the eastern edge of the town, on County Road 18, is the Elora Quarry, a swimming hole with sandy beaches surrounded by high cliffs left after limestone was quarried there in the early 1900s.

During trout season (the third Saturday in April to the end of September) anglers come from as far away as Britain to enjoy fly-fishing on a special-regulation section of the Grand River nearby. Barbed hooks and organic baits are prohibited.

For two weeks every summer (in late July and early August) Elora resounds with the music of the Elora Festival.

The festival features classical music with a choral focus, spanning three centuries from the Baroque period to the present. Outdoor concerts are held in the quarry, with musicians performing on a raft in the quarry for a rapt audience securely seated on the limestone cliffs.

Special events

I Love Country Show and Sale
(early May)

Elora Gala of Artists (late July)

The Elora Festival
(late July to early August)

The Elora Studio Tour
(late July to early August)

Annual Flower and Vegetable Show
(late August)

Elora Antique Show and Sale
(mid-September)

Trees clinging tenaciously to the sheer walls of Elora Gorge create a green mantle for this spectacular, 30-m-deep limestone chasm.

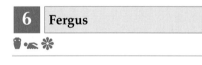

6 Fergus

Nineteenth-century limestone buildings proclaim the Scottish heritage of Fergus (pop. 6,757), a town on the banks of the Grand River. It was founded in the 1830s by Scottish immigrant Adam Fergusson and took his name.

The river provided the energy and transportation for a tannery and gristmill. These two magnificent buildings are now empty but stand on the river at the northern end of town, a reminder of the industries that harnessed the Grand and brought wealth to the town. Other handsome limestone buildings—there are more than 200 in all—include Fergusson's home, the Beatty Foundry and St. Andrew's Presbyterian Church.

The Beatty Brothers' factory now bustles with farm stalls every weekend. The Fergus Market is held inside it year-round and offers fresh local produce as well as local crafts.

Fergus is renowned for its Highland Games. Every August, contestants come from Scotland and North America, as well as Canada, to take part in highland dancing, tossing the caber, and bagpipe competitions.

During the summer, the energetic can canoe down the Grand River and over its rapids. Those who want something more leisurely can walk through the Templin Gardens along the riverside, or browse through the local craft shops.

Between Fergus and Elora is the Wellington County Museum and Archives, at one time the county poorhouse. In this limestone building, dating from 1877, local history is displayed in reconstructed pioneer storefronts and room settings in which agricultural tools, textiles, fashions, domestic artifacts and photographs of prominent citizens of the past are arranged. *Open year-round, Monday to Friday, 9:30 am to 4:30 pm; Saturday and Sunday, 1 pm to 5 pm.*

Special events
Fergus Market (Saturday and Sunday)
Highland Games (mid-August)

7 Campbellville

The tree-lined village of Campbellville (pop. 741) is a treat for both antique lovers and nature lovers. The quaint mix of 19th- and 20th-century brick and clapboard shops on the village's main street sell everything from antiques to stained glass and handcrafted furniture. The surrounding countryside has several conservation areas that abound with splendid scenery and hiking trails.

The beauty of the landscape is due largely to the Niagara Escarpment, a massive ridge of fossil-rich sedimentary rock that cuts across 450 km between Niagara and Tobermory, and rises up to heights of 500 m in some places.

Just south of Campbellville, on the Guelph Line, is the Crawford Lake Conservation Area. Its 12 km of rugged but groomed skiing and hiking trails wind through tranquil woodland and along the escarpment cliffs. From an elevated boardwalk, you can see pristine Crawford Lake, a protected stretch of water. The small lake is a rare geological time capsule. Corn pollen excavated from successive layers of the lake's sediment has helped archaeologists to date the Iroquois occupation of the area to between A.D. 1200 and 1645.

Also part of the conservation area is a reconstructed 15th-century Iroquois longhouse village surrounded by a palisade. Interpretive stations in the village describe North American Indian games and agricultural and burial practices. The Wolf Clan Longhouse has a mini-theatre, an archaeology exhibit, and a display of the daily life of the native people. *Open November to May on weekends, and daily from May to November, from 10 am to 4 pm.*

Rattlesnake Point Conservation Area lies about 7 km east of Campbellville on a detached part of the Niagara Escarpment that rises 91 m above the countryside. Stunted and spindly white cedars 700 years old, discovered only in 1988, cling to the edge of the escarpment near Buffalo Crag Lookout. From this point, you can see buffalo, grazing in a fenced compound in the Nassagaweya Canyon.

To the east of Campbellville, on the outskirts of the town of Milton (pop. 30,529), is the Ontario Agricultural Museum, with one of the largest collections of historical farm machinery in North America. Two farmsteads, an octagonal barn, an old stone schoolhouse, and other old buildings dot the 32-ha site. Interpreters in period costume show visitors how the tools and machinery were used. *Open daily, mid-May to mid-September, 10 am to 5 pm.*

Special events
Mohawk Raceway's Annual Fall Fair
(late September)

8 Rockwood

The clang of a bell and the rumble of wheels on rails can be heard in the woodlands of rural Ontario. They signal the presence of electrical streetcars from a bygone age, the treasure of the Halton County Radial Railway Museum, at Rockwood (pop. 1,391).

Most of the streetcars are more than 60 years old and are rebuilt and repaired here by volunteer craftsmen and artisans who use traditional methods and materials to lovingly bring back these beauties to their former splendor. A ticket bought at the gift shop will take you on a mile through the woods, past workshops, the turn-of-the-century Rockwood railway station and car houses. *Open daily, mid-May to late October, 10 am to 5 pm.*

For those who are not railway buffs, the village of Rockwood offers its own charms. It was originally settled by Quakers in 1821, when it was known as Brotherstown, and the village still has several old stone buildings from that time, as well as antique and craft stores.

Nearby is the Rockwood Conservation Area, rolling woodland cut through by the Eramosa River. It has unusual cave formations, potholes gouged by the spinning waters of a retreating glacier, the ruins of a 19th-century stone mill, and two millponds, now used for swimming and boating. There are also facilities here for camping and fishing.

9 Alton

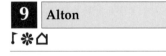

A tree-covered hill known as the Pinnacle overlooks the north end of the rural town of Alton (pop. 1,086). Once an excellent vantage point for Indian

The Millcroft Inn, overlooking a waterfall at Alton, originally served as a woolen mill.

Roads to explore:
Rustic lanes and quaint communities by the Credit River

Distance (approx.): 79 km / 50 miles

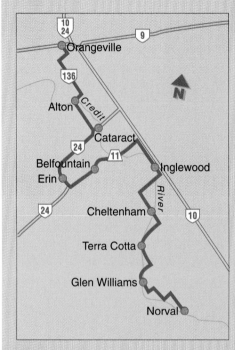

The drive from Norval to Orangeville follows the Credit Valley, lined by dense hardwood forests that explode with color in fall.

● The village of Norval (pop. 277) straddles the sparkling waters of the Credit River. It was founded in 1820 by James MacNab, a United Empire Loyalist who fled the United States. Pause by the former home of Lucy Maud Montgomery, author of *Anne of Green Gables*. The house served as manse for the neighboring Knox Presbyterian Church, built in 1878.

● Drive north on Winston Churchill Boulevard (Route 19), across the fast-moving waters of the Credit. Turn left on Mayfield Road and then left again at 20 Sideroad into the town of Glen Williams (pop. 1016), established in 1824. Stop at the Copper Kettle Pub for a bite, or stroll to the Clay Concepts Studio and Gallery for some shopping.

● Follow the main street north, then turn left on Winston Churchill Boulevard to Terra Cotta (pop. 196). The village was once known as Salmonville because of the abundance of salmon crowding the Credit at that point. Visit Terra Cotta Conservation Area, 160 ha of towering hardwood trees, marshes, and springs, to camp, hike, swim, or picnic. Or wander through the General Store and galleries dotted throughout the village. To the southwest lies the Silver Creek Conservation Area, which is cut through by the Bruce Trail.

● Continue east along King Street (Route 9), cross the Credit River and wind up the Niagara Escarpment to Mississauga Road, where on the left stand the majestic towers of the former Cheltenham Brick Works.

Cheltenham (pop. 467) was founded in the 1820s by Charles Haines, a millwright, who named it after his English birthplace. Several 19th-century buildings in the town, including the Country Store, town hall and lodge, are protected heritage buildings.

● Head north up Creditview Road to Olde Base Line Road, and turn right. The rolling hills of the red clay predominant in this area provide a spectacular view of the surrounding countryside.

● A short distance east, turn left on Dufferin Street (1st Line West), leading into Inglewood (pop. 572). Its stone quarry supplied the materials for Toronto's curbstones and historical site, Casa Loma.

● Farther north on Dufferin, turn left on Forks of the Credit Road (Route 11), which winds past the Forks of the Credit Provincial Park and into Belfountain (pop. 296). Extensive hiking trails snake in and around the village, also a popular spot for fishing. In 1910, the White Mountain Spring Water Company (later Canada Dry) bottled spring water here, eventually using it for its ginger ale. Visit the century-old general store, site of the hamlet's first tavern. Head to Belfountain's conservation area to enjoy the scenic falls on the Credit or the many historic buildings.

● Follow Bush Street west, turn right on Main Street (Highway 24) in Erin, where there are many antique and craft stores. Continue on Highway 24, then turn right at Caledon's 3rd Line West into Cataract (pop. 103), on the lip of the valley, overlooking the Credit and the beautiful Cataract Falls.

Water spills from a three-tiered pedestal, now enveloped with moss, at Belfountain.

● Double back on the 3rd Line, which becomes Road 136, and travel north through rolling countryside and Coulterville and Alton to Orangeville. The Orangeville Reservoir is the source of the Credit River. It has an abundance of fish and birds and is an enjoyable place to picnic.

10 Hockley

Wooded countryside threaded with trails for horse riding and hiking, pick-your-own berry farms, and craft studios, surrounds the village of Hockley (pop. 250). During the fall, the bosky Hockley Valley has a palette of ochers, greens, oranges and golds unsurpassed in southern Ontario.

In the village is The Driveshed, a long, two-story, dark brown frame building with a wooden awning, built as a hotel in 1837. It now houses a general store, tea shop and bed-and-breakfast. In the courtyard behind it are several little craft shops selling everything from children's clothing to handmade lace and stained glass.

Just west of Hockley Village, south of Hockley Road on the 7th Line, is the modern Cistercian Monastery of Notre Dame, built in 1983. The church and a small shop are open to the public year-round, and 10 rooms are reserved for guests on retreat. On a clear day, the view from the monastery, one of the highest points in southern Dufferin County, is among the most spectacular in the area: from this spot, you can see Lake Simcoe 65 km to the northeast.

An eye-catching weather vane in the window of a Hockley shop.

The Hockley region is a hiker's haven and, in the winter, a favorite spot of cross-country skiers. Casual hikers often walk the 12-km-long Hockley Road from Highway 10 to the village of Hockley. More serious hikers sometimes seek out the many 18th-century Ojibwa trails that crisscross Dufferin County in the heart of the Hockley Valley. The trails are not

tribes to spot the wildlife roaming the valley below, it now offers a spectacular view of farming countryside, which rolls away from it like a three-dimensional, multicolored carpet.

A tributary of the Credit River, which is known locally as Shaw's Creek, flows through the centre of town. The fast-flowing stream once provided power to the numerous mills that lined it—Alton was home to one of Canada's largest underwear manufacturers a century ago. Now the mills are silent, with windows boarded up, and the creek, quiet once more, lures nature lovers to its shady, tree-lined banks.

Dod's Mill, where a large meteorite landed in the millpond in the 1920s,

making the water boil, is now the Millcroft Inn. The rooms and dining area at the back of the inn directly overlook a rumbling mist-shrouded waterfall that plunges 7 m below. The waterfall is at its finest in winter, when it is partially frozen and the water in the stream below gleams jet black against the crisp, white snow.

Next to the Millcroft Inn is the Balloonery, where intrepid travelers can take trips in brightly colored hot-air balloons and enjoy the countryside from an unusual height.

This area has some of the best new golf courses in Canada, including the fairway at Osprey Valley, west of Alton, on Highway 136.

A touch of red and green to door and roof enlivens a weathered barn in Hockley Valley.

marked, but a map of them is available at the Mono Township offices on County Road 8. Since the trails are largely on private property, it is only courteous to get permission to walk along them from the owners.

Just west of the Second Line East, and crossing the Hockley Road, is the 780-km-long Bruce Trail. Look for white blazes on trees, fence posts, stiles, or rocks to direct you. Double blazes mean a change of direction. Blue or yellow blazes mark side trails.

Mono Cliffs Conservation Area, about 2 km north of the village of Mono Centre, is another favorite spot for hikers and cross-country skiers. The sheer dolomite cliffs that give the conservation area its name are part of the Niagara Escarpment. A dozen species of rare lichens and ferns grow on

the cliffs, along with 400-year-old stunted cedar trees.

West of Hockley, on Dufferin County Road 7, are two ski resorts—Cedar Highlands and the Hockley Valley Resort, which in summer is one of Ontario's most hilly 18-hole golf courses.

Between them, on the same road, 6.5 km west of Hockley, is the Eagle's Nest Apiary, where you can see how bees make honey. The sweet stuff is also for sale.

11 Tottenham
❋

From Tottenham (pop. 4,500), you can ride the rails into history on a 1920s, open-window passenger train pulled by a vintage steam engine. With steam hissing in the air and the haunting whistle ringing in your ears you can take a step back in time as the train

puffs through the Beeton Valley and back to Tottenham, playing tag with Beeton Creek as it winds in and out of view. Cows and sheep graze placidly in the pastures, and you may even see a blue heron lifting its huge, awkward wings in preparation for flight. *The railway runs from late May until Thanksgiving weekend, on Sundays and holiday Mondays, on the hour, from 10 am to 4 pm. The ride is about 40 minutes.*

12 Schomberg
🏺❋

At the western edge of the Holland Marsh is Schomberg (pop. 1,269). This quaint old town has many antique and craft shops that have been remodeled to reflect the past. It is also the home of the restored Schomberg Feed Mill, built in 1844. The mill served as the feed grain supplier for the surround-

Roads to explore: A Quaker temple, a Byzantine memorial
Distance (approx.): 150 km / 93¾ miles

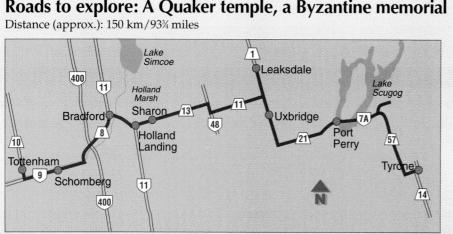

A rich concentration of Canadian heritage lies north of Toronto, from reclaimed marshland to a Quaker temple, a Byzantine-style memorial, the house of Canada's best-known author, and a 19th-century mill.

• A pleasant starting point is Tottenham. From here, head south on County Road 10 and turn left on Highway 9. Drive through Schomberg, with its antique and craft shops, and on for about 17 km to Highway 11. Turn north on Highway 11 until you reach Route 51. Branch right to Holland Landing.

• Leave Holland Landing by traveling northeast on Route 13 to Sharon, where a Quaker sect temple is situated. From the temple, take Mount Albert Side Road (Route 13) east for about 10 km, to the junction with Highway 48. Head south for 2 km, then east again on Herald Road (Country Road 11) for 15 km. Turn north onto Durham Region Road 1.

• About 1 km along, the magnificent verdigris domed roof of the Thomas Foster Memorial Temple can been seen

Holland Landing's 1848 Christ Church

through the trees surounding it. Thomas Foster was raised in Leaskdale, to the north. He apprenticed as a butcher, ventured into a successful career in real estate, served as an MP (1917-21) and then as mayor of Toronto (1925-27). He built the temple between 1935-36 as a memorial to his wife and daughter. It was inspired by the Taj Mahal in India. The Byzantine-style temple has a copper dome 18 m high; inside, 16 marble pillars support four arches, illuminated by stained glass windows. *Open June to September, the first and third Sunday afternoons. Check first with local tourist office.*

• Farther along Durham Region Road 1 is Leaskdale, where Lucy Maud Montgomery, author of *Anne of Green Gables*, lived 15 years. Her husband, Rev. Ewan Macdonald, was Leaskdale's Presbyterian minister. The site, closed to visitors, is marked with a plaque.

• From Leaskdale, head south on Region Road 1 some 10 km to Uxbridge (pop. 12,000). Here the Uxbridge-Scott Museum features a display on the life of Lucy Maud Montgomery. The town, settled by Quakers in 1808, boasts some of southern Ontario's finest farmland.

• Continue south on Uxbridge's main street until you reach County Road 21. Then head east to Port Perry, a lakeside town with old shops and boutiques.

• From Port Perry, head east on Highway 7A for 9.5 km, then turn south on Regional Road 57 for 15.5 km. Keep an eye out for a small sign reading Tyrone, and head east for 3 km. This will take you to the 19th-century Tyrone Mill (see page 215 for a detailed description).

• Head south on Region Road 14 to reach highways 2 and 401, located just north of Bowmanville.

ing farms until the mid-1980s. Now the weighing scale and antique grain machinery are still, but they are kept in gleaming condition to be seen by visitors. *Open daily, year-round, 10 am to 5:30 pm.* Farmer's markets abound in the fertile area.

The nearby Holland Marsh, once a tamarack marsh, covers thousands of hectares where Holland River flowed into Lake Simcoe. The area, named after Maj. S. Holland, surveyor general of Canada in 1791, was first settled in the mid-1800s, but was considered too soggy for farming. However, the wild marsh grass was harvested to make ropes, as well as the stuffing for mattresses. A young, energetic farmer and businessman named David Watson was the first person to suggest dredging the canal. In 1934, the marsh was drained into the canal and Holland River. Soon afterward, market gardening began on the reclaimed land. Today this farmland is renowned for the quality of its crops.

The level roads of Holland Landing are ideal for cyclists.

Special events
Agricultural Fair (late May)

13 Kleinburg

⌐ ✳ ⌂

The village of Kleinburg (pop. 1,250) may be small in size, but its stature is of international proportions. What makes it so significant is the McMichael Canadian Art Collection. The gallery, set on parkland overlooking the Humber River valley, contains the largest display of works by the Group of Seven, and other important collections of Canadian art and sculpture.

In the grounds is the studio shack once lived in by Tom Thomson, one of

PLAYING THE FOOL DOWN ON THE FARM

An old farmhouse, big red barn, outbuildings, split-rail cedar fences, and horses and cows mark Puck's Farm, which looks no different from any other farm in the Schomberg area. But stroll around looking at the sheep, pigs, goats, rams, rabbits, ducks, geese, roosters, and chickens and you will see firsthand just what is so different about it. This is a working farm for city people to see exactly what farmers do and perhaps even lend a hand.

The owners have turned the 69-ha property into what they call an entertainment farm. They named it Puck's Farm after the lovable fool in Shakespeare's *A Midsummer Night's Dream*, and also because, as one owner says, "You've got to be a fool to farm."

Depending on the season and time of day, Puck's Farm offers hayrides, sleigh rides, pony rides, and a chance to take part in sheepshearing, feeding the animals (maybe even bottle-feeding a lamb), and making butter. If your visit happens during spring planting, you are welcome to help sow seed. During corn season you can pick your own corn, shuck it, drop it into a tank of boiling water, and eat it right on the spot. All the crops at Puck's Farm are pick-your-own: sweet corn, melons, snow peas, apples, pumpkins, raspberries and strawberries. And you can eat as much as you want while picking.

It is not all about farming here, either. The farm has held a giant Easter-egg hunt (with 30,000 foil-wrapped Easter eggs), and holds a haunted hayride every year in the last week of October. Bluegrass and country music are also performed here every weekend from May to October.

Puck's Farm is located on the 11th Concession Road of King Township, some 2.5 km south of Highway 9, near Schomberg.

Canada's greatest painters of the early 20th century. It was moved from its original site in Toronto.

Visitors to the gallery can watch artists at work, attend lectures and films about art, and art workshops. *Open May to October, Monday to Saturday, 11 am to 5 pm, Sunday 11 am to 6:30 pm; November to April, Tuesday to Sunday, 11 am to 5 pm.*

The village itself invites you to wander around and to browse among the antique and craft stores. You can visit the Kleinburg Doll Museum, with a collection of 165 antique and character dolls. The lovely exhibits include Eaton Beauties, bisque dolls and a ventriloquist's dummy. *Open year-round, Tuesday to Friday, noon to 5 pm; weekends and holiday Mondays, noon to 6 pm.*

Not far away is the Kortright Centre for Conservation. Demonstrations and activities are organized there to inform visitors about conserving water, wildlife, forests, land, and energy. The highlights include a maple syrup demonstration, wildflower walks, planting for wildlife, hunting skills, and birdbox building. The centre, set in 325 ha of woodland, has a wetland boardwalk, a wind generator, and 10 km of walking and cross-country ski trails. *Open daily, 10 am to 4 pm.*

Special events

Four Winds Kite Festival, Kortright Centre (May)

Kleinburg Binder Twine Festival (September)

Groundhog Winter Carnival, Kortright Centre (January)

---

14 Sharon

❋

The focal point of the community of Sharon (pop. 2,500) is its temple. It was built between 1825 and 1830 by David Willson and his Children of Peace, a group of Quakers disillusioned with their previous form of religion. The temple is square (denoting unity and

Lea Vivot's Loveseat, *on display just outside the artist's studio, is one of a profusion of artworks for which Kleinburg is famed.*

justice to all men) with a door on each side, which is intended to show that everyone entered on an equal footing from all directions. It is three stories high (representing the Trinity) with an equal number of windows all around (amounting to 2,952 panes of glass) so that the light of the Gospel might fall equally upon all people.

In 1991, a secret compartment was found in the ark, or altar, of the temple, containing documents written and placed there by David Willson 160 years ago. Staff at the temple will tell you about them.

The temple was designated a national museum in 1992. *Open for tours from May until the end of October, Wednesday to Sunday, 10 am to 5 pm. Tours include several other buildings of historical significance.*

Special events

June Day (early June)

The Illumination (early September)

Thanksgiving Harvest Festival (mid-October)

---

15 Kirkfield

A general store and a few homes make up the peaceful hamlet of Kirkfield (pop. 300). But about 3 km north of the community is its premier attraction— Kirkfield Lift Lock, built in 1907 as part of the Trent–Severn Waterway.

The lift lock was intended for commercial traffic, but it is now used by pleasure boats. The lock raises and lowers boats a height of about 15 m in two connected water-filled chambers. The upper chamber is filled with an extra 30 cm of water, which causes it to sink downward and forces the other chamber an equal distance upward. Each chamber has huge hinged gates at both ends, holds about 1,700 tonnes of water, and carries boats up to 40 m long. It is intriguing to watch the giant hydraulic lock, which takes about 10 minutes to go through one cycle.

From the lock, boaters can go west to Canal Lake and Lake Simcoe, or south-east to Mitchell Lake, Cameron Lake, and Fenelon Falls.

The summit of the Trent–Severn Waterway is Balsam Lake, about 10 km east of Kirkfield. Balsam Lake Provincial Park has a 500-m-long sandy beach and shady campgrounds. The limestone that lines the lake protects its water from various forms of pollution such as acid rain, and keeps it relatively free of algae and weeds. The lake is good for sailboarding and fishing for bass and muskellunge. You can also cycle around the park.

On the 2.5-km-long Lookout Trail, you can see two different types of glacial origin: a ridge of glacial debris, called an esker, formed by a stream flowing beneath the ice of a glacier; and steep circular hills of layered sand and gravel, known as kames. Retreating glaciers left these deposits here at the end of the last Ice Age.

Special events
Annual Summer Festival
(early September)

Kirkfield Lock, Canada's second largest lift lock, is a key link in the Trent–Severn Waterway.

16 Bobcaygeon

At the junction of Sturgeon and Pigeon lakes, on the boat-busy Trent–Severn Waterway, is the town of Bobcaygeon (pop. 2,200). It was a fishing paradise early this century and still hosts the Canada/United States Walleye Tournament every Victoria Day weekend. In recent years, the holiday resort has become a retirement community and artists' colony.

At the north end of Bobcaygeon, on Dunn Street, is the Kawartha Settlers' Village, a large, recently created pioneer village. Turn-of-the-century log buildings and an old carriage house have been donated by families throughout the region. The village holds "heritage activities" throughout the year: winter sleigh rides, quilt-making groups, costume days, and craft classes. *Open daily from Victoria Day to Thanksgiving, 9 am to 5 pm .*

Just west of Bobcaygeon, on County Road 8, is Dunsford House, one of the area's most significant landmarks, with a beautiful view of Sturgeon Lake. Built in 1838, it is said to be one of the finest examples of two-story log architecture in existence. The great house, which originally had 12 rooms and four fireplaces, has been restored and is now a country inn. Its six large suites are furnished with period reproduction furniture.

Bobcaygeon is near the Central Ontario Toptrails, a network of snow-mobiling and cross-country skiing trails that stretches 3,000 km from Peterborough and Lindsay in the south to Bancroft and Haliburton in the north.

Also on the Trent–Severn Waterway is the village of Buckhorn (pop. 243), between Buckhorn and Lovesick lakes. Apart from boating, and trails that are maintained in winter, the village has galleries that draw art-lovers from far and wide. The Gallery on the Lake, about 2.5 km east of Buckhorn, displays works by prominent Canadian

THE ROCKS THAT TEACH

In May 1954, three geologists on a rock hunt stopped for lunch on a large flat rock. They noticed that it was pitted with marks, looked closer and saw that the indented shapes had in fact been made by human hands. They had discovered one of the largest series of petroglyphs, or rock carvings, in North America. The huge rock was covered with carvings of more than 300 symbols and 600 indecipherable images, inscribed with gneiss scrapers and hammerstones. They may be the work of Algonquian-speaking Indians who visited here between 500 and 1,000 years ago.

This site is revered by the Ojibwa of the Anishinabe Nation, who call the rocks *Kinomagewapkong* —The Rocks That Teach. No one is certain what they were used for, but the glyphs may explain the cycle of life. Tribal elders may have brought young men on the threshold of puberty to the rocks for spiritual and mythological instruction. The medicine wheel indicated that life began in the east, where the sun rises. The bright sun of midday was youth. The west symbolized old age, and the north the afterlife.

Experts believe the images include Kitchi Manitou, the Great Spirit who created the Earth, and Nanabush, a trickster with rabbit ears who was sent to teach the Indians the arts of survival. The three images shown here (top to bottom) represent a legendary water being, a mythical figure, and a moose.

Today the main part of the rock is covered by a building with a walkway that allows visitors to see up close this rich and fabulous heritage.

artists, such as Edwin Matthews, Michael Dumas, and Mary Lampman. *Open year-round, daily, 9 am to 5 pm.* And on Curve Lake Indian Reserve, nearby, is the Whetung Craft Centre and Art Gallery. It is owned and run by Ojibwa Indians, who exhibit their crafts and fine art. *Open year-round, daily, excluding Christmas week, 9 am to 5 pm; July and August, 9 am to 9 pm.*

Special events

Wildlife Art Festival, Buckhorn (mid-August))

Ontario Open Fiddle and Step Dance Contests (mid-July)

Fall Fair (early October)

---

17 Petroglyphs Provincial Park

Huge stands of red and white pine, mixed with various hardwoods, marshy wetlands and two small lakes, make up Petroglyphs Provincial Park. The park was founded in 1976 to protect a national treasure—one of the best series of Indian petroglyphs, or rock carvings, in Canada.

Trails lead past rock cairns built by the staff to mark interest points and paths, and run to the lakes and the petroglyph site itself. There is no swimming at the park, but picnic sites on the shores of McGinnis Lake have spectacular views. The park is ablaze with wildflowers in spring, and is inhabited by many small animals as well as white-tailed deer. *Open mid-May to Thanksgiving, from 10 am to 5 pm.*

18 Port Perry

Two great fires, in November 1883 and July 1884, leveled much of downtown Port Perry. The village, on the shores of Lake Scugog, had originally been a wagon stop. After the fires, it was rebuilt in the Italianate style of Victorian architecture fashionable during the

Inviting contemporary store fronts merge attractively with the 19th-century Italianate facade of Settlement House at Port Perry.

1880s. Walk along Queen Street today and you will see bay windows, turrets, and decorative wrought iron characteristic of that era. Inside the many antique and art and craft stores on the main street, wooden floors and high ceilings maintain the Victorian flavor. A self-guiding tour of Port Perry is available.

Port Perry (pop. 5,000) was the home of Daniel David Palmer, the founder of chiropractics. A historical plaque marks his birthplace in 1845 at 15238 Old Simcoe Road. There is a statue of Palmer in the lakeside park that bears his name. Palmer Park is a perfect summer spot for swimming, playing on the beach, and fishing for bass and muskie, or for ice fishing

Fun on the beach for children at Port Perry's Palmer Park

214

and skating in winter. An environmental park with a boardwalk is presently being constructed there.

A five-minute drive east from Port Perry across a causeway to Scugog Island leads to the Scugog Shores Museum Village on Island Road. A pioneer village on the grounds of a former schoolhouse (now the main museum-building) and church depicts 19th-century life in this area. Among the eight buildings are a print shop with an 1865 press that still works, and an 1860 church that is being restored using the original building methods and tools.

Guides dressed in period costume conduct tours on weekends and holiday Mondays, from Victoria Day until the third weekend in September. *Open May to September, Tuesday to Friday, 9 am to 5 pm; weekends and holidays, 1 pm to 5 pm.*

Special events

Canoe the Nonquon (early June)

Antique and Craft Show and Sale (mid-June)

Festival Days (mid-July)

Blackstock Fair (late August)

Port Perry Fair (Labor Day weekend)

Open Air Ice Palace (mid-January)

19 | Port Hope

✽ ⌂

An architectural treasure trove of period houses and commercial buildings has been lovingly restored and maintained on Lake Ontario's north shore. It is Port Hope (pop. 12,500), settled by Loyalists in the 1790s and whose early prosperity as a lake port is reflected in the fine quality of its architecture.

One of its fine dwellings, the elaborate Penryn Park, built in 1859, is used as the site of the popular CBC TV series *The Road to Avonlea*. And the town's main shopping area, Walton Street, sometimes doubles as a Victorian streetscape for film and TV crews.

History and architecture buffs could easily spend a day walking around the town. A shorter tour is to ramble along Walton Street, then south on Queen

A distant view of Port Hope's Victorian spires and dwellings hints at architectural and historical delights in store for visitors.

CIDER FROM AN OLD MILL

In the 1840s, Irish and English immigrants established the hamlet of Tyrone (pop. 250), north of Bowmansville. It was one of the first mill communities to serve the growing agricultural area around Bowmanville and Oshawa. The water-powered mill itself was built in 1846 to grind grain. It is the oldest structure of its kind still standing in Durham County. Today, the mill is used to cut lumber and, from June to September, to produces apple cider. Work is underway to set the old mill-stones in motion again, grinding wheat into flour.

Inside the mill, well-worn wooden steps lead up to a woodworking shop on the second floor. Antique tools, old flour bags, and wooden beams and floors evoke images of the past. In the store, freshly made apple cider, homemade jams, cheese, baked goods, fudge, and rock candy sticks are for sale. *Open, year-round, Monday to Saturday, 9 am to 6 pm; September to June, also Sunday, 1 to 5 pm.*

A phonograph and other collectibles crowd an antique store at Port Hope.

Street to the town hall, a two-story, red-brick, 1890s gem, which has a domed clock tower. A footbridge across the Ganaraska River takes you to Mill Street, where you can climb a set of steps, known as Jacob's Ladder. They lead to King Street, the town's first main thoroughfare, which still has much early architecture. The Bluestone, on Dorset Street East at the junction with King, is a splendid Greek Revival mansion built in 1834 and faithfully restored by its owners. Nearby, on King Street, is the 1822 St. Mark's Anglican Church, one of the last surviving frame churches in Canada, and the burial spot of Canada's first native-born governor general, Vincent Massey.

The local branch of the Architectural Conservancy of Ontario arranges tours of privately owned historic homes on the Saturday before Thanksgiving.

In early December, Port Hope celebrates an Old Tyme Christmas: local people don Victorian costume and sing Christmas carols in a candlelight procession down the main street. Afterward, it is customary to eat a Yuletide snack of roasted chestnuts and drink hot apple cider.

20 Keene

❋ ⌂

Sheep-flecked hills and fields dotted with rolled bales of hay surround the village of Keene (pop. 207). In the mid-19th century, the settlement boomed with industry, powered by the waters of the Indian River. Now, life is quieter. But the memory of its heyday survives just 1.5 km to the north, at Lang Century Village.

In summer, pioneer life is relived in this community of more than 20 restored buildings. People in period costume go about domestic work and ride horse-drawn buggies on the dirt roads past clapboard houses to the general store and post office, just as the pioneers did in the 1850s. The blacksmith hammers at his forge, and the carpenter saws and turns his wood.

The restored Lang Grist Mill, north of the village of Keene, is powered by the Indian River and still grinds flour with a millstone, as it did when it was first built in the mid-19th century.

The printer's press rolls out a weekly newspaper. On the farms, with their humble log dwellings, apples are pressed for cider.

Sheepshearing demonstrations, corn roasts, a harvest thanksgiving, and folk-music concerts by musicians and dancers are just some of the highlight events at the village. *Open daily, early May to mid-October, Monday to Friday, 11 am to 5 pm. Saturday hours, 1 pm to 5 pm; Sunday, 1 pm to 6 pm.* The visitors' centre houses an interpretive museum. *Open February to mid-December, Monday to Friday, 1 pm to 5 pm.*

Girl in period costume, Lang Century Village

Beside the Lang Century Village is the Lang Grist Mill, built in 1846 to grind flour for local and export needs. It has been restored and is working again. Nearby is the miller's house, furnished as it was in the 1860s. *Opening hours as for Lang Century Village.*

21 Brighton

This community (pop. 4,300), just a stone's throw away from Lake Ontario, was first settled by Loyalists in the late 1700s. The town's history is evident in buildings such as the Proctor House Museum, overlooking Lake Ontario. This restored merchant's mansion, dating from 1865, records life in the area in the 1860s. *Open daily, July to Labor Day, 10 am to 4 pm; Victoria Day to June, weekends only, 1 pm to 4 pm.*

Brighton's waterfront is designed for leisure and relaxation. Boats can be chartered there for fishing in Lake Ontario, where northern pike grow to a large size, the walleyes are plentiful, and salmon and trout abound in summer. Swimming, camping, and even scuba diving are popular recreations here. The town is at the western end of the Murray Canal, along which pleasure craft can cruise to enter the Trent-Severn system.

If more rigorous outdoor pursuits interest you, there is an annual wild turkey hunt in May. Participants must obtain a permit—issued by lottery—from the Ministry of Natural Resources. But if ambling about is more to your taste, Brighton has several antique and craft shops.

Brighton sits at the point where the Presqu'ile Peninsula juts out into Lake Ontario. A large part of the peninsula is occupied by Presqu'ile Provincial Park. Its French name means "almost an island." But it consists of two limestone islands, the larger of which is joined to the mainland by gravel and sandspits. The park has a wide range of habitats—forest, marshes, sand dunes, abandoned farmlands and cobble beaches—which support some 700 plant species.

Presqu'ile is a popular stopover for birds on the Atlantic and Mississippi flyways, during the spring and fall migrations. At these times the number of birds in the park is boosted to some 300 species. The park holds several waterfowl viewing weekends during the year. At other times, the birds can be seen from an observation tower on the marsh boardwalk. Interpretive programs on birding, as well as hiking and nature photography, are held in the visitors' centre in the former lighthouse keeper's home.

The park's shores have more than 2 km of white sandy beach to entice swimmers and sunbathers, and its waters are ideal for sailing, windsurfing, and canoeing. *Open daily, Victoria Day to Labor Day, 8 am to midnight; October to May, 8 am to 4.30 pm.*

Special events
Wild Turkey Hunt
(first 2 weekends, May)
Underwater Treasure Hunt (June)
Brighton Applefest (late September)

Rippling, sinuous shapes mark the burial grounds at Serpent Mounds Provincial Park.

THE MOUND BUILDERS OF ANCIENT ONTARIO

Four thousand years ago, Indians started to visit the north shore of Rice Lake in summer. Here they found wild rice and mussel beds that provided a few weeks' sustenance. On the hill overlooking the lake, they dug pits where they buried their dead with exotic possessions and objects. Burials were conducted with elaborate rituals.

For a brief time about 2,000 years ago, the Indians of Rice Lake began to build earthen mounds above the remains of their dead. Some experts believe this change was influenced by the example of the mound builders who were active at that time throughout the eastern half of the United States.

Today, the grassy mounds—the largest and best preserved in Canada—are the key feature of Serpent Mounds Provincial Park. The site was named by a 19th-century investigator who was impressed by the serpentine shape of the largest mound, which is 7 m high and 2 m wide and curves for 61 m. The other eight mounds are smaller and egg-shaped. Archaeologists have excavated the mounds and uncovered remains, pottery, shell beads, copper spears, and loon beaks. The visitors' centre displays some of these treasures and relates the history of the area.

SOUTHWESTERN ONTARIO

13
SOUTHWESTERN ONTARIO

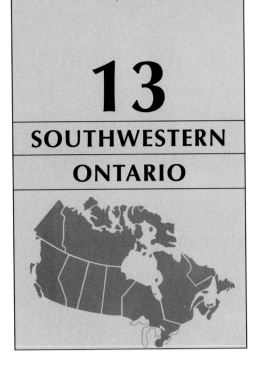

Places to see
Kingsville
Pelee Island
Petrolia
Oil Springs
Dresden
Thamesville
Goderich
Blyth Festival
Benmiller
Clinton
Bayfield
St. Marys
Port Stanley
Long Point
Sparta
Port Dover

Roads to explore
Port Stanley to Port Dover

National park close-up
Point Pelee

Previous pages:
A park scene, Goderich

N

| 0 | 20 | 40 km |
| 0 | 20 | 40 miles |

U.S.A.
CANADA

Sarnia   402   7

3
Petrolia

80   Oil City

Oil Springs
4

St. Clair River

Wallaceburg   **Dresden** **5**

40

Lake St. Clair   Chatham

Detroit River   **Windsor**

2   Tillbury

401

18

3   77   3

Amherstburg

1
Kingsville   Leamington

To Pelee Island

Point Pelee National Park

1 Kingsville

🦃🍴🥙🛶🐟🦆🌸⌂

Kingsville (pop. 6,000) is one of those agreeable communities that beg exploration. Graced with sandy beaches that are perfect for swimmers, sunbathers, and windsurfers, it is also rich in history: the French were here in the early 18th century, and the Loyalists arrived late in that century.

To appreciate the life and times of a prosperous Ontario family in the mid-1880s, visit the John R. Park Homestead, just west of Kingsville, on Highway 18.

John Park, store owner, farmer, and sawmill operator, emigrated from the United States to Upper Canada in the 1820s. His Greek Revival-style home was built in 1842 at a near perfect lakeshore location. Many special events are held here during the year, including maple syrup and blueberry festivals, and military musters. *Open daily, July and August; Sunday to Friday in late spring and early fall; Monday to Friday, Thanksgiving to Victoria Day.*

Kingsville is best known for the 120-ha Jack Miner's Bird Sanctuary, 5 km north of town, off County Road 29. John "Jack" Thomas Miner was one of Canada's greatest naturalists. Born in Ohio, in 1865, he was 13 when his family moved to Kingsville, where he worked in the family tile business. In tune with nature from an early age, he became a skilled hunter and woodsman. His brother's death in a hunting accident convinced Miner to devote himself to wildlife conservation.

About 1904, Miner began attracting ducks and geese into the natural ponds on his property. In the process, he established one of the earliest bird sanctuaries in North America. In 1917, the property was officially declared a pro-

This heated pond at Jack Miner's Bird Sanctuary is a year-round haven for migrating birds.

vincial crown reserve, a decision that eventually prompted the adoption of the Canada goose as our national bird.

Although largely self-taught, Miner wrote two books and lectured far and wide on the need for conservation. He was the first to recognize the importance of bird banding as a means of studying bird migrations.

A deeply religious man, Miner inscribed each bird band with a verse of Scripture. In this way, he was also a "long distance" missionary to Indian and Inuit hunters in the Hudson Bay lowlands, where the tagged birds spent the summer.

King George VI awarded Miner the OBE, and the week of his birth (April 10) is celebrated in Canada as National Wildlife Week. Jack Miner died in 1944.

Each year, about 30,000 ducks and geese find refuge at the sanctuary during their annual winter migration in October and November. This is the best time to see the geese. Late March is also good as the birds are returning then to their northern habitats.

To witness the awesome spectacle of "flushing," when staff at Jack Miner's walk among the birds, causing them to take to the air as one in an incredible flurry of flapping wings, plan to visit

the sanctuary in late fall, or early spring, at 4 p.m. *The sanctuary is open year-round, Monday to Saturday, 9 am to 5 pm; the grounds, 8 am to sundown. Admission free.*

Special events
Victorian Festival (May)
Migration Festival (October)
Fantasy of Lights (November to January)

2 Pelee Island

🚲🦆🛶🐟🦆🌸⌂

On the same latitude (41°N) as northern California, Pelee (pronounced *peelee*) Island lies in Lake Erie, midway between Ontario and Ohio. The island covers 4,000 ha of fertile farms, productive vineyards, and quiet, sandy beaches. The population is slightly less than 650. During summer and the pheasant-hunting season in late fall, this number may triple. But the island rarely gets more crowded than this.

Two ferries—MV *Jiimaan* and MV *Pelee Islander*—sail daily from Leamington and Kingsville for Pelee Island's main communities, West Dock and North Dock (Scudder Dock). The

The John R. Park Homestead is an example of Greek Revival elegance.

schedule varies according to the season. In summer, reservations—at least two weeks in advance—are essential for visitors with cars. The island can also be reached by air.

Pelee Island is the largest of a cluster of islands lying on both sides of the Canada–United States boundary. Although Pelee is usually said to be Canada's most southerly location, the distinction belongs to Middle Island, now privately owned.

Pelee and the other islands were formed roughly 4,300 years ago when Lake Erie's waters rose, submerging most of a limestone ridge stretching from Marblehead Peninsula, Ohio, to Point Pelee on the Ontario mainland. The ridge separates Erie's shallow western basin from the considerably deeper eastern basin.

Indians once used the islands like stepping-stones to cross Lake Erie by canoe. Pelee Island passed from Indian hands to the British crown in 1788. William McCormick purchased the island in 1823 for $500 and moved here in 1834 to establish an estate he hoped would become his family's ancestral home. One of his first acts was to build the stone lighthouse—now abandoned—whose tower dominates the northeastern tip of the island.

McCormick's descendants eventually sold some of their land to three Kentuckians, who established the island's first vineyard in 1866. To store the wine, the vintners excavated an underground rock cellar, 18 m long, 12 m wide, and almost 4 m deep. On top, they built "Vin Villa," a two-story mansion, which burned down in 1963. This was Canada's first commercial estate winery. Its walls—wreathed in wild grape vines—and the rock cellar can still be seen at Pelee's northwest tip. The story of the vineyards is told at the Wine Pavilion, part of Pelee Island Winery and Vineyards. *Open daily, seasonal hours.*

The stone lighthouse on Pelee Island's northeastern tip was in use from 1834 until 1909.

The Heritage Centre, a museum at the town hall near the West Dock, surveys the island's past. The collection includes Indian artifacts and navigational maps marking offshore wrecks. *Open daily, mid-April to November.*

Pelee Island, a stopover for migrating birds of two continental flyways, is a mecca for bird-watchers. Two vantage points—Pelee Island Nature Reserve (at the island's southeast corner) and Fish Point (at the south end)—are accessible to bird-watchers at all times. In September, they are joined by butterfly enthusiasts, who arrive to observe the migration of hundreds of thousands of monarch butterflies en route to their wintering grounds in Mexico's Sierra Mountains.

Special events
Heritage Weekend
(September)

Point Pelee

A few of the narrow sandspits in the Great Lakes have become heavily used crossroads in the journeys of birds, mammals, colonizing plants, and man. One is 17-km-long Point Pelee, an arrowhead-shaped peninsula protruding from the northern shoreline of Lake Erie. At 15 km², this southernmost tip of the Canadian mainland is also one of the smallest of our national parks.

Point Pelee is the deep south of Canada. Parts or all of 25 American states lie north of the peninsula, which is at the same latitude as northern California. The point also lies within Canada's Carolinian forest—an area that represents a quarter of 1 percent of Canada's landmass but contains 25 percent of its people. More species of plants, birds, mammals, and other fauna are found here than in any other area in the country. Unfortunately, the present forest in the Pelee area is too small to support this abundance. The park promotes projects such as planting native trees and encourages visitors to reduce their impact on this fragile environment.

The Pelee forest varies from flooded silver maple swamps to well-drained, semiopen red cedar savannas, and upland forests with thick canopies and dense undergrowth. About 40 native tree species grow in the park, and a good number of these, including sassafras, sycamore, hackberry, blue ash, and black walnut, are at the northern edge of their ranges.

The profusion of vines gives Point Pelee's forest its jungle-like look. Wild grape vines, many as thick as circus ropes, dangle from the forest canopy, and leaves and lianas of Virginia creepers cloak many hefty trees.

Certain open, arid areas are filled with prickly pear cactus, a plant bristling with needles and showy in midsummer with bright yellow flowers. The park's largest grove of honey locust, another barbed curiosity, is found near the largest cactus patch.

Two-thirds of Point Pelee is a wetland mosaic of lily-filled ponds and open water. Intertwined cattails with wiener-on-a-stick seed heads form a floating carpet over most of this permanently flooded ground, which is home to moisture-loving plants, such as the swamp rose mallow, an hibiscus rare in Canada. This "belle of the marsh" is renowned for its cotton-candy pink blossoms.

A lacework of elegant plants rises from the peaty floor of Point Pelee's lagoons. One prominent plant is the bladderwort, a delicate flower distinguishable by the many rice-size capsules attached to its whorled leaves floating underwater. The spadelike leaves of the spatterdock are found in the lee of the cattail

Visitors to Point Pelee can explore the park on boardwalks that crisscross the marshlands.

mat, and the platterlike pads of the white water lily cover the surface nearby. Both have striking flowers, but the lily's lotus-style blossom opens only in daylight.

In spring and fall, Point Pelee is one of the continent's hot spots for birds and the warbler capital of North America. The bird invasion begins with a February-through-March trickle of ducks, blackbirds, and robins. The flow increases throughout April, becoming a flood by mid-May when the migration peaks. In fall, the number of migrating birds swells with their offspring. The subtle plumage of fall birds is more than compensated for by the antics of migrating hawks and the fiery colors of Mexico-bound monarch butterflies.

PARK INFORMATION
Access: Highway 401 from Toronto or Windsor to Highway 77 south (Leamington exit). Follow road signs from Leamington South.
Visitors' centre: Located inside the park, 8 km from the entrance.
Accommodations and other facilities: Day-use park open year-round. From April to October, free, environmentally friendly transit between the Visitors' Centre and the "Tip." Group camping for organized groups by advance registration. Variety of interpretive programs and exhibits. Bicycle and canoe rentals.
Summer activities: Fishing (catch and release only, national park licenses needed, available in the park); bird and butterfly watching; unsupervised swimming in designated areas; picnicking; bicycling; walking (five nature trails); canoeing.
Winter activities: Skating by the Marsh Boardwalk; skiing; hiking.

3 Petrolia

During the late 19th century, Petrolia (pop. 4,600) was a dominant force in the Canadian oil industry. Its first oil well was brought into production in 1860. Whereas nearby Oil Springs faded away after a brief but spectacular boom, Petrolia sustained its early growth with a steady output from a large oil field.

After 1880, Imperial Oil and Canadian Oil set up refineries here. In time, multinational oil company takeovers slowly reduced Petrolia's importance. By the early 1950s, the town's production was eclipsed by the vast oil fields of Alberta.

Just outside town, Petrolia Discovery welcomes visitors to an oil field where early rigs and equipment are still used. Its 16 wells produce a small but steady flow of more than 230 barrels a month. The oil is pumped with the jerker-line devised by a Petrolia prospector, John Henry Fairbanks (1831-1914).

The Fitzgerald rig—named for another local oil pioneer, Frederick Fitzgerald—has been operating, on and off, since 1903. It is reputedly the world's largest rig. The field encompasses the original "gum beds" that first attracted prospectors to the area. *Open daily May to Labor Day; Labor Day to October 31, Monday to Friday, 8:30 am to 4 pm.*

Petrolia was said to be the wealthiest Canadian community west of Toronto. Many handsome public buildings and houses survive from its boom days. The white-brick Victoria Hall (1889) houses municipal offices and a 440-seat opera house (with a theatre company). Its designer was the architect George F. Durand, of London, Ont., who was also responsible for the 1887 Masonic Temple, St. Philip's Catholic Church (also from 1887), and the 1890 St. Andrew's Presbyterian Church. Petrolia's hospital, at Dufferin and Greenfield streets, was once "Glenview," home of oil baron "Jake" Englehart. He was one of 16 local oilmen whose merged interests became Imperial Oil.

Petrolia Discovery preserves the oil industry's primitive rigs, such as this mobile pole derrick.

Special events

Discover Petrolia Days (July)

Petrolia-Enniskillen Fall Fair (September)

Petrolia Fall Home and Town Tour (mid-September)

4 Oil Springs

The Canadian oil industry started at Oil Springs (pop. 693). The story is told here at the Oil Museum of Canada, which features working models of rigs originally used at Oil Springs. The museum's most prized exhibit is a reconstruction of the 1858 oil well drilled by James Miller Williams. It was the first

This 1860 chapel is one of six 19th-century buildings at Uncle Tom's Cabin Historic Site.

commercial oil well in North America. (The famous Titusville well in Pennsylvania was drilled one year later.).

In the early 1850s, C.N. Tripp began making asphalt here from oil skimmed from the surface of "gum beds" in nearby forests and swamps. Previously, Indians had used the oil for medicinal purposes. By accident, Tripp found underground oil while digging for water, but failed to pursue the discovery. He sold his holdings to James Miller Williams, who drilled systematically. Williams' search paid off when he struck oil in 1857.

After successfully establishing his oil well, Williams built a refinery—another first—to make kerosene, widely used for lighting. Within two years, he had five operating wells, and shipped out some 9,400 barrels of crude oil.

The news of Williams' well spread quickly. Prospectors congregated at a shanty town on the banks of Black Creek, now the site of Oil Springs. By late 1861, they had sunk some 400 wells, using the spring pole, the standard drilling rig of the day.

In January 1862, a gusher spouted explosively from a 49-m well sunk by Hugh Nixon Shaw. Some 3,000 barrels poured out each day. It took a week to cap the well, using a leather bag stuffed with flax seed. Unfortunately, that week's uncapped flood of oil polluted Black Creek and the North Sydenham River, Lake St. Clair and the Detroit River.

But the bountiful days at Oil Springs were brief. The oil flow declined or, at some wells, ceased. By the end of the 1860s, Oil Springs—the first oil capital of Canada and the world—was abandoned for nearby Petrolia.

Special events
Kite Fly (May)
Quilt Show (June)
Oil Springs Picnic (August)
Harvest Time Craft Show (October)

5 | Dresden
❀

"Farewell, old master / Don't come after me / I'm on my way to Canada / Where colored men are free." So sang black slaves escaping from slavery in the southern United States during the years between 1840 and 1860. Stopping to rest only at safe houses on the secret network known as the Underground Railroad, many of the fugitives made their way to Canada, crossing the border into southern Ontario. Here, they settled in places such as Dresden (pop. 2,600), then, as now, a peaceful, rural community on the Sydenham River.

In the half century before the American Civil War, about 60,000 fugitives reached "Canaan," as the land to the north was sometimes called. The best known of these is the Reverend Josiah Henson (1789-1881), whose early life inspired Harriet Beecher Stowe's novel *Uncle Tom's Cabin* (1851).

Henson was born a slave in Maryland. He was ordained a Methodist preacher in 1828 and, two years later, he fled to Canada with his family, crossing from Buffalo, N.Y., to Fort Erie, Ont. In 1841, Henson and a group of abolitionists bought about 80 ha of land at Dresden, where they established the British American Institute, a refuge and school for fugitive slaves.

Today, Henson's house, with its handmade square nails and its tulip-wood siding, is the centerpiece of Uncle Tom's Cabin Historic Site, 2 km southwest of Dresden off Highway 21.

Other buildings at the site include a house where newly arrived fugitives lived, and the church where Henson preached. Also displayed are implements of slavery—whips, clubs, and handcuffs. The museum's collection includes abolitionist literature, as well as different editions of *Uncle Tom's Cabin*—in its day, second only in popularity to the Bible. *Open mid-May to the end of September.*

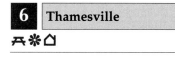

6 Thamesville

This community (pop. 1,000) on the River Thames was settled by United Empire Loyalists, who found refuge here in 1797 after the American Revolution. The town is said to be the setting for *Fifth Business,* the first novel of the Deptford Trilogy by noted author Robertson Davies, who was born here in 1913.

Two sites in the area recall the Battle of the Thames on October 5, 1813. One, honoring the Shawnee war chief Tecumseh (c. 1768-1813), is 10 km east of town on Highway 2. Tecumseh and his followers joined forces with the British and the Canadians against the Americans at the outset of the War of 1812, and were with them at the local battle. A monument marks where the Shawnee chief was killed.

Another casualty of the battle was the village of Fairfield, which the American forces destroyed. Founded in 1792, the community was a haven for another band of refugees from the United States—Moravian missionaries and their Delaware Indian converts.

In 1815 the missionaries reestablished their village near present-day Moraviantown, now on the Delaware Indian Reserve. Regular Sunday service is held in the 1848 mission church.

Fairfield Museum, at the site of the 1792 community, honors the Moravian missionaries and the Delaware Indians. *The museum, east of Thamesville on Highway 2, is open daily, except Monday, May to October. Admission charge.*

7 Goderich

The town of Goderich (pop. 7,500) is situated at the mouth of Maitland River on a bluff overlooking Lake Huron. Visitors can't help admiring its location; some refer to it as the "prettiest town in Canada."

Lighthouse, Goderich

Goderich (generally pronounced *Godrich*) was founded in 1827 by John Galt, the head of Canada Company, a land colonization corporation, and his associate, William "Tiger" Dunlop, soldier, surgeon, jour-

Bedford Hotel is one of the elegant buildings beside Goderich's leafy Court House Square.

nalist, and politician. They named the town after Viscount Goderich, then British chancellor of the Exchequer, who sold the Canada Company 400,000 ha of the Huron Tract, which stretched from Guelph to Goderich.

One of the founders' first acts was to develop Goderich harbor, still the largest on the Canadian side of Lake Huron. Dunlop is credited with the town's layout, in which tree-lined residential streets radiate from the central octagonal (eight-sided) Court House Square, the town's commercial heart.

Dunlop also supervised construction of the Huron Gaol, built between 1839 and 1842. This three-story octagonal stone structure, with 1-m-thick walls, is now a museum, but it housed prisoners up to 1972. Its most notorious 19th-century inmate, convicted murderer James Donnelly, imprisoned here in 1859-1866, was one of the Donnellys murdered by vigilantes at Lucan, Ont., in 1880. The elegant 1901 Governor's House, next to the gaol, can also be visited. *Open from May to November.*

Just a block west, the Huron County Museum has "theme" rooms, such as a dentist's office, depicting Victorian life and times. *Open year-round, except Saturdays from Labor Day to April.*

A THEATRE FESTIVAL IN A FARMLAND SETTING

Dreamland, *a 1989 musical at Blyth, was one in a succession of popular festival hits.*

Rural Ontario abounds with little-theatre and music groups that provide opportunities for local artistic expression. Blyth (pop. 1,000), some 40 km east of Goderich, is part of this tradition, but with a notable difference. Since its inception in 1975, the Blyth Festival has won national acclaim for the successful presentation of new Canadian plays. The festival was founded by director James Roy, a native of Blyth, with assistance from playwright Anne Chislett and newspaper editor Keith Roulston. It runs from June to September every year.

Festival plays often portray the issues and concerns of rural people. One of the first presentations was *Mostly in Clover,* a dramatization of Harry J. Boyle's 1961 memoir of farming life. A remote farmhouse served as the setting for Peter Colley's popular thriller *I'll Be Back Before Midnight,* produced here in 1979. Another success, Anne Chislett's *Quiet in the Land* (1981), a depiction of Mennonite family life in rural Ontario during the 1930s, went on to international acclaim.

The festival is staged at the Blyth Memorial Community Hall, built in 1919-1920 to honor villagers who had served in World War I. The hall was used for council meetings and court sessions. Local theatre groups and visiting vaudeville shows also performed here. By 1974, the hall had fallen into disrepair. The villagers rallied to save it from demolition. The following year, the festival occupied the hall with one show produced for a modest summer run.

Today, the Blyth Festival offers five premieres every summer. Notable festival playwrights include Carol Bolt, Colleen Curran, Gorden Pinsent, Lister Sinclair, Ted Johns, and Michel Tremblay.

As ticket prices for the festival are reasonable, theatregoers are advised to book in advance. Thanks to recent renovations, the stifling heat and the hard-wooden seats that once tested the mettle of even ardent festival enthusiasts have given way to air-conditioning and comfortable padded chairs.

The Huron County Marine Museum is housed in the wheelhouse of the 1907 Great Lakes freighter *J.C. Morse* (later renamed the S.S. *Shelter Bay*). The museum displays anchors, lifeboats, and other nautical memorabilia, as well as historic photographs illustrating Goderich's role in Great Lakes shipping. *Open daily from July to Labor Day, from 1:00 to 4:30 pm.*

A self-guiding tour of the heritage buildings is available from the tourist information centre and the town hall's architectural conservation office.

Special events
Festival of Arts and Crafts (July)
Annual Quilt Show and Fair (August)

8 Benmiller

❋ ⌂

There are a number of ghost towns in southwestern Ontario—once thriving communities such as St. Joseph and Wroxeter. By rights, Benmiller should belong to this company. That it has escaped this fate is due to the Benmiller Inn. Population is a case in point. The official figure is 50 but locals will tell you 150, adding, "when the inn is full."

Benmiller nestles in a wooded hollow, where Sharpes Creek meets the Maitland River. The tenacious village is named after Benjamin Miller, who set up a gristmill here in the early 1830s. The cluster of mills that followed Miller's used the water power of the local falls. By the 1970s, the village —its old mills long outmoded—seemed about to vanish from the map.

In 1974, the owners of Benmiller Inn began to restore the mills and revitalize the village. Today, the 30-ha resort complex offers accommodation in the mills

Garden settings enhance the atmosphere of the Benmiller Inn, which comprises a complex of restored early 19th-century mills.

228

that once thrived here. All are comfortably refurbished in styles suitable to their 19th-century origins.

The Woollen Mill (c. 1878) was the first restoration, followed by River Mill, Gledhill House (home of a mill owner), and Mill House. A likeness of Jonathan Miller, Benjamin's son, appears on the sign at the River Mill entrance. At 188 cm and 220 kg, Jonathan was reputedly the largest man in the country in his day.

The inn recently restored Cherrydale Farm, a six-room guesthouse. The 1829 stone farmhouse, the first building in Colborne township, was home to Michael Fisher and his wife, and their seven sons and three daughters. Fisher paid the Canada Company the equivalent of $10,000 in today's money for 2,225 ha beside present-day Benmiller.

Collectibles from the past, such as chandeliers, clocks, tabletops, and even flour sacks, form the inn's decor. The grounds are a blend of "natural" Canadian and "manicured" British, with enough flower gardens and wooded areas to suit all tastes.

9 Clinton

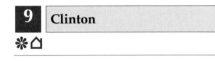

This agreeable town of 3,000 is justifiably proud of its past. Its main street is lined with handsome brick buildings, which date from between 1877 and 1884. Since 1870, Clinton's town hall with its imposing tower has dominated the local scene.

During World War II, Clinton was the "home of radar." An 11-m-wide antenna, reaching up 9 m at the corner of Mary and King streets, recalls the days when the first radar-training school in North America was here.

Another fascinating link with bygone days—the School-on-Wheels, a restored railway car—is found in Sloman Memorial Park, just outside the town. It recalls a program, in operation from 1926 to the 1960s, which used the railway to bring teachers to students

The School-on-Wheels, preserved at Clinton, brought the three R's to remote Ontario regions.

who lived in the far-off parts of northern Ontario.

A Canadian National Railway coach served both as a classroom and the teacher's living quarters. It was pulled into a siding in one of the northern settlements, where it stayed for four days at a time. Children—and the adults for night school—came by foot or sled for their schooling. Before departing, the teacher assigned homework for the train's next visit.

The School-on-Wheels was a great success. By 1938, there were seven of these schools traveling all across northern Ontario. Clinton-born Fred Sloman (1894-1973), the dean of the program, taught from its inception until his retirement in 1965. His wife and five children traveled with him. All of the Sloman children attended kindergarten to grade 12 at the itinerant school.

After Sloman's death, the people of Clinton bought his railway car—CNR No. 15089—and restored it as a museum. *Open daily from May 24 to Labor Day. Admission free.*

Special events
Klompenfeest (May)

10 Bayfield

This resort village (pop. 850) was laid out in 1832 by a Royal Navy surveyor, Capt. Henry Wolsey Bayfield, on a 600-ha site owned by his employer, the Dutch aristocrat Baron van Tuyll. It was the second community (after Goderich) established in the Huron Tract. The school built in 1836—now part of The Hut in Clan Gregor Square —is a reminder of Captain Bayfield's early settlement.

During the 19th century, the village prospered. By the early 1890s, it had a population of 595 and some 25 businesses. But it never became the vital shipping centre envisioned by its founder.

Bayfield was almost forgotten until the 1970s, when it was rediscovered by city people searching for a quiet getaway spot. Fortunately, the newcomers chose not to disturb its 19th-century essence, but confined themselves to reviving vacant homes and shops. Today, its old clapboard dwellings, sheltered by lofty chestnut trees, shine anew with fresh paint and restored fretwork.

Main Street is a delightful promenade lined with craft shops, many in restored buildings, offering pottery, lace, and even homemade fudge. It is graced with two historic inns – the yellow-brick 1857 Albion Hotel and The Little Inn, once a stagecoach stop on the Goderich-to-London route.

Bayfield also boasts two concerns reminiscent of the Victorian period. The Springbank Harness Company, south of the town, specializes in stable gear. *Open to the public on Thursdays, from 8 am to 6 pm.* Penhale's, to the north of town, makes fine carriages and landaus for Disney World and other international clients. *Open from Monday to Friday, from 8 am to 4 pm.*

Special events
Bayfield Fair (August)
Zurich Bean Festival (August)

Bayfield offers three busy marinas on one of the best and prettiest of Lake Huron's harbors.

11 St. Marys

The architecturally engaging town of St. Marys (pop. 5,400) preserves the largest concentration of 19th-century stone buildings in Ontario. The wealthy entrepreneurs of the day—notably George Carter, William and Joseph Hutton—made their money in grain and spent lavishly on mansions and public buildings. (One enterprising local businessman, Timothy Eaton, opened a store here in 1860 before moving on to Toronto, where he launched the retail empire that still bears his name.)

The grandest of St. Marys' buildings is the 1880 Gothic Revival opera house, which once seated 1,000. Long the centre of the town's social life, the three-story structure was saved from demolition in the 1980s. Renovated, it now has condominiums on the upper floors and retail and office spaces at street level.

The 1891 town hall, built in limestone and trimmed with imported red sandstone, is in the robust Richardson Romanesque style. It is a superb example of the craft of stonemasonry that earned St. Marys the sobriquet "The Stonetown."

Credit for the town's handsome appearance also belongs to St. Marys' premier architect William Williams. He designed the MacPherson Block, one of the community's first commercial buildings when it was built in the 1850s, and the 1884 Andrews Building.

Nearby quarries not only provided the limestone for St. Marys' buildings but also enriched the local economy. One of these quarries, just south of town, is now used for swimming. Some 250 m long, 75 m wide, and 12 m deep, it is said to be the largest swimming hole in the country. Abandoned in the 1930s, it gradually filled with clear, icy water from an underground spring. With no shallow end, the pool

The bright green and yellow engine and coaches of the Port Stanley Terminal Railway pull out of the Lake Erie port on an excursion trip.

St. Marys built its 1891 stone town hall in a robust style that reflected local prosperity.

is unsuitable for children and non-swimmers. *Open from June to Labor Day; noon to dusk.*

12 Port Stanley

🚤 🚂 🐟 🏖 ❄ ⌂

Main Street in this quaint fishing and resort village has a pleasing mixture of restored wharf buildings and shops with a nautical flavor. Port Stanley (pop. 2,100) sits on the north shore of Lake Erie, at the mouth of Kettle Creek.

French explorers, who passed here in the 1600s, had only good things to say about this pleasant anchorage. But the region slumbered on until autocratic Col. Thomas Talbot (1771-1853) obtained 2,025 ha on Lake Erie in 1803. The year later, Talbot granted the site of present-day Port Stanley to his friend, surveyor John Bostwick.

The village was named in honor of Britain's Lord Stanley, during his 1823 Canadian visit to Colonel Talbot. The construction of Port Stanley's harbor began in 1827. When the work was completed in 1833, the village became the port for London, 35 km to the north. Even today, the harbor remains the largest on Lake Erie's north shore.

In the early 1900s, summer visitors started traveling here on the London & Port Stanley (L&PS) Railway, which was built in 1856 to haul freight. They came to enjoy a day of swimming and picnicking by the lakeside and, later, to dance at Port Stanley's popular beach-side L&PS Railway Pavilion.

The 30-m by 60-m pavilion opened on July 29, 1926. That first night, some 6,500 people paid 15¢ admission and a nickel for every dance. Music was by the Vincent Lopez Band from New York's Ritz Carlton Hotel. The dance hall, with a 1,200-m² maple floor, was resplendent with wicker furniture and Chinese lanterns.

Roads to explore: Mills and marshes on the Erie shore

Distance (approx.): 115 km/71 miles

This picturesque drive starts at the resort village of Port Stanley. The main routes—county roads 24 and 42—skirt Lake Erie's restful shores.

● Take Elgin Road 23 north, turning east on Elgin Road 24 to Port Bruce. Go north on Highway 73 to Copenhagen, and turn east on to Elgin Road 42 for Port Burwell. Visitors can climb the village's 1840 lighthouse, reputedly the oldest wooden lighthouse in Canada, or bask in the sun on a 600-m-long white sand beach. Nearby Port Burwell Provincial Park overlooks this picturesque village.

● Turn north on Highway 19 to Vienna with its Thomas Edison Museum. *Open Tuesdays to Fridays, 9 am to 5 pm, summer only.* The inventor spent summers here as a boy.

● From Port Burwell continue on 42 past Houghton and The Sandhills, a privately owned resort, with 135-m-high sand bluffs. In the late 1800s, visitors first came here to view the bluffs—at a dime a head!

● Turn south on Highway 59 to Long Point peninsula. Waterfowl and fish abound here, and a provincial park offers camping and swimming.

● Return to 42 and pass through Port Rowan to the Backus Heritage Conservation Area. Ontario's oldest continuously operating mill is here. Built about 1798,

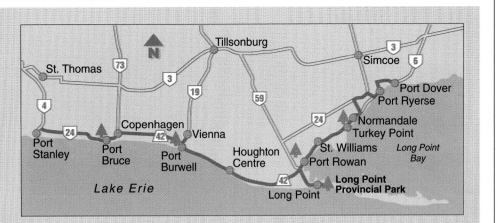

it was owned by the Backhouse family for more than 150 years. *Open Monday to Friday, and holidays. Admission charge.*

● Leave 42 at St. Williams, turning south on Haldimand-Norfolk Road 16 (Townline Road). Turn east on Lakeshore Road, past a marsh to Turkey Point. Turn south on Haldimand-Norfolk Road 10 to get to the village and the beach, and north to get to Turkey Point Provincial Park.

● Continue to Normandale on Lakeshore Road, which turns north at Mill Street. Follow this street to the Normandale Furnace site. A plaque commemorates the iron foundry built here in 1818 and said to be one of the first in Canada. American traders from across Lake Erie sought out the stoves and agricultural implements fashioned here.

● Carry on along Lakeshore Road to Fishers Glen, turning north on to County Road 10. Turn east on to to Highway 24, which you follow to Haldimand-Norfolk Road 57.

● Turn south (right) on to 57 and go to Port Ryerse. The name of the hamlet honors its Loyalist founder, Lt. Col. Samuel Ryerse (1752-1812). Stop on King Street at Port Ryerse Anglican Church, whose construction began in 1870. The white clapboard edifice bears a plaque with the story of Ryerse's life. The cemetery's weathered headstones mark the burial places of the area's first settlers.

● From Port Ryerse, a sharp right onto Nanticoke Port Ryerse Road takes you to Highway 24. Along the way, stop at Hay Creek Conservation Area, open to campers, picnickers, and hikers.

● Head north on 24 and turn east onto Radical Road and into Port Dover. Turn south on Main Street to get to the beach.

The heyday of the pavilion was the big-band era from the mid-1930s to the mid-1940s. It resounded to the music of Louis Armstrong, Count Basie, Cab Calloway, Duke Ellington, Benny Goodman, Woody Herman, Harry James, Guy Lombardo and his Royal Canadians, and Les Brown and his Band of Renown with Doris Day. During the summer, the huge windows were thrown open to let in cool night breezes. A broad promenade encircled the exterior of the hall.

Closed down in 1949, the pavilion reopened the same year with a new name: The Stork Club. When the L&PS service ended in the 1950s, the club fell

A solitary child builds a sand castle on one of Lake Erie's beaches, near Port Stanley.

on hard times, but continued to host banquets and receptions until 1968. It was renovated for band shows in 1974, only to burn down five years later.

A reminder of this colorful era, Port Stanley Terminal Rail Inc.—a revitalized descendant of the L&PS—offers 40-minute round-trips from the local station through Kettle Creek Valley to Union. *The train runs Sunday afternoons year-round; Saturday afternoons, June to October; and weekday afternoons, July and August.* There are also one-way trips and round-trips to St. Thomas.

Kettle Creek Inn, at Main and Bridge streets, built in 1849 by Squire Samuel Price as a summer home, has been a hotel since the 1920s. (Price ran Port Stanley's general store and dispensed justice from a "court" next door.)

The old jail, now a museum, and a fishermen's memorial, on the other side of Kettle Creek, can be reached by one of Ontario's few remaining lift bridges. Port Stanley offers a choice of beaches (the Big and the Little) and five marinas, all at the mouth of Kettle Creek. In summer, an hour-long harbor cruise is available on the *Kettle Creek Queen*, a paddle wheel tour boat.

Hawk Cliff, 8 km east of town, is a mecca for bird-watchers. In late September, more than 20,000 migrating broad-winged hawks a day fly over this vantage point. From August to December, nighthawks, peregrine falcons, bald eagles, loons, and Canada geese can be seen. In early October, flocks of blue jays pass overhead at the rate of 500 a minute.

Signs and shingles in a profusion of styles decorate the pleasant streets of small-town Ontario. The village pub in Sparta displays this flamboyant example.

A PENINSULA SHAPED BY RESTLESS WINDS AND WAVES

Throughout the world, there are 300 international biosphere reserves—areas where the efforts of conservation and development are well balanced. The United Nations Educational, Scientific and Cultural Organization (UNESCO) chooses the sites. One of its six Canadian choices is Long Point, which extends 32 km into Lake Erie.

Long Point peninsula has been created by the restless winds and waves that carry sand and gravel from west to east across Lake Erie. Some experts believe it has taken about 10,000 years for the peninsula to reach its present shape, but all agree that it is still changing. The widest dryland portion—Bluff Point in Long Point National Wildlife Area—measures only 4 km. The peninsula embraces a mixture of marsh, dune, meadow, and woodland. The entire south shore on Lake Erie is beach, much of which is off-limits to visitors. The north side, facing the mainland and protected from the lake, is marshland.

In 1670, French monks Dollier de Casson and Galinée became the first Europeans to set foot on Long Point. Missionaries visited from time to time, and traders

Two fishermen enjoy the calm expanse of water by the marshy shores on the north side of Long Point.

set up posts on Long Point in the early 1700s. But real settlement did not take place until United Empire Loyalists arrived late in the 18th century.

Long Point has a special appeal for bird-watchers. Some 350 bird species have been recorded here. Roughly a third of these stay to nest. In spring, bird-watchers can observe the migrating flocks from vantage points at Long Point Provincial Park. Nearby Long Point Bird Observatory bands birds and studies migration patterns.

You can reach Long Point by the Highway 59 causeway. West of the causeway, a path along the top of 2 km of dike in Big Creek National Wildlife Area provides views of the marshland. The peninsula comprises three sectors. At the base of the peninsula, a provincial park offers camping, fishing, or basking on a 4-km-long strip of beach. The outer reaches of the peninsula are accessible only by boat with restricted landing sites and use. The private Long Point Company, formed in 1866 to manage the peninsula, donated half of its holdings to the Canadian people in the late 1970s. This portion is now managed as Long Point National Wildlife Area by the Canadian Wildlife Service of Environment Canada.

13 Sparta

To reach Sparta (pop. 225), travel north on Highway 4 from Port Stanley, then east on County Road 27 at the village of Union.

The Sparta settlement was originally a Pennsylvania Quaker community founded by Jonathan Doan in 1815. The village, preserved virtually intact from the 1800s, boasts antique shops, craft shops, and tearooms. Artist Peter Robson, well-known for his watercolors of old southwestern Ontario towns, has a studio and gallery in The Abbey, a former girls' school built in 1840.

Any Sparta merchant will provide a free copy of a self-guiding tour to historic Sparta. The tour lists more than 25 historic attractions, including homes in the New England Colonial Quaker style, and the Society of Friends Cemetery, just west of Sparta. The cemetery is the burial place of Joshua Doan, a rebel in the 1837 Rebellion.

Visitors should note local shops are generally open Tuesday through Sunday in summer, but only on weekends in winter.

14 Port Dover

This fishing port brings a touch of the Maritimes to the shores of Lake Erie. The locale pleased its first visitors, the French monks Dollier de Casson and Galinée, who stayed here in 1669 while exploring the Great Lakes. Galinée praised its beauty in his journals. Today's visitors to Port Dover (pop. 4,500) add their praise to Galinée's.

The original settlement, known as Dover or Dover Mills, grew up in the early 1800s near a mill on the River Lynn, just upstream from the present Port Dover. During the War of 1812, American raiders burned down the settlement. The raid went unopposed

Port Dover displays a collection from its nautical past in a quaint harborside museum.

because local British and Canadian forces were fighting elsewhere.

Every Canada Day, a mock raid is staged. This time, the Canadians in uniforms of 1812 are at the ready. And, to the delight of onlookers, they defeat the American invaders.

After the 1812 War, the settlement was rebuilt closer to Lake Erie. The move was timely because the opening of the Welland Canal in 1825-1830 increased shipping on the lake. The settlement, with "Port" appended to its name, enlarged the harbor to handle cargoes of grain and lumber.

Although Port Dover prospered with shipping, its true maritime occupation is fishing. It was once the haven for the world's largest inland fishing fleet. About 40 boats from the port still ply Lake Erie.

At 3 o'clock every afternoon, the fleet sails back to port. The holds are laden with bass, pickerel, walleye, whitefish, and delectable Lake Erie yellow perch.

Fresh fish dinners are the specialty of Port Dover's beachside hotels and restaurants. Freshness is assured because it takes only minutes to bring the catch of the day from dock to kitchen.

Port Dover Harbour Museum, once a net shanty, illustrates the rigors of Lake Erie with records of wrecks and rescues. It also displays the latest Great Lakes fishing technology. Some exhibits are "hands on." *Open mid-May to mid-October; 10 am to 6 pm. Small admission charge.*

Special events
Heritage Parade (Victoria Day)

Canada Day (Celebration unbroken since 1867)

Summer Arts and Crafts Festival (August)

Antique Show (September)

Special activities
Peggy Jane lake cruises (May to Labor Day)

SOUTHEASTERN ONTARIO

14

SOUTHEASTERN

ONTARIO

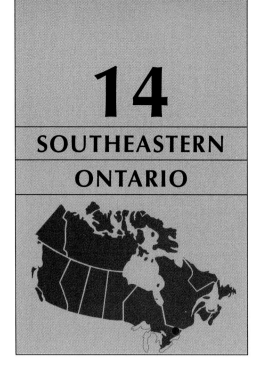

Places to see
Sandbanks Provincial Park
Picton
Adolphustown
Bath
Gananoque
Bon Echo Provincial Park
"Old Walt" at Bon Echo
Almonte
Perth
Charleston Lake Provincial Park
Athens
Merrickville
The Rideau Canal
Maxville
Williamstown

Roads to explore
Around Prince Edward County:
Picton to Point Traverse
Wolfe Island

National park close-up
St. Lawrence Islands

Previous pages:
Tay River at Perth

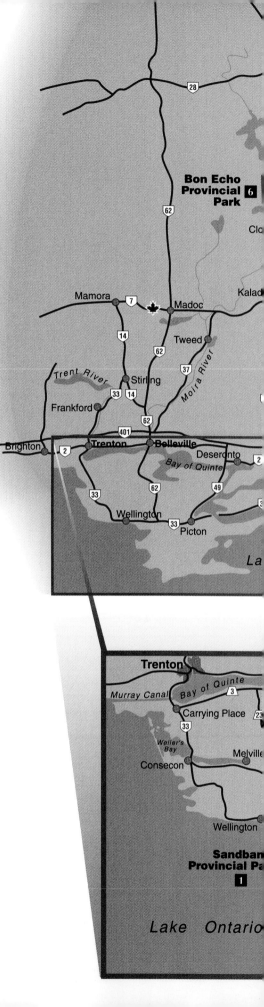

Bon Echo
Provincial **6**
Park

Clo

Kalad

Mamora **7** Madoc

14 Tweed

62 **37**

Trent River Stirling

33 **14**

Frankford

62

401

Brighton **2** Trenton Belleville

Deseronto **2**

Bay of Quinte

33 **62** **49**

Wellington

33 Picton

La

Trenton

Murray Canal Bay of Quinte **3**

Carrying Place **23**

33

Weller's Bay Melville

Consecon

Wellington

Sandban
Provincial Pa

1

Lake Ontario

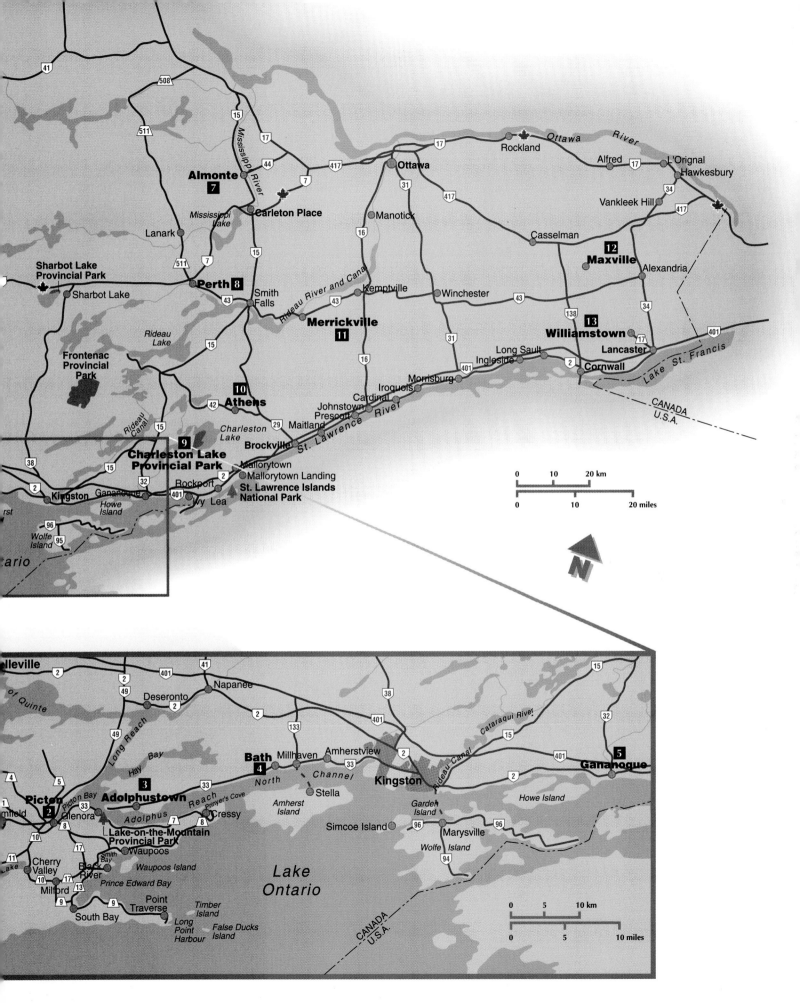

1   Sandbanks Provincial Park

Sandbanks Provincial Park in the southwestern corner of Prince Edward County contains restless, shifting dunes that can rise to heights of 25 m. It has taken more than 10,000 years of buffeting by waves and westerly winds to create this tract of dunes, which stretches 10 km along the shore of Lake Ontario.

Until the mid-1800s, the dunes were covered with grass and scrubby trees, which anchored the sand. But with the advent of farming, much of the vegetation was cut down or eaten by grazing cattle, and the sand began to drift, covering more and more land. Over the years, mature cedars, apple orchards, and farms disappeared under the onslaught of sand. To halt the "sand monster," the Ontario government reforested the problem areas in the 1920s and 30s. Also, many organizations, such as the Boy Scouts and Rotary Club, have planted cedars to prevent further encroachment. The dunes are now as stable as possible. The process of reclaiming lost land and stabilizing the dunes continues.

To explore the most spectacular golden dunes—the sandbanks for which the park is named—visit the West Lake sector. The East Lake sector also has some impressive and more accessible dunes. The 1.5-km Cedar Sands Trail in this sector winds through forested sand hills to a platform, which overlooks the Outlet River. Staircases along the trail ease your way over steep, unpredictable dunes. They move an average of 1.8 m per year toward the West Lake shoreline.

At Sandbanks Provincial Park, you can also enjoy birding—swamp sparrows, pileated woodpeckers, and marsh wrens are sighted here. The park supports a wide range of colorful

Shrubby trees and bushes anchor the shifting dunes at Sandbanks Provincial Park.

Roads to explore: Lofty cliffs and lakeshore lookouts

Distance (approx.):
115 km/69 miles

From Picton, head east on Highway 33 to Lake on the Mountain Provincial Park, perched on a limestone cliff some 100 m above Adolphus Reach. The lake was long believed to be bottomless or connected by tunnel to Lake Erie. (It is now known to be spring fed and about 60 m deep.) Pause to picnic or to stroll along the park trails. From a lookout just across from the park, gaze down at the Glenora ferry—from this summit, a lilliputian vessel—on its voyage across Adolphus Reach.

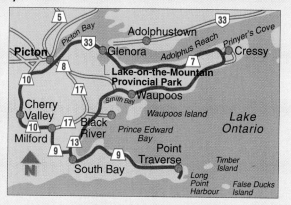

● East of Lake on the Mountain, County Road 7 leads to Cressy and dips down to Lake Ontario at Prinyer's Cove, a Loyalist landing place in the 1780s. During the Prohibition era of the 1920s and 30s, it was a smugglers' port (called Whiskey Cove) from which illicit liquor was shipped to the United States.

● At Cressy, turn west onto County Road 8, which climbs from the lakeshore to lofty cliffs. The road winds through apple orchards and farms. Just before Waupoos is Rose House, built in 1817 and now restored as the Marysburgh Museum, containing a treasure of Loyalist furniture and crafts. *Open Victoria Day to late June, and Labor Day to late September, weekends only; daily, July and August; 9:30 am to 4 pm.*

● Head southward to South Bay, and the Mariners' Museum Lighthouse Park. Built in the 1820s on offshore False Ducks Island, the lighthouse was dismantled, and reassembled here in the 1960s. *Open late May to Thanksgiving, weekends only, July and August daily except Friday, 9 am to 5 pm.*

● Take County Road 9 to Point Traverse. At its remote tip is tranquil Long Point Harbour, the tiny home port of the last commercial fishing fleet on Lake Ontario.

● Return to Picton by county roads 9 and 10. Along the way visit the Exotarium, a breeding centre for exotic and endangered reptiles. *Open mid-May to July, weekends; July to Labor Day, daily, 10 am to 5 pm.*

The lighthouse at South Bay Mariners' Museum is the second oldest on the Great Lakes.

flowering plants as well as small reptiles and amphibians. One of the more unusual creatures of the park is the burrowing wolf spider, which measures about 23 mm across and burrows holes as deep as 1 m in the sand, in which it hides during the day. (The spider is harmless to humans.)

The East Lake and West Lake sectors offer fishing for largemouth and smallmouth bass, walleye, lake trout, catfish, and perch. The waters of Lake Ontario are ideal for small-craft sailing and sailboarding.

In summer, park staff provide interpretive programs, including guided walks and slide presentations about fauna and flora, as well as children's programs. Among the most popular activities are the "spirit walks"—nightly strolls with costumed park guides who impersonate local historical figures and re-create the bygone days when the dunes in the park were the hunting and fishing grounds of native peoples.

2 Picton

In 1791, Loyalists established the settlement of Hallowell, on the north side of present-day Picton (pop. 4,235). One hundred years later it had burgeoned as a small commercial centre and port for lake steamers. Just before 1820, Hallowell's supremacy was challenged by another village called Picton (also known as Delhi), which was established across Picton Bay by a prominent local landowner, Rev. William Macaulay (1794-1874).

After years of profitless rivalry, the villages eventually merged in 1837, adopting the surname of British Maj. Gen. Sir Thomas Picton. But the old names linger on, and the original neighborhoods retain their early character: Hallowell is

Street sign, Picton

the commercial core, and Delhi a district of churches and dignified homes.

All walks through the tree-lined streets of these neighborhoods begin at the North American Hotel in the heart of town. With its two-story veranda and fanlighted entrances, this 1830 hotel was long a favorite of 19th-century travelers.

To explore Hallowell, just turn the corner onto Main Street West. You will pass the Royal Hotel, which superseded the North American Hotel in popularity during the 1880s, and well-preserved shop fronts from the boom years of the 1830s as well as the 1860s and 1870s. King Street—just one block north—is the site of the town hall (1866), the Fralick Octagon (c. 1862), and Benson/Blakely Hall (c. 1815), one of Picton's oldest buildings.

Return to the North American Hotel and walk along Bridge Street to reach Delhi. The Reverend William Macaulay endowed this area with the 1834 Greek Revival courthouse. Macaulay Heritage Park, two blocks east on Church Street, comprises its namesake's 1830 home and Old St. Mary Magdalene Church (1825-1870), now the county museum. *Open June to September, Monday to Friday (excluding Tuesday), 10 am to 4:30 pm; weekends, 1 pm to 4:30 pm. Opening times vary during the rest of the year.*

Picton's gracefully proportioned Macaulay House, built in 1830, is an outstanding example of a neoclassical-style dwelling.

The lacy trim and steeply pitched gables of Merrill House, built in 1878, are elements of Picton's early Victorian dwellings.

Delhi's reputation as the best address in Picton was eclipsed by the Town Hill area after the 1870s. Today, with its profusion of late 19th-century dwellings, Town Hill ranks with Hallowell and Delhi in architectural importance. For your walk through this area, start once again at the North American Hotel and turn onto Main Street East. Notice the towers, gables, Gothic windows, the bargeboard and delicate woodwork trim of the Victorian dwellings.

> **Special events**
> Antique Fair (mid-June)
> Quinte Flywheel Vintage Show (early July)
> Prince Edward County Quilters' Guild Show (mid-July)

3 Adolphustown

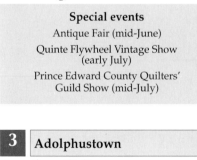

A plaque by the Bay of Quinte near Adolphustown (pop. 1,235) commemorates the landing of the first United Empire Loyalist settlers in 1784.

Reminders of the Loyalist past are everywhere in local churches, heritage homes, and museums. At Adolphustown Park, the Loyalist Cultural Centre houses a collection of Loyalist artifacts in the former residence of David Wright Allison, warden of the county and grandson of Joseph Allison, one of the original settlers.

Each room of this imposing two-story house focuses on a different aspect of Loyalist life. One room traces the change from simple wooden farming tools to metal equipment. Another displays utensils used to create the delicate moldings typical of Loyalist homes. A homey warmth pervades the craft room with its tatting, blankets, and quilts. The prized items in the glass and china room are large bowl-shaped saucers, from which Loyalist farmers hastily sipped tea before going out to labor in the fields.

The centre's reference library is extensive. Trained assistants help anyone interested in discovering their Loyalist roots. A Victorian-style tearoom is hosted by local volunteers who serve their own homebaked goods. *Open late May to Labor Day. Tuesday to Saturday, 10 am to 4 pm; Sunday, 1 pm to 5 pm.*

> **Special events**
> Spirits of Adolphustown Park (late July)
> Art in the Park (late August)

4 Bath

There is treasure to be found on a quiet stroll along the streets of the historic village of Bath (pop. 1,450). One of the oldest Loyalist settlements in this region, the town has several architectural gems.

The town offers a short, self-guiding tour to help you discover some of Bath's finely crafted dwellings. The walk begins on Main Street and takes you past 28 identified buildings built before 1861.

Admire the gabled roof of Capt. Jeptha Hawley's house on Main Street. Hawley built it in 1784, the same year he and other disbanded soldiers of Jessup's Loyal Rangers settled in the area. It is reputed to be the oldest continually occupied residence in Ontario.

The Gutzeit Estate on Main Street is another of the province's oldest homes. It was built in 1796 to mirror the colonial style of the Fairfield House (1793) in neighboring Amherstview. Both homes belonged to the Fairfield family, who settled here from Vermont. *Tours daily, July to September, 11 am to 4 pm.*

Continue on to the Bath Academy on Academy Street. It was erected in 1811 as a grammar school and public library. One of its famous professors, Barnabus Bidwell (1763-1833), was a radical politician and reformer.

Another beauty is the Bath Museum on Davy Street. Housed in an 1859 board-and-batten Gothic structure, it is known locally as the "Layer Cake Hall." It earned that name when both

The daylight passing through the Gothic windows of Bath's Layer Cake Hall once shone on both Anglicans and Presbyterians.

Roads to explore: Driving the country lanes on the largest of the Thousand Islands

Distance: 76 km / 47½ miles

South of Kingston, where Lake Ontario flows into the St. Lawrence River, is the largest of the Thousand Islands, Wolfe Island (pop. 1,097). Its name commemorates British General James Wolfe, who took Quebec City and fell at the Battle of the Plains of Abraham in 1759. With rolling farmland and quiet coves, the island is ideal for a half-day drive or a day-long bike trip.

The island is reached from the Wolfe Island ferry terminal on the waterfront in Kingston. Wolfe Island is a popular summer destination, so it is best to arrive early at the terminal. The free ferry is the only link between the island and Kingston, where most islanders work, and operates year-round, every day. The 25-minute ferry journey is a pleasant prelude to a delightful drive.

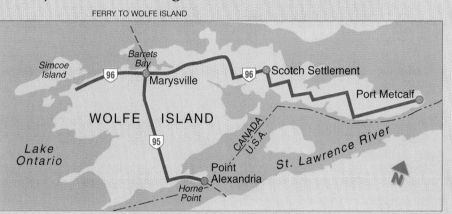

FERRY TO WOLFE ISLAND

Simcoe Island • Barrets Bay • Marysville • 96 • 96 • Scotch Settlement • Port Metcalf • WOLFE ISLAND • 95 • Lake Ontario • CANADA U.S.A. • St. Lawrence River • Point Alexandria • Horne Point • N

The ferry terminal, Wolfe Island

• As you get off the ferry, you are in Marysville, the island's hub and its only town. Head east on Route 96 toward Port Metcalf, at the end of the road. The road zigzags sharply, its views punctuated by scenic glimpses of the St. Lawrence River.

• Port Metcalf was once a real port, with a Canadian customs office that served shippers. It is now abandoned, but the spot still provides a pleasant lookout downriver toward the Thousand Islands. Howe Island is off to the left, and on the right, you may see freighters plying the shipping channel of the St. Lawrence.

• Return east through Marysville to the Simcoe Island ferry just 6 km past the village. You will see Garden Island on the way, and the Kingston skyline beyond. The ferry is a pleasant five-minute ride; much of the island is privately owned, but if you follow the only road west, the 1830s lighthouse at its end is a pleasant picnic site.

• Once back on Wolfe Island drive 6 km

to the corner of Routes 96 and 95. Turn right on 95, the main north-south artery and a favorite of cyclists. At Sacred Heart of Mary Roman Catholic Church, almost immediately on your right, you can see fine stained-glass windows.

• From the church, you can cross the island in about 15 minutes by car to Horne Point, perhaps the island's most scenic part. The route is lined with large Manitoba maples. At Horne Point, the Horne family has operated a ferry to Cape Vincent, New York, since 1802, when Samuel Horne charged a quarter to take people across in a rowboat.

• When you return to Marysville, stop to wander around it. On Main Street is the limestone town hall, built in 1859. Across from the old wharf is the General Wolfe Hotel, built in the 1880s, where you can have an elegant meal. Off Main Street is the village's oldest building, Hitchcock House, now a bed-and-breakfast, overlooking Barretts Bay.

Presbyterians and Anglicans worshiped there in the 1890s. (The Presbyterians held their services on the first floor; the Anglicans, on the second.) Today the museum attracts visitors who come to trace their Loyalist roots. *Open weekends, July to early September, 2 pm to 4 pm.*

At the marina, you can see secluded Amherst Island across the North Channel. This rural haven can be reached on the *Amherst Islander*, a local ferry. It leaves from neighboring Millhaven every hour on the half hour.

5 Gananoque

The town that calls itself "the gateway to the Thousand Islands" is a charming attraction in its own right. Gananoque (an Indian name pronounced *Ga-na-noc-way*) was settled by Loyalists in 1792. During one of the earliest skirmishes of the War of 1812, American raiders attacked the settlement and destroyed its bridge.

Down by the present bridge nestles a small red-brick pump house, now the Chamber of Commerce, where you can

Gananoque's town hall, built in 1831, was originally the dwelling of mill-owner and local notable John Macdonald and his wife.

get a brochure that takes you on a walking tour of the town of 5,200 residents. Nearby stands *Susan Push*, one of the last engines to serve on the Thousand Islands Railway, one of Canada's shortest railway lines. The 4-km route passed the town cemetery.

The town hall is an appropriate place to start the walk. It was built in 1831 by John Macdonald as a dwelling for his bride. It is considered one of the finest examples of neoclassical architecture in Ontario.

Gananoque has a rich manufacturing and commercial history, and many of the stately mansions built for its merchants have been preserved in the historic south end. Some are still private homes; others, such as the Trinity House Inn at 90 Stone Street South, have been lovingly transformed into high-quality historic inns. Built in 1859 for a Gananoque doctor, Trinity House has six lavishly furnished Victorian bedrooms, a bistro, and a small art gallery featuring the work of local artists. Guests can also stay in jail for a night if they wish to rent the town's original lockup, a renovated 1840s constabulary owned by the same people who run the inn.

Gananoque's downtown area is full of delights, including a museum housed in the Victoria Hotel built in 1840. The displays include 19th-century Canadian furnishings, costumes, and Indian artifacts. *Open June to September, Monday to Saturday, 9 am to 5 pm.* Also downtown is an antique caboose, which recalls the bygone days when passenger trains brought a steady stream of visitors and summer islanders into town.

If you're feeling energetic, you can rent bicycles and cycle the 50-km path that runs along the St. Lawrence between Gananoque and Brockville.

Down at the public docks, the Gananoque Boat Line runs daily one-hour and three-hour tours of the Thousand Islands on its triple-decker cruise ships. A handful of marinas will rent small boats to individuals or families without supervision.

On summer evenings, Gananoque presents live theatre at the Thousand Islands Playhouse, which stages comedies and musicals from mid-May to late October. The playhouse, located in a former boat clubhouse at the foot of Charles Street overlooking the river, has been called the most charming theatre in Canada. And no one disputes the claim.

Special events
Guild of Arts and Crafts Summer Fair (mid-July)

Festival of the Islands (mid-August)

Art Colony Studio Tour (mid-October)

6 Bon Echo Provincial Park

One of the impressive sights of southeastern Ontario is Mazinaw Rock, which rises more than 100 m above Mazinaw Lake. The 1.5-km-long mass, also known as Bon Echo Rock, was formed a billion years ago. Centuries ago, the Algonquin Indians decorated the surface of the mighty rock with more than 260 ochre-red pictographs of birds, animals, and people. These fragile images scattered along the rock face just above the waterline are best seen from a canoe.

St. Lawrence Islands

Man's discovery of the St. Lawrence River islands began some 9,000 years ago, shortly after the last Ice Age. Samuel Champlain was the first European to see them, in 1615. The missionaries and *coureurs de bois* called the 80-km, island-clogged stretch of river between Kingston and Brockville *Lac des Mille-Iles* ("Lake of the Thousand Islands"), and the region became an important canoe route for the expanding fur trade.

In the 1800s, the St. Lawrence islands were rediscovered when wealthy Europeans and North Americans started taking steamer trips upriver. They soon became popular vacation sites and by the early 1900s millionaires were buying the islands as sites for their summer mansions.

But year-round residents along the river wanted to maintain free access to the islands. In 1874, they petitioned the federal government to set aside some islands as parkland. Thirty years later, on land donated by a local family, St. Lawrence Islands National Park became the first federal park east of the Rocky Mountains.

Evening falls where the St. Lawrence flows by the Thousand Islands at Ivy Lea.

Today, of the 1,000 or so islands in the area, St. Lawrence Islands National Park owns all or part of 18 islands, a small mainland property around Mallorytown Landing, and 85 islet shoals. Many islands have romantic names: Camelot, Endymion, Mermaid, Beaurivage.

With their rugged character, even small islands display a great variety of habitat types. At the west end of Georgina Island, the geographic heart of the park, wind-gnarled pitch pine and white oak thrust up between boulders and rock faces. Blueberry clings to pockets of sandy soil in the lee of the sun-heated granite outcrops. Inland, protected from prevailing southwesterly winds, verdant hills and valleys are cloaked with a variety of tree species, such as red and white oak, shagbark hickory, basswood, and some ash. Shady stands of hemlock accented by white birch and alder boughs grace the island's cool north shore.

Located in a transitional forest zone, the islands mark the range limits for a variety of plants. Southern plants are represented by slippery elm, swamp white oak, winged sumac, summer grape, bur cucumber, and deerberry, one of Canada's rarest plants. Northern plants include buffalo berry, shrubby cinquefoil, hoary willow, and balsam fir.

Because of their proximity to the mainland, the islands are an ecological extension of the mainland. Wind-borne seeds and tiny insects drift on air currents from island to island. Squirrels, snakes, weasels, minks, raccoons, and deer swim among islands, stopping wherever food and shelter entice them. After the river freezes, the ice is tracked with the footprints of inter-island travelers.

At the last count there was an unsurpassed variety of 33 reptile and amphibian species in the park, from midland painted turtles to bullfrogs and water snakes. Hill Island has nine kinds of snakes. One, the endangered black rat snake, which can measure up to 2.5 m in length, is the largest snake in the country.

In mid-March each year, the river ice begins to break up. With unerring timing, great flocks of waterfowl fly in to await the thaw of rivers and lakes farther north. More than 20 species of duck and geese bide their time with courtship and diving displays. The largest rafts comprise as many as 3,000 scaup, goldeneye, or canvasback. Some 250 species of smaller birds island-hop across the northeastern rim of Lake Ontario.

The park's most famous fowl are great blue herons and wild turkeys. The noisy great blues wade through marshes, their long beaks poised to stab at unwary fish. Turkeys stay within oak-pine forests year-round. No respecters of park or international boundaries, they fly back and forth between the park's Hill Island and Wellesley, in the United States.

PARK INFORMATION
Access: Thousand Island Parkway
Visitors' centre: Mallorytown Landing
Accommodation: Mallorytown Landing has a 63-unit campground (no electrical hookups).
Summer activities: Boating, fishing, bicycling, hiking. Most islands have docking (limited to three consecutive days each), picnicking, and some camping. Boat ramp at Mallorytown Landing and a day-use area with supervised beach and picnic areas.
Winter activities: Cross-country skiing.

THE GHOSTLY VISIT OF A GREAT POET

"Old Walt,"
Bon Echo
Provincial Park

After Flora Macdonald Denison purchased Bon Echo Inn from Dr. Weston Price in 1910, she transformed it into a gathering place for artists and writers. She launched a periodical, *The Sunset of Bon Echo,* published to promote the 19th-century American poet Walt Whitman, whose work she admired. She invited Whitman devotees, including his literary executor Horace Traubel, to lecture at the inn.

In 1919, to commemorate Whitman's 100th birthday, Denison hired stonemasons to carve three lines from Whitman's *Leaves of Grass* on Mazinaw Rock across the lake from the inn. The inscription extends more than 6 m in length, and each letter is 30 cm high. Denison, whose interests embraced spiritualism, chose lines that express Whitman's view of reincarnation:

> *My foothold is tenon'd and*
> *   mortised in granite.*
> *I laugh at what you call dissolution*
> *And I know the amplitude of time.*

Whitman died in 1892 without ever having set foot in Canada, but some claimed the poet's ghost appeared at Bon Echo in the summer of 1919. Horace Traubel, who was gravely ill, came here for the dedication of the inscription in August. One night he claimed that Whitman's ghost was at his bedside. The following September, witnesses at Bon Echo claimed they too had seen the poet's apparition, which had gazed down at Traubel with a reassuring smile and nodded twice before vanishing. Three days after this ghostly visit, Traubel died.

Every year, 150,000 vacationers come to the park to hike, canoe, fish, swim, and bask on the sand beaches, and to enjoy the view of Mazinaw Rock, which has been called "Canada's Gibraltar."

The land was originally owned by Dr. Weston Price and his wife, who took a honeymoon canoe trip here in 1898. They later built the three-story Bon Echo Inn, naming it for the wonderful echo that resounds off Mazinaw Rock.

In 1910, Bon Echo Inn was purchased by Flora Macdonald Denison, a successful Toronto businesswoman with an interest in the arts. She encouraged the Group of Seven to depict Mazinaw Rock and other local scenic settings on canvas. After Denison's death in 1921, her son, the writer Merrill Denison, became proprietor. In 1936, a fire destroyed the elegant inn and ended the artistic tradition and hospitality of the Denison years.

Bon Echo Provincial Park, the largest in eastern Ontario, was created in 1965 after Merrill Denison donated his property to the province. Today the

Canoeists glide by Mazinaw Rock, "Canada's Gibraltar," Bon Echo Provincial Park.

65-km² park contains Mazinaw Lake, one of deepest in Ontario at 145 m, and several smaller lakes, such as Bon Echo, Joeperry, and Pearson. You can enjoy contemplative canoe trips on the park's smaller lakes, where motorboats are restricted. Canoes can be rented at one of several marinas on Mazinaw Lake.

There are 530 campsites (some accessible only by canoe), which are open from mid-May to Thanksgiving. For the same period, day passes are also available. The park has several hiking trails, including a 1-km-long path to the top of Mazinaw Rock. It can be reached by the *Mugwump* ferry, which crosses Mazinaw Lake. You can take a 90-minute lake cruise on the *Wanderer Too.* The ferry and cruise service operates during July and August and, weather permitting, on weekends until Thanksgiving.

Both vessels pass the "Old Walt" inscription—three lines of poetry by American poet Walt Whitman carved on the face of Mazinaw Rock near the Indian pictographs. Flora Macdonald Denison had the lines placed here to honor the poet. For a close-up view, you can visit "Old Walt" by canoe.

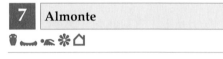

7   Almonte

This town (pop. 4,200) was named for a popular 19th-century Mexican diplomat and patriot, General Juan Almonte. The local people, however, pronounce the name in anglicized fashion—*Al-mont.*

Before the town was so exotically named, settlers were drawn to this site on the Mississippi River (a tributary of the Ottawa River) by the falls, which promised abundant waterpower. By the 1850s, Almonte was the centre of a booming textile industry, with many mills producing a variety of woolen goods from flannel to worsted.

Today the only remnant of the once-thriving industry is the Mississippi

Valley Textile Museum, a gray stone building with red-trimmed windows at 3 Rosamond St. East. The museum displays a 19th-century assembly line for making woolen garments. There is also a charming gift shop. *Admission charged only for special outside exhibits. Open mid-May to December, Tuesday to Friday, 10 am to 4 pm; Saturday, 10 am to 5 pm; Sunday, 1 to 5 pm.*

On Hamilton Street, across the river from the mill site, are several historic homes, many still privately owned. One of the most stately, Old Burnside, once belonged to James Wylie, a Scottish immigrant who was a contractor on the Rideau Canal. His Georgian mansion, with tambour entrance and six fireplaces, was built in 1835 with limestone that was quarried on the property.

There is an excellent view of the Mississippi River Falls from the lawns of the Metcalfe Conservation Area, on Main Street. The park is part of the Mississippi River Conservation Authority, which manages flood and erosion control. Next to the boat launch you can see structures such as timber walls, gabion baskets, and riprap slopes, designed to limit erosion of the shoreline. At night the falls are spectacularly illuminated.

Two of Almonte's native sons achieved international fame, and both have museums here to mark their contributions. Some 3 km northwest of Almonte on Highway 15, a wooden farmhouse named the Dr. James Naismith Visitor Centre commemorates the physical education teacher who invented the game of basketball in Springfield, Massachusetts, in 1891. Naismith, who used two half-bushel peach baskets as goals for his first game, lived to see basketball's inauguration as a world sport at the 1936 Olympics. A photographic display in the Naismith centre provides an illustrated history of the game. *Admission free, donations accepted. Open year-round, Monday to Friday, 10 am to 4 pm; Saturday, noon to 4 pm.*

The Mill of Kintail, at Almonte, is a showcase for the works of sculptor Robert Tait McKenzie.

At the Mill of Kintail Conservation Area, 10 km northwest of Almonte, stands the former summer home of Dr. Robert Tait McKenzie, a boyhood friend of Naismith. A pioneer in rehabilitative medicine and early advocate of the benefits of physical education, McKenzie was also renowned as a sculptor of athletes in bronze. In 1930, he restored the Baird Grist Mill as a studio/home. Now it is a museum displaying many of his works. *Open mid-May to mid-October, Wednesday to Sunday (including holiday Mondays), 10:30 am to 4:30 pm. The rest of the year, Wednesday to Sunday, noon to 4 pm.*

Special events

"Jam in the Hills" Country Music Festival (June)

Ice Cream Festival (mid-July)

North Lanark Highland Games (late August)

Annual Fall Fair (September)

8   Perth

In the early 1980s, Heritage Canada selected Perth (pop. 6,000) as the pilot project for its Mainstreet program. Under the watchful eye of an architect and restoration expert, the town council and local merchants were encouraged to restore buildings on Gore Street, the town's main thoroughfare.

The result is a town that looks much as it did a century and a half ago when it was settled by Scottish officers after the Battle of Waterloo and laid out with military precision on the banks of the Tay River.

A good starting-point for a tour is the town hall, built in 1863 of local cream-colored sandstone and topped later with a clock tower. Here you can pick up a brochure that outlines three different walking tours, each taking about 30 minutes.

Perth treasures its heritage buildings, such as this 1883 riverside factory, which was converted into condominiums in the 1980s.

Near the town hall, the Perth Citizens' Band, Canada's oldest town band (founded in 1867), plays concerts at the bandstand at 7:30 pm on alternate Thursday evenings during June, July, and August.

Behind the town hall, there is picnicking and swimming in Stewart Park. Across Gore Street from the town hall, you might see small pleasure boats in the Tay Basin, where once steamers plying the Rideau and Tay canals used to dock.

Also on Gore Street is Matheson House, home of the Perth Museum. The severe sandstone structure, built in 1830, has several furnished period rooms and an impressive mineral collection. Other exhibits include the pistols used in Canada's last fatal duel, fought by the Tay in Perth in 1833 between two hotheaded young law stu-

dents over a remark one made about the other's fiancée. *Open year-round, Monday to Saturday, from 10 am to 5 pm; Sunday, 1 pm to 4 pm.*

Just a 10-minute stroll from downtown is the site of the duel on the banks of the Tay. Today, the site is a campground, where swimming, fishing, and boating, rather than dueling, are the activities of the day.

Continue down Gore St. and turn right onto Craig Street to view Inge-Va. The dwelling in the neoclassical, or Colonial Georgian, style was built in 1823 by the Rev. Michael Harris, Perth's first Anglican pastor who arrived in 1819.

The house eventually became the home of Robert Lyon, the combatant who died in that last fatal duel. A later owner who had lived in Ceylon (now Sri Lanka) named the house Inge-Va,

A porcupine ambles along the Quiddity Trail boardwalk at Charleston Lake Provincial Park.

which means "come here" in Tamil, one of the languages of that country.

9 Charleston Lake Provincial Park

The landscape in Charleston Lake Provincial Park evokes northern Ontario with rocky outcrops and forests of pine, but it has the moderate climate of southern Ontario.

Centuries ago, the area was a hunting and fishing stopover for native peoples, who stayed in the rock shelters along the shore. Signs of their visits were discovered in 1976, when two park naturalists snorkeling offshore found several ancient clay pots resting on rocky underwater ledges.

The deep island-studded lake and its Precambrian granite shores and sandy beaches are home to a fascinating array of plants, fish, birds, and other animals, some of which are unique to the area, such as the harmless tree-climbing black rat snakes. Deer, raccoons, porcupines, foxes, and flying squirrels are denizens of the park's woodland. From boardwalks, you may spot beavers, muskrats, turtles, frogs, and salamanders.

At Charleston Lake, birdwatchers can sight blue herons, turkey vultures, hawks, ospreys, and loons. At night, nesting barred owls fill the air with their distinctive call.

Charleston Lake has long been known as a fisherman's paradise. Although the days are gone when you could take 100 bass in a single day, as an 1867 brochure boasted, bass, lake trout, and northern pike are plentiful enough to make an evening meal of pan-fried fish almost a certainty.

The 2,400-ha natural environment park has a wide variety of interpretive programs geared to all ages, including guided hikes, children's nature programs, and campfire presentations.

Every August, Canadian astronomer and writer Terence Dickinson visits the park to lead an evening of star-gazing, in which participants can spot distant stars through telescopes. The sessions have become so popular that some campers plan their visit to coincide with Dickinson's.

Running's Bay and Slim Bay are off limits to motorboats. For energetic paddlers (you can rent canoes here), the 20-minute portage to Red Horse Lake leads to the 52-km Gananoque Lake system canoe route. And those who like roughing it in the wild may enjoy one of the park's 10 campsites accessible only by foot or canoe. The park is also used by cross-country skiers during the winter, although trails are not maintained.

10 Athens

A proud and prosperous past lingers on every street corner in the town of Athens (pop. 900). Everywhere you turn in this Loyalist haven, you are confronted with signs of 19th-century wealth. Handsome farmsteads and century-old white clapboard houses dot the landscape. A block of three-story shops lines the main street. (Some, like the local drugstore, have been open since 1887.) And an elegant clock tower graces the post office, a symbol of civic pride.

Adding to the town's charm are 11 giant murals, brightening facades with bold colors and vivid images. They were painted in or after 1986 as part of a town beautification program.

Many of the murals depict the town's humble pioneer beginnings. In one scene, the wind buffets an apron-clad wife as she hangs bedsheets to

One of Athens' murals depicts a bygone fabrics store and a billowy Union Jack, which complements the flags on the adjacent street.

dry. In another lively mural, a turkey fair is in full swing.

Most of the community's settlers were United Empire Loyalists who came here in the late 1870s. The town was first called Dickson Corner and then Farmersville. In 1888, the name Athens was suggested by Arza Parish, a local merchant. He saw in his town a parallel with the great Greek centre of enlightenment. At the time, the town boasted a grammar school, a high school, and a training school for aspiring teachers.

11 Merrickville

One of Ontario's best-preserved 19th-century villages, Merrickville celebrated its bicentennial in 1993. Old stone buildings and stately gingerbread-trimmed heritage homes give the village of 1,000 residents a delightful romantic air. The boutiques and restaurants on St. Lawrence Street are a favorite haunt of boaters on the Rideau River, which runs through Merrickville.

A walking tour booklet with helpful photographs and map (available at most local stores) guides you around more than 30 heritage properties in the village. You can see such buildings as the City Hotel (c. 1856), now a pub, and village founder William Merrick's third house—a rambling mansion built

in 1821 and renovated many times since. Don't miss the ornate splendor of Sam Jakes Inn (c. 1861), originally a wealthy merchant's home and now a restaurant and hotel. On the corner of St. Lawrence and Main stands the carefully restored three-story Jakes Block (c. 1862). In the 1870s, it housed the largest department store between Chicago and Montreal; now it contains a restaurant and boutiques.

Three locks, now modernized, were built in Merrickville as part of the Rideau Canal system around 1830. At the east end of Main Street is a clapboard house known locally as the John By cabin. It once served as headquarters for Lt. Col. John By, who directed the building of the Rideau Canal. From a pathway running near the dam, on the Rideau River, you can see the Merrickville Blockhouse, a squat two-story structure with metre-thick stone walls, built in 1832 to shelter 50 soldiers. Now it is the village museum, with displays of military paraphernalia and re-created officers' living quarters. It is accessible from Highway 43, near the dam. *Open mid-June to Labor Day, Tuesday to Sunday, 10 am to 5 pm.*

A walk or drive north across the swing bridge takes you to the Industrial Complex Museum and the ruins of woolen mills, foundries, and factories. Plaques recall the days when giant wheels and grinding stones turned to make the village prosperous. In 1870, Merrickville had 58 industries and was larger than neighboring Perth or Smiths Falls. But when the railway bypassed the town, the village's fortunes dwindled. The fine craftsmanship of the era's stonemasons is still evident in the ruins, but the sounds of industry have been replaced by the quiet chatter of summer tourists.

Special events

Antique Show (early May)

Merrickville Fair and Steam Show
(mid-August)

Artists' Guild Annual Studio Tour
(late September)

Entrancing buildings of the Victorian era create a quaint atmosphere at Merrickville.

SIGHTS AND STOPOVERS ON AN HISTORIC WATERWAY

The 198-km-long Rideau Canal between Kingston and Ottawa was originally built in1826-32 for military purposes. The international stretch of the St. Lawrence River was vulnerable to American attack, and the canal was intended to provide a secure route in case of an attack.

Under the direction of Lt. Col. John By, more than 4,000 Royal Engineers and Sappers dug, blasted, and dammed the waterway through 200 km of wilderness. Linking lakes, rivers, flooded swamps, and canals, the project—with 47 locks, 24 dams, and 29 km of man-made channels—was completed in little more than five years. The canal was the world's first to carry steamboats. It was considered one of the greatest engineering feats of that time. But it was never used for its intended purpose. During much of the 19th century, it was used by commercial vessels.

The Merrickville Lock on the Rideau Canal

Today the Rideau Canal serves some 75,000 pleasure craft every summer, although it has changed little since 1832. Boaters still crank locks and swing bridges by hand on big winches, just as the military did when the canal was first opened in the early 1830s.

The middle stretch of the Rideau Canal has a number of attractive and little-known sights and stopping places, which are easily accessible by boat and car. One such stop is Manotick (pop. 3,200), a village of beautiful old homes and the site of three-story stone Watson's Mill (1860), which has been restored and once again produces flour. Near Watson's Mill, look for Miller's Oven, a tearoom rumored to serve the best pie on the Rideau Canal.

Just outside Kemptville, the G. Howard Ferguson Forest Station is a vast nursery with an annual production of 7 million trees. There are several excellent hiking trails within the forest station. Rideau River Provincial Park, situated near the canal some 5 km north of Kemptville, has campsites and self-guiding trails.

One of the oldest towns along the canal is Burritts Rapids, settled by Loyalists in 1793. The local Anglican Church was built in 1831. Walk along the 2-km Tip to Tip Trail, which runs the length of a man-made island past historic homes, through woodlands, and by marshlands. Downstream at Nicholson's Locks, a 400-m walk leads to the abandoned milling community of Andrewsville. At Merrickville, another historic Rideau Canal village, is the largest of the canal's four blockhouses, now a museum.

Smiths Falls (pop. 9,000) is the halfway point on the canal. Here the Rideau Canal Museum offers five floors of canal artifacts and displays, including a multi-projector slide show and 6-m-long model of the canal. *Open daily, mid-June to Labor Day, 10 am to 7 pm; May 1 to mid-June and Labor Day to October 31, Tuesday to Saturday, 10 am to 5 pm, Sunday noon to 5 pm.* Chocolate-lovers can enjoy a side trip to Hershey's chocolate factory, less than a kilometre from the canal.

The Rideau Canal from Chaffey's Lock to Lake Opinicon was once a scourge of the Royal Engineers. The swampy area was a breeding ground for malaria. Many workers who succumbed to the disease were buried in unmarked graves near Chaffey's Lock.

At Jones Falls Locks, stroll along a stone dam, more than 100 m long and 20 m high. The structure was the highest of its kind in North America, and the third-largest in the world, when it was completed in 1831. Perched on a point of land overlooking the dam is the Sweeney House, a fortified lockmaster's dwelling that doubled as a defensive structure. *Admission free. Open daily, mid-June to September, 9 am to 4 pm.* You can also tour a nearby blacksmith's forge furnished in 1843 style and, in summer, see demonstrations of the craft of forging metal for the locks and gates.

12 Maxville

⛺ ✳ ⌂

Robbie Burns' *a hundred pipers and a' and a'* converge on the village of Maxville (pop. 853) in the heart of Glengarry County. The community has been named for a local preponderance of people whose surnames begin with "Mac." Every year, Maxville resounds with the skirl of the bagpipes at the Glengarry Highland Games, held at the Kenyon Agricultural Grounds on the Saturday before the first Monday in August. The games attract pipe bands, Highland dancers, and athletes from North America, Scotland, and Australia.

The piping, drumming, and dancing competitions begin at 8 am. The big event of the day is a thrilling massed pipes-and-drums march, following the official opening at 12:45 pm. Another high point of the games is the North American Pipe Band Championships. All through the August afternoon, the hum and wail of the bagpipes ripple through the air as judges compare as many as 40 competing pipe bands.

Throughout the day, you can watch dancers kick and tap their toes to strathspeys, jigs, and reels. You can also take in the track-and-field events, the traditional Scots feats of physical prowess—the caber toss, hammer throw, and shot put. Dozens of booths sell everything from Scottish tartans and jewelry to Highland bagpipes. A hot-and-cold buffet of Scottish delicacies awaits hungry visitors at the Maxville arena.

If you plan to attend the games, book ahead. There are a few bed-and-breakfast establishments, and supervised camping for family groups is available only on the Kenyon Agricultural Grounds.

Less than 5 km northeast of Maxville is the village of Dunvegan (pop. 65), and set in a grassy field at the Dunvegan crossroads is the Glengarry Pioneer Museum.

The museum complex includes a log inn dating from 1842, a livery shed, a restored log barn and weaver's loft, and a miniature cheese factory, which will transport you back to the days of the Scottish pioneers who settled here some 200 years ago.

The inn, known as the Starr Inn in the mid-1800s, has its original bar,

A lively lass dances at Almonte, one of the eastern Ontario communities where Scottish traditions are still celebrated.

Every August, pipe bands march at Maxville, site of the Glengarry Highland Games.

wainscoting, and broad pine floors. Behind the bar is the kitchen with a fascinating array of antique utensils once used by families who farmed the rocky soil of Glengarry County for generations.

Upstairs you can browse through antique Gaelic bibles, grammar books, land registries, and 19th-century account books kept in elegant script. One debt is written off cryptically: "Debtor deceased, wife absolutely refuses to pay."

The livery shed houses a gargantuan stoning machine, and graceful sleighs. One of the sleighs was used by pallbearers, who tucked the deceased neatly under the seat. In the log barn, a dog-driven butter churn shares space with an apple juicer, a corn shucker, antique adzes and axes, horse and buggy accessories.

The loft is a weaver's loft, complete with spinning wheels, a pre-1850s loom, a quilting frame, and sewing machines.

At picnic tables outside, you can enjoy a slice of homemade pie from the cheese factory (which no longer makes cheese but doubles as a craft shop). *Open Victoria Day to late June and Labor Day to Thanksgiving, weekends only, 1 to 5 pm; July and August, daily, except Monday, 1 to 6 pm.*

The imposing walls are all that remains of St. Raphael's Church, near Williamstown.

"*Tread softly, stranger, reverently, draw near; the vanguard of a nation slumbers here.*" The words on the gate of St. Andrew's Church in Williamstown speak with pride of the role the village has played in Canada's history. Settled in 1784 by some of the first Loyalists in Upper Canada, by North West Company fur traders, and by Highland Scots, Williamstown is the cradle of history in Glengarry County.

The cemetery surrounding the 1812 stone church is the resting place of many key figures in Canadian history, such as explorer Alexander Mackenzie who named the Mackenzie River. One of the founders of the North West Company, Mackenzie donated the church bell, which is still rung every Sunday. The church windows are said to be the best examples of Palladian design remaining in Ontario.

On the western edge of Williamstown is one of Ontario's oldest homes, the historic Bethune-Thompson House. The oldest section, a log cabin built in 1784, adjoins a white stucco Georgian cottage that was added in 1804. It was the home of the first Presbyterian minister in Upper Canada, Rev. John Bethune (1751-1815), now remembered as the great-grandfather of Dr. Norman Bethune. After his death, it belonged to the North West Company explorer and mapmaker David Thompson (1770-1857), who surveyed the present border between the United States and Canada, from the St. Lawrence River to Lake of the Woods, in 1816. The Bethune-Thompson House is now owned by the Ontario Heritage Foundation. *Open year-round, weekdays, 4:30 pm to 5 pm; Sunday, 1 pm to 5 pm.*

Another place of interest is the Nor'Westers and Loyalist Museum on John Street. The two-story, red-brick Georgian building houses portraits of famous Nor'Westers, David Thomp-

St. Andrew's Church at Williamstown is the resting place of explorer Alexander Mackenzie.

son memorabilia, and an 8-m-long reproduction birchbark canoe, which was paddled from Thunder Bay to Williamstown in 1967 to celebrate Canada's Centennial. *Open Victoria Day to Labor Day, Sunday to Friday, 1 pm to 5 pm; Saturdays and holidays, 10 am to 5 pm; Labor Day to Thanksgiving, weekends only.*

Canoes are an important symbol in the village, because so many of the Nor'Westers settled here. Many of the handsome frame homes display family names on canoe-shaped signs. And

every April, Williamstown and Martintown co-host the Raisin River Canoe Race. Starting upriver at St. Andrews West, scores of canoeists race a 35-km course, and then celebrate their paddling prowess at a banquet in Williamstown.

The stone shell of the St. Raphael Church, built in 1821, dominates the quiet countryside some 9.5 km north of town. The church was destroyed in a 1970 fire. Its first pastor, Alexander Macdonell, was also the first Catholic bishop of Upper Canada.

WESTERN QUEBEC

Baskatong
Reservoir
8

Sainte-Anne-du-Lac

Rivière du Lièvre

Mont
Sir-Wilfrid

309

Ferme-Neuve
7

117

Mont-
Laurier

105

309

Maniwaki

L'Annonciation

117

Rivière

Noire

Labelle

Mont
Trembl

Réserve
faunique
de
Papineau-
Labelle

Mont-
Tremblant
Village
9

Fort William

Île
des
Allumettes

Chapeau

148

Fort-Coulonge

Île
du
Grand-
Calumet

Lac
Simon
6

Duhamel

321

Saint-Jovite

323

327

S.
Fa

Lac-Simon

Namur

Huberdeau

1
Shawville

366

Val-des-Bois

Rivière du Lièvre

323

Chénéville

321

148

Ottawa River

Quyon

105

Rivière
Gatineau

3
Wakefield

309

315

Gatineau
Park
2

Pontiac

321

Notre-Dame-
de-la-Paix

Riv. de la petite-

Nation

5
Montebello

Chelsea

50

Masson

Thurso

148

Plaisance

4
Papineauville

327

Aylmer

Hull

148

Ottawa

Réserve
faunique
de Plaisance

Grenville

Lachut

344

0   10   20 km

0   10   20 miles

ONTARIO
QUEBEC

St. Lawrence River

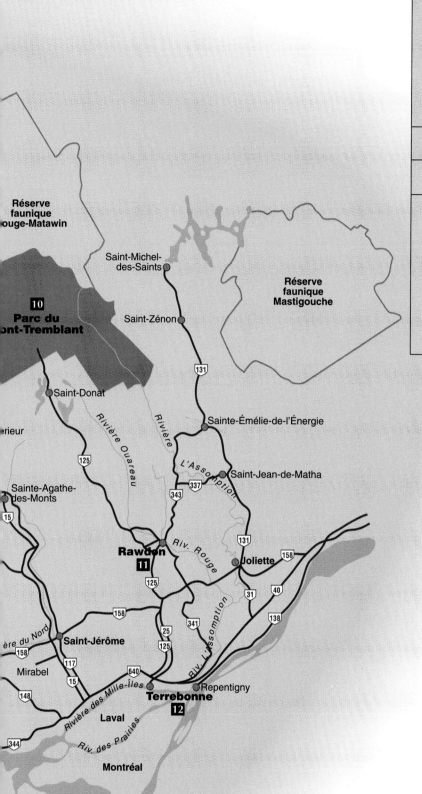

Réserve
faunique
ouge-Matawin

Saint-Michel-
des-Saints

Réserve
faunique
Mastigouche

10
Parc du
ont-Tremblant

Saint-Zénon

131

Saint-Donat

Rivière Ouareau

Rivière

Sainte-Émélie-de-l'Énergie

rieur

L'Assomption

125

Saint-Jean-de-Matha

Sainte-Agathe-
des-Monts

343

337

15

Riv. Rouge

Rawdon
11

131

158

Joliette

125

31

40

ère du Nord

158

341

138

25

125

Saint-Jérôme

Riv. L'Assomption

117

Mirabel

640

15

Repentigny

148

Rivière des Mille-Îles

Terrebonne
12

344

Laval

Riv. des Prairies

Montréal

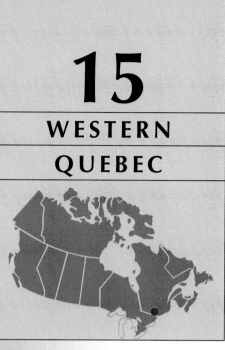

Places to see
Shawville
Gatineau Park
Wakefield
Plaisance
Montebello
Lac Simon
Ferme-Neuve
Baskatong Reservoir
Mont-Tremblant
The Lofty Lair of Windigo
Parc du Mont-Tremblant
Rawdon
Terrebonne
Île des Moulins

Roads to explore
Upper Ottawa Valley:
Hull to Fort William
Petite-Nation Region:
Montebello–Chénéville–
Saint-André-Avelin
Lanaudière: Saint-Jean-de-Matha
to Saint-Michel-des-Saints

Previous pages:
Lac Monroe, Mont-Tremblant

1 Shawville

Shawville, with a population of slightly more than 1,600, is one of the oldest English-speaking communities on the Quebec side of the Ottawa River. It was established in 1873 as a lumbering and agricultural centre, and later added brick production. The arrival of the CPR in 1886 sparked further growth. Fine Victorian dwellings and churches and the Main Street commercial blocks attest to past prosperity.

The former railway station, converted into the town museum, is located on the fairgrounds on the east side of the community. *Open only on Saturdays and holidays in July and August, and during the Agricultural Fair in early September.*

The main highlights of the Shawville Fair—the largest of its kind in the region—include a horse show and harness racing. Another popular annual event is the Pontiac Gas and Steam Association's Exhibition of turn-of-the-century machinery, held mid-August at Campbell's Farm in Clarendon, a 15-minute drive northwest of Shawville.

2 Gatineau Park

This 356-km² park stretches more than 50 km from the outskirts of Hull to the rugged highland of the Canadian Shield. It preserves a wilderness, whose predominant features are rolling, forested hills, meadowlands, lakes, and ponds. Established in 1938, the park embraces a wide range of recreational and historic attractions, which are accessible by routes 5, 105, 148, and 366. The visitors' centres are at Old Chelsea and Lac Philippe.

Gatineau Park is operated by the National Capital Commission, which provides 80 km of shared hiking and biking trails, 125 km of walking trails, 190 km of cross-country ski trails, six supervised beaches, and three camping sites. It also maintains the park's historic sites, such as the 230-ha Mackenzie King Estate. Meeting visitors' outdoor demands while conserving the park's natural resources is a major concern for the commission.

The park's hills were carved by glaciers more than 10,000 years ago. The glaciers rounded the stumps of ancient mountain range, and the meltwater filled the park's 50 lakes. After the retreat of the glaciers, a forest rooted itself on the rocky surface. Today, the park contains roughly 60 types of trees, largely hardwoods. About 100 species

Autumn colors engulf the woods on L'Île des Allumettes, an Ottawa River getaway.

Roads to explore:
The islands and hamlets
of the Upper Ottawa River
Distance: 128 km/79.5 miles

Route 148 links the small, picturesque riverside towns in the sparsely settled area northwest of Hull on the Quebec side of the Upper Ottawa River. Views of the river and the distant Laurentians create scenic backdrops for the drive.

● About 30 km west of Hull, Route 148 widens to four lanes. Turn right just past this point at Luskville's red brick town hall and follow the road to Luskville Falls. There is a pretty picnic spot just at the base of the falls.

An additional attraction here is a steep but rewarding 45-minute hike to the fire ranger's lookout atop the Eardley Escarpment, which forms the southern boundary of Gatineau Park.

● Some 10 km farther west along Route 148 is the old lumbering town of Quyon. Here you can see Granny Bean's cottage, a rivermen's stopover of the mid-1800s. One of the community's claims to fame is a visit by the Prince of Wales (later King Edward VII), who made an unscheduled stop during a tour of the Ottawa River valley in 1860.

● Follow the signs to the 100-year-old Quyon Ferry for the 5-minute crossing to Mohr's Landing on the Ontario side of the Ottawa River. The ferry operates from mid-April, when the ice breaks on the river, until the end of November.

● About 20 km farther west on Route 148 will bring you to Shawville.

● About 1 km past Shawville, turn off 148 and follow 303 to historic Portage-du-

Fort (pop. 330). Located where the old canoe route bypassed Cheneux Rapids, the town grew from a stopover on the fur trade and exploration routes to a mill town after 1850. Many of its stone buildings survive: look for the stone, one-room schoolhouse on Mill Street. Nearby Usborne House was built in 1887 by lumber baron Henry Usborne as a storehouse and later converted into a residence. On Church Street, you will see the grand Reid House (now the Pontiac Hotel), the town hall, and three old stone churches. Within easy walking distance of the rapids are a swimming beach and a picnic park.

● Continue north on 301 and 148. Take a side road to the community of Bryson, where boat rentals, river tours, and rafting excursions are available.

● At Bryson, follow the sign to Île du Grand Calumet. The island, rich in history, was the site of early Algonquin Indian settlements. Take the river road through the hamlet of Calumet to Au Bouleau Blanc, a log restaurant overlooking the Ottawa River. Nearby there is a 60-ha property that has hiking and cross-country ski trails, and rustic campgrounds. The white gravestone on the outskirts of the village commemorates a local hero, Jean Cadieux, the legendary voyageur and adventurer.

Marchand Bridge at Fort-Coulonge is one of ten covered spans in the backwoods area on the Quebec side of the Ottawa River.

● Returning to 148, head north to Campbell's-Bay (pop. 830), whose first commercial development came in the late 1880s with the CPR. Stop just north of town at a picnic site with a panoramic view of the Ottawa Valley.

● The next stop is Fort-Coulonge (pop. 1,640), settled by French fur traders in the mid-1800s. Today, it is the French-speaking centre of the Pontiac region. Two of its sites are visible from the route. The first on the right is Bryson House, built in 1854 by lumber baron George Bryson. On the left is the bright red Marchand Bridge (1898), which spans Coulonge River. At 129 m, it is Quebec's third longest covered bridge. Cross its single lane to a pleasant resting spot on the other side.

● Back on 148, turn right at the unpaved Bois-Francs Road to see the 48-m-high Coulonge Falls, where you can picnic or enjoy a stroll.

● Head west to Chapeau on Île-des-Allumettes. As you drive toward the community, you will glimpse the 38-m-high steeple of Saint-Alphonse-di-Liguori Catholic Church. This robust Romanesque structure, built in 1888, was planned, but never became, the cathedral of the Pembroke diocese.

● Travel on to Fort William, the site of a 19th-century Hudson's Bay fur trading post, where you can see the factor's house and other surviving buildings. In summer, the community offers boat rentals and a white sandy beach, perfect for swimming.

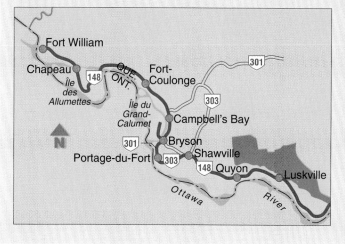

of flowers, including insect-eating sun-dews, pitcher plants, and grass pink orchids, grow on the forest floor. Bear, deer, and wolf roam the woods; beavers thrive in ponds and meadows; hawk, heron, loon, and osprey inhabit the lakes and the sky. The lakes and streams abound with smallmouth bass, northern pike, and lake trout.

During the 19th century, settlers came to the region now occupied by the park. Old mines, weathered farm buildings, and other relics of pioneer life are scattered throughout the area.

During the 1870s, wealthy Ottawans escaped to spacious summer retreats by Harrington, Kingsmere, and Meech lakes. In 1902, future Prime Minister William Lyon Mackenzie King came here and purchased his first property, Kingswood, beside Kingsmere Lake.

Later King bought Moorside and The Farm (now the residence of the Speaker of the House of Commons). For nearly 50 years the park was his summer retreat. He initiated the development of the park in the 1930s and later bequeathed his estate to the nation. Today, visitors can explore its restored summer cottages and the formal gardens, as well as the "ruins" assembled by King from demolished buildings. *Open from Victoria weekend to Thanksgiving.*

A 32-km road network crisscrosses the southern sector of the park. The Gatineau, Champlain and Fortune Lake parkways wind through the park and pass the spectacular Champlain Lookout. Just off the roads, scenic trails lead to secluded spots and spectacular lookouts. The 3-km Larriault Trail near the Mackenzie King estate begins close to Mulvihill Lake and takes you to the Eardley Escarpment, which overlooks the Ottawa Valley. The 2.5-km King Mountain Trail, also off the Champlain Parkway, leads to one of the high points in the park with a thrilling sum-mit view. You can explore Lusk Cave,

Maclaren Mill by La Pêche River recalls Wakefield's role as a 19th-century workplace.

an underground marble passage situated 5 km from Lac Philippe in the northern sector of the park. The visitors' centres at Old Chelsea and Lac Philippe will supply further information about these and many other trails in Gatineau Park.

3 Wakefield

W akefield, first settled in 1829, was the centre of a prosperous farming and lumbering community when it began attracting vacationers after the railway arrived in the late 1880s. Wakefield Bay on the eastern edge of town still draws summer visitors.

The historic treasures of this small community (pop. 250) are the Maclaren mill and museum. Built by Scot William Fairburn in 1834, the gristmill was powered by the swift-flowing La Pêche River, which runs into the Gatineau River at the heart of Wakefield. Ten years later, John and James Maclaren bought the mill, to which they added several others.

In the 1860s, the Maclarens built a Victorian Gothic mansion, overlooking their small, thriving industrial enclave. Today, the restored mill—the enclave's only surviving remnant—exhibits a working model of the mill, with descriptions of its development. Maclaren House, now a museum, tells the story of 19th-century life in this area. *Open from late June to early September.*

A summer-and-fall rail service to Wakefield revives the pleasures of bygone day-excursions. A restored 1907 steam engine, with nine passenger coaches, leaves the Hull station at Front and Montcalm streets. A 32-km journey takes about 1½ hours and includes a two-hour stop at Wakefield. In summer, the train makes one round-trip every day.

Guides on the train provide background information about the steam train and the passing villages, such as Ironsides, Tenaga, Kirks Ferry, and

On a scenic Hull–Wakefield excursion, travelers relive the excitement of old-time train travel.

Cascades. One of the highlights of the trip is watching while a large, delicately balanced turntable at the Wakefield railway terminus reverses the mighty steam engine.

Special Events
Gatineau Clog Country Music Festival, Low (early August)

Artists Studio Tours (late September)

Wakefield Craft Fair (late November)

4 Plaisance

D uring the spring, thousands of Canada geese touch down briefly at the picturesque but little-known sanctuary, Réserve faunique de Plaisance. This 27-km² wildlife reserve consists of two long and slender marshy peninsulas jutting from the north shore of the Ottawa River.

At the end of April, during the stopover of the Canada geese, the Papineau Ecological Society organizes a birding festival in the reserve. Guides are available to answer questions and direct bird-watchers to the best observation sites. A pair of binoculars and a good

camera are a must for this expedition.

The reserve has several hiking paths, including an interpretive trail that leads into the marshland, the nesting site of ducks, osprey, and tern. You can bike or walk on most of the trails, which have charming picnic spots along the way. *Open from the end of April to October 11.*

The entrances to the reserve are located just east and west of the village of Plaisance (pop. 1,080), some 20 km west of Montebello on Route 148. The visitors' centre for the park is located in the village. While you are here, look for the charming red-brick village church, which was constructed in 1902.

North of Plaisance, a seven-level waterfall, Les Chutes du Diable (the Devil's Falls), is a spectacular feature of the Petite-Nation River. (Take the right fork from Papineau Boulevard onto the Malo Concession Road, some 4 km from the Plaisance Church.)

The forest of oak and red pine that once covered this area was cleared in the early 1800s. The politician and surveyor Joseph Papineau established a pioneer community at North Nation Mills close by Les Chutes du Diable in 1805. The settlers were the first to work in western Quebec's forestry industry.

Today little is left of this lost community, but archeologists began unearthing its remnants in the early 1980s. There are nearby walking trails, picnic spots, historical interpretation boards. A lookout provides views of Les Chutes du Diable and the surrounding region of prosperous dairy farms.

5 Montebello

The heart of the Petite-Nation region is the resort and farming village of Montebello (pop. 1,240) on the Quebec side of the Ottawa River. The region was already settled by 1801 when Joseph Papineau acquired and developed the seigneury of La Petite-Nation. At one time, his thriving seigneury stretched for 30 km along the Ottawa River. In 1846, his son Louis-Joseph Papineau, lawyer, politician, and the leader of the *Patriotes* during the 1837 rebellion in Lower Canada, returned here after eight years of exile in the United States and set about building a magnificent mansion on the seigneury.

The Manoir Louis-Joseph Papineau, built in 1850, has been well preserved. During the summer, visitors are wel-

---

Roads to explore: Pristine wilds of the Petite-Nation

Distance: 84 km/52 miles

Montebello is the starting point for a drive that leads to the pristine wilderness of the Petite-Nation region and Lac Simon. The name of this region comes from the winding Petite-Nation River, which flows south from Lac Simon into the Ottawa River at Plaisance.

● Take Route 323 north from Montebello. Some 3 km outside of the village, visit the wildlife park at Domaine Oméga. Bison, European ibex, bighorn sheep, wapitis, a number of species of deer, and many small native wild creatures share this 610-ha natural habitat. A 7-km road runs through the park. *Open year-round, hours depending on the season. There is an admission charge.*

● About 18 km north of Domaine Oméga on Route 323 is Notre-Dame-de-la-Paix (pop. 750) on the Petite-Rouge River. Along the way, you cross the Petite-Nation River and pass Claude Lefebvre's strawberry farm, located just outside the community. In late June and July, you are welcome to stop and pick strawberries from Lefebvre's fields.

● Some 20 km farther north on 323, you reach Namur (pop. 500), also on the Petite-Rouge. It was founded in 1865 by Belgians, who named it after their hometown in Belgium. A pleasant side trip leads north on 323 to Lac des Plages.

● From Namur, head west 15 km on Route 315 to Chénéville (pop. 670) on the Petite-Nation. The hamlet, founded in 1857, was first named Sévigné. It was

renamed in 1885 to honor the local postmaster, Hercule Chéné.

● From Chénéville, there is a choice of side roads. Take Route 321 north along Lac Simon to Duhamel. Or continue on route 315 to Montpellier (pop. 3,000), which has an excellent golf course.

● Drive south on 321, which skirts the Petite-Nation. Visit the museum at Saint-André-Avellin (pop. 1,540). Its collection of more than a thousand items includes historic photographs and several rare 19th-century books. *Open daily, June to September.* Return to Montebello by the side road linking 321 to 323.

come to explore 20 rooms in the stone manor, which are decorated with fine period furnishings and tapestries. Other buildings on the estate include a gardener's house, a tea pavilion, and the stables. A nearby 1855 chapel contains Papineau's grave. Another estate building, the Grainerie, served as a studio for Papineau's son-in-law, the renowned architect, painter, and sculptor Napoléon Bourassa (1827-1916). *Open daily, early May to late October, 9 am to noon and 1 to 4:30 pm. Guided tours every half hour.*

A short walk from the manor along one of the flower-lined pathways on the banks of the Ottawa River leads to the Chateau Montebello, which was built in 1930 as a private resort by a Swiss-American millionaire, Harold Saddlemire. It was originally known as the Seigniory Club.

The Chateau is an impressive structure of round cedar and pine logs in a hunting-lodge style. It is said to be the largest log building in the world. During the three months of its construction, 3,500 workers used 10,000 red cedar logs from western Canada. The roof is made of some half a million shingles, all cut by hand.

This three-story log building has six wings and some 200 rooms. The main entrance opens onto an immense rotunda with a towering hexagonal stone fireplace. The remarkable wooden floors and unusual decor create a rustic but luxurious atmosphere. Nearby gardens, woods, and lakes enhance the charm of the place.

CP Hotels and Resorts bought and renovated the property in 1970, and gave the hotel its present name. In 1981, the resort gained worldwide attention when it hosted world leaders at the economic summit of the Group of Seven Nations.

During the 1930s, members of the Seigniory Club built some 50 opulent

This sunny stairwell is only one of the many pleasing corners of the Manoir Louis-Joseph Papineau, Montebello.

houses on the quiet, shaded avenues surrounding the hotel's golf course. These homes may be seen on Rue Richelieu, off route 323 heading north toward Saint-Jovite, just past the cemetery and railway tracks.

There are several excellent restaurants in the centre of Montebello. While you are here, visit the old log railroad station, which was moved in one piece to its present location. It serves as a visitors' centre and contains an historical display about the early railway days in this area. Opposite the centre is a ceramics and artists' workshop and, a little farther along the street, Galerie d'Art Lise Martel specializes in the work of Quebec artists.

Four beach chairs await the arrival of summer visitors at a sandy stretch beside Lac Simon.

6 Lac-Simon

This sparkling lake is set in the midst of a pristine wilderness. Densely wooded cliffs rise from its shores. In summer, the Lac Simon region attracts boaters, canoeists, and sports fishermen; in winter, it draws cross-country skiers and snowmobilers.

This region was once inhabited by the Theskanini Indians who were decimated by disease and driven away by their enemies, the Iroquois. In 1854, several Theskaninis, including Marie-Louise Cimon and Amable Canard Blanc, returned to the area and gave their names to Lac Simon and a large island in the middle of the lake, Île du Canard-Blanc. (At the centre of this rocky island is yet another lake.)

A one-hour drive along Route 321 on its east shore leads from the south end of the lake at Chénéville (pop. 679) to the north end at Duhamel (pop. 380). Chénéville was originally established in the 1860s as a mission post. Later it developed as a lumbering community in the midst of the rich, thick forests surrounding Lac Simon. Today it is popular with outdoor enthusiasts who like the exhilarating challenge of canoe and fishing expeditions.

At Duhamel, the visitors' centre is close to a recreational area with a sandy beach, hiking trails, and camping sites. During the winter, Duhamel welcomes some 3,000 deer that come to feed in this vicinity. Their arrival provides some fine opportunities for nature photographers.

Cyclists relax in a Laurentian glade.

The municipality of Lac-Simon (pop. 530) on the western side of the lake can be reached by a road from Chénéville. This road skirts the southwestern corner of Lac Simon and leads to the beautiful bays of Cap Ferland, Carrée, Dorée, Groulx, Manitou, Saint-Laurent, and Yell. Many of the bays are lined by attractive wooden chalets.

Special Events
Festival du chevreuil, Duhamel
(December to March)

A daring individual may enjoy the thrill of slithering down the 50-m length of Windigo Falls, where the surface has been smoothed by a perpetual sheet of water into a natural slide.

7 Ferme-Neuve

Long before the arrival of the Europeans, the Algonquin Indians knew the wild splendor of the upper Laurentian area near the present-day site of Ferme-Neuve. The Indians traveled upstream on the Rivière du Lièvre and, during the summer, camped at the foot of 783-m-high Mont Sir-Wilfrid, which was once believed to be the dwelling place of the evil spirit Windigo. The place-names in the Ferme-Neuve area reflect the Algonquin presence: Petawaga, Baskatong, Saguay, Kimkamika, and Nominingue.

The first lumber camps opened here in the mid-1830s. A large farm, known as Mountain Farm, was set up in a forest clearing. It fed and supplied the army of men and horses who worked here. By the end of the 19th century, this farm had grown to become the village of Ferme-Neuve.

This community (pop. 3,054), some 20 km north of Mont-Laurier, can be reached by route 309. The village is tucked into a bend of Rivière du Lièvre. At its heart is Lac des Journalistes, whose name commemorates a group of writers who, in 1901, raised funds to build the local school. The village church is the only one in this part of Quebec designed by French-born monk and architect Dom Paul Bellot, who came to Canada in 1937. (His best-known work is the dome of St. Joseph's Oratory in Montreal.)

The hardy residents have transformed the Ferme-Neuve region into one of the most prosperous in the upper Laurentians. The basis of local prosperity is the lumber industry, farming, and animal breeding. Some breeders have started innovative ventures. Abigest Farm, some 7 km from Ferme-Neuve on Route 309, has a mixed herd of bison, yaks, wapitis, deer, mountain goats, and llamas. You may glimpse this strange collection of creatures as you drive by the farm. (The owner sometimes opens his property to travelers, who can visit the animal enclosures.)

The beekeepers at Ferme Apicole Desrochers, 4 km from Ferme-Neuve, make fine honey and an old-fashioned honey wine, known as mead. Visitors can choose two types of mead—white or rosé (flavored with raspberry).

Other accessible sites near Ferme-Neuve are Mont Sir-Wilfrid, the second-highest Laurentian peak, and the Baskatong Reservoir. Here you can take a jet-ski journey along the Rivière du Lièvre to a dam at Notre-Dame-du-Laus. You can also enjoy a 30-km round-trip by bicycle to two 1903 covered bridges—the only twin bridges of this kind in Quebec—at Ferme-Rouge.

Special Events

Village Festival (Saturday before June 24)

Festival of the Forest (July)

Mont Laurier Canoe Race
(3rd week of July)

Agricultural Fair (August)

8 Baskatong Reservoir

At the foot of 734-m-high Mont Sir-Wilfrid, north of Ferme-Neuve, is the Baskatong Reservoir. In the Algonquin tongue, the word *baskatong* means "packed ice."

This 337-km² reservoir was created in 1927 from Lake Baskatong with the construction of the Mercier dam on the Gatineau River. Subsequent flooding covered the small lakeshore hamlet of Saint-François-Xavier-du-Baskatong Mission, which was founded in 1880. Local folk claim you may glimpse the

chapel tower of the vanished mission when the water level is low.

Today Baskatong Reservoir is a mecca for outdoor enthusiasts. Anglers will find its waters teeming with rainbow and speckled trout, doré, pike, and freshwater salmon. Boaters can choose from more than 100 tiny islands, many of which have secluded beaches. A constant wind ruffling the surface of the water makes this an ideal spot for windsurfing. Some visitors may prefer to laze in the sun on the white sand beaches bordering the eastern shore of the reservoir. Camping facilities are available at Baie-du-Diable.

9 Mont-Tremblant Village

The village of Mont-Tremblant (pop. 1,000) is a popular travel desination, located on Lac Mercier just north of Saint-Jovite at the end of Route 327. The village was founded in 1894 at the foot of 986-m-high Mont Tremblant, the highest peak in the Laurentians. The entrance to Parc du Mont-Tremblant is 3 km to the northeast.

Mont-Tremblant is a year-round resort area with charming landmarks, such as St. Bernard's Church, which is part of a ski station.

THE LOFTY LAIR OF WINDIGO

Autumn leaves of the Laurentians

Mont Sir-Wilfrid, 783 m high, ranks second highest among the peaks of this Laurentian area. (The highest is Mont Tremblant.) It is located some 20 km north of Ferme-Neuve; its name honors the Canadian Prime Minister Sir Wilfrid Laurier (1896-1911). Some local people refer to Mont Sir-Wilfrid as "the mountain of the devil." Algonquin legend says it was the lair of the evil spirit Windigo, who took possession of humans and caused the wind to howl through mountain caves.

Undeterred by Windigo's legendary presence, outdoor enthusiasts enjoy Mont Sir-Wilfrid all year round. The breathtaking view of the region and the Baskatong Reservoir rewards the hike to the summit. The spot is ideal for a picnic. (Before leaving for a picnic, pack your basket with honey and mead from Ferme-Neuve's beekeepers, and goat's-milk chocolate from the Benedictine monks at Mont-Laurier.)

At the heart of the Windigo's lair is 18-m-wide Windigo Falls. Its wild waters career along a 50-m course. The rocky surface, smoothed to form a natural water chute, frequently tempts daring individuals to hours of gleeful sliding. For those of a quieter disposition, the nature trail along the Windigo River offers a peaceful stroll.

During the winter, heavy snowfalls transform Mont Sir-Wilfrid's rugged wilderness into an exhilarating wonderland for thousands of snowmobilers who congregate here from all over the world. The mountain offers a network of 600 km of groomed trails within a radius of 40 km of Ferme-Neuve. Despite the impressive choice of trails, most snowmobilers make it a point of honor to tackle the challenging one at the top of the mountain.

The community's roots go back to 1906 when the Wheeler family came here from the United States and established a sawmill. Later the family built Auberge Gray Rocks, the area's first luxury hostelry. By the 1940s, Mont-Tremblant had established its enduring reputation as one of the foremost ski areas in eastern North America.

South of Mont-Tremblant, there are a number of charming sites along routes 117 and 323, which can be reached by way of Saint-Jovite. This part of the Laurentians, marked by gently rolling hills, was opened up by settlers at the beginning of the 1840s. The names of villages such as Arundel, Barkmere, and Weir recall the settlers' origins in England. During the 1870s, the Most Rev. Antoine Labelle began his campaign to develop this Laurentian region by encouraging French-Canadian and European settlement.

From Saint-Jovite, take Route 323 to the 1918 covered bridge at Brébeuf (pop. 660). Some 11 km farther along 323, Saint-Rémi-d'Amherst (pop. 903) is set in beautiful lake-studded countryside. A hiking trail here leads to the old fire watchtower, which offers a commanding view of the Rivière Rouge winding its way between the mountains. The village's wooden church, built in 1905 on the shores of Lac Rémi, is well worth a stop.

From Saint-Rémi, take Route 364 about 10 km to Huberdeau (pop. 777). A *Calvary* tableau on a nearby hillside is a place of pilgrimage. The tableau, built in 1910-20, is a bronzed cast-iron version of the 1892 wooden original. Each of the 27 figures of the Stations of the Cross is 2 m high and weighs more than 300 kg.

Arundel (pop. 479) is across from Huberdeau on the other side of the Rivière Rouge. This village of quaint old houses and wooden churches was established by settlers from England.

Another charming community is Weir (pop. 369), about 10 km farther south of Arundel on Route 364. This is a popular spot with rock climbers. You can return to Saint-Jovite by Route 327, a picturesque Laurentian back road.

Special Events

Symphony of Colors
(September)

10 Parc du Mont-Tremblant

Parc du Mont-Tremblant, the oldest of Quebec's parks, was established in 1894. Its 1,500-km^2 encompasses 400 lakes and 986-m-high Mont Tremblant, the Laurentian peak for which the park is named. The Algonquin Indians called Mont Tremblant *manitonga soutana* (mountain of the spirits). According to legend, the spirits made the mountain tremble when man disturbed the tranquillity of the region.

Parc du Mont-Tremblant is popular with outdoor enthusiasts. It offers year-round activities, such as camping, fishing, sailing, canoeing, swimming, skiing, and rock climbing. Anglers may choose from 120 designated lakes where they can catch at least 36 different species of fish, including speckled and gray trout in the south, and pike, doré, and smallmouth bass in the north. The park also has a thousand camping sites and numerous cycling trails of varying difficulty. There are several interpretive nature trails, and many of the lakes are easily accessible in summer for canoeing and sailing.

In winter, Mont Tremblant Park maintains more than 80 km of cross-country ski trails with several shelters and ski-waxing cabins. There is also winter camping, snowshoeing, and snowmobiling. The downhill skiing is

A panorama of Laurentian lakes and hills expands before the viewer's eyes at this lookout in Parc du Mont-Tremblant.

superb both at Mont Tremblant and nearby Gray Rocks ski centres.

The park also attracts visitors who are drawn by its scenic beauty. The most exciting time of year is the autumn, when the changing foliage becomes a spectacle of color. You can best enjoy this by taking one of the chairlifts to the park's peaks.

The Chute-du-Diable, in the park sector of that name, and the Chute-aux-Rats, on the east side of the park, offer opportunities for exciting nature photography. Hikes along the La Roche and La Corniche trails lead to the scenic valley of Lac Monroe and the Mont Tremblant peak.

In 1980, Quebec opened a forestry educational centre at nearby Saint-Faustin. Its purpose is to make the public aware of the importance of preserving forests. The centre contains roughly 15 km of interpretive and hiking trails, along which you will find specimens of the plant and animal life found in this part of the Laurentians. *Open daily, May 17 to October 22, 8:30 am to 4:30 pm.*

11 Rawdon

The early roots of Rawdon go back to the beginning of the 19th century, when this region was first settled by Irish immigrants and, later, Scots, English, and French Canadians. The town of Rawdon was officially founded in 1837. For almost 100 years, agriculture and forestry were the area's economic mainstays.

During the 1930s, the character of the community changed with the arrival of successive waves of Eastern European immigrants: Russians, Poles, Czechs, Hungarians, and Ukrainians.

Today some 16 ethnic groups live in the shadow of Rawdon's majestic pine trees. Local history and diversity are reflected in two of this community's attractive churches: the Gothic-style Anglican church, built of fieldstone in

A tiny Russian Orthodox chapel brings a touch of Old Russia to the community of Rawdon.

1857, and the blue-and-white Our Lady of Kazen, a Russian Orthodox chapel, set in a wooded cemetery (at the intersection of 15th Avenue and Woodland Road).

The best-known scenic attraction near Rawdon is Dorwin Falls, just west of town on route 341. From two lookouts beside the falls, visitors can discern the grim visage of the Algonquin sorcerer Nipissingue in the rock face.

According to legend, the sorcerer pushed the lovely princess Hiawatha into the gorge, after she rejected his advances. When her body touched the

stream, she became the waterfall where her spirit is still said to dance and sing. The Great Manitou turned Nipissingue to stone and condemned him to watch her forever.

At the Rawdon rapids, some 6.5 km north of the village on route 337, the Rivière Ouareau winds among huge flat-topped rocks, which provide secluded spots for sunbathing.

Another Rawdon attraction is Canadiana Village, which contains more than 38 restored buildings from the 19th century, including an 1835 schoolhouse and an 1888 general store.

Guides in period costumes re-create 19th-century village life and demonstrate old-time skills, such as wool-carding and weaving of the distinctive arrowed sash (*ceinture fléchée*) worn by 19th century fur traders. *Open mid-May to early September, Tuesday to Sunday. Hours vary. The village is closed Monday except on legal holidays.*

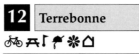

12 | Terrebonne

🚲 🛶 🏕 ⚐ ❀ ⌂

Within easy reach of Montreal, you will find many picturesque and often little-known getaways worth a day's visit. One of these spots is the Île des Moulins, located in the old section of

Terrebonne (pop. 39,700). This island, attractively situated on the Rivière des Mille-Îles, has three stone mills and a seigneurial office of the 1800s. The Quebec provincial government has used the materials and techniques of the period to restore these buildings.

A small wooden bridge links the street (Boulevard des Braves) to the Île

Roads to explore: Landmarks and legends of the Lanaudière

Distance (approx.): 70 km / 44 miles

This drive on Route 131 runs through the heart of the Lanaudière region, which stretches from Terrebonne, just outside Montreal, to the untouched wilderness north of Saint-Michel-des-Saints.

● The first stop on the drive is Saint-Jean-de-Matha (pop. 3,260), located some 35 km north of Joliette on Route 131. The village's most famous resident was the famous Quebec strongman, Louis Cyr. A statue at the parish church commemorates Cyr, who died here in 1912. The village is truly the home of the strong. Another resident, Donat Gaboury, won a place in the 1988 *Guinness Book of Records* for lifting 382 kg at the age of 81.

Within the immediate vicinity, there are two attractive sites. About 2 km south of the village on Route 131, Montagne Coupée offers mountain-bike trails. You

can drive to the summit for a superb view of the Lanaudière landscape—and, on a clear day, a glimpse of distant Montreal.

The other local landmark is the waterfall at the 30-ha Chutes-Monte-à-Peine-et-des-Dalles Regional Park, some 4 km southwest of Saint-Jean-de-Matha on 131. (Just follow the signs from the parish church.) The park is an ideal spot for picnics, nature photography, hikes, and cross-country skiing.

● After Saint-Jean-de-Matha, the level terrain with pastures and farms gives way to forested hills. Some 18 km farther north on 131, you enter Sainte-Émélie-de-l'Énergie (pop. 1,530), founded in 1870 by Jean-Baptiste Leprohon. His wife, Emélie, exhorted the settlers to work harder. The village name salutes this formidable pioneer, as well as her sainted namesake.

● The next stop on this drive is Parc des Sept-Chutes, 25 km from Sainte-Emélie. Steps built into the side of the mountain lead the visitor along the 60-m-high waterfall (Chute du Voile-de-la-mariée or Bridal Veil Falls). The falls are named for the sheer whiteness of their tumbling waters in the spring. Well-marked trails in the park may take from 50 minutes to three hours to hike. Some of the terrain is rough. But hikers will find the scenery breathtaking, particularly the

Clearings for pasture and farmland dot the Lanaudière landscape.

Mont Brossard cliffs, which rise 150 m from Lac Rémi.

● Another 15 km farther north is Saint-Zénon (pop. 1,025), which was founded in 1870. This village is located at an elevation of 750 m, the highest inhabited altitude in Quebec. The church's parking lot offers a panoramic view of the region.

● After Saint-Zénon, Route 131 runs alongside Lac Kalagamac where 15- and 30-minute hydrofoil rides are available.

● Saint-Michel-des-Saints (pop. 2,275), at the northern end of Route 131, is the last stop on this drive through the Lanaudière region. The village has been the domain of settlers, farmers, and miners since its establishment in 1864.

Close by, you can swim at the Taureau Reservoir (Réservoir Taureau), which has a long sandy shoreline. At the federal launching ramp, you can obtain permits to camp on one of its islands or bays.

An old-fashioned bandstand brightens Masson Park, just beside Île des Moulins, Terrebonne.

AN HISTORIC WORKSHOP ON AN IDYLLIC ISLAND

Île des Moulins is considered to be a major Quebec historic site, second in importance only to Place Royale in Quebec City. Since the late 1600s, the island—once a bustling industrial workshop—has passed through the hands of several entrepreneurs. The first owner, Sieur André Daulier des Landes, received the island as part of the Vieux Terrebonne seigneury from the French king Louis XIV, in 1673.

Landes seems never to have set foot in the seigneury. Nor did his successor, Louis Le Conte Dupré, who nevertheless ordered the building of Île des Moulins' first mill. In 1718, Father Louis Lepage who lived in Terrebonne obtained the seigneury. He contributed two more mills and a stone causeway linking the island and the mainland.

The wealthy Montreal fur-trade merchant Simon McTavish bought Île des Moulins in 1802. McTavish was the chief outfitter for the North West Company and set up four new mills, as well as workers' dwellings. One of the additions, the surviving 1803 bakery, supplied biscuits and conserves to the voyageurs headed west for the North West Company.

Thirty years later, the merchant and politician Joseph Masson, who made a fortune from textile manufacturing, paid more than $100,000 in cash for the seigneury. When Masson died in 1847, he had added several mills (including the 1846 gristmill) and begun work on a textile mill and a seigneurial office. Both were completed by his wife and survive on the site. A riverside park by the island honors the Masson name.

After the death of Masson's wife in 1883, Île des Moulins declined in importance, and eventually it fell into disuse. In 1974, the Quebec government acquired the island and restored its four remaining structures. This idyllic island, now an historic treasure, is a lively focus for local cultural events.

des Moulins. The first building at the entrance to the island is the "old" gristmill, built in 1846 by Joseph Masson, who acquired this property in the 1830s. Today the mill is used as the community's library.

The seigneurial office, located across from the library, dates from 1850. Its features include walls almost a metre thick and a hammered copper roof. Inside are shutters once used to retain heat in winter. The island's interpretation centre is on the main floor.

Beside the seigneurial office is the 1803 bakery, built by Montreal merchant Simon McTavish, and the "new" 1850 mill. The ground floor of the new mill has a theatre with a floating stage extending into the river. A musical show presented here four times weekly depicts events in the history of Vieux Terrebonne and Île des Moulins. In July and August, actors in period costume circulate through the park and talk to visitors about the history of the island. *The main sites are open daily, June 24 to September 1, from 10 am to 8 pm. Guided tours are available.*

Île des Moulins is an ideal spot for a picnic, a stroll, or a bicycle ride. On Sunday mornings, you can listen to classical music concerts or folk-song recitals, held here at 11 am. There is an 11-km-long walking and cycling pathway. An attractive stopping place is the dam linking Île des Moulins to neighboring Île Saint-Jean. Other activities include a guided tour of the island and a ride in a horse-drawn carriage.

Guided tours of Terrebonne are available in summer at 1 pm on Sundays. One of the stops, the 1760 house at 844 Rue Saint-François, is the oldest dwelling in the community.

NORTHEASTERN QUEBEC

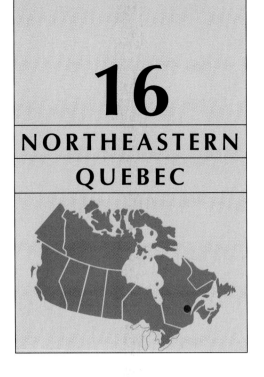

Places to see

Le Chemin du Roy (The King's Road)
Champlain
Batiscan
Sainte-Anne-de-la-Pérade
Île d'Orléans
Cap Tourmente National Wildlife Area
Les Éboulements
Saint-Joseph-de-la-Rive
Île aux Coudres
*Wooden workhorses
of the St. Lawrence*
Parc des Grands Jardins
Parc des
Hautes-Gorges-de-la-Rivière-Malbaie
Cap-à-l'Aigle and Saint-Fidèle
Port-au-Persil
Saguenay parks
L'Anse Saint-Jean
Sainte-Rose-du-Nord
Val-Jalbert
Péribonka

Roads to explore
The Mauricie Region:
Grand-Mère to Grandes-Piles
Beaupré Coast:
Cap Tourmente National Wildlife Area to
Sainte-Anne-de-Beaupré

National park close-up
La Mauricie

*Previous pages:
Port-au-Persil*

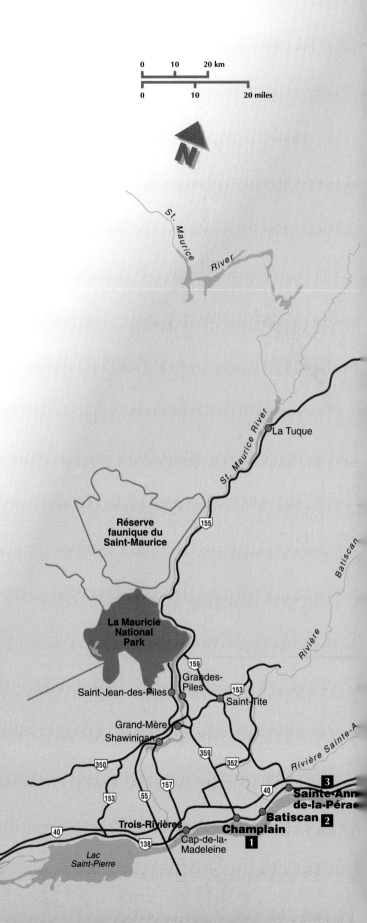

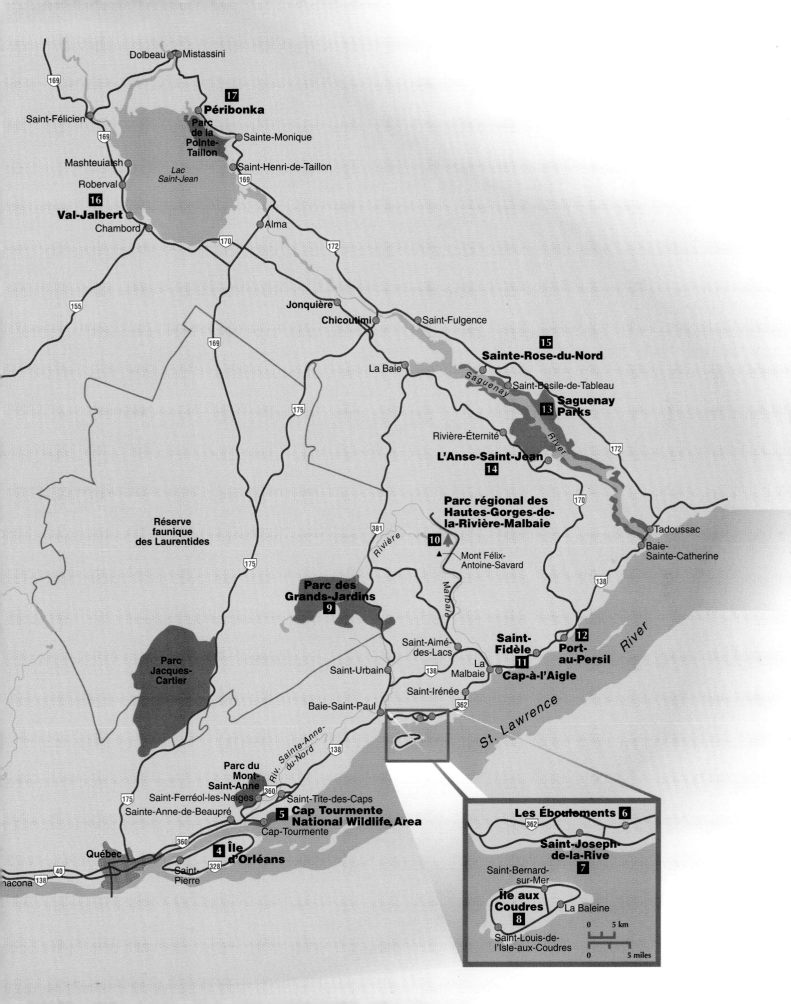

QUEBEC'S ROYAL ROAD

Sainte-Anne-de-la-Pérade's coat of arms

Route 138 along the north shore of the St. Lawrence follows *le Chemin du Roy*—the King's Road—which was built in the 1730s to link the burgeoning centres of Quebec City and Montreal. Today, the road offers a pleasing alternative to the busy Route 40 that parallels it just to the north. The most picturesque stretch lies northeast of Trois-Rivières and can best be traveled in two stages: Trois-Rivières to Sainte-Anne-de-la-Pérade and Grondines to Quebec City. The route is ideal for travelers who are looking for superb riverside views and opportunities to discover the churches, manor houses and other landmarks in some of Quebec's most charming historic villages: Champlain, Batiscan, Sainte-Anne-de-la-Pérade, Deschambault, Portneuf, and Neuville.

The *Chemin du Roy* was Canada's first year-round road. In summer, a carriage might cover the 267-km distance of this earth road in 4½ days. Travel can hardly have been restful. Some 30 wayside hostelries were built at regular intervals on the route. Here, drivers changed horses and travelers recovered before the next stage of their bumpy journey. Some of these hostelries, now restored, still stand beside the old royal road.

The presbytery at Batiscan shows the making of fine bobbin lace, one of the many traditional skills that survive in rural Quebec communities.

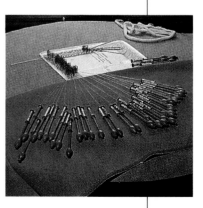

1 Champlain

∧ ⊛ ⬥ 🐟 ❋ ⌂

Once a mail-coach stop on the Chemin du Roy, Champlain (pop. 1,610) was also a fishing port in bygone days. Now its prosperity is based on agriculture. Stone houses with steep roofs line the seawall along the St. Lawrence River. Some of the owners proudly display a coat of arms. This custom began in 1979, when the village celebrated its 300th anniversary. The community also has charming wooden houses painted in pastels. The wraparound verandas are a distinctive local feature.

Champlain's Notre-Dame-de-la-Visitation Church was built in 1879 to replace a 1710 structure. Its treasured works of art include a painting of the Immaculate Conception dating back some three hundred years.

North of Champlain, you can take Route 359 to a small observatory operated by the Trois-Rivières Cégep at 300 Rang Sainte-Marie. In summer, you can spend a pleasant evening here stargazing. *Admission free. Open daily (except Mondays and Fridays, 2 pm to 5 pm, and 7 pm to midnight. The rest of the year: Friday through Sunday, 7 pm to midnight.*

2 Batiscan

🐟 ⌂

Situated east of Champlain on the Chemin du Roy, Batiscan (pop. 870) traces its history back to 1639. At 340 Rue Principale, the Vieux Presbytère (the old presbytery) is part of a picturesque cluster of church buildings.

This 1816 priest's house is located on the site of the former Batiscan seigneury, echoes a building style prevalent in the early 1700s of the French Regime. It is meticulously maintained, and its lovingly preserved furnishings blend perfectly with the architecture.

The 1816 stone presbytery at Batiscan is architectural gem on the Chemin du Roy.

More than 1,000 antiques of different styles and periods are displayed here. The main room of the Vieux Presbytère contains a mixture of objects: a pine refectory table, a three-tiered stove, a beggar's bench, an early 19th-century English-style piano, and a two-tiered armoire. Some of the other rooms have diamond-point armoires, tables and chairs in the traditional Quebec style, and a 17th-century four-poster.

The dwelling, acquired in 1983 by the local municipality, also offers summer exhibitions. *Open daily, May 1 to October 31, 9 am to 4:30 pm.*

3 Sainte-Anne-de-la-Pérade

⊛ 🐟

Sainte-Anne-de-la-Pérade (pop. 2,430) is best known for tommycod fishing, which occurs in January and February. Thousands of anglers build tiny plywood cabins on the Rivière Sainte-Anne and cut holes in the ice to fish for tommycod. A four-week festival celebrates this event. The busy schedule includes ice sculptures and parades.

As you approach the village, you will glimpse the bell towers of the neo-Gothic church. In summer, you can ex-

plore the village and discover its historic buildings, such as the Gouin (1669), Tremblay (1669), Dorion (1749), and Baribeau (1717) dwellings.

The manor house at the end of Rue Sainte-Anne was once the home of the Quebec heroine Madeleine Verchères. It is said that, in 1692, the 14-year-old girl defended her father's fort at Verchères against an Iroquois attack. Later, she married Pierre-Thomas de Lanaudière, the seigneur of La Pérade, and settled in this village, where she died in 1747.

Special Events
Tommycod Carnival
(January)

4 Île d'Orléans

Explorer Jacques Cartier gave this island its name in 1536, in honor of the Duc d'Orléans, the son of French King François I. The first settlers arrived a century later. Because so many of the churches, mills, and manor houses survive here, the Quebec provincial government has classified the entire island as an historical district—the largest in the province. A visit to the island takes visitors back to the beginnings of French settlement in North America.

Île d'Orléans is easy to travel and explore. Route 368 (*Chemin Royal*) encir-

Roads to explore: A love story of the Mauricie region
Distance: 55 km/34 miles

This drive is a must for anyone who has seen the television series *Les Filles de Caleb*, or read Arlette Cousture's novel, known as *Emilie* in English, on which it is based. The novel was inspired by the true story of two lovers, Émilie Bordeleau and Ovila Pronovost, who lived in the late 19th century. The drive starts at Grand-Mère (pop. 14,700) in the heart of the Mauricie region.

Émilie's Village, a theme park in the town of Grand-Mère, has re-created the interior of Émilie's house, the farms of Caleb Bordeleau and the Pronovost family, and the Bourdais School with sets from the television series. *Open daily, May 22 to September 13, 11 am to 6 pm.*
● To leave Grand-Mère, take Route 359 south, and follow Route 352 toward the 200-year-old village of Saint-Stanislas (pop. 1,320) where Émilie Bordeleau was born. Her parents married in the church in 1877, the year of its consecration. The couple had 10 children who grew up on Caleb Bordeleau's land on Côte Saint-Paul. At 130 Rue Principale is the house where Émilie lived after she retired from teaching; opposite,

A logger sculpted in wood swings his axe at the Village du Bûcheron.

is the forge that her father frequently visited. Several members of the Bordeleau family, including Émilie herself, are buried in the Saint-Stanislas Cemetery.
● Continue on Route 352. Just outside Saint-Stanislas, stop at Batiscan Park, as Émilie and Ovila did, to watch the rapids on the Rivière Batiscan. Drive to Saint-Séverin.
● Lucie, Émilie's best friend, lived in Saint-Séverin (pop. 1,120), northwest on Route 159. The Lafrance flour mill (1850) is located here beside the Envies River, which was formed when an earthquake shook this region in 1663. Close by is the well-preserved Lanouette mill (1878). A lovely covered bridge on the South Municipal Road is a national historic monument. The local village church was constructed in 1895 from a general stone.
● The drive continues northwest on Route 159 to Saint-Tite (pop. 2,860), a prosperous area well-known for its annual western festival.

Émilie and Ovila first fell in love here. The school where Émilie taught, a typical county school of the past century, is located at the intersection of Route 153 and Montée des Pointes. Nearby, is the Pronovost ancestral farm, and at the intersection of the Pronovost and Le Bourdais municipal roads is the farmhouse

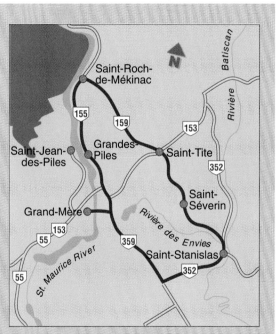

built by Ovila and his brothers. Farther along Route 150 is Lac à la Perchaude, where Émilie and Ovila often met.
● Head north on Route 159 and turn south on 155 to Grandes-Piles (pop. 420), one of the most beautiful villages in the Mauricie. At 780 5th Avenue, the Village du Bûcheron (Village of the Lumberjack) re-creates the era of the lumberjacks.
● Just across the St. Maurice River, Saint-Jean-des-Piles (pop. 600) provides access to La Mauricie National Park where much of *Emilie* was filmed. To reach the park, go to Grand-Mère and head north.

cles the island and links the six villages described here. The road also provides a succession of exhilarating views of the St. Lawrence River.

To reach the island, cross the bridge from Montmorency. Once on the island, drive east to Sainte-Pétronille (pop. 1,100), the island's smallest parish. Toward the end of the 19th century, wealthy vacationers adopted this village as a summer base. Some of their sumptuous houses can be seen as you enter the village. Rue Horatio Walker offers a view of Montmorency Falls across the St. Lawrence. (The name of the street honors the 19th-century painter who lived on the island for more than 50 years.) The 1855 wharf looks across the river to the skyline of Quebec City.

The next stop, Saint-Laurent (pop. 1,462), was founded in 1679. In the 19th century, more than 20 local shipyards (known as *chalouperies*) built rowboats (300 to 400 a year) used by islanders to cross the St. Lawrence River. Demand for the boats declined after the bridge from Montmorency was opened in 1935. The traditions of the old ship-yards survive at the Parc maritime de Saint-Laurent, where you can see boat builders at work. The island's only marina is located at the village.

You will notice that many farms in this vicinity cultivate the strawberries for which the island is famous. As you enter Saint-Laurent along Route 368, the Seigneurie de l'Île-aux-Sorciers offers bird-watching lookouts, nature trails, and man-made ponds for fishing. At the outskirts of the village, the Gosselin mill perches by a waterfall. This four-story stone flour mill, built in 1635, is now a restaurant.

Saint-Jean (pop. 960), once a seafaring community, was the heart of island life in the days before the opening of the bridge from the mainland. The 1732 church contains works by two celebrated Quebec artists of the 18th century, Jean Baillairgé and Louis-Basile David. The Mauvide-Genest manor house has a restaurant on the ground floor and a museum on the first floor. The name of the manor honors its earliest occupants, Jean Mauvide, the first doctor on Île d'Orléans, and his wife Marie-Anne Genest. *The museum is open daily, June to September, 10:00 am to 5:00 pm. Labor Day through mid-October, Tuesday through Sunday, 1 am to 5 pm.* Next to the manor house, Théâtre Paul-Hébert stages a summer season. An unusual feature of the village is the group of the Boat Pilot's houses, whose facades were decorated with yellow brick imported from Europe.

Route 368 leads to Saint-François (pop. 503). A side road leads to a rocky beach at Pointe Agentenay, the easternmost tip of Île d'Orléans, where the St. Lawrence is truly expansive. Outside Saint-François, a cross honors Jacques Cartier, and a tower offers a view of Mont Sainte-Anne and Cap Tourmente on the north shore of the St. Lawrence. The immediate vicinity offers sturgeon fishing and duck hunting in fall.

Turn east on 368 to Sainte-Famille (pop. 1,060), the oldest parish on the island, which was founded in 1661. The church, built in 1743, has a genealogical centre and a collection of religious art. Around Sainte-Famille, orchards extend from the road to the river. In season, signs invite travelers to stop and pick strawberries, apples, or corn.

As you near Saint-Pierre, you pass the house of Quebec poet and singer Felix Leclerc (1914-1988). This quaint village (pop. 1,978), once known for cheese-making, has become the island's artistic centre. It claims the oldest church in Quebec (1716-1718), which served local worshipers for the longest period. The structure, classified as an historic monument in 1954 and restored in the 1960s, is now an exhibition hall showcasing the work of some 65 local artists and artisans. *Admission free. Open daily, May through October. Hours vary.* Saint-Pierre attracts visitors to its summer theatre, Théâtre de l'Île, and its maple sugar cabins that remain open year-round.

As visitors head back across the bridge to the mainland, they often cast a last, wistful glance at the Île d'Orléans, once likened by a resident of Saint-Pierre to a "basket of flowers floating on the Saint Lawrence."

Shutters grace the sturdy Norman-style Mauvide-Genest Manor at Saint-Jean, Île d'Orléans.

La Mauricie

Sublime serenity and wild splendor sum up La Mauricie National Park, a 549-km² chunk of the Canadian Shield. Tucked among the Laurentians of central Quebec, its tree-trimmed hills ripple through a seemingly endless skein of lakes, rivers, and streams. The sluggish waters of Brodeur Stream trickle out near the park's southwestern entrance, close to Saint-Mathieu. Scarcely a kilometre along, the brook becomes a raging torrent, then foams into Lac Wapizagonke, a narrow, 12-km-long lake that all but slices off La Mauricie's western edge.

More than 150 lakes and ponds in La Mauricie conceal myriad creatures, including speckled trout. These fish swim well below the warm surface—they like their water cool. But even *namaycush*, the great lake trout, rarely penetrates the deepest of these waters where, at the height of summer, the temperature hovers around 4°C (39°F). Instead it prowls the middle depths, searching for insects and sometimes surfacing to snap up a mayfly.

An isle of sand and pine looks like a boat at anchor in Lac Wapizagonke.

Larger creatures appreciate the shallow lakeshore. Beavers work incessantly—felling trees, damming water, building and securing their lodges. Black bears roam the park, but the prudent camper looks for signs of their presence rather than the bears themselves. Claw marks on beech bark prove that this animal, unlike its grizzly cousin, can climb trees, particularly if enticed by tasty beechnuts.

Unfortunately, moose crossing signs along the scenic parkway do not guarantee a sighting, for in summer the big animals prefer backwoods swamps and small lakes. There, in solitude guaranteed by clouds of flies, the moose spends its days munching its favorite delicacy, the water lily root.

La Mauricie lies in a transitional zone between deciduous and boreal evergreen forest. Walk uphill a few steps, and bright green maples give way to somber spruce on dry, rocky hillsides. In this forest, black spruce intermingles with tamarack alongside bogs, where plants of the heather family thrive and sundews and pitcher plants lure passing insects.

Near Lac Gabet, you can follow a path beneath sugar maples, past lacy beeches, and along flower-bordered rivulets. Here, the red trillium outnumbers the more familiar white. In spring, it is accompanied by scores of yellow, red, and white flowers, all hurrying to make their seeds in the sun before a roof of leaves casts its shadow. Midsummer days bring ferns, and late summer, asters.

People first came into this area shortly after the glaciers departed 10,000 years ago. The land, left barren by the ice, reclothed itself, attracting caribou. Hunters came soon after. In 1850, loggers reached the St. Mauricie Valley and for the next 40 years they felled the area's pines, spruce, and yellow birch.

Logging has stopped in the park, of course, though most of the area was cut over at least once. Fires too have taken their toll. But the forest has simply regenerated itself. First came aspen and white birch; then, beneath them, shade-tolerant maple, yellow birch, and balsam. The rows of white spruce planted more than 50 years on exhausted farmland along the eastern bluffs of the St. Maurice River were intended to feed the region's paper factories. Inside the plantation, the air feels cool and damp. The dim light bars hopeful seeds and only moss, a fern or two, and an occasional, doomed balsam shoot is visible. Step out where a tree has fallen or a path has been cut: flowers grow underfoot, and a riot of shrubs and saplings—yew, poplar, willow, elms and basswood—reach skyward.

PARK INFORMATION

Access: Route 351 leads to a 65-km parkway in La Mauricie's southern sector.
Visitors' centre: Saint-Mathieu, 12 km south of the park entrance.
Accommodations: Three campgrounds with 517 sites; a group campsite for 60; and 187 wilderness campsites. Chalets at Lac à la Pêche are open year-round.
Summer activities: Canoeing (rentals), cycling, hiking, mountain biking, swimming. Nature walks include the 3-km Gabet and Esker/Brodeur trails.
Winter activities: Cross-country skiing, snowshoeing, camping.

A flock of geese with a thunderous flapping of wings swirl and settle at Cap Tourmente.

| 5 | **Cap Tourmente National Wildlife Area** |

During April and October, as many as 300,000 snow geese touch down at the Cap Tourmente National Wildlife Area on the north shore of the St. Lawrence River. These flocks form a large part of the world's population of snow geese. In the spring, the geese fly north to nesting grounds in the Arctic; in the fall, they head south to New Jersey, Virginia, and North Carolina.

At Cap Tourmente, the snow geese feast on bulrushes that grow abundantly in the marshes along the St. Lawrence. Visitors come here to watch the geese wheel through the sky or settle on the marshes in spectacular formations. The air is alive with the sound of flapping wings and discordant cries.

The French explorer Samuel de Champlain gave Cap Tourmente its name, after observing the winds whipping up the waters of the St. Lawrence at the base of the cape.

The Cap Tourmente National Wildlife Area was established in 1978. Two major natural regions—the St. Lawrence Lowland and the Laurentian Highland—meet here. This 22-km² wildlife area embraces a remarkable array of landscapes. It encompasses low-lying riverbanks, marshes, and agricultural land, as well as woods, cliffs, and mountains. There are 22 different kinds of trees, almost 700 varieties of plants, 30 species of mammals, and 250 species of nesting and migratory birds, including several types of wild duck.

Visitors can choose from a number of interpretive activities, including nature trails and guided tours. Some of its features include an observation tower and 18 km of hiking paths, as well as a trail for wheelchairs, which lead to the edge of the St. Lawrence River. Naturalists at the interpretive centre offer audio-visual shows, guided tours, and special student programs. *Open year-round. Interpretive activities available from mid-April to end of October, 9 am to 5 pm.*

Roads to explore: Byways of the Beaupré Coast

Distance (approx.): 36 km/22 miles

This drive along the north shore of the St. Lawrence River on Côte-de-Beaupré (the Beaupré Coast) begins at Cap Tourmente National Wildlife Area and ends at Sainte-Anne-de-Beaupré.

● Leave Cap Tourmente and head west on the secondary road toward Route 138. Stop at Saint-Joachim (pop. 1,489). The village church, built between 1771 and 1779, houses works by sculptors François and Thomas Baillairgé.

● From Saint-Joachim, take the secondary road north to Route 138. This stretch of road is called Côte de la Vieille-Miche (round loaf) because of the shape of the nearby mountains.

● Turn northeast on Route 138. Take a side road to Saint-Tite-des-Caps (pop. 1,584), named for the surrounding mountains that rise as high as 700 m. A farming and forestry village founded in the mid-1800s, Saint-Tite-des-Caps is dominated by its red granite church.

● Continue north on 138 and turn southwest on 360.

● After crossing the Rivière Sainte-Anne-du-Nord, turn left onto Chemin des Sept-Chutes, where the roaring river tumbles 130 m over a series of waterfalls into a canyon below. Visitors can enjoy 7 km of groomed hiking trails, a picnic area, and playgrounds.

● Continue on Route 360 to Saint-Ferréol-les-Neiges (pop. 1,717). The original village of Saint-Ferréol was founded in the mid-18th century. This municipality includes nearby the 64-km² Parc du Mont-Sainte-Anne. During the winter, the park becomes an international-calibre downhill ski centre, which hosts the World Cup Circuit.

| 6 | **Les Éboulements** |

The Charlevoix community of Les Éboulements (pop. 1,013) crouches on a 350-m-high plateau that overlooks the St. Lawrence. The square in front of the church at the river's edge offers a spectacular view. The village was once farther inland, but two landslides (in 1663 and 1830) swept away interven-

• Farther along 360, stop off at the Grand Canyon des Chutes-de-Sainte-Anne. This attractive site has bridges and ledges linked by footpaths alongside the 74-m-high falls. Visitors can wander the trails, take a shuttle car to view the falls, or enjoy a picnic. *Open from May to September.*

• Continue on 360 to Beaupré and take 138 to Sainte-Anne-de-Beaupré (pop. 3,300). According to legend, Saint Anne saved shipwreck victims off Cap Tourmente. A chapel dedicated to her in 1658 became the site of miraculous cures. Every year thousands of pilgrims pray at Sainte-Anne-de-Beaupré Basilica. Many arrive during the week before the saint's feast day on July 28.

ing strips of coastline. The first landslide was caused by a series of 32 earthquakes so powerful that mountains toppled and waterfalls vanished. Although the quake originated in the Saguenay region, this area of Charlevoix County was utterly reshaped.

The village name—from *les éboulement de terre,* French for landslide—commemorates these calamities. Today it is hard to believe this peaceful community was ever shaken by tremors.

It retains a rustic charm of yesteryear that delights visitors and artists.

The Manoir de Sales-Laterrière with the *moulin banal* (the village mill) and other buildings (all at 159, Rue Principale) recalls the days of seigneurial system, which was a central feature of Quebec society until its abolition in 1854. The small building on the grounds is said to have been a prison. The mill, built in the period around 1800, overlooks a 30-m-high falls. *Admission free. Open daily, June to October.*

This mill once belonged to the Tremblays, one of Quebec's largest families, whose ancestral home was Les Éboulements. Pierre Tremblay arrived here from France in 1710. At his death in 1736, Tremblay had become one of the area's biggest landowners and fathered 15 offspring. Each of Pierre's brothers, who also lived in this region, had 14 children. Today, their descendants number 100,000, including 6,400 living in Montreal.

In the heart of the village, there is a cluster of historic buildings. At the blacksmith shop (194, Rue Principale), two generations of Tremblays worked at the forge. Today an interpretation centre displays handmade tools dating

from the early 1890s. *Open daily, May 1 to October 15, 10 am to 5 pm. Guided tours available.* Next door, the blacksmith's quarters now house an art gallery. At the front, a boutique and an adjoining tearoom are open year-round. The Notre-Dame-de-l'Assomption Church, reconstructed in 1932 after a fire destroyed the original structure, has an altar piece sculpted by François Baillairgé in the 1790s.

After leaving Les Éboulements, follow Route 362 northeast to La Malbaie. Along the way, you can enjoy some of the most spectacular scenery in the Charlevoix region. The roadside stops have been carefully located at sites that evoke the scenes painted by Quebec artists, such as Clarence Gagnon, Marc-Aurèle Fortin, René Richard, and Jean-Paul Lemieux.

Special events

International Music Festival
of Domaine Forget
Saint-Irénée (June-August)

Young Artists' Symposium
Baie-Saint-Paul (August)

The quaint village mill, near the Manoir de Sales-Laterrière at Les Éboulements, is still powered by the waters of a picturesque falls.

7 Saint-Joseph-de-la-Rive

Saint-Joseph-de-la-Rive (pop. 242) occupies a narrow strip of land between the St. Lawrence and the lofty Laurentian coastline (just below Les Éboulements). The river is so wide at this point that local folk refer to it as "the sea." The maritime atmosphere and family-style inns make the village an ideal getaway for travelers who love the mighty river.

Until the early 1950s, Saint-Joseph-de-la-Rive bustled with activity generated by schooner traffic on the river. Today, the remains of grounded schooners stranded on the shore evoke this busy period. The former ship-building yard, founded in 1946, displays navigation equipment. A guide describes what life was once like for local fishermen. *Open year-round, Monday to Friday, 8 am to 5 pm.*

Across the street, the former school houses the workshops of Papeterie Saint-Gilles, the makers of fine papers. Here, the artisans use a 17th-century process to create paper from cotton pulp. Another of their products is a tinted paper inlaid with wild flowers and the leaves of ferns and maple trees. *Open year-round for guided tours, Monday to Friday, 8 am to 5 pm.*

A few steps away from the paper workshop, the general store and bakery have been owned by two Tremblay families since the beginning of this century. This is the best place to get to know local residents. A visitor rarely leaves without buying a warm, freshly baked loaf of bread.

The local church has works by sculptor Alphonse Paré, a "Way of the Cross" by Rose-Anne Mona, and a baptismal font fashioned from a huge seashell. *Admission free. Open daily, June to Thanksgiving, 9 am to 8 pm.*

A year-round ferry carrying cars and pedestrians leaves from Saint-Joseph's wharf several times a day for the 15-minute trip to Île aux Coudres. Before

The 1836 stone mill at Saint-Louis-de-l'Île-aux-Coudres still grinds grain from local farms.

the ferry service, local folk made the winter crossing of the icy St. Lawrence by canoe. They paddled and, when necessary, hauled their canoes across the ice floes. This early form of transportation inspired *La Grande Traversée*, held in January. During this event, crews of five canoeists compete in an 8-km race across the icy waters of St. Lawrence River between Saint-Joseph-de-la-Rive and Île aux Coudres.

Special Events

The Grande Traversée canoe race
Île aux Coudres--Saint-Joseph-de-la-Rive
(late January)

8 Île aux Coudres

This island was the summer home of the painter Jean-Paul Lemieux (1904-1990), who was inspired by its solitude, wide-open spaces, and perpetually changing horizons. Lemieux is best known for his evocations of bygone Quebec. The scenery on Île aux Coudres may remind some visitors of the limitless landscapes that Lemieux peopled with characters from other eras.

The island (pop. 1,442) owes its name to Jacques Cartier. During his first stop here on September 6, 1535, the French explorer found hazelnut trees (*coudriers* in French). A monument at Saint-Bernard-sur-Mer commemorates Cartier's landing. It also recalls the mass—the first in Canada—Cartier celebrated here on September 7, 1535. (A huge painting depicting this event hangs in the local church.) During the 17th century, ships on the St. Lawrence used Île aux Coudres as a stopover. The first permanent settlers—farmers to till the soil and fishermen to hunt beluga whales in the offshore waters—arrived in the 1720s.

The ferry from Saint-Joseph-de-la-Rive docks at Saint-Bernard-sur-Mer on the island's north side. A local curiosity is a dwelling of eccentric design, La Maison Croche (the crooked house), which was built only in 1963.

A 26-km-long road encircles the island, which is roughly 11 km long and 5 km wide. You can explore the island by car or bicycle. (Bicycle rentals are available here.) As you head west, you will pass through three communities: Cap-à-la-Branche, Saint-Louis-de-l'Île-aux-Coudres, and La Baleine. Along the way, you will glimpse stone houses with metre-thick walls, roadside chapels and crosses, centuries-old churches, and quaint windmills. Beached shipwrecks recall the islanders' seafaring past. The busy shipyard near the ferry dock at Saint-Bernard tells of a thriving present.

You can also take the Chemin de la Tourbière (the peat bog road) to La Baleine on the island's east side. The route passes by the peat bogs—a mainstay of the island's economy—which are harvested by vacuum equipment.

Saint-Louis (pop. 480) on the west side of the island has a number of interesting attractions. Just outside the village, a short road leads to the Cross of the Islet, which commemorates Jean-Baptiste de la Brosse, who was the first missionary to take up residence on the island.

Near the Saint-Louis Church, an 1825 water mill stands beside an 1836 windmill. (The site is unusual because it is the only place in Canada where these kinds of mills are found together.) Guides explain the mills' history and operation. If you wish, you can buy ground flour from the miller. *Open daily, May to mid-October. Hours vary.*

The museum at Saint-Louis-de-l'Île-aux-Coudres focuses on the island's history and its plant and animal life. *Open from June 20 to September 6.* The Musée des Voitures d'Eau focuses on sailing and the hunting of beluga whales in the St. Lawrence River. *Open daily, June to September.*

One of the island's oldest houses, Maison LeClerc, built in 1750, is located at La Baleine. *Open daily, June 2 to Labor Day, 10 am to 6 pm.* Some of the best inns on the island are found at La Baleine.

WOODEN WORKHORSES OF THE ST. LAWRENCE RIVER

Until the late 18th century, the St. Lawrence River was the only artery of transportation and communication between Quebec City and the small communities farther north along the rugged Charlevoix coast. The sailors and fishermen in this area used light bark canoes and, later, heavy baggage canoes and rowboats on their often perilous journeys. During the late 1700s, local shipbuilders introduced wooden schooners, which were originally equipped with sails. The 15- to 20-m-long vessels—known as *les voitures d'eau* (literally "water cars")—could carry passengers and 20 to 50 tons of cargo.

During the 20th century, the schooners switched from sails to engines, and eventually metal hulls replaced wooden ones. Large schooners transported lumber from the north shore to the paper mills of Quebec City and elsewhere along the St. Lawrence. Fishermen from the Charlevoix communities, such as Saint-Joseph-de-la-Rive and Île-aux-Coudres, found lucrative winter work in the thriving local shipyards—known as *chalouperies.*

During the 1960s, improvements in shipping brought about a decline in the demand for schooners. The Quebec filmmaker Pierre Perrault captured the last days of the schooner epoch in his documentary, *Les Voitures d'eau,* which was released by the National Film Board in 1968.

At the shipyards at Saint-Joseph-de-la-Rive, one of the major shipbuilding centres on the Charlevoix coast, you can see the grounded hulls of some of these magnificent workhorses of the St. Lawrence. The restored *Jean-Yvan* is open to visitors. The nearby sawmill, now a museum, displays navigational equipment and tools used by shipbuilders. A guide describes the construction of *les Voitures d'eau* and tells the story of the day-to-day lives of the men who sailed aboard them. *The museum is open year-round.*

In 1973, Capt. Eloi Perron established the Musée Les Voitures d'Eau in the village of Saint-Louis on the southwestern tip of Île aux Coudres. The musem documents the navigational history along this part of the St. Lawrence River. (Among the first settlers on the island were fishermen who hunted beluga whale here.) There are also displays of navigational equipment used in the past. Nearby, visitors can explore the restored schooner *Mont-Saint-Louis,* from hold to wheelhouse. *Open daily, June to September, 9 am to 6 pm. From July 15 to August 10, open until 7 pm.*

A restored schooner rests high and dry on the shores of the Île-aux-Coudres.

9 Parc des Grands-Jardins

Some of the peaks in the 310-km² Parc des Grands-Jardins top 1,000 m. The park contains vegetation similar to that found farther north in the forests of fir and spruce that border Arctic regions. In recognition of the distinctive natural features of the park, UNESCO has declared it a world biosphere reserve.

The region covered by the park was a Montagnais Indian hunting ground. The 1890s saw the establishment of private clubs, whose members came here to fish and to hunt caribou. (Hunting was banned when the caribou population declined steeply.) Eventually Quebec bought out the clubs, and established the park in 1981.

Route 381 leads to the eastern sector of Grand-Jardins, where a visitors' centre is located. This year-round park offers camping sites and chalets. Summer visitors will find opportunities for hiking, mountain biking, canoeing, rock climbing, and fishing. A 2.7-km trail at the park entrance leads to the top of 1,000-m-high Lac des Cygnes Mountain. In winter guides lead visitors to see local caribou, whose numbers are once again on the increase. The winter also brings cross-country skiers and snowshoers.

10 Parc des Hautes-Gorges-de-la-Rivière-Malbaie

Hikers who reach the heights of the Acropole des draveurs *are rewarded with thrilling vistas of the Rivière Malbaie and the peaks that rise up from the valley through which it flows.*

The scenic wonder in the interior of the Charlevoix area is the 800-m-deep gorge of the Malbaie River (hautes gorges de la Rivière-Malbaie). The gorge began as a fault in the earth's crust, which was later deepened by glaciers. Today, the peaceful Rivière Malbaie flows through the gorge whose steep walls are the highest in Canada east of the Rocky Mountains.

The gorge is one of the outstanding attractions in the 233-km² Parc régional des Hautes-Gorges-de-la-Rivière-Malbaie, which also contains some peaks more than 1,000 m high. The park, established in 1988, is the largest of its kind in Quebec. Originally, this region was the homeland of *coureurs de bois* (fur traders), loggers, and *draveurs* (the regional term for drivers who floated log booms along the river). Today it offers camping, canoeing, hiking, mountain biking, and guided nature tours. Recently, UNESCO declared it a world biosphere reserve.

A back road from the village Saint-Aimé-des-Lacs, some 10 km from Malbaie, leads to the visitors' centre at the Chalet de l'Écluse in the heart of this spectacular but remote park. The first

10-km stretch is paved, but the remaining 35-km is a narrow and winding logging road, which takes about an hour to drive.

At the visitors' centre, you can get maps and information about trails and activities, and rent outdoor equipment. One of the major attractions is an 800-m-high mountain, known as the *Acropole des draveurs* (Acropolis of the drivers). A short hike at the foot of the mountain leads to a lookout above the Malbaie River. (However, to reach the lookout, you face a climb of 250 steps.)

Another challenging 5-km hike to the top of the mountain crosses different vegetation zones. According to the elevation, each zone contains plant life found in a specific part of Quebec, from the hardwood forests of the Beauce to the bleak Arctic tundra of Ungava. At the foot of the mountain, there are maples and giant elms (you can hardly wrap your arms around them). At the next levels, evergreens displace hardwoods. Near the summit, the trees are sparse and stunted, but mosses and alpine flowers thrive.

At the top, the hiker will be rewarded with an exhilarating view of lakes, rivers, and some of the oldest mountains in the world. One of these is the Mont Félix-Antoine-Savard. The name honors the Quebec priest, educator, and writer who described this region and the arduous life of its pioneer folk in a 1937 novel, *Menaud, maître-draveur* (Menaud, Master Driver).

The Malbaie River was a favorite spot of Savard (1896-1982) and his good friend, the artist René Richard (1895-1982). Today, two riverboats—the 54-passenger *Coureur de Bois* and the 48-passenger *Maître-Draveur*—carry visitors along this quiet river to its thrilling gorge.

The departure point of the 1½-km round-trip cruise is a boat dock by the dam near the Chalet de l'Écluse. *The cruise operates daily from mid-June to mid-October. During the busy period—June 20 to Labor Day—there are six daily cruises. Hours vary.*

11 Cap-à-l'Aigle and Saint-Fidèle

The rugged coast of Quebec's Charlevoix County between Baie Saint-Paul and Baie Sainte-Catherine has long been prized by travelers for its scenic beauty. La Malbaie is one of the oldest resorts in Canada. North of La Malbaie, Route 138—the region's main highway—provides access to three entrancing and lesser known getaways by the St. Lawrence: Cap-à-l'Aigle, Saint-Fidèle, and Port-au-Persil.

Cap-à-l'Aigle (pop. 792) was a favorite vacation spot in the 19th century summer vacationers. To reach the village from La Malbaie, take Route 138 and Rue Saint-Raphaël. This farming community was once part of the old seigneury of Mont-Murray. Along the road, visitors will glimpse a thatched-roof barn, which is one of a cluster of heritage buildings. One of the treasures in the village is the tiny Anglican church, St. Peter on the Rock, built in 1872 by members of the summer community. Cap-à-l'Aigle also boasts one of the best marinas on the coast.

Some 13 km farther along, Route 138 passes through the village of Saint-Fidèle (pop. 1,180), known for its excellent cheese. The local product can be purchased at La Crémerie Saint-Fidèle on Route 138.

A side road leads from Saint-Fidèle to an ecological centre at Port-au-Saumon on the St. Lawrence. The centre, opened in the early 1970s, has a beachside aquarium, displays different fish species, anemones, crabs and mollusks, sponges, starfish, different kinds of fish, crabs and other mollusks—all examples of marine life found in the St. Lawrence River. *Open daily from June 28 to August 28, 10 am to 6 pm.*

Special Events
Triangle Sailboat Race
Cap-à-l'Aigle (late August)
Natural Science Festival
Port-au-Saumon (August)

12 Port-au-Persil

Some believe the village of Port-au-Persil was named for the wild parsley that the early pioneers gathered in this region. Others claim the name is a corruption of the word "porpoise," which was used by English settlers to describe the beluga whales that once flourished in the St. Lawrence.

Whatever the origins of its name, Port-au-Persil retains the quiet beauty that inspired artists such as Jean-Paul Lemieux and Marc-Aurèle Fortin. During their early penniless days, these artists spent summers at the village hotel and paid for lodgings with paintings, now highly valued.

The secondary road to Port-au-Persil winds down a steep coastal slope. It

A village of Port-au-Persil clusters around a scenic cove beloved by artists and travelers.

offers dazzling panoramic views before making an abrupt descent into the heart of Port-au-Persil. The village encircles a small harbor, lined by a wharf, some old charming houses, and a Presbyterian chapel built in 1897. A tiny waterfall—a delight for children—cascades into the harbor. At low water, an offshore rock dominates the scene.

In summer, visitors are welcome to the Port-au-Persil pottery, located in a converted barn. The pottery is well-known for the high quality of its products and its distinctive glazes. There is a training school associated with the pottery. A small museum of decorative arts displays the creations of some 30 Quebecois artisans. *Open daily, June to September, 9 am to 6 pm.*

Some of the pottery on display was crafted by the founder Pierre Legault, whose works are widely exhibited. Legault invented the local glazing technique, using sand, ashes from hay, seaweed and algae, and black stone to produce some magnificent effects. Every year, the prestigious Prix Pierre-Legault is awarded to artisans who experiment with glazes.

13 Saguenay parks

The lower stretch of Saguenay River is a mighty 105-km-long fjord reaching roughly from Chicoutimi to Tadoussac, where it spills into the St. Lawrence. Steep capes and headlands of the Laurentian mountains, mantled with evergreens, form the shores of the fjord.

The color of the Saguenay waters is deep amber or black because the river reaches depths of 250 m. The fjord is a mixture of fresh and salt water. The cold water from the St. Lawrence River pushes under the warmer water from the Saguenay. The marine life in the fjord is amazingly diverse. It shelters 54 species of vertebrates and 248

Headlands loom high above the Saguenay River, North America's only navigable fjord.

species of invertebrates. Some of them living in the deeper waters are Arctic species: the *Ophiopus arcticus*, which resembles a starfish, the sea worm *Nereis zonata*, and the Greenland halibut.

In 1990, the Quebec and Canadian governments created the Saguenay Marine Park to preserve all the fjord as well as a part of the adjacent St. Lawrence estuary. The park has interpretive centres at Pointe-Noire, near Baie-Sainte-Catherine, and at Cap-de-Bon-Désir, some 25 km northeast of Tadoussac.

From the footpaths and lookouts at Pointe-Noire, whale-watchers can spot belugas. Larger whales, such as the 21-m-long fin whale and the 140-ton blue whale (some are as much as 30 m long), appear at Cap-de-Bon-Désir.

In 1983, the Quebec provincial government set up the 288-km² Parc du Saguenay (which is not connected to the federal-provincial marine park). The park preserve strips of land along the south and north shore of the Saguenay fjord. The visitors' centre at Rivière-Éternité can be reached from Route 170. There are camp sites within the park. L'Anse-Saint-Jean and Sainte-Rose-du-Nord also make ideal bases for exploring this area.

One of the park's hiking trails leads to the top of 518-m-high Cap Trinité overlooking the Saguenay fjord. Here visitors will see Louis Jobin's 8-m-high statue of the Virgin Mary. The statue was commissioned in 1881 by a local businessman, Charles-Napoleon Robitaille, who believed the Virgin Mary had twice saved his life.

Another hiking trail leads to 549-m-high Cap Éternité. From here, you can glimpse three mountains on the north shore of the Saguenay—Liberté, Égalité, and Fraternité. In 1989 they were given these names to honor the 200th anniversary of the French Revolution.

Cruise ships on the Saguenay fjord are available from Chicoutimi, La Baie and Tadoussac. There are stopovers at L'Anse-Saint-Jean, Baie-Éternité, and Sainte-Rose-du-Nord. All cruises have

This miniature model of a L'Anse-Saint-Jean is displayed in the garden of the dwelling itself.

knowledgeable guides and naturalists. Many of the ships stop at the foot of Cap Trinité just long enough to pipe the strains of *Ave Maria* over the decks.

14 L'Anse-Saint-Jean

Steep mountains flank L'Anse-Saint-Jean (pop. 1,370), sometimes called Quebec's Little Switzerland. A 5.5-km road links the village on the south side of the Saguenay River with the region's main highway, Route 170. The view of the river here is spectacular.

L'Anse-Saint-Jean has conserved its traditional architecture. A heritage tour starts at the church and the town hall, and continues to several beautiful old houses. Interpretive panels explain the methods used to build local field-stone and log structures. Some houses on the tour have outdoor bread ovens still in working order. The house at 10, Rue du Faubourg was once the summer home of the Quebec painter Albert Rousseau (1890-1982).

Anyone who handles old $1,000 bills will recognize the village's best-known feature, the 1929 covered bridge over the Rivière Saint-Jean. (The bridge is depicted on the back of the bill.) In the spring of 1986, a huge chunk of ice

ripped the wooden frame from its pillars and carried it downstream for more than a kilometre. Six months' work put the frame back on its pillars.

Since 1991, L'Anse-Saint-Jean and the neighboring village of Petit-Saguenay have held an annual event called *Villages en couleurs* (Villages in color). During the event, Quebec painters depict their impressions of this spectacular spot and talk with visitors who gather to watch them at work.

L'Anse-Saint-Jean is also a good spot for salmon fishing. Other local activities include hiking, biking, and horse-riding. A 5.5-km uphill trail that starts at the Faubourg covered bridge leads to a lookout at L'Anse de la Tabatière, which rewards the effort with a stunning view of the Saguenay. Cruises and fishing expeditions on the river, camping, and cycling complete the list of local summer activities. There is a 54-site campground off Route 170.

Winter sports include skiing at Mont Édouard, which has a 450-m vertical drop, as well as snowshoeing and ice fishing on rivers. In early

Country scene, Lac Saint-Jean

L'Anse-du-milieu, one of the pretty coves at Sainte-Rose-du-Nord, nestles by the Saguenay.

spring, there are sugaring-off parties in the maple groves.

15 Sainte-Rose-du-Nord

This secluded community of 430 on the north shore of the Saguenay River spreads over hills and along three coves. The views of the river repay visitors (particularly photographers) who make the effort to travel here by car on Route 172 or by boat.

Most of Sainte-Rose is located near the dock at L'Anse-du-milieu (Middle Cove). Some intriguing landmarks include a church with forest decor (the altar is made from a large tree stump), an old presbytery converted into an inn, and a nature museum. Examples of local plant, animal, and marine life, including a shark caught in the Saguenay, are displayed here. *Open daily year-round, 8:30 to 9 pm.*

For an exceptional view of the area, climb the Chemin de la Montagne, which leads to L'Anse-d'en-haut (Upper Cove). From here, you can see both shores of the Saguenay and the village of Sainte-Rose, which, at this height, looks almost Lilliputian.

During the summer, the cruise boat *La Marjolaine* travels between Sainte-Rose-du-Nord and Chicoutimi. The departure point for the two-hour round-trip is the dock at L'Anse-du-milieu (Middle Cove). *The cruise service operates June to September.*

Visitors with a taste for curiosities will want to see Tableau, a cliff that looks like a giant blackboard. From Sainte-Rose, head for Route 172 and turn east. Take the 14.5-km dirt road leading through hilly country to Saint-Basile-de-Tableau on the Saguenay. From this viewpoint, you can look across the Saguenay River at the huge, polished rock face of Tableau.

16 Val-Jalbert

The historic village of Val-Jalbert in the heart of the Lac Saint-Jean region was a one-company town founded in 1902 by the entrepreneur Damase Jalbert. It developed around a pulp mill built on the banks of the Ouiatchouan River to take advantage of the water power from the 72-m-high Ouiatchouan Falls.

Jalbert died in 1904, but the townsite was renamed in his honor. The mill

prospered but financial difficulties forced its closure in 1927. At its peak, Val-Jalbert's population had numbered 1,000. After the closure, people moved away, and eventually the town was abandoned. For more than 30 years, Val-Jalbert was known only as a ghost town until the Quebec government acquired the site in 1960.

Today, the former convent at the town's entrance houses a visitors' centre with a permanent display of artifacts and exhibits outlining the history of the site. Near the centre are the foundations of the church, which was demolished in 1932, two years after the town officially closed.

At the commercial heart of Val-Jalbert in its heyday was the general store, which also served as a hotel. Today the restored building has a snack bar and souvenir counter, as well as several guest rooms. Several nearby structures have been converted into a craft boutique and an herb store.

The old lumber mill is at the other end of the village. Tour guides explain its operations to visitors. The mill itself has been converted into a multi-purpose hall for stage productions and exhibitions. There is also a restaurant with a terrace.

At the end of a trail that passes the old mill, a 400-step stairway leads to a lookout by Ouiatchouan Falls, which offers a view of the village and Lac Saint-Jean. You can also take a cable car up to the lookout. (Bring binoculars and a map of the area to pick out the sites.) From the lookout, you can walk to a second waterfall, Chute Maligne.

Altogether some 60 buildings in the village have been preserved or rebuilt in their original style for visitors to explore. Other restored structures include the school, the butcher's shop, and two rows of mill workers' houses.

The ghost town provides comfortable modern lodgings in some of the mill workers' houses. There are also campgrounds in the area. *The ghost town of Val-Jalbert is open daily from May 22 to September 27.*

17 | Péribonka

🚲 👣 ⛴ 🚐 ⌂

Prosperous farmland and rugged Laurentian highland surround 1,002-km² Lac Saint-Jean. Routes 169 and 170 encircle the lake and link small communites with enough attractions and events to please any traveler. At Saint-Félicien, on the fertile south shore of the lake, there is a 400-ha zoo, where visitors can ride on a small train through natural setting to view the animals. Roberval's attractions include a maritime museum and the nearby historic village of Val-Jalbert.

On the rugged north shore, you will find that Dolbeau, Mistassini, and Péribonka are small but active communities. Mistassini claims the title of the world's blueberry capital and celebrates with an annual blueberry festival in early August.

Every July, Roberval (pop. 12,300) becomes the end point for the International Swim Meet on Lac Saint-Jean. The 32-km race to Péribonka attracts some of the best swimmers in the world.

Péribonka (pop. 700) is a haven of peace where visitors can visit the Louis-Hémon Museum, which honors the French-born author of the classic novel *Maria Chapdelaine*. The museum, located some 7 km from the village, is on the old Bédard farm where the author worked briefly. The main hall, built in 1986, blends harmoniously with its rustic surroundings. It can be reached from the road by a 200-m trail bordered by white birch trees.

Near the visitors' centre is the tiny 1905 house that once belonged to Sa-

The merry masks on children add to the fun at Mistassini's August Blueberry Festival.

muel Bédard. It was here, in 1912, that the 30-year-old French visitor was hired as a farmhand. During his eight-week stay, the Bédard family noticed that Hémon wrote all the time, at the dinner table and even while he was fishing. But it was not until after his accidental death the following year in Chapleau, Ont., that the family discovered that Hémon, inspired by the lives and quiet courage of the local people, had been writing a novel about the region's early settlers. The novel first appeared as a serial in 1914. It became a success only after it was published as a book in 1921. *Maria Chapdelaine* has remained an enduring best-seller, with 120 editions in 45 languages.

Blueberries of Lac Saint-Jean

The museum displays Hémon's personal belongings and letters. *Open daily, June to September, 9 am to 6 pm. Weekdays, September to June, 9:30 am to 4 pm. (Weekends only by reservation.)*

Some of Val-Jalbert's houses, saved from ruin, accommodate visitors to this ghost town.

Special Events

La Grande Traversée internationale du Lac Saint-Jean, Roberval (July)

Les 10 Jours Western, Dolbeau (mid-July)

Le Festival du bleuet Mistassini (early August)

Agricultural Fair, Saint-Félicien (August)

SOUTHERN QUEBEC

N

0   10   20 km
0   10   20 miles

St. Lawrence

132

161

Île du Moine
Île aux Fantômes
Île d'Embarras

Lac
Saint-Pierre

132

122

Victoriaville

**Sorel
Islands 2**

Chenal du Moine

Sorel

Sainte-Anne-
de-Sorel

143

122

Drummondville

Danville

Tracy

Saint-Ours

30   **133**

Saint-Denis

20

6

Ulverton

Richmond

Verchères

Saint-Charles-
sur-Richelieu

Richelieu River

116

Ulverton R.

St. François River

Windsor

Laval

Saint-Hyacinthe

Mont-
Saint-Hilaire

137

143

Longueuil

112

Yamaska River

Lac des
Deux-Montagnes

40   **20**   Montréal

Chambly

Parc récr. du
Mont-Orford

Sherbrooke

Vaudreuil

Lac
Saint-Louis

Île
Perrot

10

Mont
Orford

ONTARIO
QUÉBEC

Canal de Soulanges

338

Châteauguay

Granby

112

Magog

5

1

Coteau-du-Lac

Saint-Timothée

Canal de
Beauharnois

Saint-Jean-
sur-Richelieu

104

Iberville

10

245

Nort
Hatl

Lac
Massawippi

Salaberry-
de-Valleyfield

Lac
Saint-François

Châteauguay R.

Lac
Brome

20

15

104

Cowansville

**Lac-Brome
(Knowlton)**
4

Saint-Benoît-
du-Lac

Ayer's Cliff
Coaticook

132

138

Ormston

133

202

Dunham
3

243

143   **141**

Huntingdon

Stanbridge
East

Mansonville

247

Beebe Plain

CANADA
U.S.A.

Highwater

Lac
Memphrémagog

Lake
Champlain

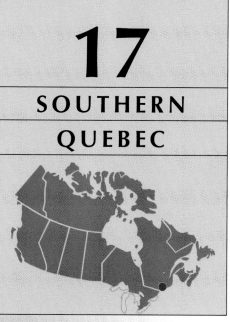

17

SOUTHERN
QUEBEC

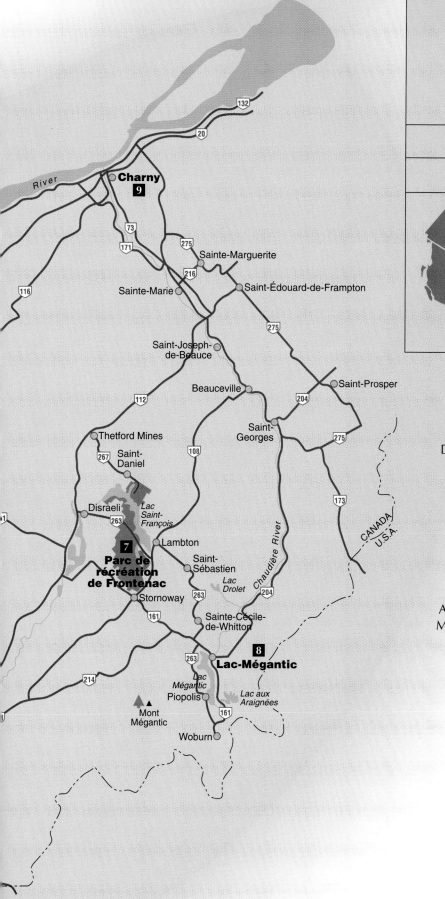

Places to see
Coteau-du-Lac
The Sorel Islands
Richelieu River valley
Dunham and Stanbridge East
Lac-Brome (Knowlton)
North Hatley
Ulverton
Parc de Frontenac
Lac-Mégantic
Charny
La Beauce

Roads to explore
Around Lac Memphrémagog:
Magog to Stanstead Plain, and
Magog to Highwater
Around Lac Massawippi

Previous pages:
Notre-Dame-des-Pins, la Beauce

1 Coteau-du-Lac

∧ ⛺ ʃ ✳ ⌂

Within easy reach of Montreal, there are a number of little-known get-aways—Île des Moulins at Terrebonne, the Richelieu River valley, and the Sorel Islands. Coteau-du-Lac (pop. 4,000) is one such getaway. It is located just west of Montreal, where the St. Lawrence leaves Lac St. François.

The name of the village comes from *coteau*, which refers to the small hill on which the first church was built. (The church is now a visitors' bureau.) A local point of interest is an 1858 flour mill, now a restaurant, which can be found just outside the village.

The history of this farming and resort community is closely linked to the various attempts to bypass the nearby dangerous rapids in the St. Lawrence and, later, to protect this stretch of the river from the threat of invasion from the United States. The first canal was built in 1750 to ease the passage of fur traders and others heading west to the Great Lakes.

In 1779-80, the British authorities, who found the earlier canal far too small and narrow for their boats, built the Soulanges Canal just below the village. This canal was orginally 300 m long and 2.5 m wide, and its three locks raised boats some 2.7 m. It was the first lock canal in North America and the forerunner of the St. Lawrence Seaway. It remained in use until the Beau-harnois canal was opened in 1845. The remnants of the canal can now be seen at the Coteau-du-Lac National Historic Site. *Admission free. Open year-round. Guided tours available daily, mid-May to late August.*

Until the 1850s, Coteau-du-Lac was an important military post and supply centre. During the War of 1812, the

Cannon, Coteau-du-Lac

British reinforced their garrisons here to repulse any attempted American advance into Quebec. They added more than 15 buildings to create a well-fortified village that could accommodate 1,500 soldiers.

Visitors to this national historic site can see the traces of some of the fortifications. Two mounted cannons appear on the grounds, and the trenches where the militia kept watch on the St. Lawrence have been restored. A reconstruction of an octagonal blockhouse, destroyed by fire in the 1830s, displays a collection of military equipment.

Coteau-du-Lac displays the skeletal frame of an early 19th-century barge, once used to carry merchandise and men through the Soulanges Canal linking Montreal and the Great Lakes.

2 Sorel Islands

🚲 ∧ ⅄ 🛶 🐟 📷 ⌂

The Sorel Islands—long a mecca for anglers, bird-watchers, duck hunters, and photographers—are located where the St. Lawrence widens to form Lac Saint-Pierre. (The Richelieu and Yamaska rivers flow into St. Lawrence at this point.)

About a hundred or so islands form a maze of waterways, whose marshes attract waterfowl from spring to fall. Here you can see congregations of bustards, snipes, marsh wrens, and common gallinules. Grande Île is said to be North America's largest breeding grounds for herons. Île du Moine is a popular site for watching shorebirds.

Some of the Sorel Islands, such as Île Madame and Île de Grâce, support fishing communities. The deep waters of Lac Saint-Pierre supply pike and sturgeon, which are served in a tasty fish stew called *gibelotte de poissons*.

A drive along the Chemin de Chenal-du-Moine is a pleasant way to explore the Sorel Islands. The road skirts one of the region's main waterways (the Chenal-du-Moine), passes quaint settlements and summer cottages, and provides access by bridge to some of the remote islands. (The drive covers a distance of roughly 30 km.)

The starting point is Sainte-Anne-de-Sorel (pop. 2,670), some 5 km east of the busy inland seaport of Sorel. The community is proud of its church, built in 1877 by architect Louis-Zéphirin Gauthier. The interior contains 14 frescoes by the painter and sculptor Suzor-Côté (1869-1937).

From Sainte-Anne, drive 3 km to Grange du Survenant, a combined summer theatre, restaurant, and pier where visitors can board a boat for a cruise through the islands. *Cruise boats offer commentary and operate from late June to early September.*

A little farther on is a cable ferry, used to transport cattle to the communal pasture on the Île du Moine. A ferry has been operating here since the first settlers arrived in the 1640s. Just down the road from the ferry, you will pass by fish smokehouses, bait traps, and fishnets hung up to dry.

The road leads to a small iron bridge that crosses over to Île aux Fantômes (ghosts island). According to legend, an abducted child can sometimes be heard crying for his father.

The Musée de l'Écriture is the next point of interest. This museum, located just beside a suspension bridge, is devoted to the works of Quebec writers. You can walk across the bridge to the

ECHOES OF OLD TURMOIL ALONG A TRANQUIL RIVER

The source of the 130-km-long Richelieu River is Lake Champlain on the Canada-United States border. The scenic river flows through a rich agricultural valley and empties into the St. Lawrence at Sorel. During the 19th century, the building of canals at Chambly and Saint-Ours transformed the Richelieu into an artery of trade. Today, this commercial traffic has ceased, and only pleasure boats ply the river in summer.

Monument to the Patriotes at Saint-Denis-sur-le-Richelieu

From the 17th century onward, the Richelieu River was the scene of conflict. Champlain ascended the river to attack the Iroquois. Before 1760, the French and English colonists fought in this area. American invaders took this route into Canada during the American Revolution and, again, in 1812.

The last conflict in this region occurred during the Rebellion of 1837-1838, when the Patriotes clashed with British authorities in Quebec. The first encounter took place at Saint-Denis on November 23, 1837, when the British forces under Col. Charles Gore suffered a defeat at the hands of the Patriotes. Two days later, the British crushed the rebels on Saint-Charles-sur-Richelieu. On November 30, Gore returned to Saint-Denis and, although the rebels surrendered, the British sacked and burned the village. The rebellion collapsed in December 1837 but revived a year later, when it was crushed again.

A drive along the east side of the Richelieu from Mont Saint-Hilaire to Saint-Ours along the stretch of Route 133, known as the Chemin des Patriotes (the Patriots Route), takes in a number of the rebellion sites.

The first stop is the 411-m-high Mont Saint-Hilaire, the highest of the Monteregian Hills of southwestern Quebec. The conservation centre offers excellent hiking, bird-watching, cross-country skiing, and snowshoeing. *Open year-round, but hours vary according to season.*

At Saint-Charles-sur-Richelieu (pop. 1,740), a monument in the waterfront park honors the rebels. Boat trips on the Richelieu are available here.

Saint-Denis (pop. 2,110), some 11 km north on Route 133, is one of the oldest villages in Quebec. Here visitors can tour the Maison Nationale des Patriotes, which describes the events of 1837-1838. This handsome 1809 house once belonged to the blacksmith, innkeeper, and merchant Joseph Masse, who was a Patriote. *Open Tuesday to Sunday, early May to late September, 10 am to 5 pm. Visits by reservation, year-round.*

Maison Nationale is the first stop on a heritage walk that passes other historic houses on Chemin des Patriotes: the Maison Cherrier (No. 639), built in 1805 and one of the oldest houses in the village; the Maison Huard with its mansard roof (Nos. 583-589); and the Victorian-style Maison Richard (No. 611). Visitors can ask at the presbytery for permission to see the richly ornamented interior of the parish church.

At Saint-Ours (pop. 1,620), you can stop by the post office, once the home of another Patriote leader, Dr. Jacques Dorion. A number of Quebec artists live and work in this pretty, peaceful village, which has an impressive seigneurial manor in its centre. The nearby Parc des Écluses borders the 1849 canal with locks and a picnic area. The lockkeepers will give visitors a brief history about the canal.

former summer home of Germaine Guèvremont (1893-1968), whose 1945 novel *Le Survenant* describes life in this region. *Open July and August, Tuesday to Sunday, 1 pm to 7 pm. Weekends only in May, June and early September.*

The road ends at the small fishing village on the Île d'Embarras. During the spring runoff, floating debris often clog the nearby river channels and cause floods. To avoid the effects of flooding, local folk have raised their dwellings high on pilings and embankments. They use the ground floors as kitchens only in summer.

On the tip of Île d'Embarras, two weathered ice houses have been converted into restaurants where you can enjoy some of delicious local dishes, such as *gibelotte*.

3 Dunham and Stanbridge East

⊕ ❄ ⌂

During the 1790s the British authorities made land grants in the form of townships to the United Empire Loyalists who fled to southern Quebec after the American War of Independence. In Quebec, the region became known as the Eastern Townships to distinguish it from the townships west of Montreal in what is now Ontario.

The Loyalist refugees were followed by Irish, Scottish, and English settlers, and, in the late 19th century, by Quebecois. Today the Eastern Townships—also known as the Cantons de l'Est or l'Estrie—is a pleasing mixture of English and French. The region—extending east from the Richelieu River valley to Lac Mégantic and south from Danville to the Quebec-Maine border—embraces a landscape of gently rolling fields, mountain peaks, and three superb lakes—Memphrémagog, Massawippi, and Mégantic. The region

A country mailbox, Dunham

is a year-round mecca for outdoor enthusiasts. It also contains some of Quebec's best dairy and livestock farms, and the most productive apple orchards in the province.

Since the late 1970s, wine making has developed in the Eastern Townships. The village of Dunham (pop. 3,226) is recognized as the centre of this small but thriving industry. (Brigham just to the north is another tiny wine-making centre.) The road between Dunham and Stanbridge East—known as the *Route des Vins* (the Wine Route)—passes through the only area in Quebec where vineyards thrive. The unusually mild local climate helps the cultivation of grapes. Vineyards here include Les Arpents de Neige, Les Blancs Coteaux, Les Côtes d'Ardoise, L'Orpailleur, and Les Trois Clochers. Visitors are welcome to tour the vineyards and to enjoy wine tastings and country-style meals.

Dunham is one of the first Loyalist settlements in the Eastern Townships. The surrounding district was the first township. It was granted to Thomas Dunn by the British authorities in 1796.

Several 19th-century dwellings of brick and fieldstone line Dunham's Main Street. Two brick houses that face each other on Main Street were built during the 1850s for two prosperous citizens: Seneca Paige, a wealthy merchant and politician, and Thomas Wood, Dunham's first mayor. (The former died without having lived in his house.) The Georgian-style house, across from the United Church (1847), has changed owners only once since it was built in 1840 by the son of Loyalist Joseph Baker.

Cottages and docks with small craft line the shaded, winding waterways of the Sorel Islands.

Another notable historic building is the offices of Small Brothers, which makes equipment for maple syrup production. (One of its inventions, the 1888 lightning evaporator, is still used to reduce the water content in the sap from maple trees.) The brick building occupied by the firm since 1893 was once Seeley's Tavern.

Stanbridge East (pop. 1,000), some 10 km west of Dunham, was also settled in the 1790s. The three-story brick Cornell gristmill—built in 1832 by Vermont-born Zebulon Cornell on the Pike River—is one of the three historic buildings belonging to the Missisquoi Museum (Musée de Missisquoi).

The ground floor of the gristmill recreates a Victorian interior, and the upper floors display traditional crafts. Hodge's Store, housed in a two-story 1843 dwelling at 20 River Street, contains merchandise of yesteryear; Bill's Barn, also on River Street, displays vintage farming equipment. Altogether the Missisquoi Museum's collection includes some 12,000 objects of historic interest. *Open daily, late May to early October, 10 am to 5 pm.*

4 Lac-Brome (Knowlton)

The town of Lac-Brome (pop. 4,824), which encircles the lake of the same name, was established in 1971 with the amalgamation of the small communities of Knowlton, Foster, West Brome, Fulford, Iron Hill, and Bondville.

Knowlton, the best known of these communities, typifies the history of the Eastern Townships. The immediate vicinity was orginally settled by Loyalists. During the early 1830s, Col. Paul Holland Knowlton

Sign for decoys, Knowlton

from Vermont settled here and established the first commerical enterprises, such a gristmill, a blacksmith's shop, and a general store.

Knowlton's enterprises spurred the growth of the village. One of the enduring local institution is the 1894 Pettes Library, the first free public library in Quebec. The imposing houses in the village reflect the prosperity of their 19th-century owners. The 1860 Drummond House (320 Knowlton) typfies the Victorian style.

Many of the 19th-century dwellings and commercial buildings in the centre of Knowlton have been converted into boutiques, art galleries, antique shops, craft stores, and restaurants. An effort has been made to retain the feeling of a village air of yesteryear. (In 1980 the community won a prestigious conservation prize, underlining the superior quality of the restoration work.)

Vacationers first arrived at Knowlton during the 1860s. The historic Lakeview Hotel dates from 1874. After 1920, wealthy Montrealers who came here by train built some of the magnificent lakeshore houses, which are still discreetly hidden behind high stone walls or thick cedar hedges.

To capture the atmosphere of yesteryear, visit Knowlton's Brome County

Many of Knowlton's shops combine contemporary flair with a pleasantly old-time atmosphere.

Historical Museum (Musée historique du comté de Brome). The complex consists of a cluster of historic buildings, including a general store, the Knowlton Academy (1854-1880), the 1854 Court House, and the 1904 Fire Hall. The museum also contains Indian, Loyalist, and military exhibits, such as a World War I German Fokker D VII aircraft. *Open Monday to Saturday, early June to late August, 10:00 am to 4:30 pm; on Sundays, 11 am to 5 pm.*

Other historic sites in the neighboring communities include the restored railway 1862 station and the 1895 red mill at Foster, the 1834 pioneer schoolhouse at East Hill, the 1864 Anglican church at Iron Hill, and the 1865 Fulford General Store. At West Brome, there is the 1860 Methodist church (now a concert hall) and Edward's General Store, once the centre of local social life. At Brome, south of Knowlton, the county fair takes place on Labor Day weekend. It has been a major local event since 1896 and retains its old-time color and flavor.

Special events
Heritage Days
Lac-Brome (May)

County Fair
Brome (Labor Day weekend)

5 North Hatley

⬛⌐💈✂⚙⛴⬛⌂

North Hatley (pop. 704), situated at the northern shore of Lac Massawippi, is one of the most popular getaways in the Eastern Townships. Its attractions include a spectacular natural setting and stately century-old dwellings. The best way to discover the charms of this village is on foot. A walking tour describing some 35 points of interest can be obtained at most local stores.

The early settlers of North Hatley included Capt. Ebenezer Hovey and the Col. Henry Cull, who built dwellings here in the early 1800s. Cull's house (550, route Hovey), dating from 1810, is the village's oldest house.

In the late 19th century, wealthy Americans, attracted to the area's natural beauty, built most of North Hatley's splendid houses in the Victorian and Queen Anne revival styles. Hovey Manor, dating from the early 1900s, was once the home of Henry Atkinson, the president of Georgia Power of At-

Hovey Manor at North Hatley is a famed hostelry of Quebec's Eastern Townships.

lanta, whose family traveled here from the southern United States by a private railway carriage every summer. The house is a copy of George Washington's 18th-century house at Mount Vernon, Virginia. The dwelling was converted into a hotel in 1950. Hatley Inn, another turn-of-the-century mansion, was originally built for the Montreal financier John Holt.

In the 1920s, local residents created the first Canadian conservation society. North Hatley is also Quebec's first heritage district, which was created to preserve local historically important sites.

The Piggery Theatre, one of Quebec's best-known English theatres, is located just off Route 108 on the outskirts of the village.

Special events

Festival du Lac Massawippi:
Sunday morning classical recitals
(May-June)
Antiques and folk art show
(mid-July)
Concerts in the park (July-August)

---

6 Ulverton

🏕🛶⌐💈⚙🚂⌂

During the 19th century, Loyalist, English and Irish settlers developed Ulverton (pop. 330), in the northern part of the Eastern Townships. By the early 1870s, local prosperity was based on the output of several mills. The only surviving remnant of that early industrial activity is the 1850 Moulin Blanchette, situated in wooded setting on the Ulverton River just outside the village. In 1906, Joseph Blanchette bought the mill for $3,500 ($200 in cash and $3,300 worth of woolen blankets, delivered over an eight-year period) and kept it operating until 1939. During Blanchette's time, the mill employed about 15 people, including children as young as 11 years old.

In recent years, the mill—the only remaining early woolen mill in Quebec—has been carefully restored. The three-story wooden structure, built on

Roads to explore: By the shores of Memphrémagog

1. MAGOG TO ROCK ISLAND
Distance (approx.): 42 km/26 miles

The first drive begins in Magog and skirts the east side of Lac Memphrémagog. (The name is an Abenaki Indian word meaning "vast expanse of water".) Take Route 247 south and enjoy a scenic 15 km lakeshore drive before reaching Georgeville (pop. 812), a hamlet founded in 1797. Stop at the village dock for a view of Elephant, Sugar Loaf, and Owl's Head mountains. The silhouette of the hills is said to represent the legendary monster *Memphré* slicing through the deep lake waters.

● Leave Georgeville, and take 247 to Fitch Bay. Cross the covered bridge over the narrow arm of the bay, and continue to Beebe Plain (pop. 1,010), a border village with an economy based on granite quarrying. (The quarries supplied the exterior stone of Saint-Benoît-du-Lac Abbey.) Four quarries and a dozen processing mills are open to the public.

● Take 147 to Rock Island (pop. 1,110), which has architectural gems: the post office, the Stanstead South United Church, and the 1904 Haskell Building, which contains an opera house straddling the Canada-United States border. At Stanstead Plain (pop. 1,100), 1.5 km north, Colby-Curtis Museum displays dolls and toys. *Open year-round, except mid-December to mid-January.*

Saint-Benoît-du-Lac with Owl's Head in the background on Lac Memphrémagog's west side

2. MAGOG TO HIGHWATER
Distance (approx.): 44 km/27½ miles

The second drive heads south along the western side of the Lac Memphrémagog to Owl's Head Mountain.

● From the visitors' centre at Magog, follow Route 112 for 3 km to Chemin du Lac (the lake road). About 10 minutes farther along this road, you will see one of this region's finest panoramas: Saint-Benoît-du-Lac Abbey with Owl's Head Mountain in the background.

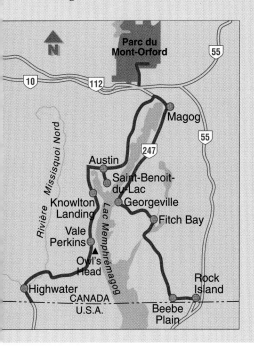

● Drive to Austin and turn south on the Fisher Road to reach the abbey. Stop at Fisher to see the 1907 Quaker-style round barn, which was built this way to prevent the devil "from hiding in the corners." Only 11 such barns exist in Quebec.

The abbey, established in 1912, was the first Benedictine monastery in Quebec. The striking design of the abbey was influenced by French-born Dom Paul Bellot, who came to Canada in 1937. At the gift shop, you can buy cider and cheeses—*Ermite* and *St. Benoit*—made by the monks. *Open year-round, Monday to Saturday, 9 am to 4:30 pm.*

● Return to the Chemin du Lac and drive south to Knowlton Landing, which dates back to 1797. This spot offers a fine view of the lake. After Knowlton Landing, Chemin du Lac becomes Chemin Owl's Head (the Owl's Head Road).

● Head south on this road to Vale Perkins, where the dock provides another lakeside vantage point. Chemin Owl's Head leads to the mountain of that name. It is said the profile of a legendary figure called Owl magically appeared on the cliff face after his death.

A trail ascends the 751-m-high summit of Owl's Head. From here, you can see Lac Memphrémagog stretching across the Canada-United States border to the south end of the lake at Newport, Vermont.

To link the drives described here, cross the border south of Highwater and take Route 105 to Newport, Vermont. From there, continue north on Route 5 to Rock Island and Stanstead Plain.

the river slope, sits on fieldstone base, which also serves as a basement. An underground channel in the basement diverts the water to an old turbine, which provides the power that still drives the mill's machinery. The mill's interpretive centre and workshops are open to the public.

You can walk to the mill from a rest area on Highway 55, or drive to the site on the Mooney to Porter roads at the western end of the village. There is an attractive picnic at the basement level just beside the river and some 5 km of walking trails in the immediate vicinity. *Open Tuesday to Sunday, early June to mid-October, 10 am to 5 pm.*

As you pass through Ulverton on Route 143, you will notice some handsome late Victorian dwellings. The 1889 house at No. 154 was once the home of the merchant James Miller. Miller's neighbor, the farmer and politician John Wadleigh, built his three-story house in 1885. Next to the Wadleigh house is the 1836 Georgian-style dwelling of Webber Reed.

At the junction of Route 143 and Chemin de l'Eglise (Church Road) is 1835 Kirkdale Hall, Ulverton's first school. Kirkdale Church, now Ulverton Church of the Saint Trinity (No. 321), was constructed in 1871. It is one of the few Gothic-style Protestant churches in Quebec to use bricks in their construction.

This Queen Anne Revival dwelling at Danville (near Ulverton) typifies a style once popular in the Eastern Townships.

7 Parc de Frontenac

The 200-km² Parc de Frontenac is a little-known getaway in Quebec's Eastern Townships, which contains deep forests, gentle hills, and peaceful lakes. The park, situated on the banks of 27-km-long Lac Saint-François, is divided into three sectors: the southern Lambton sector, the Saint-Praxède sector (north of the Lambton sector) on the west side of Lac Saint-François, and the Saint-Daniel sector on the east side of the lake. Three villages—Lambton on Route 108, Disraeli on 112, and Saint-Daniel on 267—are the respective access points to these sectors. Each sector has its own visitors' centre and offers a special range of activities.

Roads to explore: Beauty beside "deep waters"
Distance: 50 km/31 miles

Lac Massawippi lies east of Lac Memphrémagog. The Algonquin Indians who hunted and fished here called the lake *massuwippi*, meaning "deep waters." The starting point of this drive around Lac Massawippi is Ayer's Cliff (pop. 840), attractively situated at its southern end. The village's first settlers were Americans, who arrived in the late 1790s.
● From the village, head north on Chemin de la Montagne along the west side of the lake. After 7 km, take the dirt road to Les Sommets, a lookout with a fine view and a good spot for a picnic.
● Continue on Chemin de la Montagne to Sainte-Catherine-de-Hatley (pop. 1,753). At the junction with the Hovey Road, turn east (right) opposite the church. Pull over just after the curve to admire the view of Lac Magog and distant Mont Orford to the northwest.
● Follow the Hovey Road to North Hatley (pop. 750) at the northern end of Lac Massawippi. After you round the head of the lake, turn right at the second fork on Main Street to Highland Road, which cuts across a golf course. This route runs through most of this charming village.

At North Hatley, history buffs can examine the gravestones at the Old North Cemetery on the North Road. Three of the district's pioneers are buried here: the Yankee Capt. Ebenezer Hovey, the British Col. Henry Cull, and Ephraim Wadleigh, a United Empire Loyalist who came from New Hampshire. (See North Hatley, page 296.)
● Head south on Highland road, turn north on Route 143, and then take the North road to the village of Hatley (pop. 200). Local attractions include St. James Church (on Main Street), which is classified as an historic monument. Built in 1828, it is the oldest Protestant church still standing in the Eastern Townships.
● Drive west on 208 to Massawippi (pop. 460), also called Hatley West, at the junction of routes 143 and 208 west. This tiny community has a lovely view of the lake.
● Take 208 west to Ayer's Cliff. The road runs through a corridor of arching trees. This route is a little traveled in spring and fall. During these seasons, it becomes an exceptionally beautiful stretch of road, which is lined with picturesque 19th century dwellings.

Stay awhile at Ayer's Cliff. It has one of the last remaining bandstands in Quebec still used for concerts. Every year at the end of August, the Ayer's Cliff Fair takes place here. This is one of the province's oldest agricultural exhibitions dating back to 1845.

The morning mist clears to reveal the sailboats of a summer recreational club on the banks of scenic Lac Massawippi.

To end this drive on a relaxed note, leave Ayer's Cliff on Route 141 North, and stop by the roadside for a picnic alongside lac Massawippi.

This drive around Lac Massawippi Route is spectacular in autumn when the region celebrates the brilliant hues of its foliage with the *Flambée des Couleurs* festival from September 12 to October 12. For five glorious weekends, visitors have a choice of cultural activities, as well as recreational activities, such as organized mountainside walking and panoramic ski-lift rides.

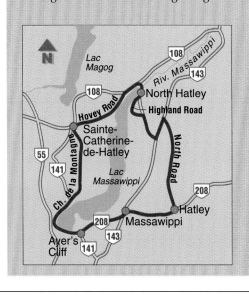

The southern (Lambton) sector, an ideal spot for canoeists, campers, and hikers, contains seven small lakes, as well as the largest bay (Baie Sauvage) on Lac Saint-François. The 8-km-long bay is a nesting and feeding area for birds. The great blue heron and the bald buzzard are denizens of this sector, and the great horned owl and the white crested falcon may also be seen here. The lakes—many are accessible by road—offer walleye, pike, and bass.

The forests in this sector are ideal for hiking. During the warm weather, you can break your walk on the Erablière Trail with a cool swim in the lake. The park's hiking trails have way stations and observation areas with explanatory signs describing the park's geology, vegetation, and animal life. An intriguing feature in the forest is a 5-km² peat bog beside a rich grove of maples. The bog contains a type of peat usually found farther north; this site is its most southerly location in North America.

The Saint-Praxède and Saint-Daniel sectors offer opportunities for swimming and windsurfing on Lac Saint-François, the third largest Quebec lake south of the St. Lawrence. In these sectors, Lac Saint-François is deep, and the water is clean and warm, often reaching temperatures of more than 26°C in summer. The Saint-Daniel Beach, located on the south bank of the Baie aux Rats Musqués, is a perfect spot to swim on a hot July day or to learn sailing or windsurfing from expert park instructors.

Visitors here usually combine different activities: canoeing or sailing with camping. The park rents canoes, sailboats, windsurfing boards, mountain bikes, and other equipment. The MJR Equestrian Centre, north of Stornoway on Route 161, supplies horses for trail riding in the park.

There are 100 wilderness camping sites, which are accessible on foot or by canoe. Each site has a fireplace and plenty of wood. The park maintains seven chalets , as well as a shelter for a group of 20 people.

8 Lac-Mégantic

The Lac Mégantic region is a little-known corner of southern Quebec. The 26-km² lake from which the region takes its name is encircled by mountains of the Appalachian range.

If you plan to visit the Eastern Townships, consider adding this region to your list of places to see. The distance between North-Hatley and the town of Lac-Mégantic (pop. 5,838) is roughly 120 km. Take Route 108 to Stornoway and turn south on 161 to Lac Mégantic. An alternative to Route 108 is the scenic and less traveled 214, which takes about the same time to cover.

The woods and waters of Lac Mégantic were the hunting and fishing grounds of the Abenaki Indians, who established a settlement here about 1700. (The name of the region comes from the Abenaki *namesokanjik*, which means "where they preserve fish.") The arrival of the railway in 1879 brought Scots, English, and Quebecois to this area. In 1885, the Scots who developed the lumber industry founded the town of Lac-Mégantic at the north end of the lake. The Quebecois came to farm, and many of their descendants carry on their forebears' traditions.

The community's architecture reflects the influence of the Scottish and English settlers. Three of its treasures are the Anglican, Presbyterian, and

Two dazzling red canoes are ready for a day's adventure on Barbue Lake in Parc de Frontenac.

Catholic churches. (The Presbyterian church, built in 1889, is now a restaurant.) A striking feature of the 1913 Church of St. Agnes is a 19th-century stained-glass window, which came from a church in London, England.

During the summer, Lac Mégantic attracts fishermen, water-sports enthusiasts, and hikers, who can explore the trails in the nearby mountains. One charming lakeside spot, the beach near Piopolis on the western side of Lac Mégantic, can be reached by Route 263. The name of the village—a combination of Latin and Greek—means "Pope's town." This village was established in 1879 by a group of French-Canadian volunteers who returned to Quebec after serving as papal guards in Rome.

The major attraction in this region is the observatory on the top of 1,200-m-high Mont Mégantic, the highest summit in Quebec accessible by road. Visitors can reach the site by heading south from Piopolis on Route 263 and turning west on 212. The low air-pollution level here makes this an ideal site for an observatory. The visitors' centre at the base of the mountain organizes stargazing expeditions on clear weekend nights. *Open daily, late June to Labor Day, 10 am to 7 pm.*

Nearby Mont Saint-Joseph is a place of pilgrimage, a small sanctuary with a chapel, and a restful picnic spot. The sanctuary was established in 1884 after local folk who had prayed to Saint Joseph survived a destructive tornado. The view from the mountain is superb.

At sunset, the observatory at the lofty summit of Mont Mégantic prepares to search for stars in the flawless night sky.

North of Lac Mégantic, Route 263 leads to the Maison du Granit (the House of Granite) on the top of 840-m-high Mont Saint-Sébastien. The site, located between Saint-Sébastien and Lac-Drolet, was a quarry from 1940 to 1950. The museum's 600-seat outdoor amphitheatre presents shows about the history of the local granite industry. (A retractable roof over the amphitheatre ensures that the show will go on even if it rains.) *Open daily, late May to mid-October, 9 am to 8 pm.*

Special events
Astronomy Festival
(July)

9 Charny

🏕️❗🐟

Charny (pop. 9,900), just across the St. Lawrence from Quebec City, traces its origins to the mid-17th century. This historic community was named after Charles de Charny, the son of Jean de Lauzon, the governor of New France. However, the town is best known for a natural attraction—Chaudière Falls.

South of Charny, the 169-km-long Rivière Chaudière rises in Lac Mégantic and flows through the long, fertile valley of the Beauce region. Roughly 6 km from its mouth on the St. Lawrence, the river suddenly expands to a width of 120 m and tumbles down a 35-m-high waterfall. The Abenaki Indians gave the name *asticou* to the churning, frothing waters in the kettlelike basin at the base of the waterfall. The French coined the term *la chaudière*—from *chaudron*, meaning cauldron—to describe the falls and its river.

At a park, just southwest of Charny, a 113-m suspended footbridge and three lookouts offer spectacular views of Chaudière Falls. There is also a roadside stop from which drivers can admire the view. The best time to see the falls is during the spring runoff, when the water level is high. In season, sport fishermen gather here to try their luck in the frothing waters at the base of the falls.

The torrent of the Chaudière Falls, Charny

A LAND OF FARMS, FLOODS, AND APPALACHIAN HILLS

The prosperous farming region of the Beauce stretches from the edge of the St. Lawrence Lowland (roughly 30 km south of Quebec City) to the foothills of the Appalachians near the Canada-United States border. The Rivière Chaudière running northward through this fertile area often wreaks havoc with its spring floods. In the fall, the maple trees on the surrounding hills glow with color. The long, narrow tracts of the farmland still recall the seigneurial system. The first seigneur, Joseph Fleury de la Gorgendière, arrived in 1736 and named the region after the Beauce region in his native France.

Route 173 links the largest Beauce communities. The economic centre, Sainte-Marie (pop. 10,500), produces the "p'tits gâteaux Vachon"—small cakes popular throughout Quebec. Travelers can visit the Vachon home and see the kitchen where Rose-Anna Vachon started her business in 1930.

Near the entrance to the town is an 1892 chapel dedicated to Saint Anne. Beside the chapel is Maison Taschereau, an imposing neo-classical building built in 1809 by the son of the first seigneur of Sainte-Marie. Elzéar-Alexandre Taschereau, the first Canadian cardinal, was born here in 1820. A little farther on is the venerable Lacroix House, one of the few stone houses in this region. In the richly forested Beauce, wood has been the traditional building material.

A tunnel of sturdy, crisscross beams supports a secure canopy for Quebec's oldest covered bridge at Notre-Dame-des-Pins.

Saint-Joseph-de-Beauce (pop. 4,350), some 20 km south of Sainte-Marie, is the administrative centre of the region. The centre of town contains five buildings, all classified historical monuments: the 1865 St. Joseph's Church (1865), the Marius-Barbeau Museum, formerly an 1887 convent; an 1890 castlelike presbytery; a 1907 orphanage; and the 1911 Lambert School. The nearby courthouse (1859), although not part of this special group, won a Canadian Building of the Year Award for the high quality of its restoration.

Beauceville (pop. 4,129), 20 km farther on, is one of the oldest communities in the Beauce. Just south of the town, stop to walk along the trails in the park beside the Rapides-du-Diable (the devil's rapids) on the Rivière Chaudière. The nearby foundations of an old mill where rock was crushed to extract gold recalls the days of the 1846 gold rush in the Beauce.

Notre-Dame-des-Pins (pop. 904), also south of Beauceville, is the site of Quebec's longest covered bridge. The 1929 span over the Rivière Chaudière is some 155 m long. Saint-Georges (pop. 20,493), some 10 km farther south, is the industrial heart of the Beauce. At the Parc des Sept-Chutes, north of town, seven waterfalls tumble into a gorge on the Rivière Pozer.

SOUTHEASTERN QUEBEC

18

SOUTHEASTERN

QUEBEC

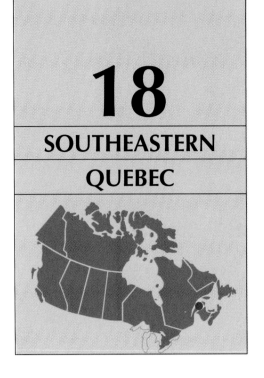

Places to see
Île aux Grues
L'Islet-sur-Mer and
Saint-Jean-Port-Joli
Cabano
Grosse Île
Île Verte
Parc du Bic
Métis Gardens (Les Jardins de Métis)
Les Portes de l'enfer (Gates of Hell)
Sainte-Flavie
Causapscal and
the Matapédia River valley
Parc de la Gaspésie
Salmon rivers of the Gaspé
Parc de Miguasha
Havre-Aubert
*Îles de la Madeleine
(Magdalen Islands)*

Roads to explore
Along the Lower St. Lawrence:
Charny to Montmagny
Along Chaleur Bay:
New Carlisle to Carleton
Magdalen Islands:
Cap-aux-Meules to Havre-Aubert

National park close-up
Forillon

*Previous pages:
Cap Bon-Ami, Forillon National Park*

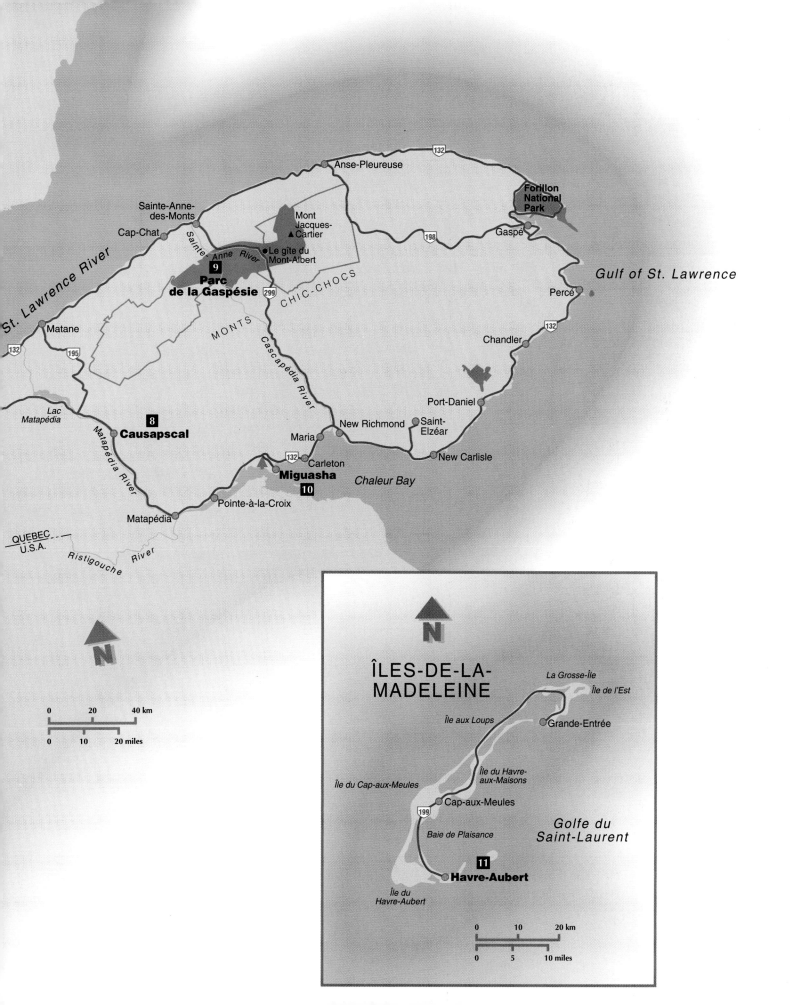

132

Anse-Pleureuse

Forillon
National
Park

Sainte-Anne-
des-Monts

Cap-Chat

Mont
Jacques-
▲ Cartier

198

Gaspé

St. Lawrence River

Sainte-Anne River

● Le gîte du
Mont-Albert

Gulf of St. Lawrence

9

**Parc
de la Gaspésie**

299

CHIC-CHOCS

Percé

Matane

MONTS

132

195

Cascapédia River

Chandler

Lac
Matapédia

8

Causapscal

Port-Daniel

Matapédia River

New Richmond

Saint-
Elzéar

Maria

132

New Carlisle

Carleton

Miguasha

Chaleur Bay

10

Pointe-à-la-Croix

Matapédia

QUEBEC
U.S.A.

Ristigouche River

N

0   20   40 km

0   10   20 miles

N

ÎLES-DE-LA-
MADELEINE

La Grosse-Île

Île de l'Est

Île aux Loups

Grande-Entrée

Île du Cap-aux-Meules

Île du Havre-
aux-Maisons

Cap-aux-Meules

199

Golfe du
Saint-Laurent

Baie de Plaisance

11

Havre-Aubert

Île du
Havre-Aubert

0   10   20 km

0   5   10 miles

Roads to explore: Along the Lower St. Lawrence

Distance: 66 km/41 miles

This drive takes travelers to the communities along the island-dotted south shore of the St. Lawrence River. At Charny (see page 301), head toward the river on the Avenue des Églises and the Chemin du Sault. Take the Côte Garneau to the Chemin du Fleuve, which provides exceptional views of Quebec City and the north shore of the St. Lawrence.

● At Saint-Romuald (pop. 10,400), cross Route 132 to reach the Cistercian Abbey (2686, Rue de l'Abbaye), where the nuns make and sell succulent chocolate. *The store is open year-round, Monday to Saturday, 9 am to 6 pm.* Return to Route 132 and cross the bridge over the Rivière Etchemin. (The name is derived from an Algonquin word, *etcmankiaks*, meaning

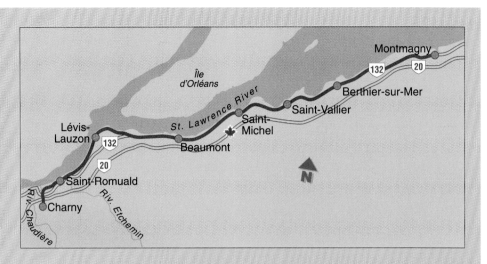

"land of skin for snowshoes.") Route 132 cuts through Lévis-Lauzon, where it is called Boulevard de la Rive-Sud.

● As you leave Lévis-Lauzon, just off Boulevard de la Rive-Sud, you will see the restored buildings of Fort de la Martinière, built in 1906, which has footpaths and an outdoor theatre. *Admission free. Open year-round.*

● Continue along the road, now Route 132. You pass Château Hearn (beside the large Hydro-Quebec pylons). The 1900 castle was once said to be haunted.

● The next stop on 132 is the village of Beaumont (pop. 2,030). The manor house of the Domaine de Beaumont seigneury overlooks the entrance to the village. The first seigneur, Charles Couillard des Islets, was the grandson of Louis Hébert, one of the first French settlers in Quebec. The village church, built in 1733, served as the headquarters for Gen. James Wolfe during the taking of Quebec in 1759.

The Beaumont seigneury's mill, built in 1821, stands on a cliff overlooking the 30-m Maillou Falls. The three-story building was originally a carding mill; later, saws and millstones were installed for cutting timber and milling grain. Visitors can buy bread and muffins baked in traditional ovens and there is a picnic area nearby.

The placid Rivière du Sud, just below the falls at Montmagny

Behind the mill, a staircase extends along the falls, offering a dramatic view and leading to the ruins of the Péan Mill. Archeologists have searched the ruins without finding the treasure of Seigneur Péan, an associate of François Bigot, the Intendant of New France in 1748. The infamous Bigot exploited the settlers during his 11 years as intendant, acquiring many ill-gotten gains. In 1759 he was sent back to France in disgrace. *Open mid-June to Labor Day, Tuesday to Sunday; Labor Day to the end of October, Thursday to Sunday. The times are 10 am to 4:30 pm.*

● At the village of Saint-Michel (pop. 1,740), about 10 km farther east, Notre-Dame-de-Lourdes grotto is a replica of the original one in France. The nearby presbytery (1739) has been restored. In summer, the picturesque village draws windsurfers and other water sport enthusiasts. Saint-Michel is also home to the Beaumont–Saint-Michel summer theatre.

● The district of Saint-Michel à Saint-Vallier is well-known for its raspberry and strawberry wines. Before heading into Saint-Vallier (pop. 1,130), take Route 132 to the Musée des Voitures à Chevaux to see 65 horse-drawn vehicles, and a collection of antique farm equipment. *Open daily, June to late August, 9 am to 6 pm.*

In Saint-Vallier, a picnic area overlooks sandbars stretching into the St. Lawrence River where flocks of snow geese rest during their spring and fall migrations.

● The last stop on Route 132 is Berthier-sur-Mer (pop. 1,280). The village has one of the finest beaches on this side of the St. Lawrence. The local church has rare gold and silver religious objects. Boats leave Berthier-sur-Mer and Montmagny (pop. 11,958), 24 km farther east, to cruise the 21 islands of the Île-aux-Grues chain.

1 Île aux Grues

🚲 🛖 🛩 ⌂

Just offshore in the St. Lawrence near Montmagny lies a chain of 21 islands, which takes its name from the 10-km² Île aux Grues. This is the largest and only inhabited island in the chain. The 200 or so island inhabitants continue the agricultural and maritime traditions of their ancestors who first settled here in the late 1670s.

The other islands in this chain include Grosse Isle, now a national historic site, and Île aux Oies. Several sandbars link Île aux Grues to the neighboring Île aux Oies, which is privately owned.

You can take a ferry to Île aux Grues from Montmagny. The ferry operates daily, from early April to late October, and the journey lasts less than half an hour. The ferry dock on the island is just 1 km from the village of Saint-Antoine-de-l'Îsle-aux-Grues.

The main road on the island passes the 1760 Painchaud ancestral home, an 1888 church, a grocery store, and an inn. Past the cheese factory (where you can buy the local product), the road reaches a former seigneurial estate. This graceful collection of buildings—a manor house, a barn, a stable, and a bakehouse—still has the atmosphere of bygone days.

The manor house, built in 1769, was renovated by Daniel McPherson, a Loyalist, who purchased Île aux Grues in 1802. The last person to live here was his grandson, Sir James McPherson Lemoine (1825-1912), the son of Julia-Anna McPherson and Benjamin Lemoine. In his time, McPherson was a well-known essayist, who was adept at writing both in English and French. The manor house, now a classified provincial historic site and the island's main attraction, was refurbished as an inn in 1986.

From the height of land near the village, you can scan the island's houses and agricultural buildings, as well as

A boat past its nautical prime is a local restaurant and a novel attraction on the Île aux Grues.

the far shore of the St. Lawrence. Here the church spire rises against the backdrop of the distant Laurentians.

Île aux Grues was originally part of the Rivière-du-Sud seigneury. The first seigneur, Charles Huault, was also the second governor of New France. The seigneur chose to live in the Montmagny area because he enjoyed hunting the geese and ducks that flocked to the marshes on the island.

Wildfowl is still hunted here, but the sandbars between Île aux Grues and Île aux Oies are now prime spots for bird-watching in spring and fall. Some 200,000 snow geese stop here during their migrations. Mallards, snipes, and blue-winged teal are some of the other denizens of Île aux Grues.

Visitors looking for a quiet getaway are likely to be captivated by Île aux Grues. Its peaceful roads are ideal for cycling, and there are spots for camping. You will eat well here, too. The island's inns have reputations for good food, and one dining place is housed in a large, beached boat.

Special events
Festival de l'Oie blanche,
Montmagny (late October)

2 L'Islet-sur-Mer and Saint-Jean-Port-Joli

🛖 🪑 ✺

The picturesque village of L'Islet-sur-Mer (pop. 1,950), formed from two seigneuries in 1677, retains its architectural heritage and maritime traditions from the early days of New France and Lower Canada. You can reach the village from Route 132, which runs along the south shore of the St. Lawrence.

Some historic buildings include the parish hall (1820), a good specimen of the Anglo-Norman style (a mixture of English Regency and Quebec elements), and the Victorian general store (1900). In the heart of the village, Notre-Dame-de-Bon-Secours Church, built in 1768 and enlarged in 1830, combines the French styles of the late 17th and 18th centuries and exemplifies local ecclesiastical architecture. Some of the best craftsmen in New

A window detail, Notre-Dame-de-Bon-Secours Church, L'Islet-sur-Mer

France contributed to the church's decor. A painting entitled *L'Annonciation* by the Abbé Aide-Créquy (1776) and a sanctuary lamp by the well-known Saint-Jean-Port-Joli sculptor Médard Bourgault complement the altar work by the Baillairgé brothers.

The Sailors' Church, built in 1834, honors local fishermen and sailors who died at sea. L'Islet's proud seafaring tradition dates from its earliest days, and the village has been called *la patrie des marins* (the sailors' homeland). It is said to have given the Canadian merchant marine almost 200 captains and marine pilots (many were sons who followed their fathers' careers), as well as countless ordinary seamen and shipyard workers.

L'Islet's most famous son, Joseph-Elzéar Bernier (1852-1934), led seven expeditions to the Arctic between 1904

Notre-Dame-de-Bon-Secours on Islet-sur-Mer typifies this region's style of church.

and 1911, which established Canadian control of the Arctic islands. To honor his memory, L'Islet created the Musée maritime Bernier (55, Rue des Pionniers est). The museum displays items from Bernier's voyages, collections of navigational instruments, and small-scale models of ships. *Open daily, May 20-September 29, 9 am to 6 pm; September 30-May 19, Tuesday to Friday only. There is an admission charge.*

Just behind the museum, visitors can climb aboard the icebreaker *Ernest Lapointe*, or the *Bras d'or*, an experimental vessel manufactured for Canada's Department of National Defense. It combines the characteristics of both submarines and aircraft.

Another attractive destination on the shores of the Lower St. Lawrence is Saint-Jean-Port-Joli (pop. 3,400), which is located some 13 km northeast of L'Islet. The community, known as Quebec's wood-carving capital, continues a tradition dating from the early days of New France. Some 50 studios (many of which are open to the public) display sculpted works of varied styles and themes: life-size religious and historical figures, landscapes, murals, and miniatures.

An impressive feature of the 1779 church is a manger scene, which was created by 17 local craftsmen. Saint-Jean-Port-Joli has two museums that display examples of the wood-carver's art. The Musée des Anciens Canadiens traces local history and contains the work of Médard Bourgault and his brothers, the preeminent carvers of Saint-Jean-Port-Joli. *Open daily, May to the end of October.* You can also visit the house of Médard Bourgault, who settled here in 1920. *Open daily from June to mid-August.* The Musée Les Retrouvailles has weaving looms, spinning wheels, agricultural and industrial equipment of bygone days. *Open late June to Labor Day.*

Special events
Chemin du Roy Festival
Saint-Jean-Port-Joli (Labor Day)

Weir traps used to catch eels line the shallows of the lower St. Lawrence River shore.

3 Cabano

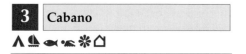

Set back from the south shore of the St. Lawrence, there is a mountainous region with wide valleys that stretches into New Brunswick and Maine. At the heart of this peaceful region is 42-km^2 Lac Témiscouata. Along its west shore are Cabano (pop. 3,390), Notre-Dame-du-Lac, and Dégelis, which offer camping and picnic sites, marinas and beaches, and fishing. To enjoy the full beauty of this remote lake, you can take a short ferry ride from Notre-Dame-du-Lac to Sainte-Juste-du-Lac on the opposite shore.

Centuries before the arrival of European settlers, Malecite and Micmac hunters and trappers camped near the present-day site of Cabano. The name in Malecite describes the temporary shelters set up by these Indians.

The present community began with the opening of the Fraser family sawmill in 1905. The 27 houses of Fraser village on the Rue du Quai are a re-

minder of Cabano's early days. The houses, built at the turn of the century for mill workers, survived a fire that destroyed much of the town in 1950.

Fort Ingall, Cabano's main attraction, was built in 1839-1842 for defense against a possible American invasion during a British-American argument over the Maine-Quebec border. The fort sheltered 200 men during the crisis. The signing of the Webster-Ashburton Treaty in 1842 ended the crisis and the fort was later abandoned.

Today, Fort Ingall has been restored. It is a provincial historic site, the only wooden military fort still standing in eastern Canada. Guides in military uniform re-create the days of the invasion threat. The fort contains a display about the naturalist and writer Grey Owl [Archibald Belaney] (1880-1938), who settled near Lac Témiscouata in the 1920s. In 1931 he moved to Prince Albert National Park in Saskatchewan. *Open daily, early June to Labor Day weekend, 9:30 am to 6 pm.*

Special events
Festival du pointu (Whitefish festival)
Sainte-Juste-du-Lac (early October)

WHERE A CELTIC CROSS RECALLS A DRAMA OF THE PAST

Between 1815 and 1941, more than 4 million people from 42 different nations passed through Quebec, a major gateway to North America. During the period between 1830 and 1860, many of the immigrants brought infectious diseases—cholera and typhus—which spread quickly through the crowded quarters of the ships crossing the Atlantic Ocean.

In 1832, the authorities, alarmed by epidemic conditions, designated Grosse Île as a quarantine station. This deserted island on the St. Lawrence was chosen because of its remoteness from the mainland population. Here ships stopped to let passengers disembark for examination.

During the first year, Grosse Île received more than 50,000 English and Irish immigrants. Every year for the next three decades tens of thousands passed through the island. Doctors issued certificates of good health to the fit, who continued on their way, and detained thousands of the sick, who died and were buried on the island. In 1847, at the height of a typhus epidemic, more than 5,000 Irish immigrants died on Grosse Île. Some 8,000 had already been buried at sea before reaching the island; another 4,500 victims were removed when the ships docked. Because the numbers were too great for the island to handle, many thousands more of the dying were sent on to Montreal. The island remained in use as a quarantine facility until 1937. Today, it has been restored as a national historic site.

You can take half-day or full-day boat excursions from Montmagny or Berthier-sur-Mer. As the boat nears Grosse Île, one of the first sights that come into view is the huge Celtic cross on a headland, which was erected in 1909 to commemorate the thousands of Irish who died at sea or on the island.

Grosse Île consists of the hotel, village, and hospital sectors. The hotel sector is the site of the old reception centre and the three hotels that provided temporary lodgings for ship passengers who disembarked here before being permitted to enter Canada. The village sector has a school, and Anglican and Catholic chapels. The hospital sector is the site of the oldest building on the island—"the lazaret"—where the gravely ill were cared for.

Today the boats from Montmagny and Berthier-sur-Mer dock at the hotel sector. From the dock, a road runs across the island and links the three sectors. About half of the 100 buildings and other island sites, such as the cemeteries, are of historical interest. *The national historic site is open from early June to early September.*

At Montmagny, the Théâtre éducatif des migrations presents a sound-and-light show about the history of Grosse Île. Another part of this musem highlights the wildfowl migrations in this region. *Open daily, April to November.*

The old lodgings for ship passengers line the shores of Grosse Île, whose scenic beauty belies past sufferings, which are commemorated by a Celtic cross (just visible on the distant hill).

4 Île Verte

The picturesque island of Île Verte lies some 5 km offshore from the village of L'Isle-Verte (pop. 1,740), which is one of the smallest communities on the south shore of the St. Lawrence. The inhabitants of the village earn their living by farming or by fishing for eels or herring. At low tide along the shore, you see the eel traps, called *pêche à fascines*, which consist of nets draped on poles. At high tide, the river sweeps the eels into the waiting nets.

At L'Isle-Verte, there are two sites worth visiting: the local Gothic-style church and seigneurial mill, both examples of traditional regional architecture. The main attraction is the *réserve faunique* (wildlife reserve), just outside the village. Seabirds and shorebirds—ducks, gulls, herons, cormorants, and plovers—nest here on the marshy riverbank.

A ferry service linking L'Isle-Verte and Île Verte operates from the beginning of May until November. It makes the 5-km crossing two or four times a day, depending on the tides. (In winter, an ice bridge connects mainland and island.) Summer visitors who wish to make just a stopover on the island are assured a five-hour visit if they arrive and leave by ferry on the same tide.

In 1773 a missionary arrived on Île Verte, which became the religious heart of the area. In the 1950s, about 400 farmers and fishermen lived here. Today it is the only island in the region with year-round inhabitants. The permanent population is less than 50, but the number triples in summer.

There is only one unpaved road on the island. Along the way, visitors will notice flocks of sheep grazing on salt marshes. (Island lamb is considered to be a regional delicacy.) One spot worth visiting is the splendid beach that curves around the north shore.

Local folk say the French explorer Jacques Cartier named Notre-Dame-

Smiling faces greet visitors on the Île Verte, a peaceful getaway on the lower St. Lawrence.

des-Sept-Douleurs, which is the largest settlement on this tiny island. The local lighthouse, the oldest on the St. Lawrence, began operating in 1809 and closed in 1972. Four generations of the Lindsay family ran the lighthouse from 1827 to 1964—a record for Canadian lighthouse keepers. (The lighthouse was honored with a special commemorative stamp in 1984.)

Today the lighthouse is also a good spot for whale-watching. The two small houses beside it are now inns. Here, guests can enjoy marvelous sunrises and sunsets, watch for beluga whales and ducks, or admire the view of nearby Île Rouge and Île Blanche.

5 Parc du Bic

The Bic region is a mixture of rocky headlands, bays, and coves, and lonely islands. Here the Appalachians touch the shores of the St. Lawrence. In his 1925 book, *Les étapes d'une paroisse* (The Growth of a Parish), Abbé J. D. Michaud offered this fanciful description of the origins of Bic's landscape: "At the time of Creation, God sent an angel to distribute the mountains He had made across the surface of the Earth. The angel's journey ended at Bic, but he still had a number of mountains left in his coat. The angel did what anyone

else would have done at the end of a hard day's work: he opened his coat and scattered the mountains at his feet. That, they say, is why there are so many mountains at Bic."

Like Michaud, local people have used poetic license in their choice of place-names: Cap Enragé (Mad Cape), Récif de l'Orignal (Moose Reef), and Île Brûlée (Burned Island). The name of nearby Île du Massacre recalls an incident in which a band of Iroquois ambushed and massacred 200 Micmac.

The 33-km^2 Parc du Bic, established in 1984, protects a strip of this coastline, which attracts artists, writers, nature lovers, and vacationers. The birds of the park include herring gulls, double-crested cormorants, and eider ducks. The offshore waters contain capelin, salmon, blue mussels, and soft-shell clams. In season, you can enjoy clam picking on the beaches. Here you will also see gray and common seals. The comparatively rare gray seal may be seen at L'Anse à l'Orignal. Within the park, the forest is a mixture of boreal and hardwood trees. Alpine, subarctic and arctic plants thrive in the maritime climate.

The visitors' centre at Saint-Fabien-sur-Mer, just west of the park, presents films and offers daily guided bus tours to the park (from late June to Labor Day). Boat excursions are also available. The park has a 6.4-km cycling path, as well as hiking trails with picnic spots. There are 140 camping sites off Route 132.

The village of Bic (pop. 3,090) is some 5 km east of the park on Route 132. You can stroll about the streets and discover the village's architectural treasures and the details of local history, which are described on panels and illustrated with photographs from bygone days.

At low tide, you walk to the nearby islands. The largest of the islands, the 14-km^2 Île du Bic, now uninhabited, is

A placid St. Lawrence River mirrors the lighthouse at Métis-sur-Mer, near Bic.

SIX GLORIOUS GARDENS IN A RUGGED GASPÉ SETTING

The 80-ha Métis Gardens (Les Jardins de Métis), some 10 km east of Sainte-Flavie on Route 132, owes its existence to Elsie Meighen Reford. Originally the site belonged to her uncle, the wealthy railway magnate Sir George Stephen, Lord Mount Stephen (1829-1921), whose plan was to build a fishing camp here when he bought the property in 1886. Two years later, however, Lord Mount Stephen moved to England, and the camp was never built.

Mrs. Reford inherited the property at the time of her uncle's death. From 1922 until 1954, she devoted her energy to creating and nurturing her magnificent gardens, which flourished in the unusually mild conditions of this particular corner of the rugged Gaspé region.

In 1961, the Quebec government acquired the Reford property and restored the gardens. Some experts rank the Métis Gardens among the greatest in the world.

A pathway of paving stones links six distinct gardens, which contain some 500 exotic and native species of perennials, annuals, bushes, and trees. The Floral Massif—at the entrance—contains perennial and annual plants, such as lupines, flowering sage, cosmos, begonias, horsetails (shave grass), and forget-me-nots.

The adjacent rock garden contains a profusion of ferns, rue-leaved saxifrage, Clayton's fern, baneberry, and alpine plants. One of the unusual features of this garden is the rare Bock's willow. This small Oriental shrub was introduced into Canada by Mrs. Reford.

The rhododendron garden showcases its namesake flower. It also puts on an early summer show of Japanese red maple, wild thyme, roses and the exotic blue poppy, the park's emblem.

The Royal Walkway recalls English gardens with its tumble of perennials, annuals, and shrubs. The timetable for this garden is as follows: arabis flowers, gold alyssum, lilac, thyme, and peonies in June; roses, larkspur, delphinium, and spiked purple lythrum (which attract ruby-throated hummingbirds); and orange sunflowers, royal lilies, and garden phlox in August.

A beautifully manicured lawn in the crab apple garden sets off a variety of ornamental plants, trees and shrubs, bent grasses, and fescues. The primrose garden displays false cypress, and silver elaeagnus. Hidden in the undergrowth are wild plants and shrubs typical of the Gaspé woods.

Visitors can tour Mrs. Reford's 37-room mansion, which stands in the midst of the garden and now houses a museum, a restaurant, and a craft shop.

Some 80 statues, created by local artist Marcel Gagnon, emerge at low tide on the shores of the St. Lawrence at Sainte-Flavie.

roughly 5 km offshore. It was once a stopping place of sailors and a base for the pilots who helped ocean-going vessels navigate the hazards on the St. Lawrence. The pilot station was closed in 1905. The name L'Anse-des-Pilotes (Pilots' Cove) recalls their former presence. During the 17th and 18th centuries, there were plans to develop Bic as a major port, because of its strategic position on the St. Lawrence, but all were abandoned.

Today vacationers may be thankful the island was left undisturbed. A number of trails wind up Mont St. Louis. From the top, you can scan the horizon and glimpse the north shore of the St. Lawrence, some 40 km away.

6 Les Portes de l'enfer

The site known as the Gates of Hell (Les Portes de l'enfer) is a 5-km stretch of the Rivière Rimouski where turbulent waters thunder down into a 90-m

This colorful rock garden is one of the peaceful corners of floral beauty at Les Jardins de Métis.

gorge. This spectacular site is located at Saint-Narcisse, some 5 km south of Rimouski. The Gates of Hell consist of five sections: the 18-m Grand-Sault waterfall; the rapids (known as la Descente aux Enfers), which are tightly enclosed by the gorge; the Petit Touladi (a fish pool); the Pinède Grise (a pine forest); and a narrow stretch of the river, the Pêche à L'Anguille, which offers opportunities for eel fishing.

The first lumber camps were established on the Rivière Rimouski in the early 1800s. Every spring, the drivers who had to manage the flow of logs floating downstream to the sawmills faced a challenging 75-km-long journey on the Rivière Rimouski.

One of the most treacherous passages was the aptly named Gates of Hell. The site figured in many tales of daring feats and lost lives on the river. But it was almost forgotten after the area's main lumber mill closed in 1964. More than 20 years later, local people developed this exceptional site, whose beauty belies its name. Today you can explore its hiking trails, footbridges, and lookouts by the falls and the rapids of the deep gorge.

7 Sainte-Flavie

At Sainte-Flavie, the gateway to the Gaspésie, a winding procession of 80 fantastic life-size statues arises from the depths of the St. Lawrence and marches ashore on a pebbly beach and through clumps of wild grass. The self-taught painter, engraver, and sculptor Marcel Gagnon, who lives by the river at Sainte-Flavie, began working on the cement and concrete figures of adults and children in the mid-1980s. According to Gagnon, the figures are emerging from the sea and the darkness to look for the light. During the summer, visitors stop to view and debate the merits of Gagnon's creation.

8 Causapscal and the Matapédia River valley

The Matapédia River, prized for its superb salmon fishing, flows south for 75 km from its source in Lake Matapédia near Amqui (pop. 4,338). It meets the Ristigouche River just above the village of Matapédia and empties into the Chaleur Bay.

Route 132 runs the length of the Matapédia Valley. Visitors crossing the valley are treated to a glorious panorama of the river, especially at sunset. In fall, red-leafed maple trees and browning elms set against a background of evergreens add colorful shadings to the mountain slopes.

The farmland in the northern part of the valley gives way to forested mountains. In 1993, the valley was named the forestry capital of Canada, because of the high concentration of lumber mills. The inescapable smell of charred wood in the Causapscal area comes from nearby sawmills, which burn lumber-processing residue in tall conical chimneys called "hells."

In summer, a common sight in the region is the sport fisherman, standing knee-high in the middle of the Matapédia River and waiting to land the majestic Atlantic salmon. The Matapédia Valley has been a major salmon-fishing centre since the first settlers arrived in the mid-1800s. In 1873, the railway magnate Lord Mount Stephen appropriated most of the land bordering both banks of the Causapscal and the Matapédia to form a huge estate. At the turn of the century, the private Matamajaw Fishing Club acquired and controlled the estate for some 60 years.

The restored Domaine Matamajaw (48, Rue Saint-Jacques) in Causapscal (pop. 2,500) displays fishing equipment and tells the history of sport fishing in the region. *Open daily, June to September, 9 am to 9 pm.*

Nearby footpaths lead to the Matapédia River, where you can watch the fishermen, or try your own luck. Les Fourches Trail leads to a particularly good spot at the point where the Matapédia and Causapscal rivers meet. Some 14 km north of Causapscal, just off Route 132, there is the 40-m-high Chutes à Philomène.

As you head south from Causapscal on Route 132, you will pass through a covered bridge at Routhierville. There are two superb roadside lookouts on

An angler casts for salmon in the swift, shallow waters of the Matapédia River.

the Causapscal-Matapedia route. At the end of 132, the hamlet of Matapédia (pop. 700) leads to the attractions of the Chaleur Bay coast in the Gaspé.

Special events

Fiddlehead Festival, Matapédia
(mid-June)

9 Parc de la Gaspésie

Route 229 cuts through the mountainous grandeur of the Parc de la Gaspésie, which covers more than 800 km² in the remote heart of the Gaspé. The northern access point to this provincial park is at Sainte-Anne-des-Monts on the St. Lawrence; and its southern access point is at New Richmond on Chaleur Bay. The road leading into the park from the north skirts the shallow, swiftly moving Rivière Sainte-Anne, one of the best-known salmon streams in this region. The visitors' centre, located within the park, is 38 km from Sainte-Anne-des-Monts and 99 km from New Richmond. The Gîte du Mont-Albert, beside the visitors' centre, provides accommodation. There are also campsites and chalets throughout the park.

The Chic-Chocs, the northern extension of the Appalachians, dominate the Parc de la Gaspésie. Here are some of

Visitors at Parc de la Gaspésie stop to wonder at the roar and rush of the Sainte-Anne falls.

OLD FISHING CLUBS AND FIGHTING SALMON

The history of Atlantic salmon fishing in the Gaspé begins with the arrival of the railway in the 1870s. Sport fishermen flocked to the Matapédia, Ristigouche, and Cascapédia rivers, which flow into Chaleur Bay. During this period, wealthy Canadians and Americans set up private fishing clubs with exclusive rights to fish in these rivers. Some of these clubs are solidly anchored in Gaspé's history. The best known include the Restigouche and Glen Emma clubs, established in the 1880s. At Causapscal, the Matamajaw Fishing Club—now the Domaine Matamajaw—started at the beginning of the century. Only the wealthy could afford to join these clubs in the early 1900s. The annual membership fee might run to $4,000—an enormous sum at that time. In the 1970s, the era of the old fishing clubs came to an end, when Quebec revoked all private leases on its salmon rivers. Today, salmon fishing is accessible to any angler who first obtains a fishing license.

The Atlantic salmon are present in sizable population along the rivers of Quebec, the Maritimes, and Newfoundland, including Labrador. The young salmon is hatched in the upper reaches of a river, and makes its way to the sea once it is fully grown—after one, two, or three years. It may spend several years at sea before returning to its parent river in autumn for spawning.

During the upstream trip, the salmon displays the fighting spirit anglers admire—it struggles against currents and rapids, and leaps up falls or salmon ladders. The fish deposit their eggs in redds, or nests, on the gravel river bed. After spawning, the Atlantic salmon (unlike its Pacific counterpart) returns to the sea. Few spawn more than once. In their final emaciated form, they are known as kelts.

Forillon

To the 16th-century Micmac Indians, the long, narrow tip of the Gaspé Peninsula was *gespeq*, "land's end". From a pebble beach at Cap Gaspé the rocky headland dove into the St. Lawrence River, just a stone's throw from the spot where a giant sea stack stood. The rock pillar was a landmark for French fishermen of Champlain's time. These mariners of old called the rock *le forillon* ("the flowerpot"), a name that persisted even after the rock collapsed into the ocean in 1851. Today, the pillar that gave the 245-km² Forillon National Park its name is but a rocky islet.

Forillon's coast on the Gulf of St. Lawrence ends in a 7-km-long wall of cliffs. During fall and winter these rock walls are empty and silent. But come April, black-legged kittiwakes, herring gulls, double-crested cormorants, and black guillemots flock back to long-established rookeries. The dark, long-necked cormorants are especially noticeable, flying to and fro with twigs and branches, building new nests, or adding new levels to large ones remaining from preceding nesting seasons.

The stout rock wall that shelters so many birds weathers constantly. Ledges crumble and quietly trickle downward while hunks of rock crash noisily to the shore below. The limestone-littered beaches draw seals who arrive in spring and remain until late autumn. Harbor seals whelp here before mid-June and gray seals come to fish and rest. Their females give birth in February—on ice floes out on the gulf.

In contrast to the summer-long flutters and cries of the seabirds, the fall silence in Forillon is shattered only periodically by the mournful calls of the gray seals. Amplified by the rock walls, the long howls echo eerily across the October landscape.

Except in the coastal cliff section, trails follow the escarpments on either side of the narrow Forillon peninsula. Visitors can observe whales including finbacks, minkes, and humpbacks from lookouts at Cap-Bon-Ami and Cap-Gaspé. It is a magical moment indeed when these creatures, spouting majestically, surface close to shore.

A beach below Cap Bon-Ami offers seclusion at Forillon.

From the shore, the Mont-Saint-Alban Trail climbs into densely wooded heights—the boreal forest of coniferous and deciduous trees—and weaves past rumbling brooks bordered by delicate overhanging ferns. Woodland carpets of bright yellow buttercups overshadow the pink-striped white flowers of the wood sorrel.

The hiker will almost certainly spot a porcupine. If the encounter is in open ground, the animal will freeze, with its spiky quills—some 30,000 in all—fully extended. Given a choice, however, a porcupine prefers to scramble up any nearby tree trunk. In the areas where spruce, fir, and white birch grow thick, moose, deer, and black bear can also be seen.

Low sand dunes and a saltwater marsh at Penouille on Forillon's southern shore support lichens, club mosses, and plants of the heather family. Capelins in great numbers arrive in June to spawn on the gravel beaches. In swarming, sparkling schools, these small silvery fish come ashore on the breaking waves of a high, lunar tide. In July and August the surface waters surrounding Forillon quiver with noisy, splashing shoals of mackerel.

Sea anemones, shrimps, crabs, urchins, sea stars, worms, squids, and shelled mollusks are among some 500 species of invertebrates identified in the waters just off Forillon. In many places, the rocky bottoms look like gardens teeming with vivid colors. On encrusted layers of pink coralline kelp, bright green or deep yellow sponges live next to blood-red starfish, green sea urchins, pure-white anemones, and purple sun stars.

PARK INFORMATION
Access: By car and bus from Highway 132.
Visitors' centre: At Penouille and midway between Rivière-au-Renard and Anse-au-Griffon.
Accommodations: 350 camp sites in 3 campgrounds plus accommodation for up to 100 persons in a campground for organized groups of 10 or more.
Summer activities: Hiking, swimming, fishing, cruises, bicycle riding, mountain biking, scuba diving, horseback riding, windsurfing and picnicking; slide shows and other family-oriented presentations at the Interpretation Centre; naturalist-conducted hikes.
Winter activities: Cross-country skiing, snowshoeing, and camping.

eastern Canada's highest peaks—many are more than 1,000 m high. The park's loftiest peak, 1,268-m-high Mont Jacques-Cartier, is visible from the St. Lawrence River, some 25 km away. The slopes of the Cartier peak shelter rare woodland caribou, Virginia deer, and moose. This mountain is located in the eastern (La Galène) sector, which also contains the impressive peaks of the McGerrigles.

The western sector of the park includes 1,150-m-high Mont Albert and the area around Lake Cascapédia. The 30-km² area at the top of Mont Albert is a lake-dotted plateau, which contains

This picturesque chalet is near the Gîte du Mont-Albert in the Parc de la Gaspésie.

mosses, lichens, and some 150 plants usually found much farther north. The park's interpretation centre describes local plant life. In summer, guides lead visitors to Mont Albert, Mont Jacques-Cartier, Lac aux Américains, and the Rivière Sainte-Anne.

The park is well-known for its hiking trails; some double as cross-country ski trails in winter. One of the most relaxing trails begins near the visitors' centre and leads to Lac aux Américains. It is an ideal half-hour walk for families or those who like a pleasant stroll before picnicking.

Some of the best trails lead along the scenic waterfalls and rapids of the Rivière Sainte-Anne. A portion of Trail 4 and all of 5, 6, 7, and 8 are level and easy to hike in all weathers.

Roads to explore: Caves, villages, and vistas on Chaleur Bay

Distance (approx.): 100 km / 62 miles

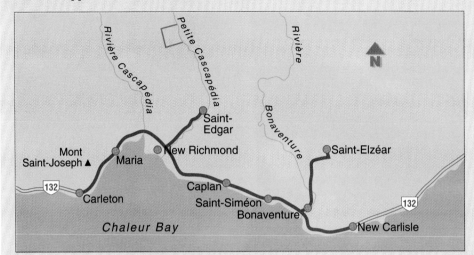

This drive through some of the communities on the southern section of route 132 in the Chaleur Bay region begins at New Carlisle (pop. 1,600), the hometown of former Quebec Premier René Lévesque (1922-1987). The town, founded by Loyalists in the late 18th century, retains the atmosphere of its British origins.

Sumptuous old houses with gabled Victorian rooflines line the streets of New Richmond. The Georgian-style Hamilton House (115, Rue Principale), built in 1852, reflects the family's American roots. Its striking features include the wide chimneys, a large foyer, an imposing central staircase, and Victorian furnishings. *Open daily, mid-June to early September, 10 am to noon and 1 pm to 4:30 pm.* The interior of the 1844 Thompson House (now a bed-and-breakfast) mixes decorative styles: French windows, neo-classical moldings, arches, and high ceilings.

● On the way to Bonaventure, spelunkers can make a detour to Saint-Elzéar to visit the Musée des Cavernes et de la Grotte de Saint-Elzéar. These world-famous underground caves are about half a million years old. The museum offers guided tours, slide shows, and a nature trail. The agile visitor can get a close look at the caves by taking a guided tour about 20 m below the earth's surface. Transportation and safety gear are provided and hiking boots and warm clothing are a must. *Open from early June to the end of October. Tours begin at 8 a.m. and last about four hours.*

The Acadians founded Bonaventure (pop. 2,500) in the mid-18th century. The

village has a distinctive Acadian atmosphere. The Musée acadien du Québec (95, Rue Port-Royal) houses an extensive collection that underlines the tremendous contribution Acadian culture has made to Quebec society. *Open daily, late June to early September, 9 am to 9 pm. The rest of the year, hours vary.*

The Rivière Bonaventure, which runs through the village, is popular with canoeists and salmon anglers. The best spot for salmon fishing is just outside town, where Route 132 passes over the mouth of the river. Be sure to obtain a local fishing permit. After fishing, you must declare your catch to the authorities.

● Continue through Saint-Siméon and Caplan, where the panoramic views of Chaleur Bay will entrance photographers.

The drive heads to the paper-manufacturing town of New Richmond (pop. 4,100). The British Gaspé Heritage Centre (351, Boulevard Perron) re-creates a village of businesses and dwellings from the period when the Loyalists and Scottish and Irish immigrants settled in the Gaspé peninsula. *Open daily, early June to Labor Day, 9 am to 6 pm.*

● Take the Saint-Edgar Road to the Chaleur Bay Forestry Education Centre, located some 10 km north of New Richmond. The centre has three interpretive nature trails. *Open daily, during the summer.* Saint-Edgar Forestry Museum on the same road has displays highlighting the evolution of the lumber industry over the past two centuries.

● Maria (Gesgapegiag) faces New Richmond across the Cascapédia River. It is one of the smallest Indian communities in Quebec, with a population of 500. Its church is shaped like a wigwam, and there is a boutique displaying Micmac arts and crafts.

● The drive ends at the picturesque village of Carleton (pop. 2,600), which, like Bonaventure, is Acadian. The scenic countryside and the magnificent local beach make this an ideal destination for the traveler who wishes to spend a few quiet days. Some of the best restaurants in the region are found nearby. The 555-m-high Mont Saint-Joseph looms over Carleton. There is a stunning view of Chaleur Bay and the distant shore of New Brunswick from the top. You can reach the top by car or hiking trail.

A gentle mist hovers above Carleton on the scenic hilly shores of Chaleur Bay.

Beachcombers search for agates and other treasures on the rocky shore of Parc de Miguasha.

There are two trails to the top of Mont-Albert. Trail 1 is ideal for less experienced hikers or those with limited time. The strenuous 20-km round-trip hike is best for experienced hikers.

The trail to the cold and windy Mont Jacques-Cartier takes about two hours. The stretch of the trail leading to the base of the mountain passes along an access road used to reach the radar base, built on the summit in the Second World War. (Wear your hiking boots and warm clothing. Even in July, temperatures at the higher levels of the Chic-Chocs may be freezing.)

The trip to the top of the mountain passes through different vegetation levels: hardwoods, mixed forest, and evergreens. Above the tree line, there is the tundra, where a few bushes and dwarf plants such as the short-leaf willow and stemless pinks hide between the rocks to shelter from the cold. At this height, you can glimpse the distant St. Lawrence.

The park offers other major hiking trails, which take several days. One such trail begins about 20 km east of Gîte du Mont-Albert at the eastern sector. It leads to the peaks of Mont McGerrigle and Mont Jacques-Cartier and ends at the top of 1,130-m-high Mont Xalibu, where the view toward Lac aux Américains is breathtaking.

10 Parc de Miguasha

Parc de Miguasha is situated on a coastal cliff on the north shore of the Rivière Ristigouche, which flows into Chaleur Bay. Although the park is only 1-km² in area, the rocks on the 8-km

Roads to explore: A glimpse of an island in the Gulf

Distance: 25 km/15 miles

For visitors newly arrived on the 100-km-long Magdalen Islands (Îles de la Madeleine) in the Gulf of St. Lawrence, all journeys begin at the busy port of Cap-aux-Meules (pop. 1,571) on the island of the same name. This commercial and administrative centre is the landing for the island's main maritime links, the car ferry from Souris on Prince Edward Island and the boats from Montreal. (The ferry service operates from April to January; the crossing from Souris takes about five hours.) Cap-aux-Meules is also an ideal base from which to explore the three other main islands: Grosse Île, Havre aux Maisons, and Havre Aubert.

This drive starts at Cap-aux-Meules and heads south to Havre-Aubert. From the ferry landing, take Route 199.

● Just 2 km along 199 is the hamlet of La Vernière, well-known for its restored 1876 church, and a restaurant, *La Table des Roys (The Table of the Kings)*.

The lovely Saint-Pierre-de-La-Vernière Church, now a classsified historical monument, is said to be one of the few remaining large wooden churches in North America. Legend says the church was built with a cargo of timber saved from a ship bound for England, which sank offshore. The following summer, another ship sent from England to collect the car-go also sank. The ship owners decided to donate the wood to the church congregation. But the bad luck pesisted: a storm destroyed framework for the church. At an inquiry into the sinking of the first ship, it was revealed that its captain in a fit of rage had placed a curse on the cargo. The villagers obtained fresh timber, had it blessed, and resumed work on the church that still survives.

● About 100 m from the church, Route 199 turns south and becomes Chemin de la Martinique. The road runs for about 10 km along a beach on the Baie de Plaisance. The marshes on the other side of the road are a refuge for birds. Past the marshes, you can eventually see Baie du Havre-aux-Basques, a rendezvous for windsurfers. Farther on, dunes on the bay side conceal another beach.

● At the first intersection, take the Chemin d'en Haut for Havre-Aubert. Less than 2 km farther on, this road overlooks a bucolic landscape and winds upward toward the Demoiselles hills. The road is the setting for brightly colored houses—blue, pink, green, and yellow—which are some of the Magdalens' most attractive dwellings on the island chain.

● About 3 km farther on, just before the road rejoins Route 199, there is an inn with a seafood restaurant, *Chez Denis à François*. Opposite the inn are the courthouse and jail, which apparently have been without "customers" for some time.

● Back on 199, turn left just before the 90° bend to visit a craft store and workshop. Its wares are made from the islands' most abundant material: sand.

● Route 199 continues alongside the La Grave pebble beach until it comes to a group of gray shingled buildings built by the first Madelinot settlers.

stretch of the Misguasha coast have yielded fish and plant fossils from the Devonian era, which occurred 350-400 million years ago.

A New Brunswick geologist, Abraham Gesner, discovered the site in 1842, and experts have studied its remains since 1880. In 1937, Quebec acted to control the unauthorized removal of fossils from the site, which is now strictly forbidden. The park was established in 1978 to preserve the site.

There are two visible rock layers at Miguasha: the upper reddish Bonaventure layer overlays a large lower grayish Escuminac layer, which is the source of the fossils. (*Miguasha* is a Micmac word meaning "red soil.")

During the Devonian period, Misguasha was a huge tropical lagoon, where aquatic creatures thrived. Here plants, mostly ferns, sometimes grew to heights of 10 m. The sediment from the rivers flowing into the lagoon eventually covered all aquatic and plant life. Later the sediment hardened into rock of the Escuminac, layer which preserved their remains to this day.

Despite millions of years of erosion and shifts in the earth's surface, the fossils at Miguasha are remarkably intact. The park's finds include some 24 fossils of Devonian fish. An intriguing specimen, *Eusthenopteron foordi*, resembles a fish, and may be a link between aquatic and land creatures. This major discovery is only one of many displayed at the park's interpretive centre.

At the centre, visitors can tour a teaching laboratory, where paleontologists extract and identify rock-bound fossils. Guides take visitors down to the beach to see the Escuminac layer. *Open daily, late June to late September, 9 am to 5 pm. Open Monday and Friday, early June and late September.*

Some experts say Miguasha's major fossil discovery, the Eusthenopteron foordi, may be a link between sea and land life.

The Miguasha headland is also worth exploring. The 20 km of quiet roads around this headland offer excellent cycling. There is also a 2-km hiking trail, which runs along the top of the cliffs and through the park.

11 Havre-Aubert

Havre-Aubert (pop. 1,000) is located on the island of the same name, the most southerly of the Magdalens (Îles de la Madeleine). The community is an ideal base from which to explore the islands. Its sweeping harbor is crowded with fishing boats and pleasure craft. A windsurfing school instructs adults and children.

At Havre-Aubert, past and present meet along the beautiful pebbly beach at La Grave (from the French *grève*). Here an historic cluster of weathered fishery buildings—used for salting and smoking fish—now house boutiques, craft shops, and restaurants. The general store has become a homey cafe where local folk and visitors meet.

In summer, visitors at La Grave can enjoy a season of plays at the Théâtre Au Vieux Treuil. The Aquarium des Îles displays local fish, mollusks, and shellfish and contains exhibits about fish-processing methods.

At nearby Pointe Shea, the Musée de la Mer displays navigation instruments, fishing equipment and artifacts from shipwrecks. *Open Monday to Friday, June 24 to September 4, 9 am to 6 pm. The rest of the year, days and hours vary.*

Special events

Lobster Festival
Grand Entrée (July)

Festival du Pêcheur
L'Etang-du-Nord
(early July)

Seafood Festival
(mid-July)

Sand Castle Contest
Sandy Hook Beach, Havre-Aubert
(early August)

Acadians' Holiday
(mid-August)

THE "MADELINOTS" AND THEIR MAGNIFICENT ISLANDS

During the 15th century, Basques and Bretons came to the Magdalen Islands (Îles de la Madeleine) in search of fish, seals, and walrus. French explorer Jacques Cartier receives the credit for discovering this chain of 16 islands: he landed at the northernmost island (Île Brion) in 1534. Samuel de Champlain stopped here 75 years later. In the 1660s, François Doublet was authorized by the French crown to colonize the islands, but he merely named them after his wife Madeleine. For the next 100 years, only mariners, fur traders, and Micmac Indians occupied the islands.

In the mid-18th century, Acadians driven out by the British from Nova Scotia and New Brunswick settled at Havre-Aubert. Although the settlers had always been subsistence farmers, now they learned to fish the sea. Some 30 years later, they were joined by more Acadians fleeing the French islands of Saint-Pierre and Miquelon off Newfoundland's southern coast. Together, they became the Madelinots—a name that has persisted to this day.

In 1787, the British crown granted the islands to Sir Isaac Coffin. The Coffin family controlled the islands for more than a century and imposed a brutal regime on the Madelinots. Many left the islands and scattered to New England, Nova Scotia, and the Lower North Shore of the St. Lawrence. In 1903 Quebec passed legislation to enable the Madelinots to buy back the islands they had worked so hard to develop.

Waves and winds have created the natural wonders of the Magdalen Islands, such as these red sandstone cliffs at Cap du Phare.

Some 15,000 Madelinots now inhabit this chain. The four largest islands—Havre Aubert, Cap aux Meules, Havre aux Maisons, and Île de l'Est—form a long, narrow 100-km-long chain in the Gulf of St. Lawrence. The islands are linked by sandbars, punctuated by coves, harbors, and lagoons, and lined with unspoiled beaches. The mighty red sandstone cliffs—the Magdalens' striking feature—are riddled with sea caves and arches. Gently rolling green farmland and pasture mantle the cliffs.

The main summer maritime link is the 5-hour car ferry between Souris, Prince Edward Island, and the port of Cap-aux-Meules, where the visitors' centre is located. The main road—Route 199—leads to most communities, byways, and scenic attractions. Local firms also offer boat cruises and bus tours.

NEW BRUNSWICK

19
NEW
BRUNSWICK

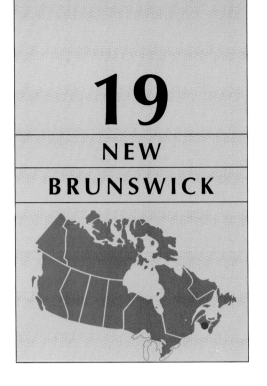

QUEBEC
NEW BRUNSWICK

Edmunston

Saint

John Riv

120

2

N

0   20   40 km

0   10   20 miles

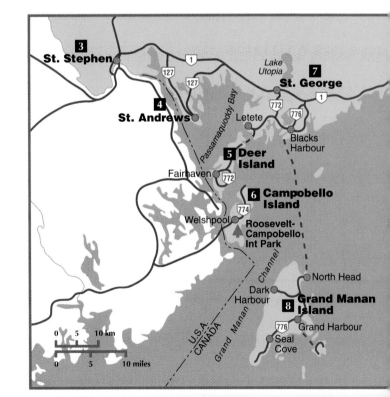

3 **St. Stephen**
127
127
1
Lake Utopia
7
St. George
772
1
776
Letete
Blacks Harbour
Passamaquoddy Bay
4
St. Andrews
5 **Deer Island**
Fairhaven
772
6 **Campobello Island**
774
Welshpool
Roosevelt-Campobello Int Park
Channel
North Head
Dark Harbour
8 **Grand Manan Island**
776
Grand Harbour
Seal Cove
U.S.A.
CANADA
Grand Manan
0   5   10 km
0   5   10 miles

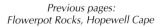

Previous pages:
Flowerpot Rocks, Hopewell Cape

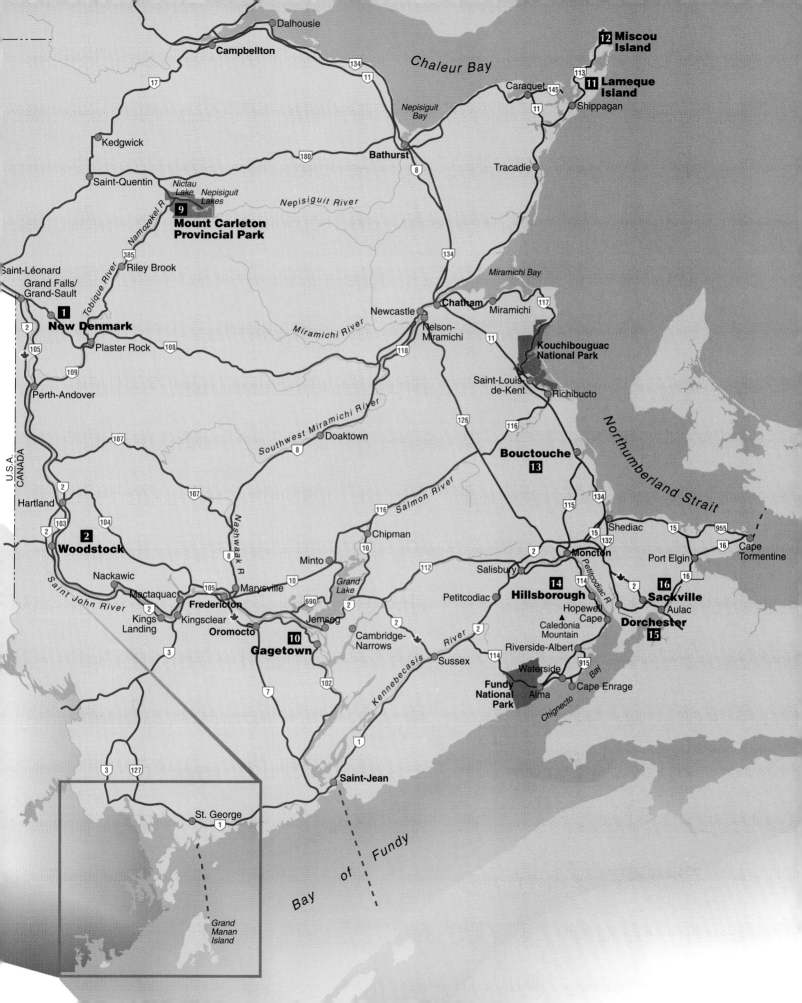

Chaleur Bay

Dalhousie
Campbellton
17
134
11

12 Miscou Island
113
11 Lameque Island
Caraquet 145
11
Shippagan

Kedgwick
180
Nepisiguit Bay
Bathurst
Tracadie

Saint-Quentin
Nictau Lake *Nepisiguit Lakes*
9
8
Namozekel R
Nepisiguit River
Mount Carleton Provincial Park

134

Miramichi Bay

Saint-Léonard
385
Tobique River
Riley Brook
Chatham
Miramichi
117

Grand Falls/Grand-Sault
Newcastle
Nelson-Miramichi
1
New Denmark
11
Kouchibouguac National Park

2
105
Plaster Rock 108
118
Saint-Louis de-Kent
109
Miramichi River
Richibucto

Perth-Andover
126

107
116
Southwest Miramichi River
8
Doaktown
Bouctouche
13

U.S.A. / CANADA

107
Nashwaak R
116
Salmon River
115
134

Hartland
Chipman
Shediac
15
955
103
2
104
10
132
15
Port Elgin
16
2
Woodstock
8
Minto
10
112
Moncton
16
Cape Tormentine
2
955
16
Salisbury
114
14
Petitcodiac R
Nackawic
2
Grand Lake
690
Hillsborough
Sackville
Mactaquac
Marysville
Petitcodiac
Hopewell Cape
Aulac
2
Fredericton
2
Caledonia Mountain
Dorchester
Kings Landing
Kingsclear
Oromocto
Jemseg
2
114
Riverside-Albert
15
Saint John River
10
Cambridge-Narrows
River
915
Gagetown
102
Kennebecasis
Sussex
Waterside
Cape Enrage
7
114
Alma
Chignecto Bay
Fundy National Park

Northumberland Strait

3
102
1

3
127
Saint-Jean

St. George
1

Bay

of

Fundy

Grand Manan Island

1 New Denmark

⊛❀⌂

A 10-km hilly stretch of Route 108 leads from the Trans-Canada Highway near Grands Falls past terraced fields and neat white farmsteads to New Denmark (pop. 362). At the top of Klokkedahl Hill, just outside the village, stop by the roadside to take in the sweeping view of the rolling countryside, where farmers prosper by growing potatoes.

New Denmark is one of Canada's first Danish settlements and one of the oldest communities of Danes in the world outside of Denmark. The promise of a hundred acres for every adult male lured the original 29 settlers here in 1872. They expected to find fertile fields ready for planting but, instead, they confronted a seemingly endless forest. With all their savings spent to reach Canada and without hope of returning to their home country, the settlers began clearing the land. One of their first achievements was to build a communal dwelling.

At New Denmark, a Danish flag fluttering by the church marks the hamlet's heritage.

New Denmark has never forgotten its early struggles or its roots. Ties to the past are visible everywhere. Mailboxes bear the names of the Jensens, Hansens, and Pedersens; signposts point to King Kristian and Applegard roads. Danish is still spoken by older residents, who pass on it to the next generation.

The New Denmark Memorial Museum displays more than a thousand treasures from the past. Some prized items include a century-old doll house decorated with tiny copies of Victorian chairs, tables, and other furnishings; handmade embroidery and lace dating back to 1879; and wooden clogs worn in pioneer days. Beside the museum, the Immigrant House re-creates the settlers' first dwelling. Another smaller building houses vintage farm equipment. *Admission free. Open daily mid-June to Labor Day, 2 to 5 pm.*

At the annual Founder's Day, held on June 19 on the museum grounds, townsfolk commemorate the arrival of the settlers. During this festival of the Danish heritage, children in traditional red and white costumes dance to folk music. At the outset of the event, the community honors its ancestors by singing Denmark's national anthem.

2 Woodstock

⋀⋔⌠⋏⋗⌂

This riverside town of 5,000 perches where the Meduxnekeag and Saint John rivers meet. The Saint John is sometimes called the Rhine of North America, in a tribute to its majestic beauty. The scenic niche occupied by the town is almost at the halfway point along the river's 673-km course to the Bay of Fundy.

Settled by Loyalists more than two centuries ago and incorporated in 1858, Woodstock is New Brunswick's oldest town. It is a place of tree-lined streets and gracious houses. Some of these fine dwellings are described in a self-guiding tour, *Woodstock Walkabout,*

Through bounteous fields, a scenic country road rolls toward secluded New Denmark.

which is available at the town's visitors' bureau.

The finest public building in the area is the Old Carleton County Courthouse at Upper Woodstock, some 5 km north of Woodstock. The local county historical society restored the structure to the days when it served as a seat of justice, a stagecoach stop, and a site for political rallies, agricultural fairs, concerts, governor's levees and military reviews. *Admission free; donations accepted. Open daily July to Labor Day, 10 am to 5 pm.*

Every July, Woodstock holds an annual fair, known as Old Home Week, a tradition for nearly half a century. Local folk now living in other parts of Canada or the United States plan vacations, family gatherings, and class reunions to coincide with the event. A parade, harness racing, agricultural square dancing, a fiddlers' contest, and woodsmen's competition are all part of the fun of the fair.

3 St. Stephen

During the first week of August, St. Stephen (pop. 4,931) stages two celebrations—a chocolate festival and a remembrance of international goodwill.

For much of the 1800s, the community was a thriving shipping and ship-building centre. The builders hauled masts down King's Street—once called King's Mast Road. In 1873, the Ganong Brothers set up their candy factory. In 1906, Arthur Ganong created the chocolate bar—a block of chocolate wrapped in paper as a snack for a fishing trip; in 1932, the company introduced the heart-shaped valentine box.

Candy making still holds sway here. Whiffs of cinnamon, peppermint, and other fragrant ingredients from the Ganong factory fill the air of St. Stephen on windy days. During the Chocolate Festival in early August, the town honors this prized commodity with chocolate dinners, contests, and other events. The Ganong factory itself is opened to visitors who can watch the candymakers at work and sample their wares for free.

The Chocolate Festival coincides with the International Friendship Festival between St. Stephen and its

Ganong candy store, St. Stephen

American neighbor, Calais, in Maine. Every year, at the opening ceremony, the mayors of the two towns meet midway on the Ferry Point International Bridge to shake hands. This gesture and the week-long celebration recall St. Stephen's refusal to fire on Calais while the British and the Americans fought the War of 1812. Instead, St. Stephen supplied its American neighbors with fireworks for the Fourth of July holiday. (In the area of practical concerns, the towns also share drinking water supply and answer each other's fire alarms.)

The Loyalist founders of St. Stephen and their descendants, as well as the local 19th-century plutocracy of timber merchants and shipbuilders, endowed the town with a legacy of gracious houses. One of the most splendid mansions, built by lumber baron James Murchie, is now the Charlotte County Museum. *Admission free; donations accepted. Open 9:30 am to 9:30 pm, Monday to Saturday, June through August.*

The local historical society offers a self-guiding driving tour to architectural treasures, such as Lonicera Hall and the Todd Mansion. The tour book is available from the Charlotte County Museum and local bookstores.

Park Hall exemplifies St. Stephen's changing history. This grand residence, built in 1866, was purchased by Ganong Brothers in 1900 and used to board their female workers—called Ganong Girls—who flocked to St. Stephen from Great Britain and Newfoundland. It is now the site of St. Stephen's University.

4 St. Andrews

This town of 1,700, situated where the St. Croix River flows into Passamaquoddy Bay, is proudly Loyalist. At the heart of St. Andrews' folklore is the remarkable foresight of the Loyalists who came here after the American Revolution in 1783. Before they fled Castine, Maine, they first dismantled their frame houses and shipped them by barge to St. Andrews. On arrival, they reassembled the dwellings on their present sites. A notable example is the green-roofed, white clapboard house at 75 Montague Street.

The Loyalists drew up an orderly town grid with six 1.5-km-long parallel streets, crisscrossed by 12 others running down to the waterfront. They honored George III (whom they had supported during the Revolution) by

A RECORD-HOLDER ON THE SAINT JOHN

In the early 1900s, 400 covered bridges spanned New Brunswick's rivers. If left uncovered, a wooden bridge rarely lasted more than 15 years. A roof and sidings protected a bridge's broad beams and trusses from rain, snow, and ice. With these improvements, a bridge might survive 80 years.

Decades of wear and weather have weakened or destroyed more than three quarters of the covered bridges in New Brunswick. Only 70 of these picturesque relics spanned its rivers in the early 1990s. The most durable specimen is the 391-m-long giant across the Saint John River at Hartland, north of Woodstock. It holds the world's record as the longest covered bridge in the world.

Seven stout piers hold the timbers of Hartland's bridge high above the Saint John River.

This privately built span was not a *covered* bridge when it opened to traffic in 1901. Nineteen years later, the spring ice floes on the Saint John River wrecked two of its rock-filled piers. The province—by that time, the owner of the bridge—built concrete piers and added the roof. On June 23, 1980, the Hartland Covered Bridge received the highest of Canadian honors: It was declared a national historic site.

In the early 1900s, covered bridges were perfect spots for kissing, cuddling, and proposing. Recently, a Toronto couple continued this romantic tradition by marrying at the Hartland bridge.

A SERENE GARDEN BY THE ST. CROIX

Morning glories, Crocker Hill

Gail and Steve Smith are the creators of Crocker Hill Studios, located on Ledge Road, 3 km east of the corner of King and Prince William streets in St. Stephen. Overlooking the St. Croix River, the 1.5-ha terraced site includes some 21 gardens, which contain more than a hundred different kinds of herbs.

In 1977, while bicycling through the area, the Smiths found the hillside site overgrown except for a clearing with a tiny, dilapidated cottage. Enchanted by their discovery, they rehabilitated the property. Steve, who is an artist and decoy maker, was the first to see its potential. Although the Smiths knew nothing about gardening, they poured energy and imagination into the creation of Crocker Hill. In the search for rare plants and wildflowers, Gail developed an abiding interest in herbs, which flourish here in abundance. The Smiths used granite, fieldstone, and blocks from old walls and foundations to build walls, terraces, steps, and benches. To enhance the mood of serenity pervading their gardens, they added quiet pergolas and vine-swathed arbors.

At Crocker Hill, you can also visit a studio where Steve paints and sculpts, and a gift shop, which sells dried herbs, tisanes, wreaths, everlasting flowers, and potpourri. *Open daily, June to September, 10 am to 6 pm. October to May, by appointment.*

naming the streets after his 15 children. Which explains why some of the streets—Adolphus or Augustus—have oddly archaic names. (The St. Andrews' courthouse displays paintings of all George III's offspring.)

Visitors can stroll about the core of St. Andrews by following a self-guided walking tour of 34 historic buildings, which has been prepared by the local historical society. (Copies of the tour and another tour of the Loyalist graveyard are available at the local visitors' bureaus.)

A list of places to see in St. Andrews should include: the Pagan-O'Neill House (1784); the Joseph Crookshank House (1785); the John Dunn House (1790); and Chestnut Hall (c. 1810).

Clapboard and shingled dwellings cluster around a quiet seaside cove at St. Andrews.

The Henry Phipps Ross and Sarah Juliette Ross Memorial Museum, at 188 Montague Street, provides a glimpse of early 19th-century St. Andrews. This brick dwelling in the neo-classical style houses a collection of fine period furniture, as well as porcelain, clocks, mirrors, and rugs. *Admission free. Open Monday to Saturday, late May to early October, 10 am to 4:30 pm.*

Greenock Kirk Presbyterian Church, built in 1824 by Capt. Christopher Scott, is said to be St. Andrews' finest building. On top of its white steeple is a sculpted oak tree—symbol of its builder's home in Greenock, Scotland.

Until the late 19th century, St. Andrews enjoyed the profits of trade with the West Indies. Just as the trade declined, townsfolk began extolling the benefits of St. Andrews' relaxing seaside location and its health-giving air, in the hope of attracting vacationers. For the wealthy, American and Canadian interests built the original Algonquin Hotel in 1889 and its successor in 1915. Today the towers of the hotel, New Brunswick's preeminent resort, rise like protective sentinels above historic St. Andrews.

Special events
Aquaculture Fair (June)
Summer Arts Festival
(early July to late August)

5 Deer Island

Every half hour, dawn to dusk, a toll-free ferry leaves Letete, south of St. George, for Deer Island. During its 9.75-km journey, the ferry plies the waterways between tiny islands at the mouth of Passamaquoddy Bay. Its destination is Butler's Point, a fishing village for two centuries, which is located at the north end of the island.

About 12 km long and 5 km wide in places, Deer Island is the third largest in the Fundy isles chain, after Grand Manan and Campobello islands. Most of the 850 residents live in the villages of Fairhaven and Leonardville. Route 772 encircles Deer Island, linking its beaches, coves, and lighthouses. (The lighthouse at Leonardville is particularly photogenic.) Offshore sights include fishing weirs or aquaculture cages (used to raise salmon and sea trout). Near Fairhaven, there are the world's three largest lobster pounds, where the crustaceans are fattened up for culinary glory.

At the island's southern tip, 16-ha Deer Island Point Park offers a view of a vast whirlpool reputed to be second in size only to The Maelstrom off Nor-

Two young fishermen delightly display their catches at Fairhaven dock, Deer Island.

way's North Sea coast. Known as "The Old Sow," the whirlpool is named for the whooshing sound it makes as its strong currents surge through the tight channel dividing Deer Island from the nearby United States mainland. The best viewing time is three hours before high tide, which occurs twice a day.

A private ferry between Deer and Campobello islands operates according to a varying schedule and only from June to September.

6 Campobello Island

In summer, a 45-minute ferry ride from Deer Island brings visitors to the busy pier at Welshpool. This village—the largest on Campobello—was founded by Capt. William Owen in 1770. For more than a century, the Owens ruled Campobello as their personal fiefdom. The house that Adm. William F. Owen built in 1835 at Deer Point is now a bed-and-breakfast inn.

At Welshpool, you can join a whale-watching excursion to explore the marine life in the offshore waters. The channel between Deer and Campobello islands abounds with minkes, finbacks, and humpbacks. An occasional visitor in these waters is the rare and endangered northern right whale.

East of Welshpool, a road leads to Herring Cove Provincial Park with its magnificent expanse of pebble beach. There are campgrounds for visitors who simply wish to stroll along the wave-lashed shore and to discover the island's beaches, cliffs, and coves. One nearby scenic spot, just behind the seawall, is the delightful freshwater pond known as Lake Glensevern.

From Welshpool, follow Route 774 to East Quoddy Lighthouse at the island's northern tip. Here a cluster of white frame buildings perches picturesquely on a rocky outcrop. It is said to be the most photographed lighthouse in Atlantic Canada.

East Quoddy Lighthouse is poised on Campobello Island's northernmost promontory.

When visitors succumb to the charms of Campobello, they can understand why United States President Franklin Delano Roosevelt called it his "beloved island." Roosevelt longed to relive the carefree times spent here at the family summer retreat at the southern tip of the island. These times began in the 1880s, when his father acquired the property, and ended in the summer of 1921, when Franklin was crippled with polio after a day's sailing.

The Roosevelts' 34-room Dutch colonial style dwelling with its green roof and shutters and red shingle siding—just a "cottage" according to them—is located at the 1,200-ha Roosevelt-Campobello International Park, maintained jointly by Canada and the United States. The park is also accessible from the mainland by the Franklin D. Roosevelt Bridge at Lubec, Maine.

Simple wicker chairs and tables furnish the interior; family pictures and childhood sketches decorate mantelpieces and tables. This imposing but cosy summer home gives the impression that the Roosevelt family has just left for the day but will return shortly. *Open daily, late May to mid-October, 9 am to 5 pm.*

7 St. George

The Magaguadavic (pronounced *Magga-dave-y*) River is the heart of St. George (pop. 1,400). The river's gorge and falls compose the community's most picturesque sight. An old red mill poised on the rocky bank completes this pretty picture. On early summer evenings, the Magaguadavic turns silver as gleaming salmon leap through the air. A fish ladder beside the falls assists the salmon in their fighting journey upstream to the spawning grounds. Visitors can watch this feat through windows in the fish ladder.

In the early 1900s, St. George gained its reputation as "Granite Town" from the red granite quarried from the surrounding hills. Canadian and American builders used the stone for major projects, such as the Parliament buildings in Ottawa and the Museum of Natural History in New York City. Orders for red granite kept local folk occupied until the output from the quarry (and the architectural taste for stone) petered out in the 1920s. Some of St. George's most imposing reminders of the red granite industry are the monuments marking the graves of the Protestant cemetery, which is one of the oldest in Canada.

If asked, older residents may tell you tales about the monster said to lurk in the depths of Lake Utopia, just north of St. George on Route 785. Some say it rivals Nessie, the monster of Scotland's Loch Ness. Both creatures are shy and rarely surface. The Lake Utopia monster first poked its head out of the waters in 1870; the last sighted in 1951. Despite the tales, Lake Utopia still draws summer visitors, who enjoy its

A wary collie stands at the entry to a weathered fish shed in Seal Cove, Grand Manan.

Roads to explore: Dulse gatherers and volcanic remains
Distance (approx.): 24 km/18 miles

From North Head, drive south on Route 776 and look for a sign pointing toward Dark Harbour on Grand Manan's west side where, according to local legend, Captain Kidd buried a treasure in gold.
● Dark Harbour, the only community on Grand Manan's rugged west side, is so named because a nearby cliff blocks the sunlight in the morning.

At low tide, local folk gather dulse. This seaweed delicacy is dried in the sun and eventually shipped across North America for sale to people who like its tangy salt flavor. If the owners of the dulse-gathering businesses are free to chat, they will regale you with tales of the sea.

● Return to Route 776 and continue to Grand Harbour (pop. 608), with its picturesque grouping of gingerbread houses and quaint stores.

Visit the Grand Manan Museum, which concentrates on the island's natural and social history, and the technologies of deep-sea fishing, shipping, and navigation.

The museum originated with a collection of 300 mounted birds that belonged to naturalist Allan Moses (1881-1953). It also has material on two famous American visitors to Grand Manan, the naturalist James Audubon and the novelist Willa Cather. Its intriguing artifacts include relics retrieved from shipwrecks on the nearby ocean floor. *Open June 15 to Labor Day; daily from 10:30 am to 4:30 pm.*

● Between the fishing villages of Grand Harbour and Seal Cove is Anchorage Provincial Park with its 81-ha bird refuge.

Near the campground, there is a sign to Red Point with its evidence of the effects of an undersea volcano that erupted some 16 million years ago. The explosion left behind greyish rocks, which are upstarts compared to the adjacent red sedimentary slabs that count their years in billions.

● At the southern tip of the island is Southwest Head Lighthouse, perched high atop a craggy headland, which is assaulted by a raging sea.

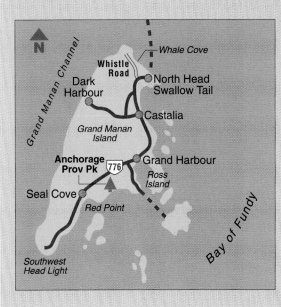

beaches and its opportunities for boating and fishing.

8 | Grand Manan Island

Some 27 km from the New Brunswick mainland is the largest and most remote island of the Fundy isles chain, Grand Manan. During the busy summer months, the first ferry leaves from Blacks Harbour at 7:30 am, and others follow—at two-hour intervals throughout the day—usually crowded with eager travelers.

As the ferry nears Grand Manan, the first sights are the high rocky outcrops, mantled with spruce and fir. On summer days, when fog envelops the island, Grand Manan may seem forbidding. But, closer to shore, just before landing at North Head, visitors glimpse the splendor of the island's cliffs, and the beauty of its coves and shingle beaches.

This 142-km² island is inhabited by 2,500 hardy individuals whose characters have been shaped by physical isolation. At North Head (pop. 800), you will hear a faint New England twang in local speech. Residents drop the *r* in words like "car," which becomes *cah,* and add the letter to words like "area" (*arear*).

The island has much to offer visitors seeking a restful setting. In 1922, the American novelist Willa Cather fled the turmoil of New York City for Grand Manan, which became her retreat and inspiration for 18 summers. Her cottage still stands at Whale Cove.

The preferred pastimes of visitors are walking or hiking along the island's scenic coastline, painting, taking photographs, whale-watching and, of course, bird-watching. Grand Manan is a major stopover for some 400 species of migrating birds on the Atlantic flyway. The abundant bird life awed the American artist and ornithologist John James Audubon during his visit to the island in 1833.

Before exploring Grand Manan, stop awhile at North Head. At the dock, visit the whale-watching interpretation centre or board a whale-watching excursion boat.

There are several attractive spots within walking distance of North Head. A quick stroll brings you to the point just east of North Head, where swallows circle the aptly named Swallow Tail Lighthouse. Just north of the village, Whistle Road leads to two rock formations at Northern Head: the ancient stone mass of Old Bishop, and the Hole-in-the-Wall, a rock buttress sculpted by wind and wave. At Whale Cove, a path descends to a beach below the 125-m-high cliffs, where seven seams of the earth's crust are visible. Some of the seams are 900 million years old. Local folk call them "The Seven Days Work" after the biblical story of creation.

Seal Cove typifies the tiny, picturesque ports along Grand Manan's accessible eastern shore.

| 9 | **Mount Carleton Provincial Park** |

New Brunswick's north-central highlands were first known to the Maliseet Indians and, later, to explorers and fur traders. In the mid-1800s, settlers drifted in to create a life of fishing, hunting, and lumbering. During the 1890s, Adam Moore and other woodsmen offered guided excursions in this unspoiled region. "Sports" eager for outdoor success came to their camps from the United States. In 1927, J. Sterling Rockefeller and Burton Moore, Adam Moore's son, organized the Nictau Fish and Game Club, which protected the highlands until 1970. At that time, New Brunswick set aside a 174-km² block in the heart of the region as Mount Carleton Provincial Park.

The largest of the province's parks, Mount Carleton embraces a mountainous wilderness containing eight lakes and the headwaters of the Nepisiguit and Tobique rivers. Two roads—routes 385 and 180—lead into the park. Because the location is spacious and remote, you can enjoy hiking, fishing, and camping in perfect solitude.

Climbers and photographers will thrill at the sweeping views from the summit of 820-m Mount Carleton, the highest mountain in Atlantic Canada. Visitors will discover plants, such as dwarf birch and Bigelow's sedge, which first appeared when the glaciers retreated from the area about 10,000 years ago. The park also accommodates an array of wildlife: deer, moose, beaver, black bear, red fox, coyote, and at least a hundred species of birds.

10 Gagetown

Townsfolk like to tell about a visiting couple who spent a summer afternoon in Gagetown and left convinced it was just like Brigadoon—the enchanted Scottish village in the 1947 musical fantasy by Alan Jay Lerner and Frederick Loewe. Bewitched, the couple returned often, discovering new delights with each visit.

Gagetown has only 630 residents, but they cooperate to bewitch as many visitors as possible. Every fall, the village hosts a county fair, a tradition for more than 150 years. Local people with an artistic bent put on an annual June craft fair with displays of everything from quilts to decoys said to fool even the smartest ducks.

Gagetown was renamed for Gen. Thomas Gage, a British commander who acquired a land grant here in 1765. Nineteen years later, the Loyalists arrived. Gagetown boasts more than a dozen sites where history was made. The handsome

Roads to explore: A lakeshore of forests, mines, and ports
Distance: 150 km/93 miles

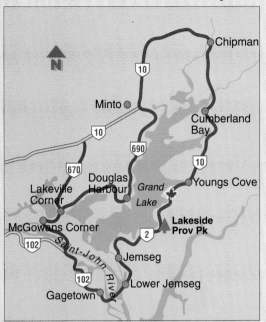

New Brunswick's largest lake, the Grand is some 34 km long and up to 10 km wide in places. It has seen every kind of vessel from Indian canoe to modern pleasure craft. During the late 19th and early 20th centuries, wood-burning paddle wheelers moved goods across the lake. Until recent times, tugboats hauled log booms bound for Saint John's mills.

● From Gagetown, take Route 102 to Upper Gagetown, where a cable-car ferry crosses the Saint John River. Head west on the Trans-Canada Highway to McGowans Corner.

● The drive around Grand Lake starts at McGowans Corner. Route 670 to Lakeville Corner leads through countryside where farms are two centuries old. Lakeville Corner is an agricultural hamlet that is also home to hobby farmers and others who work "in town."

● Take Route 690 between Lakeville and Douglas Harbour. The forested landscape is rich with shades of green in summer and glows with multicolored glory in fall. The first view of Grand Lake is from a hill overlooking Douglas Harbour, the lake's only sheltered port.

● Douglas Harbour welcomed the paddle wheelers of the past. Now it is a haven for pleasure craft from all three Maritime provinces and the United States. Some craft sail to Douglas Harbour by way of Bay of Fundy and the Saint John River. In summer, more than a hundred boats may tie up at a wharf originally built for paddle wheelers.

● Continue on Route 690 past Princess Park and Sunnyside Beach to Sypher Cove, with its picturesque eroded bluffs and caves.

● As Route 690 turns westward toward

At the village of Lower Jemseg, a prized landmark is the stone St. James Church.

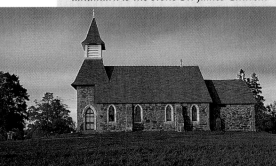

Minto, you will see a 68.6-m-high, 110-m-wide dragline chewing up the land like a hardworking dinosaur. (Mine tours are available through the Nova Scotia Coal Office at Minto.) Although strip-mining has scarred the land, more than 15 years of reclamation has helped to beautify an area where coal digging began in the 1630s. The old pits have been flooded and stocked with trout.

● Turn left to Highway 10 and head for Chipman (pop. 1,615), which was founded on lumber. New Brunswick's forests still supply the community's giant sawmill.

● Drive south through Cumberland Bay's rich farmlands. At Youngs Cove, turn right on the Trans-Canada Highway. Head for Waterborough, where a concrete wharf marks a former steamer stop, and Lakeside Provincial Park.

● Continue on to Jemseg, which becomes New Brunswick's strawberry capital every July.

● At Jemseg, turn left just before the high-level bridge and then left again to reach the road to the Gagetown ferry. About 100 m along the road, a plaque marks the site of 18th-century Fort Jemseg, built by the French. Stop to enjoy the superb view of the countryside.

● Just beyond Lower Jemseg, board the cable ferry to cross the Saint John River. On the other side, follow Highway 102 back to Gagetown.

Kouchibouguac

Kouchibouguac (the pronunciation is *koosh-e-boo-qwack*) is an anglicization of a Micmac word meaning "river of long tides." It is an apt name for this park where deep estuaries allow the Atlantic Ocean to run far inland. For Kouchibouguac is a series of strips, the outermost being a 25-km curve of sandspits and islands. Warm-water lagoons immediately inland are all bordered by salt marshes which merge with the Acadian forest. The forest contains bogs, meadows, two lakes, and numerous ponds.

Eight distinct habitats—barrier islands; estuaries and lagoons; ponds, river, and brooks; forest; open fields; bogs; salt marshes; and the offshore area—give Kouchibouguac a wide assortment of plants and animals. Not counting mosses, liverworts, algae, lichens, and fungi, for example, the park boasts more than 600 different species of plants. As well, 223 species of birds have been sighted either in the park or offshore.

Marram grass anchors the ever-shifting barrier beach islands, known locally as dunes. The three major ones are North Kouchibouguac, South Kouchibouguac, and North Richibucto. A 10-minute hike on a floating boardwalk takes visitors to the South Kouchibouguac Dune, site of Kellys Beach, and the most popular spot in the park for sunbathing, swimming, seal-watching, and birding. Anyone planning a beachcombing circuit of this island should count on spending a half-day and traveling up to 15 km.

The lagoons separating the barrier beach islands from the mainland are a snorkeler's paradise. The shallow water is clear and warm, the shore is never far away, and jungles of eelgrass conceal fascinating creatures: large eels, rock crabs, purple starfish, sand shrimp, moon snails, and beds of mussels and oysters. In the nearby meadowlike salt marshes, the chattering of savannah and sharp-tailed sparrows fills the air. American bitterns and katydids add their contributions to marsh concerts.

Red spruce, balsam fir, red maple, and paper birch are the most common trees in the park. In fact, Kouchibouguac's woodlands are typical Acadian forests, which are more or

A solitary moose ambles along a wooded road in Kouchibouguac Park.

less a transition zone between the coniferous boreal forests to the north and the deciduous forests to the south. Even among Acadian forests, however, Kouchibouguac—and indeed much of New Brunswick's Acadian shore—stands out. The most noticeable difference is the abundance of white cedars—trees that are uncommon, even absent, elsewhere in the Acadian forest.

One-fifth of Kouchibouguac's underlying sandy clay is so dense that water stagnates at the surface. This set of conditions, combined with the area's cool, humid climate, produce sedges, grasses, and strong growths of sphagnum mosses. As one set of plants dies, another growth takes its place, nourished by the displaced, decaying vegetation. In this manner, year after year, Kouchibouguac's peat lands were formed. One such area, Kellys Bog, can be reached by boardwalk. This spongy dome of multicolored sphagnum and scattered clumps of stunted black spruce and tamarack is up to 6 m at its highest points.

Most of the park's runoff flows into the St. Louis, the Black, and the Kouchibouguac rivers. These freshwater and saltwater crossroads harbor eelgrass and widgeon grass, moon snail, starfish, crab, mussel, black duck, teal, and even migrating gaspereau, tomcod, smooth flounder, trout, striped bass, salmon, and eel.

The park's best-drained sites were cleared by the descendants of the area's European settlers—Acadians, United Empire Loyalists, and immigrants from the British Isles. Many families farmed here until the park was established in 1969. The open expanses they left behind are now returning to their natural state.

PARK INFORMATION
Access: Highways 11, 134 (follow the Acadian Coastal Drive), and 117.
Visitors' centre: *Just south of Kouchibouguac village.*
Accommodations: *Open year-round, camping—but no hookups—available May to October, canteen, summer playgrounds, interpretive programs.*
Summer activities: *bird-watching, biking, hiking, boating and canoeing (rentals available), windsurfing and fishing, picnicking.*
Winter activities: *Snowshoeing, tobogganing, cross-country skiing, and winter camping.*

courthouse dates from 1837. The Anglican rectory, built six years earlier, was the work of Thomas Tilley. His son, Leonard, was born in a house built in 1786 by Loyalist Dr. Frederick Stickles. Leonard Tilley became one of the Fathers of Confederation and was eventually knighted. Which explains why Gagetown is blessed with one of those rare national historic sites, a house where a Father of Confederation was born. His birthplace, now Queens County Museum, has Loyalist and Victorian furnishings and displays about local history. *Open daily, mid-June to mid-September, 10 am to 5 pm. Saturdays and Sundays, 1 pm to 5 pm, late May to mid-June; mid-September to Thanksgiving.*

Gagetown claims what's thought to be the oldest building standing by the Saint John River. The 1761 structure—known as the Blockhouse—was once used to store rifles and ammunition. Today it houses the Loomcrofters Handweaving Studio, designers and weavers of the Royal Canadian Air Force tartan. Another riverside spot of yesteryear, the Steamers Stop Inn, recreates the spirit of the old riverboat hostelries from New Brunswick's past.

11 Lameque Island

One of the first places settled by the Acadians in the 1760s after years in exile was this peaceful island. Originally inhabited by Micmacs, Lameque Island was temporarily occupied by the French explorer Nicolas Denys in 1672.

The first five families of Acadian settlers consisted of 26 people in all. Today this 150-km² island supports roughly 10,000 people—many descended from those first families. It is one of North America's largest French-speaking islands. But it is also a world of dunes and beaches where only the waves and wind are heard.

Savoy-Landing is the first stop on the island after crossing the causeway from Shippagan on the mainland. The 26.5-km Route 113 leads to its island's largest community, Ville de Lamèque (pop. 2,000). Settled in 1790, it opted for town status only in 1983.

Route 103 skirts the west coast overlooking Chaleur Bay, passing through the "barrens" where peat moss is gathered. Six plants process, pack, and ship the peat moss for use as fertilizer, insulation, and packing material. The industry means more to the island's economy than fishing, even though it employs fewer people. The islanders refer to their home as the Peat Moss Capital and celebrate a Peat Moss Festival, usually held in July.

To explore the east coast on the Gulf of St. Lawrence, take a side road—Route 305—from Haut Lamèque. Here you'll discover picturesque fishing villages, such as Cap Bateau and Pigeon Hill. The road hugs the cliffs on the gulf shore. Near Pigeon Hill, look for the weathered wooden capstans. Fishermen once tied ropes around these posts to winch their boats ashore.

North of Ville de Lamèque, at Petite-Rivière-de-l'Île, two spires proclaim the presence of St. Cecile Roman Catholic Church, built in 1913. The church glories in vivid color as well as superb acoustics. In 1968, Father Gerard D'Astous, with help from two artists, painted the interior with religious symbols in hues of bright green, red, blue, and yellow. Every July, this "masterpiece of naive art" welcomes musicians from all over the world for the International Baroque Musical Festival, one of the highlights of New Brunswick's artistic life. The festival focuses on the performance of early music on period instruments.

At the island's northern tip, a monument commemorates French explorer Nicolas Denys. Just beyond the monument is the toll ferry to Miscou Island. In summer, the ferry leaves at half-hour intervals day and night.

12 Miscou Island

A white church set amid windblown trees comes into view as the ferry from

A collection of deep-sea fishing vessels loll in the sunlit calm of Lameque Harbor.

Lameque Island enters Miscou Harbour. The church overlooks an anchorage for the small fishing fleet, which is the island's only industry.

This restful 64-km² island—New Brunswick's Land's End—is home to about 900 inhabitants. French explorer Jacques Cartier stepped ashore briefly in 1534. Another Frenchman, Nicolas Denys, set up a trading post in the 1600s. Exiled Acadians arrived here in the 1760s, followed by Scots settlers in the early 1800s.

On the west side of Miscou Island, the 19-km stretch of Route 113 crosses fields of wildflowers to a solitary point of land reaching into the Gulf of St. Lawrence. Along the way, there are several tempting side roads. At Miscou Centre, the island's largest community, ask for Jules Road, which leads to the white beaches and the dunes on Chaleur Bay.

Slightly farther north of Miscou Centre on Route 113, a 7-km side road to Wilson's Point winds through a landscape of dune, marsh, lake, and lagoon to the shores of the Gulf of St. Lawrence.

St. John's Church near Miscou Lighthouse, Miscou Island

At the tip of Miscou Island, a tall white lighthouse sends out warning beams. Built in 1858, it is one of the oldest lighthouses in New Brunswick. Once, the lightkeepers used seal oil and kerosene to fuel its burners. Today the light does its valuable work automatically.

13 Bouctouche

Named after a Micmac word meaning "big little harbor," Bouctouche (pop. 2,367) was founded in 1784 by five Acadian families who returned here after 30 years of exile. Forestry, farming, fishing, and shipping were Bouctouche's early economic mainstays.

Today, the community is known for its prosperous oyster fishery. It is also famed for *La Sagouine*, the aging, indomitable heroine of the 1970 novel by Acadian author Antonine Maillet, whose birthplace is Bouctouche. The down-to-earth philosophy of *La Sagouine* exemplifies the experience of New Brunswick's Acadians. The actress Viola Léger has portrayed the character on stages around the world.

Le Pays de la Sagouine—a park dedicated to Maillet's creation—comprises a mainland and an island site, linked by a 305-m-long pedestrian bridge. The island re-creates life in an Acadian village in the early 1900s. Here actors impersonating characters from Maillet's novels and plays greet visitors. An Acadian restaurant and an open-air theatre for weekend musical performances are other park features. *Open daily mid-June to early September.*

Kent Museum offers another intriguing glimpse of Bouctouche's past. Built in 1880, the museum originally served as a convent and a school. In the late 1970s, Kent Historical Society con-

Buoys brighten a shingled shed on Miscou Island, which lives by fishing the Atlantic.

verted the building into a museum, which preserves a chapel created by Léon Léger, known as "the one who made wood pray." To restore the chapel in 1983, craftsmen researched the techniques used by Léger a century earlier. *Open daily, late June to early September. Monday to Saturday, 9:00 am to 5:30 pm. Sunday, noon to 6 pm.*

Special event
Shellfish Festival (July)

14 Hillsborough

This village of some 1,200 inhabitants surprises visitors with its well-preserved 19th-century dwellings. The most prized is Steeves House, now a museum that honors William Henry Steeves, one of the Fathers of Confederation, who was born here in 1814. *Open daily, June to September, 10 am to 6 pm.*

Steeves was the grandson of Heinrich and Rachel Stief, German immigrants to Pennsylvania, who moved to the Hillsborough area in 1766. Heinrich and Rachel came north with seven sons, whose descendants, now more than 150,000 strong, are scattered across North America. At Hillsborough, the Steeves (the anglicized version of Stief) office keeps track of the family's growing numbers. In summer, a jubilant fraction of the family gathers for a reunion in the village.

Riding the Salem and Hillsborough Railroad is a local attraction. A converted 1922 baggage car at Hillsborough is the terminus for the 16-km round-trip to Salem. (An adjacent railyard displays an 1898 and a 1912 steam engine.) Two 1940s diesel engines pull three refurbished passenger cars on an hour-long excursion, which passes the Hillsborough marshes along the Petitcodiac River, and traverses Weldon Creek and the 12-m-high Hiram Trestle. *Open mid-June to Labor Day in September.*

15 Dorchester

❇ ⌂

Dorchester has a proud and wistful sense of its own past. The community (pop. 1,198) was named for the British general Sir Guy Carleton, 1st Baron Dorchester, who directed the exodus of Loyalists from New York after the American Revolution in 1783 and served as governor of Quebec in the 1790s.

During the early 19th century, Dorchester was a boisterous village. Its main square was known as the "devil's half acre," whose taverns kept the place that way. The community knew the prosperities of quarrying sandstone and building the great wooden ships in the age of sail. But, by 1875, the advent of steel vessels, and an Ameri-

Roads to explore: Flowerpots, marshes and mighty tides

Distance: 118 km/73.3 miles

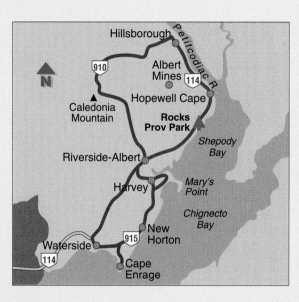

From the village of Hillsborough, head south on Route 114 to Hopewell Cape (pop. 144), where the Petitcodiac and Memramcook rivers flow into Shepody Bay and meet the tides from the Bay of Fundy. Once a shipping centre, the village has several dwellings adorned with rooftop "widow's walks," where wives anxiously watched the sea for the return of their husbands' sailing vessels. It was also the childhood home of R. B. Bennett, the only New Brunswicker to become Prime Minister of Canada (1930-35). In the centre of the village is the Albert County Museum, built in 1845 as a jail. *Open daily, June 15 to Labor Day, 10 am to 6 pm.*

● The next stop is The Rocks Provincial Park. Take a side road to the park, where you can see soft rock pillars—known as flowerpots—top-heavy with shrubbery and trees. At low tide, the reddish pillars look as though they might snap at the base and topple over on the beach. At high tide, they become tiny islands surrounded by water 14 m deep. The park is also a great place to view the Fundy tides that rise a foot in seven minutes, and 12 m in roughly six hours.

● Continue until Route 114 meets 915 outside Riverside-Albert. Follow 915 across Shepody marshes to Harvey (pop. 494).

● Take the road leading to Mary's Point and the Shepody National Wildlife Area where, in summer, thousands of tiny semipalmated sandpipers take off from the mud flats in exhibitions of synchronized flight. They stop here to feed before migrating to South America. Stroll along the trail by the edges of the freshwater dikes and marshes in the protected area.

● Return to Route 915, and drive on to New Horton, which was settled by people from Horton, Nova Scotia, who moved over as a group in 1798.

● Continue until you reach the short winding road that leads to Cape Enrage (pop. 12). The road comes to a cove and climbs a steep hill to a lighthouse on a rocky point, where many ships ran aground. Stroll along one of the trails at the top of the cliffs of red sandstone and shale. Fundy tides still eat away roughly half a metre of the cliff every year. On the beaches below, search for agate, red jasper, fossils, and ripple marks on ancient rocks. At Cape Enrage, you'll discover an abandoned lighthouse keeper's dwelling. The lighthouse now works automatically.

● Back on Route 915, continue to Waterside, where a road skirting saltwater marshes takes travelers to Route 114.

● Just past Riverside-Albert, take unpaved back country road—Route 910—that passes the 366-m-high Caledonia Mountain and returns to Hillsborough.

The Fundy tides assault the sheer cliffs of shale and sandstone at Cape Enrage.

At Dorchester, the stones of Keillor House recall a prosperous past based on local quarries.

can embargo on cut stone, undermined its economic and political supremacy.

Local stone was used to build many of the fine dwellings that recall Dorchester's once-thriving past. Keillor House was built in 1813 by Yorkshireman John Keillor. Now a museum, it features 10 rooms with 19th-century furniture. A striking feature is the three-story spiral staircase. *Open early June to mid-September, Monday to Saturday, 10 am to 5 pm, and Sunday, 1 pm to 5 pm; Wednesday to Sunday, early to late September, 10 am to 5 pm.*

The 1811 Bell Inn, reputedly the oldest stone house in New Brunswick, houses a crafts shop and restaurant. The restored Maples House once belonged to lawyer, judge and politician Sir Pierre-Armand Landry (1846-1916), the only Acadian to be knighted.

Dorchester was also the home of a Father of Confederation, Edward Baron Chandler (1800-1890), who was a politician, a judge, and a lieutenant governor of New Brunswick. Chan-

Dining room, Keillor House, Dorchester

dler had a reputation as a hearty host and raconteur. His stone house dating from 1831 still sits atop the village hill.

The invitation to dine at Chandler's lavish table—or, as the saying went, "to get your knees under Chandler's mahogany"—was a privilege accorded to Sir John A. Macdonald, Sir Charles Tupper, and other 19th-century Canadian political luminaries. Today, Chandler's house is The Rocklyn bed-and-breakfast inn, which can truly boast: Sir John A. Macdonald slept here.

16 Sackville

🎣🕊️👣❀📷⌂

In the heart of Sackville (pop. 5,740)—the site of Mount Allison University—is the 20-ha Waterfowl Park, opened in 1988. The park contains 2.5 km of trails, boardwalks, rest and view sites. Here you can see as many as 12 species of ducks, including teals and mallards, and rarer kinds such as northern shovelers and American wigeon.

The waterfowl park is a part of the surrounding Tantramar Marsh, one of four saltwater marshes that once covered the 2,000-km² region at the head of the Bay of Fundy. The marsh is the creation of Fundy's tides and a key to Sackville's history and folklore. The poet Sir Charles G. D. Roberts, who grew up at its edge, extolled the sounds of its "gossiping grass."

In the late 1600s, Acadian farmers reclaimed some 500 km² of marshland from the sea by building a system of 2.5-m-high earthen dikes—called *aboiteaux*. The dike gates opened at low tide to release river water and closed at high tide to shut out tides from the Bay of Fundy. The Acadians transformed the reclaimed land into hayfield. At one time, the Tantramar Marsh was said to be the world's largest hayfield.

During the late 1700s, settlers from Yorkshire and New England gave the region its present name. Tantramar is an anglicized version of the Acadian *tintamarre*, which describes the din of the thousands of ducks and geese that nest in the marsh. The region is a stopover on the Atlantic flyway.

One of the best views of the Tantramar Marsh is from High Marsh Road, about 4.5 km east of Sackville. From the roadside, you can look across the marsh to the weathered hay barns and a covered bridge.

Fort Beauséjour National Historic Site offers another fine view of the Tantramar Marsh. The site is located at Aulac, some 8 km east of Sackville on Trans-Canada Highway 2. It has remnants of Fort Beauséjour, built by the French (1751-1755) and captured by the British, who maintained it until after the War of 1812. The original French installation was restored when the fort became a national historic site in 1926. *Admission free. Open daily, July to Labor Day, 9 am to 5 pm; May 15 to June 30 and September 8 to October 15, 9 am to 5 pm.*

Special events

Marshland Frolics (June)

New Brunswick Fiddling Championships (June)

Atlantic Waterfowl Celebration (August)

Altantic Regional Duck Calling Championship (August)

Fundy

The Bay of Fundy stretches northeast for more than 200 km from the Gulf of Maine into Chignecto Bay and Minas Basin. Burntcoat Head, on the Nova Scotia side of the bay, is credited with the world's highest tides—a 16-m difference between high and low water. And although tides are somewhat smaller on the New Brunswick side, they still rank among the world's most awesome phenomena.

In the upper bay, these tides have created extensive salt marshes, vast low-tide mud flats, and a shoreline sculpted into sea caves and sea stacks. Fundy National Park contains samples of all these features.

Life is difficult for Fundy's beach creatures. As the water retreats farther and farther down the shore at low tide, the beach begins to dry. Periwinkle snails hide in mats of seaweeds, and rock crabs shelter in the tidal pools among silver-spotted sea anemones and pink coralline algae. Mops of knot-wrack and bladder wrack—types of seaweed common in this part of the bay—crown each rounded boulder like wet toupees.

Fundy's wide gravel flats may look devoid of life, but in the sand and under the rocks is a marine zoo. Clams hide beneath the surface of the sand--only the holes of their feeding siphons give away their whereabouts. Marine worms dig through the mud in search of prey, or build colonies with protective sandy spires.

Colonies of small barnacles form white crusts on beach boulders to which they stay anchored for life. Hidden among them are small black snails called periwinkles, tracing trails of slime over every surface they cross. They feed on the algae that coat the rocks.

The tides that mold the shoreline have another effect that is felt far inland. In summer, the cold water of the bay cools the entire coastal area, and fog regularly drifts up river valleys, reaching white fingers inland. There it encourages a lush growth of the lichens seen on trees and the ferns and mosses found on the cliffsides. Red spruce, balsam fir, white fir, yellow birch, sugar and red maples thrive in the cool humid conditions. Pine grows naturally here.

The interior of Fundy National Park is a 335-m-high plateau, where the heavy forest is broken by the odd blue lake, beaver pond, and green bog. Three main rivers drain these highlands—the Upper Salmon, the Goose, and the Point Wolfe. Damp crevices and gravelly ledges of rock walls towering high above these rivers are home to an unusual array of plants. Green spleenwort, yellow-flowered shrubby cinquefoil, primitive low selaginella and mountain club moss, dwarf bilberry with its tart, apple-flavored fruit, and a variety of grasses, sedges, and rushes are living relics of the Arctic conditions that prevailed after the last Ice Age.

During the 1800s the area that is now the park was settled and logged. Men and horses hauled the felled trees to the waterways. Any logjams that occurred enroute were broken up by men wielding peaveys. Often these men risked their lives. Colorful names were given to such difficult and dangerous sections of the region's rivers: the Keyhole on the Point Wolfe River; the Match Factory on the Forty-five River; and Hell's Gate at the confluence of the East Branch and Point Wolfe rivers.

Atlantic salmon were once plentiful in these rivers, but logging dams and mill wastes cut them off from their spawning grounds. Overfishing and poaching further reduced fish populations. In 1948, when the park was established, its rivers were barren of salmon. By 1952, the dam on the Upper Salmon River had fallen apart, and stray salmon from nearby rivers quickly moved in. During 1985, the old logging dam at the mouth of the Point Wolfe River was opened. Adult salmon—introduced as fingerlings several years before—fought their way upstream to spawning beds unused for 150 years.

Point Wolfe emerges through the trees lining a boardwalk at Fundy Park.

PARK INFORMATION
Access: Highway 114 intersects the park.
Visitors' centre: At the park entrance near Alma.
Accommodations: Hostel, motel rooms, housekeeping units, year-round camping, restaurant, book and craft shops, playground.
Summer activities: Interpretive services, evening programs (slide shows, music, and drama), campfire programs, guided walks, hiking, golfing, boating, lawn bowling, swimming, tennis, fishing, mountain biking, picnicking, bird-watching.
Winter activities: Tobogganing, snowshoeing, cross-country skiing.

PRINCE EDWARD ISLAND

20

PRINCE EDWARD
ISLAND

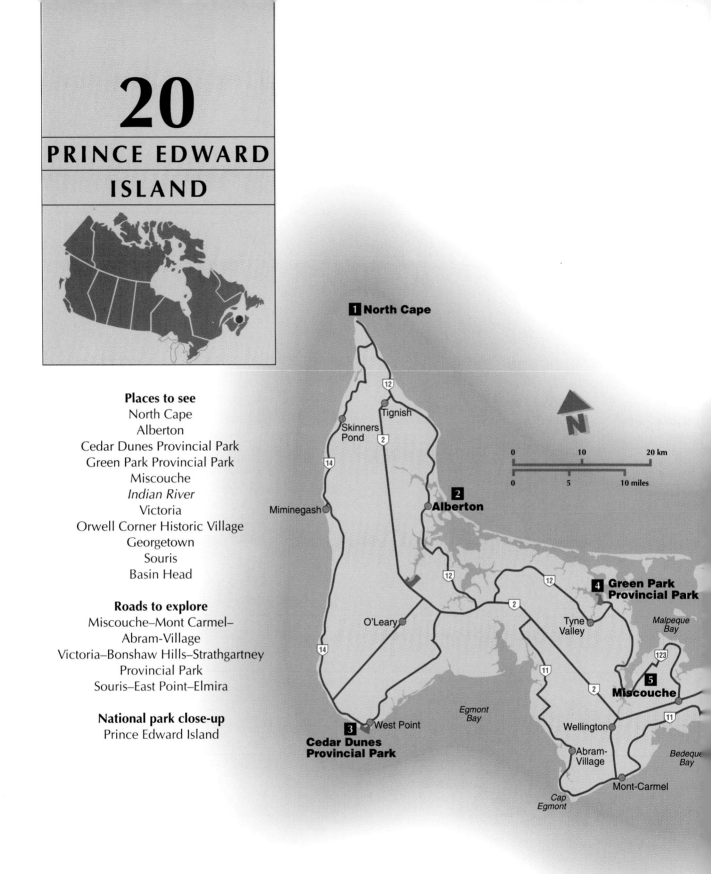

Places to see
North Cape
Alberton
Cedar Dunes Provincial Park
Green Park Provincial Park
Miscouche
Indian River
Victoria
Orwell Corner Historic Village
Georgetown
Souris
Basin Head

Roads to explore
Miscouche–Mont Carmel–
Abram-Village
Victoria–Bonshaw Hills–Strathgartney
Provincial Park
Souris–East Point–Elmira

National park close-up
Prince Edward Island

Previous pages:
Cousin's Shore, west of New London Bay

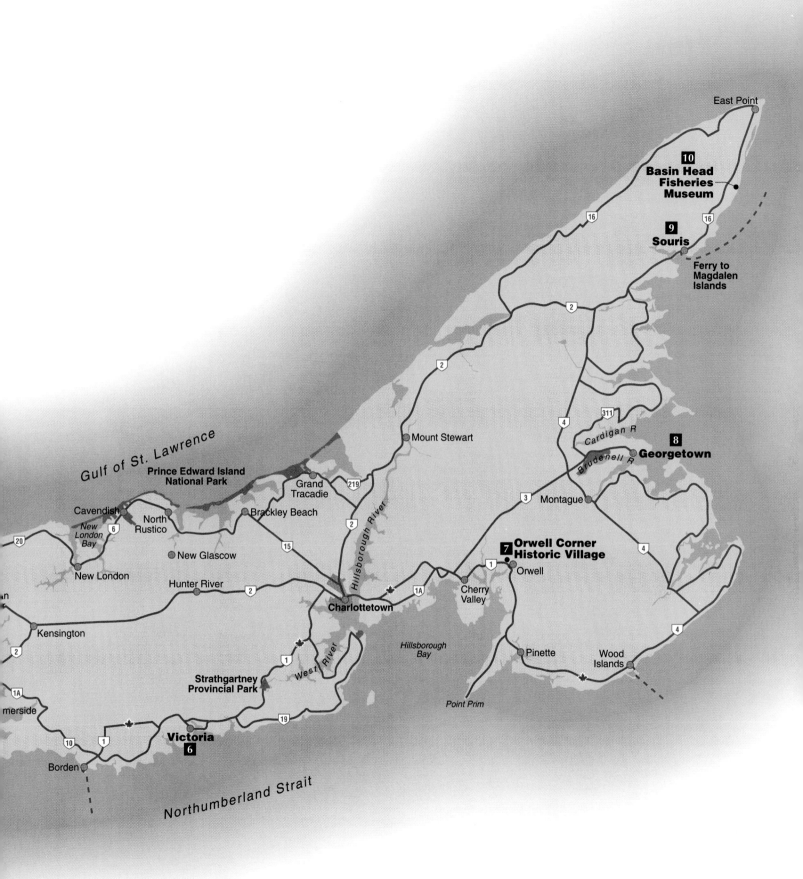

East Point

10
Basin Head
Fisheries
Museum

16

16

9
Souris

Ferry to
Magdalen
Islands

2

2

311

4

Cardigan R.

8

Brudenell R.

Georgetown

Mount Stewart

Prince Edward Island
National Park

Grand
Tracadie

219

3

Montague

4

Gulf of St. Lawrence

Cavendish

North
Rustico

Brackley Beach

_New
London
Bay_

6

New Glasgow

15

2

7 **Orwell Corner**
Historic Village

Orwell

20

New London

Hunter River

2

Charlottetown

1A

Cherry
Valley

4

Kensington

1

West River

Hillsborough River

Hillsborough Bay

Pinette

Wood
Islands

2

Strathgartney
Provincial Park

1A

19

Point Prim

merside

10

1

Victoria
6

Borden

Northumberland Strait

1 North Cape

✳ 📷

One of the longest natural rock reefs in the world is formed where the Gulf of St. Lawrence and the Northumberland Strait meet, at North Cape, the windy northernmost point of Prince Edward Island.

The 19-m-high North Cape lighthouse sends its signal 32 km across the gulf and the strait, alerting mariners to the presence of the reef. The beacon has safeguarded shipping this way since 1866.

Before the lighthouse was built, many ships foundered on the reef and disappeared without a trace. The "Ghost Ship of the Strait" continues to haunt the waters off North Cape. Many Islanders say they have seen it. Others claim they have tried to photograph it or to rescue the crew jumping from the sides of the burning vessel, but without success.

The reef is actually two reefs 60 m apart, reaching 1.6 km out to sea. During low tide you can walk out for about 80 m on the rocks. Seals often play in nearby waters, and the sea life washed up on the reef at low tide attracts plenty of waterfowl.

Below the restaurant beside the lighthouse is an interpretive centre, which displays local artifacts and tells the history of the area.

From the cliff tops, visitors can watch fishermen on horses, raking Irish moss from the beaches. This seaweed contains carrageenan, an emulsifier used in products such as ice cream, toothpaste and cough syrup. Almost half the world's supply of Irish moss comes from Prince Edward Island.

The Irish Moss Interpretive Centre at Miminegash, on Route 152, was once a fishing vessel. Now it provides slide shows and photographic displays that detail the history and processing of Irish moss. *Admission free. Open Monday to Friday, late June to late August, 9 am to 5 pm.*

The continuous wind at North Cape makes it an ideal site for wind testing. The Atlantic Wind Test Site, at the north end of Route 12, is Canada's national laboratory for wind energy research and development. Guides on the premises explain the details of the state-of-the-art wind turbines used to test wind generators as alternative energy sources. *Open daily, early July to late August, 10 am to 8 pm.*

2 Alberton

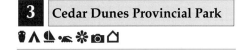

This community on scenic Route 136 is of great historical interest. In 1534, Jacques Cartier's first landing in what is now Canada was at Canoe River, where Alberton stands today. The town was named in honor of Albert Edward, Prince of Wales, who visited Prince Edward Island in 1860.

Seven churches provide services for just 1,000 residents in Alberton. The Church of the Sacred Heart is one of the most interesting. It was built in 1972 after the original 1879 church was destroyed by fire, and contains some features from the old church: a part of the altar rail, the large cross on top of the church and the smaller cross above the front entry, and the altar slab, which bears the marks of broadaxes early settlers used to hew it.

In the early 20th century, Alberton was the centre of the silver fox breeding industry. The families who bred these rare animals built elegant homes, known as "fox houses." One stands at the foot of Poplar Street. The sprawling three-story building, built around 1912, still has its original woodwork. During the summer, it is run as a bed-and-breakfast.

Behind the house are some disused fox pens, and a barn that was once the Alberton Museum. The barn became too small to accommodate the growing

Harvesting the ocean's crop, workers gather Irish moss from the rocky shores near Tignish.

collection, and a new museum was opened on Church Street, in 1980, to house it. The building was once the courthouse, built in 1878.

The new museum contains a photographic display of fox farming, as well as domestic artifacts, farm implements, books, and photographs that illustrate the history of Alberton and its inhabitants. *Open daily, except Sunday, late June to Labor Day, 9:30 am to 5:30 pm.*

On Prince William Street is Leavitt's Maple Tree Craft, where skilled craftsmen work with choice woods such as Maritime bird's-eye maple, sugar maple and curly birch, making items for sale. Visitors may wander through the workshop watching the craftsmen at work.

> **Special events**
> Prince County Exhibition
> (late August)

3 Cedar Dunes Provincial Park

At West Point, a black-and-white striped lighthouse rises above the shore of Northumberland Strait, red sand lapping at its doorstep. It is the landmark of Cedar Dunes Provincial Park, which stretches almost 2 km along the coast. The park has facilities for camping and picnicking, a supervised beach and a nature trail. Half of the park is a provincial natural area. It has old cedar trees and, on its sand dunes, rare species of plants. *Open late June to early September.*

The 21-m-high lighthouse, one of the tallest on Prince Edward Island, was built in 1875. Today, atop its distinctive shingled, tapering square tower, a modern electric light operates automatically.

Inside the lighthouse, artifacts and photographs document the history of the Island's lighthouses, concentrating mainly on the West Point light. The second floor and the Keeper's Quarters on the third floor have been turned into bedrooms for visitors—the lighthouse has nine guest rooms. Antiques and crafts decorate the rooms and museum. West Point is Canada's only active coast guard lighthouse with guest rooms. Reservations are recommended. *Open daily, mid-May to early October, 8 am to 9:30 pm. Museum admission free for diners and overnight guests.*

The building attached to the lighthouse is now a restaurant that serves Prince Edward Island's famous lobster in the shell, West Point lobster stew and steaming bowls of Island chowder.

The West Point lighthouse is a protective presence on Cedar Dunes' red sand shores.

The annual West Point Lighthouse Festival, held every third weekend in July, includes a lobster boat race. The winner receives the coveted silver Atkinson Trophy. It is said that a young Island girl, Isobel Milligan, moved to the United States more than 40 years ago, to work as a maid in a rich man's house. She married the wealthy man, a Mr. Atkinson, and later returned to the Island to donate the silver cup as top prize for the beloved boat races she remembered so well from her youth.

The festivities also include a porch party at the lighthouse, where local Islanders sing, dance, and play musical instruments.

4 Green Park Provincial Park

Take a step back into the 19th century at Green Park Provincial Park. The park preserves a shipbuilding museum and shipyard, and the gracious 19th-century home of the shipyard's wealthy owner, James Yeo.

In 1819 James Yeo was an unemployed North Devon laborer. Facing starvation at home, he emigrated to Prince Edward Island and found work in a shipyard. Between 1836 and 1890 he and his sons, William, James, and John, built 325 vessels, many of them at Green Park. When he died in 1867, a merchant, landowner, and politician, he was the richest man on the Island.

The museum exhibits ship rigs, sail making, knot tying, and information on trade routes. Films are also shown, including *Passage West*, the story of James Yeo's career.

Down at the shore is a replica of the shipyard. A partial reconstruction of a 200-tonne brigantine rests there, its keel, stemposts and sternposts ready in place, waiting for framing. The yard has two sawpits, where two workmen would have cut rough timber into 10-cm planks with long, two-handled pit saws. The man in the pit would provide the power for the cut while his partner on top guided the saw. A steam box in the yard was where the wood for the hull was soaked, to shape or curve it. The blacksmith's shop was where laborer's tools, such as axes, sledges, and hammers, were repaired.

The Yeo House, originally built by James Yeo, Jr., has been restored to its 1865 condition. Its tall centre gable, decorative eave trim, exotic cupola and veranda are typical of the mid-19th-century home. Inside, it is furnished in the style of the time.

From the third floor, adventurous visitors can climb the ladder to the windowed octagonal cupola that straddles the steeply pitched roof. The view from there is impressive; you can see,

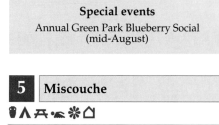

An exotic cupola crowning the gracious 1865 Yeo House encloses a widow's walk.

just as James Yeo must have done, clear to the shore where the shipyards once buzzed with activity. *Open daily, mid-June to Labor Day, 9 am to 5 pm.*

Special events
Annual Green Park Blueberry Social (mid-August)

5 Miscouche

🍴🏕️⛱️🚤✳️⛺

Soaring above Miscouche (pop. 672) are the 26-m-high twin spires of its flamboyant St. John the Baptist Church. This High Victorian, Gothic Revival church, built in only two years, from 1890 to 1892, has a lovely arched window over the main entry, and striking hood moldings over the doors. In-

---

Roads to explore: Where the flag of Acadia flies

Distance (approx.): 65 km/40 miles

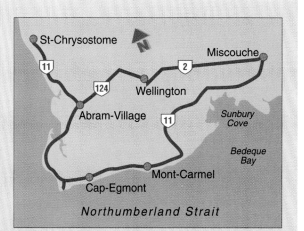

Miscouche is the starting point of this drive. Take Route 11 out of the village. Along the way, look for the Acadian flag, the French tricolor with the gold star of the Virgin on the blue stripe, which flies proudly throughout this region.

● Near Mont Carmel, the imposing twin-steepled church of Notre-Dame de Mont-Carmel, overlooks the Northumberland Strait. It is unusual in the area, being made of brick and set on a stone foundation. It was built in 1896 to replace two earlier wooden structures that burned down.

Acadian mailbox, Mont Carmel

MARTIN GALLANT

● At Mont Carmel is the Acadian Pioneer Village. A reconstructed settlement of the 1820s, it has a chapel, school, blacksmith's forge, general store, and house, all made from logs. Even the chapel's altar, candlesticks and tabernacle are fashioned from logs—Acadians had few luxuries. The Acadian restaurant at the entrance to the village serves dishes such as *fricot au poulet* (a robust chicken stew), *pâté* (a meat pie), *blé d'Inde lessivé* (hominy corn), and desserts such as *poutines à trou* (balls of pastry stuffed with apples, cranberries and raisins, served with hot sugar sauce). *The village and restaurant are open daily, mid-June to mid-September, 9:30 am to 7 pm.*

● Continue on Route 11 to Cap Egmont, and the Bottle Houses. In the mid-1970s, a retired Acadian fisherman gathered 25,000 bottles in every shape, size, and color, and with them built a chapel with an altar and pews, a six-gabled house, and a tavern. *Open daily, early to late June and early September to Labor Day, 10 am to 6 pm; late June to early September, 9 am to 7 pm.*

● Sweep north to Abram-Village, named for Abraham Arsenault, the first French settler in the district. Every year, the village hosts the Atlantic Fiddler's Jamboree, in August, and the Agricultural Exhibition and Acadian Festival, on Labor Day weekend, when the Acadians exercise their renowned musical talents and dancing skills.

● Continue on Route 11, along Egmont Bay, to the St. Chrysostome Cedar Natural Area. This 10-ha stand of original Acadian forest contains mature eastern and white cedar, white ash and white elm. The area is low-lying and wet, so wear waterproof shoes or boots.

● Return to Miscouche on Route 124, through Urbainville and Wellington.

Prince Edward Island

The whoosh and crash of breaking waves permeates Prince Edward Island National Park, a 40-km strip along the island's north shore. The park beaches are wide open to southwesterly winds. In summer, these waft by as cooling breezes; in fall, winter, and early spring they tear through the park, pushing and twisting plants and sand into new, contorted configurations.

The park encompasses sandstone cliffs, sand beaches, and rows of dunes, some soaring 18 m high. The cliffs are rusty red, colored by an oxidized iron compound, hematite. Waves, tides, and coastal currents continually reshape the beaches, alternately carrying sand out to sea and flinging it back ashore. A narrow strip of primary coastal dunes is battened down by marram grass, the sand-loving plant whose network of stringy roots anchors the mounds of sand by penetrating them as much as 6 m deep in its search for water.

But even dunes so stabilized cannot withstand heavy traffic. A footprint may seem to damage only a few blades of grass, but the slight impression it leaves can imperil an entire dune. Strong winds can now blow away the sand in the footprint and around its rim, enlarging the depression, exposing roots, and carrying away plants holding the dune together. Before long, the original depression becomes a giant hole, or "blowout." A cluster of blowouts can turn stable dunes into constantly shifting hills that drift inland. Regular blowouts contribute to the dune system's average migration speed of 1 m a year.

You can find a good example of dune migration at Blooming Point, a sandspit some 5 km long at the eastern end of the park where the dunes rise up 20 m or more. Blackened tree stumps poke through the beach sand, relics of a small forest that flourished there some 100 years ago but became a victim of the moving sand.

Blooming Point has another interesting feature: dunes coated with lichens, which are the symbiotic combination of two distinct species, an alga and a fungus. The life span of these lichens is counted in centuries; each year's growth is measured in millimetres. The hardy lichens can thrive on a minimum of nutrients and resist the most harsh weather. But the fragility of the dunes is their downfall; footsteps across a lichen-covered dune can crush decades of growth.

Wild roses, Blooming Point

Freshwater ponds and salt marshes

Some migrating dunes occasionally seal the entry to a bay or harbor, and create an enclosed pond or marsh. Only meltwater and rain replenish the water, diluting its salinity over time, thus creating a freshwater pond.

Where freshwater and saltwater wetlands are backed by fields and woods, a wide variety of bird life flourishes. Close to 300 species have been counted in the park. Whimbrels, Caspian terns, dowitchers, plovers, and sandpipers populate the beaches, sandbars, and marshes. Great blue herons with their tapering bills, snakelike necks, and impressive wingspreads are seldom out of view. The park shelters nearly 2 percent of the world's piping plover, an endangered species. This diminutive, hard-to-see shorebird lives above the high tidemark on beaches.

Prince Edward Island is too densely populated to support large animals, although foxes find adequate space and isolation within the park. Referred to as king of the dunes, the red fox burrows into sand for denning and protection. You can easily spot pups in spring and early summer when they are too young to have developed the adult fox's wariness. You may also occasionally see a silver fox wending its way through dune shrubbery. In the early 1900s two ranchers succeeded in breeding silver fox, giving birth to a pelt industy that thrived until recent years.

The first people appeared in this area some 1,500 years ago. Several nomadic tribes have passed through since; the last group, prior to the Europeans' arrival, was the Micmac, in the 15th century. One of their preferred camping sites was on Rustico Island. Waves there still uncover buried heaps of shells—remnants of the clams, oysters, mussels, and limpets that were a standard part of the Micmac's basic seafood diet.

The first European settlers in the park region were two Acadian families. British farmers moved in in the late 1700s. In 1851, a ferocious storm lashed the area, claiming hundreds of men and dozens of fishing schooners. Most of the dead were American sailors and legend has it that a local farmer gathered their bodies from what is now Stanhope Beach. He ferried them by horse-drawn cart to the old Stanhope Cemetery, where he buried them, marking their graves with the pieces of sandstone that remain to this day.

Spiky clumps of marram grass rustle in the sea breezes on the dunes of Brackley Beach, Prince Edward Island National Park.

By the late 1800s, the area's beaches were attracting American tourists from the northeastern states, and facilities were built to accommodate them. Shaw's Hotel bordering the park and park-owned Dalvay-by-the-Sea, a privately run hotel, both date from that elegant era. Dalvay-by-the-Sea was converted from a sprawling Victorian mansion built in 1896 as a summer home by Alexander MacDonald, a business associate of John D. Rockefeller.

The Cavendish Beach area developed its own élan during the same period, and had a reputation as a culturally progressive community. Lucy Maud Montgomery (1874-1942) launched her writing career while living with her grandmother at Cavendish. In 1908 she published her most famous work, *Anne of Green Gables*, still a best-selling children's story. The author set her tale at a nearby farm that belonged to some elderly cousins. Green Gables House, at the western end of the park, is now preserved. Visitors enjoy prowling its halls and imagining how the boisterous Anne, probably the best-loved character in all Canadian fiction, lived. It is open daily from mid-May to October. Places such as Anne's Babbling Brook, Haunted Woods, and Lovers' Lane are nearby. Miss Montgomery is buried in the adjoining Cavendish cemetery. Anne was the heroine in many of her 23 books.

Harvesting the gulf

From any beach in the park, and at any time of day, you might see bright white and pastel-hued fishing boats dotting the Gulf of St. Lawrence. These are cape islanders, and just about any fish or crustacean in the gulf, including lobster, mackerel, and giant bluefin tuna, is hauled aboard these craft.

PARK INFORMATION
Access: From Highway 6 at Cavendish, North Rustico, Stanhope, and Dalvay; and Highway 15 at Brackley.
Visitors' centres: Cavendish and the Dalvay Administration Office.
Accommodation and other facilities: Campgrounds at Cavendish, Rustico Island, and Stanhope; group tenting at Brackley. Hotel accommodation. Food services available in summer at Dalvay-by-the-Sea Hotel, Green Gables Golf Course Club House, and canteens at Stanhope Lane Beach, Brackley Beach, and Cavendish Main Beach. Interpretive programs.
Summer activities: Swimming, picnicking, hiking, cycling, bird-watching, tennis.
Winter activities: Cross-country skiing at Cavendish, Stanhope, and Dalvay; skating at Dalvay; snowshoeing at Cavendish, Rustico Island, Brackley, and Dalvay.

side, the soft hues from stained-glass windows bathe the handsome pews carved from ash and walnut.

Visit the Acadian Museum of Prince Edward Island, which documents the history of Acadians on the Island. These were French settlers from Nova Scotia who made their home in this region in the early 18th century. Dioramas, carpentry and farming tools, antique furniture, manuscripts, photographs, textiles, and a video presen-

tation describe the life of these people. When the settlers were deported to France and Louisiana by Britain in 1758, about 30 or so families went into hiding on the island. Portraits of many of them hang in the museum, and most of the Acadians on the island today are descended from them. The museum is also a research centre for Acadian genealogy. *Open year-round, Monday to Friday, 9:30 am to 5 pm; June to Labor Day, also Sunday, 1 to 5 pm.*

An elaborate Gothic portal welcomes worshipers and visitors to the Victorian-style St. John the Baptist Church at Miscouche.

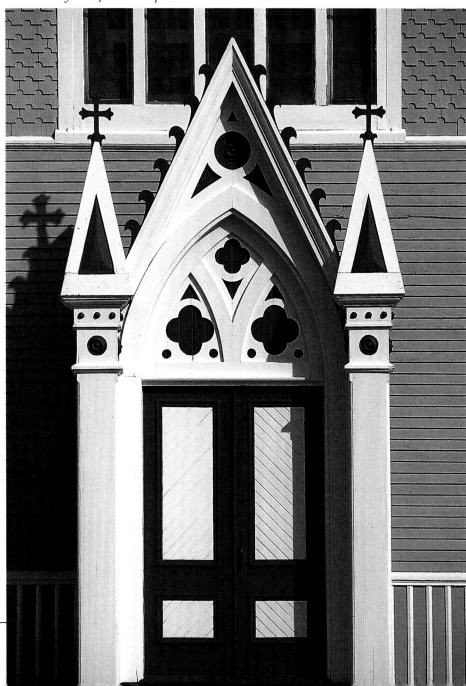

WHITE SHINGLES AND BLACK TRIM

The community of Indian River takes its name from the Micmac who lived in this area of tidal flats and low hills until 1935. Now, less than 100 people live here. Yet Indian River is still worth passing through for its magnificent St. Mary's Catholic Church, a white-painted, shingled building with its eaves and trim picked out in black.

The church, built in 1902, is a stunning interpretation of the Gothic Revival style. Its designer, William Critchlow Harris, was the most influential architect in Prince Edward Island in Victorian times. He designed 20 churches, 16 of which are still standing. St. Mary's is the largest wooden church on the Island.

An apostle of St. Mary's spire, Indian River

An impressive 39-m spire tops the round, four-staged church tower. The octagonal spire has a band of arched niches at its base. Each niche contains a hand-carved statue of one of the 12 apostles.

Harris also designed the interior of his churches. The intricate vaulted ceiling of St. Mary's Church supports the roof above the nave. The contrast between its dark cherry wood and the white pine of the church furniture gives the interior an air of simplicity and warmth. The neo-Gothic altar in the east chancel is another interior feature designed by Harris. The acoustics are excellent.

Concerts are held in the church every week during the summer.

6 Victoria

🏕️⛵🚣☀️⛺

This peaceful seaside village on the south shore of Prince Edward Island is still as charming as it was in the early 1800s. Victoria (pop. 200), having been designed in 1855 with a symmetrical, rectangular layout, is one of the few planned villages on the island. Its streets are shaded by large trees and lined with homes built before, or very early in, this century.

In the 1920s and 30s, steamers sailed from Charlottetown carrying vacationers on day-trips to Victoria. Those who wanted to stay longer could always book in at the Orient Hotel, at the top of Main Street. It was established around 1900 with 22 guest rooms. Guest books from 1926 to 1953 reveal that the hotel's guests once included vaudeville artists, prohibition officers, and even members of the Italian Air Force, whose planes were forced down in Victoria in 1933. The hotel has only eight guest rooms now.

For the last 100 years, boats sailing into Victoria's harbor have depended on the Palmer's Range Lighthouse to guide them safely into port. The light, at the entrance to the village, is still working. Visitors can climb to the top of the lighthouse or view the collection of historical photographs of Victoria in the Victoria Seaport Museum, also in the lighthouse. *Open daily except Monday, early July to early September, 12 pm to 5 pm. Admission free.*

The number of old stores is evidence of Victoria's prosperous past. The Wright Brother's Store, which was built in 1880, now houses a chocolate shop and a craft shop.

Brien's store, warehouse, and wharf were built in 1874. The building was once a bonded warehouse and was for many years the Victoria Customs House. It is now a private home, although the store has been kept in its original state. The remains of the wharf, behind the warehouse, can still be seen at low tide.

Early photos of the Victoria Village Inn show that it too was once a store. It has since been converted into a house,

---

Roads to explore: In the beautiful Bonshaw Hills

Distance (approx.): 97 km / 60 miles

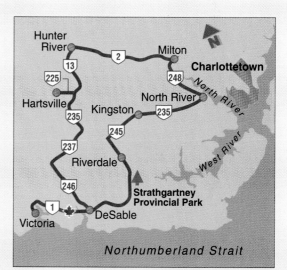

Drive east out of Victoria, across Victoria Harbour. Turn east onto the Trans-Canada Highway and continue some 4 km to DeSable.

● Take Route 246, the South Melville Road, going north. When you reach the top of the first hill, pull over to the shoulder and look to the west, out over the water. On a clear day this breathtaking view can stretch right across Northumberland Strait to the mainland.

● Turn right on Route 237, a clay road bordered by hardwoods, softwoods, and ferns. At times, the branches of the trees meet overhead to form a canopy. The road was built in 1862 and is one of the many clay roads in Queen's County.

● At the end of the road, turn north onto Route 235, which joins Route 13 about

A cottage garden in summer, Victoria

2 km along and winds through hills toward Hartsville. Near the north end of Route 13 there has been some forestry cutting and replanting, which provides a good opportunity to see some of the forestry management practices used on the Island. From here, drive on to the village of Hunter River.

● The village is in the very heart of the Bonshaw Hills and lies at the bottom of a steep river valley. The view from any of the hills around the perimeter of Hunter River is beautiful. In the village is a large working dairy farm, which doubles as a bed-and-breakfast.

● Turn east in Hunter River onto Route 2 and travel about 11 km through hills and past farms, to Milton. Head south on Route 248 to North River.

● Take a detour left onto the Trans-Canada Highway, to the causeway at North River. At many times of the year, particularly during the spring and fall migrations, the causeway is visited by many different types of waterfowl. Black ducks, goldeneye, Canada geese, and merganser are common here. Loons have been sighted as well. This is a popular feeding area for the great blue heron, and at dawn and dusk it is not unusual to see these majestic birds fishing or flying overhead.

● Return to Route 248 and turn west on Route 235, passing through Kingston. Turn south on Route 245 to Riverdale and on to Churchill, until the road meets the Trans-Canada Highway.

● Almost directly opposite this intersection is Strathgartney Provincial Park. The park borders the West River, which is excellent for canoeing or fishing. A lookout on the highway above the park has a fine view of the meandering West River.

● Continue west along the Trans-Canada Highway through Bonshaw and back to DeSable where the sandstone cliffs of the South Shore can be clearly seen.

Palmer's Range Lighthouse, more than a century old, guides sailors into Victoria's harbor and also serves as a museum.

suitably decorated in Victorian style, and is open to guests in summer.

The Victoria Playhouse, which today hosts plays, concerts, and special events, was built in 1914 by Wil Bradley, a noted local artisan. It was renovated in 1985. *Open late June to Labor Day.*

7 | **Orwell Corner Historic Village**

🍴🏕️❗🐟❄️

Walking into Orwell Corner Historic Village you may feel you have stepped back in time. Local inhabitants dressed in period costume work in the village just as the Scottish and Irish settlers did here in the late 19th century. They re-create a rural way of life that has vanished from Prince Edward Island.

In the shingle mill, an exhibition tells how men felled trees with bucksaws and axes, cut them into logs, and cleaved them into shingles to cover and protect roofs and walls from the elements. Today, equipment of the early 1900s is still used here.

At Orwell Corner, the blacksmith not only shod horses and made and repaired farm tools, he also did a bit of horse trading, advised on animal care, and when necessary, served as the community's dentist.

The general store carried everything from fabrics to fuel and bulk foods. Eggs, oats, butter, and even horsehair were brought by the farmers to the merchant in exchange for the goods he sold. The store still has its long wooden counters topped with jars of sweets, wooden cases for flour and salt, and kegs for nails.

Down the hall from the store is the post office, which was run by Dennis Clarke, the store owner's brother. The store and post office were built onto the Clarke's farmhouse, which is furnished just as if the Clarkes were still living there.

The community met in the large hall for social events and still does. In summer, these gatherings—called ceilidhs (pronounced *kaylees*), from the time of the first Scottish settlers—are held there every week on Wednesday evenings, when singers, dancers, and musicians get together for an evening of entertainment.

The Orwell Corner School, which opened in 1895, is a typical little red shingled schoolhouse. The single classroom, lit by small paned windows, still contains wooden desks bolted to the floor, the teacher's desk and a potbellied wood stove.

Scottish Presbyterians were the first religious group to settle in Orwell. In 1861 they built

Barnyard scene, Orwell Corner

St. Andrew's Presbyterian Church; services were held in Gaelic and English.

Open daily, late June to Labor Day, 9 am to 5 pm; mid-May to late June and Labor Day to mid-October, Monday to Friday, 10 am to 3 pm.

Special events
Draft Horse Show (early July)
Strawberry Fair (mid-July)
Scottish Festival and Highland Games (late August)

8 | Georgetown

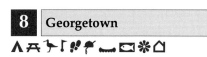

This capital of King's County lies at the end of a peninsula flanked by the mouths of the Brudenell and Cardigan rivers. Georgetown's broad streets lined with elegant old houses and more recent buildings make it a fittingly graceful place for its 716 residents.

The French, Scots, Irish, and English settlers who came to Georgetown left it with a superb architectural heritage.

Oil lamps, china and other goods of bygone days crowd Orwell Corner's general store.

A short distance into the town you will come upon the courthouse, one of the largest stone buildings in King's County. The cornerstone was laid on June 21, 1886, to commemorate Queen Victoria's Golden Jubilee. The courthouse was designed by the Island's principal architect, William Critchlow Harris (1854-1913), who also worked on St. Mary's Catholic Church at Indian River. Court is still held in the Georgetown courthouse several days each week. The King's Playhouse is next door. This 1983 reconstruction of the original 19th-century King's Theatre was also designed by Harris.

The Fanning House, on Water Street East, was built in the 1830s. Its roof has a low gable at the front, typical of houses of this style. (Georgetown has more than 50 houses with front gables of this type.) Most of the windows still have their original glass.

Georgetown's first church was Holy Trinity Anglican Church, completed in 1839. It is a simple structure, with one battlemented square tower with corner finials, and nave windows with Gothic tracery. The P.E.I. Brass Rubbing Centre is in the church basement. Centre visitors can make their own rubbings from facsimiles of medieval brasses of knights and ladies found in European churches. *Admission free. Open late June to late August, Monday to Friday, 10 am to 5 pm; Saturday and Sunday, 1 to 5 pm; or by request year-round. (Also in the basement is the Holy George English Tea Room, where you can enjoy a cup of tea with homemade bread and jam and cakes.)*

The nearby shorelines of the Brudenell and Cardigan rivers offer quiet walks and peaceful fishing spots.

Special events
Georgetown Summer Days (early July)

9 | Souris

In the early 1700s, Souris began as a base for French fishermen who crossed the Atlantic each spring to fish off the coast. Souris (French for mouse) was named after a plague of mice emerged from the forest and devoured settlers' crops, stored grain and cattle feed.

Fishing boats tie up at Georgetown harbor, one of the finest natural harbors in Canada.

Souris harbor shelters fishing and lobster boats and the ferry to the far-off Îles de la Madeleine.

Fishing is still a major resource for this community of 1500. As many as 50 draggers and lobster boats tie up each day at the local wharf from early spring to late fall.

Within walking distance from the wharf is the town's oldest church, St. Mary's, built of red Island sandstone. By the early 19th century a number of Catholic people had settled along the nearby shores. The first mass at St. Mary's was held in January 1839. The church was rebuilt twice, the last time in September 1930, as we see it today.

The sprawling Matthew House Inn on Breakwater Street overlooks the harbor. This three-story house, one of the town's first large homes, was built more than 100 years ago for Uriah Matthew, a merchant. Now an inn, it still has many of its original features, and contains period art and furniture.

The old Souris post office and customs office on Main Street is now the town hall. The exterior of the building, made from red Island sandstone, remains much the same as when it was built in 1905.

Souris spreads along the coastline of the Gulf of St. Lawrence, with stretches of white sandy beaches ideal for walking, swimming, or beachcombing. The sand in this area squeaks when you walk on it, due to its high silica content. The harbor is excellent for aquatic sports, as is the Souris River for canoeing and kayaking. A car ferry sails 134 km from the harbor to the Magdalen Islands (Îles de la Madeleine).

> ### Special events
> Souris Regatta (late July)
> Eastern Kings Exhibition
> (late August)

10　Basin Head

🍴 ⛺ 🚻 🦞 🐟 🦭 ✳️

The Basin Head Fisheries Museum lies just off Route 16, near Kingsboro, and overlooks Northumberland Strait. A

museum building, boat sheds, a box factory, and a cannery by a wharf contain displays that document the centuries-old history of fishing in the eastern part of the Island.

Roads to explore: Towering forests, swirling tides
Distance: 76.5 km/48 miles

Head northeast on Route 16 from Souris and then on Route 305, to the intersection of the abandoned Harmony Junction rail line. About 2 km beyond this point, on the left-hand side of the road, is a single lane bordered by shrubs, leading to the Townshend Woodlot. Look carefully because the lane is not that conspicuous.

● Drive along the lane as far as possible —about 2 or 3 km. At the end of the lane, take a short walk to the right to what is believed to be the best remaining example of old-growth hardwood forest on the Island. Huge maples and beeches tower over ground plants such as the provincial flower, the stemless lady's slipper. Several types of ferns and orchids, as well as many birds, are found here. The area is managed by the provincial parks department. Visitors are asked to remember the adage: "Take only pictures, leave only footprints."

● Back on Route 305, continue to Hermanville. Turn right on Route 16, and follow the north shore through Campbell's Cove to North Lake, once the centre of tuna fishing on the Island. Now tuna are seen only occasionally in the offshore waters. The scenic coastal drive continues to the East Point lighthouse.

● At this easternmost tip of the Island the waters swirl where the Gulf of St. Lawrence meets the Northumberland Strait. It is not uncommon to see scoters, old-squaws, cormorants, and several different types of gulls here. Even an osprey occasionally hovers over the water, preparing to make a swift dive for a fish. Tour the 1867 light-

Lobster pots, East Point

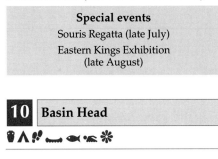

More than 10,000 years ago, Paleo-Indians came here to fish. They were followed some 8,000 years later by the Micmac, who left behind stone tools, exhibited in the museum.

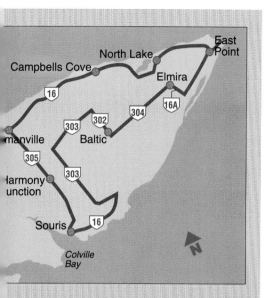

house and climb its 19.5-m-high octagonal tower. *Open daily, 10 am to 6 pm, early June to late September.*

● Continue along Route 16, then turn right onto Route 16A to visit the Elmira Train Museum. Trains no longer run on the Island but they were once an important part of Island life. Photographs of railway architecture, and schedules and fare books, chronicle the Island's railway history. *Open daily, 9 am to 5 pm, mid-June to Labor Day.*

● Take Route 304 to Baltic and turn right onto Route 302. About 3 km along, turn left along a scenic stretch of Route 303, known as Glen Road. Not far along this road a farmer's lane on the right leads into a field. Drive along the lane until you come to a path that enters the woods. This short path leads to a huge, spectacular elm, thought to be the largest tree on the Island.

● Continue along Glen Road, through the glen and onto the New Harmony Road (Route 303). In summer the road is overhung with a leafy canopy and makes a beautiful drive. On the left of the road is the New Harmony Demonstration Woodlot. Tour the site to learn about forestry practices on the Island.

● Route 303 intersects with Route 16, which will take you back to Souris.

Centuries later, French, Portuguese, and Basque fishermen sailed the Island waters. They fished for mackerel, cod, hake, herring, and smelts, and gathered oysters. Dioramas in the museum depict the fishermen at work.

From the late 1800s, the demand for lobster created a boom in canneries, and by 1903 there were 190 across the province, 53 of them in King's County. One of these canneries was the Smith Fish Cannery, which still stands near the wharf.

This cannery once processed salt fish and *chicken haddie* (canned hake), as well as lobster. Early canning equipment and labels are on display in the museum.

The boat sheds house a collection of fishing boats. In the early years, the dory was the most popular fishing

Nets, knots, rigging, old photographs, and a dory at Basin Head Fisheries Museum tell tales of life on the Atlantic a century ago.

craft, powered by a mast and sail as well as oars. It took a strong man to row a dory loaded with a day's catch back to shore. Today, these boats are pulled out only for the annual provincial dory-racing championships held in midsummer at Murray River.

When the larger, engine-powered fishing vessels were introduced, shelter and deeper water were needed. Basin Head's wharf-lined boat run was built in 1937 to accommodate them.

In the Salt Box Factory, wooden boxes were once made to pack the salt fish in. Now, local craftsmen make and sell replicas of these wooden boxes.

The museum is open daily, mid-June to Labor Day, 9 am to 5 pm. The Salt Box Factory is open Monday to Friday, March to November, and daily, July and August, 9 am to 5 pm.

Special events
Harvest of the Sea Festival
(August)

NOVA SCOTIA

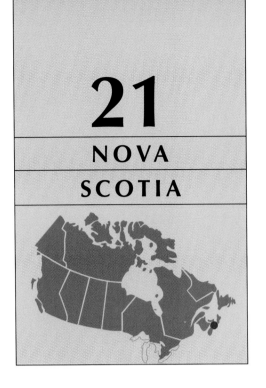

21

NOVA
SCOTIA

Places to see
Cape Sable Island
Digby
Long and Brier Islands
Bear River
Annapolis Royal
Port Royal National
Historic Park
Mahone Bay
Wolfville
Grand Pré National Historic Site
Cape Blomidon
Parrsboro
Musquodoboit Harbour
Pictou County
Isle Madame
St. Peters
Baddeck
Margaree Harbour
North East Margaree

Roads to explore
The French Shore:
Digby to Salmon River
Lunenberg to Peggy's Cove
Parrsboro to Joggins
Around Bras d'Or Lake

National park close-up
Kejimkujik
Cape Breton Highland

Previous pages:
Liscomb River, near Musquodoboit Harbour

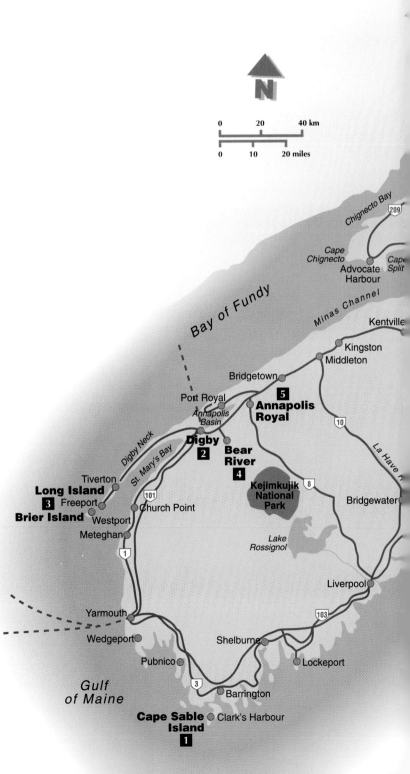

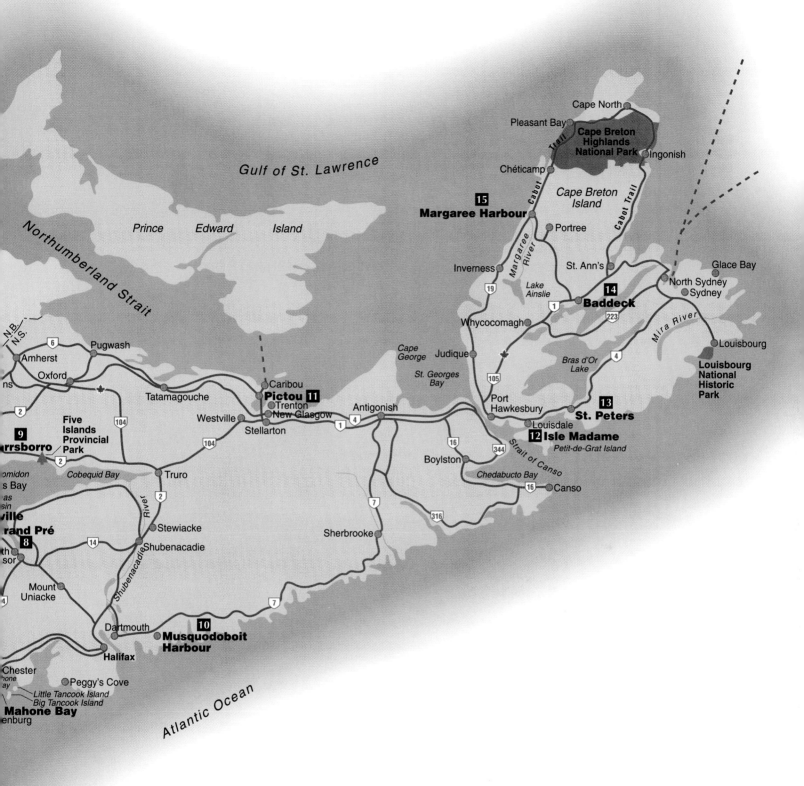

Gulf of St. Lawrence

Prince Edward Island

Northumberland Strait

Cape Breton Highlands National Park

Cape North

Pleasant Bay

Cape Breton Island

Chéticamp

Ingonish

15 **Margaree Harbour**

Portree

Margaree River

Inverness

St. Ann's

Glace Bay

North Sydney

Sydney

Lake Ainslie

14 **Baddeck**

19

1

223

Whycocomagh

Mira River

105

Louisbourg

4

Bras d'Or Lake

Cape George

Judique

St. Georges Bay

Louisbourg National Historic Park

N.B.
N.S.

6

Pugwash

Amherst

ns

Oxford

Caribou

Pictou **11**

Trenton

Antigonish

Port Hawkesbury

13 **St. Peters**

Tatamagouche

Westville

New Glasgow

Louisdale

104

Stellarton

1

4

12 **Isle Madame**

2

Petit-de-Grat Island

9
rrsborro

Five Islands Provincial Park

104

16

344

omidon
s Bay

Cobequid Bay

Truro

Boylston

Chedabucto Bay

as
sin

2

7

16

Canso

ville

River

Stewiacke

7

316

Sherbrooke

rand Pré

8

Shubenacadie

14

Shubenacadie River

th
sor

Mount Uniacke

4

Dartmouth

10 **Musquodoboit Harbour**

Halifax

Chester

Peggy's Cove

hone
ay

Little Tancook Island
Big Tancook Island

Mahone Bay

enburg

Atlantic Ocean

7

1 Cape Sable Island

Cape Sable Island, the southernmost part of Nova Scotia, is linked to the mainland by a causeway across Barrington Passage. Its main road, Route 330, does a figure-eight loop around the island, past busy wharves and boat-building shops.

At villages such as Stoney Island, South Side and Daniel's Head, fleets of brightly painted cape islanders bob on the water. These small, sturdy boats were designed in 1907 by Ephraim Atkinson. The first cape islander was built in Clark's Harbour, where Atkinson lived. Cape islanders gained fame as stable craft that handle well in shallow water. Today's boats, now made of fiberglass and powered by inboard engines, ply the waters all along our continent's North Atlantic shoreline.

Clark's Harbour (pop. 1,098), birthplace of the cape islander, is a west-coast fishing and boat-building town. Its United Baptist church (built from 1921 to 1931) is clad with smooth beach stones gathered from this and other islands. The stone walls stand on a granite block foundation. Stained-glass windows grace both floors of the two-story structure. Inside the church, ribs of polished oak beams hold the ceiling up, the same way a ship's knees support the keel.

At Centreville (pop. 316), at the middle of Highway 330's figure eight, is the Archelaus Smith Museum. Its many artifacts and displays depict the island's early maritime life. *Admission free. Open daily from mid-June to late September, 9:30 am to 5:30 pm.*

Archelaus Smith first came to the area from New England in 1760, but returned home, having decided it was no place to settle, because of hostile

A fleet of Cape Island boats anchor at Clark's Harbour, where these dependable vessels were first developed.

Indians. When Smith got home he learned that his wife and children had left for Barrington on the mainland near Cape Sable Island. Smith hastened back, expecting the worst, to find that, far from molesting his family, the Micmac had helped to take care of them. So he settled there, later moving onto the island itself, and is today regarded locally as "the father of Cape Sable Island."

The island is home to many shorebirds and a stopover for migratory birds. On quiet days, fishermen may take visitors out to the nearby islands where a highly varied birdlife thrives, especially in early fall.

Special events
Island Days (Labor Day weekend)

2 Digby

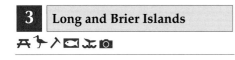

A thicket of masts sways rhythmically at the wharf in Digby (pop. 2,558), marking the presence of one of the world's largest scallop fleets. It merely adds to Digby's lovely setting, looking out on the wide Annapolis Basin and across a narrow channel to the Bay of Fundy, where the fleet fishes. The boats at the waterfront and the harbor are best seen along the seaside promenade known as Admiral's Walk.

Digby's seafaring history is told at the Admiral Digby Museum, with displays, old maps, and photographs. The museum also houses a genealogical archive. *Admission free. Open daily, late June to late September, from 9 am to 5 pm.*

The town's maritime character is even reflected in its Trinity Anglican Church, which was built by shipwrights and has a ceiling constructed like an inverted ship's hull.

Digby is known not only for its scallops, but also for its digby chicks—smoked herring—a local delicacy.

Boats can be chartered for deep-sea fishing and whale-watching, and there are facilities for boating, swimming, riding, and golf.

Special events
Digby Scallop Days (mid-August)

3 Long and Brier Islands

At the far end of a thin finger of land called Digby Neck are two islands—Brier and Long—that once formed part of the mainland.

From East Ferry (pop. 111), on the mainland, the ferry *Joshua Slocum* takes

The rock pillars of the Giant's Causeway rise from Brier Island's southern shore.

Roads to explore: Spires and a flag with a "star of the sea"

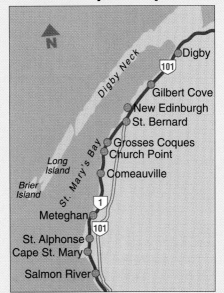

Distance: 67 km/42 miles

The eastern shore of St. Mary's Bay, known as the French Shore, is home to Nova Scotia's largest Acadian population. This coastal strip is studded with brightly colored homes. Along the road, you'll glimpse the red, white and blue flag of the Acadians, with its single star, which represents *Stella Maris*—"star of the sea"—their guiding light.

● From Digby, head south on Route 101, past Gilbert Cove lighthouse, with its original light, built in 1904, still working. *Admission free. Open daily, July to September, from 10 am to 5 pm.*
● Farther south is New Edinburgh, site of a village planned by Scottish Loyalists in 1783, but never built. Traces of the surveyed outline are still visible.
● Continue to St. Bernard, with its magnificent granite Gothic church (1910-1942). Turn west onto Route 1 to Belliveau Cove (pop. 404), with freshwater wetlands, a scenic wharf, and a marina where you can dig for clams.

● This district is said to have the largest clams on the eastern seaboard, a fact reflected in the name of the next community, Grosses Coques (pop. 357), or "large clams." It has the first cemetery established by the Acadians on Nova Scotia, and the first frame house built in the region, in 1768.
● Drive on to Church Point (pop. 318) and the tallest and largest wooden church in North America. St. Mary's was built from 1903 to 1905, with a spire 56.3 m high. Its museum houses a collection of vestments, furnishings, documents, and photographs. *Admission free, donations accepted. Open early June to mid-October, from 9.30 am to 5.30 pm.*
● Farther south is Comeauville (pop. 292), where the Acadian dish called *pâté de rapure*—made from meat or poultry and grated potatoes— first gained commercial recognition. Continue to Saulnierville, a typical Acadian village founded in 1785, with large wooden houses and an 1880 church.
● Travel on to Meteghan (pop. 890), the busiest port on the French Shore. La Vieille Maison, built in the 1820s and one of the oldest homes in the village, is now a museum, furnished in period style. Guides in traditional costume conduct tours of the house. *Open daily, late June to mid-October, 9:30 am to 5:30 pm.*
● Continue to St. Alphonse (pop. 588) whose simple church contains a grotto of the Lady of Lourdes. Nearby Cape St. Mary (pop. 131) has a breathtaking sea view. Below the cape is Mavillette Beach, a provincial park. The marsh behind the sand dunes is good for bird-watching.
● The drive ends at Salmon River (pop. 323), with its wharf, beach, and fish processing plant, clustered around the mouth of a tidal river.

traffic across to Tiverton (pop. 292), on Long Island. Just west of the village is the Tiverton Islands Museum, with displays on the history of the islands, including a model of a fish shop, and a period garden. *Admission free, donations accepted. Open daily, May to October, from 9 am to 8 pm.*

Beachcombers and rock hounds will delight in the trail to the Fundy shore, in the island's provincial park.

At the far end of Long Island is Freeport, from where a ferry crosses Grand Passage to Westport (pop. 353), the only community on Brier Island. South of the village dock is Big Cove, where a knoll overlooking Grand Passage is topped by a memorial to Joshua Slocum. Slocum, who lived in Westport, was the first man to sail alone around the world, from 1895 to 1898.

The island is crossed by three roads, which lead to three lighthouses and the picnic sites beside them, and to a bird-banding station. Brier Island is an important stopping-off point for migrating birds (as many as 300 species have been identified there). In 1988, 486 ha on the island were turned into a refuge for native and migratory species such as bald eagles, ospreys, great blue herons, and seabirds.

The variety of Brier Island's wildlife extends to its flowers, which range from common pansies to rare tiny orchids and large flowering thistles.

Offshore cruises take visitors close to whales, dolphins, and porpoises, drawn by the rich feeding grounds created by the sea surging in against the land where Fundy's great funnel begins. The cruises are run by Westport's Brier Island Ocean Study (BIOS), formed in 1984 to gather information on endangered species that inhabit the sea around this area.

On the south shore of the island is the so-called Giant's Causeway, where a series of dramatic basalt pillars rise straight from the sea.

Special events
Heritage Days (mid-August)

4 Bear River

Every day, in the morning and evening, the tide surges more than 6 m high at Bear River (pop. 900) and turns the gravel beds and eel-grassed mud flats into a silvery lagoon. The water washes under the town's houses, which are raised on frames fixed into the sides of the surrounding hills.

The local Micmac Indians called Bear River *Elsetkok*, meaning "flowing along by high rocks." It is thought that the community's present name is an anglicized version of the last name of Louis Hébert, a French settler in the 17th century. The grape vines planted by Hébert are now wild and they sprawl on the hills above the village.

The wooded valley of the Bear River once rang with the sounds of thriving shipyards.

The river's access to the sea and timber-clad hills attracted Loyalists settlers, who turned to lumbering and eventually to shipbuilding. (Many of the Loyalists were Hessian soldiers who fought with the British during the American Revolution.) In the 19th century, two big shipyards and a large sawmill prospered in Bear River. The brigs, barques, and schooners that were built on the riverbanks transported the local lumber to major American

cities, the West Indies, and the British Isles. The decline of wooden sailing ships in the 1870s led to the collapse of the industry.

The old houses in the village reveal their ingenious construction at low tide. They are grouted into the steep banks beside the river, and are supported at the rear by heavy frames of squared timber, which rise more than 12 m and are fixed into the hillsides. Many buildings extend over the water and look as though they were erected on stilts. Despite their height, at high tide the river almost reaches them. A number of houses have two-story verandas, an architectural feature unique to Bear River.

The Riverview Ethnographic Museum, on Chute Road, is said to have the largest private Canadian collection of ethnic costumes, folk art and books about costumes. The costumes, mostly from the 1800s, are from Europe, Asia, the South Pacific, Latin America, and Africa. The collection also includes garments and accessories worn by Bear River residents during the early 1900s. *Open year-round, except October, Tuesday to Saturday, from 10 am to 5 pm.*

The village also has a pretty riverside park with picnic tables, and, on the waterfront, a replica of a Dutch windmill. The Micmac Reserve near Bear River is open to visitors. At the Band Hall the Indians make and sell basketry, beadwork, and other crafts.

Special events
Cherry Carnival (late July)

Digby County Exhibition
(late August)

5   Annapolis Royal

When you walk through Annapolis Royal (pop. 634), you're strolling through nearly four centuries in the oldest surviving European settlement in Canada. In 1605 the French established a fur-trading post called Port

THE REBIRTH OF AN HISTORIC SETTLEMENT

The old royal flag of France still flies beside Port Royal's palisades and dwellings.

Just over 10 km from Annapolis Royal, Port Royal National Historic Park offers a reconstruction of the first French colony in the New World. From 1605 to 1607, the explorer Samuel de Champlain established a fur-trading post overlooking Annapolis Basin. The Micmac came here to trade furs for implements, food, and blankets. In return, they taught the colonists survival techniques.

To raise the spirits of the colony during the harsh winters, Champlain organized a social club, *The Order of Good Cheer*, which served feasts of moose pie, roast duck, and wine. Fellow colonist Marc Lescarbot wrote and produced *The Theatre of Neptune*. (The social club and the play were Canadian "firsts.")

After Champlain's departure, another band of French colonists tried to revive the settlement. But a 1613 British expedition from Virginia destroyed Port Royal. The story of Champlain's settlement lived on. The site was identified in 1911; its reconstruction was completed in 1941. Today costumed guides escort visitors through buildings faithful to the originals in most ways.

As you walk through the settlement, you almost expect to see Champlain stroll from his quarters to share breakfast with his fellow colonists or join in hearty banter in the blacksmith shop. *Admission free. Open daily, mid-May to mid-October, 9 am to 6 pm.*

Royal on Annapolis Basin. Hostilities with the British ended the life of the post. In the 1630s a second French post was built at present-day Annapolis Royal. In 1710, this post fell to the British who named it Fort Anne to honor their queen.

Fort Anne is now a national historic site. Climb the earthworks and tour the museum in the former British officers' quarters where volunteers are embroidering a tapestry to commemorate the past. *Admission free. The site is open year-round. The museum is open daily, mid-May to mid-October, 9 am to 6 pm; mid-October to mid-May, Monday to Friday, 9 am to 6 pm, closed on holidays.*

The social history of the area is recorded in many buildings in the town. The Robertson House Museum of Childhood (c. 1785) contains a collection of local childhood objects from the 19th and 20th centuries, including games, books, toys, and clothes (c. 1785). *Open early June to late September, Monday to Saturday, 9:30 am to 5:30 pm; Sunday, 1 pm to 5 pm.* A collection of Victorian costumes, furniture, and artifacts is preserved in the O'Dell Inn Museum (c. 1869). *Open early June to late September, Monday to Saturday, 9:30 am to 5 pm; Sunday, 1 pm to 5 pm.* There is also the Adams-Ritchie House (c. 1712), a restored two-story Georgian structure, and the Sinclair Inn, or the Farmer's Hotel (c. 1710).

On St. George Street, the King's Theatre, built in 1921, features live theatre and music. Farther along, the Historic Gardens offers 4 ha of theme gardens, rose gardens, and pathways, considered among the best in Canada. It even has a bountiful cottage garden around an Acadian cottage. *Open daily, mid-May to mid-October, 8 am to dusk.*

A causeway leads out of town to the Annapolis Tidal Power Generating Station, the first in North America. It harnesses the Fundy tides as they

The spires of three churches—Anglican, United and Lutheran—are reflected in the still waters at the head of Mahone Bay.

surge through Annapolis Basin, and is the only saltwater generating station in the world. *Admission free. Open May to mid-June, early September to mid-October, 9 am to 5 pm; mid-June to early September, 9 am to 8 pm.*

The causeway banks are a good place to catch striped bass and trout. Just beyond the causeway lies Granville Ferry, across the water from Annapolis Royal. On its outskirts, the North Hills Museum, a frame house built in the 1760s, contains Georgian furniture, paintings, glass, silver, and ceramics. *Admission free, donations accepted. Open mid-May to mid-October, Monday to Saturday, 9:30 am to 5:30 pm; Sunday, 1 pm to 5:30 pm.*

Special events
Farmers Market (Saturdays and Wednesdays, mid-May–mid-October)

Craft and Antique Show and Sale (late July)

Annapolis Royal Natal Days (late July–early August)

Charter Day (mid-September)

Annapolis Royal Arts Festival (late September)

6 Mahone Bay

Three 19th-century churches stand side by side looking out over Mahone Bay. On a still morning, their image, reflected in the water that glistens like polished steel in the rising sun, is highly striking. It is just one of many scenes that make Mahone Bay (pop. 1,228) such an attractive town.

German Protestants, who had been settled by the British along Nova Scotia's South Shore, founded the town in 1754. Despite these origins, the town's name supposedly comes from *mahonne*, a French word for a pirate ship. French and English settlers eventually joined the "Foreign Protestants," and their descendants launched a shipbuilding era that thrived for more than a century. This heritage is revived annually in the Wooden Boat Festival.

The past is also celebrated in the Settlers Museum in the Benjamin Begin House (c. 1850) on South Main Street. It exhibits ceramics, antique toys, and documents of the pioneer days, and has an architectural display that identifies the styles of local heritage homes. *Open from Victoria Day to Labor Day, Monday to Saturday, from 10 am to 5 pm; Sundays, from 1 pm to 5 pm.*

Mahone Bay has several antique shops, a Sunday flea market, and many craft studios that sell locally made pottery and pewter, among other goods. The Teazer Gift Shop was named for an American privateer, the *Young Teazer*, which was trapped by British warships and blown up during the War of 1812. This event has been woven into local folklore, with tales of sightings of the blazing privateer, and is reenacted in the Wooden Boat Festival.

Visit the picnic park on Edgewater Street for excellent views of the harbor, and of the Mush-a-mush River, which attracts great blue herons, ospreys, and gulls. You will find tennis courts, an outdoor pool, and a wooded park. Canoes and kayaks can be rented, and boats are available for charter.

The largest of the islands in Mahone Bay—Big and Little Tancook—can be reached by ferry from nearby Chester. No cars are allowed onto the islands, which have secluded walks and beautiful sea views.

Special events
Wooden Boat Festival (late July)

Craft Sale, Flea market and Chowder dinner Big Tancook Island (August)

7 Wolfville

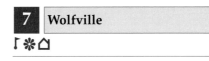

The stately university town of Wolfville (pop. 3,235) is often referred to as the cultural centre of the Annapolis Valley—and this is a place that used to be called Mud Creek. It was renamed in the 19th century, when the granddaughters of Judge DeWolf, a sheriff

Roads to explore: Buried treasure and idyllic inlets

Distance (approx.): 112 km/70 miles

The shores of Mahone Bay and its neighbor, St. Margaret's, are peppered with fishing villages—and the road that links them is fittingly called the Lighthouse Route.

Lunenburg (pop. 2,781) is Nova Scotia's most important fishing port. It was settled in 1753 by German and Swiss Protestants. Its European past is revealed in the distinctive architecture, surnames, and cuisine.

Lunenburg is the winter home of a replica of the *Bluenose*, the schooner on the back of the Canadian dime. The Fisheries Museum of the Atlantic, located on the waterfront, recalls the fishing vessels of eastern Canada and the hardy life of the crews who sailed them. *Open daily, mid-May to mid-October, from 9:30 am to 5:30 pm.*

● From Lunenburg, drive along Route 3 to the town of Mahone Bay and take the turning to the fishing, lobstering, and boat-building coastal village of Indian Point (pop. 104).

Boats at anchor idle in Chester Basin, an idyllic natural harbor on Mahone Bay.

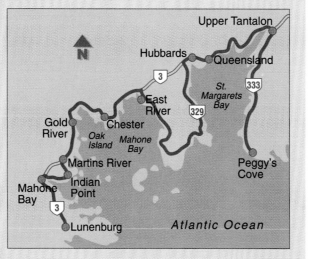

● Over the bridge, turn left inland to Martin's River, and then return to Route 3 toward the causeway to Oak Island. Since 1795, people have been searching this island for treasure that may have been buried by the pirate Captain Kidd.
● Continue along the coast, through the villages of Western Shore and Gold River, with their disused gold mines. Travel through tranquil Chester Basin to the village of Chester (pop. 1,119), set on a peninsula with idyllic inlets called the Back and Front Harbours. It was first settled by New Englanders in the late 1700s. Take the first right, a road that winds through the village, around the waterfront, and back to Route 3.
● Drive east to Graves Island Provincial Park at East Chester, a camping-picnic area with a small beach. At East River turn onto Route 329, a loop around the rugged Aspotogan Peninsula that divides Mahone and St. Margaret's bays. The road runs through fishing villages and past many sandy beaches.
● Back on Route 3, travel to Hubbards, where a lobster pound sells cooked lobster. Turn right there and drive through Queensland and Black Point.
● At Upper Tantallon, swing right on Route 333 and drive 21 km through several hamlets to the end of the peninsula and Peggy's Cove, set on a moonscape of granite ledges laid bare by the last Ice Age. Its lighthouse is now a post office and there are gift shops, galleries, and a restaurant.

and tax collector, said they couldn't bear to say they came from a place with such a name.

The town is dominated by its elegant Acadia University, established as Queen's College in 1838. Among its gracious homes is the Randall House Museum, built in 1808 and furnished accordingly. *Admission free. Open mid-June to mid-September, Monday to Saturday, from 10 am to 5 pm; Sunday, from 2 pm to 5 pm.*

The Robie Tufts Nature Centre, on Front Street, provides an interpretive display of the behavior of Wolfville's chimney swifts. These acrobatic birds gather at dusk from late May to late August, circling theatrically before darting, one at a time, down a chimney to roost for the night.

Wolfville's Wickwire Trail, a 4-km loop, runs east from the town along abandoned railway tracks. It affords a spectacular view of Minas Basin and the cliffs of Cape Blomidon.

Special events
Apple Blossom Festival (late May)
Mud Creek Days (late July–early August)

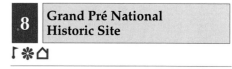

8 Grand Pré National Historic Site

A short drive east of Wolfville is Grand Pré National Historic Site. The name means "great meadow" in French, and it salutes the farmlands Acadian settlers created when they built some 8,650 m of dikes to hold out the Fundy tides. From trails on top of the dikes, you can look onto the farmlands.

Grand Pré National Historic Site, established where the Acadian village used to be from 1680 to 1755, has a French-design stone church, which contains an exhibit on the Acadian deportation in 1755. Above its entrance, a large stained-glass window, created by Halifax artist T.E. Smith-Lamothe, depicts the issuing of the expulsion orders. *Admission free. Open daily, mid-*

A fleet of canoe paddle up one of the many wooded waterways in Kejimkujik National Park, home of an unusual mixture of plants and animals.

Kejimkujik

Kejimkujik National Park preserves a 381-km^2 wilderness of gently rolling landscape, pocked with lakes and littered with rocks and bogs. Because the soil is unsuitable for farming, no one ever settled here for long.

But for at least 5,000 years, the native Micmac people were hunter-gatherers in the area, where mixed forests, berry-laden lakeshores, and plentiful game provided sustenance. They traveled lightly, by canoe and on foot, and left little to mark their passing except for a few park place-names: Peskowesk, Pebbleloggitch, Peskawa.

The first Europeans to see Kejimkujik country were probably the early French fur traders. In the late 1790s the British, desperate for timber to build warships to fight Napoleon's navy, sent surveyors deep into the wilderness to find tall white pine for the ship's masts. Some of Kejimkujik's white pines may have been used to build the ships that defeated the French at Trafalgar in 1805.

In the 1840s settlers established small farms on the hills around the park, although the forest was their mainstay, providing wood for building and, later, pulp for paper. In the 1870s, city folk from England and the United States came to hunt and fish here. Kejimkujik became a national park in 1964, just in time to save some of the spectacular old-growth hardwoods and to preserve some small cathedrals of 400-year-old hemlocks.

Kejimkujik nurtures an unusual mixture of true northern plants and animals and rare species generally found only in the southern United States. In a boggy backwater, labrador tea, a tough northerner, can be found side by side with marsh st. john's-wort, a plant common in Florida. In a quiet cove the common bladderwort may grow beside one of the rarest plants in Canada, the water pennywort. Ferns, mosses, and lichens, as well as more than a dozen species of wild orchid, thrive in the moist summer heat. Hikers can stand under the misty green canopy of an ancient hemlock forest, knowing this is one of the last of its kind.

Visitors may see deer and porcupines grazing along the roadside at dusk or dawn. There are also more reptiles and amphibians in this park than anywhere else in eastern Canada: 13 species of frogs and salamanders, five kinds of snakes, and three types of turtles, one of them (the Blanding's turtle) found only in this area of the Maritimes. During an easy, half-hour paddle up the Mersey River it is common to see 20 or 30 turtles basking in the sun.

The variety of hardwoods, softwoods, bogs, floodplains, and meadows supports about 165 species of birds such as spruce grouse and black-backed woodpeckers, and the more southerly warblers, flycatchers and wood thrushes. The many lakes and streams shelter loons, terns, and sandpipers, as well as fish.

Kejimkujik has many tales to tell visitors who picnic by its rivers, or hike or canoe through its backcountry. Even the rocks have stories to tell: 5-tonne granite boulders were shoved here as easily as pebbles by glaciers; slate rocks once lay off the coast of Africa; and rocky outcrops remain where mountains as high as the Himalayas once stood.

PARK INFORMATION
Access: Via Highway 8.
Visitors' centre: Maitland Bridge.
Accommodation: 329 semi-serviced tent or trailer sites, 47 backcountry sites.
Summer activities: Interpretation program, hiking, picnicking, biking, canoeing (bicycles, craft and life jackets can be rented at Jake's Landing).
Winter activities: cross-country skiing.

A HOME FOR A GOD ON FUNDY BAY

Red sandstone cliffs topped with thick forest rise some 200 m above red beaches on Minas Basin, a narrowing of the Bay of Fundy. These are the cliffs of Cape Blomidon, whose name is said to have evolved from "Blow me down," as seamen referred to it.

In Micmac Indian legend, this was the home of the great god Glooscap, from where he watched over his "children of light" (the meaning of *Micmac*) and the animals. To the Micmac, his smile was sunshine, his anger was thunder.

Legend says that Beaver, Glooscap's rival, defied the god by building a dam across Minas Basin. Glooscap's voice rose with the wind as his rage grew, and he shattered the dam with a club. The

Manicured farmlands cover Cape Blomidon.

remains of the dam created Cape Split, a rock formation at the extreme tip of the peninsula that sweeps out from Cape Blomidon in a great crescent.

Route 358 leads along the cape to Scots Bay, start of the Cape Split Hiking Trail. This 14-km round-trip runs through thick forest and clearings, along the peninsula's cliff tops to Cape Split, where Fundy's tides rage at the cliffs that narrow their scope. To the left of the Split, a short but challenging trail leads down to a rocky beach, where amethysts and agates can be found. Beware of the tides: rising waters can strand unwary hikers.

May to mid-October, from 9 am to 6 pm.

In front of the church is a bronze statue of Henry Wadsworth Longfellow's *Evangeline*. Although the 19th-century American poet never set foot in Nova Scotia, his epic poem and this statue illustrate the heart-wrenching experience of the expulsion and the separations that went with it. As you walk round the statue, the face changes from that of a young lover to one mourning a lover she never saw again.

9 Parrsboro

🏕🚶⛺🛶🚣⚓🛥🐟🎣🐚❄📷

The town of Parrsboro (pop. 1,634), tucked into a northern corner of Nova Scotia, is a pleasant and unhurried place, with handsome houses that go back to the prosperous times of sailing ships. Even its summer theatre has a nautical association. The Ship's Company theatre performs on a retired ferry, the MV *Kipawo*.

In 1985, Parrsboro was propelled from relative obscurity onto the front pages of the world. The sandstone cliffs near the town were discovered to contain fossils from between 240 million and 175 million years ago. This oldest collection of its kind in North America included parts of early crocodiles, large and small dinosaurs, lizards, and sharks, as well as the footprints of a small dinosaur.

In the town, the Fundy Geological Museum has displays of the area's geological history that go all the way back to the beginning of the universe and include the gems, minerals, and fossils found in the area. *Admission free. Open May to July 1, and September 1 to mid-October, from 9 am to 5 pm; July and August, from 9 am to 9 pm.*

The cluster of five islands, about 30 km east of town, on Highway 2, is said to have been created when Glooscap was throwing great chunks of rock at his rival, Beaver. Nearby is Five Islands Provincial Park, at the foot of the modest mountain called Econ-

Delicate fossils of ancient plants and animals decorate the steep cliffs near Parrsboro.

omy, an English phonetic interpretation of its Indian name.

About 6.5 km west of Parrsboro is the Ottawa House Museum, overlooking Minas Basin. It was the late 18th-century home of Sir Charles Tupper, who was the shortest-serving Prime Minister of Canada from May to July in 1896. The restored house, furnished in period style, contains displays of early shipbuilding and lumbering. *Open daily, late June to September 1, from 10 am to 6 pm.*

The museum also overlooks Partridge Island, where rock hounds gather every year for the Rock-hound Roundup, to gather the semiprecious stones such as amethyst that come tumbling off the eroding cliffs.

Special events
Parrsboro Old Home Week Festival (early July)

Five Islands Glooscap Festival (mid-July)

Rock-hound Roundup (August)

Economy Clam Festival (early August)

10 Musquodoboit Harbour

⛺🐟❄

The Musquodoboit River, a trout and salmon stream, divides Musquodoboit Harbour as it reaches the Atlantic Ocean. The Micmac name is pronounced *musk-a-dob-it*, and means "rolling down to the sea in foam," which the river still does.

Roads to explore: A mystery ship and a primeval footstep

Distance (approx.): 259 km/162 miles

The route from Parrsboro to Joggins takes you right into the western branch of the Bay of Fundy. From Parrsboro head west on Highway 209 to Port Greville, home of the Greville Bay Shipbuilding Museum, where the traditions of the region's shipbuilding past come alive in exhibits.

● Follow the winding road through mountainous terrain to Spencer's Island, the site of the mystery brigantine, the *Mary Celeste*. In 1872 she set sail for Italy, but was found abandoned near the Azores. No survivors were ever found. A lighthouse museum tells her story. *Open Wednesday to Sunday, 10 am to 6 pm.*

● Farther along, at Cape d'Or, you can peer down a precipitous cliff face at the edge of Minas Channel. Just past the cape is Advocate Harbour, with its great sweep of beach, where you can find clams and the edible seaweed called dulse. Drive on to Cape Chignecto, a wilderness of towering cliffs and rare plant life.

● Head north on Highway 209 to the mining town of Joggins (pop. 577). A short walk along the beach below its jagged rocks can yield the image of an ancient fern preserved in rock, or the footprint of some creature that lived hundreds of millions of years ago. The cliffs contain 300-million-year-old tree stumps, in one of which was entombed Hylonomus, the oldest reptile ever found. The mud-lacquered stumps, remnants of primitive plants that once thrived in lush swamps, are a reminder that Nova Scotia once lay near the equator. The Joggins Fossil Centre shows rare finds from the site. *Open daily, early June to late September, 9 am to 6:30 pm.*

● A few kilometres on is Minudie (pop. 28), with its legends about Amos (King) Seaman. The story of this poor boy who came from nowhere and became an industrial baron in the 19th century is told at the Amos Seaman School Museum. *Admission free. Open daily, July to September, 9 am to 6 pm.*

● Go on to Amherst or turn south and head for Parrsboro through River Hébert, a village where men mined coal on their knees. Drive through the Cape Chignecto game sanctuary on a gravel road to the community of Halfway River, where you join Highway 2 to Parrsboro.

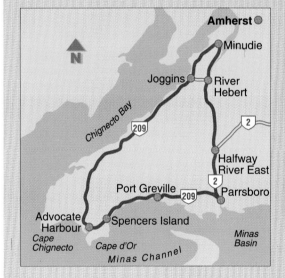

The windswept crags of Cape d'Or loom above Minas Channel.

An English settlement began in Musquodoboit Harbour in 1754. Later came Loyalists and soldiers from the American Revolution, and German Methodists. Fishing, forestry, and light manufacturing are the chief industries in the area today.

In the heart of the village of Musquodoboit Harbour (pop. 930) is the Musquodoboit Railway Museum. It is housed in a restored 1915 railway station, painted red, beside tracks now overgrown with grass. From 1915 to 1960, the Blueberry Express made daily runs from here to Dartmouth. The museum's exhibits include a caboose, a rail snowplow, an old Canadian Pacific combination passenger-baggage car, assorted baggage wagons, a pump car, and equipment used by railwaymen. *Admission free. Open daily, from mid-May to October, from 9 am to 7 pm.*

Musquodoboit Harbour is one of many communities in a chain of seaside villages along the eastern shore. Many nestle in long, narrow, rocky inlets dotted by pretty islets topped by clumps of evergreen trees and gray glacial boulders. Along the shoreline, weathered boats and fishing gear have been pulled up to dry.

At Jeddore Harbour, a red and white lighthouse guards the entrance. The

A sandpiper searching for food picks its way across wave-washed Martinique Beach.

other marker at the entrance is a huge rock called The Old Man, about 4 km out to sea. From a distance, it looks like a grizzled human figure with hunched shoulders and a huge head.

Nearby, at Jeddore Oyster Pond, the Fisherman's Life Museum displays domestic objects, an old pump organ and hooked rugs to re-create the life of local fisherman James Myers and his family at the turn of the century. Visitors to the museum can sample treats such as gingerbread served hot from the oven by ladies in period costume. *Open mid-May to mid-October, Monday to Saturday, from 9:30 am to 5:30 pm; Sunday, 1 pm to 5:30 pm.*

Martinique Beach, 10 km south of Musquodoboit Harbour, has nearly 5 km of white sand, making it Nova Scotia's longest beach. On the lee side of the sandspit, a bird sanctuary shelters a great variety of ducks as well as sandpipers and blue herons.

Special events

Eastern Shore Summer Fair
at Musquodoboit Harbour
(mid-July)

Elderbank Outdoor Recreation
Festival (mid-July)

Clam Harbour Beach Sand Castle
and Sculpture Contest
(early to mid-August)

Halifax County Exhibition
at Middle Musquodoboit
(mid-August)

11 Pictou County

A warm Scottish greeting hails visitors to Pictou County—*"Ciad mile failte,"* or "a hundred thousand welcomes." In 1773, 189 people from the Scottish Highlands arrived here aboard the ship *Hector*. Thousands more Scots immigrants followed and set the stage for Pictou's claim as "the birthplace of New Scotland." The county now has five towns—New Glasgow (the largest, pop. 10,000), Stellarton, Pictou,

Westville, and Trenton— which extend some 65 km along the Northumberland Strait.

The town of Pictou (pop. 4,500) was once an active shipping centre. In keeping with this past, a replica of the 30-m-long, three-masted *Hector* is being built at the Hector Heritage Quay, using shipbuilding methods of the 1700s. Guides in period costumes welcome visitors to the waterfront projects. *Open daily, year-round, from 9 am to 8 pm.*

A walk through the town will take visitors past many early 19th-century stone and wood houses. McCulloch House on Haliburton Road was once the home of the educator, Rev. Dr. Thomas McCulloch, Pictou's first Presbyterian minister. This handsome house was built in 1806 from bricks imported from Scotland. It has some fine original features, such as handcarved woodwork and elaborate plaster cornices. *Open mid-May to mid-October, Monday to Saturday, 9:30 am to 5:30 pm; Sunday, 1:30 pm to 5:30 pm.*

The Burning Bush Museum, in the First Presbyterian Church Hall on Prince Street, houses a collection of documents and objects relating to church history and the lives of Pictou's most famous residents. *Admission free, donations accepted. Open July and August, Monday to Friday, from 9 am to 5 pm. Saturday and Sunday, from 1 pm to 5 pm. Sunday worship at 11 am.*

Outside town, the Crombie House contains the Sobey Art Collection, which includes paintings by the Group of Seven and the 19th-century artist Cornelius Kreighoff. *Open July and August, Wednesdays, from 9:30 am to noon and 1 pm to 5 pm.*

Off Highway 376, en route to New Glasgow, is the Loch Broom Log Church, a replica of the first place of worship built by the original settlers of Pictou County in 1787. Sunday services are held there at 3 pm in summer.

The stately Stewart House on tree-lined Temperance Street in New Glasgow was built in the early 1800s. Inside

The sumptuous interior of Notre Dame de l'Assomption at Arichat, Isle Madame, reflects its past as the diocese cathedral.

On Janvrin's Island, a painter's handiwork transforms a humble boat into a sea monster.

are items that recount Pictou County's shipbuilding, mining, and social history, and a fine collection of Trenton glassware. *Open July and August, Monday to Friday, from 9 am to 4:30 pm; Saturday and Sunday, from 1 pm to 4:30 pm.*

Pictou County offers many opportunities for scenic drives and walks along lovely beaches. The beaches on Pictou Island can be reached by boat from Caribou. The county also has fine golf courses, trout and salmon to be caught in the rivers and lakes, and cod, halibut, pollock, and mackerel to be fished for out at sea.

Special events

Pictou Lobster Carnival (early July)

Festival of the Tartans, New Glasgow
(mid-July)

Hector Natal Day By the Sea, Pictou
(early August)

Hector Festival, Pictou
(mid-August)

---

12 Isle Madame

Ringed by rocky coves and picturesque fishing villages, Isle Madame thrusts out into the sea where Chedabucto Bay becomes the Atlantic. The 45.5-km² island takes its name from one of the titles of the Queen of France. It may have been bestowed by French fishermen who, from the 16th century onward, used the island as a base

while netting catches in the offshore waters. In the mid-1700s, Acadians found refuge here after their expulsion from other parts of Nova Scotia. Most of the 5,000 islanders are Acadians, whose living is still made at sea.

A bridge at Louisdale crosses Lennox Passage to the isle. Route 206 winds southward through forests until Chedabucto Bay comes into view at the village of West Arichat, once a shipbuilding and coastal trading centre.

On nearby tiny Janvrin's Island, there are beaches for digging clams and an outfitter who rents gear for scuba diving, waterskiing, windsurfing, and deep-sea fishing. The offshore waters are ideal for anyone interested in underwater photography.

Arichat, farther east on Route 206, is the most historic community on Isle Madame. To get there, take the lower road, which runs parallel to Route 206. It leads to Notre Dame de l'Assomption Church, a twin-towered wooden structure built in 1837, and once the cathedral of the diocese.

In Arichat, the LeNoir Forge on the lower road comprises a restored 19th-century stone blacksmith shop and a museum preserving Arichat's history as one of the leading ports on Canada's Atlantic seaboard. Thomas LeNoir was a blacksmith who came here from the Magdalen Islands in the early 19th century. The forge built by LeNoir supplied the Arichat shipyard with hardware and tools and eventually became the first blacksmiths' school in Nova Scotia.

Farther east is Petit-de-Grat Island, where fishing has been a way of life since the Acadians first settled here. The road around Petit-de-Grat curves around the inlets where fishing boats are anchored. The island's scenic beauty makes it a favorite spot with artists.

On the east shore of Isle Madame, on Route 320, is D'Escousse, another coastal village with a fishing tradition. Beyond the village are Martinique and a provincial park ideal for picnicking and hiking, an historic lighthouse, and a nearby yacht club with sailboat rentals available.

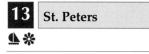

Special events

Arichat Oceanview Festival (early July)
Harbourfest, D'Escousse (early August)
Acadian Festival, Petit-de-Grat (early August)
Janvrin's Fest (late August)
Louisdale Fall Fair (late September)

13 St. Peters

For 10 years, starting in 1520, Portuguese fishermen came every spring to a settlement they called San Pedro, on a little isthmus that just barely separated the Atlantic Ocean from Bras d'Or Lake. They left because the winters were too cold.

A century later, French merchants built a small fortified settlement called Saint Pierre, and in 1650 the enterprising Nicolas Denys took it over and from it established a fur trade with the Micmac Indians. By the end of the 18th century the area had fallen to the British, who built Fort Dorchester on nearby Mount Granville. They called the settlement below it St. Peters.

St. Peters' importance grew when a canal was carved into the isthmus to help boats and people penetrate Cape Breton. The construction of the 800-m canal started in 1854. It took 15 years to dig, blast, and drill an opening 30 m wide and 800 m long through a granite hill 20 m high; to shore it up with timber and planking; and to install locks. Merchant ships plied the canal, but today it is mainly a gateway for pleasure craft heading for Bras d'Or Lake, although commercial vessels do occasionally pass through it.

The ruins of Fort Dorchester and the French supply base called Port Toulouse, built in 1713, are just to the east of St. Peters, in Battery Provincial Park. They include the remnants of the trading post of the first British settler, Lawrence Kavanagh.

The Nicolas Denys Museum, on Denys Street, has been built in the style of the explorer's 1650 fort. Its exhibits

The series of locks at St. Peters, a feat of 19th-century engineering, provide a passage between Bras d'Or Lake and the Atlantic.

Roads to explore: An island-hopping jaunt around Nova Scotia's scenic "Arm of Gold"

Distance: 185 km/109 miles

Bras d'Or Lake—its name means "arm of gold" in French—is a 1,098 km² inland sea, which almost splits Cape Breton into small isles. Only a thin strip of land at St. Peters seals off the Atlantic on its western shore. Around its sparkling waters rise highlands reminiscent of Scotland. Many lakeshore folk are of Scottish stock, and keep alive their forebears' traditions.

● From Baddeck, go west on the Trans-Canada Highway (Route 105), past the Wagmatcook Indian Reserve, home of one of four Micmac bands living on the Bras d'Or. At Bucklaw, head for Little Narrows on Route 223. Watch for bald eagles, which thrive on the bountiful fishing, open country, and clean environment. At Little Narrows (pop. 126), cross St. Patrick's Channel on a cable ferry. In three minutes you are on the Washabuck Peninsula.

● Continue on Route 223 for 30 km to Iona (pop. 120), and the Nova Scotia Highland Village, the only museum in Nova Scotia depicting the life-style of the Highland Scots. It has 11 historic buildings and offers a view of all Cape Breton's four counties. *Open mid-June to mid-September, Monday to Saturday, from 9 am to 5 pm; Sunday, from 11 am to*

6 pm; mid-September to June, Monday to Friday, from 9 am to 5 pm.

● A nearby park has a picnic area and a beach overlooking Barra Strait and the chalk cliffs of Plaster Cove.

● Take the 5-minute ferry ride across the strait to Grand Narrows. (A bridge is planned to span the gap.) Continue east on Route 223, along the shoreline of St. Andrew's Channel, through Christmas Island, popular with visitors who like to have Christmas cards postmarked here.

● Drive on to Barachois Harbour and turn off Route 223 onto the Georges River Road. Follow the road another 8 km past Georges River to the Trans-Canada Highway. From there, drive back to Baddeck, via the 731-m-high Great Bras d'Or Bridge (known locally as Seal Island Bridge). The bridge has a dramatic view of the Great Bras d'Or Channel, which links the lake with the Atlantic.

● On the other side of the bridge is Kelly's Mountain. Cape Bretoners say that

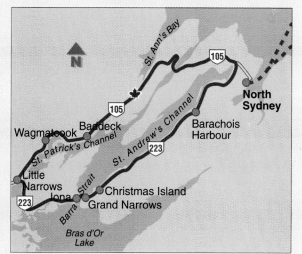

no visit to their island is complete without crossing this mountain.

To local Micmac Indians, the mountain is known as *Nukmij'nawe'nuk* (Place of my grandmother), and the place where the great god Glooscap will return. On its steep slopes are two lookout points with wonderful views. On one side you look back at the Seal Island Bridge. On the other side, you see St. Ann's Bay and the distant hills of the rugged Cape Breton highlands.

---

go back to the mid-1800s. *Open daily, June to September, from 9 am to 5 pm.*

Not far away, on Granville Street, is the Wallace MacAskill Museum. Its walls are lined with the photographs of Wallace MacAskill, a renowned marine photographer and local personality, and it contains artifacts related to his life. *Admission free. Open daily, July to September, from 9 am to 5 pm.*

On the other side of the street, about a block away, is Morrison's Store, built in 1881 by A. A. Morrison. His grandchildren Alex and Catherine now run the store, the oldest business in town.

Special events

Oceanview Sportsmen's Exhibition
(early April)

Annual Lobster Supper (July 1)

Summerfest
(first weekend in August)

14 Baddeck

∧⌐🍺🛏️🛶🐟🦞❄️⌂

A popular resort community on Bras d'Or Lake, Baddeck (pop. 995) is a stopover for yachts that sail these Cape Breton waters. It was also the summer home of Alexander Graham Bell, father of the telephone and inventor *extraordinaire*. A museum dedicated to his work is based there, at the Alexander Graham Bell National Historic Site. *Admission free. Open July 1 to September 30, from 9 am to 9 pm; October 1 to June 30, from 9 am to 5 pm.*

During the summer, a replica of the *Silver Dart* is displayed in the village. Bell sponsored the development of this airplane, which flew here in February 1909. It was the first flight by a British subject in the British Empire.

Special events

Bras d'Or Festival of the Arts
(July and August)

Bras d'Or Yacht Club Regatta,
Baddeck (August)

Highland Village Day, Iona (August)

Cape Breton County Exhibition,
North Sydney (August)

Harvest Home at the Bell Museum,
Baddeck (September)

Baddeck Handcraft Festival
(late September)

15 Margaree Harbour

🦞⌂

Once, freight for the entire Margaree Valley came through Margaree Harbour, to and from the glittering Gulf of St. Lawrence. The harbor bristled with steamers and tall ships, and the harbor

"THE LITTLE WOMAN" OF NORTH EAST MARGAREE

A weathered gravestone at St. Patrick's Roman Catholic Church in the North East Margaree Valley honors Henriette Lejeune. She was known as "The Little Woman"—the midwife who, in her time, helped bring all the local babies into the world. Many legends are associated with her. The gravestone inscription (see below) preserves one of these legends: that she was with the French at the second siege of Louisbourg in 1758.

Recent research has dispelled these stories. But it has also revealed a life as rich as any legend.

Marie-Henriette Lejeune was born at Rochefort, in France, in 1762— four years after the Louisbourg siege. The British had forced her Acadian parents to flee here from Cape Breton. Until the age of 30, she wandered first with her family and later with her first two husbands, in search of a permanent home in the New World. In the early 1790s, she returned to Nova Scotia, where she met her third husband, James J. Ross, a British soldier who had served in the American Revolution. They became the first settlers in North East Margaree Valley in 1800. She had four children, but only Joseph and Jean survived. Their descendants are still found in this area.

In the early days of the mixed English and Acadian settlement at Margaree Valley, Marie-Henriette acted as a midwife and a nurse. It was said that she was immune to smallpox, once one of the most dreaded diseases. In time, she became known to all as Harriet and, as years went by, as Granny Ross. Her husband died in 1825; but she lived on until she was 98, in 1860. Her great-grandson Thomas, who erected the gravestone at St. Patrick's, helped—unwittingly perhaps—perpetuate another legend: that she died at the age of 117.

road was lined with dozens of two- and four-horse carts ready to haul puncheons (70-gallon casks) of molasses and other goods overland to St. Ann's, a distance of nearly 100 km. Taverns rollicked with boisterous customers, and in winter men came from as far away as Judique, Mabou, and Inverness to race their horses on the ice.

Today, Margaree Harbour (pop. 128) is a small fishing community, visited mainly because it lies where two scenic drives meet—the Cabot Trail (Route 19) and the Ceilidh Trail (Route 219).

Near the bridge at the mouth of the Margaree River is the *Marion Elizabeth*, a 40-m schooner that houses a restaurant and a museum of the local ship-building and fishing industries. At nearby Schooner Village is "The Boat Who Wouldn't Float," the subject of a book of the same name by author Farley Mowat.

The dock at the harbor is lined with lobster boats and charter boats that take people out for deep-sea sport fishing, whale-watching, or bird-watching on Margaree Island.

Margaree Harbour's past still lives in the architecture of its traditional farmhouses, and the low, sturdy profiles of buildings along the waterfront. Apparently they were built this way to brace against sou'wester gales that have been known to blow cattle through ships' sails.

Wading in the swift currents of the Margaree River, fly fishermen cast for catches of salmon.

Cape Breton Highlands

Northern Cape Breton is a world of rock, wind, and water, where the cloud-tipped highlands plunge steeply to the sea. The Cabot Trail, one of the loveliest drives in North America, traverses this rugged tableland like a thin lifeline. Twisting across the 950 km² Cape Breton Highlands National Park, it links the coast of the Atlantic Ocean on the east with the shores of the Gulf of St. Lawrence on the west.

The interplay of ocean, mountain, and sky creates the 105-km trail's breathtaking scenery: an astonishing variety of sand and cobble beaches, granite headlands, hardwood valleys, coniferous woods, taiga barrens, tumultuous waterfalls, and quiet fishing villages.

Cape Breton's understructure has some of the oldest and hardest rock on earth and the stresses of a billion years of geological change can be seen throughout the park. Periods of continental collisions and massive upheaval have left steep canyons and great valleys such as the Chéticamp, the Clyburn, and the magnificent Aspy.

The filigree Beulach Ban Falls slips down steps of granite rock, Cape Breton Highlands.

When dinosaurs wallowed in fern swamps that are now Cape Breton coal, rivers flowing down from the highlands dropped silt, sand, and rock as they slowed to enter the ocean. In the hot climate of that time, shallow ocean bays evaporated, leaving deep deposits of precipitated gypsum and limestone from which ocean and weather have carved harbors for Chéticamp, Pleasant Bay, Dingwall, and Ingonish, fishing villages just outside the park.

For thousands of years, Micmac Indians had seasonal camps along the coast and major river valleys. John Cabot may have landed at Aspy Bay in 1497. By the 1520s Ingonish, then called Port d'Orléans, was a Portuguese fishing station. It later became a French settlement and was burned to the ground when Louisbourg fell in 1745.

Then, as now, storms claimed many lives at sea. But wayfarers perished inland, too, when overtaken by fierce weather on desolate trails. The death of one such unfortunate, Mary Brown, led to the establishment of halfway houses for travelers between communities. The park's mountaintop emergency cabins, furnished with stoves, are today's versions of those long-ago refuges.

In summer, greater yellowlegs nesting on the bogs screech at the passing wilderness hikers. Around them, fluffy bog cotton flutters among delicate white-fringed orchids and pink arethusa, while the carnivorous pitcher plants and sundews wait for unwary insects. On the exposed ridges, reindeer moss, wild blueberries and cranberries, and stunted tamarack barely cover the rock.

July and August are a glorious mix of hot days, cool nights, and ocean breezes. By late August there is a briskness to the sunny days and the nights turn decidedly chilly. When October comes, carpets of vivid red huckleberry and tiny gold tamarack garb the highlands. But by midmonth, the gold and red leaves begin to fall.

When winter gales roar across the taiga barrens inland, black bears tuck themselves into winter dens, and moose and deer descend to lower elevations. The high country (90 percent of the park), becomes buried in more than 4 m of snow every year.

The park's lush hardwood forests grow in steep, sheltered valleys. Except for the rippling of waterfalls, there is a deep quiet in those groves of sugar maple, red oak, yellow birch, beech, hemlock, and pine. For some 300 years, they have nurtured woodland creatures, especially in the Clyburn, Grande Anse, and Aspy valleys.

Hidden in dark canyons, often beside waterfalls where little else will grow, are Hornman's willow herb, golden mountain saxifrage, and mountain sandwort, which normally sprout in the Arctic or on western mountaintops. These arctic-alpine plants have survived in these canyons since the last Ice Age, 9,000 years ago.

PARK INFORMATION

Access: The Cabot Trail. Entry points are north of Chéticamp on the west and at Ingonish Beach on the east.

Visitors' centres: Chéticamp (open from mid-May until October) and Ingonish (year-round).

Accommodation: Year-round campgrounds at Chéticamp and Ingonish, although services may vary with the season; other campgrounds close in mid-October.

Summer activities: Bird-watching, hiking, fishing, golfing, tennis, and biking. (Some rental equipment available.) Interpretive programs. Outdoor theatre. Concerts of Acadian or Scottish folksinging, dancing, fiddling, and bagpiping.

Winter activities: Cross-country skiing, ice fishing, skating, and toboganing.

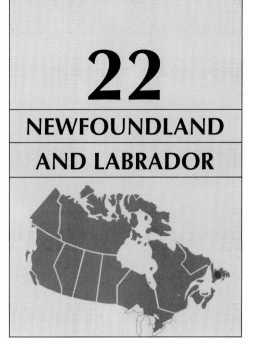

22

NEWFOUNDLAND AND LABRADOR

Places to see

L'Anse aux Meadows

St. Anthony

Red Bay

Deer Lake

Channel-Port aux Basques

Burgeo

Harbour Breton

Hermitage

Boxey

Fogo Island

Trinity

Random Island (boat trip)

The Trinity Loop

Harbour Grace

Cape St. Mary's Ecological Reserve

La Manche Provincial Park

Roads to explore

Along the Labrador Coast:

Blanc Sablon to Red Bay

Central Newfoundland:

Badger to Buchans

Around the Burin Peninsula:

Marystown–Grand Bank–Burin

National park close-up

Gros Morne

Terra Nova

Previous pages:
Hikers in Gros Morne National Park

UNCOVERING THE TREASURES OF VIKING VOYAGERS

Driven by tales of a rich, bountiful land to the west, Viking seafarers braved the mighty Atlantic in wooden, single-masted longships powered by the wind and guided by the stars. They landed at L'Anse aux Meadows on the tip of the Great Northern Peninsula of Newfoundland about A.D. 1000.

For many years archeologists searched for a site called Vinland, described in the Viking Sagas. But it was not until the 1960s that the mystery came closer to being solved. Between 1961 and 1968 a Norwegian writer and explorer, Helge Ingstad, with his wife, archeologist Anne Stine, and an international archeological team excavated L'Anse aux Meadows— its name comes from the French *l'anse aux méduses* ("bay of jelly-fish"). Their finds confirmed the site was Norse and identified it as the first known European settlement in the Western Hemisphere.

Low, grassy mounds turned out to be the lower courses of the walls of eight buildings, constructed from wood and sod. They include four workshops, three large dwellings that could each house up to 20 people, and, down at the brook, a smithy (the first known ironworks in the New World).

A model of a Viking displayed at L'Anse aux Meadows

Among the treasures recovered were a bronze ring-headed pin, a stone lamp, a small soapstone spindle whorl, the fragment of a bone needle, and a whetstone. The last three items indicate that women came with the explorers. The remains of boat nails or rivets and iron slag were also found. These were proof that the settlement was most likely a winter camp and a base for repairing ships. In summer, they probably sailed to the North American mainland.

Today L'Anse aux Meadows is a national historic park. The visitors' centre exhibits many of the items from the site, and has models and films that describe the history of the settlement. From there, a boardwalk leads to the grass-covered remains of the eight buildings. Beyond them, three sod houses have been reconstructed, furnished with cooking utensils and tools of the time.

In 1978, L'Anse aux Meadows was declared a UNESCO World Heritage Site, the first cultural site to win that title. *The site grounds are open year-round.*

1 St. Anthony

The largest town of Newfoundland's Great Northern Peninsula, St. Anthony (pop. 3,164) is famed for the Grenfell Mission. Until 1892 it was a fishing community much like any other in coastal Newfoundland. But in that year an English doctor arrived who was to change the settlement forever. He was Wilfred Grenfell (1865-1940), a representative of the Royal National Mission to Deep Sea Fishermen.

Grenfell was deeply moved by the poverty and disease that abounded on the remote Newfoundland and Labrador coasts. He returned to England to raise funds for hospitals, nursing stations, schools and a children's home. These were built, and a medical network with headquarters in St. Anthony was established. Eventually the network, linked by sea and air, stretched for 2,400 km along the Labrador coast.

This visionary also set up cooperatives, cottage industries, and a dry dock to improve the economy of St. Anthony and of the settlements on his

An immense iceberg drifts offshore near St. Anthony on Newfoundland's northern tip.

A pair of traditional snowshoes, Grenfell Museum

network. He even imported a herd of reindeer from Lapland to St. Anthony, in an attempt to diversify the region's economy. Under his guidance, St. Anthony grew from a port to a sizeable commercial centre.

Overlooking the harbor, on the west side of town, is Grenfell's home. It is now a museum, where artifacts, photographs, letters, and memoirs record his remarkable life. *Open daily, July and August, and Wednesday to Sunday, May, June, and September, 10 am to 8 pm.*

On Tea House Hill, overlooking the hospital, are the graves of Grenfell and his wife, and those who dedicated their lives to helping him.

Next to Grenfell House is the Charles S. Curtis Memorial Hospital. In the hospital rotunda are eight ceramic murals created in 1967 by the Montreal artist Jordi Bonet. They depict the story of the people of Newfoundland and Labrador and pay tribute to the work of Grenfell.

Special events
Cod Festival (late July)

2 Red Bay

Before 1977, the tiny fishing port of Red Bay (pop. 334), on the coast of south Labrador, was known for its bakeapple harvest, its red tile rock, and the whale bones on its beach. But in that year, excavations revealed it to be a site of international importance.

In the peaty ground of nearby Saddle Island, archeologists uncovered a 16th-century tryworks. There, whale blubber was rendered into oil in large, copper cauldrons and casks for storing the oil were assembled and repaired. They also found small dwellings, which housed whalers, and a whalers' cemetery, where more than 140 whalers were buried.

Roads to explore: Along the coves of the Labrador coast
Distance (approx.): 196 km/122¼ miles

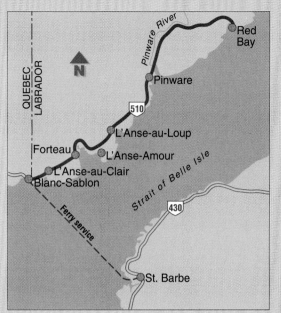

From northern Newfoundland, you can cross to Labrador, one of the remotest parts of Canada. A ferry from St. Barbe sails across the 17.6-km Strait of Belle Isle to Quebec and Labrador. It makes two round-trips a day between May and December. Icebergs and whales throng the strait in spring and summer. The ferry docks at Blanc Sablon, Quebec, near the Labrador-Quebec border.

● Head east from Blanc Sablon on Route 510, which links several fishing communities overlooking sandy beaches, in the shadow of high, craggy cliffs. The first village along the way is L'Anse-au-Clair, founded by the French in the 1700s.

● Next is Forteau, which means "strong water." It is an administrative centre for Southern Labrador. The Labrador Straits region boasts one of the best berry-picking locations in the entire province. Squashberries, blueberries, and bakeapples abound here in July and August. Forteau hosts an annual four-day Bakeapple Folk Festival in August.

● Drive to L'Anse Amour, once L'Anse aux Morts ("cove of the dead"). It is the site of a Maritime Archaic Indian burial mound, where the grave of an Indian boy and artifacts dating back 7,500 years have been unearthed.

● Outside L'Anse Amour is the Point Amour light, built in 1857. At 33 m, the limestone tower is the tallest in Atlantic Canada, and said to be the second tallest in Canada.

● Visit the Labrador Straits Museum along the way to L'Anse-au-Loup, for a glimpse of the way of life in this region in past times. L'Anse-au-Loup, Capstan Island, and West St. Modeste share a common ancestry. Their first settlers came to Labrador from England, Jersey, and Newfoundland. *Open daily, July to mid-September, 10 am to 6 pm.*

● Pinware (pop. 195), 52 km east of Blanc Sablon, was named for a large, foot-shaped stone at the mouth of Black Rock Brook. French settlers called it "pied noir" (black foot), which English-speaking residents pronounced "pinware." The community is sheltered by a 106-m-high cliff called "Ship Head," where French and English settlers concocted dye from bark to color their nets. A barking pot, used to make the dye, can still be seen at Ship Head.

There are two scheduled salmon rivers near Pinware—Pinware River and Trout Brook. The settlement of Pinware River, roughly 6 km from Pinware, is one of the best salmon fishing resorts in the country. Plump and succulent grilse and sea-run trout are the catches of the Pinware River. Runs are best in July and August. Trout Brook is a few kilometres past Pinware toward Red Bay.

● Route 510 ends at Red Bay, once the largest whaling port in the world.

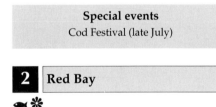

Point Amour lighthouse is the second tallest in Canada.

Gros Morne

Gros Morne (pronounced "gross morn") is one of the few places in the world where samples of Earth's outer crust and interior mantle are visible within arm's reach of each other. A showcase of some of Canada's finest natural wonders, the 1,805-km² park also contains almost every major North American rock type. Fascinating geological features take visitors back billions of years, provide evidence of continental drift, and illustrate the wondrous effects of glaciers in an island setting.

Scientists theorize that during the ancient dance of the continents, the floor of the Iapetus Ocean, which preceded the Atlantic Ocean, ruptured. Lava flowed out and chunks of ocean bed were pushed onto the edge of North America. Rock from inside the earth—harzburgite, dunite, and gabbro—was also shifted onto the edge of the continent. These are the rocks of the Tablelands, a plateau in the southwestern corner of Gros Morne. The plateau itself is a slab of the ancient ocean floor, 8 km wide by 15 km long.

Such continental meetings and separations produced landforms as varied as the stark beige barrens of the tablelands, the volcanic coast of Green Gardens, the rounded mountains of the Long Range, and the flat layers of broad coastal plain. They also created features as unusual as the Cow Head breccia. The product of massive underwater landslides along the edge of the ocean, breccia is a conglomerate of rocks and fossils from both shallow, warm seas and deep, cold waters. Such phenomena first led to the theory of continental drift.

Gros Morne fossils also present a fascinating record of eons of marine life. Beside the highway near Green Point, you can examine layers of geological history, ranging from the Precambrian to the Paleozoic eras. Just north of Green Point, near Broom Point, you can step from rocks of Cambrian times to the later Ordovician periods, and see fossil progression from trilobites, gastropods, and graptolites to more highly developed snails and clams.

Gros Morne also offers a blend of dramatic canyons, deep lakes, treeless plateaus, bogs, and lowlands. All are a legacy of ice. The deep and sinuous

An Arctic hare in summer coloring, Gros Morne

gorge of Western Brook Pond is typical of the gargantuan cuts glaciers eroded through the mountains. This immense lake, 16 km long, 3 km wide at its widest point, and 165 m deep, is enclosed by cliffs rising 656 m above its waters.

Cold ocean currents keep the weather especially cool on the Long Range Mountains, where conditions resemble those of the Arctic, and plants hug the ground to escape the bitter winds. Paradoxically, you will find some of the park's largest trees—immense spruce fir, balsam fir, and birch—in the sheltered valleys of this zone. In the lowlands, the park preserves a boreal forest of balsam fir, white birch, and black spruce. Fierce winds have contorted the tangled growth on exposed coastal ridges into a krummholz forest, also known locally as "tuckamore" or "tuck."

Gros Morne is fringed by 72 km of extremely varied shoreline. Sheer cliffs edge parts of the park. Tides sweep over cobble beaches and mud flats. Extensive stretches of dune-edged, sandy beaches outline the northernmost shore. In the Newfoundlander's colorful turn of phrase, the narrow channel separating St. Paul's Bay from the Gulf of St. Lawrence is known as a "tickle." The gentleness of the name notwithstanding, the tides surge into the bay, creating salt marshes, which are a rich food source for shorebirds migrating in the fall.

On sunny days, harbor seals bask on rocks in St. Paul's Bay, and harp seals appear along the coastline from time to time in winter. Pods of pilot whales (locally known as "pothead whales" because of their bulbous heads), minke and fin whales are annual visitors to Bonne Bay. Blue whales—the largest creatures on earth—and humpback whales have also been spotted not far from shore.

PARK INFORMATION
Access: Routes 430 and 431.
Visitors' centre: 3 km south of Rocky Harbour in the park, and Wiltondale Pioneer Village.
Accommodation: Five campgrounds, group camping.
Summer activities: Swimming, angling, boat tours, hiking and backpacking; rock climbing (you must first register your plans at the visitors' centre or with a park warden).
Winter activities: Winter camping, cross-country skiing, snowshoeing.

Ten Mile Pond is one of the fjordlike lakes of Gros Morne, which became landlocked when the earth rebounded after the Ice Age glaciers receded.

Underwater excavations disclosed remains of three large ships, a small supply vessel, and several smaller boats possibly used to pursue the whale during the kill. The most completely excavated ship was the *San Juan*, a 300-tonne galleon that sank with a full cargo of whale oil in 1565. It is the best-preserved example ever found of the kind of vessel in which Europeans colonized the New World.

From the early 1530s to the early 1600s, as many as 20 ships sailed to Red Bay each year from the Basque regions of France and Spain. Their crew hunted right and bowhead whales, rendered oil from the blubber and carried it back to the markets of Europe. Red Bay was the first industrial site in the New World and the whaling capital of the world at the time.

On the south side of Saddle Island is the whalers' cemetery. About half the graves found contained more than one individual. This fact seems to underscore the dangerous, often disastrous work of a whaler. The graves also yielded a number of garments in surprisingly good condition, including a pair of leather shoes with its ties intact, wool trousers and stockings, and a knitted cap.

An interpretive centre on the mainland of Red Bay displays the items that have been found, and shows a documentary on the excavation of a Basque whaling ship. *Open daily, July and August, 8 am to 8 pm; June and September, 10 am to 6 pm.*

Special events
Bakeapple Festival (August)

3 Deer Lake

Some of the most spectacular scenery in Newfoundland's interior is found in the Humber Valley. At the heart of this valley is the thriving town of Deer Lake (pop. 4,327). Many townsfolk depend on the logging industry that supplies the pulp and paper mill in Corner Brook, south of the lake.

The Humber Valley Heritage Museum portrays life in the area during the early 1920s. The museum is located

An Atlantic salmon leaps Big Falls in Sir Richard Squires Memorial Provincial Park.

in the Humber Development Association Building. Logging and farming tools, as well as a collection of old photographs and newspapers, are on exhibit. *Open daily, June to August, 9 am to 9 pm.*

Near Deer Lake are two picturesque places. To the north is the Sir Richard Squires Memorial Provincial Park, along a whitewater stretch of the mighty Humber River. Take Route 430 north, and branch off onto the partially paved Route 422. In July you can witness the spectacular sight of Atlantic salmon fighting their way out of the water and over Big Falls to reach their spawning grounds upriver.

South of Deer Lake the highway follows the east shore of the lake. Stop at Steady Brook and stretch your legs on a walk through a forest path that leads to a breathtaking view of 39-m Steady Brook Falls.

Special events
Hangashore Folk Festival (July)
Humber Valley Strawberry Festival (late July)
Humber Valley Agricultural, Home, and Handicraft Exhibition (late September)

Once the world's largest whaling port, Red Bay is now a snug Labrador fishing community.

4 Channel-Port aux Basques

⚓ 🐟 ❄ ⌂

Fishermen from northern Spain were the most frequent users of this small, ice-free port, from as early as 1560. Samuel de Champlain recognized the fact in 1612 and dubbed it Port aux Basques. Now it is part of Channel-Port aux Basques (pop. 5,644), the terminal for the mainland ferry from North Sydney, Nova Scotia. It is also a departure point for ferries linking Burgeo, Grey River, Hermitage, Harbour Breton, and other outports on Newfoundland's south coast.

Follow Main Street for about 2 km past the town hall to the Gulf Museum.

Established by volunteers, the museum houses several displays that explain the area and its history. Among its exhibits are a 100-year-old diving suit, and the Mushrow Astrolabe, a 17th-century navigational instrument and the first of its kind discovered in Canada. Local diver Wayne Mushrow rescued the bronze plate from one of the hundreds of wrecks lining the southwestern coast of the province. *Open daily, summer months.*

From the crest of Stadium Hill, you look down on nearby Channel, the other community that lends the town its name. Main Street runs into Legallais Street, which offers a view of Channel Head. This stone protrusion from the gulf's waters supports a vital

Roads to explore: The wilds of central Newfoundland

Distance (approx.): 75 km/47 miles

To reach the wilderness heart of Newfoundland, take Route 370 from Badger to the shores of Red Indian Lake and the Exploits River. (Badger is about 27 km west of Windsor and Grand Falls, the largest towns in central Newfoundland.) The highway, with a roadside forest of black spruce, cuts through rolling hills, wandering streams, marshes, and lakes, inhabited by moose and caribou; sightings are almost guaranteed.

● Just 12 km along is the gravel road to Millertown Junction, a former Canadian National Railway siding. Camp near the roadside, fish Joe Glodes Pond, or stroll along the old railway bed.

● Return to Route 370 and continue south to Buchans Junction, birthplace of Newfoundland Premier Clyde Wells.

● Turn left at Buchans Junction and drive to the once prosperous logging community of Millertown (pop. 158). A remnant of the early logging days remains in the form of a waterwheel that protrudes defiantly from the waters of Red Indian Lake. Stroll along the town's main street, formerly a section of railway line. Visit the Church of England, built by Scottish lumber merchant Lewis Miller in 1901, and the 1940s schoolhouse, now a museum. The schoolhouse contains pictures, documents, and objects pertaining to the logging industry, and recounts the his-

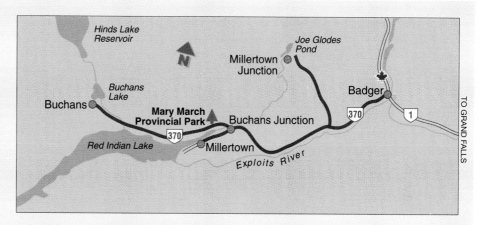

tory of the 45 Norwegian and Swedish families that settled here. *Admission free. Open daily, July and August, 12 pm to 8 pm.*

● Just 3.2 km outside the town, along the lakeshore, is a reconstructed Beothuk encampment. The Beothuks were native to the area but were wiped out by the early 19th century. Replicas of their winter *mamateeks*, or wigwams, show how the Beothuks lived, and displays explain how they prepared caribou and other types of game meat in smokehouses.

● Continue through Millertown along a 2.5-km dirt road to Exploits Dam, where a fish elevator transports Atlantic salmon over the dam to spawning grounds in summer.

● Return to Buchans Junction and drive west on Route 370 for 2 km to Mary March Provincial Park, named after a Beothuk woman captured by explorers.

Walk along the park's beach and enjoy the tranquil solitude, or take a dip in Red Indian Lake.

● Route 370 continues another 40 km to the former mining town of Buchans (pop. 1,164). Like a fortress, the town surveys the surrounding land from the top of a plateau. Its last remaining mine shaft dominates the skyline.

Visit the Miner's Museum, in the former company manager's house. Artifacts and photographs honor the 23 men killed in mining tragedies, and tell how Mattie Mitchell, a prospector, accidentally discovered the area's rich mineral deposits. Legend has it that Mitchell was boiling his kettle when he noticed the steam had melted a piece of ore, later found to contain lead, zinc, copper, silver, and gold. *Admission free. Open daily, June to mid-September, 10 am to 12 pm; 1 pm to 8 pm.*

lighthouse. Automated just a few years ago, the beacon is still surrounded by the now vacant dwellings of keepers.

5 Burgeo

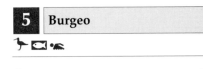

A remote community bravely facing the Atlantic, Burgeo is a fishing centre (pop. 2,400) built on an island linked to the mainland by a causeway. Just offshore lie the Burgeo Islands, the community's buffer against an aggressive Atlantic Ocean.

You can reach Burgeo by coastal boat from Channel-Port aux Basques, or take Route 480, off the Trans-Canada Highway. The 146-km road of solitary blacktop is little traveled and entirely unserviced. It is best to stock up on provisions at the turnoff near Barachois Pond Park.

Burgeo's small museum houses items that stretch back into the hamlet's distant past, loaned by local residents. The exhibits include old fishing tools and photographs of the steamboats that once traveled along the coast. *Open daily, June to September, 10 am to 8 pm.*

To the west is Sandbanks Provincial Park, the nesting site of the rare piping plover. Its sparkling beaches are claimed to be the best in the province.

A ferry from Burgeo connects it with the island of Ramea. Reservations are not needed for the one-hour voyage to the small but picturesque fishing community. However, the schedule does change with the seasons, so it is best to call ahead. Stopovers are short, so little of the settlement can be explored, unless you plan to spend a day there. A walking trail circles the 1.6-km-long island. The cruise takes you close to the rugged coastline that has claimed its share of ships and sailors.

The coastal boat also visits Grey River, one of the few true outports, or coastal fishing settlements, left in the province. The twice-weekly round-trips by the boat are the only direct contact the community has with the rest of the area.

6 Harbour Breton

Route 360, stretching from Bishop's Falls to Harbour Breton (pop. 2,418), passes through thick forest, the habitat of moose, and traces the path of the Beothuk and Micmac Indians who once lived here. Just before this solitary 223-km road ends at Harbour Breton, it sends out branches—Routes 364 and 362—to Hermitage, Boxey, and other outports on Fortune Bay.

Harbour Breton is named after the fishermen from Brittany who frequented the shores of this coast during the late 1600s. Its ties to the sea are still evident in the fish stages at Down Harbour, the oldest part of the town, and the dories that dot the bay. The two sides of Harbour Breton are connected by a bridge.

Brunette Island, in Fortune Bay, is visible from Harbour Breton on a clear day. In the 1960s, the island was the site of an ecological project. Buffalo were transported to the island to see if they could thrive on the island. The buffalo are gone now, unsuited to the habitat, although local folk say that a lone survivor still roams the island.

To explore the offshore islands, ask one of the local fishermen if he will take you on a tour of the bay. The sea offers the best view of the jagged coast, which is defined by sheer granite cliffs, deep fjord bays, and sandy beaches. Harbour Breton can also be reached by ferry from Terrenceville, to the east.

7 Hermitage

Perched on the slopes that shelter the clear blue waters of Hermitage Bay is a village settled by the French centuries ago. Hermitage (pop. 831) still has brightly painted, two-story houses once popular in outports. Local fishermen chose bright colors to ensure they could pick out their dwellings when leaving or returning home.

By the shore is a wharf, where a ferry departs for Gaultois (pop. 558), on Long Island, located on the other side

Lofty rocky slopes form a backdrop for the remote outport of Harbour Breton, which survives on a sheltered arm of Fortune Bay.

Boxey is a settlement scattered along Fortune Bay on Newfoundland's south coast.

of Hermitage Bay. The ferry runs from 8 am to 8 pm in the summer, carrying passengers as well as freight—but no cars. Travelers wishing to take the excursion to the small island can leave their vehicles behind in a parking lot just beside the wharf.

The 30-minute boat ride takes you past Little Fox Island and Fox Island. The flashing light on the western point of Fox Island guides boats through the narrow channels of the bay. If you're lucky, a passing pod of whales might breach to blow.

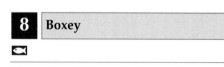

8 Boxey

As you travel along Route 363, you are greeted with the sign "Welcome to Boxey—A Piece of Heaven on Earth." The village (pop. 120) was famous in colonial days for a "spy hole" located in a rock formation. The vantage point was used to navigate boats sailing into Coombe's Cove, past the rocks in St. John Harbour.

It is said that two local fishermen, Jacob Penney and his companion Simon Bungay, were sailing to nearby Deadman's Bight to search for treasure. But the two men were distracted by spirits, who lured them aground off Boxey Head. They managed to free themselves and set sail once again, but arrived in the bight just in time to see the treasure slip behind a rock door and disappear from sight forever.

Roads to explore: Around the "boot" of the Burin Peninsula
Distance (approx.): 350 km/218 miles

Route 210 stretches from the neck of the Burin Peninsula to the colorful communities at its boot. This 140-km-long part of the drive begins at the junction of Route 210 and the Trans-Canada Highway, near Goobies. It passes through wilderness, with only one roadside community, Swift Current, which you pass through just after leaving Route 1.

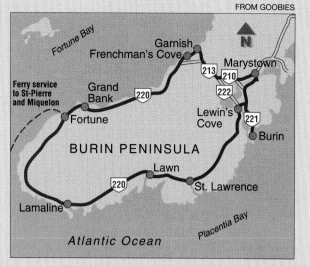

- The first stop on Route 210 is Marystown (pop. 6,739). Turn right at the traffic light. Near the light is Route 213, which passes through the quiet village of Garnish (pop. 716), with its 1885 lighthouse, and Frenchman's Cove.
- Route 213 joins Route 220 and leads to one of the peninsula's most historic towns, Grand Bank (pop. 3,528). Visit the Seamen's Museum, on the left just as you enter town. This dramatic white

Seamen's Museum, Grand Bank

building, shaped like the sails of a fishing schooner, was the Yugoslavian pavilion during Montreal's Expo 67. The museum features models of schooners and naval artifacts from years ago.

In the town, stroll along the Heritage Walk, past houses and other buildings constructed in the early 1900s.

- Just 3 km from Grand Bank on Route 220 is Fortune (pop. 2,177). From here, take the ferry across to the French islands of St. Pierre and Miquelon for a taste of Europe. On clear days, you can see the distant outline of the islands from French Island Park, farther south on Route 220.

- Continue southeast on 220 to Lamaline, and cross the causeway to Allan's Island and the Virgin Mary Grotto.
- Between Lamaline and Lawn (pop. 1,025), Newfoundland cloudberries, called "bakeapples," can be found in the marshes or are sold at roadside stands.
- At St. Lawrence (pop. 1,743), the "Echoes of Valour" monument in front of the town hall honors the 203 American sailors lost in February 1942 when the ships *Truxtun* and *Pollux* ran aground nearby. It also pays homage to miners who died from working in the community's fluorspar mines. Stop at the Miner's Museum on the Main Street. *Admission free. Open daily, late June to August, 11 am to 8 pm.*
- Drive on to Route 221, and turn right to historic Burin (pop. 2,940). At the intersection turn right onto Main Street, which leads to old Burin. The Heritage House, built around 1920, is filled with turn-of-the-century artifacts, clothing and furniture. *Open from mid-May to mid-June, and September and October, Monday to Friday, 9 am to 5 pm; late June to late August, daily, varying hours.* During the second weekend of August, the museum hosts the Burin Heritage Weekend, which features old-time music, dance, and heritage costumes.
- Take Route 210 back to Marystown.

Museum shingle, Burin

Terra Nova

Seasons merge subtly at Terra Nova National Park, the most easterly of Canada's 35 national parks. Spring on Newfoundland's northeast coast begins in late April with the breakup of ice on inner Newman Sound and the arrival of dozens of common goldeneyes, black ducks, and Canada geese. Soon the mauve blossoms of rhodora will perk up the bog browns; clumps of white paper birch will splash the evergreen hillsides with the brighter green of their unfurling leaves; and the quickening Labrador Current will drive the first glistening icebergs onto the horizon.

Whenever the weather forces the current close to shore, the bergs—some as large as cathedrals—glare white and blue, near Terra Nova's beaches. Even during the summer temperatures of 25°C, you can see them floating on the horizon.

The Labrador Current also transports a rich retinue of cold-loving ocean life, including pods of humpback and pilot whales, and solitary minke whales. These creatures swim within park boundaries, and a boat ride enables you to see some of them up close.

Newman Sound is a lovely setting for a boat excursion. Flocks of white gulls escort you as you enter the sound. And the rock arches and sea caves along its shore reveal countless seabirds—among them black guillemots and Arctic terns, and even some puffins and murres.

For Terra Nova's land life, the presence of the Labrador Current means cool summers that come late. July arrives before the flowers of the ubiquitous lambkill sprinkle open heaths with pink, and the white and gold puffs of cotton grasses mingle with the rich pink and yellow-lipped blooms of dragon's-mouth, a delicate orchid. At ground level, more than a dozen species of sphagnum moss form a quilt of yellow, green, rust, red, and brown patches.

Only 14 mammal species were found on Newfoundland when Europeans first arrived, although other animals—moose and snowshoe hares, for example—were subsequently introduced. The species of medium to large land mammals whose tracks are regularly seen in Terra Nova can be counted on one hand: moose, black bear, lynx, and otter. There are many weasels, squirrels, minks, and snowshoe hares but, like the rest of the island, the park has no porcupines, skunks, raccoons, woodchucks, or snakes. These vertebrates are scarce largely because Newfoundland is separated from the mainland by frigid salt water.

Fall weather often persists in Terra Nova into late December or early January, when snowfall starts to be heavy. September frosts weave their magic on a few red maples, turning their green foliage to brilliant scarlet almost overnight. Large-scale color changes in the broad-leaved trees take place in October when the poplars and birches turn vivid yellow, the huckleberry bushes in the fens become magenta, and the cinnamon ferns add russet hues to green alder swales. By the time the golden needles of the tamaracks have fallen to the forest floor, the first snowstorm is on its way from the west.

Summer brings the blue tint of new growth to Terra Nova's spruces.

PARK INFORMATION

Access: The Trans-Canada Highway and Route 310.
Visitors' centre: Newman Sound and Twin Rivers, mid-June to early September.
Accommodation: Campgrounds at Newman Sound (year-round), and Malady Head, for group tenting, and two primitive campgrounds.
Summer activities: Boating and canoeing (canoes and kayaks can be rented at Sandy Point); snorkeling, scuba diving; fishing; hiking; golfing; picnicking; interpretive programs; guided walks.
  Winter activities: Camping; snowshoeing, cross-country skiing, ice fishing.

9 Fogo Island

🏕 ⚓ ✳ ⌂

Just a 45-minute trip on the ferry from Farewell takes you to Fogo Island, where the villages are among the least-changed in Newfoundland.

The island was settled in the 1680s by English and Irish fishermen, who sought refuge there from French raiders and the Beothuk Indians. An isolated haven until the 20th century, its inhabitants still retain traces of the Elizabethan dialect and keep ancient customs alive.

The island's name is thought to come from the Portuguese *fuego*, meaning "fires." It may refer to Beothuk campfires seen on these coasts by Portuguese explorers who first sailed these waters in the 15th century.

After crossing Hamilton Sound the ferry docks at Stag Harbour. Follow Route 333 across this small island—25 km long and 14 km wide—through villages with quaint names, such as Little Seldom.

The route ends at Fogo (pop. 1,153), the largest town on the island. In the town is Bleakhouse Museum, in a former fish merchant's home, built in 1816. It has been restored to its original appearance and its contents recount the lives of the fishermen and merchants of the island. *Admission free. Open daily, July to September, 10 am to 7 pm.*

In the northeastern part of the island is Joe Batt's Arm, which refers to a deserter from Captain Cook's ship, which charted the coast in 1763. Route 334 ends at the fishing communities of Tilting and Sandy Cove.

Tilting is thought to have been named after the slant of the log huts built there by early settlers. It has one of the earliest Irish Catholic cemeteries in Newfoundland, dating to the late 18th century. Sandy Cove was once the summer settlement of Beothuk Indians, who migrated every year to the island from the mainland.

There are hiking trails across the island, to Lion's Den, Brimstone Head (considered by the Flat Earth Society to be one of the four corners of the Earth), Locke's Cove, and Eastern Tickle. You may come across a small herd of Newfoundland ponies, which are let loose in summer to graze on the island.

Special events

Brimstone Head Folk Festival
(mid-July)

10 Trinity

✳ ⌂

This village (pop. 328) is one of Newfoundland's oldest settlements. Trinity Bay was discovered by the Portuguese explorer Gaspar de Corte Real in 1501, and the village was first settled in 1558. By the mid-1700s Trinity was thriving with fishing and shipbuilding.

St. Paul's Anglican Church, built about 1892, is the predominant landmark. Its 31-m tower can be seen from almost any vantage point in this village. Its interior is lavish with polished wooden arches and two impressive stained-glass windows.

A monument in the churchyard honors Rev. Dr. John Clinch, who administered the first smallpox vaccines in the New World at Trinity in 1800. Clinch was an Anglican missionary and a friend of William Jenner, the discoverer of the vaccine.

A short distance north of the church is the Hiscock House, built in 1881 for a Trinity blacksmith, Richard Hiscock. It has been restored to the 1910 period; costumed guides show visitors around the house. *Admission free. Open daily, July to September, 10 am to 5:30 pm.*

South of the church is the Trinity Museum, in a "saltbox" house built in the 1880s. The museum has more than 2,000 items, such as a shoemaker's kit

The 31-m-high steeple of St. Paul's Church overlooking Trinity Bay has served as a beacon to worshipers and sailors alike.

A DAY'S EXCURSION TO IRELAND'S EYE

Random Island, at 388 km², is the second-largest on the coast of Newfoundland. Located just south of the Bonavista Peninsula, the island is encircled by Smith Sound and North West Arm—two inlets of Trinity Bay. On a map the island seems to be one of Newfoundland's ragged promontories. But a close look reveals that a tiny channel—bridged by a causeway—separates the island from the mainland.

To reach Random Island, take Route 230 from the Trans-Canada Highway to Milton. Cross the causeway and follow 231 to Petley on Smith Sound. Here you can board the *Lois Elaine II*—the only passenger boat operating regularly on the sound. The round-trip to Ireland's Eye offers a glimpse of a lost way of life on Newfoundland's coast.

The vessel sails east, passing coves and harbors that have not been called home for more than a quarter of a century. At Warrick's Harbour, the concrete pillars mark the site of an abandoned fish processing plant. At Popes Harbour, on the mainland side of Smith Sound, there are overgrown gardens with fruit and ornamental trees, surrounded by wild spruce and birch. At British Harbour, another mainland site, neglected dwellings have developed a slow lean.

After the *Lois Elaine II* leaves Smith Sound, it sails for the community of Ireland's Eye. Legend says you could see Ireland by looking through a narrow channel here. The harbor is still flanked with dwellings, their paint fading and their windows gaping wide. The church, without its spire, still watches over the abandoned settlement. The only residents are a brood of eagles.

On the trip back, the *Lois Elaine II* passes Thoroughfare, another Random Island settlement that was once the site of a fish factory that prepared herring and salmon for export. As the *Lois Elaine II* heads for Petley, travelers can glimpse minke whales cavorting in the waters of Smith Sound.

A DELIGHTFUL RUN ON AN OLD RAIL LOOP

Trinity Loop Railway Village is the only place in Newfoundland where visitors will hear a train whistle blow and the grinding of steel wheels on iron tracks. It is the last surviving section of railway in Newfoundland and the only known outdoor railway loop in North America. The village is located south of Trinity. To get there, turn right at Dunfield off Route 239.

The purpose of the railway loops is to help the ascent of trains from low to high ground. In the early 1900s, the railway engineers surveying a route for the Bonavista Peninsula branch line encountered a problem at Trinity. The distance from low to high ground was too short. The engineers realized that, if they laid the tracks straight on the incline, the grade would be too steep for the trains. The solution was to increase the distance of track. This they did by "looping" the tracks around a pond.

In 1984 the branch line was closed after the Canadian National Railway decided to abandon the Newfoundland Railway. Plans called for all the tracks, including the Trinity loop, to be torn up and sold as scrap. But local railwayman and historian Clayton Cook led an intensive one-man campaign to save the loop.

Today, a miniature locomotive with passenger cars takes delighted visitors for an excursion trip on the loop. Several locomotives and railway cars, once part of the Newfoundland Railway fleet, are preserved in the nearby Newfoundland Railway Museum. *Admission free. Open daily, mid-June to Labor Day, 11 am to 8 pm; late May to mid-June, and Labor Day to Thanksgiving, Saturday and Sunday, 11 am to 8 pm.*

from 1900, medical supplies from 1890 and cooper's tools. One of its oldest exhibits here is a book published in 1729. *Admission free, donations accepted. Open mid-June to mid-September, Monday to Saturday, 10 am to 9 pm; Sunday, 2 pm to 6 pm.*

Farther along Church Street is the Holy Trinity Roman Catholic Church, the oldest wooden church still in use in Newfoundland. Its interior has remained unchanged since it was built in 1833. The tower was added in 1880.

On Victoria Road, the high street overlooking the town, is the Green Family Forge, built in 1895 and operated until 1955. Some of the tools on display are over 200 years old. *Open July and August, Monday to Saturday, 10 am to 9 pm; Sunday, 2 pm to 6 pm.*

At the end of Victoria Road are the ruins of Lester House, built by fish merchant Benjamin Lester in 1750. Nearby is the Lester-Garland Store, the centre of Lester's empire. Trinity's history is told in the Trinity Interpretation Centre, next to Lester House. The centre is housed in a green, two-story house, built in the early 1900s. *Admission free. Open daily, July to September, 10 am to 5:30 pm.*

Special events

Trinity Festival (July)

11 Harbour Grace

✻ ⌂

In his diary entry for October 7, 1612, Englishman John Guy, first of the colonial governors, wrote: "by sailing and rowing we came to Havre de Grace as far as the Pirate's Fort . . . where we remained until the 17th of October." The "pirate" was the notorious Peter Easton, who in 1610 built a fort at Harbour Grace, from where he controlled the western North Atlantic.

Despite its nefarious beginnings, Harbour Grace grew into a thriving, respectable town, and for a long time was regarded as the island's "second capital." Unfortunately, twice in the 19th century and again in the 20th, disastrous fires razed large sections of the town. Consequently it is at the Conception Bay Museum, at the east end of Water Street, that visitors obtain their best impression of the town's colorful history. This brick and stone building was a customs house constructed in 1870 on the site of Easton's fort. *Open daily, June to mid-September, 10 am to 6:30 pm.*

Outside the museum is a plaque that honors the American aviatrix Amelia Earhart. In 1932 she flew from here in the first solo flight across the Atlantic Ocean by a woman.

On Cochrane Street is St. Paul's Anglican Church, built in 1835, the oldest stone church in Newfoundland. Farther on are Coughlan United Church, named for Rev. Laurence Coughlan, who brought the first Wesleyan mission to North America here in 1765, and the imposing Roman Catholic church of the Immaculate Conception, built in 1889.

Harvey Street leads to Carbonear (pop. 5,259), the town where Easton's lieutenant, Gilbert Pike, gave up the pirate life to settle down in domestic bliss with an Irish princess, Sheila Na Geira,

A window of the museum at Harbour Grace makes a charming frame for Conception Bay.

whom he rescued from a Dutch man-o'-war where she was held prisoner.

Special events

Harbour Grace Regatta (late July)

Conception Bay Folk Festival (late July)

Trinity-Conception Fair
(late September)

12 Cape St. Mary's Ecological Reserve

On a clear summer's day at Cape St. Mary's it is hard to know which is the more fascinating—the sight and sound of thousands of seabirds wheeling and diving, competing for food and nesting material, or the schools of humpback, fin and minke whales just offshore.

Ancient mariners who endured the frequent storms and dense fogs here named it *Capo da tormenta*, and later Capo de Sancta Maria. In 1964, Cape St. Mary's became an ecological reserve. It lies at the southwest tip of the Avalon Peninsula, just off Route 100, at the end of a 16-km road.

A 10-minute walk from the lighthouse parking lot brings visitors to within 15 m of Bird Rock, or "The Stack," a tiny sea stack rising some 76 m out of the sea and connected to the mainland by a land bridge. Here, visitors have an eye-level view of one of the largest colonies of gannets in the world. From May to September, as many as 53,000 birds, which include murres and kittiwakes, gather on the sea stack and the mainland cliffs.

The breeding cycles of these birds are tied to the presence of fish in the water, particularly caplin. These fish usually come ashore in early summer to spawn on the beaches, and it is at this period that chicks are hatched.

In summer, there is an interpretive centre at the cape. *Open daily, June to early September, 8:30 am to 5:30 pm. The reserve is open year-round.* Dress warmly since, even in summer, the weather can become cool, foggy, and windy.

Multitudes of birds crowd Cape St. Mary's cliffs, one of the world's important nesting sites.

13 La Manche Provincial Park

A long, narrow, steep-sided inlet of the Atlantic forms the mouth of the La Manche River on Newfoundland's east coast. The name, which is derived from the French word for "sleeve," is also the term used in France for the English Channel. The river and the valley it flows through form La Manche Provincial Park, established in 1966.

More than 50 species of birds have been recorded in the park, from the common loon and the yellow-bellied flycatcher to several types of hawks and sparrows. Moose, beavers, and snowshoe hares can be seen, as well as shrews and wild mink.

The 1.25-km Falls Trail takes you to the spectacular waterfall above La Manche Pond. Another 1.25-km trail leads to the abandoned town of La Manche, which was almost totally destroyed by a storm on January 25, 1966.

The park is adjacent to the Avalon Wilderness area, home of the world's largest herd of woodland caribou, comprising more than 5,500 animals.

Near the park is the Witless Bay Ecological Reserve, three islands of grassy burrows and rock faces that shelter one of the largest concentrations of seabirds in the world. They are the summer resting place for thousands of puffins and Leach's storm petrels, among others. The birds are most active during the caplin run, from mid-June to mid-July.

Our contributors

12 AROUND TORONTO

SCOTT ANDERSON
Port Perry

MOLLY HARDING
Jordan
Niagara Peninsula*

STUART JOHNSTON
Credit River valley*

KEITH KNIGHT
Bobcaygeon
Kirkfield

CAROL KOZAK
St. George

SUSAN LAWRENCE
Port Hope

DAVID MEYER
Elora

CHRIS POWELL
Alton

HARRY SULLIVAN
Puck's Farm
Sharon
Schomberg
Tottenham to
Tyrone Mill*

LISE TALLYN
Campbellville

RON TURPIN
St. Jacobs

DAVID WEBB
Hockley

13 SOUTHWESTERN ONTARIO

HEATHER BOA
Bayfield
Benmiller
Clinton

PETER EPP
Dresden
Oil Springs
Petrolia
Thamesville

DAVID GREENBERG
St. Marys

MONA IRWIN
Blyth
Goderich

IAN ROBINSON
Long Point
Port Dover
Port Stanley
Port Stanley to
Port Dover*
Sparta

DIANE SIMON
Kingsville
Pelee Island

DON WILKES
Point Pelee Nat Pk

14 SOUTHEASTERN ONTARIO

BRIAN AMARON
Charleston Lake
Provincial Park
Merrickville

JOE BANKS
Williamstown

LEE ANNE PARPART
Gananoque

MAUREEN PEGG
Perth

MARTHA PLAINE
Almonte
Rideau Canal

JACQUES POITRAS
Wolfe Island*

ED REEVES
Sandbanks Prov Pk

DON ROSS
St. Lawrence Islands
Nat Pk

JEFF WILSON
Bon Echo Prov Pk

15 WESTERN QUEBEC

KATHERINE ALDRED
Shawville
Ottawa River valley*

JEAN BELLEAU
Lac-Simon
Montebello
The Petite-Nation
Region*
Plaisance

NATALIE DE BLOIS
Baskatong Reservoir
Ferme-Neuve
Mont Sir-Wilfrid

DANIEL DESLAURIERS
Mont-Tremblant Village
Parc du Mont-Tremblant

KATHARINE FLETCHER
Gatineau Park

ERNIE MAHONEY
Wakefield

LOUIS PELLETIER
Île des Moulins
The Lanaudière
Region*
Rawdon
Terrebonne

16 NORTHEASTERN QUEBEC

PIERRE DUBOIS
Beaupré Coast*
Cap Tourmente
National Wildlife Area

MRYKA HALL-BEYER
La Mauricie Nat Pk

LISE PILOTE
Parc des Hautes-Gorges-
de-la-Malbaie
Cap-à-l'Aigle and
Saint-Fidèle
Port-au-Persil

LOUISE PLANTE
Batiscan
Champlain
Chemin du Roy
The Mauricie
Region*
Sainte-Anne-de-la-
Pérade

ANDRÉE RAINVILLE
L'Anse St-Jean
Saguenay parks
Sainte-Rose-du-Nord

PAUL-ÉMILE THÉRIAULT
Péribonka
Val-Jalbert

FRANÇOIS TRÉPANIER
Île aux Coudres
Les Éboulements
Parc des Grands-Jardins
Saint-Joseph-de-la-Rive

NIL VERMETTE
Île d'Orléans

17 SOUTHERN QUEBEC

PIERRE BRETON
La Beauce

LISE CARRIER
Charny

NATACHA CHARLAND
Knowlton

MARGARET ELLIS
Dunham

LOUISE GRÉGOIRE-RACICOT
Richelieu River valley
Sorel Islands

DANY JACQUES
Lac Massawippi*
Lac Memphrémagog*
North Hatley
Ulverton

LIZ MORENCY
Coteau-du-Lac
Nat Hist Site

RÉMI TREMBLAY
Lac Mégantic
Parc de Frontenac

18 SOUTHEASTERN QUEBEC

PAUL BEAUDOIN
Grosse-Île Nat Hist Site
Île aux Grues
L'Islet-sur-Mer

LISE CARRIER
Charny to Montmagny*

GILLES DUBÉ
Cabano
Île Verte

STÉPHANE GIROUX
Causapscal and
Matapédia Valley
Chaleur Bay*
Miguasha
Parc de la Gaspésie
Quebec's salmon rivers

CHANTAL MANTHA
Havre-Aubert
Magdalen Islands*

PIERRE MICHAUD
Jardins de Métis
Parc de Bic
Portes de l'enfer

DIANE TURCOTTE
Forillon National Park

19 NEW BRUNSWICK

RAYANNE BRENNAN
New Denmark

MICHAEL BURZYNSKI
Fundy Nat Pk

JUDY COLE
Hartland
Woodstock

CHARLENE DALEY
Lameque Island
Miscou Island

ROSS INGRAM
Gagetown
Grand Lake*

GAIL MacMILLAN
Mount Carleton
Provincial Park

CAROL-ANN NICHOLSON
Crocker Hill Studios
Campobello Island
Deer Island
Grand Manan Island*
St. Andrews
St. George
St. Stephen

EDITH ROBB
Bouctouche
Dorchester
Hillsborough
Hillsborough to
Cape Enrage*
Sackville

MICHAEL ROSEN
Kouchibouguac
National Park

20 PRINCE EDWARD ISLAND

KATE MacQUARRIE
Bonshaw Hills*
East Point*

PHIL MICHAEL
Prince Edward Island
National Park

HEATHER MOORE
Alberton
Basin Head
Cedar Dunes
Provincial Park
Georgetown
Green Park
Provincial Park
Miscouche
Miscouche to
Abram-Village*
North Cape
Orwell Corner
Historic Village
Souris
Victoria

21 NOVA SCOTIA

ROSEMARY ALGAR
Cape Breton Highland
Nat Pk

SUSAN BELLIVEAU
Parrsboro
Parrsboro to Joggins*

BILL DUNPHY
Baddeck
Bras d'Or Lake*
Margaree Harbour
North East Margaree

MILLIE EVANS
Kejimkujik Nat Pk

SUE HEBB
Bear River
Long and Brier Islands

MARGARET HENNIGAR
Lunenberg to Peggy's
Cove*
Mahone Bay

CATHY HOLMES
Cape Sable Island

JO-ANNE MacDONALD
Isle Madame
St. Peters

DOUG MacNEIL
Pictou County

SHEILA McDOUGALL
Musquodoboit Harbour

SANDRA MEERS
Annapolis Royal
Cape Blomidon
The French Shore*
Grand Pré Nat Hist Site
Port Royal Nat Hist Site
Wolfville

22 NEWFOUNDLAND AND LABRADOR

KIM BRETT
Fogo Island

WILLIAM CALLAHAN
Cape St. Mary's
Ecological Reserve
Harbour Grace
La Manche Prov Pk

BARBARA DEAN-SIMMON
Random Island
Trinity
Trinity Loop

REG HAMILTON
Badger to Buchans*

DAVE HUDDLESTONE
Gros Morne Nat Pk

LINDA NORMAN
Boxey Harbour
Deer Lake
Harbour Breton
Hermitage

SHERRY PILGRIM
Blanc Sablon to
Red Bay*
L'Anse aux Meadows
Red Bay
St. Anthony

MICHAEL ROSEN
Terra Nova Nat Pk

KEN SIMMONS
Burgeo
Channel—Port-aux-
Basques

DEBBIE SMITH
Burin Peninsula*

---

*Roads to explore

Index

Page numbers in *italics* refer to photographs. Parenthetical references identify provincial locations of parks, islands, roads, or trails, as well as the sites of museums and other points of interest. References to air, boat, ferry, and train trips are grouped under the relevant **bold** headings.

Picture credits

All photographers listed below are represented by FIRST LIGHT ASSO-CIATED PHOTOGRAPHERS (TORONTO, ONT.). The exceptions are those whose names appear in parenthesis. The positions of photographs are identified as follows: *t = top; b = bottom; l = left; r = right; m = middle.*

Cover: (© George Hunter/Comstock); **Inset** © Janet Dwyer; **Front and back endsheets** © Brian Milne; p. 5 © Darwin Wiggett, p. 6*l* © Alan Marsh, p. 6*r* © Mark Burnham, p. 7 © Dale Wilson; **Region 1** © David Nunuk, p. 21*tr* © Steve Short; **Region 2** © Alan Sirulnikoff, p. 47 © Steve Short; **Region 3** © Alan Sirulnikoff; **Region 4** © Steve Short; **Region 5** © Darwin Wiggett; **Region 6** © Darwin Wiggett; **Region 7** © Todd Korol, (p. 127 *tr* courtesy Motherwell Homestead); **Region 8** © Brian Milne, p. 134*b* © Todd Korol, (p. 135*tl* courtesy *The Banner*); **Region 9** © Dawn Goss, (p. 155*b* © Dennis Smyk), (p. 156 Industry, Science & Technology Canada), p. 161 © Brian Milne; **Region 10** © Mark Burnham, pp. 166, 166-167, and 168 © Dawn Goss; **Region 11** © Alan Marsh, (p. 183 © David Gilchrist/CPS Bruce District), p. 193*b* © Donald Stanfield; **Region 12** © Ken Straiton, (p. 214*l* Ontario Ministry of Natural Resources), (p. 215*br* Industry, Science & Technology Canada); **Region 13** © Alan Marsh, p. 224 © Grant Black, (p. 228 courtesy Blyth Festival); **Region 14** © Alan Marsh; **Region 15** © Mark Burnham,

pp. 254-255, p. 264*b* and pp. 266-268 © Kitchin/Hurst, (p. 265*b* and p. 269 © P. Brunet/Publiphoto); **Region 16** © Kitchin/Hurst, (p. 274*t* Association Touristique du Cœur-du-Québec), (p. 277 © J. Pleau/Parc National de la Mauricie), (p. 278 © Perry Mastrovito/Réflexion), (p. 278 inset © Paul G. Adam/Publiphoto), (p. 281 © Yves Tessier/Réflexion), (p. 282 Association de développement des Hautes-Gorges); **Region 17** © Kitchin/Hurst, (p. 293 © Gil Jacques/Réflexion), (p. 296*b* and p. 298 © J. Boutin/Publiphoto); **Region 18** © Kitchin/Hurst, (p. 309*b* © Robert Etcheverry), p. 319 © Stephen Homer; **Region 19** © John Sylvester; **Region 20** © John Sylvester (pp.. 342-343 © Richard Vroom), (p. 352*t* Wayne Barret/PEI Tourism); **Region 21** © Dale Wilson, (p. 361*t* Industry Science & Technology Canada), (p. 372*t* courtesy Cecile Miller); **Region 22** © Dale Wilson.

Film work: Tri-Graphics Litho Services Ltd.
Printing: Transcontinental Printing Inc.
Binding: Harpell's Press Co-operative
Paper: Westvaco

Front and back endsheets: Pembina Valley, near La Riviere, Manitoba (page 139)